S0-BME-685

THE PAPERS OF

James Madison

SPONSORED BY
THE UNIVERSITY OF VIRGINIA

THE PAPERS OF
James Madison

RETIREMENT SERIES

VOLUME 2

1 FEBRUARY 1820–26 FEBRUARY 1823

EDITED BY

David B. Mattern

J. C. A. Stagg

Mary Parke Johnson

Anne Mandeville Colony

UNIVERSITY OF VIRGINIA PRESS

CHARLOTTESVILLE AND LONDON

This volume of *The Papers of James Madison* has been edited with financial aid from the National Endowment for the Humanities, an independent federal agency, the National Historical Publications and Records Commission, and the University of Virginia. Financial support has also been provided by Founding Fathers Papers, Inc., the Packard Humanities Institute, Holly C. Shulman, and Joyce Galbraith Colony.

UNIVERSITY OF VIRGINIA PRESS

First published 2013

The paper used in this publication meets the minimum requirements
of ANSI/NISO Z39.48–1992(R 1997) (Permanence of Paper).

1 3 5 7 9 8 6 4 2

Library of Congress Cataloging-in-Publication Data

Madison, James, 1751–1836.
The papers of James Madison, Retirement series / edited by David B. Mattern . . . [et al.].
p. cm.
Includes bibliographical references and index.
Contents: v. 1. 4 March 1817–CA. 31 January 1820—v. 2. 1 February 1820–26 February 1823.
1. Madison, James, 1751–1836—Archives. 2. Madison, James, 1751–1836—Correspondence. 3. Presidents—United States—Archives. 4. Presidents—United States— Correspondence. 5. United States—Politics and government—1817–25—Sources. 6. United States—Politics and government—1825–29—Sources. 7. United States—Politics and government—1829–37—Sources. I. Mattern, David B., 1951–. II. Title.

E302.M19.2010
973.5'1092—dc22

2009017515

ISBN 978-0-8139-2849-4 (v. 1) (cloth : alk. paper)
ISBN 978-0-8139-3376-4 (v. 2) (cloth : alk. paper)

To

Penny Kaiserlian

Publisher for James Madison

Contents

CONTENTS

Preface

The documents in this volume cover the period from 1 February 1820 to 26 February 1823, during which time Madison remained at Montpelier, his Orange County, Virginia, estate, with occasional visits to friends in the neighborhood and attendance at the biannual Board of Visitor meetings at the University of Virginia. As he described his post-presidential life, Madison "devoted himself to his farm & his books; with much avocation however from both, by an extensive & often laborious correspondence (as his files shew) which seems to be entailed on Ex-Presidts. especially when they have passd. a like prolonged & diversified career in the pub. service" (Madison's Autobiography, December 1830, NjP).

The "laborious correspondence" Madison referred to included a wide range of topics, from politics and personal finance to education and the creation of the University of Virginia. Many writers sent books, articles, and pamphlets in hopes that a comment from Madison would boost sales. Most received a short, polite acknowledgment, but a few like Mathew Carey, who wrote about domestic manufactures, were treated to a substantive reply. Others sought letters of introduction, particularly to Madison's friends in Europe. And despite his well-known reluctance to do so, Madison provided many letters of recommendation to President James Monroe for friends, relations, and others, such as Tench Coxe and James Leander Cathcart, who Madison thought deserving of his patronage. Another group of letters that fell into the "laborious" category were those from people who asked for Madison's judgment on matters or activities that had taken place during his years in executive office. To these letters from Charles D. Coxe, Joseph Wheaton, David Easton, and Benjamin L. Lear, Madison pleaded a lack of memory and advised a recourse to public records. Finally, there were letters from strangers who requested from Madison pronouncements on specific measures before the public. To these Madison courteously but firmly declined to comment.

Madison wrote far more substantial letters on domestic and international politics to Monroe, who kept him abreast of events and frequently solicited his advice on matters that included the Missouri Question, the Transcontinental Treaty, internal improvements, and presidential appointments. Madison's neighbor, James Barbour, a U.S. senator, also asked for explicit advice on the Missouri Question. Madison exchanged letters with Spencer Roane on various Supreme Court decisions, such as *Cohens v. Virginia.* Richard Rush, George Joy, and Lafayette provided the latest news and opinion from Europe, and Madison commented at length to Rush on the controversy between Thomas Malthus and William Godwin on population growth.

The bulk of Madison's extensive correspondence with Thomas Jefferson in this volume deals with the ongoing construction and funding of the buildings that comprise the University of Virginia. In addition to this exchange of letters, and that with Joseph C. Cabell, the editors decided to continue publishing the minutes of the Board of Visitors meetings of the university attended by Madison as well as any report generated by the board and signed by him as a member. These documents provide a detailed picture of the slow and onerous process of building the university and maintaining political and financial support for it in the state legislature.

Readers should be aware that this volume also includes Madison's extended discussions on the importance of public education as expressed in letters to Joel K. Mead, Albert Picket, Littleton Dennis Teackle, and William T. Barry; a reiteration of his oft expressed opinion on religious freedom to Jacob de La Motta; and his comments on slavery in an exchange with Francis Corbin. Of particular note in respect to this latter subject is Madison's allegory on slavery entitled "Jonathan Bull & Mary Bull" also published here.

The appearance in 1821 of Robert Yates's *Secret Proceedings and Debates* of the Constitutional Convention spurred interest in Madison's own notes on the debates from Richmond publisher Thomas Ritchie, and elicited a passionate appeal to publish them from Madison's former brother-in-law, John G. Jackson. It also evidently inspired in Madison renewed energy for the task of editing his papers. Madison continued to express his concern for establishing an accurate account of past events by sending corrections of the historical record to Ritchie and Hezekiah Niles for publication.

Finally, there is a range of private letters dealing with financial matters and the daily routine of life at Montpelier. Given the usual vagaries of weather, plant diseases and pests, bad harvests, poor crop prices, and the difficulty of recovering debts owed to him, Madison's financial situation, though not dire, was unsettled. In addition, the plantation experienced a typhus epidemic during the winter of 1820–21 that sickened over forty people, including Madison, and killed ten. Despite this gloomy picture, the Madisons lived comfortably and continued to purchase household goods, wine, horses, and books, as well as needed items for the plantation. Montpelier remained a magnet for visitors (see the Chronology, pp. xxxiii–xxxiv, for a complete list of known visitors), and the editors have included in this volume a number of visitor's accounts published in the newspapers of the time.

Acknowledgments

The editors wish to acknowledge the assistance of a number of individuals and organizations who have contributed to the preparation of this volume: our transcriber and master of languages, Sarah Marshall, and our administrative assistant, Stacy Diggs-Allen; Racquel Yerbury, Faculty in Latin and Director of International Programs, and her Latin IV class at St. Andrew's Episcopal School in Potomac, Maryland (Rebekah Daniels, Janice Freeman, Morgan Harris, Alexander Hill, Andrew Looney, Marcus Maibach, Matthew Mitterhoff, and Alex Palmer); Thomas Chapman, Meg Kennedy, and Matt Reeves of James Madison's Montpelier; Timothy D. W. Connelly of the National Historical Publications and Records Commission; Ann L. Miller; Susan Holbrooke Perdue of Documents Compass; Holly C. Shulman of the Dolley Madison Digital Edition; Kate Ohno of the Papers of Benjamin Franklin; Jeff Looney and Lisa Francavilla of the Papers of Thomas Jefferson, Retirement Series; Dan Preston of the Papers of James Monroe; and the staff of the Papers of George Washington; Elizabeth W. Pope, Ashley Cataldo, and Dennis R. Laurie of the American Antiquarian Society; Jerome Brooks, Julie Miller, and Mary Rich of the Library of Congress; Tal Nadan, Laura Slezak Karas, and their colleagues at the Manuscripts and Archives Division, New York Public Library; the staffs of Alderman Library and the Albert and Shirley Small Special Collections Library, University of Virginia.

Editorial Method

The guidelines used in editing *The Papers of James Madison* were explained in volumes 1 and 8 of the congressional series (1:xxxiii–xxxix and 8:xxiii), in the first volume of the secretary of state series (1:xxv–xxvii), and in volume 6 of the presidential series (6:xxxii–xxxiii). These guidelines have been followed in the retirement series. Considerable effort has been made to render the printed texts as literal, faithful copies of the original manuscripts, but some exceptions must be noted. Characters and words that are missing owing to damage to the manuscript are indicated by [. . .]; those that are obscured by binding, tape, or blots, are restored by conjecture within angle brackets. Words consistently spelled incorrectly, as well as variant or antiquated spellings, are left as written; however, words that may appear to be printer's errors are corrected through additions in square brackets or followed by the device [*sic*]. The brackets used by Madison and other correspondents have been rendered as parentheses. Slips of the pen have been silently corrected, but substantial errors, discrepancies, or omissions have been noted.

Pertinent information related to the documents is set forth in the provenance notes. Notes or dockets made by various clerks, editors, and collectors through the years, have not been recognized unless germane to an understanding of the document. Postmarks are noted only when three or more days have elapsed before posting, or when used to support conjectured dating of undated letters. When the enclosures mentioned are newspapers or other ephemeral publications that would have been immediately separated from the document, the absence of such items has not been noted in the provenance.

Where identifications of persons are made without source citations, the relevant material has been taken from the *Dictionary of American Biography* or the *Dictionary of National Biography*. Wherever possible, names and dates have been verified from the *Library of Congress Authorities* (authorities.loc.gov). Letters in foreign languages are printed in full and followed by a condensed translation. The order of documents continues unchanged from previous series.

Depository Symbols

In the provenance section following each document the first entry indicates the source of the text. If the document was in private hands when copied for this edition, the owner and date of ownership are indicated. If the document was in a private or public depository in the United States, the symbol listed in the Library of Congress's *MARC Code List for Organizations* (2000 ed.) is used. (For recent updates, see http://www.loc.gov/marc/organizations/). When standing alone, the symbol DLC is used to cite the Madison Papers in the Library of Congress. Documents in the National Archives are designated DNA with the record group and in most cases a second symbol corresponding to the official classification. The location symbols for depositories used in this volume are:

CLjC	Copley Newspapers Inc., James S. Copley Library, La Jolla, California
CLU-C	William Andrews Clark Memorial Library, University of California, Los Angeles
CSmH	Huntington Library, San Marino, California
Ct	Connecticut State Library, Hartford
DLC	Library of Congress, Washington, D.C.
DNA	National Archives, Washington, D.C.
	CD Consular Despatches
	DD Diplomatic Despatches
	LAR Letters of Application and Recommendation
	ML Miscellaneous Letters
ICHi	Chicago Historical Society, Illinois
ICN	Newberry Library, Chicago, Illinois
ICU	University of Chicago, Illinois
IHi	Illinois State Historical Library, Springfield
InU	Indiana University, Bloomington
MB	Boston Public Library, Boston
MBBS	Bostonian Society, Boston
MBCo	Countway Library of Medicine, Boston
MdHi	Maryland Historical Society, Baltimore
MH-H	Harvard University, Houghton Library, Cambridge, Massachusetts
MHi	Massachusetts Historical Society, Boston
MiDbEI	Edison Institute, Henry Ford Museum, and Greenfield Village Library, Dearborn, Michigan
MSonHi	South Natick Historical, Natural History, and Library Society, South Natick, Massachusetts
MWA	American Antiquarian Society, Worcester, Massachusetts
MWiW-C	Williams College, Chapin Library, Williamstown, Massachusetts

N	New York State Library, Albany
NHi	New-York Historical Society, New York City
NIC	Cornell University, Ithaca, New York
NjMoHP	Morristown National Historic Park, Morristown, New Jersey
NjP	Princeton University, Princeton, New Jersey
NN	New York Public Library, New York City
NNPM	Pierpont Morgan Library, New York City
NUtM	Munson-Williams-Proctor Institute, Utica, New York
OClWHi	Western Reserve Historical Society, Cleveland, Ohio
PHi	Historical Society of Pennsylvania, Philadelphia
PPAmP	American Philosophical Society, Philadelphia
PWacD	David Library of the American Revolution, Washington Crossing, Pennsylvania
THer	Ladies' Hermitage Association, Hermitage, Tennessee
UkLoBM	British Museum, London
Vi	Library of Virginia, Richmond
ViU	University of Virginia, Charlottesville
ViW	College of William and Mary, Williamsburg, Virginia
WHi	State Historical Society of Wisconsin, Madison

Abbreviations

FC File copy. A copy of a letter or other document retained by the sender for his own files and differing little if at all from the final version. A draft, on the other hand, is a preliminary version of a document, typically either incomplete, varying in content or expression from the final version, or bearing marks of emendation. Unless otherwise noted, both are in the sender's hand. A letterbook copy is a retained duplicate, often bound in a chronological file, and usually in a clerk's hand.

JM James Madison.

Ms Manuscript. A catchall term describing numerous reports and other papers written by JM, as well as items sent to him which were not letters.

RC Recipient's copy. The copy of a letter intended to be read by the addressee. If the handwriting is not that of the sender, this fact is noted in the provenance.

Tr Transcript. A copy of a manuscript, or a copy of a copy, customarily handwritten and ordinarily not by its author or by the person to whom the original was addressed.

Abstracts and Missing Letters. In certain cases a document is presented only in abstract form because of its trivial nature, its great length, or a combination of both. Abstracted letters are noted by the symbol §.

The symbol ¶ indicates a "letter not found" entry, giving the name of the writer or intended recipient, the date, and such other information as can be surmised from the surviving evidence. If nothing other than the date of the missing item is known, however, it is mentioned only in the notes to a related document.

Short Titles for Books and Other Frequently Cited Materials

Ammon, *James Monroe.* Harry Ammon, *James Monroe: The Quest for National Identity* (New York, 1971).

Annals of Congress. *Debates and Proceedings in the Congress of the United States . . .* (42 vols.; Washington, 1834–56).

Annual Register. *The Annual Register, or A View of the History, Politics, and Literature, for the Year . . .* (80 vols.; London, 1758–1837).

ASP. *American State Papers: Documents, Legislative and Executive, of the Congress of the United States . . .* (38 vols.; Washington, 1832–61).

AV. *The Bible.* Authorized (King James) Version.

Bear and Stanton, *Jefferson's Memorandum Books.* James A. Bear Jr. and Lucia C. Stanton, eds., *Jefferson's Memorandum Books: Accounts, with Legal Records and Miscellany, 1767–1826* (2 vols.; Princeton, 1997).

Boyd, *Papers of Thomas Jefferson.* Julian P. Boyd et al., eds., *The Papers of Thomas Jefferson* (36 vols. to date; Princeton, N.J., 1950–).

Brigham, *American Newspapers.* Clarence S. Brigham, *History and Bibliography of American Newspapers, 1690–1820* (2 vols.; Worcester, Mass., 1947).

Callahan, *List of Officers of the Navy.* Edward W. Callahan, *List of Officers of the Navy of the United States and of the Marine Corps from 1775 to 1900* (New York, 1901).

DMDE. *The Dolley Madison Digital Edition*, ed. Holly C. Shulman (Charlottesville: University of Virginia Press, Rotunda, 2004), http://rotunda.upress.virginia.edu/dmde/default.xqy.

Evans. Charles Evans, ed., *American Bibliography . . . from . . . 1639 . . . to . . . 1820* (12 vols.; Chicago, 1903–34).

Hamilton, *Writings of James Monroe.* Stanislaus Murray Hamilton, ed., *The Writings of James Monroe . . .* (7 vols.; 1898–1903; reprint, New York, 1969).

Heitman, *Historical Register.* Francis B. Heitman, *Historical Register and Dictionary of the United States Army, from Its Organization, September 29, 1789, to March 2, 1903* (2 vols.; 1903; reprint, Baltimore, 1994).

Knox, *Naval Documents, Barbary Wars.* Dudley W. Knox, ed., *Naval Documents Related to the United States Wars with the Barbary Powers* (6 vols.; Washington, D.C., 1939–44).

Lipscomb and Bergh, *Writings of Thomas Jefferson.* Andrew A. Lipscomb and Albert Ellery Bergh, eds., *The Writings of Thomas Jefferson* (20 vols.; Washington, D.C., 1905).

Madison, *Letters* (Cong. ed.). [William C. Rives and Philip R. Fendall, eds.], *Letters and Other Writings of James Madison* (published by order of Congress; 4 vols.; Philadelphia, 1865).

Malone, *Jefferson and His Time.* Dumas Malone, *Jefferson and His Time* (6 vols.; Boston, 1948–81).

Miller, *Treaties.* Hunter Miller, ed., *Treaties and Other International Acts of the United States of America* (8 vols.; Washington, 1930–48).

OED Online. *Oxford English Dictionary*, www.oed.com.

PJM. William T. Hutchinson et al., eds., *The Papers of James Madison* (1st ser., vols. 1–10, Chicago, 1962–77, vols. 11–17, Charlottesville, Va., 1977–91).

PJM-PS. Robert A. Rutland et al., eds., *The Papers of James Madison: Presidential Series* (7 vols. to date; Charlottesville, Va., 1984–).

PJM-RS. David B. Mattern et al., eds., *The Papers of James Madison: Retirement Series* (2 vols. to date; Charlottesville, Va., 2009–).

PJM-SS. Robert J. Brugger et al., eds., *The Papers of James Madison: Secretary of State Series* (9 vols. to date; Charlottesville, Va., 1986–).

PMHB. *Pennsylvania Magazine of History and Biography.*

Riverside. G. Blakemore Evans, ed., *The Riverside Shakespeare* (Boston, 1974).

Senate Exec. Proceedings. *Journal of the Executive Proceedings of the Senate of the United States of America* (3 vols.; Washington, 1828).

Shaw and Shoemaker. R. R. Shaw and R. H. Shoemaker, comps., *American Bibliography: A Preliminary Checklist for 1801–1819* (22 vols.; New York, 1958–66).

Shoemaker. Richard H. Shoemaker, comp., *A Checklist of American Imprints for 1820–1829* (11 vols.; New York, 1964–72).

Swem and Williams, *Register.* Earl G. Swem and John W. Williams, eds., *A Register of the General Assembly of Virginia, 1776–1918, and of the Constitutional Conventions* (Richmond, 1918).

Tulard, *Dictionnaire Napoléon.* Jean Tulard et al., *Dictionnaire Napoléon* (Paris, 1987).

U.S. Statutes at Large. *The Public Statutes at Large of the United States of America . . .* (17 vols.; Boston, 1848–73).

VMHB. *Virginia Magazine of History and Biography.*

Wheaton. Henry Wheaton, *Reports of Cases Argued and Adjudged in the Supreme Court of the United States* (12 vols.; Philadelphia, 1816–27).

WMQ. *William and Mary Quarterly.*

Madison Chronology

1820

Post–7 February	John Labouchère and John Peter Insinger visit
17–19 February	Gen. Jacob Brown, John A. Dix, Edmund Kirby, and Samuel Storrow visit
23 February	JM ill with fever
March	First intimation of R. Cutts's financial difficulties
March	John P. Todd leaves for Washington
ca. 26–30 March	Thomas Todd visits Montpelier
1 April	Madisons visit Monticello
3 April	UVa. Board of Visitors meet
mid-June	Monroes visit Montpelier for a day
ca. 15 July	Levett Harris visits
ca. August	Anna Cutts and family at Montpelier
ca. August	Samuel L. and Maria Monroe Gouverneur visit
ca. 1 September	Monroes, Hays, and Maria Mayo Scott and family visit
2–3 October	UVa. Board of Visitors meet
1 November	Isaac Briggs visits Montpelier
9–10 November	Nathaniel Helme and Landon C. Read visit Montpelier
November-January	Typhus fever strikes Montpelier plantation

1821

January	William B. Lawrence and John Q. Jones visit
ca. 3 January	Richard S. Hackley visits Montpelier
ca. 30 January	Dr. T. G. Watkins visits
February	John P. Todd at Montpelier
2 April	UVa. Board of Visitors meet
ca. 15–30 April	JM away on visit to sick friend
May	John P. Todd at Baltimore
2 May	William S. Cardell visits
June	John P. Todd returns home for eighteen months
ca. 3 June	Eliab Kingman visits
ca. August	Anna Cutts and family at Montpelier

ca. 16 October	JM attacked by fever
30 November	UVa. Board of Visitors meet

1822

ca. August-September	Anna Cutts and family at Montpelier
6 August	Monroe visits Montpelier
ca. 30 September	Arthur Middleton visits Montpelier
ca. 1 October	George W. Erving visits Montpelier
7 October	UVa. Board of Visitors meet
14 October	JM purchases Cutts house in Washington
ca. 14–15 October	Monroe visits Montpelier
22 November	John P. Todd departs for Washington
ca. 23 November	John Dunn Hunter visits Montpelier

1823

February	JM ill

THE PAPERS OF

James Madison

To Thomas Mann Randolph

Dear Sir Montpellier Feby. 1. 1820

The writer of the inclosed letter[1] has thought proper to pass it to you thro' my hands. My acquaintance with him is of the most accidental & transient kind. It justifies me however in believing him to have personal worth, as well as respectable connections. Of the degree of his eccentricity you can be best informed by the two Engineers who are from his neighbourhood.

I recd. lately the inclosed newspaper from Judge Peters.[2] ⟨Per⟩haps you may think it worth while to engage Mr. Richie to republish the remarks on Hemp & Flax, when the Enquirer can conveniently spare room for them. I have seen a sample of the flax prepared in the mode & by the machinery referred to, which almost equalled Silk in its glossy fineness. With my best wishes accept Dear Sir assurances of my cordial esteem & regard.

James Madison

RC (NjP); Tr (ViW). RC docketed by Randolph as received 7 Feb.

1. The enclosure has not been found, but it was James B. Pleasants's letter to JM of 15 Jan. 1820, *PJM-RS*, 1:586–87.

2. JM probably enclosed a copy of the 6 Jan. 1820 Philadelphia *Poulson's American Daily Advertiser*, which printed a 1 Jan. 1820 letter from Richard Peters, covering an essay entitled "Hints of the Advantages of Cultivating and Preparing Hemp and Flax." There is no evidence that the piece was reprinted in the *Richmond Enquirer*.

To Francis Preston

Montpellier Feby. 3d. 1820.

I pray you My dear Sir, to be assured that I sympathize, in all the feelings which led to your letter; and that I shall learn with corresponding pleasure that your efforts have been successful in alleviating the misfortune of a brother whose amiable qualities have so long endeared him to his relatives, and made him interesting to his friends. Affectionate respects

James Madison

RC (NjP: Crane Collection). Fragment. Upper portion of letter, including salutation and dateline, is missing. Dated "Montpellier Feby. 3d. 1820." in Dolley Madison's hand. Recipient identified as Francis Preston based on Preston to JM, 30 Jan. 1820, *PJM-RS*, 1:596–97.

To Langdon Cheves

Dr Sir Montpr Feby 4 1820

Having in so recent an instance troubled you with a deviation from my general wish to decline recommendatory letters, I feel the greater awkwardness in now yielding to the request of another friend, who overrating my testimony is desirous of adding it to that of others, in making you acquainted with his standing both personally and in relation to the probable extent of his property.

F. Preston Esqr. to whom I allude, a senior brother of the late Govr Preston, is at present a member of its State Legislature and I believe a General officer of the Militia. He was formerly a Representative in the Legislature of the U. S. and regarded as a very intelligent & valuable one. Having been myself a contemporary member, I can speak with confidence on this point, and can add with pleasure that in his private character I have always held him in very high esteem as a man of the purest integrity, & the strictest honor.

Of the degree of his wealth I can not speak from personal knowlege. I have always understood and do not in the least doubt, that it is very great; made so by the addition to his own patrimony of the very rich inheritance of the Lady he married. I have understood also that his possessions are not only very extensive; but very productive also; comprehending Salt pits which are made available to the annual amount of some thousands of dollars. On this subject you will doubtless have from other sources more precise information than I can give.

Your favor of the 14. Ult[1] was duly recd. and I can not acknowlege it without an intimation that it was not wish'd that my former letter more than the present shd. put you to the trouble of an answer, nor without adding to reassurances of my high esteem, and cordial respect, my best wishes for your personal happiness & public success.

Draft (DLC).

1. *PJM-RS*, 1:585–86.

From James Monroe

Dear Sir Washington Feby 5. 1820.

I send you herewith the principal documents which have been printed since the commencment of the Session. Should any be omitted, or should there be any information on any point not touched by them, which you may desire, or [*sic*] being so advised, I will communicate it.

The Missouri question, as it is call'd, still engages the attention of Congress, & will probably do it, much longer. The result is altogether uncertain. The project was laid by Mr K.[1] The members who brought it forward last Session were the instruments. Clinton[2] it is said claims the merit of having originated it. The object is to form a new party division, turning the power which it may give, to those having the ascendancy, to all the purposes of which it may be susceptible, without much regard for its consequences in the Southern States. I doubt the policy which led to the union of Maine with Missouri, as it puts the republicans in Maine, & the Eastern States generally, in the hands & at the mercy of the authors of this scheme, and of their antagonists in that quarter. There is no one in Virga., or in that direction, of sufficient experience or force, to meet the crisis, tho many are respectable and able. I doubt whether the union mentiond, will gain one single vote on the main question; I think it more likely to lose votes on it, as the Eastern members, must in the last resort, as I presume, leave the southern, & separate the questions and admit Maine; in which case, it is possible, that their reunion, may not be effected as to all of them, on the admission of Missouri unrestraind. What effect, the daily encreasing knowledge, of the object of this project, may have, on the community, remains to be seen.

We hear nothing from Spain, and there is much cause to believe that no minister will be sent, for some months, if during the Session of Congress. Your friend

James Monroe

RC (DLC: Rives Collection, Madison Papers). Docketed by JM.

1. Rufus King (1755–1827) was a Harvard-educated lawyer who served in the Continental Congress, 1784–86, and was a Massachusetts delegate to the Constitutional Convention of 1787. A strong Federalist, King was elected U.S. senator from New York and served from 1789 to 1796, when he was appointed U.S. minister to Great Britain, returning to the United States in 1803. He stood as the Federalist vice presidential candidate in 1804 and 1808, and as the Federalist presidential candidate in 1816. As U.S. senator, 1813–24, he opposed JM's administration and the War of 1812; later, he opposed the Missouri Compromise of 1820, and was outspoken in his attacks on the extension of slavery (*PJM*, 9:73 n. 13; Robert Ernst, *Rufus King: American Federalist* [Chapel Hill, N.C., 1968], 20, 22, 44, 69, 92, 148, 217–18, 277, 286–87, 306, 320, 323–30, 351, 372–75, 393).

2. DeWitt Clinton (1769–1828), nephew and political colleague of New York governor and JM's vice president George Clinton, was a political force in New York and national politics. He served in the U.S. Senate, 1802–3, but resigned to become mayor of New York City, 1803–7, 1809–10, and 1812–15. In 1812 he was chosen by the Federalists and some Republicans to oppose JM for the presidency but lost the election by 128 electoral votes to 89. While governor of New York state, 1817–23, 1825–28, he spearheaded efforts to construct the Erie Canal, which successfully opened in 1825.

From Langdon Cheves

Dear Sir, Philada. 7 Feby 1820

I take the liberty to introduce to your Acquaintance & to recommend to your Notice Mr. John Labouchere.[1] Mr. L. has visited the United States for the Purpose of becoming Acquainted with the Country & its distinguished men, I can not therefore do him a greater favour than to make him Acquainted with you. Mr. L. is a Very intelligent & interesting Young Gentleman. He is the Son of Mr Labouchere who is at the head of the great house of Hope & Co. of Amsterdam & the Nephew of Alexander Baring[2] Esquire; And Appears to have those good feelings & favourable prepossessions towards our Country for which his Uncle has been so much distinguished. I beg leave to use the Occasion to renew assurances of the high Consideration and Attachment with Which I have the honor to be, Dear Sir, Yr. Obt St

Langdon Cheves

RC (DLC). Docketed by JM, with his note: "introducing Mr. Labouchere."

1. John Peter Labouchère (1799–1863) became a partner in the London banking firm of Williams, Deacon, Thornton, and Labouchère. His father, Pierre-César Labouchère (1772–1839), was a Dutch banker of French origin who was head of Hope & Company (Algar Labouchere Thorold, *The Life of Henry Labouchere* [London, 1913], 15 and n. 1; Tulard, *Dictionnaire Napoléon*, 1011).

2. Alexander Baring, Baron Ashburton (1774–1848), was a British financier and politician with long-standing American ties who was sent as commissioner to negotiate the United States–Canadian boundary, and signed the Webster–Ashburton treaty of 1842 (*PJM-SS*, 3:287 n. 2).

From Samuel Wyllys Pomeroy

Sir Brighton, Masssts. 7. Feby. 1820.

Having been highly gratified & instructed, by the perusal of your address to the Agricultural Society of Albemarle in may last—I take the liberty of forwarding herewith, enclosed, the last number of the Massts. Agricul. Journal; & to request your attention to a letter in that publication, on "*dairy Stock*,"[1] in which I have hinted at the expediency of introducing the practice of *Spaying heifers*, to fit them for farm & road work, as a substitute for horses.

Tho' I should esteem the Circumstance fortunate that might elicit the opinion of so great a physiologist as yourself, on the theories advanced in that paper, the inducement to this intrusion has been caused Sir, by that part of your address relating to the working of oxen instead of horses; in which the prejudices against their general use, have been very ably combated—and the 5th. objection, which is allowed to have some weight, may I believe be in a great measure removed, by recurring to what was experienced in the War of the Revolution, particularly the latter years of it; when it will appear that the principal transit of Stores & heavy Ordinance for the Armies, from New England to Virginia, was performed by *Ox teams*, to much greater advantage than could have been done with horses—& that they were more to be depended on for their punctual arrival at the destined Stations. I am in hopes soon, to be in possession of facts, collected from some of the remaining Actors in the glorious struggle alluded to, that will place the question beyond a doubt, & may when published, I presume, have a commanding influence in promoting a more general use of oxen, for the transportation of the products of the soil from the interior.

Oxen are in general use in New England, for all Agricl. operations, except ploughing among crops on land of easy tillage, they are seldom *fed with grain*, unless when under severe service—And it is the general opinion, that with judicious management, no loss of capital need ever be sustained by the farmer, for his working Stock, provided that consists of oxen. Viewing the subject as important to the Agricul. interests of the nation, you will I trust Sir, pardon this interruption of the repose, which your eminent public Services entitle you to claim. With respectful consideration I have the honor to be Sir Your Obt Srt

SAML. WYLLYS POMEROY[2]

RC (DLC). Docketed by JM.

1. Pomeroy to Josiah Quincy, 29 Dec. 1819, printed in the *Massachusetts Agricultural Repository and Journal* 6 (1820): 87–90.

2. Samuel Wyllys Pomeroy (1765–1841) was a Boston merchant who owned an estate in Brighton, Massachusetts, where he was active in agricultural experimentation. In 1832 he founded the town of Pomeroy in southern Ohio, where he invested in the coalfields in that region. He died in Cincinnati (Albert A. Pomeroy, *History and Genealogy of the Pomeroy Family* [2 vols.; Toledo, Ohio, 1912–22], 1:352; Thornton, *Cultivating Gentlemen*, 118 and n. 43).

From Enoch Reynolds

SIR. WASHINGTON CITY 8th. Feby. 1820.

In the summer of 1816, you did me the honor to subscribe for two copies of the splendid edition of the Declaration of Independence, then in hand, and now published by Mr. John Binns' of Philada.[1]

The copies are now received by me, for the subscribers which I obtained, at ten dollars each.

I have also received some in elegant frames, the prices of which including the prints and glass complete are $29. or $27.50—accordingly as they are ornamented. I will thank you to inform me whether you will receive them with, or without the frames, and to whom I shall deliver them for you. I have the honor to be most respectfully Sir Your very obedt. Servt

ENOCH REYNOLDS[2]

RC (DLC). Docketed by JM.

1. John Binns's engraved facsimile of the Declaration of Independence, within an ornamental oval formed by the seals of the thirteen original colonies and portraits of John Hancock, George Washington, and Thomas Jefferson, was published in 1818. Binns (1772–1860) was an Irish-born editor and printer who was active in Pennsylvania Republican politics and closely allied with Simon Snyder.

2. Enoch Reynolds (ca. 1776–1833), originally from Connecticut, was chief clerk, under Richard Cutts, in the office of the superintendent general of military supplies in Washington in 1816. By 1829 he was chief clerk under the second comptroller of the Treasury (*Daily National Intelligencer*, 15 Oct. 1833; *ASP, Miscellaneous*, 2:307, 310; *A Register of Officers and Agents . . . 1829* [Washington, 1830], 19).

To James Monroe

DEAR SIR MONTPELLIER Feby. 10. 1820

I have duly recd. your favor of the 5th. followed by a copy of the public documents; for which I give you many thanks. I should like to get a copy of the Journals of the Convention.[1] Are they to be purchased & where?

It appears to me, as it does to you, that a coupling of Missouri with Maine, in order to force the entrance of the former thro' the door voluntarily opened for the latter is, to say the least, a very doubtful policy. Those who regard the claims of both as similar & equal, and distrust the views of such as wish to disjoin them, may be strongly tempted to resort to the expedient; and it would perhaps be too much to say, that in no possible case such a resort could be justified. But it may at least be said, that a very peculiar case only could supersede the general policy of a direct and magnanimous course, appealing to the justice and liberality of others, and trusting to the influence of conciliatory example.

I find the idea is fast spreading that the zeal with which the extension, so called, of slavery is opposed, has with the co-alesced *leaders*, an object very different from the welfare of the slaves, or the check to their increase; and that the real object is, as you intimate, to form a new State of parties founded on local instead of political distinctions; thereby dividing the republicans of the North from those of the South, and making the former instrumental in giving the opponents of both an ascendancy over the whole. If this be the view of the subject at Washington, it furnishes an additional reason for a conciliatory proceeding in relation to Maine.

I have been truly astonished at some of the doctrines & declarations to which the Missouri question has led; and particularly so at the interpretations of the terms "migration or importation &c." Judging from my own impressions, I should deem it impossible that the memory of any one who was a Member of the General Convention could favor an opinion that the terms did not then *exclusively* refer to migration & importation *into the U. S.* Had they been understood in that Body in the sense now put on them, it is easy to conceive the alienation they would have there created in certain States. And no one can decide better than yourself, the effect they would have had on State Conventions, if such a meaning had been avowed by the advocates of the Constitution. If a suspicion had existed of such a construction, it would at least have made a conspicuous figure among the Amendments proposed to the Instrument.

I have observed as *yet*, in none of the views taken of the ordinance of 1787 interdicting slavery N. W. of the Ohio, an allusion to the circumstance, that when it passed, the Congs. had no authority to prohibit the importation of slaves from abroad; that all the States had, and some were in the full exercise of, the right to import them; and consequently, that there was no mode in which Congress could check the evil, but the indirect one of narrowing the space open for the reception of slaves. Had the federal authority then existed to prohibit directly & totally the importation from abroad, can it be doubted that it would have been exerted, and that a regulation having merely the effect of preventing an interior dispersion of slaves actually in the U. S. and creating a distinction among the States in the degrees of their sovereignty, would not have been adopted? or perhaps thought of?

No folly in the spanish Govt. can now create surprize. I wish you happily thro' the thorny circumstances it throws in your way. Adieu with affece. respects

James Madison

RC (DLC: Monroe Papers); FC (DLC). RC docketed by Monroe. Minor differences between the copies have not been noted.

1. *Journal, Acts and Proceedings, of the Convention* (Shaw and Shoemaker 49802). For JM's aid to John Quincy Adams in compiling this volume, see Adams to JM, 22 Oct. 1818, and 1 and 18 June 1819, and JM to Adams, 2 Nov. 1818, and 7 and 27 June 1819, *PJM-RS*, 1:367–68, 464, 473, 372, 465, 476.

To Enoch Reynolds

DR. SIR MONTPR. [ca. 10–29] Feby. 1820

I have recd. your favor of the 8th. inst. When I subscribed for two copies of the newly edited "Declaration of Independence,["] It is probable that I expected they would have been ready for delivery, previous to the expiration of my official term; and that one of them was intended for a piece of wall furniture in the Presidents House. I feel myself however bound to take both, and mention the circumstance only as explaining my preference of one of the Copies elegantly framed, to the 2 without frames; if it be entirely agreeable to the party interested in the sale to allow this option. Should this not be the case, I shall satisfy myself with the 2 unframed ones. In either case payment will be remitted by a private opportunity in a few days, with an intimation of the best mode of forwarding the one or the two.

Draft (DLC). Day of month not indicated; conjectural day assigned based on internal evidence.

From James Barbour

DEAR SIR WASHN. Feby 10th. 20

The Missouri question in its consequences threatens the tranquility if not the dissolution of the Union. Altho in the Senate we have a large majority against restriction yet in the House of Representatives the majority is decidedly the other way. And upon the exclusion of Slavery from the territories there is a Majority in both Houses. It has been proposed by the most moderate to compromise the question by permitting Missouri to come into the Union unrestricted and drawing a line 36½ No[r]th latitude which happens to be the dividing line between the Missouri and Arkansaw to commence on the Western limit of the Missouri and run indefinitely by that parallel and limit the introduction of Slaves to the South of that line. Every Member of the administration give it as their decided opinion that this proposition should be accepted; as do Mr Clay Mr Lowndes[1] and our most distinguished politicians. To this therefore Mr Pleasants and myself inclined. But it is opposed by King & Otis[2] and other choice spirits who wish to keep open the question for purposes it is unnecessary to State and by many also of our Southern Brethren who seem to think it is better to risk at once a dissolution of the Union than agree to a Compromise. Such also seems to be the opinion of many of our friends in the Virginia Legislature. If the question be kept open Maine will be introduced. Missouri will be excluded as also the whole territory to the West of the Mississippi will be taken from us. And King or Clinton will most probably be the next President. In this State of threatening calamity is it trespassing too much upon our acquaintance to ask of you in Strict confidence if required—to give me your advice. It is unnecessary to State how hig[h]ly I should appreciate it. If you afford it me the sooner the better. Every Subject beside is lost sight of. The public mind seems to be in that State of frenzy that forbodes the most hazardous counsels. Accept assurances of my high respect.

JAS BARBOUR

RC (DLC). Docketed by JM.

1. William Lowndes (1782–1822) was a South Carolina planter and politician who served his state in the U.S. House of Representatives, 1811–22, as a Jeffersonian Republican and strong supporter of JM's administration (Edgar et al., *Biographical Directory of the South Carolina House of Representatives*, 4:359–61).

2. Harrison Gray Otis (1765–1848) was a Harvard-educated Boston lawyer who served in the U.S. House of Representatives, 1797–1801, the Massachusetts legislature, 1802–17, and the U.S. Senate, 1817–22. An active Federalist, he was a leader in the opposition to JM's administration and the War of 1812, as well as spokesman for the Hartford Convention of 1814. In the debates over the Missouri question, he took a leading part against the extension of slavery into the territories.

To Mathew Carey

SIR MONTPR. Feby. 11. 1820

I have recd. your favor of Jany. 26.[1] with copies[2] of the addresses of the Philada Societies for the protection of the National Industry; for which I return my thanks. Such a mass of valuable information on a subject deeply interesting to the public must be acceptable even to those whose opinions would qualify some of the inferences deduced from it.

The occasion reminds me of the acknowledgements which have been long due for the volume in vindication of Ireland;[3] which you were so obliging as to send me. The delay in making them has been occasioned by a wish to give, previously, an attentive reading to a work that seemed to invite it. Other demands on my time have not even yet permitted me to do this. But I have dipped enough into your researches & observations to be satisfied of your success in shewing that the Irish Nation has been as much traduced by the pen of History, as it has been scourged by the rod of power. Be pleased Sir to accept my esteem & friendly respects

(Signed) JAMES MADISON

Draft (DLC). Dateline, salutation, and first part of opening sentence in JM's hand; remainder of letter in an unidentified hand.

1. *PJM-RS*, 1:590.

2. The unidentified hand begins here.

3. Mathew Carey, *Vindiciæ Hibernicæ: or, Ireland Vindicated; An Attempt to Develop and Expose a Few of the Multifarious Errors and Falsehoods Respecting Ireland* . . . (Philadelphia, 1819; Shaw and Shoemaker 47515).

From Edward Wyer

DEAR SIR, WASHINGTON Februy. 11. 1820.

Permit me to offer you two iron casts of Washington the well beloved,[1] which I had taken from my seal [*sic*] at Berlin last year. They are said to be good. Ever mindful of your kind attention to me during the time you was in public life, I remain Dear Sir, with all respect, Your devoted Servant. May the smiles of Heaven rest in your abode, and continue to make you happy.

EDWD. WYER

P S. If you have any commands for the North of Europe, it will give me pleasure to take charge of them when I return in June next.

RC (DLC). Docketed by JM.

1. These were probably cast-iron bas-reliefs of George Washington known as "Berlin castings," made in Germany in the late eighteenth century as memorial jewelry and fashioned as brooches, rings, or pins (Stephen Decatur, "Washington Memorial Jewelry," *American Collector* 8 [1939]: 6–7, 20).

To James Barbour

DEAR SIR MONTPR. Feby. 14. 1820

Your favor of the loth. has but just come to hand. It states that there is a decided majy. in one House agst. an unrestricted admission of Missouri, and in both for applying the restriction to all Territories West of the Mississippi: but that in a spirit of Compromise Missouri will be admitted without restriction, and the restriction as to Territories confined to the Space N. & W. of Missouri, and N. of Latitude 36.° 30.°° Between these alternatives, the latter must be obviously preferable as a lesser evil, to those who regard both as evils: it being understood of course that they dispair of a favorable change in the prospect and see no insuperable obstacles in the Constitution or Treaty.

But as the advocates for restriction yield the principle they have contended for, by such a partition, ought they not on the principle of equity, to make the partition correspond with the estimated proportions in which the common property was paid for by the two descriptions of owners.

I make these brief & hasty remarks in compliance with the wish you have intimated, and in the confidence you have authorized. Friendly respects & good wishes

James Madison

RC (NN: James Barbour Papers); FC (DLC). FC in an unidentified hand; initialed and docketed by JM: "Senator Barbour."

From Thomas Jefferson

Dear Sir Monticello Feb. 16. 20.

With this letter I commit for you to the mail a bundle of seeds, one parcel of which was sent by you to mr. Randolph for inspection. The other is seakale seed lodged here for you by Genl. Cocke. Have I returned your Vitruvius to you?[1] I am in great tribulation about it? I keep my borrowed books on a particular shelf that they may neither be forgotten nor confounded with my own. It is not on that shelf, nor can I find it. I know that I meant to return it to you on reciept of a copy of it among some books which came to hand from Paris 3. weeks ago: but not recollecting the act of returning I am uneasy & wish to know from you. The finances of the University are in a most painful state. The donation of 1820. is recieved & paid away, and we still owe 15,000 for work already done. In our reports we have always calculated on a punctual payment of the subscriptions, and were they so paid we should be perfectly at ease. But 8000.D. are in arrear on the instalments of 18.19. and that of 11,000 for 20. payable Apr. 1. Little is expected to be recieved. To us, visitors, who stand so engaged on our personal honor that Dr. Cooper's draught in Apr. or May shall be paid, it is important to give a preference to that draught, and there is no chance of doing it from the general collection. I have notified the Proctor therefore to appropriate to that the instalments of half a dozen by name whose punctuality can be counted on, to wit, the 4. visitors subscribers, mr Divers & Colo. Lindsay. This is our only security for keeping faith and honor with Cooper. My health is as usual: no pain, but low, weak, able to walk little, and venturing to ride little on account of suspicious symptoms in my legs which Dr. Watkins[2] flatters himself will disappear in the spring. I salute you with constant affection & respect.

Th: Jefferson

RC (DLC); FC (DLC: Jefferson Papers). RC docketed by JM.

1. This was probably an edition of Marcus Vitruvius Pollio, *Les dix livres d'architecture de Vitruve corrigez et traduits nouvellement en Français, avec des notes & des figures . . . Par M. [Claude] Perrault . . .* (Paris, 1684) (Sowerby, *Catalogue of Jefferson's Library*, 4:358).

2. Thomas G. Watkins (d. 1830), a Tennessee physician who settled at Glenmore in Albemarle County, Virginia, in 1817, had successfully treated Jefferson for various ailments. In the Charlottesville *Central Gazette* of 15 June 1821, Watkins announced that he was declining to practice medicine except to "wind up" cases to which he was pledged. He died in Jefferson County, Tennessee, on 2 Jan. 1830 (Bear and Stanton, *Jefferson's Memorandum Books*, 2:1369 n. 59; Silas Emmett Lucas Jr., ed., *Obituaries from Early Tennessee Newspapers, 1794–1851* [Easley, S.C., 1978], 386).

To François Barbé-Marbois

Dr. Sir [ca. 17 February 1820]

I have duly recd. the volume relating to the Equestrian State [*sic*] of Henry 4th. with one of the medals to which it gave rise for both which I offer you my thanks.

The volume is not only a valuable present to Artists, but is enriched with articles of information, which make it interesting to the curious who are not artists. I observe that it justly records your essential agency in this national monument; and, have not overlooked the fine morsel of appropriate sentiment which it was your lot to address to the reigning Prince whose name was so closely associated by the occasion, with that of his illustrious ancestor.

France is happy in having had a King worthy of the national devotion which the erection of this Statue proclaims to the memory of Henry 4. He may be regarded as a model not only to his hereditary successors under a limited monarchy, but as one also, to the other departments of the Govt. His personal virtues seem to have furnished that check & balance to his royal prerogative, which are provided by partitions of power among the Constitutional orders of the States.

I hope Sir you continue to enjoy the good health, of which you make so good a use, & that you will accept this renewed assurance of my distinguished esteem.

Draft (DLC). Undated. At the head of draft, JM wrote: "To Mr. Marbois, but not sent." Conjectural date assigned based on JM to William Harris Crawford, post–17 Feb. 1820, and nn. 2–3. François Barbé-Marbois (1745–1837) had been variously secretary of the French legation, consul, and chargé d'affaires in the United States from 1779 to 1785. As director general of the public treasury under Napoleon, Marbois negotiated the Louisiana Purchase treaty with James Monroe and Robert R. Livingston, and he wrote a history of that event that was published in Paris in 1829. Marbois was active in the chamber of peers in the French legislature, 1819–28, and served as first president of the Cours de Comptes, 1807–34. He was also instrumental in restoring the equestrian statue of Henri IV in Paris in 1818 (*PJM-SS*, 2:284 n. 3; E. Wilson Lyon, *The Man Who Sold Louisiana: The Career of François Barbé-Marbois* [1942; reprint, Norman, Okla., 1974], 118–23, 169, 171–72, 176–79).

To William Harris Crawford

DR. SIR [post–17] Feby[1] 1820

Yours of Feby 12.[2] with the medal from Ct. Marbois were duly handed to me by Genl. Browne.[3] Will you do me the favor whenever you have occasion to write to the Ct. to make my acknowlegments for this token of his polite attention, and assure him that he has a full return of the friendly sentiments & wishes expressed by him.

I learn with pleasure from Genl. Brown that you enjoy good health in the midst of your official fatigues. I hope the former will continue & that the latter will accomplish for our Country all the good which I am sure is the object of your .[4]

When do you meditate an excursion into the Country, or a trip to Georgia. In either case it need not be repeated, that Montpr. has ever the most cordial welcome for Mrs C. & yourself, to both of whom Mrs. M joins in sending sincere respects, & of every good wish.

Draft (DLC). Day of month not indicated; conjectural day assigned based on evidence in n. 3 below. At the head of draft JM wrote: "Wm. H. Crawford." On the verso, in JM's hand, are figure calculations and the words "Blankets" and "Dinah," the latter perhaps referring to his female slave of that name.

1. Here JM originally wrote, then crossed through "25."

2. The letter has not been found, however, Crawford wrote to Jefferson on the same day, informing him that "Major General Brown will deliver to you a bronze medal, struck in commemoration of the casting and erection of an Equestrian statue of Henry the 4. of France, which has been sent to me by the Marquis Marbois" (DLC: Jefferson Papers).

3. Maj. Gen. Jacob Jennings Brown, accompanied by John A. Dix, Edmund Kirby, and Samuel Storrow, arrived at Montpelier on 17 Feb. for a two-day visit (John D. Morris, *Sword of the Border: Major General Jacob Jennings Brown, 1775–1828* [Kent, Ohio, 2000], 166, 169, 217). Dix's recollection of the visit follows: "In the spring of [left blank in text] I went with General Brown on an excursion into the interior of Virginia, the chief object of which was to pay a visit to Mr. Madison and Mr. Jefferson. Our first pause was at Montpelier, the residence of the former, in Orange County. It was under his administration that the general received the commission which laid the foundation of his military reputation, and I need not say that the meeting was a cordial one on both sides. We passed two days with him, charmed with his interesting and instructive conversation, the graceful and unaffected hospitality of his wife, and the devoted attention of his son, Payne Todd. Mr. Madison was of low stature and quiet manners, and with no physical traits to mark the eminence he had attained; but his conversation, though simple and unpretending, would soon have im-

pressed one entirely ignorant of his political career with the conviction that he was a man of great intellectual power, with a large and varied experience in public affairs" (Morgan Dix, comp., *Memoirs of John Adams Dix* [2 vols.; New York, 1883], 1:58).

4. Left blank in draft.

From James Monroe

Dear Sir Washington Feby 19. 1820.

I send you by this days mail a copy of the journal of the convention which formd the fedl. constitution. One is allowed by the act of Congress to yourself, to Mr Jefferson & to Mr Adams.

Several votes were taken yesterday in the Senate on different propositions, respecting the Missouri question, & it appears that one was adopted by a majority of 4. for the establishment of a line to commence westward of Missouri, on the parallel of 36: degrees 30 minutes, & to run westward, north of which, slavery should be prohibited for ever; south of it to be permitted: Missouri & Arkansas to be admitted free from restraint. You will have seen how the members from different states voted, in the Intelligencer, of which you doubtless have a copy.[1] The terms *for ever*, I presume, are intended to operate as a restraint on new states within the line describd, as well as in their territorial condition. I have been inclind to think, that a distinction existed, under the constitution, between states & territories, as to the right of Congress to impose a restraint: that it might be done as to the latter, but after admitted, that they must have the same rights, as the original states. If this interpretation is the true one, respecting which I shall of course take the opinion of the administration, and such is also the import of the proposed clause, a painful duty may be imposed on me. I shall be glad to have your opinion on the subject.

Before the arrival of Mr King, the discussion was managed with moderation, & the zeal of that party had diminished. He infusd new ardour into it; his own exhibition has lessend his reputation for talents, & patriotism & indeed for morality. He has declard to some, in whom he confided, that it was an effort for power, & it has been intimated, confidentially, that propositions have been made to some of the members of Pena., to induce that state to unite, in this new combination. Other facts are stated, which, if true, & there seems to be no reason to doubt them, place the conduct of the leaders in this scheme in a very reprehensible light. I am inform'd, for example, that Mr Hunter[2] says, that his mind has been confirmd, in the view he has taken of the subject, from his knowledge of the origin of the scheme, & the purposes intended by it.

I really thought, after the successful termination of the late war, that our system might be considerd as having escaped all the perilous trials to which it was inevitably exposed, in its early stages. This is however a new one, of more serious character, especially should the conflict proceed, & these men be supported by the non slave holding states, than any which preceded it. All the members, now voting against their state, will probably be removd, in which case, the majority will be decidedly on that side. Mr Kings doctrines avowed immediate emancipation, & that he should consider the compact broken, if slavery was extended to Missouri. Granger[3] I am told has had much agency in this business. He is a member of the N. Yk. assembly. Your friend

James Monroe

RC (DLC: Rives Collection, Madison Papers). Docketed by JM.

1. *Daily National Intelligencer*, 18 Feb. 1820.

2. William Hunter (1774–1849), a moderate Federalist, was a Rhode Island lawyer who served in the U.S. Senate, 1812–20, where his vote in favor of the Missouri Compromise lost him his seat. Andrew Jackson appointed him chargé d'affaires to Brazil in 1834; he was soon made U.S. minister there and served until 1845.

3. Gideon Granger (1767–1822), a Yale-educated lawyer, was appointed U.S. postmaster general by Jefferson in 1801 and held the post until JM forced his resignation in 1814. Granger was a resident of Canandaigua, New York, in 1820 and served that year in the state senate (*PJM*, 17:130 n. 4).

To Cumberland D. Williams

Sir Montpellier [ca. 22] Feby 1820

I have recd. your favour of Jany. 29.[1] accompanied by the Pamphlet on the subject of a circulating medium.

I have not found it expedient to bestow on the plan proposed the attention necessary to trace the bearings & operation of new arrangements ingeniously combined on a subject which, in its most simple forms, has produced much discussion among political Economists.

It cannot be doubted that a paper currency rigidly limited in its quantity, to purposes absolutely necessary, may be made equal & even superior in value to specie. But experience does not favor a reliance on such experiments. Wherever the paper has not been convertible into specie and its quantity has depended on the policy of the Govt. a depreciation has been produced by an undue increase, or an apprehension of it. The expedient suggested in the pamphlet has the advantage of tying up the hands of the Govt. but besides the possibility of Legislative interferences bursting the fetters, a discretion vested in a few hands over the currency of the nation and of course over the legal value of its property, is liable to powerful objections, and tho' confined to a range of 5 PerCt. would still have room for a degree of error or abuse not a little formidable. The idea also of making a foreign currency depending on a foreign will, and the balance of trade always varying and at no time reducible to a certainty & precision, standards for the national currency, would not easily be admitted.

I am sensible, Sir, that these observations must have been included in your examination of the subject; and that they are to be regarded in no other light than as an expression of the respect & acknowlegement which I pray you to accept for your polite communication.

JAMES MADISON

RC (MdHi); draft (DLC). RC day of month not indicated; conjectural day assigned based on postmark: "Orange CH 22 Feby 1820." Addressed and franked by JM to Williams at Baltimore. Docketed by Williams. Minor differences between the copies have not been noted.

1. *PJM-RS*, 1:595–96.

To James Monroe

DEAR SIR MONTPELLIER Feby. 23. 1820

I received yours of the 19th. on Monday. Genl. Brown, who returned from Monticello on that evening, has been since with me, till 10 OClock today. Your letter found me indisposed from exposure to a cold wind without due precaution; and I have continued so. I write now with a fever on me. These circumstances will account for both the delay & the brevity in complying with your request.

The pinch of the difficulty, in the case stated, seems to be in the words "for ever," coupled with the interdict relating to the Territory North of Lat: 36°. 30.°° If the necessary import of these words be, that they are to operate as a condition on future States admitted into the Union, and as a restriction on them after admission, they seem to encounter, indirectly, the arguments which prevailed in the Senate for an unconditional admission of Missouri. I must conclude therefore from the assent of the Senate to the words, after the strong vote, on constitutional grounds, against the restriction on Missouri, that there is some other mode of explaining them in their actual application.

As to the right of Congs. to apply such a restriction during the *Territorial* periods, it depends on the clause specially providing for the management of those subordinate Establishments.

On one side, it naturally occurs that the right, being given from the necessity of the case, and in suspension of the great principle of self-Govt; ought not to be extended farther, nor continued longer, than the occasion might fairly require.

On the other side, it cannot be denied, that the Constitutional phrase "to make all rules &c." as expounded by uniform practice, is somewhat of a ductile nature, and leaves much to Legislative discretion.

The questions to be decided seem to be 1. whether a *territorial* restriction, be an assumption of illegimate power, or, 2. a misuse of legitimate power: and if the latter only, whether the injury threatened to the nation from an acquiescence in the misuse, or from a frustration of it, be the greater. On the 1st. point there is certainly room for difference of opinion; tho' for myself I must own that I have always leaned to the belief that the restriction was not within the true scope of the constitution. On the alternative presented by the 2d. point, there can be no room with the cool & candid, for blame on those, acquiescing in a conciliatory course; the demand for which was deemed urgent, and the course itself deemed not irreconcileable with the Constitution.

This is the hasty view I have taken of the subject. I am aware that it may be suspected of being influenced by the habit of a guarded construction of Constitutional Powers. And I have certainly felt all the influence that could justly flow from a conviction, that an uncontrouled dispersion of the slaves, now within the U. S., was not only best for the nation, but most favorable for the slaves also, both as to their prospects of emancipation, and as to their condition in the mean time.

The inflammatory conduct of Mr. K.[1] surprizes every one. His general warfare agst. the slaveholding States, and his efforts to disparage the securities derived from the Constitution, were least of all to have been looked for. I have noticed less of recurrence to cotemporary expositions of the Charter, than was to have been expected from the zeal & industry of the Champions in debate. The proceedings of the Virga. Convention have been well sifted: But those of other States ought not to have been overlooked. The Speeches of Mr. King in Massts.[2] & of Mr. Hamilton in N. York[3] shew the ground on which *they* vindicated, particularly, the compound rule of Representation in Congs. And doubtless there are many other evidences of the way of thinking then prevalent, on that & other articles, equally the result of a sense of *equity*, and a spirit of *mutual* concession. Respectfully & affectionately Yours.

JAMES MADISON

RC (DLC: Monroe Papers); draft (DLC). RC docketed by Monroe. Minor differences between the copies have not been noted.

1. Rufus King.

2. King had defended the mechanism of the three-fifths clause in the determination of representation and taxation at the Massachusetts Ratifying Convention of 1788, arguing that "it was the language of America" (*Debates, Resolutions and Other Proceedings of the Convention of the Commonwealth of Massachusetts . . . 1788* [Boston, 1808; Shaw and Shoemaker 15516], 63).

3. In his speech of 20 June 1788 before the New York Ratifying Convention, Alexander Hamilton pointed out the efficacy of the three-fifths clause, which was "one result of the spirit of accommodation, which governed the [Constitutional] Convention; and without this indulgence, no union could have possibly been formed" (*The Debates and Proceedings of the Convention of the State of New-York. . . .* [New York, 1788; Evans 21310], 11, 21, 25–26).

From Elihu F. Marshall

Friend Madison Saratoga Springs 23d. of 2 month 1820.

I hope thou wilt excuse me for intruding on thee by sending thee a copy of the "American Tutor's Assistant"[1] and requesting thee to peruse it. I should not perhaps have done it had I not considered that thou art one that feelest interested in the Literature of the United States. Therefore wilt thou be pleased to examine the Book and send me thy sentiments thereon? By complying with the above request thou wilt very much oblige Thine &c

E. F. Marshall[2]

RC (DLC). Docketed by JM.

1. Elihu F. Marshall, *A Spelling Book of the English Language: or The American Tutor's Assistant; Intended Particularly for the Use of "Common Schools." The Pronunciation Being Adapted to the Much Approved Principles of J. Walker*, 2d ed. (Saratoga Springs, N.Y., 1820; Shoemaker 2110).

2. Elihu F. Marshall (d. 1840), a Quaker born in Easton, New York, moved to Rochester, where he became a writer, printer, and bookseller best known for his spelling book (see n. 1 above). He established a weekly newspaper, the *Rochester Album*, in 1825 and published the paper until it merged with the *Rochester Telegraph* a few years later (*Pittsfield Sun*, 24 Sept. 1840; Frederick Follett, *History of the Press of Western New-York* . . . [Rochester, N.Y., 1847], 47, 49).

To Samuel Wyllys Pomeroy

Sir Montpellier (Virga.) [ca. 29] Feby. 1820

Your favor of the 7th. with the Agricultural pamphlet came duly to hand, and I offer my thanks for them.

The letter on Dairy Farms gives some interesting views of the subject. What relates to the use of the spayed Heifer in place of the Ox, is new to me. If their qualities for draught be such as seems to be attested, they furnish new arguments for making less use of that expensive animal the Horse. That their carcase will be improved for beef comports with analogy.

The case of the Ox-teems [*sic*] as used in the Revolutionary war is in point, as to the aptitude of the Ox for long trips and warm climates; and being of domestic experience & authority, may be expected to combat prejudices with more effect than evidence drawn from distant times or countries. It well merits therefore the attention you allot to it.

I have not yet read the other papers in the publication; but from the subjects of them, & the reputation of the Society, under whose auspices they appear, I regard them as promising me both pleasure & instruction. I tender you, Sir, my friendly respects

James Madison

RC (MWiW-C); FC (DLC). RC day of month not indicated; conjectural day assigned based on postmark: "Orange CH 29 Feby 1820." Addressed and franked by JM to Pomeroy at Brighton, Massachusetts. FC in Dolley Madison's hand, with JM's docket at head of letter.

Madison and Richard Cutts's Financial Difficulties

EDITORIAL NOTE

This letter is the first serious indication of Richard Cutts's financial problems, which eventually led to his bankruptcy and JM's involvement in Cutts's personal affairs.

Cutts, a former U.S. congressman (1801–12) from Saco, Massachusetts, District of Maine, had married Dolley Madison's beloved sister, Anna, in 1804. A member of a prosperous merchant and ship-building family, Cutts engaged in the business but ran into difficulties at the beginning of the War of 1812 when he lost a number of ships (Henry S. Burrage, "Richard Cutts," *Collections and Proceedings of the Maine Historical Society*, 2d ser., 8 [1897]: 1–7, 10, 24–25, 29). JM, who enjoyed an affectionate and trusting relationship with Cutts, appointed him to the position of superintendent general of military supplies in 1813 (*PJM-PS*, 5:123 n. 3). Cutts held that post until 1817, when President Monroe named him second comptroller of the Treasury (*Senate Exec. Proceedings*, 3:92–93).

Cutts launched a number of speculative ventures immediately after the war, using his own funds and those of Dolley Madison, JM, and John Payne Todd. The first amount he borrowed from JM that we have evidence for was in excess of $5,000 (Cutts to JM, 23 Aug. 1816 [MHi]). In April 1817 Cutts signed a promissory note to JM for $7,500 and gave a receipt for a loan of $4,000 more (Promissory Note from Richard Cutts, 4 Apr. 1817, *PJM-RS*, 1:25). Also in that month Dolley Madison loaned an undisclosed amount of John Payne Todd's money to Cutts on his promise that "he would make double if allowed the use of the Money on speculation." This unsecured loan was bitterly recollected later by John Payne Todd (undated memorandum in John Payne Todd's hand, ibid., 25 n.).

In addition, in the presidential years and thereafter, Cutts often acted as JM's agent in Washington during the latter's absence from the city (JM to Cutts, 27 Aug. 1816, MHi). It is likely that Cutts and JM had a reciprocal lending arrangement and called on each other from time to time when their funds were short or extraordinary calls for cash were made on them (see JM to Cutts, 23 July 1817, *PJM-RS*, 1:93–94).

By October 1821 Cutts was in court for default on a note for $2,000; because of his nonpayment of the court's judgment, goods and chattels for that amount were seized in May 1822 by order of the circuit court of the District of Columbia (District Court to Tench Ringgold, 27 May 1822, DNA: RG 21, U.S. District Court of the District of Columbia, box 278, NC-2, entry 6, case papers #79). It was probably sometime between October and May that Dolley Madison wrote Cutts about "the threatening situation of your affairs," pleading with him to secure to her "*all* the *mony lent you*, in a *House*, *Lots*, or some other property, *in case*, you have at this unlucky moment to part with what you possess in Washington." She assured him that he might "⟨*a*⟩*fterwards* command *this* sum, with all that could be ⟨r⟩aised from every source, to *rescue*, or to enrich you, from more fortunate speculations" (NjP: Crane Collection). This Cutts failed to do.

Later, Dolley Madison would recall to her former brother-in-law, John G. Jackson, another of Cutts's creditors, that Anna Cutts "& 4 of her children ware with us last summer, when they flattered themselves with the prospect of a rise in city property & B. Stock & that they would have been able to pay all, & save a fortune—but *she* was entirely ignorent of the extent of his embarisments, or the individuals who would suffer by her Husbands losses" (Dolley Madison to Jackson, 29 Nov. 1822, Mattern and Shulman, *Selected Letters of Dolley Payne Madison*, 247, 404).

The sale of "all his household Furniture" took place at Cutts's house on 5 November 1822 (advertisement of "Marshal's Sale," *Daily National Intelligencer*, 1 Nov. 1822). Dolley Madison had arranged to buy most of the furniture through an agent, Col. George Bomford. Of the $853.06 brought by the sale, Bomford spent $679.31 (List of items bought at the sale of Richard Cutts's furniture, 5 Nov. 1822, DNA: RG 21, U.S. District Court of the District of Columbia, box 278, NC-2, entry 6, case papers #79). In December 1822 Dolley wrote Anna Cutts with the following instructions: "you will tell Colo B. that it is necessary for *him* to write *me* the *transaction* to have the Deed made in my name as well as to transfer *his controul* of the furniture The negro girl, cow, & &. to me so that I may directly reply, by *rects.* or what else he may direct me, as a legal proceeding" (owned by Mrs. George B. Cutts, Wellesley, Mass., 1982). This was done and the purchased items were held in trust for Anna Cutts with Andrew Stevenson as trustee (Trust Fund for Anna Cutts, 2 Apr. 1823 [owned by Charles M. Storey,

Boston, Mass., 1961]). In June 1824 another trust for Anna Cutts was established out of $1,200 in funds provided by her sister, Lucy Washington Todd, and others (Trust Agreement for Anna Cutts, 12 June 1824, Mattern and Shulman, *Selected Letters of Dolley Payne Madison*, 255).

In the meantime, Cutts had advertised the sale of house lots he owned in Washington for public auction in August 1822, but the sale was postponed, first to 20 October, then to 7 November (*Daily National Intelligencer*, 15 and 19 Oct. 1822). By then any hope of liquidating assets and remaining solvent was at an end. Cutts wrote JM on 12 October 1822 that he was ready to declare bankruptcy. JM replied on 14 October that he regretted "most sincerely, the circumstances which compel you to take the step you meditate, as the only resort under the pressure of your debts. I wish it were more in my power to aid you in your distress. Short crops, low prices, and other causes limit my present means, & suggest caution as to future engagements." He went on to say that he had, however, determined "to risk a purchase of the House & lots from the Bank as is proposed," so long as the property titles were clear and Cutts agreed to "appropriate a reasonable portion of your [Cutts's] Salary to a discharge of the debt to the Bank." JM asked Edward Coles to investigate the title and financial arrangements, which he did, reporting in some detail the history of Cutts's financial transactions (Coles to JM, 30 Oct. 1822). On 4 November 1822 JM purchased from the Bank of the United States through Cutts's trustee, Richard Smith, the house on Lafayette Square, where Cutts and his family lived, and additional lots, for $5,750 plus interest, to be paid in four equal installments over four years (JM to Cutts, 4 Nov. 1822; Burrage, "Richard Cutts," *Collections and Proceedings of the Maine Historical Society* 8 [1897]: 25).

Richard Cutts's bankruptcy proceedings awakened an army of creditors who saw JM's purchase of the house and lots as a dodge for Cutts to escape his fiscal responsibilities (notice of bankruptcy, *Daily National Intelligencer*, 22 Oct. 1822). JM was made a party to at least two lawsuits for debt recovery, one of which, despite JM's plea of noninvolvement, carried on until 1828, the other into 1831 (Answers to Charles Edmonston, 1828 [owned by Charles M. Storey, Boston, Mass., 1961]; JM to Nicholas Van Zandt, 31 Oct. 1826, DLC; JM to Richard Cutts, 29 Mar. 1831, NjP: Crane Collection). JM was also faced with requests to intervene with Cutts by friends who had been hurt by Cutts's recklessness (Dolley Madison to John G. Jackson, 29 Nov. 1822, Mattern and Shulman, *Selected Letters of Dolley Payne Madison*, 247; William Thornton to JM, 2 Sept. 1823, DLC).

The Cutts family remained in the house on Lafayette Square, paying rent to JM after Cutts had finally paid off his debts in 1829. That year, however, Cutts suffered another reverse when he was removed from office in the Treasury Department in a wholesale purge of the federal bureaucracy by President Andrew Jackson (JM to Richard Cutts, 13 June 1829 and 19 Mar. 1831, NjP: Crane Collection; Mattern and Shulman, *Selected Letters of Dolley Payne Madison*, 398).

To Richard Cutts

DEAR SIR MONTPR. Mar. 1820

Yours of the 21st. Ult:[1] came duly to hand. I thank you for your attention to the expected papers from Judge Washington. It was not my intention to trouble you with an application to him, but merely to receive & forward the papers which he was to put into your hands.

I have sincerely sympathized with you in your pecuniary difficulties. Whatever inconveniencies may have resulted to myself from them, will be compensated, if the delay in remitting my funds, has essentially aided in saving your own. It will be doubly agreeable if the recruited state of the latter should at no distant day enable you to prepare me for a contingent object which may call for all my disposable resources. In the mean time, I shall be glad if a moment of leasure should make it convenient, to intimate the amount which will be ultimately due. I write this by Payne, whose communications will take the place of all I could add, excepting the assurances I beg you to accept of my constant affection and most sincere wishes for your success & happiness.

JAMES MADISON

RC (MHi).

1. Letter not found.

To James Monroe

DR. SIR MONTPR. Mar. 1820

My nephew R L. Madison has turned his thoughts to the new acquisition expected from Spain on our S. Frontier, and wishes an official situation there which may be convenient for the time and improve his future prospects for a growing family. The reluctance I feel in speaking on all such occasions is heightened on this by the personal relation which may be supposed to bias me. Leaving to other sources therefore the more general information requisite, I will not permit myself to say more than that I consider him as not deficient in talents & that to these have been added a tolerably good education. However agreeable it must of course be to me to see his interests promoted, I can neither expect nor wish it farther than his pretensions may bear the test applied to those of others, and than public considerations will authorize.

Draft (DLC).

To Nicholas Van Zandt

[ca. 1 March 1820]

J Madison presents his respects to Mr Vanzant,[1] with an acknowlegement of the receipt of the acct. of Mr. Clark.[2] After a lapse of eight years from the original date, and a silence for three more, it could not but be unlooked for. It might fairly be presumed that the Newspaper for which the charge is made, was like sundry others, never subscribed for; being voluntarily sent to the Executive of the U. S. from motives other than pecuniary, and not countermanded from respect to the motives. Mr. V. will however oblige J. M. by asertaining whether the paper in question was subscribed for; whether any previous acct. was ever sent; or whether there is ground for inferring that the delays have been occasioned by circumstances sufficiently explaining and justifying them. If the result of the enquiries impose, in the judgement of Mr. V., the slightest obligation, the acct. will be satisfied by an immediate remittance. J. M. & Mrs. M beg Mr. & Mrs. V. to be assured of their sensibility to the kind expressions conveyed in Mr. V.s note,[3] & of the continuance of their best wishes for the happiness of both.

FC (DLC). Undated; conjectural date assigned based on internal evidence and the fact of JM's illness in late February 1820. In Dolley Madison's hand; docketed on verso by JM.

1. Nicholas Biddle Van Zandt (1780–1863), formerly of New York, was married to Martha (Maria) Wood Southall Van Zandt, a cousin of Dolley Madison, and served as John Beckley's principal clerk, 1805–7, when Beckley was clerk of the U.S. House of Representatives and librarian of Congress. Defeated for the clerkship in the first session of the Tenth Congress, and passed over as librarian of Congress in 1807, Van Zandt became a clerk in the General Land Office in Washington, from which he wrote *A Full Description of the Soil, Water, Timber, and Prairies of Each Lot, or Quarter Section of the Military Lands between the Mississippi and Illinois Rivers* (Washington, 1818; Shaw and Shoemaker 46631). He also served as a justice of the peace in the District of Columbia (Smith et al., *Papers of Andrew Jackson*, 7:259 n.; Dolley Madison to Maria Van Zandt, 29 Aug. 1807, *DMDE;* Edmund Berkeley and Dorothy Smith Berkeley, *John Beckley: Zealous Partisan in a Nation Divided* [Philadelphia, 1973], 239, 264, 265 n. 28, 278 and n. 21; William Cabell Bruce, *John Randolph of Roanoke, 1773–1833* [2 vols.; New York, 1922], 1:308; Charles S. Bundy, "A History of the Office of Justice of the Peace in the District of Columbia," *Records of the Columbia Historical Society* 5 [1902]: 281).

2. The reply to JM's inquiries, through Van Zandt, by Darius Clark, the Bennington, Vermont, publisher and editor of the *Green-Mountain Farmer* (later, the *Vermont Gazette*) has not been found. JM described it, however, in his letter to James Monroe, 7 Apr. 1821 (Brigham, *American Newspapers*, 2:1072, 1074–75).

3. Letter not found.

From George W. Featherstonhaugh

Sir Duanesburgh State of New York March 1. 1820.

I have the honour to enclose to You An Address from the Board of Agriculture of the State of New York to the County Societies of the State.[1]

Permit me Sir to request for the Board a printed Copy, if it has been put into the pamphlet Form, of Your eloquent and truly philosophical Address upon Agriculture, which we have Seen only in the publick Papers.

I have also to express a wish on the part of the Board to open a Correspondence with the Agricultural Associations of the State of Virginia, upon all occasions which promise advantage to the Agricultural interests of America.

I have the Satisfaction to add that the institution of our Board of Agriculture, the first and only one I believe in this Country; is a very popular measure here, and that a Bill is now before the Senate of this State, having passed the Assembly, to Extend the provisions of the Act for ten Years. I have the honour to remain Sir With a true respect Your most obt & hble Servant

G W Featherstonhaugh[2]

RC (NN). Docketed by JM.

1. *Address of the General Committee of the Board of Agriculture of the State of New-York, to the County Agricultural Societies, for 1820. With Accompanying Documents* (Albany, N.Y., 1820; Shoemaker 2478). JM's copy, with Featherstonhaugh's presentation inscription, is in the Madison Collection, Special Collections, University of Virginia Library.

2. George William Featherstonhaugh (1780–1866) was an Englishman who married Sarah (Sally) Duane and settled in Duanesburg, New York, near Albany, in 1808, where he farmed on a grand scale. He promoted the idea of a New York state board of agriculture and became its secretary once it was established in 1820. A member of the American Philosophical Society, Featherstonhaugh cultivated an interest in geology and mineralogy throughout his life, accepting an appointment as a U.S. geologist in 1834. Featherstonhaugh remained a British citizen, however, and in 1844 he was appointed British consul at Le Havre, France (Edmund Berkeley and Dorothy Smith Berkeley, *George William Featherstonhaugh: The First U.S. Government Geologist* [Tuscaloosa, Ala., 1988], 1, 13–14, 17, 18–19, 21, 26, 114, 207–8, 271, 317).

From George Joy

Dear Sir, London 1st March 1820

It is so long since I received your last letter,[1] that, tho' carefully preserved, it is out of my immediate reach; and it would take a longer time to get at it than the occasion requires, seeing it's substance, as well as that of your more remote Correspondence is too interesting to be at any time beyond my powers of reminiscence. I am greatly obliged by your efforts in my favor; I assure you, I have more satisfaction in the unsuccessful attempt on your part than I should have had in succeeding without it.[2] Give me a Judge, whose motives for his own Conduct are pure—if he err it will be in my favor; but on the point of intention I am bold to say, he will not err by consulting the mirror in his own breast. I speak of my endeavours to serve my Country without prejudice to the essential interests of any other. The quantum has been small: I wish it were more extensive, and it would have been—I mean that of my endeavours—had the opportunity been given me. The enclosed Correspondence will shew how the business of my appointment in Holland has terminated.[3] There let it rest.

I have always thought that in polemics a man should attend to what is said or written on both sides of the question, and not idly turn his back upon the Arguments opposed to the opinion he may be inclined on a first impulse to espouse; but rather give them a preference in the labor of investigation to counteract the Bias to which we are all subject. Yet, when he has retired from the Duties of active Life, he may be indulged in the perusal of Authors of opinions congenial with his own; which is certainly the more agreable amusement. I therefore send you a work with which I have lately become acquainted;[4] and which I hope you will find an interesting pastime in alternate readings between your Lady & yourself; tho' I must protest (if it fall to your Lot to read the note at the foot of page*[5]) against your robbing the Geese of the Emphasis to place it on the word similar. I dont charge you with many facetia in this gender; yet I remember your recommending the interpolation of a word to produce an effect on an irritable enthusiast of Shakespeare by the name of Myers. I had found what appeared to me sufficient for this purpose in the preface to my Del Pino, where the Author in commending the Language which he could hardly commend too much, whatever might be said of his Grammar, observed of certain Spanish writers—Cervantes, I suppose—perhaps Garcilesso or Lope de Vega, that they were the most sweet Swans from whom Corneille and others in France, and Shakespeare in England had embellished their performances.[6] You advised me to read "surreptitiously embellished &c" and Myers bounced like a parched Pea.

A jocis ad seria:[7] what a state is Spain in at this moment! What a state has she been in for the profitable adjustment of our Concerns! I hope this will be yet effected, peaceably effected, with the Minister now on his way to the U.S. before the Nation shall assume an attitude less favorable to the attainment of our rights. The Insurrection has a formidable appearance—as respects Spain herself any Change must be for the better. I have no Idea of her recovering her Colonies; yet even there there is a portion of the Leven that is hostile to freedom. The monstrous Combination of Church and State has it's ramifications in everything that is or ever was Spanish—for as to the King—(he seems to have no friends; but I am not without a Spice of Compassion for his manifold infirmities;)—what can he desire in which the happiness of the nation is not identified with his own? There are many discordant interests to consult; and he has been a weathercock, but perhaps the wind has blown too strong for him. He went to Spain—so said Lord Castlereagh when badgered by the opposition; and he may be believed on this point, since every crowned head, and every minister at the Congress could have contradicted him if it were otherwise—he went to Spain in the serious intention to confirm the Constitution of the Cortes. But he had not reached his Capital when he was surrounded by Priests and Grandees and others, who persuaded him that it was not the will of the nation. Now if I am afraid to say, against the current of opinion that this was true; I am not prepared to go with the stream in asserting it's falsehood. I wrote you on the first burst of the Spaniards against the usurpation of Buonapartè[8] that it was not liberty they were seeking, but the restoration of Past miserable phantoms of a theocratico-monarchical vice-regency to which they were still the Dupes. The Conduct of their Allies was in no way calculated to eradicate this notion. They hated the English; confounding the Licentiousness of the Soldiery with the theoretical principles of a free government. From the sample before their Eyes they were not likely to fall in love with the System; and they were easily persuaded that these were the effects of an heretical apostacy from the true faith. A few men there may have been among them of sufficient strength of mind to break the Chains of Kingcraft and Priestcraft; and such may have caught the glimmerings of the Light shining in darkness in the neighbouring nations; but the general darkness of their own comprehended it not—so that altho' Lord Erskine is unhappy in brutifying them in Edinburgh[9] at the moment when Quiroga's Proclamation is circulating in London;[10] he is only speaking the Language that most men have spoken, and would continue to speak, but for the tardy Evidence of the March of mind having beat up some recruits in Spain; because, like the food for powder here, they could endure their distresses no longer.

But will the Revolution succeed? I say yes. Such at least is the Preponderance of my opinion—not because the Nation was prepared for it at the time of Ferdinands return; but because of the miseries that they have endured from the opposite System. Adversity has taught them wisdom. What obstructions it may meet, is a question for time to decide. There is the Nemesis of Porlier[11] to appease, and not a few living Victims; and the subjects of the most Catholic King are not specially imbued with christian meekness—on the other hand there will be no Crusade in favor of Ferdinand to excite his subjects to murder him; and he may thus escape the fate of the good Louis XVI—moreover he has a retreat open on the ground abovementioned; and surely there will be some one to remind him of it. The speech of Lord Castlereagh will corroborate his averment;[12] for it is in print, and in a very positive style; tho' I dont find it so generally remembered as it ought to be. I would jog his memory—pauvre Diable, if I were near him. Kingship has been a bad trade of late—they are neither better nor worse than we; and have as much need of all our Charities as the poorest of their subjects have of theirs. The thing beginning with the Army savours somewhat of Imperatorial Elections; but I trust that military Mania are on the decline—true it is they have floated much on the Brain of late; and Buonaparté succeeded for a time in substituting the enthusiasm of martial Glory even for that of Liberty; but the Epidemic is abating in Europe. God forbid that it should rage in our Country. Sad indeed would be the falling off, if a Nation that "Sprung forth a Pallas armed & undefiled"[13] should suffer the Principles that nerved her Arm, to be obscured in the false glare of an Ignis fatuus.[14] The Proclamation of Quiroga, by making the People paramount, says as little however for imperial as for regal usurpation—mais nous verrons.[15]

I shall rejoice to hear from you at your leisure; and a Letter directed to me at No 13 Finsbury Square, or to Mr: Rush, will always find me whether in or out of town; and I shall be happy to be of any use to you; resting always, very faithfully Dear Sir, Your friend & Servt:

G. Joy

P. T. O.

Enclosed

G. Joy to the Secry. of State 4th Novr: 1817
Chargé d' Affaires, at Brussells to G. J. 30 June '19
G. J. to Do. 13 July '19 Extract
Do: to Sec. of State 16th Do.—Do.

To compleat this Correspondence in respect to this Object, there is wanting an Extract of a Letter from Mr: Adams that crossed mine of the 4th Novr: 1817 which is not at hand; but which advised my going to Rotterdam &ca.—see foot of Extracts[16]

In a separate Parcel
Life of Colo: Hutchinson by his Widow 2 Vol: 8vo

RC, two copies, and enclosures, two copies (DLC: Rives Collection, Madison Papers). First RC postmarked "Norfolk VA May 10"; docketed by JM. Second RC in a clerk's hand, except for Joy's emendation, signature, and note: "Duplicate . . . Original with two Octavo Volumes sent under cover to Chas. Mallory Esqre. Collector Norfolk ℘ ship Comet." Minor differences between the copies have not been noted. For enclosures (20 pp.), see n. 3.

1. JM to Joy, 15 Aug. 1817, *PJM-RS*, 1:100–101.

2. In the second RC, the following sentence appears here: "Your appreciation of my humble services is a source of gratification which you know how to estimate."

3. Joy enclosed two copies of the following letters: (1) Joy to John Quincy Adams, 4 Nov. 1817, giving his reasoning for wishing the post of consul general in Holland, discoursing on European politics, and opining on U.S. relations with European powers; (2) Alexander H. Everett to Joy, 30 June 1819, requesting of Joy whether he would be taking up the post of consul at Rotterdam as Consul Wambersie at Oostende had expressed an interest in it; (3) Joy to Everett, 13 July 1819, relinquishing the post at Rotterdam in favor of Wambersie; and (4) an extract of Joy to Adams, 16 July 1819, noting that Joy had been willing to go to Rotterdam, but he "should have very soon demanded a successor." For the history of Joy's interest in the post, see his letters to JM of 10 May and 17 June 1817, *PJM-RS*, 1:45–46, 61–62.

4. Lucy Apsley Hutchinson, *Memoirs of the Life of Colonel Hutchinson . . . With Original Anecdotes of Many of the Most Distinguished of His Contemporaries, and a Summary Review of Public Affairs* . . . , 3d ed. (2 vols.; London, 1810).

5. Joy placed an asterisk here and at the bottom of the letter's last page wrote: "*I cannot find this in the present Edition; and the Editor, notwithstanding his assurance (preface page v) has, no doubt, suppressed it; but I read it in the large paper Quarto in Wiltshire—it is indeed very trite; but, having noticed, I must give it to prevent the trouble of a research. I think it is an extension of the note b at the foot of page 277 V. 1 of this Edition. Vizt. that it was probably suggestd by the Author, who was a great reader of the Classics, and probably remembered that a similar watchfulness of the Geese saved the Roman Capitol."

6. Hipólito San Joseph Giral del Pino, *A New Spanish Grammar; or, The Elements of the Spanish Language* . . . , 3d ed. (London, 1787), xv.

7. *A jocis ad seria:* from jokes to serious matters.

8. In a letter Joy wrote to JM on 17 Sept. 1808, he noted in regard to the Spanish uprising against the French that "instead of a People rising to assert their own rights, the metaphorical standard of an absent Crown was set up; and at this time or shortly after it appeared that they were dedicating Victories to the holy Mother of the true Prince of Peace, by some modern title which I had never before heard, and have already forgotten" (DLC).

9. At a dinner given for Thomas Erskine, first Baron Erskine of Restormel (1750–1823), in Edinburgh on 21 Feb. 1820, Lord Erskine remarked to the assembled guests that "if he [Ferdinand] had stuck by the Cortes, he would have saved his empire in South America; and if he established it even now, the danger in Spain would be, that the people would still be not sufficiently free, having been brutified so long by the despotism to which they have submitted" (*Times* [London], 1 Mar. 1820).

10. Antonio Quiroga (1784–1841) was a Spanish army officer and veteran of the Napoleonic wars who, along with Rafael del Riego y Núñez, launched an uprising in 1820 that eventually forced Ferdinand VII to accept the Constitution of 1812. Quiroga issued many proclamations, but Joy is probably referring to that of 5 Jan. 1820, in which Quiroga called on the army to rise against "a tyrannical and arbitrary Government, which disposes at will of the properties, the existence, and the liberties of the unhappy Spaniards" (*Biographie universelle* [1843–65 ed.], 34:675–76; *Times* [London], 16 Feb. 1820).

11. Juan Díaz Porlier (1788–1815) was a Spanish army officer who fought as a guerrilla general against the French army, 1808–13. Disappointed in the postwar political situation, he led his troops in 1815 from Coruña in an attempt to unseat Ferdinand VII, but the insurrection failed, and Díaz Porlier was condemned and hanged (Rodolfo G. de Barthèlemy, *"El marquesito" Juan Díaz Porlier: "General que fue de los ejercitos nacionales . . ." [1788–1815]* [2 vols.; Santiago de Compostela, Spain, 1995], 1:17, 31, 65–68, 355, 2:444, 449–53, 542, 547, 585, 588).

12. Joy may have been referring here to Lord Castlereagh's defense of Ferdinand VII and British policy toward Spain in reply to a motion of 15 Feb. 1816 by Henry Brougham,

requesting British intervention against the king of Spain and his measures (*Times* [London], 16 Feb. 1816).

13. "Can tyrants but by tyrants conquered be, / And Freedom find no champion and no child / Such as Columbia saw arise when she / Sprung forth a Pallas, armed and undefiled?" (George Gordon Byron, "Childe Harold's Pilgrimage," stanza 96, lines 856–59, in Jerome J. McGann, ed., *Lord Byron: The Complete Poetical Works* [7 vols.; Oxford, 1980–93], 2:156).

14. *Ignis fatuus:* something that confuses or misleads.

15. *Mais nous verrons:* but we shall see.

16. This paragraph is omitted from the second RC. The note continues: "if I wished for Consular Emoluments, or the like—to this I considered my said Letter as furnishing a reply; and it was to this last, among others, that a reply was promised on the annexed Conditions; but time is above being made, and that which is ready made will halt for no one; but glides on

"ut Unda impellitur Unda Urgeturque prior venientem, urgetq. priorem. [as wave is pushed on by wave, and as each wave as it comes is both pressed on and itself presses the wave in front] (Ovid, *Metamorphoses* 15.180–82 [Loeb Classical Library, 2:376–77])—it has therefore never yet brought me the promised Communication."

From Noah Webster

Amherst, Hampshire County,
Sir, in Massachusetts. March 1st. 1820.

Your letter without date, but bearing the post mark Jany. 18. 1820,[1] & addressed to me at New Haven, reached me while in Boston attending the legislature, at their late Session. You will see by the place of the date of this Letter that I reside in Massachusetts. I did not answer your letter while I was in Boston; as I had not with me the letter of which you request a copy. I trust this circumstance will be accepted as an apology for the delay.

I know not, Sir, where a copy of the "Sketches of American Policy" can now be obtained. I have a single copy only, bound with other pamphlets.

I have one Copy of Pelatiah Websters "Dissertation on the Political Union & Constitution of the thirteen United States," published in 1783. but it is bound with other pamphlets. He wrote also "Essays on Free Trade & finance" in 1780—but I do not find them among my pamphlets. By advertising for them in Philadelphia, they may perhaps be obtained. The former is the pamphlet for your purpose.

In my letter to you Augt. 20. 1804. I observe an error, in suggesting that you brought forward in 1785 the proposal for a new frame of government—instead of saying that you brought forward a proposition for a Convention of Commissioners to frame commercial regulations—which measure was carried into effect.

Inclosed is a copy of your letter which I have compared with the original—one word only being illegible—is left blank.

That your remaining days may be rendered useful in illustrating the history of the great events which have distinguished the last half century, in many of which you have been personally concerned—& that you may enjoy great satisfaction in beholding the rising greatness of our common country is the sincere wish of Sir, your most Obedt Servt

N WEBSTER

RC (DLC: Rives Collection, Madison Papers). Docketed by JM.

1. *PJM-RS*, 1:588.

From Jethro Wood

ESTEEMED FRIEND POPLAR RIDGE CAYUGA COUNTY 3 mo 2, 1820

Amongst the materials for domestic manufactures *flax* occupies an important place. The manner of preparing it however, in this Country is very imperfect; and inconsequence the value of the Crop is variable and uncertain. The process of *water* roting whether it has been owing to the great care which is necessary both in respect to *time* and the manner of *handling* it in that soft state or whether it has been owing to other Causes, has never been generally introduced; and from that of *dew rotting*, the fibre is not only often obtained harsh and weak, but sometimes it is totally lost in the snows of winter.

Impressed by these Considerations the President of the Cayuga County Agricultural Society has requested me to ask for such information as thou may possess on the subject of dressing flax *without roting*.[1] We have seen specimens which were prepared in this manner, much superior in both softness and strength to the Common material; but the result of our enquiries into the minutia of the process has not been satisfactory. Every detail relative to this business will be interesting. Please direct to Poplar Ridge Post Office. I am very respectfully thy friend

JETHRO WOOD[2]
Corresponding Secretary of said Society

RC (DLC). Docketed by JM.

1. Retting flax stalk is the process by which the flax fiber is separated from the woody material and softened, usually by steeping in water (John Warnes, *On the Cultivation of Flax; The Fattening of Cattle with Native Produce; Box-Feeding; and Summer-Grazing*, 2d ed. [London, 1847], 116–18).

2. Jethro Wood (1774–1834) was a New York farmer and inventor who is best known for his improvements to the cast-iron plow, which were widely adopted.

From William S. Cardell

Dear Sir, New york 4th: March 1820

Though my name is signed individually to the enclosed circular[1] you will not, unknown to you as I am, consider me as acting without the concurrence of the first Scholars and the first citizens in this vicinity. The subject is considered as resting on its own merits or I should have asked a distinguished gentleman personally acquainted with you to enclose my letter.

There is a particular anxiety in organizing such an institution to give it all the weight of character and talent possible. Mr: Jefferson is requested to accept the Presidency. Should he decline from age or any other circumstance, the wish is unanimous and we hope it will not be considered as asking too much to request, that the Society may have the Sanction of your name as President, or as first vice President, should Mr: Jefferson accept. His answer is daily expected.

Your opportunities, Sir have been very great for knowing the leading scholars of our country. You will confer a particular favour by mentioning the names of such gentlemen, particularly in the Southern and western states, as you think most likely to be creditable and useful as members of such an institution. With the highest Consideration and respect I am yours

W. S. Cardell[2]

RC (DLC). Docketed by JM.

1. The enclosure, a two-page printed circular dated 25 Feb. 1820, invited the recipient to join in creating an American Academy of Language and Belles Lettres, designed to "guard against local or foreign corruptions" of the English language, to "correct such as already exist, to settle varying orthography, determine the use of doubtful words and phrases, and generally, to form and maintain as far as practicable, an English standard of writing and pronunciation" (DLC: Madison Collection, Rare Book and Special Collections Division).

2. William S. Cardell (d. 1828), author of readers and spellers for schoolchildren, was one of a number of grammarians in the 1820s who sought to rescue written and spoken English from polite usage, arguing that reason, and not custom, should be language's arbiter (*Daily National Intelligencer*, 15 Aug. 1828; Kenneth Cmiel, *Democratic Eloquence: The Fight Over Popular Speech in Nineteenth-Century America* [New York, 1990], 76).

To William S. Cardell

Sir [post–6] Mar. 1820

I have recd. your favor of the 4th. inclosing a printed copy of a circular address on the subject of a "National Philological Academy."

The object of such an Institution well recommends it to favorable attention. To provide for the purity, the uniformity, & the stability of language, is of great importance under many aspects; and especially as an encouragement to genius & to literary labours by extending the prospect of just rewards. A universal and immortal language is among the wishes never likely to be gratified: But all languages are more or less susceptible of improvement and of preservation; and none can be better entitled to the means of perfecting & fixing it, than that common to this Country & G. Britain, since there is none that seems destined for a greater & freer portion of the human family. This consideration alone makes it desirable, that instead of allowing this common tongue to be gradually fashioned into distinct ones, or even to diverge into different dialects, there should be at least a tacit co-operation in perpetuating its identity by a joint standard. No obstacle on the side of G. B. can arise from the present ascendancy of British over American literature and population. Whilst it must be flattering to both nations to contemplate the prospect of covering with their posterity & their language, a greater space on the earth, than any other nation, it is obvious that a few years will transfer the ascendancy to the U. S. with respect to the number of people, and that a period of years, may be calculated to have a like effect as to the number devoting themselves to scientific & literary pursuits.

From this view of the subject you will not doubt my cordial wishes for the success of the projected Academy, nor the sense I have of the honorary relation to it, held out to me. Foreseeing at the same time, as I can not but do, that in accepting it, I should be a nominal functionary only, and in the way of some other choice which might justify the distinction by the services due from it, I must hope to be excused for requesting that my name may not be proposed as suggested by your partiality & politeness.

I know not well what to say in answer to your request of names worthy of being associated in the proposed Institution. I am not sure that any occur to me at present who are not sufficiently known to the public; nor can I lose sight of the risk of doing injustice by omissions of which I should be unconscious. I shall not be backward nevertheless in contributing any future aid on this head, which my better recollections, or further information, may put in my power.

Draft (DLC). Day of month not indicated; conjectural day assigned based on internal evidence and Cardell's 4 Mar. letter to JM, postmarked "Mar 6."

To George W. Featherstonhaugh

Dear Sir June [7 March] 1820

I have recd. your favor of the 1st. inst; with the pamphlet, containing the "Address from the Board of Agriculture of the State of N. York to the County Societies."

I thank you, Sir, for the Communication. The Address seems happily calculated as well to dissuade from the fallacious pursuits which have been so extensively injurious, as to cherish a zeal for the one most essential to the public prosperity; and which gives at the same time the best assurance of individual success.

It is truly gratifying to see the interest now generally taken in Rural Economics. The extent in which the State of N. York has patronized the study & practice of them is highly creditable to its liberality, and merits the more attention as it forms a ground of instructive comparison with the experiments left by other States to the unaided associations of patriotic individuals. Thus far the experiment in the latter form has a promising aspect with us. But it is of too recent a commencement for any final inference with regard to its comparative success.

I shall deposit the publication for which I am indebted with the Board to which I belong; not doubting that it will readily accept the proffered correspondence with that of N. York. I have as little reason to doubt a similar disposition of the other Societies within the State.

I can not at present send you the Document requested in a Pamphlet form. As soon as I can procure a copy, it shall be put under a cover and forwarded. Be pleased to accept &c &

J M.

FC (DLC). Incorrectly dated June 1820. Corrected date based on the RC, dated "[7] Mar. 1820," offered for sale in the *Gerard A. J. Stodolski, Inc., Catalogue Two* (Manchester, N.H., [1993]), and Featherstonhaugh to JM, 1 Mar. 1820.

From Tench Coxe

Dear Sir Philada. March 7. 1820.

During your investiture with the office of President you were so good as to confer the appointments of Midshipman on two of my Sons. One of them, Henry Sidney Coxe on the return of Peace was induced by me to withdraw as I feared the influence of the severities of the service, would certainly deprive the family, his father & himself of his life. His symptoms were decidedly hectic. I induced him to yield to parental anxiety, and he has ⟨hired?⟩ with an extensive shipping house, which built, equipt and dispatched every variety of vessels to India, the Pacific, the Levant & other ports, and has acquired much of that intimacy with navigation, building & equipping vessels, officers and seamen of our commercial marine, and all those things in regard to the mercantile business *on the ocean*, which are excellent preparations for the naval service. His health is restored and confirmed. His attachment to the navy is uninterrupted and increased. He has prevailed on me to consent to his return to his old station or accepting a new appointment as it may be offered or granted. I have addressed the President, the Secy of the Navy & his principal assistant requesting his restoration to the warrant granted him in 1815; or may be ⟨regular?⟩ a new appointment. His impressions of the most respectful attachment which in common with very many old friends he knows I cherish for your person and character has occasioned him to hope that you would communicate with Mr. Monroe on the subject. These occasions for aid in life seriously remain, on which ground and your general knowledge of the course of my life have determined me to submit his request with my own to your consideration. Whatever may appear proper to be done will have the best effect if done at an early day. The obvious advantage of the old warrant and station renders it very desireable to have that allowed, which he still possesses, uncancelled.

Since I trouble you, my dear Sir, with a letter let me first present my most respectful and my affectionate remembrances to Mrs. Madison: and then give you a little view of my latter sentiments, feelings, opinions & course.

I have been deeply impressed with the delicacy, importance, and high inconveniencies of the agitation of the *Missouri question*. I cannot perceive the right and power of Congress to impose the restriction upon her in the constitutional form; especially within the limits [of] the Louisa. cession. The policy of the friends of the Africans should be to promote their diffusion, in order to facilitate and render safe, at the earliest day, their gradual abolition. Many of our lawyers, of both parties, disbelieve in the right of Congress to impose the restriction and numbers of our citizens, who have attended to the constitutions & their legal foundations refused to sign the petition for the restriction. In regard to the Africans an idea, of late has much interested me. I wish they may adopt the African colonization plan with success, but I do not expect from that operation any material or extensive advantages. They will not go. Their friends will not subscribe except it be to send slaves back. But let this and every other measure to diminish their numbers be adopted. Among others the idea presented in the enclosed paper signed Columbus[1] has induced me to devote an evening to the concoction of it. You will find it in *the Recorder* pages 132 & 133 under the signature of Columbus. The paper has been selected because it has a very confined circulation, and I wished not to agitate the subject with any public excitement. If I could shave money I would have printed on a folded sheet, 100 or 200 copies for use among the most discreet and influential. I shall give perhaps one or two more guarded numbers. It may be best to divide, or to promote such settlements, in the interior counties of each state.

During the last year, I found my interest in the subject of *the vine* encrease. You will remember or perceive, in the introductory letter to Mr. Gallatin, prefixed to the digest of the returns of manufactures by the Marshals in 1810, some printed notices of the vine and its fabrications.[2] I have agitated the subject with the french here, who came out in consequence of the revolutions of 1814 & 1815. They probably determined on the Alabama vine operation in consequence.[3] I presented them and their American connexions with this work at an early day after their arrival. During the last year I extended my enquiries, and published my facts, arguments, and considerations, in the national intelligencer in 8 numbers, in the Months of November or December 1819, and Jany 1820, under the signature of "*a friend to the National Industry*."[4] My caption was ["]Thoughts concerning the grape vine, and its wines, brandies, salts, and dried fruits" or something like that title. You may have seen the numbers. I have convinced myself, that tho our cotton sold in the highest year, in our ports for shipment & home consumption for 42 millions of dollars, and will bring in this year perhaps 20.000.000 Drs. yet our capacity for the vine, is actually much more valuable, than what cotton has yet proved in money. France, I feel convinced, has not a better climate for the vine than ours is & is becoming by clearing and draining: and we have vastly more soil to spare to it. Yet to France, according to Rozier edited and enlarged by Chaptal,[5] the vine & its various fabrications abovementioned, are worth 100 millions of our dollars. I beg leave to recommend to your consideration and that of your agricultural society, the serious examination of my facts, and a scrutiny into my arguments as they appear in those papers.

The numbers are all in my hands, and I could print 1000 copies on the pamphlets of them, in 32 pages each for 100 dollars, if it were subscribed. I used to do these things and have spent 1000 dollars in my time in that sort of useful publication, always presenting them to the right persons, but I cannot now spare or find the money. It is a matter of the deepest importance to our agriculture to strike out new objects of cultivation to prevent redundance. If so much industry were not applied to the Cane, Cotton, Indigo, Rice, and Tobacco, our grain & cattle & orchard farming would be deeply injured. The cheapness of foreign labor in Hindostan, South Russia (on the black sea) Italy &c will try us severely. Russia shipt from the black sea, in a year since the peace, 16.000.000 of bushells of wheat, raised by people paid 25 dollars ℔ ann: for a farmers, his wifes & his childrens wages they finding themselves in house, bed & board. The superiority of our manufacture of flour is our great present protection. The distillery & brewery the next support of grain.

Our manufactures have had a share of my close attention. I remain convinced that they are not, in general, in need of more protection than necessary revenue drawn from foreign goods does and will (wth. the charges of importation[)] give them. This is proved by our shipping no raw material (no iron, hides, skins, flax, hemp, silk, wool, rags, or lead) in the last returned year. All were and are manufactured. All are too high to be shipt to any foreign country. Cotton alone is redundant. It is to be considered, whether upon mere agricultural policy, we ought not to force the manufacture of any landed production, of which we cannot find Consumers abroad. You know, Sir, my opinions concerning the ultimate influence of India cotton produced where labor of man is 3 to 5 cents ℔ diem, without bed or board; a man, plough, and cattle the man finding himself and cattle, can be hired at four pence sterling ℔ day. The power of machinery to consume cotton is perfectly well known. I consider my mind as having progressively reached sound & strong ground, it appears, from the necessity to aid redundant & depressed production like cotton; and tobacco and grain, and the perishable like fruit or the orchard, & on the other hand from the absence of the necessity to force the manufacture of those articles of which [we] cannot produce enough, such as wool, flax, hemp, skins, iron, lead rags and silk. On these last when foreign the necessary revenue being imposed, gives the manufacturers very considerable encouragement, such as no one thought of [in] 1789. Agriculture, the laborer, the improver, the industrious, the frugal cannot wisely be burdened to promote more rapidly our great & growing manufactures.

Spain, the letters about which of Jan. 3. 5 & 6 here are surely serious,[6] is not in a way to be troublesome to us. Their naval Arsenal at Carracas near Cadiz is their best and most necessary at this moment. The army of Andalusia is disjointed as to the Crown, and embodied anew by the patriots. I wish their wise King had been wiser with the Cortes & with us. I have the honor to be dear Sir your most faithful servant

T. Coxe

RC (DLC). Docketed by JM.

1. Coxe's essay, "Civilization," signed "Columbus," published in the Philadelphia *National Recorder*, 26 Feb. 1820, called for the establishment of a "new Africa," government reservations for African-Americans in the remote western territories of North America (Cooke, *Tench Coxe*, 515 and n. 18).

2. Coxe referred here to the section on wine and grape cultivation in his *Statement of the Arts and Manufactures of the United States of America for the Year 1810* (Philadelphia, 1814; Shaw and Shoemaker 31257), 39–40.

3. On 3 Mar. 1817 JM signed into law an act granting a group of French Bonapartists, including a number of military officers of high rank, four townships in the Creek Cession in the Alabama Territory, "for the encouragement of the cultivation of the vine and olive." By 1822, few of the original participants in the Vine and Olive Colony, as it was known, had settled there, and most had abandoned their grants (Rafe Blaufarb, *Bonapartists in the Borderlands: French Exiles and Refugees on the Gulf Coast, 1815–1835* [Tuscaloosa, Ala., 2005], 48, 117–18).

4. Coxe's essays on wine cultivation appeared in the *Daily National Intelligencer* on 6, 10, 13, 16, and 19 Nov., and 2, 15, and 31 Dec. 1819.

5. Coxe referred here to one of the many editions variously titled of Jean-Antoine-Claude Chaptal et al., *Traité théorique et pratique sur la culture de la vigne; avec l'art de faire le vin, les eaux-de-vie, esprit-de-vin, vinaigres simples et composés . . .* (2 vols.; Paris, 1801).

6. Letters and a journal from Spain of those dates announcing the army revolt against Ferdinand VII, originally published in the *Philadelphia Gazette*, were reprinted in *Niles' Weekly Register* 18 (4 Mar. 1820): 1–2.

To James Monroe

DEAR SIR MONTPR. Mar. 15. 1820

Whilst I was in the Government at Washington, Henry Sidney Coxe, a son of Mr. Tench Coxe, was appointed a Midshipman. On the return of peace, ill health, brought on by the severities of the service, and the advice of his father prevailed on him to retire. His father states that his health is now re-established, and that his attachment to the navy having never ceased, it is the wish of both, that he could resume his former Station, or be gratified with a new appointment; for which his latter situation in an extensive shipping House is supposed to have rather cultivated than impaired his qualifications. I am equally aware that difficulties may attend the case, and that your personal dispositions may be as favorable as public considerations will allow; and that I ought on these as well as other accounts to make an apology for troubling you with a word on the subject. But having been long acquainted with Mr. Coxe, and with his indefatigable labors, I believe I may truly say, with his important services, on occasions deeply interesting to his Country, I could not decline this expression of good will to him, and to his son, who if my impressions be correct, was found by his character & conduct, to have well justified the appointment he formerly received.

As I know not that I shall have a better occasion, I will take another liberty for which another, & perhaps a greater apology is due. Burwell Randolph a son of Mrs. D. M. Randolph,[1] has been some time at Washington in the hope of finding employment in some of the public offices. You are apprized of all the circumstances which naturally excite within a certain sphere, an interest in behalf of both the Mother & the son who is represented as adding to a fitness for employment, a laudable anxiety to discharge his filial debts, by contributing to the support of the family of which he is a member. In saying that a peculiar apology might be due for this obtrusion, I had in view the circumstance that appointments such as that in question, are extraneous to your functions. But as opportunities sometimes occur, in which a knowlege that a candidate was thought favorably of by the President, might properly turn the scale in the hand of the appointing functionary, I have ventured on what it was wished that I should intimate. I do it however in this as in all cases with the reserves dictated by my knowlege of the delicacy of your situation, and my ignorance of the rival pretensions before you.

The public prints announce that your youngest daughter has just made her choice of a son in law for you.[2] So many circumstances concur in assuring Mrs. Madison & myself of her success in pleasing her parents as well as in providing for her own happiness, that we offer without stint, our congratulations on the event to all to whom they are due. Health & prosperity

James Madison

RC (UkLoBM); draft (DLC). Minor differences between the copies have not been noted.

1. JM had appointed Burwell Starke Randolph (1800–1854) a midshipman in the U.S. Navy in 1815, but a fall left him crippled and he was forced to resign in 1817. He was the son of Mary (Molly) Randolph Randolph (1762–1828), the sister of Thomas Mann Randolph and wife of David Meade Randolph. After her husband's bankruptcy in 1808, Mary Randolph opened a boardinghouse in Richmond. In 1820 she moved to Washington to live with her son, William Beverley Randolph, who was employed as a clerk in the Treasury Department. She published *The Virginia House-Wife*, one of the first American cookbooks, in 1824 ("Randolph Family," *WMQ*, 1st ser., 9 [1901]: 250; Callahan, *List of Officers of the Navy*, 452; Jonathan Daniels, *The Randolphs of Virginia* [Garden City, N.Y., 1972], 247–48; Mattern and Shulman, *Selected Letters of Dolley Payne Madison*, 411).

2. Maria Hester Monroe married her cousin, Samuel L. Gouverneur of New York, President Monroe's private secretary, in a private ceremony at the President's House on 9 Mar. 1820 (Ammon, *James Monroe*, 405, 407; *Daily National Intelligencer*, 11 Mar. 1820).

From Martin Van Buren

Sir, Albany March 15th. 1820.

An election of a chief magistrate for this state of more than ordinary interest is approaching. The Republican members of our Legislature have nominated Daniel D. Tompkins[1] as their candidate for that station. A leading motive (independent of his fitness for the station) which has induced to this selection, was a strong desire in the people of this state, to renew the expression of their gratitude for the distinguished services rendered to his country by the Vice President during the late war—a war by the successful prosecution and honorable termination of which, the public welfare was so much promoted & our national character elevated. As the greatest efforts have been made and are making to detract from his merits in this particular, it is deemed but just by the meeting which has nominated Mr. Tompkins, that the evidence of his devotion to the cause of his country at that eventful & highly interesting period, should in its fullest extent be submitted to the people.

The difficulties—the embarrassments—& the responsibilities of his situation as Chief magistrate of this state in the fall of 1814 are well known. We are informed that an opportunity was at that time presented to him to extricate himself from those embarrassments with credit & honor by accepting a seat in the national cabinet tendered to him by you, but that from a consciousness of being best able to serve his country in the station confided to him by the people, he declined your flattering offer and persevered in labours from which the public cause received the greatest aid, and in consequence of which he has been subjected to the most virulent and unmerited reproaches.

As chairman of the meeting at which Mr. Tompkins was nominated, I am requested respectfully to solicit from you, for publication, a copy of the correspondence between yourself and the Vice President on this Subject.[2]

We are not aware that any objection exists to a compliance with our wishes. Should you however think otherwise, we trust our error in this particular will be attributed to its true source—a strong solicitude to do ample justice to a citizen for whose services New York cherishes sentiments of the warmest gratitude, and for whom she is proud to acknowledge respect.

Be pleased to accept, Sir, in behalf of those for whom I act, their acknowledgment of the invaluable services you have rendered to your country, and the expression of their lively solicitude for your future health & happiness. With great respect & esteem, I have the honor to be Your obedient & very humble servant

M. V. Buren[3]

RC (DLC). In a clerk's hand, signed by Van Buren. Cover addressed by Van Buren to JM at "Orange Court-house Virginia." Docketed by JM.

1. Daniel D. Tompkins (1774–1825) was governor of New York, 1807–17, and vice president of the United States, 1817–25. A strong supporter of JM's administration and the War of 1812, Tompkins bolstered his state's war effort with his personal fortune but bitterly disappointed JM by refusing the president's offer to become secretary of state in 1814 (*PJM-PS*, 5:134 n. 2; Ray W. Irwin, *Daniel D. Tompkins: Governor of New York and Vice President of the United States* (New York, 1968), 1, 54–55, 134–35, 167, 180–81, 196, 210–12, 305).

2. JM's letters to Tompkins of 28 Sept. and 18 Oct. 1814, and those of Tompkins to JM of 6 and 8 Oct. 1814, the latter in the form of an extract, along with JM's cover letter to Van Buren of 27 Mar. 1820, were published in the *Daily National Intelligencer*, 25 Apr. 1820.

3. Martin Van Buren (1782–1862) was a New York lawyer and politician who served as U.S. senator, 1821–28, as governor of New York, 1 Jan. to 5 Mar. 1829, as U.S. secretary of state, 1829–32, and subsequently as vice president, 1832–36, and president, 1836–40 (Sobel and Raimo, *Biographical Directory of the Governors*, 3:1075–76).

From Martin Van Buren

DEAR SIR, ALBANY March 15th. 1820.

The friends of the Vice President deem the publication of the correspondence I have referred to, important, but he feels a delicacy to permit its publication without your consent. To meet the circumstance of your not having the letters in your possession, I take the liberty of enclosing copies which have been taken from the Vice President's letter book. I am fully aware, Sir, of your aversion to connecting yourself at this time with the party politics of the day, and did I consider the expression of your opinion on the merits of Governor Tompkins' services during the late war as having, in the least degree, that tendency, I should be the last person who could be induced to impose on you the necessity of declining it. But thinking otherwise, I will throw myself on your indulgence in suggesting the high gratification, which that portion of our citizens who look to their conduct during that most interesting period of your administration, as the proudest of their lives, would derive, from learning that the services rendered by the Vice President to his country during the war, are as highly estimated by you as they are by them.

Permit me, Sir, to repeat in this note my veneration for your public character, and the devotion with which I am Your very obedient and very humble Servant,

M. V. BUREN

RC (DLC); draft (DLC: Martin Van Buren Papers). RC in a clerk's hand, signed and addressed by Van Buren. Draft docketed: "Dr Private letter to Mr Madison." Minor differences between the copies have not been noted.

To Tench Coxe

DEAR SIR MONTPELLIER Mar. 20. 1820

On the receipt of yours of the 7th. I dropped a few lines to the President on the subject of your son. I did it however rather in compliance with your desire, than from a doubt that his own dispositions would be as favorable as circumstances will permit. I sincerely wish that nothing in those may oppose the object you have so much as so justly at heart.

I am glad to find you still sparing moments for subjects interesting to the public welfare. The remarks on the thorney one to which you refer in the "National Recorder," seem to present the best arrangemt for the unfortunate part of our population whose case has enlisted the anxiety of so many benevolent minds, next to that which provides a foreign outlet and location for them. I have long thought that our vacant territory was the resource which in some mode or other was most applicable and adequate as a gradual cure for the portentous evil; without however being unaware that even that would encounter serious difficulties of different sorts.

I had noticed the views published in the National Intelligencer on the culture of the Vine, and conjectured the source to which they were to be credited. I heartily wish they may engage the same public attention, and with the same success as distinguished the efforts in behalf of the article of Cotton: but it can scarcely be hoped that a progress equally rapid will take place in the case of the vine as was experienced in the other. I believe I have heretofore expressed my anticipation of a decreasing market for all our great staples for exportation, and of the consequent necessity, of directing our labour to other objects. The vine would add a very important one, as you have shewn, to the manufacturing substitutes. With respect to these I concur in the opinion which I take to be yours, that the zeal of some of their advocates has pushed them beyond the practicable & eligible limit; whilst others have run into the opposite extreme, by allowing no exceptions to a just theory. A middle course difficult to be defined, and more difficult to be made the basis of a compromise in the National Councils & in the public opinion, would in this as in most cases, be the advisable one. After all I fear the greatest obstacle to domestic manufactures lies where it has not been sufficiently adverted to, and where it will be found most difficult to overcome it; I mean, in the credit which the foreign capital gives in the sale of imported manufactures. Our manufacturers giving little or no credit to the retail merchants, these must do the same to the consumer. The importing merchants, by the credits they enjoy, enabling the retailers to grant correspondent indulgences, the foreign fabrics readily exclude or supplant the domestic in the general consumption; notwithstanding the preference due to the quality & price of the domestic. I am led to believe that apart from the difference between the credit & cash sales, the market for the domestic would rapidly extend itself. There seems to be an additional circumstance not friendly to the household branch more than to our Spinning Establishments. The sale of yarns being of less importance to the retail merchants through the Country, than that of imported stuffs, they are not interested in favoring the household Looms by keeping on hand the spun material.

It is proposed in Congress, I see, to invigorate the Statutory contest with G. B. for a reciprocity in the W. Inda. trade, in which the address of the latter has thus far parried the measures on this side.[1] Perseverance in counteracting her Protean expedients can not fail of ultimate success. But the peace & plenty now enjoyed in Europe, and still more the supplies attainable from Canada, and from the contiguous parts of the U. S. now become so productive, *through* Canada, may render the contest more obstinate than might have happened at periods when the dependence of the Islands on our exports was more acutely felt. Be pleased to accept my best wishes and be assured of my great esteem & respect.

James Madison

RC (Sotheby's, New York, N.Y., 1990); FC (DLC). RC docketed by Coxe. FC in Dolley Madison's hand; emended and intitialed by JM, with his note "(Copy)," and docket "Tench Coxe Esqr." Minor differences between the copies have not been noted.

1. On 10 Mar. 1820 Rufus King submitted two resolutions to the U.S. Senate. The first would have extended the restrictions of the navigation act passed in April 1818 to Bermuda and all the British colonies in the West Indies. The second would have banned foreign goods imported from Bermuda and the British West Indies as well as New Brunswick, Nova Scotia, and Newfoundland, that were not "truly of the growth, produce, or manufacture, of the province, colony, or place from which the same shall be directly imported into the United States" (*Annals of Congress*, 16th Cong., 1st sess., 489, 491–92). These measures were aimed at British regulations that targeted U.S. commerce. For a detailed discussion, see Benns, "Study No. 56: The American Struggle for the British West India Carrying-Trade," *Indiana University Studies* 10 [1923]:64–70).

From Robert Slaughter Jr.

Sir, Culpeper. 20th. March 1820

You will no doubt be surpris'd on reading this and at the same time think it assuming in me to be thus intermedling in other peoples affairs in which I have no concern but the motive I hope will be taken in its proper point of view and plead an apology.

The Death of the late Mr. Alexr. Shepherd[1] has I am afraid left his family (which now too frequently happins) in a very distressd situation. From what information I have the Widow and 5 Children will have for their support only her Dower right in 700. Acres of Land.

Communicating with her on her future prospects she seems quite disponding not knowing of any friend she can in confidence look up to for aid in her present distressd situation.

The Negroes are all on sale as you may observe in the Herald.[2] There is among them two families of Negroes consisting of a Man his Wife and two Children each. With these two families of Negroes and her Land she flatters herself she wd be able to support herself & Children in tolerable Comfort.

The purport of this is solliciting your friendly aid to the family. Feeling a confident hope that yr friendly aid will be extended to them as far as yr convenience will admitt of.

A line on or before the day of sale on the Subject will be a favor as I am trying to make friends to buy these two families of Negroes for the Widow and Children. With sentiments of Esteem & Respect Dear Sir yrs Obt. Servt.

R. Slaughter Jr[3]

RC (DLC). Addressed to JM at Orange, and marked "Mr Wm D Clarke." Docketed by JM.

1. Alexander Shepherd (1770–1819) was a Culpeper County, Virginia, planter. His wife, Elizabeth (Betsy) Conway Madison Shepherd (ca. 1780–1850), whom he married in 1798, was the daughter of JM's brother, Francis (*Daily National Intelligencer*, 9 Oct. 1819; Chapman, "Who was Buried in James Madison's Grave?," 259).

2. The advertisement by William Shepherd for the sale of "about 30 likely Negroes" set for 30 Mar. 1820 at Culpeper Court House was published in the Fredericksburg *Virginia Herald* on 1 Mar. 1820.

3. This was probably the Robert Slaughter Jr. who was appointed a justice of the peace for Culpeper County, Virginia, in 1783, and who also served as a trustee of Stevensburg Academy, which opened in 1802, and as a vestryman of St. Mark's Parish (Scheel, *Culpeper*, 62–63, 68; Green, *Genealogical and Historical Notes on Culpeper County, Virginia* [1989 reprint], 1:90).

From Bushrod Washington

Dear Sir Mount Vernon March 23. 1820

Since my return from Washington the trunk in my possession, containing letters to & from the General, has been carefully examined, and the enclosed have been taken from the bundles found in it. Not doubting but that a much larger number of your letters are in the trunks at Richmond, I have written to the Chief Justice to request that he will in the course of the summer look over those bundles and enclose to me all that he can find from you to the General. Those now enclosed are dated 4 Jany 90—6 april 89—24 Octr. 93—29 Jany & 1 Decr 96.[1]

As soon as I receive those from Richmond, they shall be forwarded to you or to Mr Cutts—I am very respectfully Dear Sir Your Mo. ob. Servt.

Bush. Washington

RC (DLC). Docketed by JM.

1. For the letters of JM to George Washington, 6 Apr. 1789, 4 Jan. 1790, 24 Oct. 1793, and 1 Dec. 1796, see *PJM*, 12:49–50, 466–67, 15:129–31, 16:418–19. JM's letter to Washington of 29 Jan. 1796 has not been found. At some point in his retirement, as an aid to compiling a complete collection of his papers, JM composed a list of thirty-nine letters "from G. Washington to J.M. on the files of the *former* and not of J.M." and "from G.W. to J.M on the files of the latter & not of G.W.s" (DLC: Rives Collection, Madison Papers; 1 p.).

From James Pleasants Jr.

DEAR SIR WASHINGTON 25th March 1820

The enclosed letters & documents[1] have been put into my hands through the agency of Robert S. Rose,[2] at this time a member of the N. York legislature. A perusal of them will give you at once a view of the object they have in view. Your answer is solicited at as early a moment as your leisure will admit, as their election takes place early in April. Be pleased to direct yr. answer to Smith Thompson[3] esqr. Secty. of the navy at this place, who will forward it immediately. Your goodness will excuse the liberty I take in troubling you on this not very pleasant subject to one in your situation. I am with the greatest respe[c]t yr obt. &ca.

JAMES PLEASANTS JR.

RC (DLC).

1. The enclosures were probably Martin Van Buren's two letters to JM of 15 Mar. 1820, covering a correspondence between JM and Daniel D. Tompkins, at this time vice president of the United States and a candidate for the governorship of New York in the April 1820 elections.

2. Robert Selden Rose (1774–1835) was born in Amherst County, Virginia, but moved to New York state in 1803. He was a member of the state legislature, 1811, 1820, and 1821, and served in the U.S. House of Representatives, 1823–27, and 1829–31.

3. Smith Thompson (1768–1843) was a New Yorker and a graduate of the College of New Jersey, who served as secretary of the U.S. Navy, 1819–23. He resigned that position to become associate justice of the U.S. Supreme Court, a position he held until his death (Paolo E. Coletta, ed., *American Secretaries of the Navy* [2 vols.; Annapolis, Md., 1980], 1:123, 127).

From Edward Coles

MY DEAR SIR ENNISCORTHY March 26. 1820

I enclose you a receipt for the 10$ you sent by me for the Agricultural Society of Albemarle.[1]

I presume Judge Todd will be with you by the time this will be received. I beg you will urge him to come by and pay me and my friends here a visit. He will make us all particularly happy by doing so. I propose to set out for the West on Monday or Tuesday (the 3 or 4 of April) and should be very much gratified indeed to have the pleasure of his society on the journey. It will not be much out of his way to come by this—we are here but one days journey from Staunton. I have paid him so many visits in Keny. that I have, I think, a right to expect him to go a little out of his way to visit me. With my best regards for Mrs. M. I am most truly and sincerely your friend

EDWARD COLES

RC (ICHi). Docketed by JM.

1. Coles had recently been to Montpelier and described it thusly: "I paid a visit of 4 or 5 days last week to Mr. & Mrs. Madison. It was a most charming visit. They were to me among the happiest days of the year. They were both remarkably well and happy—looking as young as they did ten years ago" (Coles to Richard Cutts, 26 Mar. 1820 [IHi]).

To Martin Van Buren

SIR MONTPR. Mar. 27. 1820

I have just recd. your communication of the 15th. in which my consent is requested to the publication of my correspondence in 1814, with the V P. of the U. S. then Govr. of N. Y. on the subject of his proposed nomination for the Department of State. There being nothing in that correspondence which I could possibly wish to be regarded as under a seal of Secrecy, I can not hesitate in complying with the request.

As most delicate in relation to the vice P. as well as becoming to myself, under existing circumstances, I forbear to add for publication, any further expression of the high sense which I have always entertained of his exertions & services during the period of the late war, and which were so generally applauded throughout the nation.

The transcripts are returned with the interlined correction from the papers in my possession of a few immaterial errata, the effect probably of the copying pen. I am not able to lay my hand on the first letter from me of Sepr. 28. 1814; but I cannot doubt the sufficient exactness of the copy now returned. Be pleased Sir to accept assurances of my esteem & respect.

Draft (DLC).

To Thomas Jefferson

DEAR SIR Mar. 31. 1820

Judge Todd accompanied by one of his sons being on his return thro' your neighbourhood will call to pay his respects to you. His great worth justly entitles him to this introduction to your recollections.

I propose to be with you tomorrow evening. Mrs. M. will not lose the opportunity of making a visit to the ladies of Monticello. Yours allways & affecy.

JAMES MADISON

RC (NjP).

From Edmond Kelly

SIR COLUMBIA TEN april 1820

I this day read the presidents last message[1] wherein (agreeable to a wish of the rusian Emperor) he recommends it to congress to deferr any resolution to occupy E Florida untill as I suppose it shall be convenient to Ferdinand to signify how he has or will dispose of it—very probably to England for an armament and money to subdue the south An. colonies or some of them. I consided [*sic*] the non ratification of the Treaty a finesse—the effect of a secret understanding with the british Ministry for that purpose—the seemingly Confidential Communications of Lord Castleah. to Mr Rush[2] plainly indicate that propositions to that effect were made but his Lordship is more a diplomatist than to discover the secret intentions of his govt respecting them—& should the exhausted & desperate situation of the Spanish Monarch induce him to sacrifice all that british Avarice Can expect from them or covet & should he as I think he will dissemble procrastinate & finally anull the treaty of Don Onis & deliver E Florida to England—she will by that means get the Command of the Gulf of Mexico & possess that position from which the U States are most Vulnerable. I am clearly of opinion that in such event she may gain by artifice & Intrigue what her armies cannot effect—that E Florida will become the rendezvous of the ambitious disaffected & traiterous citizens of the U S—that she will divide & disunite the states & finally reconquer & reduce them under her govt. Selfpreservation requires that such an Enemy should be excluded your Territory—that E Florida should be possessed peopled & Fortified by native Citizens with the lest possible delay. I acknowledge that much respect ought to be given to any matter which the Empro Alexander proposes—

that moderation & a sense of honor & Justice elevates him as much above the other Kings in merit as he is their superior in power & that England would not decline for one hour to war with Amca could she secretly prevail on him to Coalesce for that purpose that she wishes to make him the pivot of all military Movements & rest her hopes of Conquest on his disposeable force—satisfied of all this I yet think so wise & Just a monarch could not expect that America shall neglect & Omitt to provide for her own safety & that 60 days or so long as a final answer can be had from Madrid should only Intervene between the resolution of Congress to annex E Florida to the U States & its being possessed & garrisoned by American Troops—the present Opportunity to ensure the safety of the republic & secure her Internal tranquility is too favorable to be neglected—there are other Considns. that urge it—suppose Spain becomes a limitted monarchy ruled by Ferdinand & the Cortes—or suppose Charles the 4th restored & the Cortes established (& either event is not improbable) will he or the Cortes consider themselves bound to ratify the acts of his son to whose usurpation & Incapacity will be attributed the Misfortunes of Spain—by no means—it is therefore to be hoped that no insidious Ingenuity shall influence Congress to abandon a measure of such Vital Importance and on the execution of which the Integrity of the republic depends.

It is much to be regretted that Mr Adams should give that fine Country beyond the Missisipi in Exchange for Florida.[3] That Country alone exclusive of spanish spoliations is in Value more than an Equivalent—the Integrity safety & security of the republic might Justify the sacrifice if Insisted on as a sine qua non but the necessity for it did not in my opinion exist. I Imagine that for cotton sugar & perhaps for Coffee too the Tery Ceded to Spain is unequaled by any other belonging to the U S—this is a grevious loss—as in a little time it might supply the Republic with these articles instead of taking poisoned sugars Rum &ca from the W India Islands in Exchange for flour & other provisions and necessaries. Specie would be had for them—for these reasons I Imagine a repurchase of the Ceded Teritory ought to be an object of Imediate attention with a provident & an honest Executive did it actually exist (but which I doubt)—under the treaty I consider spain entitled to it but should she make War for Florida & put Ama. to the expence of defensive operations I do not Know any other Circumstance that could in Justice render it retributable or recoverable except a repurchase for cash which I Imagine would now be accepted.

I have read 2 thirds of Genl Jacksons Meml[4] no more being published here—the first part of it is substantially a Lawyars Demurrer which admitts the facts but objects that the proceedings are erroneous & Contrary to practice—it Contains attempts to recriminate & very decided & unreserved defiance of the Legislative body—but admitts that his character will be Injured if the report is adopted & to avert this by an appeal to Magna

Charta he calls on the Orangemen to aid & extricate him & deceive the republic—in fact he with ominous Warning Identifies the Career of Madness & Folly as he calls it of the french democratic Govt and its transient & short duration with that of the american Govt. but in all their proceedings & Documents & accusations of traitors nothing was exhibited so indecent & insulting as his Meml which if Evidence was wanting contains Indisputable evidence of his own guilt—in fact his referring to the british Magna Charta is both a call on the Orangemen to aid & Extricate him and an audacious threat to overthrow democracy which I think from him is madness for he is no tactitian & does not even understand discipline [(] that is if I may Judge of his military Knowlege from the discipline & parades of his nashville Guards)—to elucidate the fact that his Meml contains Internal Evidence of his Guilt it is only necessary for me to remind you that Magna Charta is considered the foundation of what is called british Liberty—that the battle of Runemeade enabled the Barons to extort certain privileges from King John which were partially enjoyed untill the Stewarts attempted to resume them but their expulsion gained from Wm. the 3d and secured the bill of rights or as it is considered the british Constitution which all the Orangemen are sworn so that Magna Cha⟨rta⟩ the bill of rights & the glorious & Immortal Memory of Wm. the 3d prince of Orange & Nassau is the theme of every Orangemans praise these Orangemen were first formed in Ireland into societies to oppose & defeat the United Irishmen of whom they were the executioners & Comprised all the unprincipled ruffians whom the hope of robbery & pillage could attach to the party of the british ascendancy or oligarchs & the crown & deservedly stigmatised as bloodhounds & all of them as I sayed are Sworn to fidelity to the british Constin to the sistem of places innumerable pensions sinecures & unlimitted taxation such is the british [*illegible*] & these Infernal bloodhounds are all sworn to establish it and subvert American Independence for which services they are to receive Innumerable forfeitures &ca. &ca. &ca. this may be relied on a corect Outline from which any one can Judge of the present state of things & the necessity for Florida—in short that audacious traitor Jackson has made Apostacy the condition for promotion & patronage & I expect the American Govt will shortly have to disband a disaffected army or anticipate disastrous effects unless it will remove from Command without delay an audacious traitor who is in this manner disseminating disaffection apostacy & treason & who has made considerable progress to sap & undermine the republican Edifice & I think unless the resolution of the Legislature removes him from Comd they will endanger the freedom & Independence of the republic—the numbers that have Joined an orange Lodge he has branched out here in Columbia is surprising it is managed or mastered by a Doctor Horatio De priest a Virginian now there & in his absence by a Mr Dale a store Keeper a Mr

Surgeon John B Hayes[5] & the quelling of the troubles in England has given our Orn. confidence & brought them into a reaction which renders the removal of Jackson from Command Indispensibly necessary—the tranquilised state of England renders such precaution & Vigilance necessary the Zeal & Confidence of these bloodhounds and robbers in Jackson & success is increased & increasing they now find officially too that the british Oligarchs by their friends Agents & Dependants secretly caused that ferment Commotion & alarm in England which they the oligarchs subsequently made Laws to tranquilise & suppress Cromwells and Wms. nobility dread the Idea of retribution. Mr Addington the present Lord Sidmouth[6] was my uncles friend—his patronage for this poor man alarmed them they drove the british Ignorant poor into insurrection Intimidated the Minister gained their point and made Laws to punish Insurgents the Conversation of Hunt[7] & the parson & the Examination of the printer before the Lord Mayor of London & his Lordships advice demonstrates these facts which every Intelligent Briton Knows but like the Misteries of Ceres of old cannot divulge such is the conduct of the United Irishmen—Contemptible dupes Very respectfully

Edmond Kelly

RC (NN). Addressed by Kelly to JM: "late president U States City of Washington Virginia or Elsewhere," and franked. "City of Washington" has been crossed out and "Orange C H" interlined above. Docketed by JM. Damaged by removal of seal.

1. Kelly referred to James Monroe's message to Congress of 27 Mar. 1820, transmitting letters from U.S. ministers in Russia and in Spain, respecting the non-ratification of the Transcontinental Treaty concluded by the United States and Spain and conveying "the strong interest which His imperial Majesty [Alexander I] takes in promoting the ratification of that treaty." Monroe requested Congress to discuss "whether it will not be advisable to postpone a decision on the questions now depending with Spain until the next session" (Hamilton, *Writings of James Monroe*, 6:117–18).

2. Kelly may have been referring here to Lord Castlereagh's August 1819 assurances to U.S. minister Richard Rush that Great Britain had done nothing to prevent the ratification of the treaty between the United States and Spain (Powell, *Richard Rush*, 144).

3. For the terms of the Transcontinental Treaty between the United States and Spain, signed 22 Feb. 1819, in which Spain ceded all its territory east of the Mississippi River (that is, East and West Florida), and the boundary between U.S. and Spanish possessions west of the river was fixed at the Sabine River, north to the Arkansas River and then by 42° north latitude to the Pacific Ocean, see Miller, *Treaties*, 3:3–18.

4. On 23 Feb. 1820 Rufus King presented Andrew Jackson's memorial defending his actions in the Seminole War to the Senate. The memorial was in response to a 24 Feb. 1819 report of a Senate committee headed by Abner Lacock of Pennsylvania that condemned as dishonorable Jackson's invasion of Florida and his execution of two British subjects (Robert V. Remini, *Andrew Jackson and the Course of American Empire, 1767–1821* [New York, 1977], 375–76). For the memorial and supporting documents, see *Annals of Congress*, 15th Cong., 2d sess., 2308–2350.

5. Horatio Depriest was a physician and one of the first lot holders of Columbia, Tennessee, as well as a director of the Columbia Bank, established in 1819. Edward W. Dale was a

Columbia merchant and original lot holder in the city, who purchased his property in 1808. He promoted the Planters' Bank, which opened in 1838. John B. Hayes (d. 1868), originally from Virginia, was a physician who served as an alderman of Columbia in 1839. He married Ophelia, the sister of U.S. president James K. Polk (*Century Review, 1805–1905, Maury County, Tennessee* [Columbia, Tenn., 1905], 14, 43, 46, 51, 75).

6. Henry Addington, first Viscount Sidmouth (1757–1844) entered Parliament in 1784 and held the speakership from 1789 to 1801, when he became First Lord of the Treasury and prime minister in a new administration. The Addington ministry fell in April 1804. He held a variety of cabinet posts from 1806 to 1809, and then became home secretary in 1812, a position he kept until 1822. During those years he took severe measures to quell rioting and unrest by Luddites and the poor, and as the discontents of the working class became politicized in the years after 1817, Addington's severity culminated with the introduction in Parliament in 1819 of the repressive Six Acts. He retired from the ministry in 1824.

7. Henry Hunt (1773–1835) was a farmer and reformer who advocated annual parliaments, universal sufferage, and vote by ballot. Unsuccessful in his bids for election to Parliament, Hunt was a regular organizer and speaker at popular reform meetings at Spa Fields (1816), Palace Yard (1818), Smithfield (1819), and St. Peter's Fields (1819). At the latter place the meeting was broken up violently by mounted militia and became known as the Peterloo Massacre. Hunt was arrested, tried, and convicted for his part in the meeting and sentenced to two and a half years in prison. He was elected to Parliament in 1830 and served until 1833.

Minutes of the Board of Visitors of the University of Virginia

1820. Apr. 1.

A special meeting of the Visitors of the University having been called in the month of February to be held on this day Apr. 1. signed by Th: Jefferson, James Madison, Chapman Johnson, Joseph C. Cabell, James Breckenridge & Robert Taylor, and duly notified to John H. Cocke to whom no opportunity had occurred of presenting it for his signature, the sd. Th: Jefferson and James Madison attended accordingly, but not constituting a Quorum, no proceedings took place.

TH: JEFFERSON Rector.

Ms (ViU: Jefferson Papers, Special Collections). In Jefferson's hand.

To Isaac Coffin

DR. SIR MONTPR. VIRGA. Apl. 2. 1820

I have been so fortunate as to procure for you, 3 wild Turkies, two Goblers and one hen.[1] I regret that I could not double the latter also, but all my efforts have failed. The solitary Gobler in a Coop by himself, is several years old, is very large, and has the finest plumage I have ever seen on a Turkey. The pair in the other Coop are of the last year's brood, and not a forward one. They will grow therefore. They promise to be stately birds, and have all the characteristics of the genuine stock. All the three have been partly domesticated, and have on that account the better chance to bear the transportation. They will be sent in a day to the Consul at Alexa. as you desired with a suggestion of the stores & precautions necessary at sea. I wish they may arrive as safe as those heretofore sent, and that they may prove less erratic & more prolific. Mrs. M. charges me to include her in the friendly respects, & all the good wishes which I pray you accept from your Obed Servt.

J. M.

Draft (DLC).

1. For the correspondence between JM and Coffin relating to wild turkeys, see Coffin to JM, 17 May and 22 Dec. 1817, and 10 June 1819, and JM to Coffin, 1 Oct. 1819, *PJM-RS*, 1:47, 177–78, 466, 519–20.

Minutes of the Board of Visitors of the University of Virginia

Apr. 3. 1820.

At a meeting of the Visitors of the University of Virginia at the said University on monday the 3d. of April 1820, present Thomas Jefferson, James Madison, James Breckenridge, John H. Cocke, and Joseph C. Cabell.

Resolved, that the Visitors of the University accede to the loan of $40,000. authorized by a Resolution of the President and Directors of the Literary Fund of 23d. March 1820.[1]

Resolved, That the aforesaid sum of $40,000. shall be applied as follows viz.

1st. to the payment of the debts of the University. 2d. to the completion of the buildings now on hand.

Resolved, that the balance that may remain of the $40,000. after accomplishing the two objects last specified, together with the annuity of the year 1821. after deducting the interest that will be due on the loan from the Literary Fund, be applied towards the erection of three other pavilions & their accessory dormitories.

Resolved, That the committee of superintendence be authorized to borrow of the Presiden⟨t⟩ and Directors of the Literary fund, or should that be impracticable, from any other quarter, the further sum of $20,000.

Resolved, That the aforesaid sum of $20,000. together with any balance of the preceding sums as may remain on hand, and the annuity of the year 1822, after deducting the sum due for interest on monies borrowed, be applied towards the erection of buildings of accomodation on the Eastern Back Street.

Resolved That the Committee of Superintendence be authorized & required to propose to the President & Directors of the Literary Fund a postponement for one year of the period of commencement of the installments of the principal borrowed of the said Fund.

Resolved That in the event of the agreement of the President & Directors of the Literary Fund to the postponement of the installments of principal as last mentioned, any balance tha⟨t⟩ may remain on hand of the aforesaid sums of money, together with the annuity of the year 1823, after deducting the sums due for interest, be applied towards the erection of buildings of accomodation on the Western Back Street.

Resolved, that Thomas Jefferson be appointed Rector of the University for the ensuing four years.

Resolved That Thomas Jefferson, and John H. Cocke, be appointed a committee of superintendence.

Resolved, That the Committee of superintendence be authorized to communicate to Doctor Thomas Cooper the delay & uncertainty now unavoidable in regard to the time of opening the University, and to make such change in the contracts with him as to them may seem advisable.

Th: Jefferson rector

Ms (ViU: Jefferson Papers, Special Collections). In Joseph C. Cabell's hand; signed and dated by Jefferson.

1. As one of the visitors of the University of Virginia, JM signed for the loan, "to the payment whereof, well and truly to be made, we bind ourselves and our successors, to the said President and Directors and their successors" (Resolutions of the President and Directors of the Literary Fund, 25 Mar. 1820 [ViU: Jefferson Papers, Special Collections]).

From Francis Preston

Dear Sir City of Washington. April 5th 1820

I am thus far on my return from Phila. with a sad heart being totally disappointed in the object of my journey there—and shall have to witness the innevitable consequence of seeing my misguided and unfortunate brother reduced from affluence to indigence—but notwithstanding this deplorable result I shall always regard with the best feelings of gratitude and friendship your kind and friendly letters to Mr Cheves and myself.

Mr Cheves was polite and friendly and I am confident was sincere in the wish to accommodate me had it been consistent with the rules of the institution over which he presides.

I could not pass without making to you my Dear Sir my acknowledgements for your kindness and tendering to you and my much Esteemed friend Mrs. Madison my sincerest esteem. Your friend & very Hble Sert

FRANS. PRESTON

RC (NN). Docketed by JM.

To James Patton

[6 April 1820]

I have been desired by Admiral Sr. Isaac Coffin to commit to your care some wild Turkies, to be forwarded by you to Liverpool. He has I presume apprized you of this circumstance; and that they are to be addressed to the care of Ths. & Wm. Earle & Co. at that place. I propose to send the Turkies, a male & female in one Coop & a Male in the other to the steam boat at the mouth of Potom; Creek which they will probably reach early next week, with directions that the Coops be delivered according to the orders from you on the arrival of the Boat, which is to make no charge on you for freight to Alexa. The Turkies are fine & genuine samples; and it will be very agreeable to the Adml. to recieve them as safe, as he did two others sent him the year before the last. You will be able I hope to find a favorable conveyance before the season is too much advanced. I need not suggest the necessity of a plentiful Store of food, such as Maize, Oats or rye; or rather of a portion of each, at least of the two first. Fresh water will also of course be a daily allowance; and protection as much as possible agst. the drenching effect of the salt water in rough weather. A little gravel put into the Coops from time to time will also be material.

Draft (DLC). Undated; conjectural date assigned based on Patton's 10 Apr. 1820 reply to this letter. James Patton (d. 1824) was an Alexandria merchant and lawyer who served as British vice-consul, 1816–24 (Miller, *Portrait of a Town: Alexandria*, 279; Miller, *Artisans and Merchants of Alexandria*, 2:22–23).

From James Patton

SIR, ALEXANDRIA 10th. April 1820

I have just received your favor of the 6th. instant advising of your being about to forward to my care some wild Turkies by the steam Boat via

Potomac Creek at the request of Admiral Sir Isaac Coffin, to be addressed from hence, to the care of Messrs. Thos. & Wm. Earle & Co. of Liverpool. When they reach this, you may rely on the utmost care, and attention being paid to them in my power, and I have only to express my regret that they have not come sooner as several large Vessels have been dispatched from this to that Port this season, and I fear no other opp'y is likely to offer soon, in which case would it not be adviseable to send them on to Norfolk, If any Vessel is going from thence. I have not heard from the Admiral on the subject, having however the pleasure of his acquaintance it will afford me great satisfaction, If I can aid, in having them safely transported. Your directions as to food & treatment will be duly attended to. Be pleased to accept of my best Wishes for the Health & Happiness of you & yours in which Mrs. Patton most cordially Joins and I remain With true regard and respect, Dear Sir, Your very faithful, Humble servant

James Patton

RC (DLC). Docketed by JM.

From Thomas Jefferson

Dear Sir Monticello Apr. 11. 20.

Our brewing for the use of the present year has been some time over. About the last of Oct. or beginning of Nov. we begin for the ensuing year, and malt and brew 3. 60 galln casks *successively*, which will give so many successive lessons to the person you send.[1] On his return he can try his hand with you in order to discover what parts of the processes he will have learnt imperfectly, and come again to our spring brewing of a single cask in order to perfect himself, and go back to you to try his hand again on as much as you will want. You will want a house for malting, which is quickest made by digging into the steep side of a hill, so as to need a roof only, and you will want a haircloth also of the size of your loft to lay the grain on. This can only be had from Phila. or N. Y. I sett out for Bedford the first of next week to be absent till the 1st. week in May. I will give you notice in the fall when we are to commence malting and our malter and brewer is uncommonly intelligent and capable of giving instruction if your pupil is as ready at comprehending it. Ever & affectionately yours

Th: Jefferson

RC (DLC); FC (DLC: Jefferson Papers). RC docketed by JM.

1. For JM's experiments in substituting beer for whiskey for his slaves, see Ketcham, "An Unpublished Sketch of James Madison by James K. Paulding," *VMHB* 67 (1959): 436.

From Mark Langdon Hill

SIR WASHINGTON April 17th. 1820.

When I came to this City for the first time at the commencement of the present session, I intended to do myself the honor to call and pay my respects to you & President Jefferson & pass by the way of Williamsburg to see my friend Col. Basset;[1] but oweing to the press of business and the procrastinated time of adjournment, will oblige me to return home, without enjoying the pleasure intended.

This I deplore the more, because during your administration, I was in the minority of the Senate of Massachusetts, where, during the late war, we had to contend "with principalities & powers,"[2] and at times, not without some fears for our personal safety; this with other considerations has created a sympathy & feeling, which I cannot well describe.

Mr. R. Cutts of this City, who was a native of the same town with myself, I often see with his Lady, and who are, with their family, now enjoying good health.

I take the liberty to send you for your perusal & amusement a letter written by Mr. Jefferson to Gov. Langdon,[3] who was an uncle of mine, and with whom you were well acquainted, but he has gone to "the land from whose bourne no traveller returns."[4]

I asked permission of Mr. Jefferson to publish the letter at some proper time, but his answer, which I also enclose for your perusal,[5] is in the negative; of course I am strictly bound to comply with his wishes, and I have suffered no copy to be taken thereof, but one at the request of President Monroe.

After you shall have perused, I will thank you to return them to this City to Your most obedient hume. Servant.

MARK LANGDON HILL[6]

RC (DLC). Docketed by JM.

1. Burwell Bassett (1764–1841) served in the Virginia legislature, 1787–89, 1793–1805, and 1819–21, and in the U.S. House of Representatives first as a Jeffersonian Republican, 1805–13, 1815–19, then as a Jacksonian, 1821–29.

2. "For we wrestle not against flesh and blood, but against principalities, against powers, against the rulers of the darkness of this world, against spiritual wickedness in high places," Eph. 6:12 (AV).

3. The letter was Thomas Jefferson to John Langdon, 5 Mar. 1810, in which Jefferson excoriated the British government for both its hereditary monarchy and its policies (Lipscomb and Bergh, *Writings of Thomas Jefferson*, 12:373–79).

4. "The undiscover'd country, from whose bourn / No traveller returns," Shakespeare, *Hamlet*, 3.1.78–79 (*Riverside*).

5. Hill requested Jefferson's permission in a letter of 28 Mar. 1820. Jefferson replied in the negative on 5 Apr. 1820, noting that the letter "was written in warm times, and is therefore

too warmly expressed for the more reconciled temper of the present day" (DLC: Jefferson Papers).

6. Mark Langdon Hill (1772–1842), a resident of Maine, served in the Massachusetts legislature as a Republican, 1797–1808, 1810, 1813–17, as a Massachusetts member of the U.S. House of Representatives, 1819–21, and as a member from Maine, 1821–23. He was appointed collector of customs at Bath, Maine, in 1824.

To Mark Langdon Hill

Dr. Sir [post–17] apl. 1820

I have recd. yr. favor of the 17. enclosing 2 letters from Mr. Jefferson, one to the late Govr. Langdon, the other to yrself, and a copy of your printed address to yr. Constts. on the Missouri question.[1] The letters I return as you desired. Mr. J. was very right I think in not assenting to the publicn of his letter to yr. uncle.

I was myself, intimately acquainted with yr. Uncle, and cheerfully concur in all the praise Mr. J. bestows on him. He was a true patriot, & a good man; with a noble way of thinking and a frankness & warmth of heart, that made his friends love him much as it did me in a high degree, & disarmed his enemies of some of the asperity indulged towards others.

The candid view you have given of the Missi. question is well calculated to assuage the party zeal which it generated. As long as the conciliatory spirit which produced the Constn. remains in the mass of the people and the several parts of the Union understand the deep interest which every part has in maintaining it, these stormy subjects will soon blow over, and the people on the return of calm, be more disposed to consider wherein their interests agree, than wherein their opinions differ. The very discords to which they find themselves subject even under the guardianship of a United Govt. premonish them of the tempestuous hostilities which await a dissolution of it. I did not know that I had so much personal concern in the length of the Session, as I find I had by its effect on your intended visit. I well know how much room there is for a sympathetic recollection of the political scenes thro wch. we have passed, and shd. have found the pleasure of seeing you increased by the tranquil review wch. our conversations might have taken of them. I cannot but hope that a future oppy. will repair the disappt., and that It may still be in my power to express to you, under my vine & fig tree, the esteem & friendly respects of which I pray you to accept this paper assurance at Washington.

Draft (DLC). Day of month not indicated; conjectural day assigned based on Hill's 17 Apr. 1820 letter to JM.

1. Mark Langdon Hill, *Fellow citizens of the state of Maine, the Missouri question having excited unusual interest . . . induces me . . . to assign the reasons for the vote I gave on that occasion . . .* (Washington, 1820; Shoemaker 1584). JM's copy is in the Madison Collection, Rare Book and Special Collections Division, Library of Congress.

From James Patton

SIR ALEXANDRIA 18th. April 1820

Since I had this pleasure under date the 10th. instant, I have received yours of same date with its inclosure for Admiral Sir Isaac Coffin as also the Turkies. They appear in high condition and their fixtures well calculated to protect them on the Passage across the Atlantic. No oppy. yet offers from this to Liverpool, and I fear none will soon so that I am anxious to hear from you whether it would not be adviseable to send them to Norfolk or New York without delay. The Bacon Hams as mentioned to me in a letter from Mr. H. Farish have not come to Hand. I hope they will in a day or two cast up. The Turkies came separately. The Cage with two the first day and the Cock the second the finest Bird of the kind I ever saw. I shall watch the steam Boat to day and If the Barrel of Hams should cast up, I shall add a postscript. I remain With true regard and respect Dear Sir, Your very faithful Hbl servant

JAMES PATTON

P. S. I have just seen the Captain of the steam Boat who tells me that He brought up 2 Barrels Hams, this Morning directed to Mr. Cutts, and that He delivered the same to his Order. These I presume are what Mr. Farish thought were to my care. Yours &c

JP

RC (DLC). Docketed by JM.

To John S. Barbour

DR. SIR Apl. 21. 1820

I recd. in due time your favr. of Jany. 27.[1] apprizing me of the rents due by Mr. Ward, & of the oppy. you expected, of ascertaining the real extent of the land embraced by the Mortgage of Mr. Strode. I did not advert then to an expression since observed in your letter, which may imply that your prosecution & exposé of the case, might depend on my intimating a desire to that effect. Shd. this be a condition, I beg leave to remove it, by a request that you will be good eno' to continue your attention to the business as far as it may be necessary to obtain for me whatever may of right be mine. I will thank you also whilst endeavoring to recover the disappearing 100 Acres, to drop me a line of information, as to the prospect of prompt payment of the liquidated amt. of rents by Mr. Ward.

To these requests, I must add a particular one that You will assure Mr. Strode that I have never doubted the integrity of his intentions, or that he will still aid as far as he can in effectuating the object of justice, and that he continues to enjoy my friendly wishes.

Draft (DLC).

1. *PJM-RS*, 1:590–91.

To Moses Hoge

Revd Sir Montpr. Apl 22. 1820

I have recd: a printed Copy of the Laws of Hampden-Sidney College;[1] to which is prefixed a list of the Trustees among whom I find that my name is honored with a place. I can not be insensible to this mark of respect & confidence: But as my distance from the Institution, with my advanced life and the ordinary incidents to it, leave me no prospect of being more than a nominal member, I am sure I shall be readily excused for not accepting an appointment which could have no other effect than to exclude some one more worthy of the trust, because more capable of fulfilling its obligations. I pray the Board at the same time to be not the less assured of my cordial wishes that the College may be instrumental in doing as much good to the present & succeeding generations as I am persuaded is the object of those who administer & patronize it.

Draft (DLC). Moses Hoge (1752–1820) was a Revolutionary War veteran and ordained clergyman, who ministered to a church in Shepherdstown, Virginia (now West Virginia), from 1787 to 1807. Hoge was elected president of Hampden-Sydney College and professor of theology in 1807, and he remained in that post until his death.

1. *Laws of Hampden Sidney College* (Richmond, [1819]; Shaw and Shoemaker 48145). JM's copy is in the Madison Collection, Rare Book and Special Collections Division, Library of Congress.

To Martin Van Buren

DR. SIR [post–25 April 1820]

I find by a newspaper just come to hand that the publication of the correspondence with Govr T. in 1814. is preceded by that or rather part of that between you & myself.

I cannot but regret that my intention in this particular was not rightly understood. My hasty letter was written under the impression that nothing would go to the press but the original correspondence, with at most an intimation that it had been ascertained that on my part there was no desire that there shd. be under any seal of secrecy on it. Writing under this impression, I did not distinguish between the letter from you as chairman & that in your own name; to the latter of which the terms of mine were indeed more particularly adapted than to the other.

I have not yet seen any comments on this publication: but am apprehensive of inferences from the face of it that I furnished the copies of the origl. correspondence which I shd have thought of doubtful propriety at least, if I cd. have readily done it, and that I publickly volunteered for the occasion ⟨a⟩n extra testimony of my high sense of the merits of the Vice President; which ⟨w⟩d. not have accordd, with the aversion I ought to feel at any thing like in[. . .] party politics, and which is commensurate with the manifest impropriety of it.

I have thought it p[. . .] to ⟨trouble?⟩ you with these remarks, in full confidence that you will in the mode you may deem best, controul such inferences as I have alluded to, by letting it be publickly known, that they are erroneous, which I presume may be done without a publication of this letter.

Draft (DLC). Undated; conjectural date assigned based on the assumption that JM had recently seen his published correspondence with Daniel D. Tompkins and Van Buren in the *Daily National Intelligencer*, 25 Apr. 1820 (see Van Buren to JM, 15 Mar. 1820, first letter, and n. 2, and second letter). At the head of draft JM wrote: "For Mr. Van Buren, but not sent, there appearing to be no occasion for the explanation." Extensively damaged by mold.

From John S. Barbour

DEAR SIR FREDERICKSBURG May 1st. 1820

Your late favour[1] reached me in due time. The Chancellor entertained great doubts upon the subject of the rents which had been received by Mr. Berkely Ward. He directed an argument from the Bar, which was made on Friday last and this day he has delivered his opinion. The Court decrees that you are entitled to the rents from filing the Bill of foreclosure, and upon this basis you have recovered Eighty Dollars and half the Costs, for the other half you have a Decree agt. Mr. Strode. For this amount of rents Execution will issue after the rising of the Court, upon which the Deft Ward will have the power to give a forthcoming bond, and may thus delay payment until after the next term of the Chancery Court. Upon inspecting the Courses &c laid down in the Deed from Mr Strode to yourself I perceive that the lands embraced within those boundaries will equal the quantity indicated by Mr S.

If my memory serve me, Mr. Strode said to me, that he held under one of three brothers who jointly inherited the Lands of which 162 acres was the third portion; The entire tract was in the form of trapezium which being carelessly divided, (and for the want of Mathematical Skill, the division was made as if it were a Square) gave to this lot you now own, a quantity much less than you are legally entitled to have. Knowing that Mr Strode coud more easily & satisfactorily correct this error of allotment, I had forborn to take any step in it, until I had the aid of his personal attendance. This assistance I was promised from him about the period I wrote you last, but it has been retarded because of a severe paralytic affliction from which he is now so far recovered as to promise me a visit in the progress of this month. So soon as he arrives I will adopt immediate measures to obtain for you that which is of right, yours. From everything I have learned on the subject I cannot doubt, but that your right to the larger number of acres (say 162) is clear & indefeasible. With Sentiments of Highest Respect and Esteem Yrs

JNO. S. BARBOUR

RC (DLC). Docketed by JM.

1. JM to Barbour, 21 Apr. 1820.

From William J. Coffee

SIR, MONTICELO May 3. 1820

I have taken the Liberty of Inclosing you Small Acct which I Shall be much favord by recving in a few days when I Shall Call on my way home.[1] Sir I Am with Much Respect and Esteem

W: J: COFFEE

RC (DLC).

1. On 25 May 1820 JM made out a receipt, which Coffee signed: "Recd. of James Madison fifty dollars seventy five Cents: being in full for Models & Busts made for him" (CSmH). For

the busts of JM, Dolley Madison, and John Payne Todd modeled by Coffee, see his letters to JM of 4 July 1818 and 23 Dec. 1819, *PJM-RS*, 1:297, 575.

From Hazlewood Farish

DEAR SIR FREDG. 3 May 1820

The box for Mr. Cutts has been delivered to me, & shall be immediately forwarded to Washington. I am very Respy Dear Sir Your mo: ob. St

HAZLEWD. FARISH

RC (DLC).

From James Monroe

DEAR SIR WASHINGTON May 3d. 1820

Our troubles with Spain are not ended, nor is it possible to say when they will be. It was hoped and presumed that this minister[1] would have been authorisd to settle every difficulty, but it appears that he came, simply, to ask explanations, and report those given to his government, to amuse, and procrastinate as his predecessor had done. He admits that he is personally satisfied, as to the causes which prevented the ratification of the treaty, but has neither power, to surrender the territory, or do any other act, which would give security for the future, not even to declare, that his govt. will be satisfied. He demands a stipulation, that the UStates will not recognize the So A: colonies, untill they shall be recognized by other powers. I shall lay the result before Congress in a few days.

My family were very thankful for yours & Mrs Madisons kind attention, in regard to our daughter Maria. She and Mr Gouverneur are on a visit to his family at N. York. Mrs Monroe has been in very delicate health for some weeks, & is still so, owing to the fatigue incident to the winter, to which she has found herself unequal. We all desire our best regards to Mrs Madison. Your friend

JAMES MONROE

RC (DLC). Docketed by JM.

1. The new Spanish minister, Gen. Francisco Dionisio Vives (1755–1840), arrived in Washington on 9 Apr. 1820 and left two years later to become captain general of Cuba, 1823–32 (Bleiberg, *Diccionario de historia de España*, 2d ed., 3:1030–31; Cunningham, *Presidency of James Monroe*, 106).

From Elkanah Watson

SIR NEW YORK. (SAY ALBANY) 3d May 1820

Having terminated my Canal and agricultural Labours, I take the liberty to enclose for your acceptance a work just published comprising a historical view of these objects.[1] I am with profound respect

E WATSON

RC (DLC). Docketed by JM.

1. Elkanah Watson, *History of the Rise, Progress, and Existing Condition of the Western Canals in the State of New-York . . . Together with the Rise, Progress, and Existing State of Modern Agricultural Societies . . .* (Albany, N.Y., 1820; Shoemaker 4187).

From Alexander Tunstall

COLLECTOR'S OFFICE NORFOLK May 10th. 1820.

Alexander Tunstall[1] will attend with pleasure to the directions of Mr. Madison respecting a package containing two Books, which was received yesterday, per the ship Comet from London, directed to the care of Charles K. Mallory Esqr.[2] He has no knowledge of the Cost of the Books, & therefore is unable to ascertain the duty on them.

RC (DLC: Rives Collection, Madison Papers).

1. Alexander Tunstall (1787–1868), deputy collector of the Norfolk customhouse, was appointed inspector of the customs at Norfolk in 1832 (St. George Tucker Brooke, "The Brooke Family of Virginia," *VMHB* 14 [1907]: 438; Philemon Gatewood to Richard Rush, 12 Dec. 1825, and Louis McLane to Conway Whittle, 23 Oct. 1832, DNA: RG 56, Letters to the Collector, Norfolk, 1800–1833).

2. Charles K. Mallory (1781–1820) was a Virginia legislator and lieutenant governor of the state during the War of 1812. In 1814 JM appointed him customs collector of Norfolk and Portsmouth, and he held this post until his death (*PJM-PS*, 5:44 n. 4; *Senate Exec. Proceedings*, 2:450; Charlottesville *Central Gazette*, 29 Apr. 1820).

To Elkanah Watson

May 12. 1820

I have recd. Sir[1] the little volume on Canals & Agricl Societies[2] wch. you have been so obliging as to send me.

The subjects of the publication, with the source from which it proceeds, sufficiently recommend it to the perusal which I shall take the first convenient leisure for giving it. In the mean time, I offer you my thanks with the renewed expression of my esteem & my friendly respects.

Draft (DLC); letterbook copy (N: Elkanah Watson Papers). Draft written at the foot of Watson to JM, 3 May 1820. Minor differences between the copies have not been noted.

1. The letterbook copy has "from Mr Steele" here. This was Daniel Steele (1772–1828), a bookbinder and bookseller in Albany, New York, and the publisher of Watson's "little Volume" (Daniel Steele Durrie, *Steele Family. A Genealogical History of John and George Steele, (Settlers of Hartford, Conn.) 1635–6, and Their Descendants* . . . (Albany, N.Y., 1862), 22.

2. See Watson to JM, 3 May 1820, and n. 1.

From Thomas Jefferson

DEAR SIR MONTICELLO May 17. 20.

As the measures which were adopted at the last meeting of our visitors were of a very leading character[1] I have thought it proper to inform our absent colleagues of them; and have delayed the communication only until I could add what has been done under the resolutions of the board. As this latter information has not been received by you, I inclose you my letter to General Taylor[2] for perusal and pray you, when read, to stick a wafer in it and put it into the post office. You will excuse this economy of labor, as from the stiffening of my wrist, writing is become slow & painful. I have moreover such another letter to write to mr. Johnson,[3] and a good part of it to Genl. Breckenridge.

My general health is mended, altho' I do not gain strength. I am obliged to continue bandages, altho' under their pressure the swelling is kept down, yet it returns on omitting them. I salute you with constant & unchangeable friendship.

TH: JEFFERSON

RC (DLC); FC (DLC: Jefferson Papers).

1. For the authorization to build "three other pavilions & their accessory dormitories," see Minutes of the Board of Visitors of the University of Virginia, 3 Apr. 1820.

2. Robert Barraud Taylor (1774–1834) was a Norfolk lawyer, a veteran of the War of 1812, and a member of the original board of visitors of the University of Virginia, serving from 1819 to 1822 (Tyler, *Encyclopedia of Virginia Biography*, 2:188–89). For Jefferson's letter to Taylor of 16 May 1820, see Lipscomb and Bergh, *Writings of Thomas Jefferson*, 15:252–56.

3. Chapman Johnson (1779–1849) was a Staunton, Virginia, lawyer and state legislator who was a member of the original board of visitors of the University of Virginia, serving from 1819 to 1845. He was rector of the university, 1836–45 (Tyler, *Encyclopedia of Virginia Biography*, 2:197; *Manual of the Board of Visitors of the University of Virginia, 1998* [Charlottesville, Va., 1998], v).

From John Rhea

Sɪʀ, Wᴀsʜɪɴɢᴛᴏɴ 17th. May 1820.

I did anxiously desire to have visited You as I passed through on my way home, and had anticipated the pleasure of seeing Mrs Madison and Yourself—but some business in Tennessee requires my attention as soon as possible. The late has been a long session of Congress, and there has been some troublesome business—inclosed is a copy of a speech and of a circular letter, which please to accept.[1] In the circular I have stated some opinions relative to agriculture commerce and Manufacture—which I trust will have Your approbation. I am with sincere esteem Your obt sert.

Jᴏʜɴ Rʜᴇᴀ

RC (DLC). Docketed by JM.

1. Rhea enclosed a pamphlet entitled *Debate on the Spanish Treaty, in the House of Representatives* (Washington, 1820; Shoemaker 2996), which included a copy of his speech on the Spanish treaty given on 4 Apr. 1820, and a circular letter to his constituents, dated 8 May 1820. JM's copy of the pamphlet is in the Madison Collection, Rare Book and Special Collections Division, Library of Congress. Rhea's speech is printed in *Annals of Congress*, 16th Cong., 1st sess., 1776–81; his circular letter is printed in Cunningham, *Circular Letters of Congressmen*, 3:1115–21.

From Mason Locke Weems

Vᴇʀʏ Hᴏɴᴏʀᴅ & Esᴛᴇᴇᴍᴅ Sɪʀ Fʀᴇᴅʀɪᴄᴋsʙɢ May. 18. 1820

I send by the stage a copy of what the Critics in these things call "*A very interesting history of the Great French War*"[1]—in all its ramifications, I presume, of numbers, moods, Cases &c &c! This Copy belongs to your modest & worthy Son P. Todd Esqr who subscribd to me for it, last winter. I can't conclude without adding my fond hopes that Doctr. Hunter[2] has had the honor to amuse yourself & very Amiable Lady, this Inclement Spring, with the welcome flowers of his finely colouring fancy. You know I dont pretend to talk or write much before you, save to get ideas & information but I must needs say of this same Doctr. Hunter, that I know no luxury beyond that of reposing myself, when weary, on some refreshing green under trees made vocal by Natures Songsters & her rustling gales, and perusing his Enchanting pages.

On returning home I found after a long search, the letter you did me the honor to write to me relative to Marion.[3] I thank you much for it. We are about to Steriotype that little Vol. I am preparing a little affair that I hope will divert you—["]against Dueling"[4]—with Caricatures that wd not dishonor, Bunbury or even Hogarth[5]—all American. Wishing that you & yr Excellent Partner may, e'er long, gaze with extacy on the "*Sacred Group*" of Infant Angels dulce rident, dulce loquent,[6] in the pleasant halls of Montpelier, I remain Most Esteemed Sir Yours,

M L Weems

The bundle too late for this Stage, but left at the Stage Office.

RC (DLC). Docketed by JM.

1. Edward Baines, *Baine's History of the Late War, between the United States and Great Britain: With a Critical Appendix, &c. by Ebenezer Harlow Cummins* (Baltimore, 1820; Shoemaker 186).

2. For Henry Hunter, see Weems to JM, 22 Jan. 1819, *PJM-RS*, 1:404 and n. 3.

3. JM to Weems, 16 Feb. 1819, ibid., 418–19.

4. Mason Locke Weems, *God's Revenge against Duelling, or, The Duellists Looking Glass . . .* (Georgetown, D.C., 1820; Shoemaker 4233).

5. Henry William Bunbury (1750–1811) was an English amateur artist and caricaturist. William Hogarth (1697–1764) was an English artist best known for his satirical engravings of contemporary life.

6. *Dulce rident, dulce loquent:* sweetly smiling, sweetly speaking. Weems refers here to the last two lines of an ode of Horace: "dulce ridentem Lalagen amabo, dulce loquentem" ("I will love my sweetly laughing, sweetly prattling Lalage"). Weems may have chosen this allusion to flatter JM, since the moral of the ode is that "from the Righteous Man even the Wild Beasts Run away" (Hor., *Odes* 1.22.23–24 [*Horace: Odes and Epodes*, Loeb Classical Library (1978 reprint), 64–65]).

To Benjamin Silliman

Sir Montpellier May 26. 1820

I owe many apologies for not sooner recollecting that I was a subscriber for the first year of your Scientific Journal. I now inclose $5. which can not be more than I ought to pay for the numbers I have recd. of that valuable publication. Should it be less, be so good as to let me know. I sincerely wish you success in the prosecution of the work, and regret that the considerations which limited my engagement to a single year do not permit me to renew it. Be pleased to accept Sir my esteem and friendly respects

James Madison

RC (ViU: Madison Papers, Special Collections).

¶ From Thomas Jefferson. Letter not found. *2 June 1820.* Enclosed in Dolley Madison to Lewis J. Cist, 4 July 1842 (DLC: Dolley Madison Papers).

From Benjamin Silliman

SIR NEW HAVEN June 9. 1820.

I learned with some mortification that my printed circular relative to the Journal of Science had been forwarded to you—which was contrary to my intentions. I beg leave however to return my thanks for your very handsome treatment of the subject & to acknowledge the receipt of the 5$ enclosure.

I hope you will not think me presuming if I take the liberty of forwarding the 1st. No of Vol 2 (recently from the press)[1] & the remainder of that Vol whenever it shall appear requesting you to receive them as a mark of my respect, & disclaiming any additional remuneration, & any obligation on your part to continue the work. I remain with very great respect Your very oblgd & obt hble Servt

B SILLIMAN

RC (DLC). Docketed by JM.

1. Silliman referred to his *American Journal of Science, and Arts*. In 1818 he had sent JM a prospectus for this new journal (see Silliman to JM, 3 Mar. 1818, *PJM-RS*, 1:227–28 and n. 1).

From Thomas Sumter Jr.

SIR RIO DE JANEIRO 9 of June 1820

Having by chance obtained in this distant part of the World from the Artist who took it 20 years ago, a portrait of Mr. Jefferson[1] which is said by conoisseurs to be admirable for its execution, and which I think is the best likeness I have ever seen of him; I am convinced, if neither they nor I are mistaken on these points, that there are many persons in the U. States who have higher claims to the possession of it than I can boast of; and, also, that no one can have a better claim to possess and preserve it than yourself. For this reason I do myself the honor, and you, Sir, the Justice, of offering this picture to you: and if it be accepted, I shall content myself, on parting from it, with the good fortune of having found an accidental opportunity of giving both to Mr. Jefferson and Mr. Madison one small proof of my veneration for the public & private virtues, and the personal friendship, which have so long united them in public & in private life; and which, in my estimation have entitled them to be regarded by their countrymen as their best and safest models in the pursuit of public and private reputation.

I hope there is nothing like flattery in this manner of expressing or proving my sentiments of gratitude towards such men—should any such intention be suspected, it would be too severe a punishment to me for the presumption which I may be, more justly, accused of having indulged myself in. I pray you, Sir, to offer to Mrs. Madison my respectfull compliments and remembrance; and to accept of them yourself in addition to the high esteem & regard with which I do myself the honor of subscribing myself your faithfull and humble Sert.

Tho. Sumter Junr.

RC (DLC). Docketed by JM. Cover (the verso of which is the draft of JM to Andrew Ramsay, 13 Aug. 1820) addressed by Sumter to JM and marked: "Hond. by the care of John Graham Esqr. Minstr. Plenipy. of the U.States at the Court of Rió de Janiero." Enclosed in Andrew Ramsay to JM, 5 Aug. 1820.

1. The Jefferson portrait referred to was a crayon sketch done in 1801 by an artist named Bouch. An engraving by Auguste Desnoyers taken from the sketch became the most familiar image of Jefferson in France of its day. In 1892 information was published about this work, possibly from a label on its reverse: "For James Madison, Esq., late President of the United States. From Rio de Janeiro, 1820. This picture was in the possession of James Madison at the time of his death. It was sold with the residue of his effects, which then formed part of the estate of Mr. Todd . . . at Vendue, and bought by Mr. John H. Lee, of Orange, Virginia, and by him sent to me (Dr. R. C. Moffat) in May, 1858, in very perfect condition." The drawing is still in the hands of a descendant of Reuben C. Moffat of Brooklyn, New York (Thomas K. Murphy, *A Land Without Castles: The Changing Image of America in Europe, 1780–1830* [Lanham, Md., 2001], 87; Lance Humphries, Montpelier Foundation researcher, email message to editor, 15 Jan. 2010).

To John Quincy Adams

Dear Sir. Montpellier June 13. 1820.

I have received and return my thanks for your polite favor[1] accompanying the copy of the printed Journal of the Federal Convention transmitted in pursuance of a late Resolution of Congress.[2]

In turning over a few pages of the Journal, which is all I have done, a casual glance caught a passage which erroneously prefixed my name to the proposition made on the 7th. day of September for making a Council of six members a part of the Executive branch of the Government. The proposition was made by Col: *George Mason* one of the Virginia delegates, and seconded by Doctor Franklin. I cannot be mistaken in the fact: for besides my recollection which is sufficiently distinct on the subject, my notes contain the observations of each in support of the proposition. As the original Journal, according to my extract from it, does not name the mover of the proposition, the error I presume must have had it's source in some of the extrinsic communications to you; unless indeed it was found in some of the separate papers of the Secretary of the Convention; or is to be ascribed to a copying pen. The degree of symphony in the two names *Madison* and *Mason* may possibly have contributed to the substitution of the one for the other.

This explanation having a reference to others as well as myself, I have thought it would be neither improper nor unacceptable. Along with it, I renew the assurance of my high esteem & cordial respects.

James Madison.

FC (DLC); draft (DLC). FC in John C. Payne's hand.

1. Letter not found.

2. On 22 Apr. 1820 Charles Pinckney "offered a joint resolution directing the Secretary of State to transmit one copy of the Journal of the Convention, which formed the Federal Constitution, to each of the members of that Convention, who are now living." The resolution passed the House of Representatives on 24 Apr. and the Senate on 5 May (*Annals of Congress*, 16th Cong., 1st sess., 673, 1947–48, 1951). For the printed journal, see John Quincy Adams to JM, 22 Oct. 1818, *PJM-RS*, 1:367–68, 369 n. 1).

From Levett Harris

Sir Philadelphia 15. June 1820

After having spent fourteen years of my life in the Service of my Country, and having had so distinguished a Share in the establishment of our Relations with the Emperor of Russia, I returned to the US under a full conviction of enjoying, as I felt I deserved, the countenance & Confidence of my Government at home, as I had done abroad. But I had not been long here, before I was apprized by Mr. Adams Secretary of State, that he was in possession of Certain reports which implicated my Consular Character, and which he made known to me as he Stated, with friendly dispositions toward me and with a View of Enabling me to afford Such explanations on the Subject as I might think proper.

To this Communication I immediately replied, and I have good Reason to know that the explanations furnished, were at the time Satisfactory to every body, except perhaps Mr. Adams, who since his Return from Europe, has evinced on my Subject, an inexorable & an unceasing ill will, and which his Credit has been employed to extend even beyond the limits of his Department.

A Young man of the name of Lewis, almost a Stranger to me, brother to an american trader established at St Petersburg, arrived here last Autumn, and uttered in the Shape of Anonymous hand Bills, which he clandestinely and industriously circulated both here and at Washington, a new edition of the Self Same Calumnies which had been previously Reported to me by Mr Adams.

I immediately instituted a Suit against this libeller,[1] and to the astonishment of every body here did it Soon afterwards appear that he was upon a footing of intimacy and of friendly Correspondence with the Secretary of State; and that an union of feeling and of action existed between them on the occasion.

A Conduct so Extraordinary and the same time, so unworthy, necessarily excited in me and my friends the liveliest indignation. It was deemed expedient however to Remain silent on this discovery. Mr. Adams, in his active determination to defeat all my supposed views of further advancement in the diplomatic Service, having been led into the wildest indiscretions, I was encouraged to wait the Slow but certain issue of Events, and especially of the law, in the Suit I had just commenced.

It is now ascertained that it may be of importance to me to proceed to Russia, in order to collect evidence necessary to this prosecution. I have therefore Resolved, and have deemed it an imperious duty to lose no further time in making you fully known to the conduct observed towards me in this conjuncture, and to leave you ignorant of nothing, either as to the merits of this Transaction, or the machinations of my enemies.

You will witness in these disclosures the manner in which the honor of the Executive Government has been committed, and how the man, whom you Sir protected and promoted, and whose acts, far from having dishonored Your Administration, are full of Evidence to the Contrary, has been treated by one, who owes, I have it in my power to prove, a no inconsiderable Share of his present Credit to my Successful efforts in the public Service.

As I am hence, exceedingly anxious to have as early an interview with you, as it may be agreeable to you to honor me with, I shall Repair to Montpellier, the moment I am apprized of the time that it will be most Suitable to you to Receive me.

Mr Jefferson having taken also a prominent interest in the course of my public life, and feeling I flatter myself, no little concern in my future Welfare I have deemed it equally due to your predecessor Sir in the presidency to address him a letter of a Corresponding tenor of the present. I am With Sentiments of the most profound Respect, Sir, Your most Obedient & Very humble Servant

LEVETT HARRIS

RC (NN). Docketed by JM.

1. Harris's suit against John D. Lewis for publishing a pamphlet entitled *Consular Corruption*, which accused Harris of accepting bribes, came to trial in February 1827. Harris, who sought $100,000 in damages, was awarded $100. For a description of the case, see Nagel, *John Quincy Adams*, 273–74.

From William Maury

My Dear Sir, Richmond 19 June 1820

I received, & thank you for your very friendly letter to me at Charleston last year,[1] which set my mind at ease, as you would accept no apology for a Merchants interference with Agriculture.

This letter relates only to my proper department, it is to ask you to ship your Crop (which I am informed is now in Fredericksburg), on board the Arethusa, a remarkably fine coppered Ship, now loading at Bermuda Hundred to my Fathers address—she will sail 1 August, which will insure its arrival in good order.[2]

Since my last, I have been over the Upper Counties of Georgia where I met a number of old Virginians. Of course I felt at home, particularly as many were acquainted with my Father, so that I think the *old Man* would find more pleasure in visiting his Native County than he supposed.

If you would ask him & *offer quarters* for himself & Daughter, I really should not be surprized at his coming over on a visit next Spring, she is coming, & as she is the only one, I hardly think he would *trust* her with any but himself.

I saw about a fortnight ago a Mr Insinger[3] who told me he had received much pleasure from his trip & visit to yourself & Mrs Madison, to whom pray present my respects, & In hopes of doing that personally in 3 or 4 weeks I have the honor to be With high respect Your obedient servant

William Maury

RC (DLC). Docketed by JM.

1. JM to William Maury, 24 Dec. 1819, *PJM-RS*, 1:575–76.

2. In a letter of 20 July 1820 from James Maury in Liverpool to William Maury, the former wrote: "I thank Mr. Madison for his intended consignment. I have had Tobo from him" (Maury, *Intimate Virginiana*, 9).

3. John Peter Insinger, a young member of the Amsterdam merchant family, accompanied John Labouchère on his visit to JM in February 1820 (Langdon Cheves to JM, 7 Feb. 1820; John Quincy Adams diary, 15 Feb. 1820, MHi: Adams Papers; Marten G. Buist, *At Spes Non Fracta: Hope & Co. 1770–1815* [The Hague, 1974], 551 second n. 4, 647 n. 3).

From George Alexander Otis

Philadelphia, 215 Market Street. June 20. 1820

The translator of de Pradt's Europe for 1819.[1] hopes it may find acceptance as an apology for addressing So distinguished a fellow Citizen as the twice elected Chief Magistrate of the only free Nation.

The writer also begs permission to offer the first Volume of his translation of Botta,[2] which if it should be so fortunate as to meet the approbation and merit the high patronage of the late President of the United States of America, cannot fail of Success. A word of encouragement from such a source would indeed be more precious than fame and its Surest presage. This history having been for Eleven years the delight of Europe, it seemed a little surprising to the writer on his return to America, after an absence of four years to find that no translation of it existed in the English language. It is true that five different individuals have thought of it and made the attempt, but have been discouraged before getting through the first volume. The Writer begs many pardons for the great liberty he has taken to enclose his proposals, which if Mr. Madison should deign to approve the design and this Specimen of its execution, he will promote the accomplishment by recommending to the gentlemen of his vicinity. With the truest veneration, I have the honour to be, his most humble servant

GEO. ALEX. OTIS[3]

RC (DLC). In a clerk's hand, signed by Otis. Docketed by JM.

1. Dominique de Pradt, *Europe after the Congress of Aix-la-Chapelle; Forming the Sequel to the Congress of Vienna*, trans. George Alexander Otis (Philadelphia, 1820; Shoemaker 2842).

2. Charles Botta, *History of the War of the Independence of the United States of America*, trans. George Alexander Otis (3 vols.; Philadelphia, 1820–21).

3. George Alexander Otis (1781–1863) was a Boston merchant. Besides Botta, Otis translated *The Tusculan Questions of Marcus Tullius Cicero* (1839) (*San Francisco Bulletin*, 23 July 1863).

From John Quincy Adams

DEAR SIR, WASHINGTON 21. June 1820.

I have had the pleasure of receiving your Letter of the 13th. instt. The error in the printed Journal of the Convention, by which the motion on the 7th. of September for the establishment of a Council of State, is ascribed to you, is in the original list of yeas and nays, taken at the time by the Secretary, who probably in the hurry of writing made the mistake which you suggest of your name instead of that of Mr. Mason.

I am apprehensive that upon examination of the volume you will find many other errors and inaccuracies, some of which will be traceable to the same source as this, and the others to the imperfection of all the assiduity, with which it was my intention to exhibit all the evidence that did exist at this Department of the proceedings of the Convention. If without intruding too much upon your leisure, I could take the liberty of requesting that you would take the trouble to examine the volume throughout, and to minute all the passages where your recollection or your notes would detect an error, it would confer a new and valuable obligation upon me, and might enable me to correct hereafter the misapprehensions which may be entertained, in consequence of those errors, which have crept into the compilation from the manner in which the materials for it were necessarily collected and arranged. I am with the highest, Dear Sir, your very humble and Obedt. Servt.

JOHN QUINCY ADAMS

RC (MiDbEI); letterbook copy (MHi: Adams Papers). RC in a clerk's hand, signed by Adams; docketed by JM.

¶ To Levett Harris. Letter not found. *21 June 1820.* Offered for sale in John Heise Autographs, Catalogue A (1921), item 26. This letter was probably the one listed for sale in Stan. V. Henkels Catalogue No. 836 (2 Feb. 1900), item 4, as to an unidentified correspondent.

From Frances Wright

SIR WHITBURN SUNDERLAND June 28th. 1820

The Tragedy of Altorf, a copy of which I presume to request your acceptance,[1] was favourably received, some time since, in the Theatres of New York and Philadelphia. The kindness which, as a young and unknown Author, I then experienced, has added sentiments of heartfelt gratitude and affection to that admiration which I had previously conceived for the people of America, from the consideration of their history, their excellent laws and liberal constitution.

I must apologize Sir, for thus intruding my sentiments upon one with whose name and reputation I am alone Acquainted. But on these Sir, it is—upon your name which is connected with that of your country, and your reputation which has spread beyond it, that I rest my excuse.

It was the many engagements incident to my sudden return from America to England, at the call of friendship, that prevented me from presenting to Mr Madison at an earlier period a little work which had been so fortunate as to receive the approbation of some of his countrymen. I am Sir, with the highest respect, your most obedient servant

FRANCES WRIGHT[2]

RC (DLC). Docketed by JM.

1. Frances Wright, *Altorf, a Tragedy* (Philadelphia, 1819; Shaw and Shoemaker 47790). The play was about the Swiss struggle for independence.

2. Frances Wright (1795–1852) was a Scottish-born writer and social reformer whose first visit to the United States in 1818–20 led her to write *Views of Society and Manners in America* (London, 1821). On her second visit to the United States in 1824, she toured the country with Lafayette and visited JM. Their conversations about slavery led to a correspondence. Wright's experimental community, Nashoba, in Tennessee, established in 1825, was a plan to test ideas of emancipation. Between 1828 and her death, Wright edited the Indiana *New Harmony Gazette*, which later became the New York *Free Enquirer*, and lectured to a public scandalized by her advocacy of equal rights for women, free love, and birth control, and her attacks on organized religion. Jefferson's granddaughter, Ellen Coolidge, reacted with characteristic disapproval when she wrote in 1829 that "Frances Wright has arrived in Boston to deliver a course of lectures which I hope no body will go to hear." About Wright's views on the immorality of marriage, she wrote that "I fear the people here are scarcely advanced enough to relish the doctrine, & Miss Wright will probably not be noticed by any modest woman" (Ellen Wayles Randolph Coolidge to Virginia Randolph Trist, 21 July 1829, ViU: Correspondence of Ellen Wayles Randolph Coolidge, Special Collections).

From Levett Harris

SIR, PHILADELPHIA 29. June 1820.

I return You my acknowledgments for Your very kind Reply of the 21st inst[1] to the Letter I had the honor to address You on the 15th.

I purpose leaving here in All next Week for Monticello, on a Visit to Mr Jefferson, whose Stay there, he writes me is limited to about two Weeks, and I shall thence Repair to pay my Respects at Montpellier. I beg You to Accept in Advance the Renewed Assurances of my most profound Respect and Veneration

LEVETT HARRIS

RC (NN). Docketed by JM.

1. Letter not found.

To James Maury

DR. SIR [ca. July 1820]

I send you by the present Conveyance 8 Hhds of Tobo. as noted in the Margin. The greater part is I believe of prime quality notwithstanding the season which was remarkably unfavorable. The rest, tho' inferior is better probably than the generality of the shipments this year. The whole is reported by the Inspectors, as put up in the best order & neatest manner. Out of the proceeds Be pleased to send the following articles. Fredericksburg you know is the port nearest to me. Mr. Mackey[1] has promised to take the proper steps for having the Tobo. ensured.

Two pieces of fine Irish Linin—Two ditto of fine Sheeting—Twelve pair mens silk stockings Six pair of them white & six black. Four pieces of furniture Chintz, of lively colours—with fringe to suit it, all, for bed & windows of the same room. One ps. fine Cambrick Muslin for dresses one ps. fine linen Cambrick for shirt ruffles—one Sett Ivory handle Knives & forks—say four dozn. 2 dozn. large & 2 ditto small—2 Carving ditto.

Draft (NN: Arents Tobacco Collection). Undated; conjectural date assigned based on information in JM to Robert Mackay, 1 Sept. 1820, Mackay & Campbell to JM, 4 Sept. 1820, Maury & Latham to JM, 13 Sept. 1820, and JM to James Maury, 20 Feb. 1821. Written above JM's draft is the list of articles partially in Dolley Madison's hand.

1. Robert Mackay was a Fredericksburg merchant, former mayor, and partner of Mackay & Campbell to whom JM consigned the sale of his agricultural productions from 1820 to at least 1823 (John T. Goolrick, *Historic Fredericksburg: The Story of an Old Town* [Richmond, Va., 1922], 156).

From Joseph Wheaton

ILLUSTRIOUS SIR WASHINGTON CITY July 1st. 1820

The enclosed copy of a Statement (correctly made,) is some evidence of the truth of the memorial presented to the House of Representatives United States in N. York when you was a member of it,[1] and which with your aid gave me the appointment of Sergeant at Arms to that Honorable Body, with that memorial and the enclosed Statement, and your personal knowledge of me for thirty years past, with much of my exertions in the late war, I am induced to ask the favor of you, of a letter or certificate, of your Sense of my conduct as came within your information during that war, Both in the Black Swamps of ohio the Siege of Fort meigs upon Sandusky and in Virginia.[2] I have Children & Grand children am descending the down hill of life, and it would be very gratifying to me, to have Something from you, which they may read and look upon—With the Homage of my Heart I have the honor to be, Illustrious Sir, faithfully, your Obedient Servant

JOSEPH WHEATON[3]

RC and enclosure (DLC).

1. The enclosure (2 pp.; docketed by JM), is a copy of a deposition addressed to Wheaton from William A. Rind, 24 Apr. 1820, attesting to a conversation Rind had had with Wheaton's brother in 1815, in which the latter observed that he supposed Wheaton had been a second time disinherited by his father for "fighting against your King and family

for the damned Yankee rebels." Wheaton's original memorial, addressed to the Senate and dated 6 Apr. 1789, petitioning for government employment, attested to his service in the Continental Army and his personal circumstances (DNA: RG 46, Applications for Jobs, 1A–G1).

2. For Wheaton's detailed reports of his experiences during the War of 1812, see his letters to JM of 10, 23, 29, and 31 Dec. 1812, 3 and 8 Jan., 10, 12, and 26 Feb., 26 Apr., and 1 May 1813 (*PJM-PS*, 5:496–97, 521, 532–33, 537–38, 549–51, 564–65; 6:9–11, 14–15, 72–73, 241–43, 273–74).

3. Joseph Wheaton (d. 1828) was a Revolutionary War veteran from Rhode Island. He was appointed sergeant at arms of the U.S. House of Representatives on 12 May 1789 and served until 1807. In April 1813 he was commissioned a captain and deputy quartermaster general in the U.S. Army, was promoted to major the next year, and served until January 1815 (Abbot et al., *Papers of George Washington: Presidential Series*, 5:328 n.; Heitman, *Historical Register*, 1:1022–23).

To George Alexander Otis

Sir — Montpellier July 3. 1820

I have received your favor of June 20. & with it the translated Copies of Pradt's Europe for 1819, and of the 1st. vol. of Botta's History of our war of Independence. Be pleased to accept my thanks for both.

The literary reputation of the latter Author, with the philosophic spirit & classic taste allowed abroad to this historical Work justly recommended the task in which you are engaged, of placing a translation of it before American readers; to whom the subject must always be deeply interesting, and who can not but feel a curiosity to see the picture of it as presented to Europe by so able a hand. The Author seems to have the merit of adding to his other qualifications much industry and care in his researches into the best sources of information; and it may readily be supposed that he did not fail to make the most of his access to those in France not yet generally laid open. A compleat view of our revolutionary contest, involves transactions in & out of the Cabinets of the several nations who directly or indirectly participated in it, which time may be expected more & more to disclose.

I sincerely wish Sir that you may meet with all the encouragement due to your laudable undertaking; which besides the gratification it will afford to readers in general, will enable the more critical part of them to mark & correct errors which all the care & candor of Mr. Botta may not have avoided, and which either do injustice or not full justice to the American cause & character.

I shall endeavor to give an oppy. for subscribing your proposals, to such of the individuals in my vicinity as are most likely to make use of it. The number would be small under more favorable circumstances. Under those now felt every where, I can not venture to expect any sensible aid to the publication. With respect & good wishes

JAMES MADISON

RC (owned by Harlan Crow Library, Dallas, Texas, 2008); draft (DLC). Minor differences between the copies have not been noted.

To Joseph Wheaton

SIR MONTPR. July 6. 1820

I have just recd. your letter of the 1st. instant. Your wish that your descendants shd. possess a just & favorable view of their ancestor is natural & commendable. There are others whose knowlege of your character & public services being more special may enable them to do more justice to your object than I can do. What I can say with truth & with pleasure is that in originally favoring your appointment to the place you held under the H. of Reps. I was governed by satisfactory evidence of the sacrifices both of interest and of the ties of blood which you made to the cause of your country, and of your gallantry in fighting its revolutionary battles. I can add that in your conduct during the late war many instances fell within my information of a zealous activity in promoting its operations very creditable to you both as a Citizen & a Soldier. I tender you Sir my respects & best wishes

J. M.

Draft (DLC).

From Peter Cardelli

EXELLANCE 19 Juillet 1820

J'ai expedie deux bustes pour Votre Exellance au potomac crik dans le memme endrois que j'avais envoye; les Autres—Un c'est celui *de Mr. Jefferson*—et l'Autre de *Mr. Clay* ils ont une preparation que l'on peut toujour les laver.

Je suis pret a partir bien tot; mon intention est de faire un grand tour jusque à la nouvelle Orleans et eax Quantoqui en debitent mes Ouvrajes; mes forses sont bien petittes je cherche à m'eder comme je peut. Pardonez ma Liberté et plain d'Estime et Respect je suis les tres humble Serviteur

PR. CARDELLI

P. S. Ma direction est to Mr Adams Secr. of States.

CONDENSED TRANSLATION

Has sent two busts for JM to Potomac Creek, the same place that he sent the others. One is of Jefferson and the other of Clay. They are prepared so that one can always wash them.

Is ready to leave soon; his intention is to make a grand tour as far as New Orleans and Kentucky, while offering his works for sale; as his means are quite small, he looks for ways to help himself however he can.

RC (DLC).

From Lafayette

MY DEAR FRIEND, LA GRANGE July 22d 1820

I Have not Had for a Long time the pleasure to Hear from You,[1] and Beg You not to Leave me in this painful privation of Your Correspondence. It Has been Lately my fate to be entangled in a Long, boisterous Session; where much has been Said in favour of liberty, but much Has been perpetrated against it. Yet upon the whole I do not know whether the talkers Have not Had the advantage of the doers. Individual liberty, liberty of the press are Suspended. A mode of election already strangely aristocratical Has been Replaced by one infinitely more So; Yet Such is the general Sense, that even now government is not Sure of a large majority, and a minority from which they Can not Exclude Certain popular Members, Carries with in the great Weight of the nation. Revolution and Counter Revolution are in presence. The King and Ministers Hitherto Seeming to form a kind of third party are now oppenly with our adversaries; in this Struggle of ours, the foreign Nations, divided also under the banners of Right and privilege, take a Very warm interest, as if they instinctively felt that their fate, in this respect, is principaly depending on the issue in france. The Emancipation of Spain, and lately that of Naples are, in return, Heartily Welcomed by us. There exists a Sympathy of liberalism throughout Europe Which, after Having Appeared in the first Years of the Revolution, Had been Checked by the Excesses, follies, and Crimes of the Ensuing period, by the ill policy of the directory, and the Ambition, Conquests, and despotism of bonaparte; but now it Has Revived Again, and is cherished with great Care. I do not know whether our debates are related in the American papers; But finding Under my Hand what I Said on a late occasion which Has Since been printed, I inclose it as a Specimen of our parliamentary prattle, or rather as a Criticism of our Situation with the opposite party.[2]

Now I am returned to La grange where I Have Reunited the Several branches of the family Excepting, and this is for mr. Todd's Remembrance, my eldest grand daughter Celestine Latour mauburg, who Has been of late Very Happily married. Such is my Reluctance to give Up the pleasure of farming that I Have attempted Continuing the Trade in Spite of eight months attendance at the House; a frequent Correspondence and the choice of a Very good Head Servant Have Well Seconded my inclinations. Happy I Would be, My dear Madison, to Receive You at La grange, Happy to find myself Under Your Virginia Roof. Let us at least write oftener to Each other and believe me forever Your affectionate obliged, and Constant old friend

LAFAYETTE[3]

My best Respects to all friends within and out of Your family.

RC (PHi).

1. JM had last written Lafayette on 10 May 1816 (NNPM), which Lafayette had answered on 18 Aug. 1816 (PHi).

2. *Opinion de M. de Lafayette, député de la Sarthe, sur la projet de loi relatif aux élections. Séance du 27 mai 1820* (Paris, 1820).

3. Marie Joseph Paul Yves Roch Gilbert Du Motier, marquis de Lafayette (1757–1834), the young man who so captivated George Washington and American hearts while fighting in the American Revolution, had weathered the French Revolution and ensuing years of Napoleonic rule to emerge as a political force in the French legislature, where he became the focus of opposition to the crown. Lafayette made a triumphant tour of the United States in 1824–25, where he twice visited JM at Montpelier (Tulard, *Dictionnaire Napoléon*, 1016–18).

To Reynolds Chapman

DR. SIR July 24 1820

I have recd. yours of the 20th.[1] I shall be content with whatever arrangements may be made with Ambrose Madison on the subject of Milly.[2] Yrs Affe.

J.M

Draft (ViU: Special Collections). Reynolds Chapman (1778–1844) was clerk of the Hustings and Superior courts of Orange County, Virginia. He married JM's niece, Rebecca Conway Madison, the daughter of William Madison and Frances Throckmorton Madison, in 1802 (*Daily National Intelligencer*, 20 Feb. 1844; Chapman, "Who was Buried in James Madison's Grave?," 254, 262).

1. Letter not found.

2. Milly was one of JM's slaves, and probably the same who was conveyed to John Payne Todd by Dolley Madison in 1844. She would have been about sixteen years old in 1820 (Mattern and Shulman, *Selected Letters of Dolley Payne Madison*, 372).

From George Watterston

Dr. Sir, City of Washington Augt. 4th. 1820

I beg you to accept the accompanying copy of a little work of mine, published a few winters ago.[1] With most of the characters delineated in it, you are, I believe, well acquainted & will therefore be enabled to judge of the truth & correctness of the Sketches. I have it in contemplation to undertake a history of your administration, which I conceive to be the most interesting period, except the revolution, of [the] American story. Could I be so fortunate as to obtain your aid in explaining the more obscure events of that time, & in furnishing such other information as might be useful & important; it would not only render me more competant to the task, but the work itself, more interesting. Cotemporary history has been objected to, but I think it is from that source, the future historian is the best enabled to obtain his facts & to select his matter. My respect for your character may indeed make me somewhat too partial; but I shall always endeavour to keep in view the course an impartial historian should ever observe, when he writes for the edification of posterity.

Be so good as to make my respects to your excellent lady; may you both enjoy long life & happiness, as you must enjoy, the gratitude & respect of a generous & enlightened nation. I have the honor to be very respy Yr. obt servt.

Geo Watterston[2]

RC (DLC). Docketed by JM.

1. George Watterston, *Letters from Washington, on the Constitution and Laws; With Sketches of Some of the Prominent Public Characters of the United States. Written during the Winter of 1817–18* (Washington, 1818; Shaw and Shoemaker 46708).

2. George Watterston (1783–1854) was a lawyer who practiced for a time in Hagerstown, Maryland. After a tour of the West Indies in 1810, he wrote the poem, *The Wanderer in Jamaica* (1810), which he dedicated to Dolley Madison. In 1813 he became editor of the *Washington City Gazette*, and in 1815 JM appointed him librarian of Congress. Watterston served in that position until President Jackson removed him in 1829. During those years he published a number of novels, including *The L . . . Family at Washington; or, A Winter in the Metropolis* (1822). After he left the library, Watterston edited the *National Journal* and wrote newspaper and magazine articles, some of which were published in the *Southern Literary Messenger*. He helped found the Washington Botanical Society, the Columbian Horticultural Society, and the Washington National Monument Society (Julia E. Kennedy, *George Watterston: Novelist, "Metropolitan Author," and Critic* [Washington, 1933], 1, 2–3, 6–7, 8–9, 10, 15, 56–57).

From Andrew Ramsay

Dear Sir, City of Washington 5th. August 1820.

Mr. John Graham arrived at my house on the 23d. ultimo from Rio de Janeiro, in extreme ill health, and is now greatly worse—indeed, becoming weaker and weaker every day. His liver is seriously affected, and with it, a severe bowel complaint, which has reduced him to a mere skeleton. We are under the most serious apprehensions as to the result, and unfortunately, his brother Mr. George Graham[1] is now absent on a short visit to Kentucky.

Mr. Graham requested me this morning to put under cover the enclosed letter from Mr. Sumpter, and to say with his very best wishes and regards to you and Mrs. Madison, that the engraving of Mr. Jefferson, mentioned in the letter, he will have forwarded in whatever way you may be pleased to direct. On his arrival here he flattered himself with the prospect of an excursion to the Springs, in which event, he had promised himself the pleasure of making you and Mrs. Madison a visit at Montpelier.

Mrs. Ramsay joins me in best regards to Mrs. Madison and yourself. I have the honour to be With the greatest respect & esteem Your Mo. Obed. St.

Andrew Ramsay[2]

RC and enclosure (DLC). RC docketed by JM. The enclosure was Thomas Sumter Jr. to JM, 9 June 1820.

1. George Graham (ca. 1772–1830) was a veteran of the War of 1812 from Dumfries, Virginia, who served as chief clerk in the War Department, 1814–18. In 1818 he was sent as a special agent to Texas. He was president of the Washington branch of the Second Bank of the United States, 1817–23, and commissioner of the U.S. land office, 1823–30 (Tyler, *Encyclopedia of Virginia Biography*, 2:180; *Niles' Weekly Register* 12 [16 Aug. 1817]: 399).

2. Andrew Ramsay (ca. 1771–1828) was a clerk in the paymaster's office of the War Department. He was married to John Graham's sister, Catherine (*Daily National Intelligencer*, 20 Dec. 1828; *A Register of Officers and Agents . . . 1827* [Washington, 1828], 75; Jackson and Twohig, *Diaries of George Washington*, 6:336 n.).

From Jacob De La Motta

Dear Sir. Savannah, Georgia August 7th. 1820

The services of those who have acted well for their Country, can never be requited; and in a government like ours, the retirement of the first magistrate and relinquishment of his exalted station; does not lessen the respect that the people should, at all times entertain for him. Under this impression, and believing that you have ever been, and still continue to be, liberal in Your views of a once oppressed people; and confident that you would cheerfully receive any information, appertaining to the history of the Jews in this country; have been induced to solicit your acceptance of a discourse, pronounced on the occasion of the Consecration of the New Synagogue recently erected in our city.[1] I am aware it contains nothing worthy attention, except a few facts in relation to the Jews. And I am imboldened to this act, not only from respect, but for the liberality you possess. Allow me the honor of considering myself very Respectfully Your Obt. Hume. Servt.

JACOB DE LA MOTTA[2]

RC (DLC). Docketed by JM.

1. Jacob De La Motta, *Discourse Delivered at the Consecration of the Synagogue of the Hebrew Congregation, Mikva Israel: In the City of Savannah, Georgia, on Friday, the 10th of Ab, 5580, Corresponding with the 21st of July, 1820* (Savannah, Ga., 1820; Shoemaker 986).

2. Jacob De La Motta (1789–1845) was born in Savannah, Georgia, but spent most of his life in Charleston, South Carolina. He received his medical education in Philadelphia and held a commission as surgeon in the U.S. Army during the War of 1812. He was active in local politics and was a contributor to the scientific and literary discourse of his time. Among the many community and charitable organizations of which he was a member and officer, he was secretary of the Medical Society of South Carolina, 1825–35 (Thomas J. Tobias, "The Many-Sided Dr. De La Motta," *American Jewish Historical Quarterly* 52 [1963]: 200–219).

To Jacob De La Motta

SIR MONTPELLIER [post–7] Aug: 1820

I have received your letter of the 7th. inst: with the Discourse delivered at the consecration of the Hebrew Synagogue at Savannah, for which you will please to accept my thanks.

The history of the Jews must for ever be interesting. The modern part of it is at the same time so little generally known, that every ray of light on the subject has its value.

Among the features peculiar to the political system of the U. States, is the perfect equality of rights which it secures to every religious sect. And it is particularly pleasing to observe in the good citizenship of such as have been most distrusted and oppressed elsewhere, a happy illustration of the safety & success of this experiment of a just & benignant policy. Equal laws protecting equal rights are found as they ought to be presumed, the best guarantee of loyalty & love of country; as well as best calculated to cherish that mutual respect & good will among Citizens of every religious denomination, which are necessary to social harmony and most favorable to the advancement of truth. The account you give of the Jews of your

Congre[g]ation brings them fully within the scope of these observations. I tender you, Sir, my respects & good wishes

James Madison

Draft (DLC). Day of month not indicated; conjectural day assigned based on De La Motta to JM, 7 Aug. 1820.

Montpelier, the Seat of Mr. Madison

[9 August 1820]

Leaving Fredericksburg on the Rappahannock, you travel in a westerly direction through the county of Spotsylvania, to Orange Court House, about five miles from Montpelier. The country between Fredericksburg and the eastern foot of the South Mountain, is, with the exception of the flats on each side of the streams, rather sterile, and the soil composed of a white gravelly clay, which gives it an appearance not altogether inviting. The moment, however, you reach the foot of the South Mountain every thing changes like magic. It is but crossing a little stream two yards wide, and the soil becomes of a deep orange colour, which gives its name to the county of Orange. Here every production of a Virginia farm flourishes, and the fields of wheat and corn indicate that this singular soil, which conveys rather an idea of poverty, possesses great fertility. A few miles now bring you to the Court House, which is in the midst of a little village, beautifully situated and commanding, from the windows of the principal Inn, the view of a fine variegated country to the north and west, bounded by a cluster of mountains, inclining to the eastward, and shutting the view in that direction.

From the Court House to Montpelier, after quitting the main road, you pass through a deep forest, from which you emerge, all at once, to a view of the house and plantation. The effect is peculiarly striking, and the sudden contrast creates both surprise and pleasure. The House is composed of a centre embellished with a fine doric portico, and two wings of lesser height, with flat roofs and a railing around them. In front is a lawn, in which are scattered a number of fine trees—beyond this an extensive open field nearly a mile in extent, and bounded on all sides by a thick wood, over which the eye passes without interruption till it rests on the distant horizon, which is formed by the Blue Ridge. In the rear is another lawn, at the extremity of which, and ascending abruptly to a little stream, is a grove of the finest black walnuts.

Seated on the western declivity of the South Mountain, though much nearer the bottom than the top, the piazza commands a fine prospect of woodland scenery, bounded in every direction by mountains. In front the Blue Ridge passes from north to south with the regularity of an artificial wall; on the right the mountains appear more varied and picturesque in their outlines, and to the left, the jutting promontories of the South Mountains, here and there, present a view of different country seats. The whole situation, with its surrounding scenery—its woods, mountains, and evening skies, is altogether singularly striking, though it wants a view of water. The Rapidon [*sic*], a branch of the Rappahannock, passes within a few miles, but is every where hid by the majestic forests.

Here, out of the way of intrusion from all except those who come out of the high road on purpose to visit him, Mr. Madison passes a life of repose, though not of useless idleness. His plantation is large, and he pays particular attention to agriculture, riding out generally twice a day to observe the progress of his rural domain; neither obtruding himself upon the public attention, as if he was apprehensive his country would forget his services, nor retiring from action when he can be useful, either by his political experience or his agricultural skill. He reads a good deal, but writes few letters, and, if he should live twenty years longer, will probably not outlive his reputation, by any public exhibition of weakness or vanity. The wisdom of age consists, in a great degree, in husbanding that glory and honor and affection, which rewards the toils of youth and manhood; not in attempting to increase them by new exertions that only display the ravages of time. The mind sometimes outlasts the vigour of the frame, as the lamp may be broken yet the light remain. But this is not the general course of nature, and it ought occasionally to be remembered, that there is a prodigality sometimes in age, as well as in youth, which is equally fatal to the hopes of both.

It has never fallen to my lot to see a great public character so completely abstracted from public life, or so devoted to rural enjoyments and rural occupations. He seems to have forgotten that he ever directed the destinies of this great republic, and has settled, gracefully as well as happily, into the most respectable, if not the happiest, of all human characters—an independent farmer. Hospitable, kind, and benevolent, without ostentation, every thing about the house indicates a plentiful exuberance of all the real comforts of life; and, without effort, every visiter [*sic*] is made welcome.

It is among the beauties of our system of government, that these examples are almost always present to us, of virtuous statesmen, who, after having exhibited a striking picture of public virtue and public services, retire to the shades of private life, there to exhibit another example not less useful and illustrious—that of an unambitious citizen, who has tasted the sweets of authority, without losing his relish for those of rural life. It is gratifying to the pride and the heart of an American to behold such a man in such a situation; since it is a proof of the excellence of that system under which power does not corrupt, or public station unfit for private happiness. In viewing Mr. Madison, reposing in retirement, and busying himself with the employments of the ancient patriarchs, one cannot help reverting to his previous life, and recalling his exertions and his services.

In tracing his long and noble career, we always find him grappling, with the strongest adversaries, and identified with the most important measures of the government, foreign and domestic. At first we see him engaged in supporting the pillars of this great confederation—advocating, in conjunction with Hamilton and Jay, the adoption of that constitution which has borne us aloft almost to the pinnacle of prosperity, and advocating it in a manner worthy of the subject, worthy of his coadjutors, worthy of himself. Following his course, we next see him supporting with equal force of reasoning, those famous propositions of 1794, which, though then defeated, have since been made the great basis of our foreign policy. Then, as Secretary of State, we see him defending his country's rights, vindicating her honor, and triumphantly establishing a good cause by unanswerable arguments. From this we follow him to a station from whence he conducted the nation through a war of difficulties unparalleled, against a powerful foreign foe, and powerful internal faction, leaving the nation in the possession of her rights, and the full enjoyment of her glory, respected by those who before contemned her spirit and despised her resources.

Last of all, we see him retire with dignity from a situation which he had supported with firmness, to the enjoyment of an useful and honorable age, unsullied by superannuated vanity, and unruffled by even a wish to obtrude himself again upon the attention of his country, which will not, he knows, forget him. Should he ever see this unstudied effusion, the writer hopes he will receive it as a testimony of affectionate respect, such an one as, now that he no longer rewards or punishes, a great man, may receive without blush, and an honest man offer without degradation.

"Montpelier, the Seat of Mr. Madison," Communications, *Daily National Intelligencer*, 9 Aug. 1820.

To George Watterston

DR SIR MONTPR. Aug 10. 1820

I have recd. your favor of the 4th. accompanied by a copy of "the letters & sketches &c." I had seen & read these as they successively issued from the press. I thank you for the collected form in which they now appear. Not venturing to pronounce on the likenesses of the portraits, particularly those of which the originals are least known to me, I can only pay a just tribute to the apparent capacity of the pencil furnishing them.

On the other subject of your letter I am still more restrained by the personal concern involved in it. I allow myself only to say, that whatever errors may be seen or supposed in the Ex: administration of the federal Govt. whilst in my hands I feel not only a consciousness of pure intentions; but indulge a persuasion that it will not suffer from a candid & full review: And in that persuasion it can not be dissatisfactory to me, that the task shd. be undertaken by one who to every advantage of access to the ordinary sources of information, adds that of personal opportunities of judging in some cases, & who joins to both a determination not to permit his pen to swerve from the line of impartial History. How far I can aid your materials by explanations of events not otherwise attainable is a point on which some reserve may be imposed on me. I can feel none in assuring you that it will in no instance be so, by any distrust of the depository into which the explanations would pass. With this assurance be pleased to accept that of my friendly esteem & good wishes

J. M

Draft (DLC).

To Richard Rush

Dr. Sir Montpellier Aug. 12. 1820

In acknowledging your favor of Sepr. last, an interval between that date & this, presents itself which would call for apology, were I less sure that you would put no misconstruction on it. The truth is, I well know your time must be so engrossed with objects more important than my correspondence, that I am unwilling to multiply its interferences; notwithstanding the temptations I feel in the pleasure which your letters afford me.

I thank you much, my dear Sir, for your kindness in procuring the posthumous works of Gibbon, and the continuation of Eustace, by Sr. R. Hoare. The latter I have not yet found it convenient to look over. The former has recreated not a few of my leisure hours. I have to thank you also for the copy you were so good as to spare, of the pamphlet relating to the Holkam Estate. It contains some instructive, and many amusing pages. I was surprizd to see stated as expedient, the substitution of *dotting*, for *turfing*.[1] I had practised the former for several years on a small scale, without regarding it in the least as a new idea.

The scene you are witnessing in the case of the British Queen,[2] so agitating on the local theatre, is regarded not without curiosity at this distance. The Ministry seem to be entangled in their own web: and Monarchy itself may well dread the tendency of such specimens, in the present temper of the world, and with the contrast of an uncorrupted Republic giving full relief to such deformities. This consideration, I presume, accounts for the general anxiety to stifle the enquiry in its birth.

You see that the evasive resorts of the B. Parliament agst. the retaliatory Acts of Congress, have produced a further effort to force a reciprocity in the W. Inda. trade.[3] I heartily wish you may be able to negociate the controversy into a just & amicable settlement, for the benefit of both parties. Resting as the claims of Congs. do, on the soundest of principles, and united & committed in the contest as all parties here now are, no retreat on this side can be expected on the other; notwithstanding the advantage it may have at this postponed epoch, makg. the British ⟨W.⟩ Indies independent of direct supplies from the U. S. particularly by supplies, thro' Canada, from the districts now so productive, on the Lakes and the St. Laurence. It has always appeared to me, that the B. Govt. had no plausible plea for the course it has pursued. The rule of reciprocity, the only admissible one, between independent nations, evidently forbade it. The very principle of Colonial Monopoly gives no countenance to it: that principle excluding all commercial intercourse, between a Colony & a foreign country, other than through the parent State, and being abandoned the moment a *direct* intercourse is opened in national vessels. The colonial ports in this case are assimilated to other ports of the same nation opened to such intercourse: and are brought of course within the same rule of reciprocity. Nor is there any truth in the plea, so much urged on the British side, & too often admitted on ours, which refers to the practice of other European nations having colonies. The general practice of these nations, conformably to the colonial principle, is to shut the colonies, agst. all direct trade with foreign countries. But it is equally their practice, whenever they find it requisite to suspend the principle, by opening the colonial ports to a foreign trade, to respect the principle of reciprocity, by allowing to foreign vessels the same carrying privileges with their own. If there be any exception, it is of recent date, and probably an effect of the British practice instead of a precedent for it.

You will learn with pleasure that the seasons of the present year are proving abundantly fruitful throughout our whole country. For want of adequate markets however, particularly for the esculent grains, the surplus will not give the desired relief from the pressure felt by so large a portion of the people. This must be the work of time & economy; aided by professional & household manufactures. The latter abridges the expenditures of individuals; and both, the amount to be paid to foreign nations. There are glimpses it would seem, in late Parliamentary discussions, of some approaching relaxation of the system which precludes the sale of British products, by refusing to purchase those of other Countries. In so plain a case, the error of the system can not permanently resist the increasing light on all subjects of political economy. But it is so common to find a long interval between the discovery and the correction of a false policy, that other remedies must be relied on, for the difficulties felt here.

Mrs. Madison & myself are much gratified by the promise of Mrs Rush & yourself, to give us an oppy. of welcoming you both in due time, at Montpr. We shall do it, with the same affecte. feelings, with which we now jointly tender our great respect, & all our best wishes.

J. M.

Mrs. M. desires me to mention, that she committed to Mr. Astor a long letter for Mrs. Rush; which he may have retained untill he should pass from the Continent to England.

Draft (DLC).

1. In Edward Rigby's pamphlet, *Holkham, Its Agriculture, &c*, the author noted that the agriculturalist Thomas William Coke recommended a process he called "inoculating," in which arable land was converted to pasture. By this practice, small squares of grass or turf were transplanted in a plowed field in winter, leaving bare patches between them. In the spring, grass seed was sown on the bare spots, and over the course of a year, the grass gradually extended to cover the entire field (4–5).

2. Caroline of Brunswick (1768–1821) married George, Prince of Wales, in 1795. The two became estranged soon after, and by 1814 Caroline was living abroad. On the ascension of her husband to the throne as George IV in 1820, she became queen of Great Britain. Her return to London in that year provoked a Parliamentary enquiry into her conduct while abroad and a public trial in the House of Lords. A bill of pains and penalties, if passed, would have exiled Caroline. The trial, held between August and November, sparked enormous interest and ended with riots and popular demonstrations in support of the queen until the ministry finally withdrew the bill (Thea Holme, *Caroline: A Biography of Caroline of Brunswick* [London, 1979], 6, 30–32, 57, 189–92, 194–96, 205–6, 211, 217).

3. In May 1820 Congress passed an act supplementary to the Navigation Act of 1818, closing U.S. ports to British vessels coming from any British American colony, including Lower Canada, New Brunswick, Nova Scotia, Newfoundland, and the West Indies. This act was in response to a British law of 1818 that had created free ports in St. John and Halifax, thus encouraging U.S. ships to carry products for the West Indies to those ports (Benns, "Study No. 56: The American Struggle for the British West India Carrying-Trade," *Indiana University Studies* 10 [1923]: 66–67, 70–71).

To Andrew Ramsay

DR. SIR MONTR. Aug. 13. 1820

Your favor of the 5th. did not come to hand till yesterday. The same mail brought the melancholy event[1] for which it wd. have prepared me. I had so high an esteem & so true an affection for the friend who is no more that I partake deeply in the grief felt for his loss. Mrs. Madison was equally sensible of his great worth, and joins in my feelings as she does in cordial regards for the most distressed of his mourners to whom we wish that our sincerest condolence may be duly made known.

May I ask the favor of you to have the article from Mr. Sumter committed in a secure State to the Steam boat, under an address to the care of Mr. Farish of Fredg; noting to me whatever expence may be involved in the case.

Mrs. M. charges me with her particular regards for Mrs. R & yourself; to which I beg that the addition of mine may at the same time be accepted.

Draft (DLC).

1. JM placed an asterisk here and in the left margin wrote: "*death of John Graham."

To Thomas Todd

My dear Sir Montpellier Aug. 13. 1820

I have just been favored with yours of July 26:[1] & thank you much for your kind attention to the subject of the Legislative Journals of Virga. The copy borrowed from Mr. Littell[2] to whom you will be so good as to make my acknowlegements, shall be carefully preserved & returned; as shall be your fragment for 1788[3]; if desired. I have myself a part of the Journal for 1777 viz from May 5. to May 22. All my efforts here to obtain copies of these documents have failed, such is the rate at which they perish. I inclose a list of the copies I possess,[4] the remains of the compleat setts I once had. I should be glad, as opportunities occur, without too much trouble or expence, to fill up the chasms; I should be particularly so to get the Journals of the H. of D. or even of the Senate for 1784-5-6-7. But I do not say so, without a protest agst. your doing more in the case than merely availing yourself of any *casual* opportunity.

I am sorry I have no recollections that throw light on the question stated by Mr. Littell; nor have I probably any printed sources of information not within his own reach. Could any "official act of the B. Govt." alter the boundaries of a County fixed by a Statute of the Colony?

After a severe & threatening drought, fine rains have given us flattering prospects in our fields of Corn & Tobo. Our Wheat Crops came in before the drought had much affected them, and were on the whole good. Indeed we learn from all quarters that the year will be uncommonly productive.

The Markets however are such that the farmers will not be relieved from their difficulties by the supplies they have for them. The planters are a little better off, the demand & price of Tobo. being somewhat more favorable. Should the present season continue to be good, the growing crop may reduce them to a level with their farming brethren.

Mrs. M. wrote two days ago to Mrs. Todd. I have therefore nothing to add but assurances on my part of the sincerest affection to her & yourself; and the expectation we indulge, notwithstanding all discouragements, of being able to embrace you both in the course of the Autumn. Truly & respectfully yours

James Madison

RC (NjP: Crane Collection); draft (DLC). Minor differences between the copies have not been noted.

1. Letter not found.

2. William Littell (1768–1824) was a Kentucky lawyer and writer on politics, history, and the law. He is best known as the compiler of the multivolume *Statute Law of Kentucky* (1809–19).

3. JM wrote "1778" in draft.

4. In place of "I possess" in the RC, JM wrote "which I find among my own papers" in the draft.

From Thomas Jefferson

Dear Sir Monticello Aug. 13. 20.

I recieved yesterday the inclosed Letter proposing to me an interposition which my situation renders impracticable.[1] The gentlemen of my family have manifested at times some opposition to mr. Nelson's elections: which has produced an intermission of intercourse between the families: and altho' I never took the smallest part in it, and nothing but what is respectful has ever passed between mr. Nelson and myself, yet I cannot but feel the ground too suspicious to venture on the experiment proposed. And indeed the thing is so delicate that I know not whether any ground, however cordial, could render it safe, but of this you will be the best judge as to yourself, for which purpose I inclose you the letter. I suppose myself it is impossible that a Virginian can be elected and that mr. N's competition would only defeat Genl. Smith's election and ensure a Northern and unfriendly choice.

Our buildings at the University go on so rapidly, and will exhibit such a state and prospect by the meeting of the legislature that no one seems to think it possible they should fail to enable us to open the institution the ensuing year. I salute mrs. Madison & yourself with constant affection & respect.

TH: JEFFERSON

FC (DLC: Jefferson Papers).

1. The enclosure was Samuel Smith to Jefferson, 2 Aug. 1820 (DLC: Jefferson Papers), in which Smith requested Jefferson's and JM's help in dissuading Virginia congressman Hugh Nelson from vying for the position of Speaker of the U.S. House of Representatives in Smith's favor. Smith believed that in a three-way contest between himself, Nelson, and John W. Taylor of New York, that he and Nelson would split the southern vote, ensuring a win for the antislavery Taylor. While Nelson did not run, William Lowndes of South Carolina did, and after twenty-two ballots, Taylor was elected Speaker (John S. Pancake, *Samuel Smith and the Politics of Business: 1752–1839* [University, Ala., 1972], 155).

Monticello and Montpelier

DEAR SIR: [15 August 1820]

You request me to give you some account of my late excursion to Virginia. I comply with the request, but am sorry to observe, that the time occupied in making it was too short to enable me to take those views of the country through which I passed that are necessary to render any description pleasing or satisfactory. The observations, however, I had the power to make, in my rapid journey, I submit to your examination, with a hope that they may be found not entirely destitute of interest. . . .

Having visited this illustrious patriarch [Thomas Jefferson], we could not resist the inclination to call upon his friend, and the friend of his country, Mr. Madison. The natural scenery around this gentleman's residence is also rich and magnificent. The building is of brick, ornamented in front with a Roman portico, and opening, from a saloon behind, into a beautiful lawn, from which, through an artificial vista, you have a view of the range of mountains, called, from their appearance, the Blue Ridge. Groves of forest trees, extensive spots in cultivation, and the waving line of stupendous mountains, are constantly presented to the eye from this elegant retreat.

Montpelier, the residence of Mr. Madison, is about 25 miles from Monticello, situated in Orange county, so called from the Prince of Orange, and about 5 miles from the Court House and the little village in which it stands. His farm is extensive and well improved; the soil, though of a deep orange, is rich and productive; and he seems to want no convenience that might contribute to his comfort or add to his happiness.

It is amidst those isolated mountain habitations that the social affections of our nature become more durable and vigorous, because, being less liable to distraction, they are more concentrated. It is in situations like these that man feels the dignity of his nature, and the happiness of which he has been made susceptible. Nature spreads before him her beauties; masses of verdure surround him; his foot softly presses the green lawn that has been furnished as his carpet; his eye plays over the ever-varying landscape; his ear is regaled by the melody of the grove; and he breathes an air as pure as his heart, and as gentle as the current of his feelings.

Oh, rus! quando te aspiciam?[1]

In such sequestered retirements the heart acquires a purity and innocence that nothing can destroy, and the happy inhabitant contemplates the objects around him with a pleasure that it would be difficult to describe. He beholds in the rising sun the grand epoch of creation, and sees in his descent, when he paints the clouds with a thousand colors, and gilds the summit of the trees that veil his retreat, the last scene of life, in which the projects of ambition and the pomp and trophies of greatness are "ingulphed in an abyss that never restores its prey."[2]

We found Mr. Madison in good health, very cheerful, and very happy. His person, you know, is small, and his countenance grave; but it is soon illuminated when he enters into conversation, and the ease and fluency with which he speaks, gives to what he says a charm that cannot be resisted. His deportment has the same ease and dignity in private, as it had in public life, and the former politeness of his manners, and hospitality of his heart, are still recognised and felt by all who have the happiness to visit him in his delightful retirement. In this retirement he devotes himself to the innocent pursuits of agriculture, and, like the patriarch of Monticello, he seems to manifest a degree of delight at the idea of having honorably freed himself from the cares, the burdens, and the miseries of government. It is certainly a spectacle of no ordinary grandeur to see those who have revolved in the highest spheres of life sinking down into the bosom of society, without a sigh of regret, or an effort to "cast one longing, lingering look behind."[3] The relinquishment of power is not often attended with the enjoyment of happiness. The splendor which surrounds the head of him who wields the destinies of a nation has been considered too alluring and attractive to be abandoned without reluctance and regret; but in the instances this country has furnished, it may be safely averred, that pleasure, rather than pain, has been felt by those who have yielded up the "rod of empire."[4]

"It is seldom (says Gibbon) that minds long exercised in business, have formed any habits of conversing with themselves; and, in the loss of power, they principally regret the want of occupation."[5] But, like Dioclesian, both Mr. Madison and Mr. Jefferson have preserved their taste for the most innocent, as well as natural pleasures, and their hours, like those of that Roman emperor in retirement, are sufficiently employed in reading, planting and cultivating their farms, to exclude the miseries of indolence, and the horrors of *ennui.* The residence of both Mr. Jefferson and Mr. Madison, is the residence of taste and elegance, and to both may be applied, with peculiar aptitude, the lines of the poet of nature;

An elegant sufficiency—contentment,
Retirement, rural quiet, friendship, books,
Ease and alternate labor—useful life,
Progressive virtue, and approving Heaven.[6]

W.[7]

Extract of "Monticello and Montpelier," Communications, *Daily National Intelligencer*, 15 Aug. 1820.

1. "*O, rus, quando ego te aspiciam!*": "O rural home: when shall I behold you!" (Hor., *Satires* 2.6.60, in *Horace: Satires, Epistles and Ars Poetica*, Loeb Classical Library [1970 reprint], 214–15).

2. The writer borrowed most of this paragraph from Ferdinand Marie Bayard, *Voyage dans l'intérieur des États-Unis . . .* (Paris, 1797), 32–33: "Il jouit le soir d'un spectacle aussi beau, et plus instructif peut-être que celui du matin: c'est la descente de l'astre du jour, qui, laissant après lui des traces de sa lumineuse présence, dore et teint de milles couleurs les somets des arbres qui voilent sa retraite. Ce flambeau de la nature semble, en s'éteignant chaque jour, vouloir nous rappeller la dernière scène de la vie, et le terme où les projets ambitieux, les trophées, les grandeurs et leur pompe s'engloutissent dans un abîme qui ne rend pas sa proie."

3. "Nor cast one longing ling'ring look behind?": Thomas Gray, "Elegy Written in a Country Church-Yard," in Austin Lane Poole, ed., *The Poems of Gray and Collins* (1919; reprint, London, 1961), 95.

4. "Hands, that the rod of empire might have sway'd": ibid., 93.

5. Edward Gibbon, *The History of the Decline and Fall of the Roman Empire* (7 vols.; London, 1896–1902), 1:387–88.

6. James Thomson, "Spring," in J. Logie Robertson, ed., *James Thomson: Poetical Works* (1908; reprint, London, 1971), 46.

7. This was possibly written by George Watterston, the novelist and librarian of Congress, who visited Jefferson at Monticello in July 1820 (Watterston to Jefferson, 4 Aug. 1820, DLC: Jefferson Papers) and very likely took in Montpelier as well.

To James Monroe

DEAR SIR MONTPR. Aug. 29. 1820

Mr. Governeur gave us to understand that we should have the pleasure of seeing you & Mrs. Monroe about the first or second week in Sepr. Be so good as to drop a line saying as nearly as you can the precise time. Mrs. M. & myself have a little visit to make in the neighbourhood, which can be executed with equal conveniency a little sooner or later, and which we shall hasten or delay, so as to ensure our being at home at the time of your arrival. We hope Mrs. Monroe's health is perfectly re-established and you will be able to gratify us with a stay of some days on your return, besides the time necessary to make up for what your late haste deprived us of. With our affece. respects for you all. Yrs.

James Madison

RC (DLC: Monroe Papers). Docketed by Monroe.

From Andrew Ramsay

Dear Sir, City of Washington 30th. August 1820.

I had the honour to receive your letter of the 13th. instant, and to communicate its contents this morning to Mrs. Graham, who returned to my house yesterday, after a short visit to her relations in Maryland. To a mind filled with deep affliction, and to the family throughout, your friendly and affectionate expressions of condolence at the death of Mr. Graham, together with Mrs. Madison's, excited feelings of much comfort and gratification.

The day preceding Mr. Graham's death, and the date of my letter communicating his illness, he expressed himself with the utmost warmth & affectionate regard for you and Mrs. Madison; that there was no man he was more sincerely attached to, nor one that he held in higher estimation than yourself.

The Revd. Mr. Hawley[1] left this City a few days since for Culpepper and Orange, to whose particular care I committed the engraving of Mr. Jefferson. I thought this a much safer and better mode of conveyance than by the Steam Boat as you requested.

Mrs. Graham and Mrs. Ramsay charge me with their particular and affectionate regards for Mrs. Madison and yourself, in which I beg to be included. I have the honour to be With real respect & esteem Your Obed. St.

Andrew Ramsay

RC (DLC). Docketed by JM.

1. The Rev. William Hawley (d. 1845) was a veteran of the War of 1812 who served as the second rector of St. John's Church in Washington from 1817 until his death (Van Horne, *Papers of Benjamin Henry Latrobe*, 3:892 n. 9).

From Richard Rush

DEAR SIR. LONDON August 30. 1820.

The Mr Keilsall to whom the enclosed letter is addressed,[1] I have not, by all the inquiries which it has been in my power to make since I came to London, been able to find out. I therefore return it, not without regret at my disappointment, which however is lessened by the excuse which the act of returning it affords me of writing to you.

The last time I had that pleasure, was, if I recollect right, in September last, when I forwarded Gibbon's posthumous works, and Hoars Italy. I do not know if the latter author any where speaks of Italian *witnesses.* But it is plain, that, here in England, they are falling into bad repute. This trial of the queen continues, day by day, to monopolize the publick attention, deluging the country with loads of indecency in a manner that is, perhaps, without parallel. How it will end in itself, or what may grow out of it in all other respects, no one can say. Whatever may have been the queens aberrations, (and as yet there would appear to be no proof of them but by Italian witnesses who confess that they are in most bountiful keeping,) the supposed harshness with which she is treated has had the usual effect of stirring up zealots in her cause. The common people have embarked their passions in it, and the wave seems to gather as it rolls. It has given to dissafection a new and animated ralying point, and increased for the time being its numbers. For myself, however, I do not anticipate any very serious commotions. The truth obviously is, that this is essentially a military government. The regular army is too strong for the unarmed millions, who would otherwise not allow the government to stand for six months; and while the government has the direction of the army, the latter will continue to be paid, and the former supported by the bayonet in its authority. That this state of things will be very permanent, I do not think probable; but I believe it to be an accurate description of them at the present juncture. I renew to you, dear Sir, now, as at all times, the assurances of my invariable affection and respect.

RICHARD RUSH

RC (PHi: Richard Rush Papers). Docketed by JM.

1. JM to Charles Kelsall, October 1817, *PJM-RS*, 1:136. See also Rush to JM, 2 May 1818, and nn. 1–2, ibid., 249–51.

To Robert Mackay

Dr. Sir Montpr. Sepr. 1. 1820

I inclose a Bill on Mr. Maury for £100 Sterling which will cover your advance[1] of $300. and leave a balance of ,[2] which if convenient I shall be glad of by our Court day for this month. I have ventured to draw for that much, as the bill is at 60 days & as I rely on the quality of the Tobo. I have sent, and the amount of the ensurance, to make the payment safe. I have written for a few articles, to come out of the proceeds, of the Tobo. which in case of its deficiency will not be sent, or be provided for by a draft on me. Friend[l]y respects

J. M

Draft (DLC).

1. Here JM wrote and then crossed out "to me."
2. Left blank in draft.

From Charles Pinckney

Dear Sir Charleston September 2 1820

I have long intended to write to you but somehow or other have neglected it—it is a long while since we have seen each other—within a few days it will be 33 Years the day we dined together on signing the Constitution[1]—what changes have taken place since & in my opinion, one of the worst to us is that we are so much older than we were then—for in spite of all that the divines & philosophers may tell us I am honest enough to confess that I think old age is not the most comfortable state in the world—most other inconveniencies may be remedied or palliated but this cannot—it is a state which grows worse every day & he must indeed be a philosopher who can bear it without some times sighing & wishing he was young again. On my asking him if it was true Doctor Franklin has frequently told me it was that he had often said he wished to live his life over again—"that it had been a good world to him & his life a successful one & that he should like to live it over again."[2]

Do not suppose however that these sombre reflections arise from my being particularly pressed yet by either the weakness or inconveniencies of age, for excepting an accident to me in returning from Congress, I have thank God enjoyed In the last twenty Year's an uncommon share of health—my residence in Europe absolutely renewed me. I was not sick one moment while there. Madrid is certainly equal to any climate on Earth. I never found it one day too hot or too cold there & indeed the Experience I had of every part of Europe I visited convinced me, that that was the Portion of the Globe which the Creator intended as the residence of the White Skin & that to each part of the Earth he gave a Skin & Hair suited to the Climate.

I hope you have enjoyed Your health also & will live yet many years in continued usefulness to Your Country. If I am to judge of your residence by the name you have given to it, it must be a very healthy one—in going to Italy I went through the South [of] France & visited Montpelier whose situation & Climate I found to answer the Description given of it. I staid there near a week & in one of my walks seeing the name of *Izard* in large golden letters over a book shop, curiosity led me into it to enquire of the owner about his name & family—he said he had heard that one of them had emigrated about 100 Years agoe to America but he knew nothing of them & that all that were there were like himself poor & mechanics. You recollect an old Friend Mr Izard in Congress & his unusual haughtiness[3]—how do you think he would have liked this account of the Origin of his family? I will now go to more important subjects & congratulate You on the increase & ease of our Country in every thing that can make it great, free & of course happy since I saw you—this I always knew would soon be the case & used to tell them so in Europe—but they never would believe it—they always had the idea (to use Cevallos's Expression)[4] that we were a people in the Woods & that as soon as we increased in numbers We would separate into small confederacies & therefore used to think very little about us. Unfortunately Graham who you sent me as my secretary had got the same notion into his head & all I could do I could never persuade him to the contrary. In the affair of the Deposit at New Orleans[5] I never saw any one more astonished than he was when late one Evening I brought him home the King's order to open it as he was convinced they never would do it & did not care a farthing about what We said.

And now let me ask you what is Your Opinion about Our affairs with Spain should she refuse to ratify the treaty—shall we take Florida, or what shall we do—give me Your opinion freely—do you not recollect my consulting with you on the affair of the Misissipi treaty in 1786 recommended by Mr Jay when you were not in Congress & at Elsworths[6] & is not a little extraordinary I should still have the opportunity to do so, about our affairs with the same nations at so distant a period.

Let me also have Your Opinions fully & freely on the Tariff Question—this favor I ask pro bono publico,[7] as I am obliged very reluctantly to go once more to that dreadfully cold & bleak Place Washington[8] & shall have to give Opinions & Votes on it if I live as my Constituents in Charleston are meeting to express their abhorrence of it—by the by what do you think of those gentry at the northward on the Missouri & Tariff & other questions of that sort—& of our old friend Rufus[9]—come I ask you as a great favour to write me your opinions freely on those subjects & *particularly such as will come before Congress—they shall be considered sacredly confidential by me.*

As I suppose You take both the National Intelligencer & Niles' Register, You have seen my opinions on the Missouri & on the nature & importance of the State Governments to the Union strengthening it as they increase.[10] I wish to give them on the Tarif & if necessary on the affairs with Spain & then to be done—my constituents were very anxious I should be a Candidate for reelection & I should have been reelected without an opponent—but I find the trouble of going there—the long absence from my home & friends & the dreadfully rigorous Climate where the Thermometer is 6 to 8 degrees below Zero & 40 degrees colder than Charleston make it not only prudent but indispensable to decline it. Of the 200 members nearly that compose Congress there are now only four or five who were there when I was last a member in 1801—General Smith, Mr King, Mr Macon,[11] Mr: Dana & Mr: Randolph[12] & probably Mr Otis. Of the Members who signed the Constitution only 7 are alive & 3 of them, nearly half from what is called "the Unhealthy South Carolina.["][13] I hear You are soon about to Give us the history of the Convention & all the Speeches of the members. Lowndes mentioned something about it to me the other day—is it so—the sooner the better & when will it be. I am anxious to hear from you after You get this—to prevent accidents please send *a duplicate* of your letter & direct it to me in Charleston South Carolina. With affectionate regard & best Wishes I am always dear Sir Yours truly

CHARLES PINCKNEY

When you see Mr Jefferson please Remember me very affectionately to him—as his name was very repeatedly mentioned in Congress as favourable to the Tarif & manufacturers, I intend to write to him on it[14] as Newton[15] was the only Virginian who voted for it.

RC (DLC). Docketed by JM.

1. George Washington noted in his diary entry for 17 Sept. 1787 that after the signing of the Constitution, "the business being thus closed, the Members adjourned to the City Tavern, dined together and took a cordial leave of each other" (Jackson and Twohig, *Diaries of George Washington*, 5:185).

2. "Hitherto this long life has been tolerably happy; so that, if I were allowed to live it over again, I should make no objection, only wishing for leave to do, what authors do in a second edition of their works, correct some of my *errata*" (Benjamin Franklin to Catherine Greene, 2 Mar. 1789, in Jared Sparks, ed., *The Works of Benjamin Franklin; . . . With Notes and a Life of the Author* [10 vols.; Boston, 1836–40], 10:387).

3. Ralph Izard (1742–1804) was an immensely rich South Carolina planter and politician who was educated in England and served as an American diplomat in Paris, 1776–80, and as a member of the Continental Congress, 1782–83. Izard was very influential politically in

South Carolina, where he served in the General Assembly, 1783–90, and as a Federalist in the U.S. Senate, 1789–95 (Edgar et al., *Biographical Directory of the South Carolina House of Representatives*, 3:371–72).

4. Pedro Cevallos Guerra (1764–1840) was Spanish minister of state when Charles Pinckney served as U.S. minister to Spain, 1801–5 (Bleiberg, *Diccionario de historia de España*, 2d ed., 1:819; *PJM-SS*, 2:24, 9:xxiv).

5. In 1802 Spain closed the port of New Orleans to American goods being shipped down the Mississippi River despite the fact that the right of deposit was guaranteed to the United States by the 1795 Treaty of San Lorenzo. For the Spanish act and the American response, see *PJM-SS*, 4:xxv–xxix.

6. Pinckney referred here to the period between the last week in July and the first week of August 1786, when JM was visiting New York City during the sitting of Congress there. Under discussion in Congress at the time were the Jay-Gardoqui negotiations for a treaty between the United States and Spain in which the free navigation of the Mississippi River was an item of contention. JM stayed at the boardinghouse of Vandine Elsworth at 19 Maiden Lane (*PJM*, 9:71 n. 5, 91 n. 3, 260 n. 2).

7. *Pro bono publico:* for the public good.

8. For Pinckney's 1819–21 term in the U.S. House of Representatives, see Marty D. Matthews, *Forgotten Founder: The Life and Times of Charles Pinckney* (Columbia, S.C., 2004), 130–37.

9. Rufus King.

10. For Pinckney's speech in Congress on the Missouri Question, see *Niles' Weekly Register* 18 (15 July 1820): 349–57.

11. Nathaniel Macon (1758–1837) was a North Carolina planter and veteran of the Revolutionary War who was a powerful Republican presence in the U.S. Congress, serving in the House of Representatives, 1791–1815, and as its Speaker, 1801–7, and in the Senate, 1815–28. He opposed JM's candidacy for the presidency and ranged himself with the "Tertium Quid" faction of the Jeffersonian Republicans (Powell, *Dictionary of North Carolina Biography*, 4:185–86).

12. John Randolph (of Roanoke) (1773–1833), a Virginia planter and politician, served in the U.S. House of Representatives, 1799–1813, 1815–17, 1819–25, and 1827–29, and in the U.S. Senate, 1825–27. A powerful voice for the Republican party during the first Jefferson administration, Randolph openly opposed JM for president in 1808 and opposed the War of 1812. He briefly served as U.S. minister to Russia in 1830 (Bruce, *John Randolph of Roanoke*, 1:3, 155, 169, 177, 222, 253, 306, 325, 358, 368, 426, 444, 448, 462, 472, 505, 542, 553, 634, 638, 646, 2:46).

13. There were eight signers of the U.S. Constitution still living when Pinckney wrote—JM, Jared Ingersoll, Jonathan Dayton, Rufus King, William Few, Pinckney, Charles Cotesworth Pinckney, and Pierce Butler. The last three were from South Carolina.

14. Pinckney to Thomas Jefferson, 6 Sept. 1820 (DLC: Jefferson Papers). In this letter Pinckney wrote: "I have lately written Mr. Madison but as [it] is reported he is about to go to Europe on a vesel he will not recieve it." Perhaps Pinckney had seen the notice in *Niles' Weekly Register* 19 (2 Sept. 1820): 13, that "a Cork paper of the 27th June, announces the arrival in Ireland, of Mr. *Madison*, late president of the United States, for the purpose of taking a tour through that country!"

15. Thomas Newton Jr. (1768–1847), a Republican from Norfolk, served in the U.S. House of Representatives, 1801–30, and 1831–33 (*PJM-SS*, 4:152 n. 2).

From Mackay & Campbell

Dr. Sir, Fredericksburg 4 Septem. 1820.

Your favour 1st. inst. to our prior,[1] covering your sett of exchange on Maury & Latham for £100 Sterlg. is before us. Seven weeks ago we Valued on these Gentlemen for £150 Stg. on account your 8 Hhd's Tobacco & on account 8 Hhds of our own, Shipped per Scipio, Capt. Drummond, from Jas. River. Our Bill was made under the supposition that we were to Value for proceeds your Tobo. as well as our own; but as you have sent us this Bill, (& have made other appropriations of the remaining proceeds) we will forward it to M. & L. to be placed to your debit & our Credit, with a request that the proceeds of your Tobo. may be placed to your Credit. When the matter will Stand as you wish—We will either bring or Send to next Court the Money requested.

Liverpool letters of 27th. July mention that wheat had advanced 6/. ℔ quarter in London, in consequence of unfavourable weather for eight days & our flour was here enquired for in Liverpool at a Small advance.

Tobacco of good quality was also in better demand, but inferior Sorts were quite neglected. We are Dr. Sir With much respect, Your friends & Servts.

Mackay & Campbell

Flour $4.
Wheat 75–77¢.

RC (DLC). Docketed by JM.

1. Letter not found.

From Thomas Ewell

[Circular.]

Sir: Washington, [6] September, 1820.

I take the liberty of directing this to you, to ask your encouragement of an establishment designed to promote medical science, by the means of relieving the diseased poor around us. There is not in our country a population equal to that of this city and Georgetown, (exceeding twenty thousand,) which has not some medical institution for the relief of the sick. In addition to the number of poor common to such a population, there are many more arising from the resort of strangers to the seat of government. It is not to be denied, that many cases of severe suffering, even of death, have occurred, from the want of an Hospital in Washington.

Although anxious to make this establishment, I am not unconscious that many philanthropists believe that hospitals have done more harm than good. But the fact is, that the injuries have proceeded from those who planned them. Splendid buildings have been erected, chiefly to display the vanity of the founders. It appears always to have been forgotten that the best means of relieving the sick is to accommodate them in the manner to which they have been accustomed. Instead, therefore, of a large house, of crowded rooms, generating and diffusing the foulest atmosphere, there should have been small and detached buildings, such as the inhabitants of hospitals are accustomed to at their homes. It is from this view that I propose to establish the Columbia Hospital, on some square convenient to the City and Georgetown, which shall be selected by the majority of the contributors.

The regulations of the establishment will be such as are believed to be unexceptionable. Its government and use of funds are to be conducted exclusively by the clergymen of the county, who will monthly meet for the management. The medical department will be as exclusively under the direction of the regularly qualified physicians of the City and Georgetown; and every clergyman, physician, and contributor to the Hospital, shall have the right of ordering the admission of any sick person deemed a proper object.

In order to add to the utility of this institution, a part of it will be assigned for a lying-in-hospital, where women will be instructed in the duties they should perform to each other in childbed; a school from which much good may be expected.

Should you approve of this establishment, I hope you will be pleased to request the gentlemen of your particular acquaintance to join in the subscription, and to return this to me as soon as convenient. Respectfully, your obedient servant,

Thomas Ewell.[1]

Printed circular and printed enclosure (DLC: Madison Collection, Rare Book and Special Collections Division). Day of month not indicated; conjectural day assigned based on a letter from Thomas Ewell to Thomas Jefferson, 6 Sept. 1820, enclosing this circular (DLC: Jefferson Papers). Docketed by JM. The enclosure (1 p.) is a prospectus for the establishment of "Columbia Hospital. Outlines of the Institution designed, in the least expensive and most expeditious way."

1. Thomas Ewell (1785–1826) of Dumfries, Virginia, was a physician who studied with, among others, Benjamin Rush in Philadelphia. From 1808 to 1813, he was a naval surgeon in Washington, where he married Elizabeth Stoddert, daughter of Benjamin Stoddert, a former secretary of the navy. In addition to his medical practice, he wrote several treatises, including the popular *American Family Physician* (1824), and managed the family property, including an apothecary shop in Washington and a gunpowder mill near Bladensburg, Maryland (*PJM-PS*, 4:323 n. 2). For Ewell's dispute with the Navy Department over the quality of his gunpowder, see Ewell to JM, 10 and 20 Jan., 21 and 23 May, and 27 July 1813, ibid., 5:565–66 and nn., 598–99 and nn., 6:327–28 and nn. 2–4, 336–37 and n. 1, 477–81 and 482 nn. 5–10 and 13–14.

From Bernard Smith

DEAR SIR. NEW BRUNSWICK N.J. Sepr. 6th. 1820.

Having voted against the proposed restriction on Missouri, attempts are making to prevent my re-election to a seat in Congress. This question is not generally understood and the *restrictionists* are actively employed in endeavoring to destroy the popularity of those who opposed the measure.

In 1804, you appointed me to a situation in the Dept. of State, which I held for Six years. Soon after my return to this State, I was appointed Post-master of this City, and Surveyor of this Port. In 1816, you did me the additional honor to appoint me one of the Comrs. for receiving Subscriptions to the National Bank.

Altho' I have not understood that my opponents charge me with not having faithfully discharged the duties of these several offices, I am however of opinion that a letter from you, expressive of your approbation of my official conduct while you were at the head of the Dept. of State, and of the Genl. Govt., would, at this crisis, be of essential service to me. Should you favor me with a few lines, it would greatly increase the obligations I already owe you, for the patronage & friendship I experienced from you at an early period of my life, and which was continued untill you retired from the helm of State.

Accept of my best wishes for a continuance of your health, and may you long live to experience the gratitude of the American people. With much esteem & respect, I remain Dear Sir Your obedt. Servt.

B: SMITH[1]

RC (DLC). Docketed by JM.

1. Bernard Smith (1776–1835) of New Brunswick, New Jersey, was employed by JM as a clerk in the State Department, 1804–10, served as postmaster of New Brunswick, 1810–19, and as a member of the U.S. House of Representatives, 1819–21. He was appointed register of the land office at Little Rock, Arkansas Territory, in 1821, and later also served as secretary to the governor of Arkansas, 1825–28 (*New Hampshire Patriot and State Gazette*, 24 Aug. 1835; *PJM-SS*, 7:81; Lewis Condict and others to James Monroe, 23 Nov. 1811, DNA: RG 59, LAR, 1809–17, filed under "Smith, Bernard").

To Bernard Smith

DR. SIR [13 September 1820]

I have just recd. yours of the 6th. inst. Knowing nothing that could in the least detract from the respect & confidence of which you have had successive marks from me, I should always be ready to bear the testimony, requested under circumstances not liable to be misconstrued or misrepresented. How far those under wch. it would not be given are of that character I can not but think may deserve consideration of us both. The people of the States are naturally & justly jealous of external interferences, & particularly so on occasions when they are exercising their elective rights; and any thing from me to be publickly used on the approaching one to which you refer, would be the more likely to awaken that feeling, as it involves it seems, a great political question on which a local bias might be alledged or suspected to be charged on me. With this view of the subject, I think I do not err in supposing that I consult your advantage not less, than what concerns myself in leaving the result in the present case to the merit which heretofore procured the suffrages of your Constts. and to their intelligence & liberality in appreciating yr. discharge of the trust committed to you.

I thank you Sir for the very kind wishes you have expressed, and beg you to be assured of a Sincere return of mine for a long & prosperous life

Draft (DLC). Undated; conjectural date assigned based on the letter's acknowledgment in Smith to JM, 20 Sept. 1820.

From Maury & Latham

Sir, Liverpool. 13 Sep 1820

We beg leave to inform you that by the Scipio, Capt Drummond, for Norfolk, we shipped the goods you directed should be purchased, and consigned them to Mess Moses Myers & Son, requesting them to receive Mess Mackay & Campbells instructions respecting them. We judged it best to send them to Norfolk as there may be no vessel from hence to the Rappahannoc this twelvemonth. We must apprize you that we have sent no German Oznaburgs, as they are not to be had here, and if we were to send a bolt of Scotch Oznaburgs the quantity is so small that the bounty would be lost, and you might in that case buy it much cheaper in Baltimore. We sent a piece of yellow lining for the Curtains, altho not order'd, as they could not be made up without lining.

We have also to inform you that we have sold 7 Hhds of your Tobo. viz. 1 @ 4¾—5 @ 5d. & 1 @ 5¼. The average of fair James River leaf is about 5½, altho very fine brings as high as 8d. There are now 8000 Hhds here, & several cargoes expected. The price of James River leaf 3¼ @ 8d. strips 3½ @ 6½. Rappahannoc leaf 3. 5½ strips 3¼ @ 5d & no favorable change looked for.

American flour sells @ 24/–25/pbl. and no chance whatever of the ports opening this year. Wheat has sold @ 8/3 ℔ bushl. of 70 lbs. We have the honor to be Sir, Your faithful & obt Serts.

MAURY & LATHAM

RC (DLC). Docketed by JM.

From George Hay

DEAR SIR, LOUDOUN OAK:HILL Sept: 18. 1820.

When I left Montpelier, I did not imagine that we should bring away more than we had carried. I find however, that three books belonging to the library, and a fourth belonging to Mr. T's[1] room, were transferred from the apartment to which Mrs. Scott[2] was conducted, to Mrs. Hay's chamber, and stowed away by her maid among her baggage. This petty larceny was not discovered until several days after our arrival here. The three books are Allens theology,[3] Sheridans rhetorical grammar,[4] and the quarterly review No 43.[5] The fourth book is an unbound duodo. Vol: of Footes farces:[6] the "taking and carrying away" of which, I shall contend, if Mr. T. shall commence a prosecution against us, is not only not a larceny, but no offence whatever: the farces contained in the same, being utterly without value. It is true that I have read but very little of this volume: but that little has convinced me, of what I had not suspected, that Foote is a wretched plagiarist. He borrows without Ceremony from Le Sage, and Boccacio,[7] and is manifestly incompetent to manage what he has thus unfairly acquired.

I regret now, as we had this additional burthen, that I did not avail myself of your polite offer as to "les ordonnances:"[8] the safe location of which in *the bag*, would have necessarily excluded the volumes which found their way there. I shall return them by the mail in a short time.

Fearing that the review may be missed, I have thought it proper to apprise you of its Situation. I am, with very great respect Yr. mo: ob: Srt.

GEO: HAY

P.S. Tuesday Oct: 9th. 1820.

Perhaps it is not quite polite to Send a letter of So old a date; & I should not Send it, if I had time to write a new one. We are all at this moment in the hurry of preparation for an early journey tomorrow. A letter from N.Y. received by this days mail, hardly leaves us any hope of Mr. Gouverneur's[9] recovery. He has had a fever without intermission for 25 days. A few days ago he was better: he has since relapsed.

The books (Mr. Benton) the manager here will Send in two or three detachments.

RC (DLC). Docketed by JM.

1. John Payne Todd.

2. Maria Mayo Scott (1789–1862), daughter of John and Abigail De Hart Mayo, was the wife of Gen. Winfield Scott. Her son, John (1819–20), died during their visit to Montpelier and was buried in the Madison family plot (Allan Peskin, *Winfield Scott and the Profession of Arms* [Kent, Ohio, 2003], 64–66, 70, 264).

3. This was probably Ethan Allen, *Reason the Only Oracle of Man, or A Compenduous System of Natural Religion. . . .* (Bennington, Vt., 1784; Evans 18322), generally known as Allen's Theology, or Allen's Bible.

4. Thomas Sheridan, *A Rhetorical Grammar of the English Language . . .* (Philadelphia, 1783; Evans 18184).

5. JM subscribed to the London *Quarterly Review* until February 1823 (JM to Edward Everett, 18 Feb. 1823).

6. This could have been any volume of the many multivolume editions of *The Dramatic Works of Samuel Foote* (London, 1754–78).

7. Alain-René Lesage (1668–1747) was a French novelist and playwright. Giovanni Boccaccio (1313–75) was an Italian writer and author of the *Decameron* (1353).

8. René-Josué Valin, *Nouveau commentaire sur l'ordonnance de la marine, du mois d'août 1681 . . .*, new ed. (2 vols.; La Rochelle, France, 1776).

9. Samuel L. Gouverneur (1799–1865), of New York, was president James Monroe's private secretary and Mrs. Monroe's nephew. He married the Monroes' younger daughter, Maria Hester Monroe, in 1820. Gouverneur served in the New York state assembly in 1825, and was postmaster of New York City, 1828–36 (Baltimore *Sun*, 12 Oct. 1865; Ammon, *James Monroe*, 405, 407, 547; Marian Gouverneur, *As I Remember: Recollections of American Society during the Nineteenth Century* [New York, 1911], 256–57; *Catalogue of Officers and Graduates of Columbia University from the Foundation of King's College in 1754* [New York, 1916], 96).

From Bernard Smith

DEAR SIR NEW BRUNSWICK Sepr. 20th. 1820.

I have recd. the letter which you did me the honor to write to me on the 13th. inst.

The reasons which you give, for not wishing publicity to be given to your opinion as to the manner in which I discharged my official duties, while you were at the head of the Govt., are satisfactory. It is gratifying to me to learn, that you "should always be ready to bear the testimony requested, under circumstances not liable to be misconstrued or misrepresented." For this friendly assurances [*sic*], I pray you to accept of my sincere thanks.

The excitement respecting the Missouri question, is still kept up here, by certain ambit[i]ous individuals who whose [*sic*] object it is evidently to gain elevation & office. Two of my Colleagues (Bloomfield & Kinsey)[1] and myself, are denounced, and a short time will determine whether we shall be the victims of intrigue & popular delusion or not. I have the honor to be very respectfully, Dear Sir, Your obedt. & very Hble. Servt.

B SMITH

RC (DLC). Docketed by JM.

1. Charles Kinsey (1773–1849) was a Maryland-born paper manufacturer who served in New Jersey state politics after his removal there and carried on the paper industry at various New Jersey locations throughout his life. Kinsey was a member of the U.S. House of Representatives, 1817–19, and 1820–21, and served as judge of the court of common pleas and of the Orphans' Court of Bergen County, New Jersey, 1830–45.

¶ From James Monroe. Letter not found. *22 September 1820.* Offered for sale in *The Collection of Autographs of Hon. James T. Mitchell* (Stan. V. Henkels Catalogue No. 731 [1894], 77).

From Edward P. Page

[ca. 2⟨4?⟩ September 1820]

[. . .] I am greatly encouraged to find that what I have been zealously contending for has recently been maintained by the Revd. Holland Weeks[1] of Abingdon Massachusetts. A council of Presbyterian ministers have excommunicated him for entertaining similar dangerous heretical opinions to mine. Glory to God Babylon is on fire he declared before his judges "there is not a single truth remaining in the old church, but, what is falsified." The editor of the "Boston recorder" a religious paper seems alarmed that men should be exercising their *reason.*[2] Aye, & reason will shew them before long that Dr. Franklin was after Divine magic when he found the magic circle of circles (12 the central number) & square of squares.[3] And sir, however you may smile as all the world at present does—divine magic or the power of immortality on *earth* & of working miracles will revive with men. It is man's prerogative. The Arts & Sciences progress. Light develops light. 'Tis to recover what we have lost & that by the full reaction will effect it. By man came death. By man will come life. Mankind is Jesus Christ. The Universe is the Temple. Down with partition walls & contend for a free circulation of air. Universal free masonry is the life of the world. The sooner it comes the sooner your fathers will re-appear & you & yours become immortal on this globe. There is a final restoration of all things & death is not an eternally dead soul eternally tormented—no such nonsense. We are rewarded according to our de⟨e⟩ds & works. Creatures of time do not die everlastingly and yet be alive in hells hottest damnation's fire for offences committed in *time.* No Devil God. God is Love, & Wisdom, Love, *Justice.* To create that he might everlastingly torment would but ill comport with his attributes—and I hesitate not to affirm that all Christendom (perhaps Quakers & one or two others excepted) make God a Devil in every hideous sense of the word by construction. He made all things, & blessed be him & all his handy works—for nothing was created in vain. I pray you lift the veil as much as possible from off the eyes of the Jew-Xians that they may be as good as Turks. Yours respectfully

EDWARD P. PAGE[4]

Partial RC (DLC). Undated; conjectural date assigned based on postmark "Marietta Sep 2⟨4?⟩" and JM's docket. Addressed by Page to JM: "Late President of the United States Virginia," with "Orange CH" added in an unidentified hand. First page extensively damaged.

1. Holland Weeks (ca. 1768–1843), a graduate of Dartmouth College in 1795, was installed as the pastor of the First Church of Christ of Abington, Massachusetts, in 1815 and continued there until 1820, when he was tried before a council of ministers and dismissed for preaching and holding opinions "embracing the system of Emanuel Swedenborg." Weeks was ordained in the New Jerusalem Church and moved to Henderson, New York, where he farmed and ministered to a small church (Benjamin Hobart, *History of the Town of Abington, Plymouth County, Massachusetts, From its First Settlement* [Boston, 1866], 115–29; Franklin B. Hough, *A History of Jefferson County in the State of New York, from the Earliest Period to the Present Time* [Albany, 1854], 170).

2. The *Boston Recorder* was a weekly religious newspaper published under various editors from 1816 until after 1820. At the time of this letter, Nathaniel Willis was editor and sole proprietor (Brigham, *American Newspapers*, 1:341). For the newspaper's report of the council's deliberations at Abington, see the *Boston Recorder*, 2 Sept. 1820.

3. For Benjamin Franklin's mathematical inventions, his "magic circle of circles . . . & the square of squares," see Franklin's two letters to Peter Collinson, [1752?], and editorial headnotes, Labaree et al., *Papers of Benjamin Franklin*, 4:392–400.

4. Edward Postlethwayt Page (ca. 1782–1857), a native of Great Britain, emigrated to New York City about 1807, before moving to Marietta, Ohio, where he lived for nearly forty years. Known to himself and his friends as the "High Priest of Nature," Page's eccentricities extended to an attempt to create a new religion, the "Union Concentric Society of light," and the publication of a monthly in 1831–32 entitled the *Reminiscence of Nature, and Clew to Bible Astrology, by the Recess of the Equinoxes According to Fluxions.* His claim to have squared the circle gained him a certain notoriety and even provoked a sketch in a piece on "Monomaniacs" in the *Knickerbocker:* "The latest example of inveterate monomania is furnished in the person of Mr. Edward Postlethwayt Page, who has been passing the winter and spring in Philadelphia and New-York. He seems to have gone mad on the subject of figures; for, on every topic not encumbered with numerals, he speaks with an ease and gentlemanly propriety, which would astonish any one. . . . But drop a word respecting time, or space, or numbers, and his intellect is off in a tangent, among squares, and cycles, plannets, billions, trillions, sextants, and terms, negative, positive, and mean. He has wasted a fortune in printing wild, incomprehensible handbills in support of his system, and is still journeying over the country, boring the people with his harmless theories" (*Ironton Register*, 4 June 1857, http://www.lawrencecountyohio.com/node/227; *Notes and Queries: A Monthly of History, Folk-Lore, Mathematics, Literature, Art, Arcane Societies, Etc.* 18 [1900]: 159; the *Manchester Iris: A Literary and Scientific Miscellany, Published Weekly in the Years 1822 & 1823* [2 vols.; Manchester, England, 1822–23], 1:87; Edward Postlethwayt Page, "The Theory of Celestial Periods," *Niles' Weekly Register* 47 [22 Nov. 1834]: 182; "Monomaniacs," the *Knickerbocker, or New-York Monthly Magazine* 5 [1835]: 524–25).

From Edmond Kelly

Sir — Columbia Ten 26th Septr 1820

I hope you are perswaded that no wish to catch at popularity Induced me to write my former letters—that is the road usually traveled by obscure demagogues whose object it is to exalt themselves, and I wd. deserve contempt had I been actuated by any such motive—every days experience verifies the truth of Lord Mansfields observation that the applause of the mob is not always the meed of merit,[1] and is so veering, so capriciously lost that the best patriots & those that approach nearest to human perfection seldom retain it long and in truth I would not wish to be suspected to be a Candidate for that sort of popularity or envied it by the meanest demagogue or dullest Editor in the union. My motive was a different one. I found that a Conspiracy Organised by british agents for Cromwells & Williams nobility (but in which the present ministers who are not of the Orange party had no share) to anihilate American Independence and enslave this country to England was Identified with their efforts to extinguish my right to my family property—which was usurped by some of that party before & after the revolution of 1688—thus circumstanced I own I felt interrested in opposing it. I did so & that party has done all that poisonous & sanguinary bloodhounds could do against me—and also all that avaricious mercenary Traitors alured by promises of shareing in their countries pillage could with safety attempt. I hope I have Contributed to expose and defeat their designs and I have the pleasure to find they are for the present foiled—but altho my efforts to resist british despotism & robbery & its fatal effects did not emanate soley from that pure motive of public good which actuates true & great patriots & in which personal Interest & self preservation has no share I yet hope that I am not undeserving that protection which the constitution I suppose extends to every honest & well behaived man in the Commy. that merits it. I mention this in reply to a charge of favoritism I perceive to have been artfully and insidiously made & I beg leave to observe that partiality to any one on whom fraud is practised or attempted to be practised is consistent with the purest exercise of Justice which protects & secures every man his rights & property, and that in this instance a resistance to british Intrigue was a civic duty & not an act of prejudice or partiality—and to certain Impostors sent to America to Claim Estates in Ireland that as America can neither legislate Judicate nor adjudicate for Ireland—Title duly certified to have been proved in a court of Justice in Ireland is necessary to be produced here to entitle any such claimant to any rents or mesne rates of Lands to which claim is made that may have been transmitted here from that country but that it would be contrary to Justice & to every duty of Republicanism to pay it away as a quantum meruit[2] to the favorite gallants of a british princess for meretricious favors & services—even & altho such claimants or gallants should in the Opinion of their british patrons possess patriotic Virtues & perfections that would qualify each & every of them from Wil Snip to John Bull to be a grecian Archon & a roman Consul.[3]

My last letter[4] (& I suppose many others) was written in such an inexcuseable hurry that it was after puting it in the post office I recollected some gramatical Errors & assertions that required explanation particularly respecting what I mentioned of Genl Jackson. I am yet of the same opinion that he is not a tactition & could not with any force the American Orangemen could procure him subvert the freedom of the Republic if Opposed by an experienced Officer & tactitian yet I am perswaded he is a daring and a dangerous Conspirator & that his patronage & influence has heretofore been exerted to encrease Orangemen in & out of the American Army & that his removal is necessary to preserve the public peace & damp or check the hopes of that extensive asso. of Conspirators to which he belongs—& I further think that $500 or one thousand dollars would induce some needy orangeman from time to time to Discloze such particulars as would enable the Legislative department to counteract their designs.

Genl Jacksons Interference in legislative proceedings here[5] on the loan office bill for the purpose of arraying the poorer against the wealthier Classes (a matter specially recomd by british Instructions (& our Governors Message is in Conformity to such Instructions) Irritated this state legislature & tended to facilitate the passing of that unconstitutional law—let it be recollected that Moreau[6] gained his greatest successes when he was a determined traitor—that his object was to become popular & to increase his fortune and to avail himself of the first favourable Oppy to Overthrow the french Republic—and should not that be a warning to the American Republic. Mr Monroe will not interfere—under his admn. a state of liberty is a state of Licenciousness—a liberty as Mr Locke says for every one to do as he list[7]—the Violations of the Constitution—by the robbery of the national branch bank at Ohio—& the robbery of it in Philadelphia appear to be matters of Indifference to him[8]—that Institution which well managed would consolidate the capital of the Republic and in the event of war prevent the necessity of sending money to foreign countries as Interest for loans he permitts a british party to pillage with Impunity because I suppose a national bank in aid of Industry and Domestic manufactures would prove fatal to the hopes of England—to rob an Individual is death but to rob the public or the nation is meritorious—such services must endear him to the british Ascendancy or Oligarchs & perhaps ensure his reelection. Surely such a man & Genl Jackson cannot disagree.

I consider Mr Monroes delivering up the possession of East Florida to Spain & his subsequently declining to occupy it under the authority of congress as done to give the spanish Govt an Opportunity at some more convenient time to interest monarchs in his favor to form a coalition to preserve it for it is only by a Coalition & an Invasion of the U States the british party expects to become the American aristocracy. E Florida which would be an invaluable acquisition to the US as a marine & military position he appears resolved shall not belong to the Amn Republic. One objection is that it is an arid Sand-but that might be the best defence against an invadeing Enemy—it is supposed never to have defrayed the expences of its govt. & if Spain loozes her colonies as is not improbable will be useless to her but is of Vital Importance to America to protect the gulf trade & exclude foreign Enemies. He has risked the Transferr of it to England the enemy of Liberty and of mankind this to say no worse of it was an error which if the british ministers were of Cromwells Oligarchs would have before this time caused a war in which he is as much disappointed as in sending Mr Campbell[9] to Rusia—instead of a pecuniary compensation for this arid sand he & Mr John Adams[10] tho both Lawyars illegally agreed to barter away the most precious part of Mr Jeffersons Acquisition that part of Texas within Loisiana which wd supply America with Coffee sugar & such other west India Island produce as would enable the U States to receive cash for their exports to these Islands and thus contribute materially to the prosperity of the US—this invaluable Territory is agreed to be transferred in liew of a barren Sand. It is not presumeable that these Gentn being Lawyars did not know such transferr unconstitutional and Inju⟨ri⟩ous to America. Mr Trimble[11] of Kentuckeys arguments are so clear & conclusive that it is not possible such a sacrifice will be permitted. In truth no man that has yet spoken on that subject shewed equal ability & were he appointed Negotiator de novo the treaty of Don Onis[12] being Voided by the nonfulfillment of its Terms &ca. he would not sacrifice the Interests of the American Republic—my Zeal to defeat the hopes Intrigues & Designs of England to enslave America & perpetuate her present ruinous monopoly in British Manufactures and Colonial or west india Island produce will excuse my Zeal and Interference in this affair Whether my Ideas of its importance are correct or not Mr Madison and Mr Jeffn. are the best Judges of & if correct it is hoped the affair will Interest them to interfere & if possible prevent a sacrifice so injurious to the best interests of the Republic.

I perceive that Merchants concerned in that ruinous business the importation of british Manufactures who are in fact british factors & Collectors of what may be considered british Revenue have prepared petitions to Congress against domestic manufactures and protecting duties on imports of it[13] and also that the Tobacco planters of Virginia apprehensive that in such Event England will retaliate by rejecting their Tobacco have also prepared a petition against D Manfs & protecting duties[14] which is no more than what might be expected & Verifies the Poets assertion

> that all men are true to their own private ends
> tho false to their Country its laws & their friends[15]
> &ca. &ca.

but supposing for argument sake that the Custom house entries & returns of England & America would not shew that American Imports from there exceed considerably her Exports (& I believe the Contrary to be the fact). If it is clearly Manifest & indisputably true that the Importation of british Manufactrs brings to England the cash that ought to Circulate in America for domestic Manufactures to be wrought here by resident Manufacturers surely a trade so Injurious to the Republic so degrading to american Intellect such a Veto of american Industry and all Industrious habits and such a source of wealth to those who subsidise all European Kings to crush every appearance of rational freedom to perpetuate their exclusive monopoly cannot be permitted—it cannot be possible that in Justice to the Republic at large the Interest of the Import Merchants & Tobacco planters Can preponderate against the Interest of the U. States Collectively—it is scarcely possible to suppose it. I admitt the Import Merchants will looze by restrictions &ca. but I deny that the Tobacco planters will. Tobacco will always have a sure sale in Europe but should it even be rejected there the Land that yeilds Tobacco will yeild grain and as there is no probability they will be Injured by this measure the sophisticated petition of Col Taylor will it is hoped be rejected.[16]

It will have another good Effect. The Hartford Conventn supposes that a seperation of the New England states either as an Independt Republic or as a british Colony would invest them with its revenues and that in the event of such a Change they would be the permanent Ministers or the permanent Executive of that Country—their supporters are the Mercantile Interest which expects to have the Import trade in british Manufactures perpetuated & secured to them. These two leading Interests are agreed & doubtless under Implied Contracts to each other to plunder & pillage the Country & divide the booty between them so much so that not a Vagrant Pedlar from that quarter comes here to vend goods that is not an Orangeman & a politician & in their own phraise not blind—do an act of Justice to the Republic & youl prevent this Intended seperation & prese[r]ve its Integrity. Establish domestic Manufactures & let resident Manufactures circulate as they must do for support & necessaries their proportions of the cash receivable for domestic Manufactures & store Keepers must do the same thing and you will at once destroy the hopes of that detestable band of Conspirators against their countrie's prosperity—destroy their Iniquitous Monopoly & domestic Industry will prosper in the same ratio—it will abolish the stimulus to disaffection treason & seperation & as Mr Emmett of New York in his pamphlet of the Philosopher sayed (but in which he unfortunately for human nature had refferrence to the Guillotine) cut off their Monopoly and you will *cut of[f] the cause from which both the evil & the exaction flows* & which is the cause of the present general scarcity of money in America & of her Embarrassment.[17]

But it may be sayed this pecuniary Embarrassment is not confined to America—it extends to Europe & is equally felt there. I admitt it. England has heretofore monopolised the productive trade of southern Europe—her Merchandise & Manufactures brought her the circulating & dispozeable cash of Portugal & Spain & their Colonies & of America &ca &ca. For her the spaniard & the Creole worked the mines of Mexico & Peru to whom Gol[d] & Silver was as dross Compared with british fine Scarlet cloth & other fineries—that source of british wealth felt considerable Interruption. England alarmed at the danger that threatened her Monopoly drew the bullion from the british banks & sent it to the north of Europe in subsidies—it is plenty there but these causes have made it scarce in the british dominions and in America—that is the cause of the Embt felt in England but the Excessive Importations of british Merchandise & Manufactures is the cause of the scarcity of money in America—it is in Vain for Messrs. Floyd & Williams[18] to sound an alarm in congress to the friends of England & the Orangemen on this subject. British monopoly is ruinous to America—its further Continuance will cause national Bankruptcy or Insolvency. These Infatuated Individuals themselves must suffer by it. Temporising expedients may check its progress but cannot ultimately avert that fatal event.

You have read with surprise England subsidising all European Monarchs to restore Charles the 4th and the french army no sooner expelled than she proposed a Briton for their King. Such acts of perfidy & duplicity are peculiar to England—she subsidised & fought to preserve her Monopoly & could do it better by having a briton on the throne of Spain than a Bourboon (Spanish Merino wool & Spanish Iron being the most necessary of all her Imported Materials). The answer of the Marquess De Ossunna[19] was worthy of a noble Spaniard *that Spain would not be governed by any Usurper* given on the part of the Nation & Nobility prevented any further attempt at Negotiation the Kings would not permitt it unless agreeable to the spanish people & there it droped—with the same Views & motives Lord Cochrane[20] is privately permitted to Join the south American patriots & supplies of men & arms are suffered to be furnished With a View of securing the friendship of the patriots & a sale for british Merchandise—thus you may perceive England has acted the deceitfull double dealer when the mistaken world considers her Magnanimous—such is britain—a modern Carthage—in Joseph Bonapartes Reign England sent such an abundance of her Manufactures to south America as alarmed that people—the patriots laid such a high duty on them that the supercargoes & agents were Obliged to sacrifice their goods at auction and the produce only defrayed their Expences & paid the duties—thus it is evident England professes herself the friend of both parties—of the Spanish King & of the patriots but will take part on that side where her Interest preponderates—& untill events decide on which side it is she will prudently remain in utrumque paratus.[21] On the whole I think England has seen her best days—should Congress sanction Mr Jeffersons great plan or design of opening a Communication with asia by the Columbia River & the pacific Ocean & indeed the absence of that great man from the public councils is a real national loss—& should America Manufacture for herself and I think the Cortes will soon have their wool & Iron manufactured at home the ship of british Monopoly will looze her Main anchor—will drift down the Current of adversity & be wrecked on the shore of mediocrity & probably find as Goldsmith sayed of Venice, that her former greatness was Phletoric [*sic*] Ill.[22] I am with the utmost respect &ca.

EDMOND KELLY

My next letter will be written next week will contain the state of british parties the cause of the Continentall Changes in Spain & Insurrection in France &ca. I expect Mr. Madison will find it Interresting.

RC (NN). Addressed by Kelly to JM "late Presidt US at his Country residence Washington City State of Virginia." Postmarked "Columbia T 30th. Sepr." Damaged by removal of seal.

1. Kelly may have been referring here to Lord Mansfield's speech in Parliament of 9 May 1770 on a bill relating to the privilege of Parliament: "It has been said by a noble lord on my left hand, that I likewise am running the race of popularity. If the noble lord means by popularity, that applause bestowed by after ages on good and virtuous actions, I have long been struggling in that race, to what purpose all-trying time can alone determine; but if that noble lord means that mushroom popularity that is raised without merit, and lost without a crime, he is much mistaken in his opinion" (William Cobbett, *The Parliamentary History of England from the Earliest Period to the Year 1803. . . .* [36 vols.; London, 1806–20], 16:977).

2. *Quantum meruit:* "as much as he has deserved" (*Black's Law Dictionary* [9th ed.], 1361).

3. William Snip was a Philadelphia merchant tailor in "Slender's Journey," a poem by Philip Freneau (Fred Lewis Pattee, ed., *The Poems of Philip Freneau, Poet of the American Revolution* [3 vols.; Princeton, N.J., 1902–7], 2:340).

4. Kelly to JM, ca. 29 Jan. 1820, *PJM-RS,* 1:591–95.

5. For Andrew Jackson's opposition to the creation of a state loan office in Tennessee designed to mitigate the effects of the financial crisis of 1819, see Smith et al., *Papers of Andrew Jackson,* 4:375–76.

6. Jean-Victor Moreau (1763–1813) was a French revolutionary general whose battlefield success, at Hohenlinden (1800) and elsewhere, for a time rivaled that of Napoleon. Jealous and suspicious of Moreau's popularity with the army and the French public, Napoleon had Moreau arrested and tried for conspiracy. Condemned to a two-year prison term in 1804, Moreau was subsequently banished to the United States, and arrived there in 1805. He and his wife settled in New Jersey, near the falls of the Delaware River, and wintered in New York City. Moreau returned to Europe in 1813 and joined the allied armies of Russia, Prus-

sia, and Austria in a campaign against Napoleon; he was mortally wounded at the battle of Dresden (*Biographie universelle* [1843–65 ed.], 29:256–62).

7. Here Kelly refers to John Locke's rebuttal of Robert Filmer's definition of freedom. It is not "a liberty for every one to do what he lists, to live as he pleases, and not to be tied by any laws"; liberty is "to have a standing rule to live by, common to every one of that society, and made by the legislative power erected in it. A liberty to follow my own will in all things where that rule prescribes not, not to be subject to the inconstant, uncertain, unknown, arbitrary will of another man" (Locke, *Two Treatises on Civil Government*, 202).

8. On 17 Sept. 1819 the state of Ohio executed a law imposing a $50,000 tax on the branch Bank of the United States at Chillicothe, Ohio, an action in defiance of the decision of the U.S. Supreme Court in the case of *McCullough v. Maryland* (*Niles' Weekly Register* 17 [2 Oct. 1819]: 65).

9. George Washington Campbell (1769–1848) was a Scottish-born, Princeton graduate who moved to Knoxville, Tennessee, and began practicing law in 1798. He was elected to the U.S. House of Representatives as a Jeffersonian Republican in 1803 and served until 1809. After a brief turn as a judge on the Tennessee Supreme Court of Errors and Appeals, Campbell was elected to the U.S. Senate in 1811, where he served until JM appointed him secretary of the Treasury in 1814. He resigned after eight months in office and returned to the Senate in October 1815, leaving when President Monroe appointed him U.S. minister to Russia in 1818, a post he held until 1820. He returned to Tennessee where he involved himself in banking and land speculation, and his last public office was a seat on the French Spoliation Claims Commission, 1832–35 (J. Jefferson Looney and Ruth L. Woodward, *Princetonians, 1791–1794: A Biographical Dictionary* [Princeton, N.J., 1991], 341–50).

10. John Quincy Adams.

11. David Trimble (1782–1842), born in Virginia and educated at the College of William and Mary, was a War of 1812 veteran and a Kentucky Republican who served in the U.S. House of Representatives, 1817–27 (*Biographical Encyclopaedia of Kentucky* [1980 reprint], 293). Trimble's speech in the House opposing the Adams-Onís Treaty was delivered on 4 Apr. 1820 (*Annals of Congress*, 16th Cong., 1st sess., 1756–68).

12. For the Adams-Onís Treaty of 1819, see *PJM-RS*, 1:410 n. 2.

13. For the memorial of the "merchants and inhabitants of Salem," Massachusetts, 31 Jan. 1820, see *Annals of Congress*, 16th Cong., 1st sess., 2335–48.

14. For the "remonstrance of the Virginia Agricultural Society of Fredericksburg against the attempts . . . to increase the duties upon foreign goods," 3 Jan. 1820, and the "memorial of the United Agricultural Society of Virginia," 17 Jan. 1820, see ibid., 2296–99, 2323–27.

15. "Most Men will be true to their own private ends, / Though false to their country, religion, and friends;" were lines taken from Fable 4, "Of the Town in Danger of a Siege," in Daniel Fenning, *The Universal Spelling-Book: or, A New and Easy Guide to the English Language* (London, 1767), 41–42.

16. A memorial to Congress, "presented and read by Col. *John Taylor*, of Caroline," was "unanimously adopted" by a "united meeting of Farmers and Merchants" in Fredericksburg on 12 Aug. 1820. The memorial, under a 29 Aug. dateline, was published in the *Daily National Intelligencer*, 2 Sept. 1820.

17. Kelly may have been referring here to *A Demonstration of the Necessity of a Legislative Union of Great Britain and Ireland, Involving a Refutation of Every Argument Which Has Been or Can Be Urged against That Measure. By a Philosopher* (Dublin, 1799), 38. "The philosopher would tell such a people [the Irish] that the true mode of redress is not by coldly declaring that it is only obliged to pay a certain tribute, and the exaction is an *innovation:* but by boldly dissolving altogether that CONNEXION between the ruling and the subject state, from which both the tribute, and the exaction flow." The author of this pamphlet was said to be Thomas

Addis Emmett's good friend, William James MacNeven (*British Critic, for January . . . June 1799* 13 [1799]: 200).

18. Lewis Williams (1786–1842), a graduate of the University of North Carolina, served in the U.S. House of Representatives, 1815–42 (Powell, *Dictionary of North Carolina Biography*, 6:211). For the speeches of John Floyd and Lewis Williams, 29 Apr. 1820, against the tariff, see *Annals of Congress*, 16th Cong., 1st sess., 2140–45.

19. The Osuna family of Osuna, Andalusia, was one of the richest and oldest noble families in Spain. Don Francisco de Borja Téllez-Girón y Pimentel (1785–1820), was the tenth duke of Osuna (Albert Boime, *Art in an Age of Bonapartism, 1800–1815* [Chicago, 1990], 253; Antonio Marichalar, *The Perils and Fortune of the Duke of Osuna* [Philadelphia, 1932], 82, 84–85).

20. Thomas Cochrane, tenth Earl of Dundonald (1775–1860), was a British naval officer and member of Parliament whose political outspokenness and alleged involvement in a stock exchange fraud, despite a distinguished service record in the wars against France, earned his dismissal from the Royal Navy in 1814. Cochrane became admiral and commander-in-chief of the Chilean navy in 1818 and assisted in the liberation of Chile and Peru from Spanish rule. He left the Chilean service in 1822 to enter that of Brazil in which he served until 1825. In that year he accepted the command of the embryonic Greek navy but was unable to muster a respectable force before the end of the Greek war in 1827. For the next several years Cochrane attempted to be reinstated in the Royal Navy and was finally successful in 1832, being gazetted rear admiral. He was appointed Rear-Admiral of the United Kingdom in 1854 (Donald Thomas, *Cochrane: Britannia's Last Sea-King* [London, 1978], 16, 74, 97, 119, 177, 217, 227, 243–44, 274, 277, 279, 291, 294–95, 313, 318, 322, 339, 341).

21. *Utrumque paratus:* prepared for either.

22. "And late the nation found with fruitless skill / Its former strength was but plethoric ill" (George Birkbeck Hill, ed., *Goldsmith, The Traveller* [Oxford, 1888], 8).

From Edmond Kelly

SIR, COLUMBIA TENNESSEE Septr 30th. 1820

The conclusion of my last letter was an opinion that if America should manufacture for herself & if Spain should manufacture her own Merino wool & her Iron (& both are unequaled in any other part of the world) that the ship of british Monopoly will loose her Main Anchor—will drift down the current of Adversity & become a wreck on the shore of Mediocrity. This I believe probable but it is so like rant that I regrett the Editors of the Washn City Gazette & of the Natl Intellr. do not Know it as it would afford them a fresh subject for Criticism Aspersion & abuse which they are liberal of where the british Govt requires it—they appear to me to be earning the loaves & fishes in the gift of that Govt. The Editor of the Gazette is either a furious Orangeman or a pensioned printer & very probably both—he is as Violent scurrilous & aspersive as Cromwells hereditary banditi is under the Orders of his Majesty—and Mr Monroes Printer is gradually and cautiously laying aside his Visor & not only gets warm but angry because I have the presumption to resist british Influence & Intrigue or object to being harassed & robd. by scotch Irish John Bull—he being licenced by his Majesty to do so—& lest censure & criticism should not be sufficient he brings ridicule to his aid. In a recent attack he says—we are sworn foes to Empiricism &ca. &ca.[1] Then follows the wound of a pitch-fork—& the ointment that healed it which was the identical Ointment used by Don Quixote &ca. Yes sir or sirs ye have told a true tale so plainly that he that runs may read it—ye are sworn Orangemen and forsworn Traitors, and enemies to the Enemies of England and of Mr Monroes republican Monarchy. Ye dispense falsehood and suppress truth and gladly fill up your paper with Col Taylors Petition Against American Manufactures and with every other Essay that ridicules patriotic efforts to promote establish & protect them. Ye well Know that remitting large balances yearly to England for her Manufactures Over and above the amount of the national exports will cause national Insolvency—which will cause—discontent & anarchy and these ye expect will be the precursors of the political dissolution of the federal union and then a republican Monarchy will be a matter of Course—and the Tobacco Planters—the Importers of british Manufactures & the Anglo American Orangemen with Mr Monroe & his confidential printer at their head will be Joint Gainers by the reestablishment of the british royal authority and also Joint sharers in the spoils of a plundered nation—the surplus goes to his Majesty & his favorites &ca. &ca. & it appears your oaths of office cause so little scruple or Impediment that ye think with the Poet

oaths are but words and words but wind
too feeble Implements to bind[2]

An other Natl Intelligencer tells Duane[3] that they the Nl. Ir. Editors do not Keep watch on the Tower (evidently the london Tower) from which I inferr that one is a royalist & the others Aristocrats & that where the contest for pillage & robbery is between royalty and aristocracy the Editors of the Nl Intr Keep their watch under the pillars of the Constitutional Monarchy—Vizt. on the side of the oligarchs. Conspirators will sometimes disagree & probably Duane expects to be Kings printer—the others with more confidence repose in the stronger party—these Editors made figures from 1 To 20 in that piece of Duanes and in their reply to it correspondent figures by way of Index[4]—this was the mode used in the french Emperors paper—the Monituer in its replys to the abuse of the british papers—he was soon after dethroned & sent to Elba and by adopting the same method the Editors of the Nl Intr give the british Oligarchs to understand that the overthrow of the American Govt is fixed and that according to Genl Jacksons Memorial to Congress[5] its mad Career will soon be at an end—they did this in a manner as unintelligible as free Masons signs to those that are not Masons but in my opinion as clearly as a signal from a Tellegraph to the british Govt. I suppose Mr Monroes reelection is determd on is certain & that the execution of the conspiracy is Identified with it & afterwards to be attempted—be that as it may—if the conspiracy succeeds it is probable they will triumph over Duane, but as in such event there will be places and pensions & sinecures for them all I suppose there will be no duelling between them.

And here I shall make one observation on the petitions of the Merchants & Tobacco planters—it occurrs to me that the present question is not whether America shall become the rival of England in making & exporting Manufactures as insidiously suggested by Interrested persons, but whether she shall manufacture for herself and thereby retain in circulation at home the cash she remitts every year to England for british Manufactures, which question may be clearly and simply decided on the principle that it is more economic and less expensive for an American farmer to raise or buy One hundred pounds of Cotton of the Value of twenty dollars & get his women & servants to Manufacture it into sufft cloth for his family than to pay from 8 to 12 dollars per yard at a store for british broad cloth for the male part of his family & proportionately for printed Cottons & Muslins for his females—his family clothing will not be less from store than 150 dollars a year & he wd save by home made cloth 130 Dollars which with other expences deducted from his crop is a serious reduction and which sum or the greater part of it is remitted to England there to Circulate—add to her capital or be subscribed in the loan towards a subsidy—but as such things must be had as cloths of that Kind Cannot be dispensed with, let him give that sum to resident Manufacturers and a large proportion of it will return to him again for provisions produce and Necessaries. The part that does not will Circulate & what does not circulate will add to the accumulating Capital of the Republic & instead of pecuniary Insolvency & ruin caused by excessive Importations & remittances for them to England the republic will attain to Enviable prosperity—returns for Exported Tobacco may be in cash west India Island produce or in some thing more beneficial than british Manufactures and the permanent Circulation of cash will by this means exceed the most sanguine Expectations.

There is an other more important document I feel it necessary to attempt an explanation of but which will be better understood on reading my next letter on the origin progress Interest & policy of Cromwells party in England & Ireland. It is an extract from the Edinburgh Review copied into the Intelligencer[6] a paper subservient to the Views & Interest of the same british party (the Ascendancy) and much read in America.

That great party whom the antient families of England & Ireland were at differt periods robbed & ruined to enrich gets Outrageous whenever there is any Scrutiny or agitation of its Titles to the properties thus acquired &

Which the descendants of the ruined Roman Cc. party having preserved the tradition of frequently agitate—unfortunately it is this agitation of their Titles that causes conspiracies & Insurrections & even facilitates revolution in Europe and also the encrease of the Orange party in America and the consequent Zeal of those Incendiaries who burn your Cities—the Kings of southern Europe are all roman Catholics & on all occasions partial to the descendants of those roman catholic families that Cromwell & the Revolution & the penal laws ruined—british Influence is by means of the british Mercantile Interest unlimitted in Europe—almost every great Mercantile house in England having a branch Or an Agent in Spain and Portugal—it is extensive in America but the more Ignorant the more credulous & the easier overcome by persuasion—by means of this great influence through the mercantile interest whenever british Titles are agitated Conspiracies are promoted & Insurrections and burning of Cities are the inevitable consequence—that desperate & vindictive party the Oligarchs has recourse to these Violent means to divert public attention from itself & its ill gotn property and to chastise & punish those it considers inimical to its Interest. This is become its sistematic & fixed principle—it is also a fixed principle with this party to arrest by all practicable means the progress of Improvement & Manufactures in other countries such advances being supposed to endanger british Monopoly. Therefore to promote foreign conspiracies Insurrections Convulsions Conflagrations & Civil War under pretence of friendship & philantrophy, is deemed a great national advantage. England is benefited by the idleness superstition Ignorance and despotism of surrounding nations. Her monopoly the source of her wealth is based on the permanence of those Lazy idle habits resulting from superstitious bigotry and Despotism—for these combined reasons she never failed to give a deadly blow to the progressive Industry & Improvement of any country she profits by whenever she has an opportunity of doing so—but it now appears there is a change of Sistem resolved on—her passions or her alarms overcame her prudence. The Oligarchs would rather preserve their Estates than Mercantile Monopoly—& to counteract the influence of the r C Kings & Clergy & punish them for their hostile partiality is secretly endeavouring by Revolutions to promote the Creation of an unive[r]sal Aristocracy partial to her Interest & Consequently opposed to the british & Irish roman C Interest but in this the Oligarchs are Mistaken—the Spanish Aristocracy or Legislature will promote the Manufacturing Sistem which will ruin the british Woollen Manufactures—no man has a higher Sense of honor than a spanish Gentn. He considers himself as good a Gentn as the King tho not so rich & will not make common cause with Cromwells party whom the world considers unprincipled & Villianous upstarts.

Before the union of Ireland to England the Oligarchs appointed a majority of the house of Coms. by means of their borroughs. Their Tenants to these Bors. (which are but small country Villages Chartered several Centuries back) pay their rents quarterly and dare not refuse to vote for whomsoever their Lordships nominate—that Majority has heretofore protected their Interests—but the Irish union & the Ingenuity of Mr Pitt[7] enabled him and his Successors in office to Outvote them—however the great mass of Influence in England still remains on their side. By means of these boroughs their Immense Estates & Connections & by their Influence they can convulse or quiet the country at will—they are the Constitutional pillars who can support or overturn the Monarchy. After the Irish Union Mr Pitt acted Independently of them—but his almost imediate death atoned for his imprudence—he was fond of wine and was poisoned. Mr Fox took the same high ground. His referrences to the antient Nobility of England were considered cuting reflections on Cromwells party. He also drank wine and was poisoned & Lord Castlereagh is now become so irritable & Cuting to them that I Expect his remains will soon be hearced to Westminster Abbey—he has already got two doses & I am Mistaken if he Survives the third dose. I considered these digressions necessary to shew them as they are.

The danger to the crown of increasing the power of that great party has hitherto excluded it from Ministerial offices—this exclusion makes it popular—by its connections Agents & dependants it manages the mob as it pleases—it secretly promoted the late insurrectn in England & after it gained its point ordered the mob to desist and shout for the queen[8]—the unfortunate Napoleon was long hostile to this great party but the frequency and facility with which it formed Coalitions against him alarmed him—he temporised—he identified the protection of his germanic Confedn on the Rine with protection of the immense properties of the british Oligarchs & with a view to avert future danger through policy became a seeming friend—he was as disappointed in the Oligarchs as in his father in law—they were more insinsere than he was—their Votes and influence were always against him.

The patronage of Charles the 4th of Spain for the Irish catholics rendered him very obnoxious to the british Oligarchs—who secretly encouraged Napoleon to seize & imprison him. Charles was a good auld & peaceable King and a Man of strict honor & deserved a better fate—& thus have the Oligarchs destroyed two Very obnoxious Enemies. It is certain that both these men Owe their reverses to british Influence & Intrigue. Ferdinand Knew it was alarmed at it and it was with a view to counteract british influence that he restored the Inquisition the popish & protestant priesthood being confirmed Enemies. He expected through the popish priesthood to arrest the further progress of british Influence & Intrigue—the act was a bad one tho the motive was good—however he was disappointed from which you will perceive that so much perfidy was never before practised by any party not so little suspected—it is certain that it secretly sanctions & promotes the perpetration of Crimes that have never been exceeded with such consummate Judgment secrecy & caution as not to be suspected—every stupid blockhead atributes its perfidious artifices & wiles to Ministers who seldom descend to refutation tho frequently innocent & yet these are the Demons whose Influence the Edinburgh Review wishes to extend throughout America.

It appears from that Review[9] that this diabolical party lately got so angry with America as in Effect to threaten war—the Review cautioned Jonathan not to be too fond of glory or that he wd be taxed as the british are & beginning with Locomotion then Enumeration of brit[i]sh taxes followed (in Terrorem).[10] I actually did suppose it tantamount to a declaration of war—but the next Review rescinded the threat & contained a proposal for an aliance offensive and defensive between the people of England and America. By which british people is not meant the exorbitantly taxed B Farmers the famishing laborers and Manufacturers or the Independt Intt. but the Tenants to their Lordships immense Estates & to their Lordships bors. who pay their rents quarterly & dare not disobey any mandate of their Landlords under pain of Ejectments and Evictions (and who on all such occasions are obliged to personate the contented & happy people of England) and also the great Mercantile Interest whose Zeal and subservience to the Govt which protects its universal Monopoly is proportioned to its gains and to its extensive Influence in America—both of these descriptions of persons are completely under the Controul of the british Oligarchs. By this attempt to conceal Wolves under sheeps clothing the Review seeks to spread their Influence over all America—& should America be deceived by this lure—& should british Influence increase the present convulsed state of Europe shews what will be its effects on America—the first effect of it will be to Impress poor illiterate Renters with a belief that the wealthier classes the proprietors of the soil are avaricious oppressive Tyrants that the laws are partial to the wealthy & that their speculations purchases & acquis[it]ions are destructive of every hope poor renters could have to get comfortable wealthy or better their conditions—this discontent will cause animosities Divisions and Insurrections and it is by such dissentions divisions & perhaps seperation of the union that the british Royal authority will be attempted to be reestablished. I forgot to mention that british Emissaries & Agents encourage wealthy men to become Orangemen Aristocrats and Consequently Lords Earls &ca. as much as they do the poor they first drive into Insurrection against the rich—these discontents make the poor the dupes and victims to british Intrigues artifices & perfidy. They become the agressors of the rich Which class is obliged to take shelter under royal authority & a standing army to protect itself from Violence robbery and assassination—so it has been hitherto in Europe and such is intended to be the effect of british Influence & Intrigue on America. I have witnessed all this in Ireland. I believe it prevailed in France & other places—the british maxim is Divide et Impera[11] and should british influence increase here it will be found as it was in those places I mentioned. Disjuncti perdemur.[12]

This perfidious party has been Known by its pernicious influence & intrigues to betray Sects Communities & Governments into dishonourable conduct & afterwards not only to disown disavow & condemn it but even to represent such conduct in so odious a light to Kings as to Induce them to coalesce which otherwise might not have happened—their influence is poison. Their intrigues are death—to exclude them from America is safety—their further increase is political ruin—dissention seperation & slavery—& the crafty Scotchman who Edited the Scotch Review is a Villianous Incendiary & an Enemy to mankind.

By any thing I sayed I do not exculpate the present royal family particularly the King & the duke of York from participating in the guilt I attempted to depict—they are as destitute of true honor & honesty as the most worthless of human beings—my next letter will contain two anecdotes of the King which I think will give a clear Idea of his principles & understanding—heretofore a prodigal profligate rake with no bounds to his extravigance & on other occasions (perhaps it was at the instigation of the Oligarchs) evincing a disposition to Avarice & fraud not equaled by the Jew in Shakespeares Merchant of Venice—the princess Mary is notoriously Known to be a Vagrant wandering prostitute at the instigation of the Oligarchic party who has spent a great part of her life in the practice of every vice that can degrade a female & debase a human being as prone to adultery and Incest as a she goat or shee ass—she selects her favourites in Ireland (from a wish to rule the mob) from the subaltern officers of the houghers[13] (persons who slaughtered the sheep & Cattle of good patriots but had not Courage to Join the Irish Insurgents or the french Invaders under Humbert)[14] & whose manners are as course & Vulgar as her conduct is loose and dissolute—from which you will perceive that Ministers are often obliged to conform to the Kings will in order to Keep their places and to sanction matters they neither Originate nor approve, and on the other hand to temporise with the Oligarchs to preserve a Majority in the House of Commons and Keep the Country in peace—and that the greater part of that abuse with which stupid Demagogues pelt them is in reality merited by the Kings and the Oligarchs but which it would be as imprudent & Impolitic as they deem it beneath them to refute—but tho I do not think they always sanction and promote the conspiracies Conflagrations & Insurrections imputed to them tho I believe Lord Castlereagh & Mr Canning to be what the world Calls Men of honor as to their private Conduct & Lord Liverpool the soundest statesman in England I am satisfied they would feel it an Imperative duty to take advantage of any favourable opporty. to Enslave America and that they would not hesitate to Make the attempt should the Orange Lodge sistem introduced here increase the british party so as to render success probable—from all of which you will perceive that under whatever disguise british Influence is introduced here it increases party animosities and divisions & is so extremely dangerous to the peace and Independence of America that Neutrality alone is safety.

I may be mistaken & yet I consider Mr. Monroe a Traitor who knows he is suspected—a hypocrite whom policy & necessity obliges to dissemble—secretly exerting his influence & the presidential patronage to increase the british party and to betray the countries Independence to a foreign despotism—how dangerous it is to have such a man supreme Governor & Generalissimo of all America during all the Intervals between the sitings of Congress & subject to no controul check restraint or responsibility—an other President is best Judge of. I am induced from that considn to think an Amendment to the Constitution necessary—in fact that some thing like the british privy Council is necessary—that it should be a Council of Elders composed of all those that were Presidents and of the Judges of the supreme Courts at Washington that this council should be stationary there during the Intervals between the sitings of Congress and also form a part of the Senate during the siting of Congress & that the members of this council should hold their places for life and that no act of the presidents should be legal or Valid during such Intervals without the assent & Consent of this Council or a Majority of it (for it might happen that an Orangeman might be one of it). Isolated Individuals coming from the remotest parts of the republic often require the aid of such a resident experienced Council—sevl centuries may not produce such presidents as Genl Washington & Mr Jefferson & Mr Madison & a salutary check & Constitnl restraint will be wanted for some of their successors—this & the Election of President by a Majority of the state Legislatures wd prevent british Agents from becoming Electors of P[r]esidt and really the Ignorant populace is so liable to be duped by british artifices & by Corrupted Demagogues that some such Amendment is necessary. I am with the utmost respect

EDMOND KELLY

RC (NN). Addressed by Kelly to JM "late presidt US at his residence state of Virginia Washington City." "Washington City" has been crossed out and "Orange C.H." written below in an unidentified hand. Postmarked "Columbia T 7th. Oct."

1. Kelly referred here to the piece entitled "The Edinburgh Review," printed in the *Daily National Intelligencer*, 14 Aug. 1820.

2. Samuel Butler, *Hudibras* (Dublin, 1732), part II, canto 2, lines 107–8.

3. William Duane (1760–1835) had engaged in journalism in India and London before moving to Philadelphia, where he succeeded Benjamin Franklin Bache as editor of the *Aurora*

General Advertiser. A passionate republican, Duane was a forceful voice in local, state, and national politics until his retirement from the newspaper in 1822.

4. The editors of the *Daily National Intelligencer* published two pieces from the Philadelphia *Poulson's American Daily Advertiser* along with a lengthy reply on 15 Aug. 1820.

5. For Andrew Jackson's memorial to the Senate, to which Kelly probably referred, see Kelly to JM, April 1820, and n. 4.

6. Kelly may have been referring to an article in the *Daily National Intelligencer* of 4 July 1820 entitled "Illustration of British Affairs. Extracts from the Number of the Edinburgh Review, for January, 1820."

7. As part of the agreement that resulted in the union of Great Britain and Ireland in 1801, Prime Minister William Pitt (1759–1806), on behalf of his government, compensated eighty-four borough-holders who had been disenfranchised by the act.

8. For the trial of Queen Caroline, and popular support for her cause, see JM to Richard Rush, 12 Aug. 1820, and n. 2.

9. Kelly refers here to an "extract from a late number of the Edinburgh Review" that was published in the *Daily National Intelligencer,* 19 May 1820.

10. *In terrorem:* as a warning.

11. *Divide et impera:* divide and conquer.

12. *Disjuncti perdemur:* disconnected, we shall be lost.

13. *Hougher:* "One who houghs or hamstrings; in Ireland, a member of an association of law-breakers who arose in 1711, and practiced the houghing of cattle; afterwards identified with the Whiteboys" (*OED Online*).

14. French general Jean Joseph Amable Humbert (1755–1823) led an invasion of Ireland in 1798 that was to support a general uprising against British rule. After its failure, and his capture and exchange, Humbert held commands in Switzerland and Saint-Domingue. A strict republican, Humbert became disillusioned with Napoleon, who had exiled him to Brittany, and fled to the United States, arriving in New Orleans about 1814. He fought against the British once again at the Battle of New Orleans, attempted to organize a filibustering expedition into Mexico some time later, and taught school in New Orleans until his death.

Minutes of the Board of Visitors of the University of Virginia

[2 October 1820]

At a meeting of the Visitors of the University of Virginia, at the University, on monday 2d. of Octr. 1820, present Thomas Jefferson, James Madison, Robert B. Taylor, John H. Cocke, and Joseph C. Cabell;

The Board proceeded to the consideration of the Annual Report, and not having time to go through with the same, adjourned to tuesday 3d. October.

Ms (ViU: Jefferson Papers, Special Collections). In Joseph C. Cabell's hand.

Minutes of the Board of Visitors of the University of Virginia

Oct. 3. 1820.

At an adjourned meeting of the Visitors of the University of Virginia, held on 3d. October 1820, present Thomas Jefferson, James Madison, Robert B. Taylor, John H. Cocke and Joseph C. Cabell;

The Board approved the arrangement made by the Committee of Superintendence relative to the annulment of the contract with Doctor Thomas Cooper.

Resolved, that From & after the first day of October 1820, the compensation to the Bursar of the University for his services, shall be at the rate of one per cent on the amount of disbursements.

Resolved, that Joseph C. Cabell be & he is hereby desired & authorized to examine and verify the accounts of the preceding years not already examined and verified.

Resolved, That the Committee of Superintendence be authorized to enter into negociations, with the following persons, with the view of engaging them as Professors of the University,

viz: Mr. Bowditch of Salem

and Mr. Tichenor of Boston.

Resolved, That in the negociations with Mr. Bowditch & Mr. Tichenor, the committee be authorized to offer the compensation hereinafter specified—viz:

1. Apartments.

2. A Salary of $2000 per annum.

3. A fee of $10. for each student engaged to attend the Lectures of the Professor.

4. If the aggregate amount of the Salary and of the fees of tuition, should fall short of $2500, in either the first, second, or third year, the deficiency to be paid out of the funds of the University.[1]

The following report was agreed to

To the President and Directors of the Literary fund.

In obedience to the act of the General assembly of Virginia, requiring that the Rector & Visitors of the University of Virginia should make report annually to the President & Directors of the Literary fund (to be laid before the legislature at their next succeeding session) embracing a full account of the disbursements, the funds on hand, & a general statement of the condition of the sd. University, the sd. Visitors make the following Report.

The General assembly at their last session of 1819.20 having passed an act authorising the sd. Visitors, for the purpose of finishing the buildings of the University, to borrow the sum of 60,000. D. and to pledge for repayment of the sd. sum and interest, any part of the annual appropriation of 15,000. D. heretofore made by law, the board of Visitors at their semi-annual meeting of April last proceeded to the consideration of the sd. act, and of the authoritie⟨s⟩ therein permitted to them. They were of opinion, in the first place, that it would be most expedient to compleat all the buildings necessary for the accomodation of the Professors & Students before opening the institution, as the maintenance of that, when opened, by absorbing all it's funds, would leave nothing to compleat what might yet be requisite for the full establishment called for by law.

On view of the accounts rendered by the Bursar and Proctor, they found that with the aid of the loan authorised (if the commencement of it's instalments for repaiment could be suspended four years) and of their annuity during the same time, they might accomplish the whole of the buildings of accomodation, for the Professors and students according to the estimates heretofore made of their probable cost, of which the following statement presents a summary view.

1820 Apr. The existing debts are		10.000
To compleat the 7. pavilions & 31. Dormitories on hand		18,000
To build 3. more pavilions & 24. Dormits. to compleat the lawn		27.600
To build 3. Hotels & 25. Dormits. compleating the East back street		19,000
	74,600	
1821. To build 2. Hotels & Proctor's house, & 25. Dormits. compleatg. West backstreet		19.000
		93.600

Means.		
1820. Apr. Loan from the Literary fund of		40,000
1821. Jan. 1. Annuity of 15,000. D—2400. int. of 40,000 D.		12,600
Additional loan of		20,000
1822. Jan. 1. Annuity of 15,000.D—3600 D int. of 60,000		11,400
	84,000	
⟨1⟩823. Jan. 1. Annuity of 15.000 D.—3600. int. of 60,000		11,400
		95,400

They therefore proceeded to negociate a loan of 40,000.D. from the President and Directors of the Literary fund reimbursable by 5 instalments of 14,244. D. a year beginning on the [2] day of April 1824. and afterwards a 2d. loan of 20,000. D. reimbursable by like annual instalments, commencing from the day when the others should end.

On this view of their resources the Board proceeded to authorise their Proctor to enter into contracts for the completion of the buildings already begun & for the erection of those still wanting, so as to provide in the whole, 10. Pavilions for the Professors required by law, 5. hotels for dieting the Students, & a 6th. for the use of the Proctor, with 104. Dormitories, sufficient for lodging 208. students; and they instructed him to make, in his contracts, effectual provision that the whole shall be compleated in the autumn of the ensuing year 1821. At that time therefore the buildings of accomodation for the Professors & Students are expected to be all ready for their reception, and the institution might then be opened, but that the remaining engagements for the buildings & the reimbursement of the sums borrowed from the Literary fund will require the whole revenue of the University for 7. years to come that is to say until the [3] day of April 1828.

In the statement of expenditures & means of the University it will be percieved that we have not taken the private subscriptions into account. Of these 2079.33 D of the 1st. instalment, 3914.13 D. of the 2d. & 8217.09 of the 3d. are still due; & the last amounting to 10,666.50 will become due on the 1st. day of April next. But of these some loss will be occasioned by the distresses of the times; & the residue, from the same cause, will be so tardy & uncertain in the times of it's reciept, that the Visitors have not thought it safe to found on it any stipulations requiring punctuality in their fulfilment. They have thought it more advisable to reserve it as a Supplementory & Contingent fund, to aid the general revenue, as it shall be recieved, and to meet casualties unforeseen, errors of estimate, and expences other than those of meer building.

In the Report of the Commissioners who met at Rockfish gap on the 1st. day of Aug. 1818. it was stated that "a building of somewhat more size in the middle of the grounds may be called for in time, in which may be rooms for religious worship under such impartial regulations as the Visitors shall prescribe, for public examinations, for a Library, for the schools of music, drawing and other associated purposes." The expences of this building are not embraced in the estimates herein before stated. It's cost will probably be of about 40,000. D. and it's want will be felt as soon as the University shall open. But this building is beyond the reach of the present funds. Nor are these indeed adequate to the maintenance of the institution on the full scale enacted by the legislature. That body, aware that Professors of desirable eminence could not be expected to relinquish the situations in which they might be found, for others new, untried, and unknown, without a certainty of adequate compensation, confided to the discretion of the Visitors the salaries which should be stipulated to the Professors first employed. But the annuity heretofore appropriated to the maintenance of the University cannot furnish sufficient inducement to ten Professors, of high degree each in his respective line of science; and yet, to employ inferior persons, would be to stand where we are in science, unavailed of the higher advances alread[y] made elsewhere, & of the advantages contemplated by the statute under which we act.

If the legislature shall be of opinion that the annuity already apportioned to the establishment and maintenance of an institution for instruction in all the useful sciences, is it's proper part of the whole fund the Visitors will faithfully see that it shall be punctually applied to the remaining engagements for the buildings, and to the reimbursement of the extra sum lately recieved from the general fund: that during the term of it's exclusive application to these objects, due care shall be taken to preserve the buildings erected from ruin or injury, and at the end of that term, they will provide for opening the institution in the partial degree to which it's present annuity shall be adequate. If, on the other hand, the legislature shall be of opinion that the sums so advanced in the name of a loan, from the general fund of education, were legitimately applicable to the purposes of an University, that it's early commencement will promote the public good by offering to our youth now ready and waiting for it, an early and near resource for instruction, and, by arresting the heavy tribute we are annually paying to other states and countries for the article of education, and shall think proper to liberate the present annuity from it's engagements, the Visitors trust it will be in their power, by the autumn of the ensuing year 1821. to engage and bring into place that portion of the Professors designated by the law, to which the present annuity may be found competent; or, by the same epoch, to carry into full execution the whole objects of the law, if an enlargement be made of it's participation in the general fund, adequate to the full establishment contemplated by the law.

The accounts reciepts, disbursements and funds on hand for the year ending with the present date, as rendered by the Bursar and Proctor of the University, are given with this report, as is required by law.

TH: JEFFERSON Rector

and the board adjourned without day.

TH: JEFFERSON Rector

Ms (ViU: Jefferson Papers, Special Collections). In hands of Joseph C. Cabell and Thomas Jefferson.

1. Cabell's hand ends here; the rest of the manuscript is in Jefferson's hand.
2. Left blank in ms.
3. Left blank in ms.

From Joseph Delaplaine

Dear sir, Philadelphia 11 Octobr 1820

At the request of the author,[1] I have the honour of transmitting to you, for your kind acceptance, a volume of poetry,[2] for your good opinion of which, I know he would feel much gratified.

An elementary book for the use of schools,[3] new in its design & arrangement, will be issued from the press by the same author, in a fee [*sic*] months; at which time I shall have the pleasure of sending to you a copy. With very high regard, I am, dear sir, your very obed. St,

Joseph Delaplaine

RC (DLC). Addressed by Delaplaine to JM. Docketed by JM.

1. Charles Mead was the principal of the Franklin Academy of Philadelphia (Albert Picket and John W. Picket, *The Academician, Containing the Elements of Scholastic Science and the Outlines of Philosophic Education* [New York, 1820], 143).

2. Charles Mead, *Mississippian Scenery; A Poem, Descriptive of the Interior of North America* (Philadelphia, 1819; Shaw and Shoemaker 48656).

3. Charles Mead, *The School Exercise, Containing a Course of Lessons, in Which the Various Branches of Education are Introduced as Subjects for Reading in Schools* (Philadelphia, 1820). An extract of JM to Delaplaine, 12 Feb. 1822, was included among the "recommendations" in the second edition of this work (Philadelphia, 1823; Shoemaker 13275).

To Isaiah Thomas

Montpellier (Virga). Ocr. 12. 1820

J. Madison presents his respects to Mr. Thomas,[1] with his acknowledgments for the copy of the Transactions of the American Antiquarian Society,[2] and his best wishes for the success of an Institution, the valuable objects of which are so well explained and recommended in the early pages of the Volume.

RC (MWA: Isaiah Thomas Papers).

1. Isaiah Thomas (1749–1831) was a printer, and publisher of the *Massachusetts Spy*, first in Boston and later, from 1775, in Worcester, Massachusetts. There he established a printing company that published a wide variety of titles, and that at its height employed 150 people and included printing presses, five bookstores, a paper mill, and a bindery. He retired in 1802, though retaining ownership, and devoted himself to other business interests and philanthropy. In 1812 he founded the American Antiquarian Society and became its first president, an office he held until his death (Clifford K. Shipton, *Isaiah Thomas: Printer, Patriot and Philanthropist, 1749–1831* [Rochester, N.Y., 1948], 2, 18–19, 32, 51–55, 63, 65–66, 67–70, 81–82, 84).

2. *Archæologia Americana: Transactions and Collections of the American Antiquarian Society* (Worcester, Mass., 1820; Shoemaker 92).

From Joel K. Mead

Dear Sir. Washington City 12th. Octr. 1820

I must rely upon the object I have in view to plead my apology for the freedom I take in obtruding upon your leisure this note. I have for some years viewed with some solicitude the want of an institution for the instruction of indigent youth of native genius and talents in the higher branches of literature, the sciences and the liberal arts. I mean more particularly those, who, having received the first rudiments of Education, discover strong natural genius or talents, or a particular aptitude, inclination or taste for some branch of human knowledge, and who are destitute of friends able to afford them the necessary means of instruction; to be selected from any and every part of the nation where they may chance to be found. It will not be contended, that talents are confined to the affluent, or virtue to the wealthy. The poor have equal pretentions to them by nature as the rich. The only difference appears to be in the advantages afforded by Education. It is also generally admitted that knowledge is power, and the general defusion of it equalizes power, and affords the best protection to our political liberties and moral freedom. I do not hazard much is [*sic*] saying that all of our large towns and cities, produce, at least, one individual in every five or ten years, capable of rendering great service to the public, of promoting our literature, or of extending the limits of our knowledge, if proper means were provided, and care taken to instruct them, according to their capacities, in what is already known. To be the humble instrument in founding an institution, to be devoted to this object by suggesting a plan to procure the necessary funds and to devote my future exertion to the accumulation of the means and to aid in the application of them is what I have been desirous of for some time past. I have formed a little project by which it seems to me the necessary funds may be raised, and successfully applied; and which I will suggest in brief, and request your opinion and such remarks as you may be pleased to make.

In the first place I propose to form a society for the purpose of founding the proposed institution, who will pay a certain sum annually, say five dollars, which I am convinced may readily be done, and I doubt not will in a few years become very numerous. Then to apply to congress for an act to authorize the society to raise a certain sum annually, by lottery—say 30 or 40 thousand dollars pr ann. for ten or twelve years. I have no doubt but even the latter sum may be raised every year in this way untill completed;

and if so, then in a very few years the society may have an institution in successful opperation, and if proper care be taken in the investment of the funds, a permanent revenue secured for its future support.

The question now presents itself, how shall the contemplated funds be vested, and where shall the institution be located? From the reflections I have given the subject I am of opinion that thirty or forty thousand acres of the public lands should be purchased, some where in Ohio, Indiania, Illinois or Missouri; where it can be had to the greatest advantage, keeping in view the eligibility for the location of the institution, the firtility of the soil with other advantages, such as timber and water &c. I am not fully informed, but believe that the public lands may be had in one of the states above named, of the first quality, for a little more than the minm. price. At the minm. price 50,000$ will pay for 40.000 acres. If this be purchased let there be 4 or 5 thousand acres reserved for the institution, to be cultivated under the direction of the society for the support of the institution in provisions, clothing &c. The residue may be surveyed into lots suitable for farms, say of 250 or 300 acres each and every other one leased to individual[s] who would settle on, and improve them; and as an inducement, let them be rent free for 7. years, and after that subject to an annual rent forever. Or let them be sold on a credit payable in installments, and if not paid for according to agreement, then to revert to the society with the improvements. This would probably soon introduce 50 or 60 good settlers in the compass of a few miles in extent. The improvements they would make would greatly increase the Value of the reserved lots; perhaps two three or four fold. These might be disposed of as circumstances may render expedient.

Upon the supposition that 30,000$ can be raised per Ann. then at the end of two years a proper person may be sent out to purchase the land, have it surveyed, and preparations made for a settlement. The funds that will be in hand will justify the society in sending out, under a suitable superintendent, at least 20 good labourers; active smart young white men, enough of whom may be obtained from the north and East for about 100$ pr Ann. and who will themselves probably become settlers in a few years. I have not sufficient data to enable me to go into an accurate calculation of the number of acres these 20 labourers would be able to clear and cultivate per Ann. nor do I think it necessary at present. In the next year the necessary buildings for the institution might be commenced, and as 30 or 40,000$ would be coming into the treasury of the society every year, it is not unreasonable to suppose that an institution may be in opperation in 4 or 5 years, and which may be increased according to circumstances.

From this bird's eye view you will be able to perceive my plan and judge of it[s] practicability and expediency. It is on these I am desirous to obtain your opinion before I proceed any farther. I am the more solicitous on this subject, because I have no wife or children, good or bad to engage my attention, and probably I never shall have. I want something to engage my attention in which more than myself are concerned. I have somewhere read that one of the Ancient philosophers, I think Pythagoras, taught that every useless man, is a dead man, and ordered that when any of his deciples became weary of studying to make themselves useful to others, they should be regarded as dead, and have tombs erected to them with suitable inscriptions as warnings to the living.[1] I know of no way in which I can better deserve a place among the living than by devoting my attention to the service of those who are in need of assistance. I am Sir, with much respect your obedient humble servant

JOEL K. MEAD[2]

RC (DLC). Addressed by Mead to JM, and franked. Docketed by JM.

1. "If any one of the Disciples, after having led this Life for some time, come to grow weary of it, and return'd to his first Condition, all the others regarded him as a dead Person, made his Obsequies, and rais'd him a Tomb, to shew, that if a Man, after having enter'd into the Ways of Wisdom, turns aside and forsakes them, 'tis in vain for him to believe himself living, he is dead" (André Dacier, *The Life of Pythagoras, with His Symbols and Golden Verses. Together with the Life of Hierocles, and his Commentaries upon the Verses* [London, 1707], 26).

2. Joel K. Mead had been the editor of the Washington weekly *National Register*, 1816–18. By 1823 he was editing the *Mercantile Advertiser* in New Orleans, and in 1832 he was operating the lottery office there. There is mention of him in Texas in 1843 (Joel K. Mead, *Washington, February, 1819. Sir, more than six months have now elapsed Since I disposed of . . . the national register . . .* [n.p., 1819]; Carolyn E. DeLatte, ed., *Antebellum Louisiana, 1830–1860* [2 vols.; Lafayette, La., 2004], 2:85; Colleen Fitzpatrick, ed., *1832 New Orleans City Directory* (New Orleans, 2000), 58; Harriet Smither, ed., "Diary of Adolphus Sterne," *Southwestern Historical Quarterly* 35 [1932]: 324).

To Bushrod Washington

DEAR SIR MONTPELLIER Ocr. 14 1820

In fulfilment of my promise I return the letters to General Washington which you were so obliging as to forward to me.[1] I should have done it sooner but that I had hoped to return at the same time the letters expected from Richmond. Will you permit me to recall your attention to the latter portion (which I believe will comprize the letters I could most wish to obtain) that the Chief Justice[2] may not lose the opportunity of a recess for looking them up. Be assured always of my high esteem & my cordial respects

JAMES MADISON

RC (NN: Emmet Collection); FC (DLC).

1. See Bushrod Washington to JM, 23 Mar. 1820.

2. John Marshall, chief justice of the U.S. Supreme Court, had written his five-volume *Life of George Washington* (Philadelphia, 1804–7) with the aid of Washington's voluminous papers, a part of which he still held at this time (Johnson et al., *Papers of John Marshall*, 6:219–26; Marshall to James A. Hamilton, 9 Mar. 1822, ibid., 9:201).

To Joel K. Mead

Ocr. 16. 1820

I have recd. your letter of the 12th. inst: & I can not speak too favorably of the object which employs your thoughts or of the disinterested zeal with which you devise means for accomplishing it. Of those which have occurred you ask my opinion. I wish it were better entitled to the confidence, you seem to attach to it. Such as it is I give it with the candor, which I can not doubt you will approve, however it may be wanting in any other recommendation.

An essential reliance is placed on a lottery & a Society (incorporated of course) under the authority of Congress. To the first there will be serious objections of a moral nature with some: & of a constitutional nature with others. To the second constitutional objections will be urged of a still more decided cast.

Should none of these objections prevail, and the lottery be successful to an adequate extent, the conversion of the pecuniary fund into a large landed estate as proposed would involve others which could not but be allowed peculiar weight. A socie[t]y formed of scattered members, as with a trust in which they wd. not be personally interested, and that trust at so great a distance, and consisting of farms on leases, would scarcely be exempt from mismanagemts. of a ruinous tendency. Whatever might be the purity & activity of the founders, & their first Agents, relaxations of zeal, in their successors, with multiplying opportunities for collusions & other abuses, would speedily ensue. Nothing has been found more difficult in practice, than to guard charitable Institutions agst. mismanagements fatal to their original objects. In England, where they have abounded in every form; late investigations[1] have brought to light a degree & a generality of the perversions of these endowments into sine cures & corrupt jobs, which suggest every where the utmost precaution agst. such evils; a task which will always be more difficult in proportion to the complexity of the plans, and the number, the dispersion, and the distance of those who are to be concerned in the superintendance & conduct of them.

Some provision for selecting & educating youths who possess genius & virtue, without the means of doing justice to the gifts of nature seems equally due to individual merit, and to the public welfare. The difficulty lies in devising the plans at once most practicable, and most effectual. Perhaps a limitation of the efforts, in the first instance at least, to the sphere & patronage of the local Authorities would promise most success. Constl. difficulties wd. then be avoided, a greater simplicity in the plans & responsibility in the execution of them, attainable. And an emulation in that as is taking place in other instances, might produce finally the most eligible provision for the object in view. A provision for selecting boys of uncommon promise, and carrying them forward as their merits might develope themselves, through the successive grades of education, was at an early day incorporated into a diffusive system [of] education proposed for this State.[2] But it has never recd. a legislative sanction.

I have only to add to these hasty remarks, a request that they may be regarded as merely addressed to yourself, and a tender of my respects & good wishes

J. M

Draft (DLC).

1. For the Brougham investigation into abuses of charitable organizations, see Detatched Memoranda, ca. 31 Jan. 1820, *PJM-RS*, 1:613, 624 n. 52.

2. JM referred here to a bill drafted by Thomas Jefferson entitled "A Bill for the More General Diffusion of Knowledge," which was introduced into the Virginia General Assembly in 1778, 1780, 1785 (by JM), and 1786, and considered but defeated each time (Boyd, *Papers of Thomas Jefferson*, 2:526–33, 534–35 n.).

From Charles D. Coxe

Sir, Sidney, near Pittston N. Jersey October 20th 1820.

On the dismissal of Lieut Col. Gale[1] from the Marine Corps, The officers have alledged to me, through my friend Mr. Pleasonton[2] of the Treasury Department, that, as they do not conceive I have resigned my commission in that Corps, *they would be very glad of my being placed at the head of it;* to which the date of my Commission would entitle me.

I conceive it now to be in your power to do me a kindness as well as an act of justice. You know the circumstances attending my being left at Tunis by my commanding officers Captain Dent & Commodore Campbell in 1806,[3] and my subsequent appointment as Consular agent by Mr. Lear.[4] The latter gentleman approving of my conduct promised to use his endeavours to obtain me the appointment as Consul, on receiving which, I was to have resigned my military Commission, and not otherwise.

I was suffered to remain several years there without any answer. I at length received a letter from the then Secretary of the Navy (Paul Hamilton Esq.)[5] dated the 15. June 1809, informing me that *"my long absence was complained of by the officers junior to me in rank,"* and desired me to inform him *"whether it was my determination to remain at Tunis or not?"* If I chose to remain he "thought it proper I should transmit to him my military Commission in the Marine Corps"—or if I should *"prefer holding my military Commission"* to return immediately to the U. States. I answerd Mr. Hamilton stating to Him the cruel dilemma in which I was placed leaving my fate entirely in the hands of Government, implicitly relying on it's justice. This answer *he never acknowledged to me his having received or accepted* from which I concluded that he had alter'd his mind about the necessity of my resigning. I retain'd my Commission in my own hands, not doubting that justice would be done me by the President on my return (in case I should be superseded in the Consulate at Tunis) and that my military Commission would remain valid. From his requesting me to inform him "whether it was my determination to remain at Tunis or not"—I naturally concluded the thing was understood between the heads of the Depts. of State and the Navy, and that the choice of remaining was left to me; for I could hardly suppose Mr. Hamilton would on his own authority, without an understanding with the Secretary of State (under whose orders I was acting as Consular agent,) risque leaving the Consulate unrepresented, when there was such a large amount of American property consigned to my care, which I could not abandon without evident risque, before being regularly relieved, I found myself constrained and forced to remain where I was, and to leave my fate in the hands of Government.

On my return to Washington, I paid my respects to you, and stated the very disagreeable situation in which I was placed, after having served my Country so long, during an absence of more than *ten years*, under so many discouraging circumstances, and with the express approbation of my superiors. You were good enough to say that you had always considered me as attached to the Marine Corps, and that you had appointed a Consul to succeed me under the idea that I wished to return to my post. I do not pretend to recollect your precise words, but I understood that fully to be your meaning. And, again, when my Consular accounts were sent to you from the Dept. of State for inspection, you returned for answer in a note,[6] as near as my recollection serves me, that you did not think several charges ought to be allowed to me, *as I was an officer in the Marine Corps and not a regularly appointed Consul*, which I believe you will recollect.

The letter of Mr. Hamilton to me, therefore, I had every reason to believe was written without even the knowledge of The President, and that its object, (to force from me an involuntary resignation) was abandoned by him, as all the officers I met at Washington with Colonel Wharton,[7] disclaimed having any hand in it. The officers now alledge that they would be very glad to see me take my rank at the head of the Corps, the truth of which The President has it in his power to ascertain. As I was placed at Tunis before Mr. Munroe came into office, my case did not come immediately under his notice. I have therefore taken the liberty to write to you on the subject, cherishing the fervent hope, you will have the goodness to address a line to The President in my favor on this occasion, as I have never entertained a doubt of your willingness to do me justice as far as is in your power. I beg leave to solicit the honor of an answer as soon as your convenience will permit, and with my best wishes for the health and happiness of yourself and amiable Lady, to whom, I pray you will present my most respectful regards, I have the honor to remain, With the highest Esteem and respect, Sir, Your most obedt. humle Servt.

CHARLES D: COXE[8]

RC (DLC). Docketed by JM.

1. Anthony Gale (1761–1842) was born in Ireland and came to the United States in 1793. He was commissioned in the Marine Corps in 1798, served in the Quasi-War and the Barbary Wars, and commanded the Marine Barracks in Philadelphia, 1801–3 and 1807–17. Gale was Marine Corps Commandant from 1819 to 1820, when he was dismissed for "habitual drunkenness." He moved to Kentucky in 1826, where he "lived out his days there in poverty and ill health" (Allan R. Millett and Jack Shulimson, *Commandants of the Marine Corps* [Annapolis, Md., 2004], 45–53).

2. Stephen Pleasonton (ca. 1776–1855), originally from Delaware, was a career bureaucrat who was employed as a clerk in the State Department, before its move to Washington, and throughout JM's tenure as secretary of state and president. By 1820, Pleasonton had become fifth auditor of the Treasury, and he held that post until his death (Baltimore *Sun*, 2 Feb. 1855; Syrett and Cooke, *Papers of Alexander Hamilton*, 22:283; *PJM-SS*, 1:349–50 and n., and n. 2; *A Register of Officers and Agents . . . 1829*, 22; *ASP, Miscellaneous*, 2:308).

3. For the death of James Dodge, U.S. chargé d'affaires at Tunis, and the subsequent appointment of Coxe as acting chargé by Master Commandant John H. Dent, see Coxe to JM, 8 Dec. 1806, Knox, *Naval Documents, Barbary Wars*, 6:491–92. Hugh G. Campbell was commodore of the Mediterranean squadron, 1806–7 (ibid., 435; Christopher McKee, *A Gentlemanly and Honorable Profession: The Creation of the U.S. Naval Officer Corps, 1794–1815* [Annapolis, Md., 1991], 184).

4. Tobias Lear, U.S. consul general at Algiers, confirmed the appointment of Coxe as acting chargé d'affaires "till the pleasure of the President shall be known," Coxe to JM, 8 Mar. 1807, Knox, *Naval Documents, Barbary Wars*, 6:511. Lear (1762–1816), a New Hampshire native and Harvard graduate, had been private secretary to George Washington. Thomas Jefferson had appointed him commercial agent at Saint-Domingue and in 1803, consul general at Algiers, a post he held until 1812. In 1814 JM appointed Lear accountant to the War Department, and he remained in that office until his suicide in October 1816 (*PJM-SS*, 1:13 n. 5; *PJM-PS*, 2:413 n. 3; Hartford *Connecticut Mirror*, 21 Oct. 1816).

5. Paul Hamilton (1762–1816) was a Revolutionary War veteran, state legislator, and governor of South Carolina, 1804–6. In 1809 JM appointed him secretary of the navy, and he served in that position until his resignation in 1812 (Sobel and Raimo, *Biographical Directory of the Governors*, 4:1391–92).

6. Letter not found.

7. A member of a prominent Philadelphia merchant family, Franklin Wharton (1767–1818) was Marine Corps Commandant, 1804–18 (Millett and Shulimson, *Commandants of the Marine Corps*, 36–44).

8. Charles Davenport Coxe (d. 1830) was appointed commercial agent at Dunkirk by Thomas Jefferson on 6 Jan. 1802 but declined the post; for his reasons, see Coxe to JM, 21 Apr. 1802, *PJM-SS*, 3:150. He was commissioned a second lieutenant in the Marine Corps on 18 Nov. 1805, promoted to first lieutenant in March 1807, and resigned his commission 18 Sept. 1809. In the interim he had been selected by the commander of his ship, John H. Dent, to be acting U.S. chargé d'affaires at Tunis in December 1806, and he was confirmed in that post by Tobias Lear in March 1807. He served at Tunis until 1813. Nominated U.S. consul at Tripoli on 13 Dec. 1825, and confirmed by the Senate six days later, he held the post until his death (*Senate Exec. Proceedings*, 1:400, 402, 459; Callahan, *List of Officers of the Navy*, 684; Coxe to JM, 8 Dec. 1806, and Coxe to John H. Dent, 3 Mar. 1807, Knox, *Naval Documents, Barbary Wars*, 6:491–92, 509–10; *Senate Exec. Proceedings*, 2:347, 3:449, 456).

From Thomas W. Maury

DEAR SIR. ORANGE CT. HOUSE 23rd. October 1820

My relation Mr. Wm. Maury of Liverpool will in a short time commence a long tour thro Kentucky, Tennessee & Mississippi, and from thence to New-Orleans. Being now absent on a tour to the eastward, and expecting to have no leisure on his way thro Virginia, he has requested me by letter, to ask the favor of you to give him letters to a few of the distinguished gentlemen in those states. If you should find it convenient to do so, I must ask the favor of you to forward the letters by mail to me at Charlottesville. I should most certainly have done myself the pleasure of waiting on you in person, but am compelled to be in Milton at 10. oClock tomorrow morning. Respectfully Yr. mo: obt.

TH: W. MAURY[1]

RC (DLC). Docketed by JM.

1. Thomas Walker Maury (d. 1842) was a lawyer and school teacher in Albemarle County, Virginia (Maury, *Intimate Virginiana*, 325–26).

From Maury & Latham

SIR LIVERPOOL. 24 Oct 1820

We beg to hand Accot sales of your Tobacco pr. scipio, with your Accot Currt. balance £35..12..5. due to you. By the next vessel for Virginia we shall ship the 10 sacks of Salt which you wish for.

Mess MacKay & Campbell handed us your dft for £100. on us, & which we shall accordingly appropriate to them if such is your wish—it will in that case leave a balance of £64.7.7. against you, exclusive of cost of 10 sacks Salt.

We have thought that the annexed report of our markets, might be interesting to you, and we have the honor to remain sir Your mo obt humble Sts.

MAURY & LATHAM

[First Enclosure]

Account Sales of 8 Hhds of Tobacco received p Scipio S Drummond from Virginia on account of Mr Madison—vizt:

1820
Sept 11 By James Galan for 3 Hhds
No C y lb.
IM
19 12. 2. 19—lb. 17 shrinkage
21 12. 1. 21 " " Nett d
22 11. — 26. " " or 4047 lb @ 5d — 84 6 3

" 12 " W Anderson 2 Hhds
18 12.1. 18—17 or 1373 @ 5¼ — 30 — 8

23 12.1 5—17 or 1360 @ 5 — 28 6 8

" 13 " Bromfield & Co. 1 Hhd
24 11. 3. 15—17 1314 @ 4¾ — 26 — 1

" " " W Anderson 1 Hhd
20 11. 3. 15—17 1314 @ 5 — 27 7 6

" 21 " John Johnson 1 Hhd
17 12.—23—17 1350 @ 4½ — 25 6 3

£221 7 5

Charges

Aug 1 To Insurance on £190 @1¼ pct: & policy 12/- 2. 19. 6
" 24 " freight @ 50/- p hhd & primage 5 p cent 21, —. —
" landing charges 10/- p hhd — 4, —. —
" fire insnce 4/- postage of remces: 5/5 — 9.5
" Commission including Brokerage & risk of debt on — £221.7.5 @ 4 p cent
8. 17. 1 37 6 —

Nett proceeds due in Cash 23 Jany: 1821
£184 1 5

Errors Excepted
Liverpool 27 Sept. 1820
Maury & Latham

J M 8.	402.	1500.	138.	1362
	403.	1520.	134.	1386
	404.	1550.	140.	1410
	405.	1470	136.	1334
	406.	1528.	137.	1399
	407.	1420.	135.	1285
	408.	1510.	132.	1378
	409.	1450.	130.	1328
				10866

Ware House Charges
Nine Dollars & three Quarters

Dr Mr. James Madison in Account Current & Interest to 23 Jany. 1821 with Maury & Latham

1820		
Aug 14	To Invoice JM 1 Box p Philip Tab	18 2 9
"	To do. sundries do.	128 4 6
Sept 27	To postages	— 1 4
"	To Interest ℔ account	2 — 5
"	To Balance carried down	35 12 5
		£184 1 5
Octo 14		101 2 — 5
		2 — 5

Cr.

1820		
Sept. 27 By Net Proceeds JM 8 Hhds Tobo. ℔ Scipio		
	184 1 5	1821 Jan 23
	£184 1 5	
By Balance brought down	35 12 5	1820 Jan 23

Errors Excepted
Liverpool 27 September 1820.
Maury & Latham

RC and first enclosure (DLC); second enclosure (DLC: Rare Book and Special Collections Division). RC addressed to JM; postmarked 23 Dec. at New York, and franked. Docketed by JM "Ocr. 23. 1820." The second enclosure (1 p.) is a printed circular letter from Maury & Latham, dated 23 Oct. 1820, with an appended "Prices Current of American Produce."

To Joseph Delaplaine

DEAR SIR MONTPR. [ca. 31] Ocr. 1820

I have recd. your note of the 11th. with the little poetical volume of Mr. Mead; for which I desire that my thanks may be accepted.

It is so long since I indulged myself in this species of reading, that I can the less venture to pronounce on the merit of the performance. From a hasty glance over it, my attention was caught by passages, which appeared well to accord with the inspiration of the subject.

I take this occasion to ask the favor of you to send me the manuscript papers containing memoranda relating to myself,[1] in which I am apprehensive there may be some inaccuracies; and the two pamphlets, the one on the British Doctrine concerning neutral trade;[2] the other entitled "Political Observations."[3] Of the former I have no copy left, and the latter has corrections, which I wish to apply to a copy on hand. Yrs with respect & good wishes

JAMES MADISON

RC (ViU: Special Collections); draft (DLC). RC day of month not indicated; conjectural day supplied from cover marked: "Orange C H Octr. 31st 1820." Addressed by JM to Delaplaine at Philadelphia, and franked. Docketed by Delaplaine.

1. In a letter to JM of 26 Feb. 1816 (DLC), Delaplaine had requested "a few facts of your life—*Birth, parentage, Education—profession. Offices* &c &c" for use in writing JM's biography for *Delaplaine's Repository of the Lives and Portraits of Distinguished American Characters*. JM complied, sending Delaplaine a three-page memorandum that he acknowledged in his letter to JM of October 1816 (DLC). This sketch of JM's life, entitled "Memorandum sent Sepr. 1816, to Mr. Delaplaine at his request," was edited and expanded by additional notes to a fourth page during JM's retirement (NjP).

2. This was JM's lengthy pamphlet, *An Examination of the British Doctrine, Which Subjects to Capture a Neutral Trade, Not Open in Time of Peace* (Shaw and Shoemaker 10776), which JM wrote in the fall of 1805 and distributed to members of Congress in January 1806. For a summary of the contents and JM's motives for writing it, see Ketcham, *James Madison*, 442–44.

3. For JM's pamphlet, *Political Observations*, dated 20 Apr. 1795, see *PJM*, 15:511–33 and n.

From Thomas Read

VERY DEAR Sir, 1 Novemr. 1820.

This will be handed by Mr. Helme a late Graduate of Brown University in the state of Rhode Island, who at this time lives with me in the Character of a family teacher of the languages &c. Mr. Helme, has at this time a small Vacation & he & my young son Landon C. Read[1] are visiting the upper country for amusement and instruction. Any civilities which you may please to shew them sir, will be acknowledged, both by them & by me.

This sir is a liberty which I trust you will readily pardon from me who am not intimately acquainted with you.

Tho' Sir I had the honor in the year 1799 & 1800 to be a member with yourself in the Virginia legislature, when the great struggle for liberty was made, & when the resolutions called *Madisons*[2] was received; which Resolutions, no doubt gave birth to the political preponderance which has since prevaled in the United states.

Any assistance, which you may render Mr. Helme & my son in viewing the upper Country will be acknowledged with Unusual thankfulness by Very dear sir Yr. mo. obt. & Hble St.

THOMAS READ[3]

RC (DLC). Docketed by JM.

1. Landon Cabell Read (b. 1803) was the son of Thomas Read and his first wife, Anne Haskins (Alice Read, *The Reads and Their Relatives . . .* [Cincinnati, Ohio, 1930], 296, 304). Read and Nathaniel Helme did visit Montpelier on 9–10 Nov. 1820, and Helme's recollections of the visit were first published in the *Providence Patriot* and republished on 13 Jan. 1821 in the Amherst, N.H., *Hillsboro' Telegraph:* "You will of course suspect that our curiosity could not be gratified before visiting the illustrious *Patriort* [sic] *of Montpelier*, Mr. Madison, whom, I am also happy to say, we found in good health. The view from Mr. Madison's residence is variegated and delightful; his person though small, is highly interesting; an amiable gravity and dignity sit enthroned on his brow; affability & politeness characterize his deportment. The paintings in his house are elegant; his dress is black, his hair powdered and tied behind. Mrs. Madison is a very pleasant, accomplished lady. We dined, supped, lodged and breakfasted with Mr. Madison; and having taken leave of our hospitable hosts, departed on the 10th inst."

2. For JM's Virginia Resolutions, see *PJM*, 17:188–90.

3. Thomas Read (1768–1834) of Ash Camp, Charlotte County, Virginia, not to be confused with his uncle, Col. Thomas Read (1741–1817), longtime county clerk, served with JM in the Virginia House of Delegates, 1799–1800 (Read, *Reads and Their Relatives*, 296–99, 541–42; Swem and Williams, *Register*, 52).

Isaac Briggs's Account of a Meeting with Madison

[1 November 1820]

"11 mo. 1—Fourth day of the week. This morning, I went 5 miles to Montpelier, the se⟨at⟩ of James Madison, and arrived there before either James or his wife had proceeded from their lodging-room; Of course, I was there long before breakfast was ready. I remained here the whole of this day, and both James Madison and Dorothy entertained me with much friendly conversation, as well as with the hospitality of their magnificent mansion. Dorothy enquired much about Deborah Stabler and Margaret Judge with expressions of esteem, and warmly and particularly about my daughter, Mary, and whether she was married. James asked to walk and see his garden; I did so. It is a large one, and in a state of fine cultivation. He enquired much about the tenets and princip⟨les⟩ of Friends; and pressed me closely with questions on what he conceived to be difficult points, such as "The Trinity," "Predestination," &c. &c. I took the ground that the whole object, scope and tenor of Scripture has, ever had, and ever will have in view Principles and not persons—that, by a literal construction and with reference to *pers⟨ons⟩* we should meet with numerous difficulties and apparent contradictions, one inspir⟨ing⟩ penman contradicting another and contradicting himself—but that, keeping in v⟨iew⟩ the highly figurative and metaphoric language of the writers of Scripture and of our Savior himself, of whom it is said, "Without a parable spake he not unto the⟨m,"⟩ and considering the object to be *principle,* the wisdom and prudence of the world and all literary pride laid low, and the mind brought to that state of humility, simplicity and dependence, aptly and beautifully figured by the Babe, enough will be revealed for every purpose of Salvation—difficulties and intricacies would disappear—all would become plain, harmonious, and consistent, to the sincere and humble enquirer, who has no human system to support. On these grounds, I endeavored to answer his questions and explain his difficulties; and, at last he confessed himself quite satisfied on every point."

Extract of RC (MdHi: Briggs-Stabler Papers). The RC is a copy of Isaac Briggs to Hannah Briggs, 7 Nov. 1820. Isaac Briggs (1763–1825) was a Quaker who settled in Sandy Spring, Maryland, after graduating from the University of Pennsylvania. His interest in science led to his election to the American Philosophical Society in 1796. A frequent correspondent of JM's during the latter's service as secretary of state, Briggs surveyed parts of the Louisiana Purchase lands between 1803 and 1807, and laid out the post road from Washington to New Orleans. Later in life he worked as an engineer on several canal projects, including the Erie Canal (*PJM-SS*, 4:1 n. 2; *PJM-PS*, 4:386 n. 1).

To Charles D. Coxe

Sir — Montpellier Novr. 7. 1820

I recd. yesterday only your letter of Ocr. 20. postmarked Philada. Nov. 4. It would give me pleasure to render you any service in which I might be justified by my recollections. But the attention required by other objects during my official period, with the subsequent lapse of time, will well account for my not being now able to throw any light on the circumstances to which you refer. Nor with respect to the conversation mentioned do I retain any definite impression of the ideas meant to be expressed in it. If you remember rightly the tenor of my note, on your consular accounts, filed I presume in the proper Dept. it will be a proof that at the date of the charges objected to, you were deemed an officer in the Marine corps. I will drop a few lines to the President[1] as you request. But they can add nothing as you will perceive, to his means of appreciating your case. Of his disposition to do justice in it no doubt can be entertained.

I thank you as does Mrs. M. for the good wishes you have expressed. Be pleased to accept a return of ours.

James Madison

RC (MH-H); draft (DLC). RC addressed by JM to Coxe at "Sidney near Pittstown New Jersey," and franked. Minor differences between the copies have not been noted.

1. JM to James Monroe, 8 Nov. 1820.

To James Monroe

Dear Sir — Novr. 8. 1820

I have just recd. a letter from Chs. D. Coxe, appealing to my recollection on certain points, and requesting a line from me to yourself. To let you see what has passed, I inclose his letter to me, and a copy of my answer.[1] The former you will be so good as to return. I presume the views of the case to be gathered from authentic sources will[2] readily decide the question of his actual official relations. Of his personal qualities and accomplishments, my impressions are favorable: affecty. & respy. Yours

James Madison

RC (DLC: Monroe Papers); draft (DLC). RC docketed by Monroe.

1. See Charles D. Coxe to JM, 20 Oct. 1820, and JM to Coxe, 7 Nov. 1820.
2. In the draft JM wrote "must."

From Tench Coxe

My dear Sir   Philada. Nov. 12. 1820.

In consequence of *a very kind* letter of the 13th Ulto. from Mr. Jefferson,[1] in which he recognizes me as one he is pleased to stile *"a fellow laborer indeed, in times never to be forgotten,"* & to treat me as a long tried public and personal friend, I have been led to reply to him, in considerable latitude. I was, at the moment of the receipt of his letter, meditating an application to Mr. Monroe for some one of the appointments, which will be vacated by the act of Congress of last Session, terminating certain classes of Commissions, which have been held by the present incumbents *four years or more.*[2] The labors to which Mr J. alludes contributed (to my utmost) to maintain that great public cause; which was revived with full effect by this state in 1799, and the Union in 1801. I lost, by those exertions, fr[i]ends, relations, office, means of life. I will not give you, Sir, the anguish of details. Nor do I want Sinecures or pensions. I wish only for an unambitious employment, as a mark of confidence, a mean of comfort, and to facilitate those voluntary exertions in politics and *the national oeconomy* of our expanding country, to which Mr. Monroe, and you and Mr. Jefferson have ever given your countenance in public and your approbation, in scenes of private confidence. The cotton ca[. . .], that of the wine grape and the olive, and domestic manufactures, especially, would give me a pension or an office in many countries. Even now, time, labor, expence and deeply anxious thought are daily given to the vast and awful subject of our black population, the mismanagement of which may too easily *prostrate* our fairest hopes, public and private. You may see under the signature of "*Greene*" in the Intelligencer,[3] a short series of papers particularly intended for Pennsylvania & the North, which I have lately prepared from an irresistible sense of duty. My calls and impulses of this kind are numerous & incessant: contributions various & frequent. I ask the favor of you to communicate with Mr Monroe upon my subject, and if you can, with some proper members of the Senate. They are much changed. Some of them know me well, and act always as friends. My stand against the career of L & D[4] were founded *on opportunities to know the ground they were going to take, and the ends at which they aimed.* The Aurora has fully explained itself. The views of former years are now displayed, and shew that the rights of property, the public order, the state rights & privileges, and *all that is requisite to the prosperity of the south* would be put at hazard *to accomplish the election of a particular candidate.* The constitution of the Union, and the treaty of Louisiana would be executed on *different* principles, in the cases of *different* new states. *Equal* rights among the members of ⟨o⟩ur confederacy would be *practically denied.* In a case where the majority of lawyers and judges believe Congress cannot restrict, the restricted state, considering the wrong to be extra-constitutional, that is extra conventional, would resort to that *ultima Ratio*[5] of all governments, which results from the departure of the parties from municipal and federal institutions, and entering upon ground purely & absolutely international. As we have grown in Numbers and extent, such objects of attention & anxiety have not decreased. Men are yet wanted, who are willing to defend these great & growing objects. The conduct of men in times past are the pledges of their future course.

If your opinion of the services I may have rendered, and those which my remaining strength may enable me yet to render, should justify an *early* interposition with the gentlemen I have refered to, or some of them, I will only assure you, I will be as I have been. In all events, my minute knowledge of the wisdom and the virtues of your private & public life can never fail to inspire me with the most perfect confidence in all your thoughts, your words and your actions in public scenes and in the bosom of private friendship.

That Heaven may bless you, as you have deserved, will be mixed with the parting orisons of your unalterable friend

Tench Coxe

RC (DLC). Docketed by JM.

1. Thomas Jefferson to Tench Coxe, 13 Oct. 1820, DLC: Jefferson Papers.

2. "An Act to limit the term of office of certain officers therein named, and for other purposes," 15 May 1820, *U.S. Statutes at Large*, 3:582.

3. A piece in the *Daily National Intelligencer*, 13 Nov. 1820, signed "Greene," contained a proposal for the strict enforcement of the ban on the international slave trade as well as a plea for a reasoned discussion about the condition of American free blacks.

4. For the struggle of Tench Coxe, Michael Leib, and William Duane for control of the Pennsylvania Republican party, see Cooke, *Tench Coxe*, 438–48.

5. *Ultima ratio regum:* the last reasoning of kings (i.e., an appeal to violence).

From Francis Corbin

Dear Sir The Reeds. Nov. 13th. 1820 Wh: Ch: Po: Off:

In the early part of September I intended to have done myself the Honor and pleasure of paying my respects to you and to Mrs: Madison. But, just about that time, I heard that you had a great deal of company—Mrs. Mayo[1]—Mrs. Scott & c.—and, therefore, fearing that my visit might be inconvenient, at that juncture, I postponed it. Since then Mrs. Corbin has added a 7th Son to my before numerous family, and my Son Robert being gone to Philadelphia to see his Brother Francis Porteus and to bring his Sister home, I am fast moored for the present year. It is a hard matter for us Virginians with large families, who subsist on our Estates, (and who of us can subsist *off* of them, or even *on* them now?) to know when we can leave them with prudence. We are, of necessity, rooted to the Soil. This I have always considered as a formidable practical objection to the Fedl. Const. because we can never have such a representation in Congress as the State is capable of affording, nor, extensive as our Territory is, even in the State Legislature. Confinement, at my time of life, I should not regret, if it did not deprive me of the pleasure of seeing you & a few others. I am happy, however, to hear from my friend Mr. Andrew Stevenson[2] that you and Mrs. Madison enjoy good health, and, what is rare in these times, good Spirits. God grant that you both may long continue to enjoy both! My Spirits, I confess, with all my Stoicism and constitutional *gas*, are very much depressed, and my health, consequently, impaired. The total absence of all Dividends from the Bank of the U.S. for 18 months, and the reduction of them in other Banks, together with the melancholy fall in the price of Corn, wheat and Tobacco, occasioned in *some* measure by a *too sudden* and *most impolitic* reduction of our Currency, have compelled me to strike, not my top gallant Sails only but my Top Sails, and if the Storm continues, will compel me to scud under bare Poles. That the Storm will continue, I very much fear. I see no prospect of it's cessation. The Sky is dark and gloomy all around us. There is no where any thing to cheer us, unless Europe should be again convulsed, which, in Christian charity, we ought not to wish—or unless we boldly acknowledge the independence of such of the Governments of South America, (Chili for instance) as seem to be able and willing to maintain their independence, and this, I think, in Christian Charity and good policy we ought to do. We have nothing to fear from the Holy Alliance. Not one of the "Legitimates" have a dollar to go to War with, and least of all to engage in a War against Liberty. The people, all the world over, are combustible, at this moment, on this Subject. The smallest Spark will set them in a blaze. Nor are we without our "Sufficit quantum"[3] of igneous matter. Black Spirits and yellow so mingle with white Spirits from Maryland to Missouri, that I cannot but augur ill of all that has been said and done, and that will yet be said and done on the Subject of Slavery. We are certainly, My dear Sir, in a very unsettled State at present. Nor will the late portentous change in St. Domingo[4] contribute to render our situation *better*. Slaves, except in the Sugar and Cotton Countries, have become so expensive, so vexatious, so unmanageable & so unprofitable with all that nine rational men out of Ten are sick of them. If I could see my way clear to any *safe* and moderately productive mode of investing the proceeds of my property here, I would, old as I am, migrate to the free North, where my Sons, uninfluenced by false Pride, might engage in honest pursuits for an honest livelihood. Here we have nothing but the Profession of the Law, and this, in addition to it's being a meagre and miserable Profession, is, generally speaking, a vile and vicious one.

What, My dear Sir, is to become of us? The Fedl. Govt. as well as the State Governments seem to me to be on the Eve of Bankruptcy. The *Sacred* Sinking fund must be again violated, and new Loans must be again resorted to. Where is this to End? Shall the Tariff be raised? Then we shall be visited with Dean Swift's Arithmetic.[5] Shall we venture upon Direct Taxes, and always odious Excises? These Evils, I suspect, will never be tolerated except in time of War and urgent necessity, Nor even then without a corresponding augmentation of Paper Currency in some shape or other. But we must retrench! Retrenchment in the Fedl. Governt. will avail nothing unless followed by retrenchment in our State Governments, in our County Governments, in our Parish Governments, and in our Families. Nor will even this suffice. When the Treasury of a single State can be robbed of $155,000 with impunity, as is the case here,[6] and our Citizens can be plundered by the Knaves who have managed our Banks to the amount of millions, and with impunity too, what have honest men to hope for? To pay taxes is to pour Water through a Sieve. That the morals of our people have inconceivably deteriorated, are daily deteriorating more and more, and require instantaneous reformation, by some means or other, is now manifest to all. But by what means can they be reformed? By Laws? Ah me! "Quid vano proficiunt leges sine moribus?"[7] Laws which are opposed to the customs and usages of a people are a dead letter; they are never and can never be executed, and for obvious reasons, because customs and usages are themselves the supreme Law, paramount all others. Some years ago several conspicuous characters in this County were presented for gaming. The greater part of the Grand Jury were conscious that they themselves and many others had been engaged in the same sport, they accordingly made presentments by *Scores*. General Minor[8]—Good Soul! Who, as the vulgar phrase is, "had got his grog aboard" addressed the Judge thus—"O come, Judge, what does it signify? We Virginians, you know, will drink and game. Let the Law then go to sleep." The presentments were all dismissed. They were *too numerous* to be tried!!

Well! My dear Sir, Events have now verified my suggestions to you last year. Slavery and Farming you now *feel* are incompatible with one another. The latter can only prosper in a Country exempt from the former and with a *dense* population. This can never be where there is domestic Slavery. Our non-effectives consume all that our effectives make. The profits of my Estate will not do more this year than pay the expences of it, our burthensome Taxes included. I suppose yours will hardly do more. This is the case with most people who have not the benefit of navigation. I really do not know how we are to work thro' our difficulties.

I expected to hear what the President would say to day, but no Speaker being chosen, his Message did not arrive. Mr. Lowndes will probably be chosen to day—so that we may hope to see it tomorrow. With my fervent wishes for your continuing health and happiness and for Mrs. M's also, and with my sincere Esteem & Respect I am, Dr. Sir, your much obliged & Obt. St.

FRANCIS CORBIN

P. S. My friendly regards if you please to Mr. Todd. Why will he not visit us in these Regions below?

RC (DLC). Docketed by JM.

1. Abigail De Hart Mayo (1761–1843), the daughter of John De Hart, a New Jersey delegate to the Continental Congress, was the wife of Col. John Mayo (1760–1818) of Richmond, the builder and owner of the Mayo Bridge over the James River (*Catalogue of the Loan Exhibition. Under the Auspices of the Old Dominion Chapter, Daughters of the American Revolution* [Richmond, Va., 1897], 5; Timothy D. Johnson, *Winfield Scott: The Quest for Military Glory* [Lawrence, Kan., 1998], 74–75; Peskin, *Winfield Scott*, 64–65; *PJM*, 16:134 n. 6).

2. Andrew Stevenson (1785–1857), a graduate of the College of William and Mary, was a lawyer who served in the Virginia House of Delegates, 1809–16, and 1819–21. In 1816 he married Sarah Coles, a second cousin of Dolley Madison. Stevenson also served in the U.S. House of Representatives, 1821–34, the last seven years as Speaker, and as a loyal supporter of Andrew Jackson. Appointed U.S. minister to Great Britain, 1836–41, Stevenson served as a member of the Board of Visitors of the University of Virginia, 1845–57, and was rector at his death (Francis Fry Wayland, *Andrew Stevenson: Democrat and Diplomat, 1785–1857* [Philadelphia, 1949], 1, 6–7, 10, 13, 21, 40–41, 44, 56, 74, 112, 196–97, 235, 237, 243).

3. *Quantum sufficit:* a sufficient quantity.

4. A divided Haiti had been embroiled in a civil war since 1806. With the death of Henri Christophe, the self-styled king of northern Haiti, in October 1820, Jean-Pierre Boyer, the head of the republic in the south, brought the country under one rule (Robert Debs Heinl Jr. and Nancy Gordon Heinl, *Written in Blood: The Story of the Haitian People, 1492–1995* [Lanham, Md., 1996], 119–53).

5. In an essay entitled *An Answer to a Paper, Called a Memorial of the Poor Inhabitants, Tradesmen and Labourers of the Kingdom of Ireland* (Dublin, 1728), Jonathan Swift wrote: "when any Comodity appeared to be taxed above a moderate Rate, the Consequence was to lessen that Branch of the Revenue by one half, . . . in the Business of laying heavy Impositions, two and two never made more than One" (ibid., 9–10).

6. For the embezzlement of the Virginia state treasury by its treasurer, John Preston, see Francis Preston to JM, 30 Jan. 1820, *PJM-RS*, 1:596–97 and n. 1.

7. *Quid vano proficiunt leges sine moribus* is a reworking of *quid leges sine moribus vanae proficiunt:* "Of what avail are empty laws, if we lack principle," Hor., *Odes* 3.24.35–36 (*Horace: Odes and Epodes*, Loeb Classical Library [1978 reprint], 254–55).

8. John Minor (1761–1816) was a lawyer and veteran of the Revolutionary War and the War of 1812, who made his home at Hazel Hill in Fredericksburg (Tyler, *Encyclopedia of Virginia Biography*, 5:847).

From Richard Rush

Dear sir, London November 15. 1820.

Your acceptable favor of the 12th of August, reached me about a month ago.

I fear that this government will continue deaf to every expostulation that can be addressed to it on the subject of the West India trade. In the negociation of 1818,[1] when Mr Gallatin was here, we made the attempt with all earnestness to prevail upon them to give up their narrow doctrines, but to no effect; whilst separate exertions on my part since have been as fruitless. We have urged upon the ministers all the points so often and ably taken in our state papers of past date, as well as such others as more recent times may have made applicable, in maintainance of our reasonable claims; but they have been met by silence, or by answers that have been refuted before. They will not consent to any enumeration by name of all the ports in the West Indies which we claim to be opened to our vessels; or that our trade with their colonies on the continent and Bermuda, should be as confined as that which they say they would be willing to let us carry on with the Islands direct; or that the duties on articles to be sent to the Islands in our ships should be the same (and not higher) as on the same articles when imported into the Islands from their own North American colonies. So long as they continue to refuse their consent to these points, not to speak to others, it is plain, as a moments examination of them would show, that all reciprocity of navigation would be but nominal on our side. The truth is, that it is the clamours of their Nova Scotian and Canadian subjects that cause the ministry to hold on to their errors, so contrary to the more enlightened notions that are fast spreading over the commercial world. A political motive has also its weight, for the delusive opinion is fostered here, that their North American colonies may be so strengthened as to become at no very distant day, effective barriers to our power. The great increase of the trade of those colonies, under the influence of extraordinary encouragements, helps to extend this opinion. It employed in 1819 three hundred and forty thousand tons of British shipping, timber being nearly the exclusive article of carriage. This amount of tonnage has been growing up most rapidly since 1814. It then stood at little more than one hundred thousand. It will decline as fast whenever the timber trade of the north of Europe is opened to this country.

The trial of the queen having ended in the overthrow of the bill of pains and penalties against her, it becomes a question whether the ministry will be able to withstand the popular clamour that may be expected to burst forth against them. As yet I see no sufficient grounds for believing that there will be a change, and I have never thought, since the first month after my residence here, that we have any reason to wish a change. It is true, that the present ministry will not open the West India trade to us, or settle impressment, or any of the other disputed points between the two countries that are only laid by for a time. But where, we may ask, has been the British ministry that would? Upon the whole, I do not recollect any ministry that has shown better dispositions towards us, if as good, at any one period since we have been a nation, as Lord Castlereagh and his associates, speaking always of the time that has elapsed since the termination of the last war. The idea of more friendly feelings towards us from the Whigs, is, I think, imaginary, notwithstanding all that is said by their Edinburgh advocates, in the review of Mr Walsh's appeal.[2] The Whigs are essentially aristocratick, perhaps the more highly so at this day from their long exclusion from power; and the dread which they now seem to have of being identified with the Reformers, perhaps drives them farther off from our republicanism than even the tories, who have no such dread. Witness Lord Greys denunciation of the principles of our constitution at Newcastle, two years ago.[3] Witness what Mr. Tierney,[4] their leader in the house of commons, has said of us of late in that house. Witness the speeches of one and all of the party in both houses of parliament, and even that of Sir Robert Wilson[5] who is a Reformer on the affair of Arbuthnot and Armbrister, and on the Florida treaty. The Whigs from the days of the stamp act, have been defending our cause only as it has been connected with their own here. Take from them that incentive, and my belief is, that we shall be disappointed if we ever calculate upon any other feelings from them than those of coldness, not to say hostility. There is no party in England favorable to us. All dislike us. The most that we shall ever get in England is, here and there, the good will of insulated individuals. But it is the *fashion* of the nation, and the feeling of all parties in it, as parties, to scoff at us. I repeat, that, in my opinion, if we expect a better ministry for us than the present, we shall most probably be disappointed, should any change take place.

You will have perceived, that the monarchs of Russia, Austria and Prussia are assembled at Troppau.[6] France and England have each a representative there also. The late changes in Spain, Portugal and Naples, so favourable to popular rights, form the objects of this new Congress. What is likely to result from its deliberations, I have, as yet, no sufficient lights for predicting. A loan of forty millions of rubles has lately been obtained by Russia from the Barings and Hope, and Austria has obtained a smaller one, about three millions sterling, from the Rothchilds. These are facts rather leading to the conjecture, that at least some military preparations are in contemplation. I remain, dear sir, with constant and affectionate respect, and with all the friendship that I may be allowed to express, your faithful and attached servt.

Richard Rush

RC (PHi: Richard Rush Papers). Docketed by JM.

1. For the Anglo-American negotiations that culminated in the Convention of 1818, see Rush to JM, 13 Dec. 1818, *PJM-RS*, 1:391–92, and n. 5.

2. See the review of Robert Walsh Jr.'s *An Appeal from the Judgments of Great Britain* in the *Edinburgh Review* 33 (1820): 395–431. There the reviewer drew a distinction between the Tories and their publications, "a party in this country not friendly to political liberty, and decidedly hostile to all extension of popular rights" (ibid., 399), and the Whigs, "another and a far more numerous party . . . who are . . . friends to America, and to all that Americans most value in their character and institutions" (ibid., 400–401).

3. Charles Grey, second Earl Grey (1764–1845) was a Whig member of Parliament from Northumberland, 1786–1807, First Lord of the Admiralty, and then foreign secretary, 1806–7, and a member of the House of Lords from 1807 until his death. He was prime minister from 1830 to 1834 and under his auspices the Great Reform Act was passed in 1832 (E. A. Smith, *Lord Grey, 1764–1845* [Oxford, 1990], 7, 9–11, 100, 108, 132, 258, 277–78, 306–7, 324). For Lord Grey's speech at the annual Fox dinner at Newcastle on 31 Dec. 1818, see the *Newcastle Courant*, 9 Jan. 1819.

4. George Tierney (1761–1830) was a Whig member of Parliament, 1789–90 and 1796–1830 (Thorne, *History of Parliament: The House of Commons*, 5:384–98).

5. Sir Robert Thomas Wilson (1777–1849) was a member of Parliament from Southwark, 1818–31, who supported reform and generally voted with the Whigs (ibid., 5:604–6).

6. The conference at Troppau, Silesia, in October 1820 was one of several meetings the Allies held to discuss the means of opposing revolutionary changes in Europe. The protocol adopted by Austria, Russia, and Prussia, but not signed by Great Britain or France, required that any state that had undergone a revolution would be summarily dismissed from the European alliance, and if that state posed a danger to any of the others, the signatories would combine, "by peaceful means, or if need be by arms," to return that state to the alliance (John Acton, *The Cambridge Modern History* (13 vols.; 1902–12; reprint, Cambridge, 1969), 10:27–29).

From James Monroe

Dear Sir Washington Novr 16. 1820

You will receive by this mail a copy of the message[1] in which I have endeavourd, to place our institutions in a just light, comparatively with those of Europe, without looking at the latter, or even glancing at them by any remark. The state of our finances is I presume more favorable, than was generally supposd. It seems probable that it will improve in future, the quantity of goods which flowed in immediately after the peace, having been in a great measure exhausted, new supplies will be called for.

The contest for the chair, and the result, indicate a disposition to revive the Missouri question, in the temper displayd in the last Session.[2] The clause in the constitution of that State, authorising an inhibition of free negroes from emigrating into it, is understood to be that which will more particularly be laid hold of. Unfavorable presages are form'd of the result. It is undoubtedly much to be regretted that the State furnished any pretext for such a proceeding. It is urgd by some favorable to the immediate admission of the State into the union, that as the Constitution repealed all parts of State constitutions, repugnant to it, then in force, so it will nullify any part of the constitution of a new State, which may be admitted, it being necessary, that the incorporation should be complete in every article & clause, & the same, as to the new as well as to the original States, & not a compact, or treaty, between separate communities, as it would otherwise be: that Congress in its legislative character can make no compact, which would deprive the Supreme court of its right to declare, such article in the constitution of the new State void: that if however it Had such right, a declaration by Congress disapproving that clause & protesting against it, would deprive it of such sanction & leave it subject to the decision of the court.

Mr Correa has saild, without giving the names of the judges whom he denounced, as having disgracd their commissions, in a letter to the Secretary of State, before his visit last summer to Virga., or of the officers, as having servd on board Artigan privateers.[3] His tone having alterd, on his visit here, after his return from Virga., it was inferrd, that he had made those denunciations, and demanded the inst[it]ution of a board, to liquidate claims, against the UStates, for prizes made by Artigan privateers, without a due knowledge of the subject, & that the change was imputable to the light which he derivd from his friends in that visit. Apprehending however that his application, had been made known to the minister of Spain, & might be the ground of a similar demand, by way of sett off against our claims on Spain, securd by two treaties, Mr Adams wrote & requested to be furnished with the names of the judges & officers denouncd by him, making at the same time a protestation against his claim of indemnity, as being contrary to sound principles, & to the usage of civilized nations. The letter was in a style very conciliatory, to which however he gave no answer.

Mr Coxe's letter[4] shall be returnd as soon as receivd from the Secry of the Navy. With our best regards to Mrs Madison, I am sincerely your friend

JAMES MONROE

RC (DLC: Rives Collection, Madison Papers). Docketed by JM and marked by him, probably at a later time: "Missouri question."

1. Monroe enclosed *Message from the President of the United States to Both Houses of Congress, at the Commencement of the Second Session of the Sixteenth Congress. Nov. 15, 1820* (Washington, 1820; Shoemaker 3902). The message is printed in Hamilton, *Writings of James Monroe*, 6:155–58.

2. John W. Taylor (1784–1854), a New York lawyer and member of the U.S. House of Representatives, 1813–33, was elected Speaker on 15 Nov. 1820 in a contentious election on the twenty-second ballot (*Annals of Congress*, 16th Cong., 2d sess., 437–38).

3. The "Artigan privateers" were corsairs who carried commissions issued by Gen. José Gervasio Artigas of the Banda Oriental (present-day Uruguay) enabling them legally to attack both Portuguese and Spanish ships (Peter Earle, *The Pirate Wars* [London, 2003], 213–14). Many of these privateers were outfitted in U.S. ports, particularly Baltimore, where the thriving business was encouraged, or at least winked at by government officials, much to the bitterness of the Portuguese minister, José Corrèa de Serra. Monroe's insistence that Portuguese claims against the United States for seizures by privateers be settled in court rather than by a commission led to angry exchanges between Corrèa de Serra and the Monroe administration (Ammon, *James Monroe*, 436–37).

4. See Charles D. Coxe to JM, 20 Oct. 1820, enclosed in JM to Monroe, 8 Nov. 1820.

To James Monroe

Dear Sir Monpr. Novr. 19. 1820.

Yesterday's mail brought me your favor of the 16th. with a Copy of your message: the only one reaching me; no newspaper containing it having come to hand. The view you have taken of our affairs can not but be well received at home, and increase our importance abroad. The State of our finances is the more gratifying as it so far exceeds the public hopes. I infer from the language of your letter that the contest for the chair terminated in favor of Mr. Taylor, and that it manifested a continuance of the spirit which connected itself with the Missouri question at the last session. This is much to be regretted, as is the clause in the Constitution of the new State,[1] which furnishes a text for the angry and unfortunate discussion. There can be no doubt that the clause, if agst. the Constitution of the U.S. would be a nullity; it being impossible for Congress, with, more than without, a concurrence of new or old members of the Union, to vary the political equality of the States, or their Constitutional relations to each other or to the whole. But it must, to say the least, be an awkward precedent, to sanction the Constitution of the new State containing a clause at variance with that of the U.S., even with a declaration that the clause was a nullity. And the awkwardness might become a very serious perplexity: if the admission of the new State into the Union, and of its Senators & Reps. into Congress & *their participation in the Acts of the latter* should be followed by a determination of Missouri to remain as it is rather than accede to an annulment of the obnoxious clause. Would it not be a better course to suspend the admission untill the people of Missouri could amend their Constitution; provided their so doing would put an end to the controver[s]y and produce a quick admission at the ensuing Session. Or if the objections to this course be insuperable; may it not deserve consideration, whether the terms of the clause, would not be satisfied by referring the authority it gives, to the case of free people of colour, *not citizens* of other States. Not having the Constitution of Missouri at hand, I can form no opinion on this point. But a right in the States to inhibit the entrance of that description of coloured people, it may be presumed, would be as little disrelished by the States having no slaves, as by the States retaining them. There is room also for a more critical examination of the Constitutional meaning of the term "Citizens" than has yet taken place; and of the *effect* of the various civil disqualifications applied by the laws of the States, to free people of Colour.

I do not recollect that Mr. Correa had any direct or explicit conversation with me on the subject between him & the Govt. It is possible that my view of it might have been inferred from incidental observations; but I have no recollections leading me to the supposition, unless inference was made from a question touched on concerning the precise criterion between a Civilized & uncivilized people; which had no connection in my mind with his diplomatic transactions. What may have passed with Mr. Jefferson I know not.

I find that Mr. Tench Coxe is desirous of some *profitable* mark of the confidence of the Govt.[2] for which he supposes some opportunities are approaching; and with that view, that you should be reminded of his public career. I know not what precise object he has in his thoughts, nor how far he may be right in anticipating an opening for its attainment: and I am aware both of your own knowlege of his public services, and of your good dispositions towards him. I feel an obligation nevertheless, to testify in his behalf, that from a very long acquaintance with him, and continued opportunities of remarking his political course, I have ever considered him among the most strenuous and faithful labourers for the good of his Country. At a very early period he was an able defender of its commercial rights & interests. He was one of the members of the Convention at Annapolis. His pen was indefatigable in demonstrating the necessity of a new form of Govt. for the nation; and he has stedfastly adhered, in spite of many warping considerations, to the true principles and policy on which it ought to be administered. He has also much merit in the active and efficient part he had in giving impulse to the Cotton cultivation, and other internal interests; and I have reason to believe that his mind and his pen continue to be occupied with subjects closely connected with the public welfare. With this impression of the services he has rendered, I can not but own, that any provision, that would be proper in itself, and contribute to make his advanced age, more comfortable than it otherwise might be, would afford me real pleasure. Of its practicability, I do not presume to judge.

In looking over the bundle of my letters to Mr. Jones I find one dated in Decr. 1780,[3] containing a Statement of what passed in the Old Congress, relative to the proposed Cession of the Mississippi to Spain, corresponding *precisely* with my recollection of it as explained to you. I was disappointed in finding that my letters are limited to that year. My correspondence run through a much longer period, of which I have proofs on hand, and from the tenor of the above letters, and my intimacy with him, I have no doubt that my communications were often of an interesting character. Perhaps the remaining letters or a part of them may have escaped your search. Will you be so good as to renew it whenever & whereever the convenient opportunity may admit.

What is become of the *secret* journals of the Old Congress,[4] and when will the press give them to the public?

A fever, of the Typhus denomination, which has for some months been rambling in this district of Country, has lately found its way to this spot. Out of 14 patients within my precincts, 5 have died, 2 only have perfectly recovered, and among the rest the major number are very ill. New cases also are almost daily occurring. I have sustained a heavy loss in a young fellow who was educated in Washington a Cook, and was becoming moreover a competent Gardener. I am suffering also much from the protracted illness of the man charged with my farming business, which exposes the several crops not yet secured to great neglect & waste.

We have heard nothing particularly of Mrs. Monroe's health, which we hope has been fully restored. We have the same hope as to Mr. Governeur, who Mr. Hay informed me was dangerously ill. With our best wishes for you all, be assured of my affectionate respects.

JAMES MADISON

RC (DLC: Monroe Papers); FC (DLC). RC docketed by Monroe. FC in John Payne Todd's hand, with JM's emendations and note at head of letter: "President Monroe Novr. 19. 1820." Minor differences between the copies have not been noted.

1. Article 3, section 26 of the Missouri Constitution provided that it would be the duty of the legislature "as soon as may be, to pass such laws as may be necessary, *First,* to prevent free negroes and mulattoes from coming to, and settling in this state, under any pretext whatsoever" (*Niles' Weekly Register* 19 [23 Sept. 1820]: 52). This provision was seen as directly violating article 4, section 2 of the U.S. Constitution: "The citizens of each state shall be entitled to all privileges and immunities of citizens in the several states" (Robert Pierce Forbes, *The Missouri Compromise and Its Aftermath: Slavery & the Meaning of America* [Chapel Hill, N.C., 2007], 108, 110).

2. See Tench Coxe to JM, 12 Nov. 1820.

3. Despite JM's note that the letter to Joseph Jones was dated "Decr. 1780," the description of the letter better conforms with his letter to Jones of 25 Nov. 1780, *PJM*, 2:202–4.

4. *Secret Journals of the Acts and Proceedings of Congress, from the First Meeting Thereof to the Dissolution of the Confederation, by the Adoption of the Constitution of the United States* (4 vols.; Boston, 1820–21; Shoemaker 4058).

To Frances Wright

Madam Montpellier Novr. 20. 1820.

I received very lately your letter of June 28th. with a Copy of the Tragedy of Altorf. I had not before seen it, although its favorable reception on American Theatres had made it Known to me. This reception is the best species of proof that its dramatic structure is well calculated to give force to the just & lofty sentiments of patriotism by which the performance is distinguished. No better praise can be given to genius than that it selects such Subjects for the exertion of its powers. And it is honorable for the Country in which such subjects & sentiments find the greatest number of responsive bosoms. I tender you Madam, my thanks for your polite attention: and permit me to add my wishes that your talents may continue to be successfully employed in rendering the Muses auxiliaries to the cause of virtue & liberty. With great respect

(Signed) James Madison

FC (DLC). In John Payne Todd's hand, with JM's docket on verso.

To Tench Coxe

Dear Sir Montpellier Novr. 24. 1820

I have recd. your letter of the 12th. and written one to the President, which will remind him of your successive services to your Country, and convey my sense of their merit and value. Being in no correspondence with any of the present members of the Senate, I feel myself less at liberty to do the same with them; especially as there may be some delicacy in anticipating a nomination from the Executive. I will however drop a few lines in confidence to one of the Senators from this State.

I am glad to find that you have not relinquished your watchfulness over our public affairs, or your efforts to give fair & consistent views of important subjects evolved in the progress of them. This can best be done by those who know best, as well the genuine[1] spirit & scope of our political Institutions, as the history of the proceedings under them. I see every day errors afloat which prove how much is unknown or forgotten, of what is essential to a just and satisfactory comment on politics of the times. Facts even the most easily traced, when not remembered, seem in many instances to be entirely misunderstood or misapplied. Among these none is more remarkable than the allegations issuing from so many sources agst. what is called the Southern ascendency. Certain it is that there never has been a time (nor is there likely to be one) when there has not been a minority of Southern votes in both Houses of Congress. It is equally certain, that in the first period under the existing Constitution, when the most precious fruits of it were gathered, the ascendancy was elsewhere, and not in that section. Nor is it less certain, that if during subsequent periods, the Southern opinions and views have generally prevailed in the national councils, it is to be ascribed to the coinciding opinions and views entertained by such a portion of other sections, as produced, in the aggregate, a majority of the nation. The ascendancy therefore was not a Southern but a Republican one, as it was called and deemed by all, wherever residing, who contributed to it. But I am not only overstepping my intended limit, but repeating what is better understood by no one than by yourself.

In looking over my pamphlets and other printed papers I perceive a chasm in the "Debates of Congress["] between Mar. 4. 1790, (being the close of No. III of Vol IV. by T. Lloyd)[2] and the removal of Congs. from Philada. to Washington. May I ask the favor of you, if it can be done without difficulty, to procure for me the means of filling the chasm. I should be glad also to procure a pamphlet "Sketches of American policy by Noah Webster," published in Philada in 1784 or 5; and another "Pelitiah Webster's Dissertation on the political Union & Constitution of the 13. U.States" published in 1783 or 4. Both of them have disappeared from my Collection of such things. Pardon the trouble of these requests, and be assured always of my best wishes & cordial respects

James Madison

RC (owned by David Barton, Aledo, Tex., 2007); FC (DLC). RC addressed by JM to Coxe at Philadelphia, and franked. Postmarked 28 Nov. at Orange Court House. Docketed by Coxe. FC in John C. Payne's hand, with JM's emendations and note at head of letter: "To T. Coxe"; incorrectly dated 4 Nov. 1820. Minor differences between the copies have not been noted.

1. FC has "general" here.

2. Thomas Lloyd (1756–1827) reported the debates of the First Federal Congress, taking shorthand notes of the members' speeches and printing them in the weekly *Congressional Register*. JM had criticized Lloyd's work as often inaccurate and Lloyd himself as intemperate and lazy, but in retirement he conceded that the speakers' ideas could most often be understood from Lloyd's renderings (*PJM*, 10:375 n. 1; 12:63–64).

To James Barbour

Dear Sir Novr. 25. 1820

Altho' I know not that any occasion will arise making it pertinent to bring the political career of Mr. T. Coxe to your attention, I can not in justice to my recollections of it refuse my testimony as to the credit to which he is entitled. I am not unaware that he may have political & perhaps personal enemies who do not speak, as I think, of him. But facts cannot be impaired by opinions.

Mr. C. was one of the Convention at Annapolis [in] 1786 where he was regarded as a sound politician as particularly enlightened on subjects of commerce, and as a man of literary accomplishments. His pen was ably and indefatigably employed in defending & recommending the Constitution proposed by the Convention of 1787. And he has stedfastly adhered, in spite of many considerations, some of a very trying sort to the principles and policy in Administering it which Ultimately had the sanction of the nation. He has the merit also of an elaborate & distinguished work vindicating at an early day our Commerce agst. its foreign foes: and of contribut[i]ng an important impulse, thro' the press, to the Cultivation of Cotton, since become the primary staple of our exports; not to mention instructive efforts in favor of other Cultivations, which by degrees may prove valuable additions to our agriculr. prosperity. With this view of his pretensions, combined with a long and intimate acquaintance, I cannot but own, that any provision for him that wd be proper in itself, & contribute to make his advanced age more comfortable than it otherwise might be wd. afford me real pleasure; and I take the liberty of saying so not forgetting at the same time, that it may be most delicate to do it in confidence, in order to avoid an apparent anticipation where I can have no warrant for it.

Draft (DLC).

To George Joy

Dr. Sir Montpr. Novr. 25. 1820

I hope you will not infer from the date of this that I am retaliating on the lapse of time between my last,[1] & yours of Mar. 1. which with its inclosures & the Memoirs of Mrs. Huchinson came to hand safely; the former how ever not expeditiously & the latter very tardily. This delay was occasioned chiefly by a misconception between me & the Collector at Norfolk where the 2 vols. were landed and a considerable time elapsed also before I cd. make it convenient to enjoy the opporty. of perusing the literary present for wch. I was to thank you. This I have done, and on the whole, with pleasure; notwithstanding the tediousness of some of its details to one ignorant of the personalities & localities described, altho' sufficiently acquainted with English history to be entertained even with the minuter features connected with the more important transactions, or which bespeak the manners of the age.

I have looked over the copies of your correspondences put under the same cover with your letter. It will be most consistent with my political demise to substitute for remarks on such subjects, an assurance that I retain all the sentiments & good wishes for you which I have from time to time expressed.

The course of events in Spain seems to be fulfilling your auguries of her success. Her example seems indeed to be quite prolific. Naples avows that parentage for her revolutionary movement. And Portugal no doubt, owes hers to it. At this distance we can form but an imperfect judgment of the prospects in those & the other Countries into which the flame may spread, and still less can we venture to pronounce on the general & permanent result. The task is perhaps not very easy to those who have much better data for calculating the precise dangers from within, or the probable dangers from without. We have however a flattering faith in the lights now shining in the political firmament; whilst we sympathize with the progress of true liberty every where, with our best wishes that its triumphs may be as little stained with blood as possible.

In G.B. the public attention, we observe continues to be engrossed by the investigation, not now it seems "the delicate" one into the conduct of the Queen.

The reflexions produced here, turn chiefly, as you wd. conjecture on the advantage of a Govt. free from the possibility of such phænomena. It is certainly a period when Kings & Queens might be expected to be rather on their Ps. & Qs. than inviting the criticisms & comparisons with which Geo: & Car: are supplying the Enemies of hereditary power.

Here we are, on the whole, doing well. The surface of public affairs is likely to be somewhat ruffled by a renewal of discussions concerning the admission of the Missouri "Territory," as a State into the Union. The question was settled, and as was hoped, finally at the last Session of Congs by a spirit of amity & accommodation. And it is to be hoped that this spirit may again prevail. In other respects the political calm is little threatened. The question of a new Tariff is most likely to affect it; but it will not do [so] seriously; no great constitutional point being involved in it. If the manufacturers shd. fail entirely in their efforts & hopes for further encouragement from the law, they will experience it from the cheapness of food, of raw materials, and of labor also; so long at least as our agricultural staples are not needed or are rejected by our foreign Customers. It is evident that if we can not sell, we can not buy; and that if we do[2] get supplies from abroad, we must provide them at home, for which the labor turned off from the soil will be a ready fund.

What pinches the community most at this moment is the failure of Bank credit to debtors who relied on a continuance of discounts; & the prodigious fall of prices for crops on which the great mass of debtors relied for paying their creditors. So extensively do these causes operate that no bidders are found at compulsive sales of property; which of course become sheer sacrifices, giving birth to a variety of remedial expedients for evils which time and patience must cure. With esteem & friendly respects

J. M.

Mrs. M. reminds me that her thanks are to be added for the share you allotted her in the perusal of Mrs. H. She continues too much of a Quaker to relish some of the Theological tenets of this lady: but admires much her devotion as a wife & her generous sentiments, as well as the fine talents visible through an undisciplined Idiom, and an antiquated fashion of thinking.

Draft (DLC: Rives Collection, Madison Papers).

1. JM to Joy, 15 Aug. 1817, *PJM-RS*, 1:100–101.
2. JM evidently left out the word "not" here.

To Lafayette

MONTPELLIER Novr. 25. 1820

I have received, my dear friend, your kind letter of July 22 inclosing your printed opinion on the election project. It was very slow in reaching me.

I am very glad to find, by your letter, that you retain, undiminished, the warm feelings of friendship so long reciprocal between us; and, by your "Opinion," that you are equally constant to the cause of liberty so dear to us both. I hope your struggles in it will finally prevail, in the full extent required by the wishes and adapted to the exigences of your Country.

We feel here all the pleasure you express at the progress of reformation on your Continent. Despotism can only exist in darkness; and there are too many lights now in the political firmament, to permit it to reign any where, as it has heretofore done almost every where. To the events in Spain & Naples, has succeeded an auspicious epoch in Portugal. Free States seem indeed to be propagated in Europe as rapidly as new States are on this side of the atlantic: Nor will it be easy for their births or their growths, if safe from dangers within, to be strangled by external foes, who are not now sufficiently united among themselves, are controuled by the aspiring sentiments of their people, are without money,[1] and are no longer able to draw on the foreign fund which has hitherto supplied their belligerent necessities.

Here, we are, on the whole, doing well, and giving an example of a free system, which I trust will be more of a pilot to a good port, than a Beacon, warning from a bad one. We have, it is true, occasional fevers; but they are of the transient kind, flying off through the surface, without preying on the vitals. A Government like ours has so many safety-valves, giving vent to overheated passions, that it carries within itself a relief against the infirmities from which the best of human Institutions can not be exempt. The subject which ruffles the surface of public affairs most at present, is furnished by the transition of the "Territory" of Missouri, from a state of nonage, to a maturity for self-Government, and for a membership in the Union. Among the questions involved in it, the one most immediately interesting to humanity, is the question whether a toleration or prohibition of slavery westward of the Mississippi, would most extend its evils. The humane part of the argument agst. the prohibition turns on the position, that whilst the importation of slaves from abroad is precluded, a diffusion of those in the country, tends at once to meliorate their actual condition, and to facilitate their eventual emancipation. Unfortunately the subject which was settled at the last session of Congress by a mutual concession of the parties, is reproduced on the arena, by a clause in the Constitution of Missouri; distinguishing between free persons of colour, and white persons; and providing that the Legislature of the new State shall exclude from it the former. What will be the issue of the revived discussion is yet to be seen. The case opens the wider field, as the Constitutions and laws of the different States are at variance in the civic character given to free people of colour; those of most of the States, not excepting such as have abolished slavery, imposing various disqualifications which degrade them from the rank & rights of white persons. All these perplexities develope more & more, the dreadful fruitfulness of the original sin of the African trade.

I will not trouble you with a full picture of our economics. The cessation of neutral gains, the fiscal derangements incident to our late war, the inundation of foreign merchandizes since, and the spurious remedies attempted by the local authorities, give to it some disagreeable features. And they are made the more so, by a remarkable downfal in the prices of two of our great staples, breadstuffs & Tobacco, carrying privations to every man's door, and a severe pressure to such as labour under debts for discharging which, they relied on crops & prices which have failed. Time, however, will prove a sure physician for these maladies. Adopting the remark of a British Senator applied with less justice to his country at the commencement of the revolutionary contest, we may say, that "Altho' ours may have a sickly countenance, we trust she has a strong constitution."[2]

I see that the bickering between our Govts. on the point of tonnage, has not yet been terminated.[3] The difficulty, I should flatter myself, can not but yield to the spirit of amity, & the principles of reciprocity, entertained by the parties.

You would not, believe me, be more happy to see me at laGrange, than I should be to see you at Montpellier, where you would find as zealous a farmer, tho' not so well cultivated a farm, as laGrange presents. As an interview can hardly be expected to take place at both, I may infer from a comparison of our ages, a better chance of your crossing the Atlantic, than of mine. You have also a greater inducement in the greater number of friends whose gratifications would at least equal yours. But if we are not likely to see one another, we can do what is the next best—communicate by letter what we would most wish to express in person, and particularly, can repeat those sentiments of affection & esteem, which, whether expressed or not, will ever be most sincerely felt, by your old & stedfast friend

James Madison

RC (NNPM); draft (DLC). RC marked "No. 53." by JM. Docketed by Lafayette: "Answered july 1er." Minor differences between the copies have not been noted.

1. Draft adds "of their own" here; crossed out in RC.

2. The quotation comes from *The Whole of the Celebrated Speech of the Rev. Dr. Jonathan Shipley, Lord Bishop of St. Asaph* . . . (Newport, R.I., 1774; Evans 13624), 18.

3. At the time of the Bourbon restoration, France had levied heavy tonnage duties on non-French ships, to which the United States objected. In 1820 Congress passed similar duties to be levied against French ships, which the French believed contravened the Louisiana Purchase Treaty. The terms of the treaty had granted them most-favored-nation status. The conflict was not resolved until the Franco-American commercial treaty of 1822 equalized duties and provided a schedule for their eventual elimination (Elizabeth Brett White, *American Opinion of France: From Lafayette to Poincaré* [New York, 1927], 65–67).

To Francis Corbin

Dr. Sir, November, 26, 1820.

I had the pleasure of receiving, a few days ago, your favor post-marked the 18th,[1] in lieu of the greater pleasure with which I should have received you *in propria persona*.[2] I am sorry you so readily yielded to the consideration which deprived us of it in September. The addition of your company would have been felt no otherwise than as an ingredient highly acceptable to that you would have met here, as well as to Mrs. M. and myself. For a day or two, indeed, you might have been involved in the common distress occasioned by the hopeless and expiring condition of the little son of Mrs. Scott; but even that drawback might not have taken place within the period of your visit.

You complain of the times, which are certainly very hard; but you have a great abatement of your comparative suffering in your paper funds, notwithstanding the suspension of their current productiveness. This is but a *lucrum cessans*.[3] How many are feeling the *damnum emergens*[4] also! Besides, in the event of a necessary sale of property, (certainly not your case,) the paper property is the only sort that can find a tolerable and certain market.

Whilst I condole with you, therefore, on the hardships in which you participate, I must congratulate you on your escape from a portion which afflicts others. The general condition of these is truly lamentable. If debtors to the Banks, nothing can relieve them but a renewal of discounts, not to be looked for: if owing debts, for discharging which they have relied on crops or prices, which have failed, they have no resource but in the sale of property, which none are able to purchase. With respect to all these, the times are hard indeed; the more so, as an early change is so little within the reach of any fair calculation.

I do not mean to discuss the question how far *slavery* and *farming* are incompatible. Our opinions agree as to the evil, moral, political, and economical, of the former. I still think, notwithstanding, that under all the disadvantages of slave cultivation, much improvement in it is practicable. Proofs are annually taking place within my own sphere of observation; particularly where slaves are held in small numbers, by good masters and managers. As to the very wealthy proprietors, much less is to be said. But after all, (protesting against any inference of a disposition to underrate the evil of slavery,) is it certain that in giving to your wealth a new investment, you would be altogether freed from the cares and vexations incident to the shape it now has? If converted into paper, you already feel some of the contingencies belonging to it; if into commercial stock, look at the wrecks every where giving warning of the danger. If into large landed property, where there are no slaves, will you cultivate it yourself? Then beware of the difficulty of procuring faithful or complying labourers. Will you dispose of it in leases? Ask those who have made the experiment what sort of tenants are to be found where an ownership of the soil is so attainable. It has been said that America is a country for the poor, not for the rich. There would be more correctness in saying it is the country for both, where the latter have a relish for free government; but, proportionally, more for the former than for the latter.

Having no experience on the subject myself, I cannot judge of the numerical point at which congratulations on additional births cease to be appropriate. I hope that your 7th son will in due time prove that in his case, at least, they were amply called for; and that Mrs. C. and yourself may long enjoy the event as an addition to your happiness. Mrs. M. unites with me in this, and in every assurance of respect and good wishes to you both.

Madison, *Letters* (Cong. ed.), 3:193–94.

1. Corbin to JM, 13 Nov. 1820.
2. *In propria persona:* in person.
3. *Lucrum cessans:* profit ending.
4. *Damnum emergens:* loss arising.

From Joseph Milligan

Dear Sir [ca. 28 November 1820]

I have taken the liberty to enclose a letter for Mrs Madison[1] also to send through the post office a small book for her subscription it is addressed to you when it comes to hand please be so good as to hand it to her.

I have had the misfortune to be under the Necessity of selling of[f] my stock for the benefit of my creditors so that my business has been suspended for 18 months past I am now about to resume the printing & publishing part of my business and amongst the first things that I wish to do is to publish a new & correct edition of Jefferson notes on Virginia I have written to Mr. Jefferson on the subject[2] & expect his answer next week; I will print a 3rd Volume of Malthus on Population if I meet with sufficient encouragement ⟨amo⟩ngst the Members of Congress its to have refferences to the two first Volumes. In the 3rd Volume Mr Malthus has drawn his conclusions and finished his whole theory If I put it to press I will let you know with best wishes for Your health & happiness I am sir with respect yours

Joseph Milligan

RC (DLC). Undated; conjectural date assigned based on Milligan's explanation in this letter of the suspension of his business, and by comparison with Milligan to Thomas Jefferson, 27 Nov. 1820, DLC: Jefferson Papers. Docketed by JM.

1. Letter not found.
2. Milligan to Jefferson, 27 Nov. 1820, DLC: Jefferson Papers.

From Thomas Jefferson

Dear Sir Poplar Forest Nov. 29. 20.

The inclosed letter from our antient friend Tenche Coxe came unfortunately to Monticello after I had left it and has had a dilatory passage to this place where I recieved it yesterday and obey it's injunction of immediate transmission to you. We should have recognised the stile even without a signature, and altho so written as to be much of it indecypherable. This is a sample of the effects we may expect from the late mischievous law vacating every 4. years nearly all the executive offices of the government. It saps the constitutional and salutary functions of the President, and introduces a principle of intrigue & corruption, which will soon leaven the mass, not only of Senators, but of citizens. It is more baneful than the attempt which failed in the beginning of the government to make all officers irremovable but with the consent of the Senate. This places every 4. years all appointments under their power, and even obliges them to act on every one nominatim. It will keep in constant excitement all the hungry cormorants for office, render them, as well as those in place, sycophants to their Senators, engage these in eternal intrigue to turn out one and put in another, in cabals to swap work, and make of them, what all executive directories become, mere sinks of corruption & faction. This must have been one of the midnight signatures of the President, when he had not time to consider, or even to read the law: and the more fatal as being irrepealable but with the consent of the Senate, which will never be obtained.

F. Gilmer[1] has communicated to me mr. Correa's letter to him of Adieux to his friends here, among whom he names most affectionately mrs. Madison and yourself.[2] No foreigner I believe has ever carried with him more friendly regrets. He was to sail the next day (Nov. 10.) in the British packet for England, & thence take his passage in Jan. for Brazil. His present views are of course liable to be affected by the events of Portugal, & the possible effects of their example on Brazil.

I expect to return to Monticello about the middle of the ensuing month and salute you with constant affection and respect.

Th: Jefferson

RC (DLC: Rives Collection, Madison Papers); FC (DLC: Jefferson Papers).

1. Francis Walker Gilmer (1790–1826) was born at Pen Park, an estate near Charlottesville, Virginia, and educated at the College of William and Mary. He read law under the direction of William Wirt, and practiced in Winchester, Virginia, and then in Richmond, until he was deputed by JM and Jefferson to search for professors in Europe for the nascent University of Virginia. That task accomplished, in 1825 Gilmer was appointed the university's first professor of law, but illness prevented him from taking the position (Richard Beale Davis, *Francis Walker Gilmer: Life and Learning in Jefferson's Virginia* [Richmond, Va., 1939], 1–2, 34–39, 73–74, 93–94, 124, 198, 249, 253).

2. "Do not forget that pure and virtuous soul of Montpellier and his Lady" (José Corrèa de Serra to Gilmer, 9 Nov. 1820, ibid., 142–43).

From Edward Caffarena

Sir Genoa Decr: 1820.

In answer to your favor dated Novr: 1st: 1817[1] I had the honor to present my respects in June 1818;[2] confirming by duplicate last Year the same, & not finding myself honor'd with an answer, I suppose they must have been lost. I hope You will excuse me if I intrude for a third time to express my sentiments, that it never was my intention to offend You Sir, in forwarding the Statue of Napoleon, and hope you will excuse the Liberty. Your desire is to know the price of the same, the original cost was $90.. as you can verify by Mr: Causici who is at present employ'd in Washington.

Permit me Sir to make you observe, that I do not ask the worth of this price [*sic*], leaving the decision agreable to your Pleasure.

Mr: John B. Sartori[3] of Trenton, New Jersey, my intimate good friend, has the charge of those few concerns, that I may have in the U.S., and you may Sir settle the whole with the same, as with myself. I shall in all times feel happy to receive your commands. While I have the honor to remain Sir Your Most Ob & Hble Servt:

EDWARD CAFFARENA

RC (DLC). Docketed by JM.

1. *PJM-RS*, 1:148–49.
2. Letter not found.
3. John Baptiste Sartori (1765–1853), a native of Rome, Italy, emigrated to Philadelphia in 1793. In 1797 he was appointed U.S. consul to the Papal States, though he returned to the United States in 1801 after deputizing his father in the position. He settled in Trenton, New Jersey, in 1803 on an estate he called Rosey Hill, where he manufactured pasta and played a prominent role in the life of the city. He was instrumental in building St. John the Baptist, the first Catholic church in New Jersey, in 1814, and in 1817 he established a calico printing factory on his estate. He returned to Rome in 1832 (Richard W. Hunter, Nadine Sergejeff, and Damon Tvaryanas, "Trenton Textiles and the Eagle Factory: A First Taste of the Industrial Revolution," (http://trentonhistory.org/Documents/EagleFactory.html; *PJM-SS*, 1:256, 2:340; John D. M'Cormick, "Catholicity in New Jersey," *American Catholic Historical Researches* 14 [1897]: 46).

From John Tayloe

MY DEAR SIR, WASHINGTON. Decr. 1st. 1820

The concerns of the Steam Boat Washington have been hitherto so injudiciously conducted, that the Stock has, so far from being valuable as we were authorised to expect, been until now so unproductive, that I flatter myself you will concur with me, that an additional effort should be made to promote its interest.[1]

Should I have the honor to possess your good opinion of my zeal and discretion in the advancement of its views, being now a Director of The Company, I shall feel myself flattered in voting as your proxy at the ensuing election of a board of Directors, and take the liberty of enclosing to you the requisite form.

Mrs Tayloe and myself request you will do us the favor to present us in the most cordial terms to Mrs Madison. I have the honor to be, dear Sir, with great respect, Your friend & Very Ob. Servt.

JOHN TAYLOE[2]

P.S. The Election for Directors is to be held on Thursday next, the 7th. Inst.

RC (DLC). Docketed by JM. Below the postscript, JM drafted his 4 Dec. 1820 reply.

1. The Potomac Steam Boat Company, organized in 1813 by Benjamin Henry Latrobe, operated the steamboat *Washington* on the route between Washington and Aquia Creek near Fredricksburg. The $40,000 ship was built in New York under the direction of Robert Fulton in 1813 but owing to the War of 1812 did not make its maiden voyage until 1815. Competition with the Alexandria and Norfolk Steam Boat Company drove the Potomac company out of business in 1822 (Donald G. Shomette, *Maritime Alexandria: The Rise and Fall of an American Entrepôt* [Westminster, Md., 2003], 105–7, 112–13).

2. John Tayloe (1772–1828), owner of Mt. Airy, a large Virginia plantation, maintained a townhouse in Washington called the Octagon House. This elegant home was used by the Madisons as their residence after the President's House was burned in 1814 (*PJM-PS*, 1:290 n. 1).

From Andrew Stevenson

DEAR SIR, RICHMOND Decr. 3 1820.

Immediately on my return from the mountains this fall, I seized the first opportunity to fulfill the promise I gave you, in endeavoring to obtain the documents desired & am sorry to say that owing to causes not within my controul, I have as yet been unsuccessful. Mr. Randolph[1] is not only willing, that you should have any letters which you may wish in his possession, but expresses much solicitude to oblige, & has repeatedly promised to make the necessary search amongst his father's papers: He is however *fond of his* ease & as the mass of old papers is very considerable & in a state of utter derangement, he is (I imagine) fearful to undertake it. I have offered to save him the trouble & make the examination myself, & would so with pleasure, but he refuses, & repeats his determination of doing it himself. We must however make the search between us ere long, & the result shall be immediately Communicated to you. I very fortunately succeeded in laying my hands on the letter of Mr Bland to Mr. Jefferson & now inclose you a copy of it.[2] No journal can be found here of the years wished, except those in the clerks office of the House of delegates, & *there 20 duplicates;* I have written to my friend Judge Fleming[3] to know if he has them, & if so to loan them to me. Should they not be obtained, I will if you desire it, have such parts of the journals transcribed as you may need, or will borrow them of Mr Munford,[4] for such time as you may wish. Any assistance I can render you in this or any other matter will be most cheerfully afforded & I hope by you freely commanded.

We shall certainly expect to see you & yr. dr. lady with us this winter according to promise & we shall be disappointed & mortified if you do not come. My good wife desires to be affy. remembered to yourself & Mrs. Madison, but I tell her to speak for herself, which she says she will do on the other side of the paper.[5] I tender to Mrs M my most respectful & affe. regards & beg you to accept the same from dr. sir Yr fd. & obt. sert.

AND: STEVENSON

RC (ViU: Special Collections).

1. Peyton Randolph (1779–1828), the son of JM's good friend Edmund Randolph, was a Richmond lawyer and official reporter of cases before the Virginia Court of Appeals (*PJM*, 4:147–48 n. 2; *New-Bedford Mercury*, 9 Jan. 1829; *Richmond Enquirer*, 12 Feb. 1829).

2. See Theodorick Bland to Thomas Jefferson, 22 Nov. 1780, Boyd, *Papers of Thomas Jefferson*, 4:136–38. A transcript of this letter can be found in the Madison Papers, Library of Congress, certified by William Munford, 30 Sept. 1820.

3. William Fleming (1736–1824) was educated at the College of William and Mary and practiced law. He served in the Virginia House of Delegates, 1776–79, for a short time in the Continental Congress in 1779, and as a judge on the Virginia Court of Appeals, 1780–1824, where he was president from 1809 until his death (David J. Mays, "William Fleming, 1736–1824," *Proceedings of the Thirty-Eighth Annual Meeting [of] the Virginia State Bar Association* [Richmond, Va., 1927], 426–35).

4. William Munford (1775–1825), a graduate of the College of William and Mary, was a Richmond attorney, a member of the Virginia House of Delegates, 1797–1802, of the Senate, 1802–6, and of the Council of State, 1806–11. He was clerk of the House of Delegates thereafter until his death. His translation of Homer's *Iliad* was published in 1846 (Rufus Wilmot Griswold, *The Poets and Poetry of America* [New York, 1873], 78–79).

5. Sarah Coles Stevenson to Dolley Madison, 3 Dec. 1820, *DMDE*.

To Richard Rush

DEAR SIR Decr. 4. 1820

Since my last which was of Aug: 12. I have been favoured with yours of Aug: 30. with which was returned my letter to Mr Keilsall; whose evanishment is not a little remarkable. Notwithstanding the trouble given you by that letter, I am not deterred from relying on your goodness to have the two now inclosed forwarded to the parties. To one of them the direction is so precise that it will readily find its own way.[1] To the other, Miss Wright,[2] the direction is as particular as her letter to me enabled me to make it. This lady is the Author of a Tragedy "Altorf" said to have been favorably received on the Theatres of Philada. & New York.

I can add little I believe, to what our public prints will give you concerning our Country. A great pinch thro' the greater part of it is felt by the mass of the people, occasioned by the discontinuance or contraction of Bank discounts, and by the unexampled fall in the prices of produce. Flour an article so extensively the main resourse is as low as 4 dollars per barrell, and in this State does not exceed 3½. It has been even lower than that, and from the account of crops abroad, & the great ones at home a further depression is apprehended. The general embarrassment produced by these causes, is multiplying injurious or abortive experiments for relief.

Congress have not yet engaged in any of the subjects most likely to bring on a fermentation. A very painful one is apprehended from a renewal of that relating to Missouri. The Tariff is another not a little pregnant with animated discussion. But it divides the nation in so checkered a manner, that its issue cannot be very serious; especially as it involves no great constitutional question. The Manufacturers also, should they fail entirely in their hopes from Congress, will experience much encouragement from the cheapness of food, of materials & of labour resulting from the cessation of the foreign demands. It is unlucky that a greater degree of mutual concession on this subject is not likely to prevail in the national Councils, and in the public mind. Instead of increasing it might then mitigate the alienation threatened by the Missouri controversy. With a renewal of the sincerest regards of Mrs. M. and myself for Mrs. Rush, I tender you my dear Sir, my high & affece. respects

JAMES MADISON

RC (PHi: Gratz Collection); FC (DLC). RC addressed by JM to Rush: "Envoy Exty. & M. Pleny. &&c." Cover docketed by Rush, with his note: "The Missouri Compromise question. / The tariff." FC in Dolley Madison's hand, with JM's emendation and docket. Minor differences between the copies have not been noted.

1. This was probably JM to George Joy, 25 Nov. 1820.
2. JM to Frances Wright, 20 Nov. 1820.

To John Tayloe

Decr. 4. [1820]

I have just rec'd yours of Decr 1. & inclose the proxy paper signed. I have hitherto been content to let my little interest in the Steam boat be decided without my participation, & shd. have been so on this occasion.

Draft (DLC). Written below postscript of Tayloe to JM, 1 Dec. 1820, where it is marked "Decr. 4. Answer."

From George Alexander Otis

Sir, Philadelphia Decr. 5. 1820

I beg your acceptance of my warmest acknowledgements for the kind interest which you were pleased to express for the success of my enterprise on receipt of my first Volume.[1] The second, which I have now the honour to address to you, I have laboured with all the care of which I am capable. And shall feel still dubious whether with Success until I have the opinion of the highest authority in my Country. I intreat that you will express it as to my translation in point of Style, and as to the Author, in respect of exactness. The interest of your testimony is only balanced by that of Mr. Jefferson, who has already indulged me in the same favour.[2] It is of infinite importance to the public that the true character of a book making such bold pretensions Should be known. The Authority on which it rests will be established forever if you should find it as unexceptionable as Mr. Jefferson has done. But from some remark, in your respected letter to which I refer, I was apprehensive you might have discovered in the first volume some ideas which did "injustice or less than justice to the American cause and character." It would oblige exceedingly if you will point me to them; As I contemplate in case of a second edition to publish notes. With that profound respect which I cannot but feel I have the honour to remain sir Your most obliged and most Obedient Servant.

George Alex. Otis

P.S. I pray for permission to publish your letter.

RC (DLC). Docketed by JM.

1. See JM to Otis, 3 July 1820.
2. Thomas Jefferson to Otis, 8 July 1820, DLC: Jefferson Papers.

From Edmond Kelly

Sir Columbia Ten Decr. 6th 1820

Persons influenced by the british Govt have made such efforts to misrepresent me that I deemed it necessary to explain my motives for these Coms. & thereby to shew their necessity—& as it is now evident that I am opposed to all demagocical pursuits, that my object is to preserve a proper subordination to the laws & to expose & defeat british Incendiary Emissaries engaged in factious inflamatory & seditious practices I hope further appology is unnecessary, & that those Gentn. whom the falsehoods of british Intriguers had induced to suspect me are now Aware of the deceit—that their suspicions are groundless & that John Bull my principal Accuser is the most unprincipled Incendiary Bully of the Squad attached to british Court prostitutes. Royal patronage recommd him to Govr. McMinn.[1] A family Connection was agreed on & Jacks first experiment was the petition to free the Tenn blacks[2] which Knowing it wd be rejected he hoped would drive them into insurrectionary Outrage. Disappointed in that he & Govr McMinn were more successfull in an other Experiment on renters & those who hold short Leases—in his last Message the Govrs newly created philantrophy denounces all who bought at public sales as grinding oppressors of the poor, & in the conclusion of it he says the good of the poor is connected with the success of his political Course.[3] This sentiment worthy of a Cromwell or usurper is bare faced hypocricy for he sold extensive tracts of the Land got from the Indians [(]sufft. to provide for a large proportion of the poor he affects to pity) to wealthy Individls. & thus perpetuated the dependence of renters on them—he sold a ten thousand acre tract to a man with whom I had dealings & who promised me some accomn. at half price & on a credit for Influence but as I spurned every advice & Insinuation the bribe was ineffectual. Then comes the loan office bill which appropriates half a Million in stock or shares of 5000 dollars each[4]—the holder of a share doubtless obtained on a Mortgage of 600 or 1000 acres is entitled to a credit of 5000 dollars more in the loan office—this paper money being useless except in payment for Land will be applied to buy up this land which will be taken by the Governors party & friends—the $5000 in stock & the $5000 allowed to be borrowed by each stockholder Covers the entire Million—the dividend of the discounts pays all Interest the sums discounted not over $500 to each Individual are unprovided for, & the public is defrauded Of the Land which Vests in John Bull & the Governors newly created Aristocracy & the tax on Land is so low that it will not Inconvenience this party to hold those Lands in forest and thus effectually stop the progress of Agriculture & Improvement. Such is John Bull & the Governors remedy for public distress here and yet an Infatuated Ignorant populace believes these Demagogues are patriotic honest men.

In my last letter but one[5] I made an erroneous statement namely that the method of making figures in the nation[a]l Intelligencer in reply to Duane is similar to the method used by the french Monituer in its replies to british newspr abuse which I since recollected was not the fact & as I deem it as improper to wrong or bely the natl Govt printer as it would be for him to mislead or deceive the nation I freely make this acknowledgement—but in other respects if not criminal he is very culpable. Col. Taylors Memorial against domestic Manufactures[6] and every production of the friends of british Mony to ridicule them Vizt D. Ms.[7] were not only published but strenuously advocated & surely a more ruinous sistem nor a more Impudent attempt to deceive could not be made—if the Custom house returns or entries should not ascertain this fact the Millions of men Composed of servants tradesmen Merchants &ca. expensively dressed in british Manufacture (& whose labor produces nothing for Exportation) Wd Convince the most superficial Observer that the money paid for their dresses & Decorations & those of their women would if retained in Circulation prevent public distress or Insolvency & that supposing all Criminality out of the question to sacrifice the remedy for this public distress to reconcile the british party to the presidents reelection or to prevent oposition to it is the reverse of patriotism. I have long since mentioned that the point & the nic are the watch words by which Orangemen recognise each other, & the meaning of nic is to ridicule and nicname their Enemies & from that Circumstance I Inferred that the nic name of Don quixote & the ridicule of the paragraph stated by me to benefit the british royal favorite was attributable to the Orange sistem—he has since Identified the success of Genl Boyer[8] of Hayti with that of the meanest schemer & Vagrant ruffian attached to the british Court prostitutes & named pat or paudeen Gibbins now proxi or locum Tenens[9] for John Bull. This fellow for his dexterity is patronised by the King. He has also sayed that the queen sanctioned the Views of demagogues & that if a Change should take place in England he would not wish to see the queen in the whirlwind of reform—he is the first that ever applied the epithet of Demagogue to Earl Grey, Sir Francis Burdett, Mr Hobhouse[10] & their Compatriots—these men were not exceeded for patriotism & private & public Virtue by any of those that appeared in Rome when a Virtuous Commonwealth & if the queens case afforded the only oppy that could offer of expressing the public will for reform and of dislike for a man as execrable for his Vices as for his bad Govt it did not Justify the man who would Commute his national honor & natl Interest to secure the Election of his principal to stigmatise them as demagogues. If Lord Chatham had now lived I presume he would be declared by the natl Intr to the American people as much a Demagogue as Earl Grey but no Educated man will be dece[i]ved by such aspersions. Nothing but reform or foreign Conquest which I perceive meditated on the European Continent as well as on the American Can save England from a gradual decay—an abolition of the borough Charters which send Members to parlt. An abolition of all places & pensions and trienial parliaments would save England—but if the English wait untill the Troops are engaged in a Continental war or Coalition war & then abolish the Regal authority the expulsion of the Tarquins had not a more beneficial effect on Rome[11] than such a Change would have on England and the frequency of Coalitions renders such an event desireable to every good Republican. Newtrality is prudent & necessary but an abuse of pure patriotism & Exalted Virtue is extremely improper.

I have read an other preface of Col Taylors entitled Construction construed, the rights of the states Violated by Congress &ca.[12] This man appears to have 3 objects in View. The first is to promote discontent to disunite & Detach the states from the union. The 2d is to afford the british Govt correct Information of America to enable it to prepare & mature Insurrectionary plans for America as I have no doubt are done for France. And the 3d is, as an Incendiary Bully to Intimidate Congress into some Concessions to the Royal favorite John Bull which it appears by his first preface Parlt refused him—is it possible that no one will reply to it.

It appears that the Edinburgh Review is the Oracle of Cromwells Oligarchs & of the Crown. The extract I lately read from it of the state of France the prejudices & antipathies of the french peasantry & people &ca.,[13] shews that it is the work or report of a british Emissary specially sent & that it is in Contemplation to drive them into Insurrection and then by force of the Bayonets of the Holy Alliance to partition France. England formerly held Maine Aquitaine Toura[i]ne Anjou & Normandy—she needs them again and as the Idea of french Invincibility which the french Revoln established is found to be erroneous an other Insurrection and A Simultaneous Movement of the Armies of the holy Aliance will Cause that rival of England to experience the fate of Poland and to be partitioned Among them & politically Anihilated.

The Spaniards appear to be more Cautious—the song of Genl. Riego at the Theatre[14]—Gulp it down dog—& I wonder it was not Guelp it down seems to be of british Texture or dictation—it was an attempt to drive the spaniards into Insurrection to establish a Democracy & then to bring on the alies wd. be a matter of course—british hopes of a contest between the spanish King & his subjects are Vanished—& his Conseqt expulsion is also hopeless. The princes of England are disappointd. The wool of Spain is indispensibly necessary to the british woollen Manufacture but which Spain (if the King has any sense) may find use for. Some calamitous Commotions alone can relieve or dissipate the apprehensions of the british Govt. and it is only by the destruction & Robbery of surrounding nations that the british Govt can Mitigate or avert the dangers that threaten it. These dangers that Govt is puting all the elements of destruction & deceit in motion to avert her present disturbed state and her attention to her European continental Intrigues is the cause of that supiness and moderation observable in the anglo American british party. In fact England knows the most hostile Cooperation of that party could not in the field render her single handed against America successfull and she anxiously waits the encrease of it. England bottoms her hopes of Conquest in America on discord civil dissention & attempts at a disunion of the states and on the discontent which the public distress occasioned by the excessive Importations of british Manufactures will cause in America—for these reasons it is Important to refute such seditious Inflamatory & traiterous pamphlets as the preface purports Col Taylors is so as to prevent the Credulous &

Ignorant from being betrayed and deceived by it into fatal Errors—it is Important that the press should not at this period deceive. I have stated the reasons for my disapproval of the Conduct of the natl Intelligr—perhaps I was hasty in my first opponion but I have no hesitation in saying the Editor of the Washington Gazette is as attached to the british Govt as the Editor of the London Courier—such men are dangerous & do not deserve Countenance.

In the foregoing attempt to elucidate the secret designs & policy of the british Cabinet & of Cromwells Oligarchs I forgot one material Observation namely the last will & advice in it of General Kellerman[15] to the french people to adhere to the Bourboons & that the safety of France required it—the Marshall was correct. He judged from facts. The Orange Lodge sistem was Introduced in France in Buonapartes time & made progress. Those sworn & formed into societies are of course as much attached to the british Govt. as American Orangemen. Cromwells Oligarchs being the authors and principals of this association they transmitt to their foreign societies such secret Information & Insts. as they deem it necessary either to prevent despondency Elevate their hopes or promote british Intrigues. In some such way did Marshall Kellerman discover the Intention of the british Govt to drive France into Insurrection & then to bring on the holy Aliance by one simultaneous movement to partition that ill fated Country between them under a pretence that such a partition Can alone keep her quiet and preserve the peace of Europe & the Marshalls will & the advice in it is the result of his Marshall Kelrs discovery & was the Effect of a pure & patriotic Love of his Country—superficial thinkers might suppose it proceeded from temporising motives or a predilection for arbitrary sistems—but it was in reality an admonitory warning to guard against a foul Conspiracy which would reduce frenchmen to the Condition of slaves & effectually anihilate their political Existence—such is the Enemy America has also to guard against—such secretly premeditated Murdrous designs betray hostility and Misantrophy to Mankind & Merit the Considn of the Genl Govt of America—my Idea of Establishing Domestic Manufactures without infringing on the Congressional revenue to any large amount as it sayed not to be very abundant & other matters I deem Important towards defeating the designs of England shall be the subject [of] my next letter. I am with the utmost respect &ca.

EDMD KELLY

PS I lately read of a woollen broad Cloth Manufacturer near new York who makes cloth superior to british Cloth because it is all made of Merino Wool—this man & such others as there may be deserve no limitted Encouragement—funds if necessary to encrease their business to increase their Machinery & to enable them to supply Congress with such superior cloth of national manufacture would be but a well merited Compliment & would be on the part of Govt a good Example to the nation—such of these men as have passed the Ordeal of british Compe[ti]tion deserve national aid & Legislative Encouragement to enlarge their works & carry on business on an Extended Scale if they have Capacity to do so—but that Encouragement to Englishmen who carry it on on the most extended scale to Emigrate here is what I believe—and I hope it will not be supposed that I advocate national Manufactures in America from any motive of ill will or Misantrophy to british Manufacturers meritorious for their Industry—my resentment is against the Govt that harasses & persecutes me & my Opinion is that Manufacturing & Commercial Monopoly upholds that obnoxious and oppressive Govt which I wish superceded so as to facilitate the overthrow of that destructive monster & I am Convinced when that happens that british oppression excessive taxation & british burthens will disappear—that Manufacturing & Commercial Industry will revive & that the british people will then be happy.

RC (NN). Addressed by Kelly to JM "late president US at his residence in the state of Virginia City of Washington," and franked. "City of Washington" has been crossed out and "Orange C.H. V" written beneath in an unidentified hand. Postmarked 25 Dec. at Washington. Docketed by JM.

1. Joseph McMinn (1758–1824), who served in the 1796 Tennessee constitutional convention, in the state militia, and in the first eight sessions of the state legislature, was governor of Tennessee, 1815–21 (Nancy Boswell Kincaid, "Joseph McMinn . . . ," in Charles W. Crawford, ed., *Governors of Tennessee, 1:1790–1835* [Memphis, Tenn., 1979], 97–99, 114).

2. In the fall of 1819, the Tennessee legislature received thirty-five petitions demanding the gradual abolition of slavery in the state. The committee to which the petitions were referred proferred a resolution that would eliminate the requirement of security for those slaveholders who wished to free their slaves, but the legislature rejected the resolution (Chase C. Mooney, *Slavery in Tennessee* [Bloomington, Ind., 1957], 66–67).

3. For Governor McMinn's message to the Tennessee legislature, 26 June 1820, see Robert H. White, ed., *Messages of the Governors of Tennessee* (10 vols. to date; Nashville, 1952—), 1:579–88.

4. The state loan office bill, proposed in the special session of the Tennessee legislature convened to deal with the worsening financial crisis in the summer of 1820, established a loan office (bank) that was empowered to issue paper money, that is, banknotes on personal security. The bill was opposed vociferously by the banking interests of the state (ibid., 593–612).

5. See Kelly to JM, 30 Sept. 1820.

6. John Taylor of Caroline, "Fredericksburg Memorial" of the farmers and merchants of Fredericksburg, published in *Niles' Weekly Register* 19 (2 Sept. 1820): 5–7. For a summary of its contents, see Murray N. Rothbard, *The Panic of 1819: Reactions and Policies* (1962; reprint, Auburn, Ala., 2007), 230–31.

7. Domestic manufactures.

8. Jean Pierre Boyer (1776–1850), born on the island of Hispaniola and educated in France, fought in the army of General Charles Leclerc against Toussaint L'Ouverture but

joined forces with Jean-Jacques Dessalines and Henri Christophe after learning that the French intended to restore slavery in Saint-Domingue. Boyer succeeded Alexandre Pétion as president of the Republic of Haiti (the southern portion of the country) in 1818 and united the country under one president on the death of Christophe in 1820. He ruled Haiti until his ouster in 1843 (John Edward Baur, "Mulatto Machiavelli, Jean Pierre Boyer, and the Haiti of His Day," *Journal of Negro History* 32 [1947]: 307–20, 347–49, 352).

9. *Locum tenens:* one who holds the place of another, as in deputy or substitute.

10. Benjamin Hobhouse (1757–1831) was a member of Parliament, 1797–1818, a voice often in opposition to the government and in support of parliamentary reform (Thorne, *History of Parliament: The House of Commons*, 4:209–11).

11. The Roman monarchy ended in 509 B.C. when Tarquinius Superbus was overthrown and the Tarquin family was expelled from Rome. The leaders of the revolt set up the Roman Republic (T. J. Cornell, *The Beginnings of Rome: Italy and Rome from the Bronze Age to the Punic Wars (c. 1000–264 BC)* [London, 1995], 215–16).

12. John Taylor [of Caroline], *Construction Construed, and Constitutions Vindicated* (Richmond, Va., 1820; Shoemaker 3407).

13. The extract Kelly referred to was a review of several French books on commerce, industry, and agriculture under the heading "Comparative Skill and Industry of France and England" in the *Edinburgh Review* 32 (1819): 340–89.

14. For a description of the incident in the Madrid theater in which insurrectionist and constitutionalist general, Rafael del Riego, "behaved with the greatest indecorum, singing songs, etc.," among them one in which the king of Spain was referred to in these terms: "*Gulp it down, dog,*" see the *Daily National Intelligencer*, 27 Oct. 1820.

15. François-Étienne-Christophe Kellerman, duc de Valmy (1735–1820), a marshal of France, commanded the army that repulsed the allies at Valmy in 1792 (Tulard, *Dictionnaire Napoléon*, 1002–3).

From George W. Featherstonhaugh

SIR, FEATHERSTON PARK. DUANESBURGH. NEW YORK. Decr 7. 1820

I had the honour of recg. at its time the Pamphlet You kindly took the trouble to Send me.[1]

The Board of Agriculture is about publishing a volume of Memoirs, and I have charged myself with the Superintendance of the Work. Being desirous of making it acceptable to the Publick, and as useful as general Circumstances admit of, I would to that end insert Your Address to the Albermarle Society, if it is agreeable to You; but I shall by no means do it without Your permission. I have therefore to request the favour of an answer on the receipt of this Letter, as it is intended to publish the Volume on the next Meeting of our Legislature, early in January 1821.

If you approve, I beg also to Know whether You desire any Alteration to be made in any part of it, as Your wishes shall be exactly complied with.

At Page 9. Paragraph 4th. it is stated, that the Supposition of the various organized bodies in Nature, consisting of the same Elements "requires more proof than has yet been offered."[2] It is undoubtedly true that there are many simple bodies called Elements, to the amount of forty or fifty: Yet these are solid bodies, and are called Elementary, because they have not hithert⟨o⟩ Yielded to chemical agency. I frankly State however that I apprehend all the important vegetable bodies have been reduced to the four or five gaseous Elements which are *now thought* to form the constituents of all the parts of Nature as we observe it. Under this view the bod[y] of all Plants is to be considered as composed of the same Elements; and the varieties in forms and qualities of Bodies as established by the various Physiology of Plants. Thus the Sap which runs through a Pear Stock, would if permitted produce Pears; but meeting with a Graft at the end of the Branch differing in its physiological Structure from that it has passed through, it is, having passed through the Leaves, modified, and then carried down the Vessels of the Bark; and at every Stage of its progress down, deposited in the cellular Substance, where it is elaborated after the Law of the peculiar Physiology it is Subservient to: and its elaborated Elements thus become a part of the body whose growth it first assists—viz. the Apple Graft. On its further descent to the main Pear Stock, it is operated upon in the same manner there—only it assists in forming the physiological Structure of a Pear. The reason why the Apple and Peach cannot be nourished by the same continuous Sap, is I imagine because their internal mechanism totally differs—which is the Case with Plants having cortical Seed Vessels, as Apples—and Crustaceous ones as Peaches, Plums, Almonds, &c.

From the simple gaseous Elements, another Argument may be devined for the indiscriminate Application of Manures. Some Vegetables are so peculiarly organized as to be incapable of assimilating Certain Constituent parts of Manures: these being rejected, the Manure is said not to be proper for the Plant. Yet I imagine that rejected portion if further reduced to its remote Elements, could in that form be assimilated by the Plant which rejected it in its Compound State. Fossils and acids Effect reductions of that Kind.

I ought to apologize for intruding these remarks, and I offer the obvious motives which have suggested them, as my apology; for the Spirit of Criticism in Europe has not been hitherto favourable to the productions of this Country; and I could not solicit the permission of making use of Your Address, without feeling at the Same time it was my duty to point out, a portion of it, which I thought, might furnish grounds for ill natured remarks. I have the honour to remain Sir With the most respectful Consideration Your obt. hble. St

G W FEATHERSTONHAUGH

RC (NN). Docketed by JM.

1. For JM's *Address to the Agricultural Society of Albemarle*, see *PJM-RS*, 1:260–83.
2. *PJM-RS*, 1:264.

From Joseph M. Sanderson

Dear Sir — Washington City Dec. 9: 1820.

I have taken the liberty of sending to your address the first volume of the Biography of the Signers to the Declaration of Independence.[1] Should you find any thing in it worth the perusal, I will thank you for your recommendation, & as the succeeding volumes are published, I shall, with your permission, forward them to you.

As the work is intended to perpetuate the lives of men distinguished for their patriotism and virtues, & as its excellence will, in some measure, depend upon the contributions of their cotemporaries, I hope it will not be considered improper, the application I make for any facts in your possession. The anxious solicitude for presenting the work to the publick in the best Shape, will serve as an apology for this request. With great respect, I remain Your humble servant

Joseph M. Sanderson[2]
Publisher

RC (DLC). Docketed by JM.

1. John Sanderson et al., *Biography of the Signers to the Declaration of Independence* (9 vols.; Philadelphia, 1820–27).

2. Joseph M. Sanderson, John Sanderson's brother (see n. 1 above), was a Philadelphia printer who acquired the newspaper *Aurora* in 1822. By 1823 he had been appointed superintendent of the Merchants' Coffee House, and in 1834 held the same position for its successor, the Merchants Exchange. In 1837 Sanderson operated the Merchants' Hotel at Fourth Street between Market and Arch. He introduced the first cab in Philadelphia (*Times, and Hartford Advertiser*, 26 Nov. 1822; *Independent Chronicle and Boston Patriot*, 20 Dec. 1823; Samuel Hazard, *Hazard's Register of Pennsylvania* 13 [1834]: 12; *A Guide to the Lions of Philadelphia . . .* [Philadelphia, 1837], 54; Nicholas B. Wainwright, "Diary of Samuel Breck, 1839–1840," *PMHB* 103 [1979]: 504 and n. 16).

To Thomas Jefferson

Dear Sir — Montpellier Decr. 10. 1820

Yours of Novr. 29. came to hand a few days ago. The letter from T. C.[1] is returned. I had one from him lately on the same subject, and in consequence reminded the President of his political career; dropping at the same time a few lines in his favor to our Senator Mr. Barbour. I sincerely wish something proper in itself could be done for him. He needs it and deserves it.

The law terminating appointments at periods of four years is pregnant with mischiefs such as you describe. It overlooks the important distinction between repealing or modifying the office, and displacing the officer. The former is a Legislative, the latter an Executive function. And even the former, if done with a view of re-establishing the office and letting in a new appointment, would be an indirect violation of the Theory & policy of the Constitution. If the principle of the late Statute be a sound one, nothing is necessary but to limit appointments held during pleasure, to a single year, or the next meeting of Congress, in order to make the pleasure of the Senate a tenure of office, instead of that of the President alone. If the error be not soon corrected, the task will be very difficult: for it is of a nature to take a deep root.

On application thro' Mr. Stephenson, I have obtained from the Legislative files at Richmond, a Copy of Col: Bland's letter to you, for which I gave you the trouble of a search last fall.[2] The letter being a public, not a private one, was sent to the Legislature, according to the intention of the writer. It contains what I expected to find in it; a proof that I differed from him on the question of ceding the Mississippi to Spain in 1780.

This will wait for your return from Poplar forest; accompanied I hope with evidence of the good effects of the trip on your health. Affectionately & truly yours

James Madison

RC (DLC); FC (DLC: Rives Collection, Madison Papers). RC docketed by Jefferson "recd. Dec. 22."

1. Tench Coxe.
2. For Theodorick Bland's letter, see Andrew Stevenson to JM, 3 Dec. 1820, and n. 2.

From Francis Walker Gilmer

Dear Sir. Richmond 10th. Decr. 1820

I received some weeks ago from our excellent friend Mr. Corrêa, his farewell to Virginia, and to all whose kindness has made it dear to him. It was natural that the friendship with which you had honored him, and the repeated civilities he had received from you, should be remembered when he was about to leave our country. He especially charges me, to preserve in your memory, the sentiments of esteem which he will ever cherish toward you; and the sense of his thanks for the many attentions he has received at Mt. Pellier. It not being likely that I shall have the pleasure to see you, I inclose you his letter,[1] which you will be good enough to return, when you have read it.

I send you also a little treatise[2] which I wrote during my visit to Albemarle in the summer. The subject is becoming important, from the argument on the other side circulating every day, without opposition. It is time the fortress should be defended. With great respect & esteem your ob. Ser.

FRANCIS W. GILMER

RC (DLC). Docketed by JM.

1. For the enclosed letter, see Thomas Jefferson to JM, 29 Nov. 1820, and n. 2.

2. *A Vindication of the Laws, Limiting the Rate of Interest on Loans; From the Objections of Jeremy Bentham, and the Edinburgh Reviewers* (Richmond, Va., 1820; Shoemaker 1393). For a discussion of this pamphlet, see Davis, *Francis Walker Gilmer*, 312–21.

From James Barbour

DEAR SIR WASHINGTON Dcr. 13. 20

Your favorable recommendation of Mr. Coxe[1] has interested me much in his behalf And I have already pressed his claims on the President who entertains for him a high respect and possesses every disposition to do something for him the first favorable opportunity. You will see by the papers that on yesterday the resolution for the admission of Missouri passed the Senate 26 to 18. Mr. Macon (as my old Father is wont to say) got his back up on account of Eatons proviso[2] in itself a perfect milk and water thing or the vote would have been 27-17. Otis & Stokes[3] being both absent and of different Sentiments would not tho present have altered the majority. Our real Strength therefore is 28 to 18.

Its fate in the House of Representatives is said to be uncertain. On the contrary I have personally always believed and Still do that they will admit Missouri. The only question is who shall be the 'scape goats of their party. Time and circumstance will furnish them. We are in daily expectation of the arrival of Mr Forsyth—whose private letters are more favorable than his official as to the ratification of the Treaty.[4] Judging by those we have strong hopes of a ratification. France is obstinately foolish about our commercial intercourse and has set up the strange pretension that our law of the last session has violated the treaty of Louisiana in so far as the port of New Orleans is concerned[5]—Contending that equality in that port was forever Gu[a]ranteed with the most favored nation and therefore she had a claim to the same favor indulged to Great Britain of which she was deprived by the law above alluded to—And pretends as I understand to make it a *sine qua non*. Our Government has placed it on the foot of the general rule of a discrimination between privileges gratuitous and for equivalents—And have intimated thro Mr Gallatin if this be insisted on Mr Neuville's trip here will be worse than useless. Accept assurances of my respect and friendship.

JAMES BARBOUR

RC (DLC). Docketed by JM.

1. See JM to Barbour, 25 Nov. 1820.

2. On 6 Dec. 1820, U.S. senator John Henry Eaton of Tennessee offered a proviso to the resolution for admitting Missouri as a state, "that nothing herein contained shall be so construed as to give the assent of Congress to any provision in the constitution of Missouri, if any such there be, which contravenes that clause in the Constitution of the United States, which declares that 'the citizens of each State shall be entitled to all privileges and immunities of citizens in the several States.'" The proviso was defeated, 24-21, the next day. Eaton offered the proviso again on 11 Dec. 1820, once the Missouri Resolution had been reported to the Senate, and it passed. Nathaniel Macon of North Carolina moved to recommit the resolution so that Eaton's proviso could be struck out, but that motion failed and the resolution passed to its third reading (*Annals of Congress*, 16th Cong., 2d sess., 39, 41–42, 43–45, 99–100, 102, 115–16).

3. Montfort Stokes (1762–1842), a Revolutionary War veteran from Virginia, settled in North Carolina in the 1780s. He held a number of local and state offices and served in the U.S. Senate, 1816–23, and as governor of his state, 1830–32. Appointed chairman of the Federal Indian Commission by President Andrew Jackson in 1832, he supervised Indian resettlement to west of the Mississippi River. He subsequently moved to Fort Gibson, Indian Territory (now Oklahoma), where he served as subagent and agent to various Indian tribes until his death (Sobel and Raimo, *Biographical Directory of the Governors*, 3:1125–26).

4. For the Adams-Onís Treaty of 1819, see *PJM-RS*, 1:410 n. 2.

5. For the Franco-American disputes over commercial discrimination, see JM to Lafayette, 25 Nov. 1820, and n. 3.

From Ebenezer H. Cummins

Dear Sir Baltimore 13th Decr. 1820.

I beg leave to address to you an English history of the late war, with a few critical notes by myself.[1] It has many merits. My opinion of it is fairly set forth in the advertisement prefixed: but I would be gratified to receive yours in the most conscientious sincerity; and especially of the character of so much as I have appended to the British performance.

I would respectfully request that you will remember me to your amiable and excellent lady, for whom in all relations I have ever cherished the most unqualified regard. I pray that our common heavenly father may bless the evening of your life with health, happiness, and the comforts of this world, and finally receive you into his own society. Yr. Mo Obt. St

Ebenezer H. Cummins[2]

RC (DLC). Docketed by JM.

1. *Baine's History of the Late War, between the United States and Great Britain: With a Critical Appendix, &c., by Ebenezer Harlow Cummins* (Baltimore, 1820; Shoemaker 186). This volume was the first American edition of Edward Baines's eponymous work.

2. Ebenezer Harlow Cummins (ca. 1780–1834) was a North Carolina native, whose family moved to Georgia, where Cummins became a lawyer. He served in the U.S. Marine

Corps and wrote to JM at least twice applying for government jobs with no success. After leaving the service, Cummins settled for a time in Georgetown, D.C., where he was part-proprietor of the newspaper *Spirit of 'Seventy-Six* in 1813. In December of that year he launched his own paper, the *Senator*; it ceased publication in April 1814. Cummins subsequently moved to Baltimore, and then to Philadelphia, where he became part-owner of the *True American* in December 1817; the last issue was in March 1818. While in Philadelphia, he published *A Summary Geography of Alabama* (1819). Cummins then settled in Washington where he was a correspondent for the New York *Journal of Commerce* (*Baltimore Patriot & Mercantile Advertiser*, 20 Jan. 1834; *Senate Exec. Proceedings*, 2:248; *PJM-PS*, 3:390, 391 n. 1; Brigham, *American Newspapers*, 1:94, 2:955).

To Francis Walker Gilmer

Dear Sir — Montpellier Decr. 18. 1820

I have received your favor of the 10th. inclosing the letter from Mr. Correa, for the perusal of which you will please to accept my thanks. I am glad to find that he leaves our country with so many cordial feelings: and I can not but value highly the share allowed me in such, by one, not more distinguished by the treasures of his capacious mind, than by the virtues and charms of his social life.

I am to thank you also for the little treatise in vindication of the Usury laws. The arguments you have marshalled on that side must be respected by those most zealous on the other. They will a[t] least agree that you have seconded them by very interesting appeals to the sympathies of benevolence.

It has occasionally occurred to me, as worthy of consideration whether a limitation of the legal interest in favor of the distressed & inconsiderate, might not admit exceptions where a higher rate would be advantageous to the borrower as well as to the lender. That there are such cases cannot be doubted, and if exceptions in favor of them could be duly guarded agst. abuse, by official formalities, & even by disinterested sanctions founded on satisfactory explanations, the space would be much narrowed for differences of opinion. How far the excepted cases would be of sufficient extent to justify the departure from a uniform rule, is another point requiring more investigation & reflection, than I have bestowed on it.[1] With great esteem Yrs.

James Madison

RC (CLU-C); draft (DLC).

1. In a letter to Dabney Carr, Gilmer commented on JM's response: "Mr. Madison to whom I sent a copy wrote a longer letter—concurring with us too in the main but tinctured with the political mysticism which I ever thought belonged to his mind. Rely upon it, his

views are neither great nor distinct—objects loom because of the haze about them. He admits needy borrowers should be protected, but thinks that those not impelled by necessity should not have the benefit of the exception. His exception to the exception, is about as practicable, as Gullivers, for setting a dial on a weathercock. It is in short, little less than sheer nonsense—and his idea about it as he himself has expressed it, is downright absurdity. I was struck as I have ever been at the contrast between his way of thinking and that of Mr. J. There is no comparison between the two men. Madison I hear was logical in debate. But in every thing I have seen from him, his logic is artificial & shallow. In conversation he is a disputatious polemic; but I think by no means a powerful adversary. He is however as much superior to his successor as he is inferior to his predecessor" (Gilmer to Carr, 15 Jan. 1821, Vi).

From Mackay & Campbell

D Sir Fredericksburg Decr. 18. 1820.

Some time since we recd. a letter from Messrs. Maury & Latham dated 30th. Septr. in which we find the following, "The balance in our hands due to Mr. Madison is £35.12/5—having sold his Tobo. & Shipped the goods he ordered. We can pass that Amount to your credit on account of Mr. Madison's dft for £100. This would leave £64.7/7. Of course if Mr. Madison wishes it we will pass this also to Your credit & his debit, but probably When he reviews his account he may choose to arrange it otherwise." To which we Replied that we would consult with you on the Subject. Please say how you wish this matter arranged, so that we may make our entries accordingly. With much Respect, Yr. mo. ob. Sts.

Mackay & Campbell

RC (DLC). Cover docketed by JM.

From James Monroe

Dear Sir Washington Decr 18. 1820

We have just receivd a letter from Mr Rush of the 20th of october, communicating one from the Spanish ambassador in London to him, of the preceding date, stating that he had been informd confidentially that the Florida treaty had been ratified.[1] It does not appear that the information had been imparted to him, from Madrid or London or by whom. It being possible that it might have been receivd from some person at London, & founded on report only, & not true, we have thought it best to say nothing about [it] here. You will therefore receive it in confidence.

I intended to have written you more fully on our affairs here, but am prevented by calls to which we are subject, & must submit to. With affectionate regards of my whole family to Mrs Madison yrs.

James Monroe

RC (DLC). Docketed by JM.

1. Richard Rush recorded in his 20 Oct. 1820 diary entry: "This morning I receive information from the Spanish Ambassador, of the ratification of the Florida treaty, and forthwith communicate it to my government, sending the dispatch to Liverpool to go by the first ship, for the chance of conveying the information to Washington, before it can arrive direct from Madrid" (Richard Rush, *Memoranda of a Residence at the Court of London*, 342).

From John H. Wood

Worthy Sir, Albemarle Decr. 22nd, 1820.

I am induced from many considerations to address you in a manner which may [be] a surprise; but it is cheifly at the instance of my mother,[1] with whom you have been well acquainted. The influencies to this address it is surperfluous to mention, the contents of this letter can the better tell, but a word to the wise.

I will deem it proper to premise, that the small pecuniary aid I am about to ask, would be most willingly afforded by my mother cou'd it be done without the Sale of a negro to which she is extremely averse, & indeed make it a matter of conscience. I wou'd give ample Security for the loan of a few hundred dollars, say from 2 to 500 for six or twelve months.

The 2 or 500$ wou'd be prefered inclosed by the Servant, or in one or two months hence at which time a bond with Sec[u]rity for whatever Sum your goodness wou'd name, wou'd be brought over ready filled up with some known character.

I might tell you of the great value of money in this county, & how the favor wou'd be appreciated by myself and most excellent parent, & that I shou'd regret exceedingly sacrificing of my negroes who are of the valuable kind (Watermen) but this wou'd be entirely unnecessary. My mother has been repeatedly disappointed in receiving no visit from Mrs. Madison (our relation) whenever she came to the county. She entertains a most sincere attackment [*sic*] for yourself, & the warmest affection for *her* who was once so kind to her youngest daughter during her visit to her cousin in 1801 in Washington,[2] as also for her repeated kindnesses to Mrs. Stras[3] & daughters in your Presidency. She, My Mother, desires her most affectionate regard to Mrs. Madison & high esteem for yourself in which permit me to unite. With due consideration I am Yrs. most respectfully

Jno. H. Wood[4]

RC (DLC). Docketed by JM.

1. Wood's mother, Lucy Henry Wood (d. ca. 1826), was the sister of Patrick Henry, and thus a distant relative of Dolley Madison (Woods, *Albemarle County in Virginia*, 347; Mattern and Shulman, *Selected Letters of Dolley Payne Madison*, 10).

2. This was possibly Jane Wood.

3. John Wood's sister, Martha Wood Southall Stras (1768–1834), was the wife first, of Stephen Southall (1757–1799), and second, of George Frederick Stras (1746–1811), a French emigrant whom she married around 1801. The family lived thereafter in Georgetown, D.C. Martha Stras had three daughters by her first husband, two of whom, Lucy Henry Southall Cutts and Maria Wood Southall Van Zandt, married men of reputation in Washington society (Bear and Stanton, *Jefferson's Memorandum Books*, 2:923 n. 20; James P. C. Southall, "Concerning the Southalls of Virginia," *VMHB* 45 [1937]: 286, 288).

4. John H. Wood was the son of Valentine and Lucy Henry Wood (Woods, *Albemarle County in Virginia*, 347).

To George W. Featherstonhaugh

SIR Montpellier Decr. 23. 1820

I received on the 20th. your letter of the 7th. inst. The Agricultura[l] paper to which it refers, being already in print, is of course subject to any further publication, without my consent: And I regard the asking it as a special mark of your politeness; the more so as it was intended to give me an opportunity of rectifying the errors into which I might have fallen. That there may be more of these than have occurred to either of us, is probable and that the passage you have pointed out, may be particularly exposed to unfriendly criticism, your suggestions ought to make me aware. I have not however, if there were time, the means of consulting the most recent works on Chymistry, and adapting what was advanced to the most approved of them. I must leave it therefore as it is; with a wish that if the paper should be inserted in your Agricultural Memoirs, it may be accompanied with whatever notices may be necessary to shew that its errors are those of an Individual only, and no wise chargeable on a defective State of Chymical knowlege in our Country.

It was far from my purpose, to enter into the depths of the question concerning the formation & food of plants. I had in view merely to infer from the vast variety of dissimilar objects in the organized departments of nature, that they could not all be composed of a few ingredients precisely the same in all. I could not reconcile either with a physical possibility, or with the apparent economy of nature, a supposition that these few distinct ingredients, whether designated by the names of elements, atoms, molecules, or gasses, could produce so great a profusion of heterogeneous existences; that they could be indiscriminately fitted for the composition & structure of each of them; and consequently that the entire mass of organizable matter might be converted into a single species of plants, the potatoe for example, and thence exclusively into the human species feeding on it.

It seemed to be more reasonable to distrust the results of Chymistry, or rather the adequacy of its decomposing and discriminating powers; and to suppose that the very few gazeous substances may themselves be further divisible, as a solar ray has been found to be by a prism; that other substances elude altogether the analysing processes, as the gasses formerly did; or that there are other elementary substances, not only undiscovered, but undiscoverable, sufficient in number & variety to form by their combinations with each other, and with those already known, the system before us, with all its diversified organizations & appearances.

In attempting to solve the problem relating to the composition, mechanism, and growth of vegetables, we must either suppose that three four or five elements, simple and immutable in their essence, are susceptible of combinations sufficiently multiplied to produce the vegitable system; or that other and more numerous elements remain to be added to them; or that the vegitable organs possess a transubst[ant]iating power by which one element can be changed into another. Among these alternatives, the first & the last seemed to have least claim to our assent.

I am very sensible, Sir, that I have glided into a train of ideas too hasty and too crude for even a private letter: and that they need an apology much more than was called for by the observations in your letter; which had sufficient interest to recommend them to attention, and the frankness of which could have no other effect than to enhance the respect & esteem of which I tender you assurances.

James Madison

RC (DLC, series 7, box 1); draft (DLC). RC cover sheet addressed by JM to Featherstonhaugh at "Featherston Park Duanesburgh New York," and franked. Docketed by Featherstonhaugh. Postmarked at Orange Court House, 26 Dec. 1820. Minor differences between the copies have not been noted.

From James Monroe

Dear Sir — Washington Decr 23d. 1820

The question as to the admission of Missouri into the union, which is still depending, will probably not be decided untill after the holydays, & the decision is then quite uncertain. You have I presume seen a proposition of Dr Eustis, for admitting her, after a certain day, provided, in the interim, the obnoxious clause in her constitution shall be stricken out.[1] Should this fail, it is understood, that it will then be proposed, to admit her, with a declaration, that that clause is unconstitutional & void. In the last resort, the resolution of the Senate will be taken up & decided on.[2] From what I hear, the prospect of its passage is fairer, than that of either of the other propositions, and I am much inclind to the opinion, that in some mode or other, the State will be admitted. This impression is however form'd, more from general considerations, than from any thing, that is seen or heard here. I can not believe that this question, can be managed, in a way, to shake our union, & hence I conclude that the sentiment in favor of that bond, & of our system of government generally, will cause a reaction, like what we have seen in other cases, that will depress anew, all those who have taken the lead in the opposition, & thus favor the admission. The party are best traind here, and in consequence, this is the last ground, on which it will be broken. The southern & western members have acted with more judgment, this session, than the last; there has been less excitement of feeling, & more appeal to good motives, in the body of the people, in States differently circumstanc'd, now, than then, & I think with good effect. The whole responsibility, is now on those, who have rejected the State, & if nothing occurs, to weaken the sentiment in favor of union, in the body of the Eastern people, it must, I think, operate here, in a way to secure the admission of the State.

We have nothing respecting the ratification of the Florida treaty since my last,[3] except an intimation from General Vives, that he had great confidence, derivd from letters from his govt., that it would be ratified.

The Secret journal[4] is in the hands of a printer at Boston, & will be publishd correctly, according to the record, as soon as possible. It had accidentally been mislaid, by one of the Clerks, during the last Session, & not found untill after my return here, which caused a corresponding delay.

I most heartily wish that some thing could be done in favor of Mr. Coxe.[5] I concur with you in the favorable opinion, you have expressd of his merit, but it will hardly be possible to remove any one from office in Phila., to provide for him, & I do not think that he would go elsewhere. There is another case, of a person of great merit, & who has strong claims, on us, personally, as well as on the public for whom I should be happy to make some provision, I mean Dr. Eustis; but will it be possible to exclude young Dearborn[6] in his favor?

All my interesting papers, including those of our late friend Judge Jones, are in Albemarle; when I return there I will make another search for your letters to him not included among those already deliverd to you.

I have been much concern'd for sometime, at the situation of Mr Cutts, & embarrassed what part to take in regard to him, in consequence of the representations, which have been made to me officially, on his subject.[7] Knowing your connection with & friendship for him, I feel it incumbent on me, to state to you in confidence, what has passd on his subject.

Mr Crawford stated to me last Session, that Mr Calhoun, was dissatisfied with his conduct, & wished him removd. He added, that he thought, that he would make a formal complaint to me to that effect. To this, I gave all the discouragment in my power, in my conversation with Mr Crawford; & in communication with Mr Cutts, who seemd to be aware, of his situation, I said all that I could, without adverting in the most remote manner, to the above, to stimulate him to a diligent & laborious discharge of his public duties, and as I hoped & thought with effect. He stated with great candour his private distresses, & consequent depression of mind, as the causes, of any omissions which might be imputed to him, but assurd me that he would fail in nothing which it might be in his power to perform. I heard no more *directly* on the subject untill yesterday, when Mr Crawford called on me again, and repeated on the part of Mr Calhoun, his fix'd opinion, that the business of his dept. had sufferd & was suffering, in the hands of Mr Cutts. Mr Calhoun's wish, (as Mr. C intimated), was, to have him plac'd in some other Station, & not to leave him unprovided for. It has been expected for sometime, that the worthy Dr Tucker[8] would be taken from us. He is still very much indisposd, & the hope of his recovery slight. Mr C. intimated that Mr Calhoun suggested, in case of the loss of that worthy character, the transfer of Mr Cutts to the vacant place; but he doubted, as I do, the sanction of the Senate to it. I do not know that you can do any thing in this case, nor do I mention it with that view. You may perhaps be able to give him hints, that may be useful, to him, without exciting suspicions of the motive. I shall sustain him, while in my power which I hope it will be, so long as I remain in office, but this you know must depend altogether on his conduct. Very respectfully & sincerely your friend

James Monroe

RC (DLC: Rives Collection, Madison Papers). Docketed by JM.

1. William Eustis's proposed joint resolution of Congress was presented in the House of Representatives on 19 Dec. 1820 (*Annals of Congress*, 16th Cong., 2d sess., 679). It was published in the *Daily National Intelligencer*, 20 Dec. 1820.

2. The resolution "declaring the admission of the State of Missouri into the Union" was reported to the Senate on 29 Nov. 1820, passed on 12 Dec. 1820, and sent to the House of Representatives for concurrence (*Annals of Congress*, 16th Cong., 2d sess., 26, 118–19).

3. Monroe to JM, 18 Dec. 1820.

4. For the secret journals of the Continental Congress, see JM to Monroe, 19 Nov. 1820, and n. 4.

5. For JM's recommendation of Tench Coxe, see JM to Monroe, 19 Nov. 1820.

6. Henry Alexander Scammel Dearborn (1783–1851) was the son of Henry Dearborn, JM's colleague and former secretary of war during both Jefferson administrations, and collector of the port of Boston and Charlestown thereafter. In 1812 when Henry Dearborn became a major general in the U.S. Army, JM appointed Henry A. S. Dearborn to be collector, and he held that position until 1829 (*PJM-PS*, 3:488 n. 4).

7. For the "situation of Mr Cutts," see Madison and Richard Cutts's Financial Difficulties, March 1820 (Editorial Note).

8. Thomas Tudor Tucker (1745–1828), a graduate of the medical school of the University of Edinburgh, settled in Charleston, South Carolina, and represented that state in the Continental Congress, 1787–88, and in the U.S. Congress, 1789–93. He was treasurer of the United States from 1801 until his death (*PJM*, 5:273 n. 3).

From Edmond Kelly

Sir Columbia Ten. 24th Decr 1820

My last letter[1] concluded my thoughts on the necessity of creating national manufactories of all the articles Imported from England—of puting them into operation, & of substituting a revenue for that pernicious one they Yeild so as not to injure or Embarrass the public service, as the only measure that can avert Impending national Insolvency—Expell foreign (british) influence & destroy the hopes of the disaffected—and my Idea of the necessity of such measures arises from a consciousness that England Calculates that a continuance of the present Importations of her manufactures will bring her all the Current Cash and also all the Capital of America—will cause Amn. national Insolvency—general discontent & Imputations of Incapacity & Inattention Against the Genl Govt for permitting foreign monopoly & peculation to Impoverish the country—and a state of anarchy that will cause a disunion of the states and facilitate or ensure her designs of a reconquest of America. The policy of England & the condition of American affairs shews the Conclusion correct—in all this I sayed nothing new—nothing but what the greatest statesman America produced foresaw. Mr Jeffn. is the creator & patron of American Manufs. Could he be but for 4 years presidt he would advance America a Century in Manufactures & the arts & thereby perpetuate her independence. In truth his retirement is a loss that under present existing Circs cannot be supplied.

The next question in Importance is the trade to India for Nankeens & womens ware and to China for Teas &ca. for both of which I suppose money is transmitted with the exception of a little Ginseng to china. The trade to India is another branch of british Monopoly. England has drawn all the treasures of the Maritime States of India by taxes & exactions & by the exclusive supply of her Manufs. She is now necessarily the Sole gainer by Indian exports & trade—the produce of which goes to british Merchants, to the british King & the Oligarchs & Nabobs which with the profits on british Amn Monopoly is applied as often as oppy offers to subsidize the northern Kings, to suppress every attempt of Other nations at freedom &

Consequent Industry lest such Industry should Interfere with british universal monopoly—which is fatally restrictive of human happyness & an effectual Veto to Improvement. It is therefore hoped the Genl Govt of America will in a manner lest calculated to alarm no longer sanction principles so oppressive to Mankind or aid a monopoly so universally pernicious & ruinous as to keep the world in a hopeless state of bondage & which is not less Injurious less menacing & less perilous to other nations than to America herself—it is the Hydra of despotism which it becomes the duty of rational Enlightened freemen to expell & that peace security & permanence of freedom will result from this Expullsion is the most rational & probable Conjecture & surely if one Legislative act which Violates no compact or Treaty can effect this great object & render the Monster ⟨Innosious?⟩ such an act of humanity will not be less beneficial to America than it will be gratefull and usefull to Mankind.

In short this trade to India & China that great & patriotic statesman Mr Jefferson also attempted to render profitable by projecting settlements on the shores of the pacific Ocean & on the banks of the Misouri & Columbia Rivers—forming settlements on their banks establishing Furr Companies & Exporting the furrs to China. As nothing can be more nationally Important after D Manufactures I beg leave to submitt my Idea of the Cheapest & quickest mode of accomplishing this great object.

Instead of reducing the Army to increase it or raise a supplementary force which shall be entitled only to half pay & by being furnished with Corn & other Necessary seeds shall after the first year support itself on Mr Secretary Calhouns plan[2] each soldier to be entitled to 160 acres after 3 years service in the vicinity of the post he served at and every settler who would settle under protection of such posts to be entitled to 160 acres or 640 if a Married man with a family. But as the savages will probably be hostile the most experienced officers should be selected for this service—half the men might be Employed in Labor one fourth on Guard & in readiness & the other 4th. to relieve in rotation—in case of savage hostility the horses might mount troops of Cavalry which any residt Englishman or Irishman who served in the british Cavalry could teach the sword Exercise & to ride & drill & also for light artillery both of which in them open Prairie Countries would be equally usefull & Decisive & which horses when no such Military service should be required would be usefull in ploughing the soil—for this purpose there ought to be a reservation of 2 sections of Land round each fort to stand in the Center—settlers on the outward Lines—soldiers to be furnished with the different artificial Grasses necessary to raise horses & hogs & the necessry quantity of stock which the danger from wild animals & the Indians wd. render it necessary to Confine in Enclosures as near the forts as possible—red clover is the best pasture for hogs & horses tho fatal to cows—also Oats for horses—should the subaltern officers be obliged to Oversee the work each man could Cultivate & raise ten acres of wheat & 8 of Corn & his half pay would get him a horse & necessaries. Each soldier would by such a regulation Consider himself an Armed Citizen & I Imagine that if such regulation extended to the Army in all remote posts in the Interior that double the number could be supported with as little expence as the present number now is & that those only doing Garrison or such like duty in Charleston Harbour Battery & such places of the same description on the sea coast should be excepted or exempt from the regulation—that is on full pay. And really the reduction of the army except for improper Conduct does not now appear to be necessary or prudent—a well regulated efficient army & a scientific & Experienced staff cannot under present existing Circs be dispensed with & is the best internal police—the force which defends the Frontiers—protects the Citizens & may ultimately & Eventually preserve the Union.

When I first suggested the necessity occupying of E Florida & annexing it to the U States—the british Orange party was geting numerous—was Confident Violent & Menaceing. I feared that the Spanish King would give it to England for aid against South America and that England intended to attempt a reconquest of the US by Wellington &ca. & E Florida being the most advantageous position to England that it would be a dangerous act of Imprudence for the US to risk the probability of such an event—& that self preservation rendered it necessary to anticipate & avert it—tho E F has not been transferred to England it is evident that my suspicions were well founded—it is now evident that the british Govt has dissembled—& has Influenced the spanish King not to Cede Florida for what purpose it is unnecessary to state—it further appears that an anxiety for political Existence induced the spanish Cortes to temporise—to side with England & court her perfidious protection lest she should influence the holy Alliance to restore the Inquisition In truth Spain is not Ignorant of the Intrigues of England—tha[t] Lord Cochrane's Armament & all the force raised for south America in England was secretly Connived at & permitted by the british Govt. to secure a Market for her manufactures & that England has kindly Instructed the south Amn. Minors in the art of Smelting—from which it is evident that the british Govt has prevented the ratification of the Florida treaty—had America permitd Armaments agst Mexico as England did agst other parts of South A. Spanish forces would ere now be expelled that Continent—but as the annexing of Florida to the US can alone give Maritime & Internal security the adoption of Mr Trimbles Sentiments on that subject is the correct course[3]—that is the settlement of the sugar & Coffee Country from Orleans to the Spanish Line—the rejection of Don Oniss Treaty & Annexing east Florida to the US in Lieu of Compn for the seizure & Detention of Amn. property and giving a pecuniary Equivalent to Spain for the difference & not a Territorial One. As it is evident it is England & not Spain that meditates secret hostility against America a further postponement of effectual measures to provide for national security is imprudent.

I Cannot conclude this letter without an observation of a private nature—among the ruffians Influenced & bribed by the british Govt. to pelt & abuse me is one of the name of Daniel in Dublin who is one of the self elected Legislating Committees of United Irish which succeeded the ruined One. My mistaken partiality for this corrupted Demagogue at an early period brought him into business & practice—it enabled him to steal Twenty thousand pounds of my money out of bank in sums of ten thousd each. One ten thousand he was obliged to refund but the other ten thousand he was permitted to retain on Condition of aiding the Royal cause & pelting & abusing me—he is no relation of mine. He is a meere Interloper in my business a british Court prostitute pioneer & a Legal Drudge as destitute of Genius as a Waggon horse is of speed & only repeating Mr Pitts Experimental Insts to prostitutes & their satelite bloodhounds which Coming from a Jacobin has more weight than from an Orangeman & is despised by the Gentn of the Irish Bar for his avarice and Meaness. I am with all possible respect &ca.

EDMOND KELLY

Cromwells Oligarchs are not more deceitfull than these Jacobin Committees are—their principles are the same & an explanation of them in some future letter will excite horror & detestation.

RC (NN).

1. Kelly to JM, 6 Dec. 1820.

2. At the behest of Congress, the secretary of war, John C. Calhoun, prepared a plan for the reduction of the army that kept its organization intact while cutting the number of enlisted men (Merrill D. Peterson, *The Great Triumvirate: Webster, Clay, and Calhoun* [New York, 1987], 93–95). The "Report of the Secretary of War on the Military Peace Establishment," 12 Dec. 1820, was published in the *Daily National Intelligencer*, 18 Dec. 1820.

3. For Kentucky representative David Trimble's speech in the House opposing the Adams-Onís Treaty, see Kelly to JM, 26 Sept. 1820, and n. 11.

To Ebenezer H. Cummins

Decr. 26. 1820

I have recd. Sir your favor of the 13th. with a copy of the American Edition of Baine's Hist: of the late war, to which I have given a hasty perusal.

The work does not bespeak historical talents of the highest order, but it is a respectable performance; and merited a republication here, by the degree of research & candor appearing on the face of it. That it contains errors, some very gross ones you have well shewn by your remarks in the appendix. It was the more proper that corrections should accompany an American Edition, as they may reach the attention of the Author, and give to his respect for truth an oppy. of doing more justice to it in another Edition.

Mr[s]. M. as well as my self, is much obliged by the kind wishes you express for us, and we offer a joint return of them with respect

J. M

Draft (DLC).

To James Monroe

DEAR SIR MONTPELLIER Decr. 28. 1820

I have recd. your two favors of the 18 & 23 inst. The prospect of a favorable issue to the difficulties with Spain, is very agreeable. I hope the ratification will arrive witht clogs on it; and that the acquisition of Florida may give no new stimulus to the spirit excited by the case of Missouri. I am glad to learn that a termination of this case also is not despaired of. If the new State is to be admitted with a proviso, none better occurs than a declaration that its admission is not to imply an opinion, in Congress, that its constitution will be less subject to be tested and controuled by the Constitution of the U.S. than if formed after its admission, or than the Constitutions of other States now members of the Union.

It is a happy circumstance that the discussions renewed by the offensive clause introduced by Missouri, are marked by such mitigated feelings in Congress. It augurs well as to the ultimate effect which you anticipate. The spirit and manner of conducting the opposition to the new State, with the palpable efforts to kindle lasting animosity between geographical divisions of the nation, will have a natural tendency, when the feverish crisis shall have past,[1] to re-unite those who never differed as to the essential principles and the true policy of the Government. This salutary reaction will be accelerated by candor and conciliation on one side, appealing to like dispositions on the other. And it would be still further promoted, by a liberality with regard to all depending measures, on which local interests may seem to be somewhat at variance, and may perhaps be so for a time.

Your dispositions towards Mr. T. Coxe are such as I had counted on. I shall regret, if it so happen, that nothing can properly be done for him. I feel a sincere interest in behalf of Docr. Eustis. The expedient at which you glance would I suppose be in itself an appropriate provision: but I am sensible of the delicacy of the considerations which I perceive weigh with you.

I wish he could have been made the Governour of his State. It would have closed his public career, with the most apt felicity.

Is not the law vacating periodically the described offices an encroachment on the Constitutional attributes of the Executive? The Creation of the office is a Legislative Act: The appointment of the officer the joint act of the President & Senate: The tenure of the office (the Judiciary excepted) is the pleasure of the P. alone, so decided at the commencement of the govt. so acted on since, and so expressed in the commission. After the appointment has been made, neither the Senate, nor H. of Reps. have any power relating to it; unless in the event of an impeachment by the latter, and a judicial decision by the former; or unless in the Exercise of a legislative power by both, abolishing the office itself, by which the officer indirectly loses his place. And even in this case, if the office were abolished, merely to get rid of the tenant, and with a view, by its re-establishment, to let in a new one, on whom the Senate would have a negative, it would be a virtual infringement of the Constitutional distribution of the powers of Government. If a law can displace an officer at every period of 4 years, it can do so at the end of every year, or at every session of the Senate, and the tenure will then be the pleasure of the Senate as much as of the Presidt. and not of the P. alone. Other very interesting views might be taken of the subject. I never read, if I ever saw, the debates on the passage of the law, Nor have I looked for precedents which may have countenanced it. I suspect that these are confined to the Territories, that they had their origin in the ordinance of the old Congs. in whom all powers of govt. were confounded; and that they were followed by the new Congs. who have exercised a very undefined and irregular authority within the Territorial limits; the Judges themselves being commissioned from time to time, and not during good behavior, or the continuance of their *offices.*[2]

Feeling a deep interest in the welfare of Mr. C.[3] his situation as intimated by you gives me much pain. I have ever regarded him as a sound patriot and honest man; and there are certainly few who have made greater sacrifices of private interest to public objects. His property was of a kind that suffered most from our commercial laws before the war, and finally from that event. He nevertheless firmly concurred in all the measures to which he owes his present distresses. Of these I have been generally, but not particularly apprized. The danger which threatens his official resource, now I presume his only one, was quite new to me. As it is occasioned, not by any impeachment of his character, but some cause which I should hope is removeable by an increased energy, with the aids he has under him, I would fain infer that this remedy will be applied, on his being made sensible of its necessity. He & his friends are much indebted for the kindness you feel for him, and particularly for the salutary conversation You had with him, and which it is possible you may have an opportunity of enforcing. I thank you myself for your suggestion as to an interposition in some shape from me. I shall make the attempt, witholding every clue to the origin of it, and precluding every idea of its being other than a most friendly one. Another Station, for which he might be better fitted in the present state of his anxieties, would be the most happy expedient for him. How far this is practicable I do not venture to judge.

The fever still continues to distress us. A death took place 3 days ago. Another is not improbable in a day or two. And there are several other cases of great illness. New cases also occur faster than compleat cures. As yet the white family escape, except that of the overseer, who with his wife & 3 of his children have been very ill, but are getting well. Yrs. affy.

James Madison

RC (DLC: Monroe Papers); partial FC (DLC). RC docketed by Monroe. Partial FC in John Payne Todd's hand, with JM's note: "President Monroe Decr 28. 1820," and another, possibly added at a later date: "Consl. limitation of tenure of office." The missing portion of the partial FC was intentionally omitted by JM. Minor differences between the copies have not been noted.

1. JM, possibly at a later date, interlined "sed" above "past" in the RC.
2. Partial FC ends here.
3. Richard Cutts.

From Tench Coxe

Dear Sir Philadelphia Decr. 28. 1820

I should have replied sooner to your last favor,[1] but I had hoped to find some of the debates &ca, for the ten years, which you do not possess. I am sorry I have not yet succeeded, and I fear the rarity of them and the constant purchases by young & rising public men, foreigners, libraries &ca. may disappoint me. I will however keep your wishes constantly in view.

The Missouri case has contributed to prevent my reply to your last favor. I have paid it the attention due to its influence upon the public interests, happiness and fame. I find it difficult to get my matter brought before the public from Washington to Maine. I have taken up the subject from 1774 to this time. All the papers are in Binn's democratic Press.[2] My materials have been historical, constitutional & statutory; and I have satisfied myself, that as the black & colored people were not, in 1774. 1776. 1781. (the Confederation) 1787 the date of the constitution, parties to our social compacts (provincial or state) so that cannot *have entered* or *be admitted* without *grave and customary form*. I shew that they are excluded now in the states; and I took, before the meeting of Congress, much ground similar to that in two Intelligencers, in a speech of Mr or Judge Smith,[3] in the Senate U.S., for

South Carolina. I have also made some mild and calm addresses to the Quakers under their ecclesiastical stile *"The friends of Truth."*[4] I cover a proof copy of one of these papers to shew the vein in which I have written, and wish when you write Mr. Jefferson, you may amuse him with the perusal of it. All my copies have been sent to Washington.

The practical comments on this case of the blacks, under the broad words of our Pennsa. constitution[5] are deeply impressive. Our *electors* are all *citizens* paying taxes. We have *native* blacks and yellows, *not taxed lest they should apply to vote*, excluded by the Commissioners from *all juries and from arbitrations;* by *law* from the Militia; by *the courts* from all retail sales of wine & distilled spirits; from the benefit of *tuition* ordained, without notice of color, for *"the poor, gratis"* but tho arranged under a law *not excluding blacks & yellows*, so dispensed by *eminent quakers*, *members of the abolition society*, *that* no black or mulattoe *has ever* been admitted!

My letters, two of this day, from each side, at Washington, carry an air of determination to support Missouri on the one part, and on past fears from the overzeal of Pennsa. on the other part, which are not comfortable but do not alarm me. *I know* that many here have been convinced by the discussions since the Autum[n] of 1719,[6] that *fully enfranchised black and colored citizens* cannot be *created and maintained* as they generally stand as to qualifications. I am convinced this opinion prevails among respectable members of the abolition society. Yet some are for an abolition, *without compensation*, of all Pennsa. slaves and servants of 28 years, of slave parents, increasing the free suddenly, at a moment of Haytian civil war, extensive black & red armaments in Spanish & Portuguese America, and of great embarrassment from our own 200.000 free colored people. Our share of these people has become in Philadelphia a messy, increasing *unmanagable* evil, in the opinions of men of all politics, all churches, all conditions in life, especially the active members of our city institutions. We consider the state of things much worse, as to the blacks & mulattoes in the city of New York, from whose workhouses, common Gaols and penitentiaries we have detailed accounts. The great question here now is, how and where can they be disposed of with justice and policy. I believe therefore the intrinsic difficulties in the happy management of the free people of color has damped precipitancy in emancipation. *The case demands the United efforts of our hearts and minds.* Tho I have left myself but a line to acknowledge my sense of your kind exertions on the subject of my request, I beg you to believe that it is *deep* and *real.* I have the honor to be with perfect respect and attachment, as ever, most faithfully yours

T. Coxe

RC (DLC). Docketed by JM.

1. JM to Coxe, 24 Nov. 1820.

2. Coxe's seven essays entitled "Considerations respecting the Helots of the United States, African and Indian, native and Alien, and their descendants of the whole and the mixed blood" and signed "A Democratic Federalist" were published in John Binns's Philadelphia *Democratic Press*, 25 Nov.–22 Dec. 1820. For a discussion of their content, and that of those mentioned in n. 4 below, see Cooke, *Tench Coxe*, 512–16, and 513 n. 15.

3. For Sen. William Smith's 8 Dec. 1820 speech on the admission of Missouri, see *Annals of Congress*, 16th Cong., 2d sess., 51–77.

4. Coxe's six essays under his pseudonym "A Democratic Federalist" and entitled "To 'The Friends of Truth'" were published in the Philadelphia *Democratic Press*, 25 Dec. 1820–8 Jan. 1821 (Cooke, *Tench Coxe*, 513 n. 15). JM's copy of No. XII in the series, printed 4 Jan. 1821, is in the Library of Congress, Madison Papers, series 7, box 2, newspaper file.

5. Article 3, section 1, of the Pennsylvania Constitution of 1790 defines the qualifications for voting in state and local elections (John H. Fertig and Frank M. Hunter, comps., *Constitutions of Pennsylvania. Constitution of the United States* [Harrisburg, Pa., 1916], 188).

6. Coxe probably meant to write "1819" here.

From Thomas Mann Randolph

Dear Sir, Richmond December 28. 1820

My Brother in Law Mr Hackley informs me that he will shortly be in the neighbourhood of your Country Seat, and I ask of him to wait upon you with my homage, which it has, for such a number of years, been my pride to be allowed to pay. His long residence in the Peninsula, and his excellent understanding, and habit of observation, may perhaps enable him to afford you interesting conversation for an evening. It would be gratifying to him, for ever, to have it in his power to engage your attention, or excite enquiries from you, upon any subject which his travels have given him the opportunity of becoming acquainted with. My warm attachment to him gives me great concern in his prosperity, but I am not fully informed of his present views. As no doubt however their direction must be towards Publick affairs, in some situation suitable to his capacity, and habits of business, I take the liberty to express the gratitude which would be felt by all his numerous friends, if you were to favor him with the communication of any sentiments you might entertain of a nature to be usefull to him in such respect.

My Wife who is with me at present renews to Mrs Madison and yourself her assurances of friendship. With the most affectionate attachment I am Dear Sir your most obedt.

Th M Randolph

RC (DLC). Cover marked by Randolph: "By favor of R. S. Hackley Esqr." Docketed by JM.

From William Davis Robinson

SIR, WASHINGTON December 28th. 1820

I take the liberty of sending you by mail a volume of my memoirs of the Mexican Revolution,[1] which I request you will do me the honor to accept, and I shall be much gratified to learn that any thing containd therein compensates for the trouble of perusing it.

My career in life has not afforded me many opportunities of exploring the walks of literature, hence the style of the volume in question may be objectionable to the eye of the Critic, but as I disclaim all pretensions to the character of an Author, I trust my fellow Citizens will view with indulgence any errors in point of literary composition. Respectfully I have the honor to subscribe myself Your obedt. Servt.

WM. DAVIS ROBINSON[2]

RC (DLC). Docketed by JM.

1. William Davis Robinson, *Memoirs of the Mexican Revolution: Including a Narrative of the Expedition of General Xavier Mina. . . .* (Philadelphia, 1820; Shoemaker 3035).

2. William Davis Robinson (b. 1774) was a Philadelphia merchant and adventurer with commercial ties to Caracas and other places in Latin America. In 1816 he entered Mexico to lend his support to the revolutionaries but was soon imprisoned by the Spanish authorities and held for three years, first at Vera Cruz, and then at Ceuta in North Africa (Eduardo Enrique Ríos, *Robinson y su aventura en México*, 2d ed. [Mexico City, 1958], 5, 27, 38, 40; Samuel Flagg Bemis, *John Quincy Adams and the Foundations of American Foreign Policy* [New York, 1949], 488 n. 17).

To Mackay & Campbell

MESSRS. M. & C Dcr. 29. 1820

I have recd. yours of the 18th. & have delayed the answer a few mails hoping for a letter from Messrs. M. & L. of a like date with their last to you. The last to me was of Sepr. 13, at which time the whole of my Tobo. had not been sold, and the invoice of the goods sent me not inclosed. Perhaps a letter for me may be in the Country & you can give me some account of it. The Tobo. seems to have sold lower, & the articles shipped to have cost more than I had estimated. For the balance due, it will be agreeable to me if so to you, to stand your debtor, rather than have a remittance to make to Liverpool. With much respect

J. M

Draft (DLC). Written on the verso of cover of Mackay & Campbell to JM, 18 Dec. 1820.

To George Alexander Otis

SIR MONTPELLIER Decr. 29. 1820

Your letter of the 5th. came safe to hand, with the 2d. vol: of the translation of Botta's History, for which I am ⟨anew to offer⟩ my thanks.

Without a more careful reading of the two volumes, and comparison of them with the original, than has been permitted by other demands on my time, I could not express any opinion as to the merits of the translation that would be worth your acceptance. Of the original work the high character seems to be sufficiently established. And as far as a limited examination of your version will warrant, I cheerfully concur in the judgment that it is entitled to all the encouragement, which I hope you are receiving. The Style of a translation can rarely observe at once the exact fidelity due to the original, and all the elegance of which the translator's language is susceptible. This remark is made merely in reference to the difficulties you have to encounter, and not to imply that you have not adequately surmounted them.

The remark you cite from my former letter was not prompted by any particular instances of a failure in Mr. Botta ⟨to do justice to our⟩ Country; but by the general probability of errors which he could not easily escape, and which might be ascertained among ourselves. The probability in this case is the greater as new light on important measures of the revolution, must from time to time be brought forth, from sources not opened at the date ⟨of his⟩ work, or not then known to him.

My letter of July 5.[1] was not written for publication; but there is nothing in it I believe, which forbids any use of it you ⟨may⟩ think proper.

I find that my conjecture was but too true, as to the little prospect of subscriptions to your work in this neighborhood, at the present period. A Gentleman not of it desires that he may be set down for copies of your volumes as they come out. You will address them to "Andrew Stephenson, Richmond Virginia." With respect

JAMES MADISON

RC (MSonHi); FC (DLC). Some words on RC are illegible; words in angle brackets are supplied from the FC. FC in John Payne Todd's hand, with JM's note: "Otis Geo: A."

1. JM's letter to Otis was dated 3 July 1820.

From George Alexander Otis

Sir, Philadelphia 4th. January 1821

I beg to acknowledge the receipt of your respected letter of the 29th Ulto. and to return my grateful acknowledgements for the honour you have done me in naming my enterprise to Mr. Stephenson; to whom I shall request my Agent in Richmond to deliver a Set.

I pray you to accept Sir my Sincere thanks for the permission to make your letter of 5th July[1] public, and for your benevolent wishes of Success to my undertaking. The high character of Botta's History is indeed sufficiently established with those who have read it in the language of the author, and can admit his apology, of the example of the ancient Historians, for factitious Speeches; and whose Self-love personal or local, is not wounded by the praises he bestows, as I think, with justice.

But one of your revered predecessors in the first rank among freemen; and one whose opinions carry great weight in New England, though he is so kind as to wish well to the Success of my labours, yet has candidly written me, that "he thinks he discerns too manifest a disposition in Botta to bestow the laurels on the Southern States which ought to decorate the brows of the Northern.["] "I will mention one instance," he continues, "which you may attribute if you please to my vanity. The speeches of Mr Richard Henry Lee and Mr. John Dickinson upon the question of independence are gross impositions on mankind.["] ["]I encourage however the propagation of the work on all occasions, though it appears to me too much like Davilas History of the Civil War in France, which although it may compare as a composition with Livy, Thucydides or Sallust—and although it professes a wonderful impartiality—yet is as manifestly an apology for Catharine de Medicis, and the Cardinal de Lorraine as Humes History of England is for the Stuarts." Such are the doubts and suspicions of the venerable John Adams.[2] To which I have the mortification to add the sentiments of the leading members of the immediate government of the University of Cambridge, near Boston, Who are among the editors of the North American Review. The Rev. Professor Edward Everett[3] writes me as follows: "Sir I feel it my duty candidly to state to you our impressions, with respect to this work and your translation of it, as Subjects of notice in our Journal.["] "In the first place, it was on every ground, the unanimous feeling of those concerned in conducting the N. A. Review, that no notice should be taken of it, if it were not Such an One, as would be favorable to the interests of the work, and gratifying to your feelings.["]

"As you are concerned only in the translation, simply to have commended that, without expressing a high opinion of the *work itself*, would have been rather prejudicial than favorable to the enterprise.["] "To make the review of your translation, therefore, of Service to you, it would have been necessary to go further, and commend the work itself.["] "This would be to be done, on two grounds; either as a work comparatively speaking of merit, and remarkable as the production of a foreigner, and entitled to a place in the collection of documents relative to America; or as a work worthy of being made a popular manual of Revolutionary History. The latter, we do not consider it, for besides many positive errors, the Author has not penetrated, at all, into the Genius of our Institutions. No foreigner could be expected to do it, without long residence here. His whole work, from this cause, wears a Strange foreign air; and is marked often with vagueness and inconclusive generalities, from the Author's ignorance of the precise character of our Civil and political institutions. To have stated and enforced this, would have been doing your work what little harm our Review is able to do any work; and it would have been a poor compensation to you, to have bestowed upon the translation the commendation of which, as I have said we consider it worthy. I should feel gratified, if you would infer from this Statement, what is the real truth, that in refraining from a notice of your work we acted chiefly out of friendship for you.["] "If you wish to have it reviewed as *a translation alone*, or, in general, that we should discuss the merits of the history, you may depend on its being done with perfect fairness, and as favorably to your enterprise as conscience admits."

I beg pardon for offering so long extracts, but they serve to show that in New England, I have much more to fear for the Author, than the Translation.

The charge above laid against Botta of not having penetrated into the Genius of our institutions, is what I am most solicitous to rebut, and your Authority, who so materially contributed to founding them, would be peremptory and irrefragable. With the highest veneration, I beg leave to subscribe myself, Sir, Your Obliged Humble Servant,

George Alexander Otis

RC (DLC). Docketed by JM.

1. Otis meant JM's letter to him of 3 July 1820.

2. John Adams made a similar complaint to Thomas Jefferson in 1815, who replied that "Botta, as you observe, has put his own speculations and reasonings into the mouths of persons whom he names, but who, you and I know, never made such speeches" (Adams to Jefferson and Thomas McKean, 30 July 1815, and Jefferson to Adams, 10[-11] Aug. 1815, in *The Adams-Jefferson Letters: The Complete Correspondence between Thomas Jefferson and Abigail and John Adams*, ed. Lester J. Cappon [2 vols.; Chapel Hill, N.C., 1959], 2:451, 452).

3. Edward Everett (1794–1865), a graduate of Harvard College, was briefly minister of the Brattle Street Church in Boston, before accepting the chair of Greek Literature at Harvard in 1815. He spent the next four years in Europe, the first two in studies at the University of Göttingen, and became the first American to receive a Ph.D. In 1819 Everett returned to Harvard, where in addition to his professorship, he was editor of the *North American Review*, 1820–24. A pronounced gift of oratory led Everett into politics, which

provided opportunities for him to serve in the U.S. House of Representatives, 1825–35, as governor of Massachusetts, 1836–40, as U.S. minister to Great Britain, 1841–45, as secretary of state for four months in 1852–53, and as U.S. senator, 1853–54. He was president of Harvard College, 1846–49. He first met JM in 1814 in Washington, and the two carried on an important correspondence in JM's retirement (Paul Revere Frothingham, *Edward Everett: Orator and Statesman* [Boston, 1925], 4, 13–14, 23–25, 33–35, 38, 41, 60, 61, 67, 87–89, 125–26, 128–29, 149, 153, 179, 185, 261–62, 270, 297–98, 326–27, 340, 361, 470).

From John H. Wood

Worthy Sir, Albemarle Jany 5th. 1821.

Permit me to thank you for your polite and friendly Answer to my letter.[1] My application was certainly predicated on the presupposition that whatever relief you cou'd grant me consistently with engagements & obligations (of which we all are surrounded) wou'd have been done with willingness.

On addresses for pecuniary aid I shou'd always be entirely *indisposed* to afford any, cou'd I suppose the embarrassmt to have originated in extravagance and dissipation. My truant days (thank heaven) are over and gone. It is chiefly the affliction of my unfortunate wife for more than two years that has a little enthrald me for the present, but shou'd I meet tolerable luck this year I expect to be entirely freed from pecuniary wants.

When ruminating on the embarrassm'ts of Life, it is not unfrequent that my mind is Struck with one of the finest pieces of Morallity contained in any paper of the Spectator. Father, says a youth, "thy fortune is a very wretched if there be not another *World*"—true, son! And what is thine if there be another?[2]

My venerable mother (wou'd that I was worthy to be her son) seems to feel all the respect & veneration due to yr. exalted virtues & talents, & that sincere affection so eminently due to Mrs. Madison, her relation; to whom with yourself, I beg leave to subscribe myself most sincerely

Jno. H. Wood

RC (DLC). Addressed by Wood to JM, and franked. Cover marked "Milton Va 20 Jany." Docketed by JM.

1. Letter not found.

2. "A lewd young fellow, seeing an aged hermit go by him barefoot, 'father,' says he, 'you are in a very miserable condition if there is not another world.' 'True, son,' said the hermit, 'but what is thy condition if there is?'" (Joseph Addison and Sir Richard Steele, *The Spectator* [8 vols.; Philadelphia, 1803; Shaw and Shoemaker 5090], 8:84).

To James Monroe

DEAR SIR MONTPELLIER Jany. 6. 1821

Mr. Hackley called on me a few days ago on his way to Washington. I found him very intelligent and of agreeable manners. He observed a commendable delicacy in the part of his conversation, which touched his personal hopes from the Government; but it was not concealed that he aspired to some provision under its patronage. He will doubtless be, if he has not already been, more explicit & particular at the seat of Govt.

I can add nothing to what you know of the public career of this gentleman; and as to his actual standing at large, I must be less competent to judge than you probably are. Of his capacity for public service, I derived a higher opinion from the opportunity afforded by his visit than I had previously formed. But what I took up the pen chiefly to state, & what may be less known to you, is that he is on the best footing with Mrs. H's[1] highly respectable connections & friends, who profess a particular esteem for him; and taking a warm interest in his welfare, wd. be much gratified by any beneficial marks of the confidence of the Governt. In making this circumstance known to you, and in adding that I should of course, sympathize very sincerely in any result favorable to him and his family, I am not unaware that private wishes, are always under the controul of public considerations, and that a casting weight only can be allowed them, when an equilibrium occurs in the latter. Mr. H. I find indulges a persuasion that he will have the benefit of this weight in the friendly dispositions both of yourself and the Secretary of State. Health & success

JAMES MADISON

RC (DLC: Monroe Papers).

1. Harriet Randolph Hackley was a sister of Thomas Mann Randolph, Thomas Jefferson's son-in-law.

To William Davis Robinson

SIR Jany. 6. 1821

I have recd. your favor of Decr. 28. accompanied by a Copy of your "Memoirs of the Mexican Revolution." As I can not at present find leisure to go thro the volume, I make an offer at once, of my thanks for your obliging attention.

So little is known of the late events & of the actual State of things in Mexico, which well deserve to be known, that accurate information as to both must be particularly acceptable to the people of the U.S. who take so deep an interest in the destinies of that neighboring section of the American hemisphere, and I am led to ⟨b⟩elieve that accounts at once accurate & authentic are no where so likely to be found as in the work you have just given to the public. I promise myself therefore much pleasure in the perusal of it. I may add that from the few pages into which I have dipped, there wd seem to be less occasion than you have presumed for the apologies you offer for its literary execution. Be pleased to accept my respects & my good wishes.

J. M

Draft (DLC).

To Thomas Jefferson

Dear Sir Montpellier Jany 7. 1821

In The inclosed[1] you will see the ground on which I forward it for your perusal.

In the late views taken by us, of the Act of Congress, vacating periodically the Executive offices,[2] it was not recollected, in justice to the President, that the measure was not without precedents. I suspect however that these are confined to the Territorial Establishments, where they were introduced by the Old Congs. in whom all powers of Govt. were confounded; and continued by the new Congress, who have exercised a like confusion of powers within the same limits. Whether the Congressional code contains any precedent of a like sort, more particularly misleading the President I have not fully examined. If it does, it must have blindly followed the territorial examples.

We have had for several months a typhus fever in the family, which does not yield in the least, to the progress of the season. Out of twenty odd cases, there have been six deaths, and there are several depending cases threatening a like issue. The fever has not yet reached any part of our White family; but in the Overseers, there have been five cases of it including himself. None of them however have been mortal. Health & every other blessing

James Madison

RC (DLC). Docketed by Jefferson "recd Jan. 11."

1. JM enclosed Tench Coxe to JM, 28 Dec. 1820.

2. For the congressional act, see Tench Coxe to JM, 12 Nov. 1820, and n. 2.

To Robert Mackay

DR. SIR Jany 7. 1821

An accident to the Saw of my Sawmill requires a new one immediately, the season being now favorable for using it. Will you be so obliging as to have a good one chosen, & held ready for the application of Mr. Howard's waggoner, who will be down very quickly after this reaches you. If he shd fail, I will authorise some other waggoner to bring up the Saw.

The sickness in my family and other circumstances have suspended the carr[i]age of my flour to Market. As you can estimate the prospect of prices better than I can at this distance I must leave it with your discretion, to dispose of what may be on hand or hereafter arrives at whatever moment you may judge most favorable. Be so good as to drop me a Sketch of the state of Accts. between us. Yrs. with friend[l]y respects.

J. M

Draft (DLC).

From James Barbour

DEAR SIR WASHINGTON Jany 8th. 21

I understood when at your house that you were in want of a good riding horse. In consequence when I returned here, having found the one I had bought of Mr Johnson[1] the writer of the within a very fine one I mentioned to him your wish. In answer he returned me the enclosed note.[2] If you think proper to avail yourself of his offer and should choose either of the horses and signify which to me I will advance the money for you here which you can restore me on my return to Virginia. Most respectfully Your Friend

JAMES BARBOUR

RC and enclosure (DLC). RC addressed by Barbour to JM, and franked. Docketed by JM. For enclosure, see n. 2.

1. Francis Johnson (1776–1842) was a Virginia-born, Kentucky lawyer who served in the U.S. House of Representatives, 1820–27.

2. The enclosure is Francis Johnson to Barbour, 8 Jan. 1821 (2 pp.), offering two "good riding Horses" for sale, one for $150, the other for $100. "The latter is the best pacer, the Other trots & paces both—they are some thing above 15 hands high. Mr. Madison may send down and have either or both of them taken up to his house and try them, if he Chooses so to do—and return either or both if he should not like them.

"I know them both to be servicable Horses. The bay Horse Lance I have rode for more than two Years—when in order he is a remarkable fine horse and is Shewy & pleasant to ride, a little head Strong when kept from exercise for some time, but has no tricks, and requires a stiff bitt. The Other Horse Bob perhaps the tallest, is a very gentle pleasant horse to ride, he is Six Years old next Spring & the Other 7. as well as I now recollect."

From Tench Coxe

DEAR SIR PHILADELPHIA Jan. 8. 1821.

I have heard of a collection of the debates in Congress between 1790 and 1800, which are to be shewn to me and will at least direct my searches and attention. Perhaps want of money, which exists in the case, may occasion a sale. If it should I shall make the terms known to you.

Our state after 41 years, and with only 700 to 800 slaves in 1810 are about to pass a final abolition act, paying every owner a value by arbitration or a jury as he may prefer, if they do not accept the slave at his value. As our law of 1780[1] gave nothing for value or damage and this is to give it by a bill drawn by a counsellor at law of our abolition society it makes the states with many slaves safe and free from the ruinous and disorganizing pretense that there is in our states & union no property in slaves. I have carefully conferred with one of Philadelphia county senators, who moved the resolution at Harrisburg and with the counsellor who in cooperation with Mr. Rawle their president, drew the pending bill. Pennsa. having 3800 slaves in 1790 has spread her slow gradual abolition of slavery over a period of 41 years tho joined on the east west & north by states with few slaves.

I have on my table a 12th number of my series of papers, which I enclose for your amusement.[2] The last N. 13 will appear to morrow. The emphatic manner, in which I maintained in all of them the rights of property, to which the abolition as a general consideration feel the greatest respect, has I am satisfied convinced such men as Messrs. Rawle, Sargeant, Binny,[3] Ingersoll & Morgan that no law could be advocated by men of their characters, which did not provide full & prompt payment.

I shall be glad after you have satisfied yourself with the enclosed, if you will cover it to him with my respects. I wish as long as I shall live that the details of my conduct and the grounds of it may be known and understood by you and by him.

The English quarterly review in a tract upon Germany undertakes to give a concluding paragraph, wch. will be translated into the German in Hanover and circulated through that interesting Empire defaming us for having refused *in Congress* the abolition of Slavery in Missouri; while "despotic Russia" is abolishing slavery.[4] We are cultivating in New York & Pennsylvania, and shall send a full reply. It will be published here on the first dearth of foreign Intelligence. I have endeavoured also in drawing it to throw in sedatives for the Missouri agitations. Great Britain is not popular among the old unappostate revolutionary men North of Maryland nor with the constitutional, republican or democratic interest there, and we believe that they are much changed since the first hasty feelings on the Missouri case.

If Spain has really ratified our Florida treaty, her abolition of the papal & ecclesiastical pomp, wealth, luxury, despotism, and general march in Europe with her moderation in S America renders her truly and deeply interesting to us and all other real friends of civil & religious liberty. I should not be surprized if she expressed her dissatisfaction at the treatment Austria seems to contemplate of Naples, & many in France would be pleased at her interfering in like manner.

You have seen with comfort that our exports by the return to Sept 30. 1820 amount to almost 70,000,000. The first year of this government was 18,000,000. The œconomy of money, of expenditures public & private and generally our encreased prudence on the pecuniary subject are working wonders for us. I have the honor to be with perfect respect dear Sir yr. most obedt h Servt

TENCH COXE

Genl. Hiester[5] has appointed but two officers, his Secretary & Attorney General. He had urgent federal applications of abilities and weight; but did not give them either of those important offices. Mr. Gregg[6] you know Mr. Elder[7] is also a Democrat. Mr. Hiester will not be separated from the republican administration of the Union and Mr. Mo[n]roe has his entire confidence and decided attachment.

RC (DLC). Addressed by Coxe to JM, and franked. Docketed by JM.

1. For Pennsylvania's Gradual Emancipation Act of 1 Mar. 1780, see Paul Finkelman, *Slavery and the Founders: Race and Liberty in the Age of Jefferson* (Armonk, N.Y., 1996), 83–85, 189 n. 10.

2. For Coxe's pseudonymous essays under the title, "To The Friends of Truth," see his letter to JM, 28 Dec. 1820, and n. 4.

3. Horace Binney (1780–1875), a graduate of Harvard College and a Federalist in politics, was a Philadelphia lawyer and legal writer who held a number of state and municipal offices before serving a term in the U.S. House of Representatives, 1833–35 (Charles Chauncey Binney, *The Life of Horace Binney, with Selections from His Letters* [Philadelphia, 1903], 2, 22, 28, 38, 48, 49, 54–55, 57–59, 72, 100, 104, 131, 437).

4. "State of Society, &c. in Germany," *Quarterly Review* 23 (July 1820): 454.

5. Joseph Hiester (1752–1832), a Revolutionary War veteran and five-term Pennsylvania state assemblyman, served in the U.S. House of Representatives, 1797–1805, and 1815–20. In 1807 Hiester was appointed a major general in the Pennsylvania militia. He was governor of Pennsylvania, 1820–23 (Sobel and Raimo, *Biographical Directory of the Governors*, 3:1298–99).

6. Andrew Gregg (1755–1835), a veteran of the Revolutionary War, served in the U.S. House of Representatives, 1791–1807, and in the U.S. Senate, 1807–13. In 1820 he was appointed secretary of the Commonwealth by Governor Hiester, and three years later he ran

unsuccessfully for governor of Pennsylvania (William Henry Egle, *Pennsylvania Genealogies; Scotch-Irish and German* [Harrisburg, Pa., 1886], 246–47).

7. Thomas Elder (1767–1853), a Harrisburg lawyer, was attorney general of Pennsylvania, 1820–23 (Charles P. Keith, *The Provincial Councillors of Pennsylvania Who Held Office between 1733 and 1766 . . .* [Philadelphia, 1883], 203).

From Andrew Stevenson

Dear sir, Richmond January 8 1821.

Your favor of the 10 ulto[1] I recd in the course of the mail, & owe you an apology for not answering it sooner; but the truth is that what with personal indisposition, & professional & Legislative duties, I have not had an opportunity of doing so, until today. Since I last wrote you Mr. R. & myself have made the promised search amongst his father's papers,[2] for yr. letters, & I am pleased to say, tht I have obtaind *abt. one hundred & forty* in number, embracing the entire period of time between '82 & 90. Altho' I have looked into them all, I cannot say they contain *all* you wish & expect, inasmuch as many are written in *Cypher*, & the Cypher not filled out by Mr. R., & of course their contents wholly unintelligible to me. I have sent them to you by mail, having carefully put them up with my own hands, & received an asurance from the Postmaster tht there wd. be no risque in sending them. I hope they will reach you safely. I also send you the *new work* of Jno. Taylor of Caroline, upon the Constitution,[3] of which I spoke when I was last up. Altho' I am conscious my dr. sir, that you need no arguments at this day, *to convince* or *enlighten* you, on the important subjects which it discusses, & I ought probably to ask pardon for the liberty I now take in sending it to you & asking yr. opinion of its merits, yet I cannot but think, that it will give you pleasure to see the true principles of our *Gov't* & *Constitution* so well understood, & ably discussed, & the standard of the good old republican doctrines of '98 '99 so triumphantly unfolded & displayed. It is believed by the most enlightened people here, to be a work peculiarly interesting at this time to the public, & eminently calculated to do good, in arousing the people of the union, from the fatal apathy into which they have sunk, upon the important subject on which it treats. I am too unequal myself to speak of the style of this work, you know the author, & his manner of writing pen; there are certainly many parts of it, *obscure* & *quaint*, tho' freely & fearlessly written; but possibly this is well, for if with such powers & lights, as the author possesses, he had the style & power of composition of Tom Paine, the consequences might be [*illegible*] in the fear of a revolution. For my single self, I do not hesitate to express the opinion, tht if his work does not lay a *foundation* deep in public opinion, & produce some active & beneficial result, the constitution is gone & the

States will soon sink into the gulph of consolidation. Indeed, Virginia is now almost the only State in the Union, who *seems to feel* on *this subject;* & to her glory it may be said, that she is the only one of her sisters who seems disposed to maintain the worship *of the principles of* the revolution & *those of '98; undefiled.* These are *my opinions,* & for their free expression, I know I shall be excused; feeling assured that you will receive them as the evidence of a cordial disposition towards the most friendly & respectful sentiments.

We regret much the disappointment, in not seeing you & Mrs M. this winter; for be assured my dr Sir, there are none on Earth, we should be more delighted to see under our humble roof than you *two.* I trust we shall yet be gratified. I beg leave to say to Mr Todd, tht I hope his engagemts, will not prevent his coming amongst us, according to promise. With sents. of perfect esteem & regard I am most respectfully Dr. sir Yr. fd hbl. srt

AND: STEVENSON

RC (CSmH).

1. Letter not found.

2. For JM's desire to retrieve his correspondence with Edmund Randolph through the aid of Peyton Randolph and Andrew Stevenson, see Stevenson to JM, 3 Dec. 1820.

3. For John Taylor of Caroline's *Construction Construed, and Constitutions Vindicated,* see Edmond Kelly to JM, 6 Dec. 1820, n. 12.

From William S. Cardell

DEAR SIR, NEW YORK 12th. Jan 1821.

The literary institution on which I before had the honor to address you[1] has become organised with very encouraging prospects. The enclosed circular which is in part an amplification of my former letter explains the outlines as far as it was thought proper to form them by anticipation.

The officers elected are His Ex. J. Q. Adams President. Judge Livingston, Judge Story[2] Hon. William Lowndes, V. Presdts. Alex. McLeod D.D. Rec. Sec.[3] John Stearns M.D.[4] (President of N.Y. State Med. Society) Treasurer. Counsellors—Chancellor Kent,[5] Daniel Webster, Boston. Bishop Brownell, Con.[6] J. M. Mason D.D. Joseph Hopkinson, N.J. P.S. Du Ponceau LL.D. Phil. John L. Taylor, C. Justice N. Car.[7] H. Clay, Kentucky. Washington Irving, now in London. There are 2 vacancies. Doct. Smith[8] of William & Mary College will be elected to fill one and probably the President of Dartmouth or Bowdoin College,[9] the other.

We have returns, generally cordial and able, from the officers elected except that from Mr. Clay we have not heard.

Among other transactions of the Society Sir, it is made my duty respectfully to communicate to you their unanimous election of you as an Honorary member.

The other Honorary members are Hon. John Adams, Thomas Jefferson, James Munroe, John Jay, C.C. Pinckney and John Trumbull.

In electing as honorary members of this new Society those citizens who have passed thro all forms and degrees of honor which a nation could confer, our scholars could not of course suppose they were imparting any additional dignity; but it was the highest tribute of respect in their power to offer, and the cordial approbation expressed by those distinguishd men gives to the institution the means of additional usefulness to our country.

In the expectation of forwarding in a few days a printed schetch of proceedings, I forbear, Sir, to trouble you with further details at this time. Accept, Sir, the assurance of my highest respect.

W. S. Cardell Cor. Sec.
Am. Acad. of Lan. & Belles Lettr⟨es⟩

[First Enclosure]

Dear Sir, New-York, October 1, 1820.

Your attention is respectfully requested to an association of Scholars for the purpose of improving American literature. This association, though yet at its commencement and unknown to the public, has been the subject of an interesting correspondence for some months past; and it is believed will not be deemed unimportant as connected with the best interests of our country.

To settle at once a point on which some difference might exist, it is not designed, independent of England, to form an American language, farther than as it relates to the numerous and increasing names and terms peculiarly American; but to cultivate a friendly correspondence with any similar association or distinguished individuals in Great Britain, who may be disposed to join us in an exertion to improve our common language.

The objects of such an institution which directly present themselves, are, to collect and interchange literary intelligence; to guard against local or foreign corruptions, or to correct such as already exist; to settle varying orthography; determine the use of doubtful words and phrases; and, generally, to form and maintain, as far as practicable, an English standard of writing and pronunciation, correct, fixed, and uniform, throughout our extensive territory. Connected with this, and according to future ability, may be such rewards for meritorious productions, and such incentives to improvement, in the language and literature of our country, and in the general system of instruction, as from existing circumstances may become proper.

These objects will not be thought trifling, by those who have spent much time in the cultivation of literature, or attended to its influence on society. Such persons need not be told how directly they are connected with our progress in general knowledge, or our public reputation; or that their influence may extend from social to national intercourse, and to our commercial prosperity. Perspicuity in language is the basis of all science. The philosophy that professes to teach the knowledge of *things*, independent of *words*, needs only to be mentioned among enlightened men to be rejected.

Most of the European nations have considered the improvement of language as an important national object, and have established academies, with extensive funds and privileges, for that purpose. An interference of the government has, perhaps, been omitted in England, from a singular and rather accidental reliance on the acknowledged superiority of a few leading individuals; and so long as all the literature in the English language had its origin and center in London, there was less danger in thus leaving it to the guidance of chance. Science may be comparatively recluse; but literature is social; and American scholars, spread over 2,000,000 square miles, are not to be drawn to a virtual and national association, without the form.

It is very properly said of France that its literature has frequently saved the country when its arms have failed. The advantages resulting to that nation, from the exertions of a few academicians, have been incalculable, and may serve to show, in some degree, what such a confederacy of scholars is capable of performing. The effect of their influence was not barely to elevate France in the literary world, and to improve its learning within itself; but to extend their language throughout Europe; to introduce, at the expense of other nations, their books, their opinions, and, in aid of other causes, their political preponderance. The Philological Academies of Italy and Spain, though unaided by the same powerful co-operation, have effected very great improvements in the language and literature of their respective countries. The great work now performing by the German scholars, in addition to what they have before done, is a noble example to other nations, and calculated to elevate the condition of our nature. With how much greater force does every consideration connected with this subject, apply, in a free community, where all depends upon the virtue and intelligence of the great body of the people.

Without dwelling a moment on invidious comparisons between England and the United States, the time appears to have arrived, in reference to ourselves, when, having acquired a high standing among nations, having succeeded in a fair trial of the practicability and excellence of our civil institutions, our scholars are invited to call their convention and to form the constitution of national literature.

We have some peculiar advantages in an attempt to establish national uniformity in language. Happily for us, our forefathers came chiefly from that part of England where their language was most correctly spoken, and were possessed of a good degree of intelligence, according to the learning of that time. Though in a country as diversified as ours, there are, from various causes, many particular corruptions, we hardly find any thing that can properly be called a provincial dialect. We have at present no very inveterate habits to correct, where gross barbarisms, through large districts, are to be encountered. The attempt therefore, seasonably and judiciously made, presents a prospect not only of success, but of comparative facility. Our scattered population seem only to want from a competent tribunal, a declaration of what is proper, to guide them in their practice. The present appearances are more favorable than the most sanguine among the projectors of the plan dared to predict. There is the best reason to expect the general concurrence of our distinguished literary men in favor of a measure which promises so many advantages, so nationally important in its principles and effects, and to which so little can be objected. It is deemed unnecessary at present to dwell minutely on the details of the plan, which probably will not be difficult to settle, if the leading principles are generally approved. It is equally useless to enter upon a train of arguments to prove the advantages of such an association under the present circumstances of our country. The commanding influence of literature upon national wealth and power, as well as morals, character, and happiness, especially in free communities, will not be doubted by those whose minds have been most directed to this interesting branch of civil policy. Perhaps there never has been, and never may be, a nation more open to the influence of moral causes, than the American Republic at the present time. In every country truly free, public opinion is in effect the governing law; and public opinion, and all the complicated interests of society, greatly depend on the state of national literature. That independence which is our boast must consist in the proper independence of the mind. Without contemning the experience of past ages, we ought not too slavishly to follow the path of others. It is enough to respect the Europeans as honorable competitors, without regarding them as absolute masters. American ambition should aspire to noble objects, if we mean to rise to excellence: for, besides that the imitator is almost necessarily inferior to his model, the old world can furnish no model suited to the circumstances and character of our country. We are a world by ourselves. Our privileges, resources, and prospects, are of the highest order. Happily exempt from hereditary despotism or bigoted hierarchies, from jealous and powerful bordering nations; the professed advocates of rational freedom, the world may justly claim from us an example worthy of such a situation and such a cause. Our numbers and wealth are greater than those of England were, when the last of her splendid colleges was erected; we may have the learning of Europeans in common stock, with an exemption from their burdens, and the highest eminence which others have attained, ought to be the American starting point in the career of national greatness.

And is there any thing impossible, or even particularly difficult, in reducing these ideas to practice? Without expecting to render human nature perfect, or to fix an unalterable standard for living language and literature, may there not be some regulation which will place the decisions of the wise in preference to the blunders of the ignorant? When can a more favorable time be expected, to correct the irregularities yearly multiplying upon us, and becoming more and more embodied with the literature of our country? Why should chance be expected to accomplish, what, from its nature, can result only from well-regulated system? It would indeed be imprudent to attempt too much. Sound discretion will point out a middle course between a wild spirit of innovation and a tame acquiescence in obvious error. Language is too important an instrument in human affairs to have its improvement regarded as useless or trifling. Of all the objects of national identity, affection, and pride, national literature is the most laudable, the most operative, and the most enduring. It is to the scholars of antiquity we owe all we know of their statesmen and heroes, and even their distinctive national existence. In the long train of ages their tables of brass have mouldered away, and their high-wrought columns crumbled to dust. Cities have sunk, and their last vestige been lost. The unconscious Turk half-tills the soil manured with decayed sculpture: but the monuments of genius and learning, more durable than marble and brass, remain the subject of undecreasing admiration and delight. The fame to which great minds aspire, is, to soar above the local contentions of the day, and live to after ages in the esteem of their fellow men. The thought of this animates the patriot's hope and nerves his arm, in danger, toil, and want. Shall it not be the ambition of Americans to proclaim the honor of their benefactors, and transmit the glory of their country to the latest age of the world? We are not here to awe the ignorant by the splendor of royal trappings, but to command the respect of the wise and good by moral greatness. These objects are neither above the capacity, nor beneath the attention, of our countrymen. They are interwoven with our individual happiness, our national character, and our highest interests. When we survey this vast assemblage of States, independent, yet united; competitors in useful improvement, yet members of one great body; the world has never prepared such a theatre for the exhibition of mental and moral excellence: and if the men of all ages, whom we most delight to honor, have made it their chief glory to advance the literature of their respective countries, shall it be degradingly supposed, that, in this favored land, either talents or zeal will be wanting in such a cause? If it is said, that Americans have not paid that attention to education which the subject demanded; it is true; and neither justice nor sound policy requires us to disguise the fact: but has any fatality ordained that the people most interested in diffusing the light of instruction, *must* be degraded in the republic of letters? Much irritation has been produced by the observations of foreign writers upon the learning and intellect of our countrymen. We ought not to waste time in idle complaint on this subject. Is there not in America enough of genius, of scholarship, and of patriotic spirit, if properly organized and conducted, to raise our literary character above the influence of any combination abroad? Shall our numberless blessings remain an unprized possession? Will foreign pens maintain and elevate American character? Is it not time to make a *national* stand in the *moral* world, as the expositors of our own principles, the vindicators of our institutions, and, under a Beneficent Providence, the arbiters of the destiny of unborn millions? Even if, contrary to all human expectation, such an association should fail in its objects, would it not justly be said, '*magnis tamen excidit ausis*'?[10]

It is not intended to bring the society before the public by a premature and unnecessary parade, but to make it known chiefly by its practical good.

The following is a general outline of the institution alluded to, subject of course to such variations as may be thought to increase the prospect of its utility.

To be called "The American Academy of Language and Belles Lettres."

Its prime object is to harmonize and determine the English language; but it will also, according to its discretion and means, embrace every branch of useful and elegant literature, and especially whatever relates to our own country.

To be located in the city of New-York, where accommodations will be furnished free from expense.

To commence with fifty members; maximum number, one hundred and twenty. More than that would lessen the credit of membership, and diminish rather than increase its authority.

Members to be divided into three classes. Resident, who reside in or near New-York; Corresponding, those whose distance prevents their regular attendance; and honorary, those at home or abroad, whom the body may think proper expressly to admit as such: but, perhaps, it will be thought best to make very few honorary members in the United States. The only reason for making a difference between resident and corresponding members, is to give to the latter all practicable privileges and facilities in communicating their opinions, propositions and votes in writing, as a compensation for the difficulties of personal attendance. In questions requiring a ballot, the written opinions and wishes of distant members are taken as votes on all points to which they directly relate. As most of the questions likely to arise will relate to written language, and as few of them will require haste in the decision, there will be a particular fitness in arriving at a general result through the means of the various opinions in writing.

It will be a standing request, though not absolutely required, that each member shall, within one year after his admission, deliver personally, or by writing, a discourse upon some subject relating to language or general literature, or to the situation and interests of the United States.

The Society, when organized, will send a respectful communication to such literary gentlemen in the British dominions as may be thought proper, explaining to them the design of the establishment, and inviting their co-operation. Public policy, as well as general convenience will point out to them the importance of improving our language, facilitating its acquisition to foreigners as well as native citizens, and preserving its uniformity throughout the extensive regions where it now does, or hereafter may prevail.

The *Modus Operandi* should be the result of the joint wisdom of the body, when formed; but almost every disputed point in language, and in ours they are very numerous, may be made a CASE, subjected to rule as far as possible, and brought to a decision, endeavoring to have this decision concurrent between the British and ourselves.

But besides the acknowledged corruptions which prevail in the language of this country, our peculiar institutions and circumstances; our discoveries and improvements, have given rise to a large class of new words, *Americanisms*, if the critics please; necessary to express new things. To adopt and regulate these is not to alter the English language; but only to supply its deficiencies. This is particularly a work of our own. It is also important that attention should be paid to the numerous names of places, French, Spanish and Aboriginal, which are daily becoming incorporated with our literature, and concerning which so much diversity at present exists.

The unprofitable disputes among teachers and the authors of elementary books, who are often very unskilful advocates of their opposing systems, and whose arguments tend only to increase a difference which ought not to exist, would be in a great degree obviated. The *professors of* RHETORIC *and* LOGICK, *in our best universities, should at least agree in spelling the names of the important sciences they teach.* Our numerous youth would then be left free to pursue the straight course to the knowledge of a language which might be, not only strong and copious, but, to a far greater extent, regular and fixed. In addition to other advantages, there cannot be a rational doubt that such an institution may have a beneficial influence in exciting emulation and national concert, in our literature in general, and that many might be drawn to this interesting subject, who are now less profitably and less honorably employed in other pursuits.

The object here contemplated is certainly of sufficient national importance to merit an adequate fund from the public. Should this fail, it would be improper to lay a burdensome expense on the members. Expenditures to any considerable amount are not considered indispensably necessary; for though individuals may not be able to accomplish all that may be desired, much may be done at a moderate actual expense. Twenty-five dollars at the admission of a member, and two dollars a year afterwards, though trifling to some, is considered enough to impose by any imperative rule.

The only objections which have been made to the proposed plan, are on the ground of its practicability. The difficulties alleged are, the superiority of the British in literature; the contempt with which they will look on our institutions and offers of correspondence; the prejudices of our own people in their favor, and the consequent necessity of waiting for them to lead the way. These difficulties, if correct to the extent that some of our citizens seem inclined to admit, show at least the necessity of TRYING to produce a favorable change. If in literature and science we are greatly inferior to any other people, it is not because we are deficient in natural, political, or moral advantages, or have not as strong reasons as any nation ever had to encourage letters; but because we have hitherto neglected any general or systematic means for their advancement. The arguments are fallacious which attempt to find in the circumstances or dispositions of our people any disqualification for the highest mental attainments. American genius and enterprise properly directed, may as well be displayed in the highest walks of literature and science as in any thing else. One difficulty is our scholars, as such, have very little intercourse, and have too long been strangers to each other. *Homo solus imbecilis.*[11]

Concert will excite a generous emulation. This, upon the plan proposed, will operate upon a vast and highly reputable field; it will be identified with the national character and the dearest interests of a great and rising people, and cannot fail to produce excellence and command patronage and respect. The bare circumstance of exciting attention to the subject is an important point gained. '*Aude et faciat.*'[12] A colonial servility in literature is as unworthy of our country as political dependence. The necessary limits of this letter forbid a course of reasoning upon the subject: it may be thought proper to give a fuller exposition in a pamphlet form. The general principles explained above are deemed sufficient as the basis of preparatory arrangement.

Among the respectable persons consulted respecting the proposed institution, the sentiment, as far as ascertained, is very general and zealous in its favor. It is designed to carry it into effect with as little delay as sound discretion, in refererence to character and advantageous arrangements for a favorable commencement will admit.

The constitution formed for the Society[13] is purposely a very short one, intended chiefly as the basis for a commencement. A body of scholars, associated for the laudable object of promoting the literature of their country, many of them very familiar with public proceedings, will need fewer legal rules than a bank or a state. Whatever may be the deficiencies of this constitution, experience will be more competent to supply them than any wisdom of anticipation.

From the peculiar circumstances of our country, the institution will have no guide in any thing which has gone before; but liberal criticism will make some allowance for the difficulties necessarily attendant on first attempts. The same regular progress will not be expected in an untrodden field as on a well travelled road; but in pursuing a noble object with good intention, there is the consolation that those best qualified to judge are least inclined to condemn. If our beginning is a small one, so was that of the Royal Society of London; and we can have no reason to dread more obloquy from the illiberal, than they received.

Very generous subscriptions, by a number of gentlemen who are not expected to be members, are volunteered, *pro patria*,[14] and there is an encouraging prospect for funds. If among the variety of character in our country, there is a portion too ignorant, or too grovelling, to depart from their own narrow views of immediate gain, it is hoped that, among ten millions of people, there are enough possessed of talent to estimate, and spirit to maintain, an institution whose aim is to promote the best interests and lasting honor of the United States. In such a cause it is deemed unnecessary for the institution to solicit pecuniary aid, farther than by a fair exposition of its principles and objects. The subscriptions are to be a free-will offering upon the altar of our country: yet it will be no less creditable to the society, than just in itself, to hold in grateful remembrance and transmit to future generations, the names of those generous citizens who, by their donations, become at once, the patrons of learning and the vindicators of the American name. It may be one of the good effects of this society to bring patriotic generosity more into fashion, by causing it to be more honored. In behalf of the Association, Sir, I have the honor to be, Very respectfully and truly yours,

William S. Cardell

RC (DLC); printed enclosures (DLC: Madison Collection, Rare Book and Special Collections Division). RC addressed by Cardell to JM, and franked. Cover docketed by JM. For second enclosure, see n. 13.

1. See Cardell to JM, 4 Mar. 1820.

2. Joseph Story (1779–1845) of Marblehead, Massachusetts, graduated from Harvard College in 1798 and practiced law in Salem. He served in the U.S. House of Representatives

for one term, 1808–9, as a Jeffersonian Republican, and several terms in the Massachusetts legislature. JM appointed him associate justice of the U.S. Supreme Court in 1811, and he served in that capacity until his death. A prolific legal scholar, Story was also professor of law at Harvard, 1829–45.

3. Alexander McLeod (1774–1833), Scottish-born Reformed Presbyterian minister, came to the United States in 1792, and settled near Albany, New York. He graduated from Union College in 1798. McLeod accepted a call to the ministry for the united congregations of New York and Wallkill in 1803 and held that position until his death (Samuel Brown Wylie, *Memoir of Alexander McLeod, D.D., New York* [New York, 1855], 13, 18, 22, 54, 518).

4. John Stearns (1770–1848), a graduate of Yale College in 1789, trained as a physician in Philadelphia and began practice near Waterford, New York, in 1793. He was a founder of the Medical Society of the State of New York, and was its president, 1817–20 (Howard A. Kelly, *A Cyclopedia of American Medical Biography* . . . [2 vols.; Philadelphia, 1912], 2:403–4).

5. James Kent (1763–1847) of Dutchess County, New York, graduated from Yale College in 1781 and practiced law in Poughkeepsie, and later, in New York City. He was appointed judge of the state supreme court by John Jay in 1798, and chief judge of the court in 1804. From 1814 to 1823 Kent served as chancellor of the New York Court of Chancery. He also was professor of law at Columbia College, 1793–98, and 1823–26. Kent is best known for his *Commentaries on American Law*, which went through many editions.

6. Thomas Church Brownell (1779–1865), a graduate of Union College in 1804, taught at his alma mater, 1805–17, rising to professor of rhetoric and chemistry. He received his doctorate in divinity from Columbia and Union in 1819, and was consecrated bishop of Connecticut that same year. Brownell was the founder of Trinity College in Hartford, Connecticut (William Stevens Perry, *The Episcopate in America: Sketches, Biographical and Bibliographical, of the Bishops of the American Church* . . . [New York, 1895], 45).

7. John Louis Taylor (1769–1829), an English-born lawyer from North Carolina, was appointed judge of the superior courts in 1798, becoming chief justice in 1811. He was first chief justice of the North Carolina Supreme Court, 1819–29 (Powell, *Dictionary of North Carolina Biography*, 6:11–12).

8. John Augustine Smith (1782–1865), a graduate of the College of William and Mary in 1800, was educated in England as a physician, practicing first in Virginia and then in New York City. He was among the first faculty members at the College of Physicians and Surgeons in 1807. Smith was elected president of his alma mater in 1814 and served until 1825, when he returned to New York and his former position on the faculty of the College of Physicians and Surgeons. He became president of the college in 1831 and retired in 1843.

9. At this time Daniel Dana was president of Dartmouth College, and William Allen was president of Bowdoin College.

10. *Magnis tamen excidit ausis:* it fell, having nevertheless dared great things.

11. *Homo solus imbecillus:* a lone man is weak.

12. *Aude et faciat:* dare and it will be done.

13. Also enclosed was a one-page printed "Constitution of the American Academy of Language and Belles Lettres," dated 15 June 1820, and signed by Cardell and four others.

14. *Pro patria:* for country.

From Thomas Jefferson

Dear Sir Monticello Jan. 13. 21.

I return you mr. Coxe's letter[1] without saying I have read it. I made out enough to see that it was about the Missouri question, and the printed paper told me on which side he was. Could I have devoted a day to it, by interlining the words as I could pick them out, I might have got at more. The lost books of Livy or Tacitus might be worth this. Our friend would do well to write less and write plainer.

I am sorry to hear of the situation of your family, and the more so as that species of fever is dangerous in the hands of our medical boys. I am not a physician & still less a quack but I may relate a fact. While I was at Paris, both my daughters were taken with what we formerly called a nervous fever, now a typhus, distinguished very certainly by a thread-like pulse, low, quick and every now and then fluttering. Dr. Gem,[2] an English physician, old, & of great experience, & certainly the ablest I ever met with, attended them. The one was about 5. or 6. weeks ill, the other 10. years old was 8. or ten weeks. He never gave them a single dose of physic. He told me it was a disease which tended with certainty to wear itself off, but so slowly that the strength of the patient might first fail if not kept up. That this alone was the object to be attended to by nourishment and stimulus. He forced them to eat a cup of rice, or panada, or gruel, or of some of the farinaceous substance of easy digestion every 2. hours and to drink a glass of Madeira, the youngest took a pint of Madeira a day without feeling it and that for many weeks. For costiveness, injections were used; and he observed that a single dose of medicine taken into the stomach and consuming any of the strength of the patient was often fatal. He was attending a grandson of Mde. Helvetius,[3] of 10. years old at the same time, & under the same disease. The boy got so low that the old lady became alarmed and wished to call in another physician for consultation. Gem consented. That physician gave a gentle purgative, but it exhausted what remained of strength, and the patient expired in a few hours.

I have had this fever in my family 3. or 4. times since I have lived at home, and have carried between 20. & 30. patients thro' it without losing a single one, by a rigorous observance of Gem's plan and principle. Instead of Madeira I have used toddy of French brandy about as strong as Madeira. Brown preferred this stimulus to Madeira. I rarely had a case, if taken in hand early, to last above 1. 2. or 3. weeks, except a single one of 7. weeks, in whom, when I thought him near his last, I discovered a change in his pulse to regularity, and in 12 hours he was out of danger. I vouch for these facts only, not for their theory. You may, on their authority, think it expedient to try a single case before it has shewn signs of danger.

On the portentous question before Congress, I think our Holy alliance[4] will find themselves so embarrassed with the difficulties presented to them as to find their solution only in yielding to Missouri her entrance on the same footing with the other states, that is to say with the right to admit or exclude slaves at her own discretion. Ever & affectionately yours

TH: JEFFERSON

P.S. I should have observed that the same typhus fever prevailed in my neighborhood at the same times as in my family, and that it was very fatal in the hands of our Philadelphia Tyros.

RC (DLC: Rives Collection, Madison Papers); FC (DLC: Jefferson Papers).

1. Tench Coxe to JM, 28 Dec. 1820, with its enclosure.

2. Richard Gem (1717–1800) was physician to the British embassy at Paris and an associate of Thomas Jefferson there. It was Gem who provoked Jefferson to write his famous letter, "the earth belongs in usufruct to the living," which led to JM's rebuttal (*PJM*, 11:414 n. 1, 13:18; Boyd, *Papers of Thomas Jefferson*, 15:384–86, 391–92).

3. Anne-Catherine de Ligniville, Madame Helvétius (1722–1800), widow of the French writer, Claude-Adrien Helvétius, was well-known for the literary salon she hosted for decades in Auteuil outside Paris (Jean-Paul de Lagrave, Marie-Thérèse Inguenaud, and David Smith, *Madame Helvétius et la Société d'Auteuil* [Oxford, England, 1999], xi, xii, xiii, xviii, 1).

4. By "Holy alliance," Jefferson meant the Federalists, led by Rufus King, who were blocking Missouri's entrance into the union.

To Joseph M. Sanderson

SIR MONTPELLIER Jany. 15 1821

I have recd. your letter of Decr. 9. with a copy of Vol. I of the Biographical work in your hands, for which I return my thanks.

The Object of the work is such as must be highly interesting to the public; and the undertaking it at an early day is necessary to do justice to the memories of the men who signed the immortal act which made us a nation.

Not having found it convenient as yet to examine more than the "Life of Hancock," and that but slightly, I cannot pretend to judge of the entire merits of the volume. What I have read appears to be executed with fidelity & candor, and to bespeak literary talents in the author. At the same time it is incumbent on me not to suppress the remark, that he some times indulges a luxurience of fancy more than is required for ornament, or permitted perhaps by the simplicity and neatness suited to biographical composition. It may well be expected however that the progress of the work will be marked by the improvements for which the capacity of the author can not be doubted.

I wish I could venture to promise a contribution to the materials you wish to collect. I did not participate in the federal Councils at the Epoch of the Declaration of Independence. And what of an interesting nature I may happen to know in relation to any of its signers, is for the most part what is attainable from public sources or better private sources of information.

Being disposed to reduce rather than extend my subscriptions for new publications, especially such as require a lengthened period for their execution, I must ask the favor of you to enter on your list of subscribers, instead of my name, that of "John Payne Todd," to whom the vols. will be delivered as they successively arrive.

Draft (DLC: Rives Collection, Madison Papers).

From Peter Stephen Chazotte

SIR PHILADELPHIA 15th. Jany. 1821.

I have the honour of sending to you, a Pamph[l]et,[1] containing Facts and Observations, on the policy of immediately introducing the rich culture of coffee, cocoa, vines, olives capers, almonds, &a &a in East Florida, and in the southern States, and which, I flatter myself, you will do me the honour to accept, and give to it a moment's perusal. On a subject of such national, importance, the opinion, of your Excellency will be received with perfect defference and respect. I have the honour, respectfully, to subscribe myself Your Excellency: Most Obedt. & humble Servt.

PR. STEPHEN CHAZOTTE[2]

RC (DLC). Docketed by JM.

1. Peter Stephen Chazotte, *Facts and Observations on the Culture of Vines, Olives, Capers, Almonds, &c. in the Southern States and of Coffee, Cocoa, and Cochineal, in East Florida* (Philadelphia, 1821; Shoemaker 4966).

2. French-born Peter Stephen Chazotte owned coffee and cocoa plantations in Saint-Domingue in the 1790s until he fled in 1798 for Charleston, South Carolina. He returned to the island in 1800 but left for good in 1804, eventually settling in Philadelphia, where by 1811 he was running a French and English seminary and boarding school. In 1821 he led an exploring party to East Florida on behalf of an association of Franco-American families who wished to settle there and grow coffee, but the association was unsuccessful in its attempt to purchase land near Key Largo and dissolved in 1822 (Canter Brown Jr., "The East Florida Coffee Land Expedition of 1821: Plantations or a Bonapartist Kingdom of the Indies?" *Tequesta* 51 [1991]: 8–17; Philadelphia *Poulson's American Daily Advertiser*, 21 Sept. 1811).

From Lynde Walter and Others

SIR BOSTON 15 Jany 1821

At a meeting of a number of Gentlemen friendly to a Bankrupt Act, it was voted that you shd. be respectfully requested to use your influence, with your friends in Washington, to obtain its passage, at the present Session of Congress; & we were appointed a Committee to convey to you the sense of the Meeting, of the great influence which your exertions, either by letter or in any other way, in favor of so benevolent an object, might have to promote the measure.

While engaged in a pursuit so indispensably necessary, for the welfare & for the liberty of a vast body of our most valuable & most efficient Fellow-Citizens, we need no apology in presenting the subject to your attention; you whose life has been devoted to obtain the same results, in a thousand different shapes. Accept the assurance of our high regard.

LYNDE WALTER
JOHN MACKAY
P.P.F. DEGRAND
N.G. CARNES
Committee

RC (DLC). Docketed by JM.

1. Lynde Walter (1767–1844) was the son of a Boston Tory who settled his family in Shelburne, Nova Scotia, during the American Revolution. Walter returned to Boston in 1800 and became a prosperous merchant (Joseph Edgar Chamberlin, *The Boston Transcript: A History of Its First Hundred Years* [1930; reprint, Freeport, N.Y., 1969], 9; William B. Sprague, *Annals of the American Pulpit . . .* [9 vols.; 1857–69; reprint, New York, 1969], 5:228 n.).

2. John Mackay (d. 1841) was a wealthy Boston merchant and sea captain who, beginning in 1815, backed financially a number of Boston piano makers, including Alpheus Babcock, Thomas Appleton, and Jonas Chickering. In 1830 he formed a partnership with Chickering, providing business and sales expertise and investment capital, as well as importing rare and exotic woods (H. Wiley Hitchcock and Stanley Sadie, eds., *The New Grove Dictionary of American Music* [4 vols.; London, 1986], 3:150–51).

3. Peter Paul Francis Degrand (ca. 1780–1855), a native of Marseilles, arrived in Boston around 1803, and began a merchant banking business. In 1819 he launched the *Boston Weekly Report*, a compendium of public sales and ship arrivals, which he continued for ten years. Degrand was known for his financial acumen and his civic and philanthropic activities (Holmes Ammidown, *Historical Collections* [2 vols.; 1877; reprint, Bowie, Md., 1996], 2:445 n.).

4. N. G. Carnes was a Boston dry goods merchant (*Columbian Centinel*, 13 Oct. 1821).

To Tench Coxe

Dear Sir Montpellier Jany. 17. 1821

I recd. a few days ago your favor of the 8th. inclosing a paper signed Phocion.[1] Your own papers inclosed in your two preceding letters have been forwarded according to your suggestion.[2]

I have looked over the paper of Phocion. It indicates intelligence and acuteness in the writer, and no inconsiderable fairness, in facing, at every point, the subject he discusses. In his charges against me of inconsistency, he errs in identifying me with Mr. Hamilton in the opinion given in the 77th. No. of the Federalist, "that a removal from office required the concurrence of the Senate."[3] It was never understood that the parties to that work were answerable, each, for all the sentiments expressed in papers written by the others. To those acquainted with the circumstances under which the work was carried on for the press, it was manifest that a mutual privity even, was not always possible. The latter part of the work on the Executive and Judiciary Departments, including No. 77. were written after I left N. York for Virginia.

In the view P. gives of my opposition at first, and my assent afterwards to the Bank, he has not adverted to the grounds of the assent, as explained at the time. It implied no change of opinion as to the original construction of the text of the Constitution. It implied the contrary; the assent being founded on the principle that a certain character & course of precedents had the effect of fixing the meaning of Constitutions as well as of laws. Altho' this is denied by some, it was not contested in the case of the Carriage tax;[4] those who regarded it as equally with the Bank a breach of the Constitution, having acquiesced in the decision on that point, tho' not so extensively sanctioned as the decision in the case of the Bank. Phocion may have been misled perhaps by the view given of this change by the Supreme Court, in their late judgment on a case involving the constitutionality of the Bank.[5]

It is remarkable that the power of removal from office, though of such material agency, excited so little attention, whilst the Constitution was under discussion. It seems to have presented its important aspects, for the first time, at the first session of Congress, when the establishment of the Executive Offices was on hand. The debates on that occasion will shew,[6] to a certain extent at least, the different reasonings in support of the different opinions on the subject. In the final decision, experience seems to have produced a universal concurrence. What indeed would become of the efficiency or even practicability of the Executive trust, if every officer from the most confidential downward, who might be favored by a single vote more than ⅓ of the Senate, could, in defiance of the President and a single vote less than ⅔, hold his place till the delays of an impeachment could reach him. If ever there was a case where the argumentum ab inconvenienti,[7] ought to turn the scale, this was surely one.

If I understand, from a perusal not very critical, the doctrine and arguments of this writer, he supposes that "Executive Power," as distinct from Legislative & Judiciary power, depends wholly on constitutional modifications. That it is subject to Constitutional distributions is certain. But that it is a substantive power distinct in its nature from others, can not be denied, whatever difficulty there may sometimes be, in marking the dividing line between them. The language of the State Constitutions and Declarations of Rights, recognizes this substantive character of the Executive, as well as of the Legislative & Judiciary powers.

If, as seems to be contended, no power not expressed, belongs to the Executive, because expressed powers only are delegated to the federal Government, to whom does the removing power belong? Not to either of the other Departments, for it is not expressed among their powers. It must consequently, as not belonging to any, result to the States or to the people. To say that it results to the President & two thirds of the Senate, is not only to take off the wheels of the Govt: but to adopt a constructive power represented as inadmissible.

The difficulty is certainly not lessened by the distinction taken between high crimes & misdemeanors, and minor offences. The distinction take[s] away the impeaching remedy even, for the latter, without leaving the remedial power of removal. Such consequences from the doctrines of P. make me almost suspect that I have not rightly caught his meaning.

The remarks into which I have run, are as you will see not in a form for the press. I have no doubt that the flaws in the paper will be much better exposed by others, if the task be called for in relation to the Constitution of Pennsylvania. As the paper affects myself merely, I am content to leave its criticisms to themselves, without imposing the trouble you so kindly offer, of pointing out their fallacies. I am neither so blind nor so vain as to claim an entire exemption from the changes of opinion, or from the argumentative inaccuracies & inconsistences, incident to a very long course of political life; & to a participation in a great variety of political discussions, under many vicisitudes and varying aspects of the subjects of them. A comparative exemption, is as much as I dare aspire to; and this I ought to presume will not be refused, if I should be found to have a title to it.

I am glad to learn that the temper of all parties is assuming so much calmness on the subject of Missouri. The views of it, latterly presented to the public, according to the specimens you have sent me could scarc[e]ly fail to have such an effect. If all the States are not in Glass houses, none of them, it appears, are within Stone Walls.

The attention you keep up to my request as to the debates of Congress for a certain period obliges me very much. As you say nothing of Noah Websters "Sketches" or Peletiah Websters "Dissertation" I conclude they are not to be procured. Health and every other blessing

JAMES MADISON

[Enclosure]

For the Democratic Press. Remarks on the Constitution of Pennsylvania, More particularly on the Power of Appointment and Removal. *Addressed to the Legislature of the State.* No. III.

Having briefly shown the extent of the Governor's influence over the officers of his appointment, and hinted at a principle by which his power might be plausibly claimed, we shall proceed to examine whether this power of removal may not be constitutionably denied to the executive and subjected to the discretion of the legislature.

The constitution of the State is not silent on this important subject. It has provided in the most explicit terms for the removal from office of all incumbents who shall misbehave themselves. By article 4th section 4. "The Governor and *all other civil officers* under the commonwealth shall be liable to impeachment for any *misdemeanor* in office. But judgment in such cases shall not extend further than removal from office and disqualification to hold any office of honor, trust, or profit under this commonwealth."

There is a marked difference between the constitutions of the United States and of Pennsylvania, on this point. When it is considered the latter was modelled on the former, and is mutatis mutandis written in the same terms, this difference cannot be supposed accidental and without consequence. By the constitution of the United States art. II. sect. 4th. It is provided that "The President, Vice President, and all civil officers, shall be removed from office on impeachment for, and conviction of, treason, bribery, or other high crimes and misdemeanours." This clause in the ordinary import of language, and the common rules of legal construction, does not embrace all misdemeanours. The words "*high* crimes and misdemeanours" are used in contradistinction and in opposition to, crimes and misdemeanors, of ordinary character, unaggravated in their nature. And the word "other" would be believe be [*sic*] construed by every judicial bench in the country to mean offences, of the same grade and character as those specifically named. Taken in this sense the Pennsylvania convention of 1790, did not consider the clause sufficiently comprehensive to embrace all causes for which removal from office should take place, abandoning therefore the discriminating words used in the constitution of the United States it has adopted phraseology which includes every degree of malversation; subjecting the officer to "impeachment for any misdemeanor in office," under the constitution of the United States, the power of removal, might have been assumed by the executive, as implied in the power of appointment, with greater color of reason, than, it could be assumed by the Governor under the constitution of Pennsylvania. The power to remove by impeachment might be considered with propriety as not reaching, many offences, the commission of which render the removal of the officer desirable. As that constitution, then had not provided for the removal of officers thus offending the general responsibility of the executive for the faithful administration of the laws, might appear to carry with it the right to remove, unfaithful officers.

But the power of removal is exercised by the president, in its full extent, embracing all officers appointed by him, by and with the advice of the senate. Whence does he obtain this power? Is it assumed, as incidental to the power of appointment? But, the president removing at his pleasure, does not appoint at his pleasure. He does not possess the totality of the power of appointment. The senate participates in its exercise: the President and Senate form the appointing power. Here then is a new case, not depending on the principle generally assumed, that the power of appointment to, includes the power of removal from, office. Though this principle should be taken as incontrovertable, it will not solve the case before us, and we must resort to other principles.

This important question has undergone a thorough discussion, and has been viewed in all possible aspects by the House of Representatives of the U. S. and in that august body, produced a most extraordinary diversity of opinion. It came before them at the first session, after the adoption of the federal constitution, on a resolution offered by Mr. Madison in the committee of the whole, "that it is the opinion of this committee that there shall be established, an executive department to be denominated the department of foreign affairs; at the head of which there shall be an officer to be called the secretary to the department of foreign affairs, who shall be appointed by the president, by and with the advice and consent of the senate; and to be removeable by the president." Immediately on the presentation of this resolution, the words "who shall be appointed by the president by and with the advice and consent of the senate," were stricken out on the ground, that "the constitution had expressly given the power of appointment in the words there used." The resolution as amended after much debate was carried, with an understanding that an opportunity would be offered for an ample discussion of the power of removal, which was denied to the president, by several members on many grounds. On the 15th of June, 1789, the question came again before the House, on the bill for establishing an executive department, to be denominated the department of foreign affairs. A more interesting animated, and argumentative debate, is not to be found in our congressional annals, than, that which arose on this occasion. The first clause of the bill after recapitulating the title of the officer and his duties had these words, "To be removeable from office by the president of the United States."

The power to remove from office was generally admitted to be lodged, in the gen. gov. but to what br[a]nch it was constitutionally given, was a point, producing great collision of opinion. There were however some gentlemen, who denied, that the power of removal from office, for mere misdemeanour was at all given by the Constitution, and who opposed every attempt of Congress to intermeddle with it, until further power had been given by the people, by an amendment to the Constitution; this class was not numerous, and it was soon overpowered by the number of its opponents, if not by the force of their arguments. Those, who believed, that the power was given by the Constitution, assigned very different reasons for their faith. By one section it was said that, the power of removal in all cases, belonged to the Senate, by virtue of the clause relative to impeachments, and that, the Constitution having pointed out that mode of dismissal from office, none other was admissible. By a second it was contended, that the power to remove was co-incident with and dependent upon the power to appoint: and that, the power of appointment being vested in the President and Senate therefore, the power of removal could be exercised only by them conjointly. A third section argued, that, as the power of removal was not expressly given by the Constitution, to the President or the Senate nor to the President and Senate; but that as the necessity of the power was apparent and the Legislature, having the right "to make all laws necessary and proper for carrying into execution the foregoing powers and all other powers vested by the Constitution" the power of removal belonged to the Legislature, embracing, the President, Senate, and House of Representatives, who might dispose of it as they should deem most advantageous to the people. This opinion was sustained, by many able speakers, and swayed the House in their decision of the question. For most of those, of the last section, we have to enumerate, who contended for the power of removal in the President alone, supported their position by this argument, that although it should not be conceded that the Constitution gave the power to the President, yet it must be admitted that the Legislature possessed it, and might bestow it on the President. It is true however, that some contended boldly, for the right of the President, under the Constitution, independently of the Legislative power: But not one of those were over willing to pass the bill, without the clause granting the power of removal of the Officer to the President. Mr. Madison who led the way on the President's Constitutional power, to appoint, at first availed himself of the foregoing argument, th[o]ugh he afterwards disclaims reliance upon it, because the Legislature might choose to vest the power elsewhere than in the President. As the opinion of this Gentleman and his associates in the argument, most materially interferes with our views on this subject, we are constrained to review the reasons on which it is founded. That we approach this task with diffidence and awe will not be doubted. The opinions of the man, who contributed so greatly to the formation of the Constitution, and to the organization of the government under it, and who justly obtained, the confidence of the Country, must always be assailed with great disadvantage. Our own convictions almost yield to the force of his name; and we fear that the voice of reason's self, would be doubted when opposed to his. Will it be permitted us before we advance to this unequal warfare to attempt to clear the way by remarking that this great man's opinions even on constitutional points, are not infallible, and that however maturely formed, they do not always resist the magic influence of expediency.

If the power claimed for the President, by Mr. Madison, be a constructive one, and we think it can bear no other name, the inference must not be drawn that Mr. M. is at all times friendly to constructive powers. In the XIIth No. of the Federalist, he combats this doctrine manfully, and on the principles which be there laid down, he in the year 1791 resisted the incorporation of the United States Bank. In addition to the reasons he drew from the specific enumeration of powers in the constitution, he gives one that we would think was conclusive and insurmountable in his own mind at least. On the floor of Congress, Mr. [M.] declared, "That the power to grant charters of incorporation was in the original plan reported by the committee to the convention among the enumerated powers granted by the 8th section of the first article of the constitution; but that after three days consideration and ardent debate in that body, it was stricken out, as a power improper to be vested in the general government." In the face of this declaration and of this fact, Mr M. as President of the United States sanctioned an act incorporating the Bank of the United States. Again, the Federalist is deemed a text book on the constitution, in the composition of which Mr. M took a considerable part, and is generally supposed to have seen and approved, all communicated to the public under the signature of Publius. The 77th number of that work, treating of the President's power to appoint, commences thus, "It has been mentioned as one of the advantages to be expected from the co-operation of the senate in the business of appointments that it would contribute to the stability of the administration. *The consent of that body would be necessary to displace as well as to appoint.*" The Federalist we all know, was written to enforce the acceptance of the Federal constitution by the several states. It was written principally by Messrs. Madison and Hamilton, who were members of the convention which framed that constitution, and therefore the presumption that their exposition of that instrument, was in the sense in which it was conceived, is founded in strict justice to them. Yet immediately after the adoption of the constitution, a construction is given to it by Mr. M. contrary to the one published to induce its adoption. We do not mean to be understood, that Mr. M. stated at any time what was not his real opinion. But we would be understood to mean that, Mr. M in the change of his opinion in the two cases we have cited, convicted himself of error, and we urge that conviction against the *Prestige* of his name and character. With this preparation we proceed to offer impartially, the foundation of Mr. M's. argument in favor of the constitutional power of the President to remove from office.

On the introduction of his resolution, Mr. Madison, defended it, on the ground of the responsibility of the executive, arising from the nature of his office; and urges strongly the expediency of imposing on the President, the responsibility for the conduct of all officers in the department. He does not attempt to prove the constitutionality of the power he contends for, until the propriety and practicability of this responsibility is shaken by the arguments of his opponents, in the debate on the passage of the bill for establishing a department for foreign affairs. It is opinion that the Constitution gives this power to the President, he avows is the result of an intermediate examination, and that "it does not perfectly correspond with the ideas which he entertained of it from the first glance." The passages of the constitution on which he relies, are the first sentence of Art. II. sec. 1. "The executive power shall be vested in a President of the United States of America," and the concluding sentence of section III. of the same article, "He (the President) shall take care that the laws be faithfully executed, and shall commission all the officers of the United States." He then contends, that removal from office is an executive power, and therefore belongs to the President; and that it being the duty of the President to take care that the laws be faithfully executed, he must necessarily have the power to remove those who execute them unfaithfully.

The construction given to these passages of the Constitution, we think we shall shew clearly is not warranted by them. That they are given in terms so general, as to admit of great latitude of construction, if they stood unconnected with other parts of the constitution, we admit, but that they would justify precisely the meaning here given to them, is not so obvious. If the words "the executive power shall be vested in a President of the United States of America," stood alone, in order to assign to them any meaning, it would be necessary to define the "executive power." In a certain sense, these words are understood by all. They mean a power to execute the laws. But the degree of power depends on the form of government and the extent of the grant. It varies from the whole power of the state, to the most incons[i]derable part. In governments approximating to despotism, the executive power is paramount to every other; in those approaching to democracy, it is feeble, and of little consideration. There is every degree of this power between the *maximum* and *minimum* of the scale. Even in the United States, where the general basis of the state governments is the same, there are various degrees of this power. Now, what is the grant conveyed by the words "executive power," as used in the Constitution of the United States. 'Tis not a despotic power; for that would render useless all other parts of the Constitution. It cannot be the executive power exercised by the King of Great Britain, for we have abjured the government of Great Britain and created one for ourselves. It cannot be that given to either of the several states; for there are no means by which we can ascertain from [which] it was borrowed. Then if it be neither of these, it must be that executive power given by the constitution of the United States, and the passage we have quoted should read, "The executive powers *given by this constitution* shall be vested in a president,["] &c. If then this be the true reading, we have not advanced a step by the use of this passage, in dete[r] mining the power of the President to remove from office. For though we should admit the power of removal to be an executive power, it does not appertain to the president unless given to him by the constitution. If this opinion need additional support, it will be found in the consideration. That the general government is altogether a factitious one, that it owes its existence to the concessions of the several state sovereignties and that it has no other power save that delegated to it—On the subject of constructive powers we would appeal from Mr. Madison construing the constitution, to Mr Madison defending it. The fear that powers not expressly given by the constitution, might be obtained by implication, formed one of the many objections to its adoption, by the several states. This objection was particularly urged against the clause, authorizing Congress "to provide for the common defence and general welfare of the United States." To remove this dread Mr. Madison in the same number of the federalist from which we have already made an extract, expresses himself thus: "It has been urged and echoed, that this power amounts to an unlimited commission to exercise every power which may be alledged to be necessary for the common defence and general welfare. No stronger proof could be given of the distress under which these writers labor for objection than their stooping to such a misconstruction. (Has experience shewn this to be a misconstruction?) What color can the objection have, when a specification of the objects alluded to, by these general terms immediately follows; and is not even separated by a longer pause than a semicolon? If the different parts of the same system ought to be expounded, so as to give meaning to every part which will bear it, shall one part of the same sentence be excluded altogether from a share in the meaning; and shall the more doubtful and indefinite terms be retained in their full extent, and the clear, precise expressions be denied any signification whatever? For what purpose could the enumeration of particular powers be inserted, if these and all others were meant to be included in the preceding general power? Nothing is more natural or common, than first to use a general phrase, and then to explain and qualify it by a recital of the particulars. But the idea of an enumeration of particulars which neither explain nor qualify the general meaning, and can have no other effect than to confound and mislead, is an absurdity which as we are reduced to the dilemma of charging either on the authors of the objection, or on the authors of the constitution, we must take the liberty of supposing, it had not its origin with the latter."

Now may we not ask, is there an argument here used against constructive powers in congress, that does not apply with equal force to such power in the President. Is not the passage relied on by Mr. Madison a "general phrase?" Is it not followed by a "recital of particulars" by an enumeration of powers in the very article of which it forms the commencement? Does not the sentence which Mr. Madison pronounces on the "author of the objection" recoil upon himself?

PHOCION.

RC (DLC). RC docketed by Coxe, with his note: "about Fedt." For enclosure, see n. 1.

1. The enclosure was printed in the Philadelphia *Democratic Press*, 9 Jan. 1821.

2. See JM to Thomas Jefferson, 7 Jan. 1821, and n. 1.

3. For Federalist No. 77, see Cooke, *The Federalist*, 515–21. In the words of Alexander Hamilton, "it has been mentioned as one of the advantages to be expected from the co-operation of the senate, in the business of appointments, that it would contribute to the stability of the administration. The consent of that body would be necessary to displace as well as to appoint" (ibid., 515).

4. For the tax on carriages, which JM opposed as unconstitutional, see JM to Thomas Jefferson, 1 June 1794, *PJM*, 15:340–41 and n. 2. For a previous use of the analogy of the carriage tax with the Bank of the United States, see JM to James Monroe, 27 Dec. 1817, *PJM-RS*, 1:190–91.

5. For the opinion of John Marshall in the case of *McCullough v. Maryland* before the U.S. Supreme Court, see JM to Spencer Roane, 2 Sept. 1819, *PJM-RS*, 1:500–503, 504 nn. 1–2.

6. For a summary of the debate and JM's speeches in support of the removal power of the president, see *PJM*, 12:55–57, 170–74, 190, 225–29, 229–30, 244–45, 254–56, 290, 291.

7. *Argumentum ab inconvenienti:* "an argument from inconvenience; an argument that emphasizes the harmful consequences of failing to follow the position advocated" (*Black's Law Dictionary*, 9th ed., 122).

To George Alexander Otis

SIR MONTPELLIER 17 Jany. 1821

I received some days ago your letter of the 4th. instant. However favorable my general opinion may be to the History of Botta, I could not undertake to vouch for its entire exemption from flaws, such as are charged on it, without a more thorough examination of the work than I have made, or than other calls on my time will now permit me to make. It is indeed quite presumable, that at the early date of his undertaking, a defect of materials may have betrayed him into errors of fact; and that as a foreigner, he has not always penetrated the character of a people, fashioned as the American has been by so many peculiar circumstances; nor comprehended fully the mechanism and springs of their novel and compound system of Government. It is not the less true however, that his history may have a value justly entitling it to all the attention claimed for it from the American Public. If it cannot be regarded as a popular Manual, it may aspire to the merit of being nearly a cotemporary work, by an Industrious Compiler, who was capable at the same time of viewing our revolutionary transactions & events with a philosophic eye, and describing them with a polished & eloquent pen.

I know not any source from which Botta could have taken a tincture of partiality for one more than for another portion of our Country. He was probably led to put his fictitious and doubtless very erroneous Speeches for and against Independence into the mouths of Mr. Lee and Mr. Dickinson, by his discovery that the former was the organ of the proposition, and the latter the most distinguished of its opponents. It is to be regretted that the Historian had not been more particularly acquainted with what passed in Congress on that great occasion. He would probably have assigned to your venerable correspondent[1] a very conspicuous part on the Theatre. I well recollect that the reports from his fellow labourers in the cause from Virginia filled every mouth in that State, with the praises due to the comprehensiveness of his views, the force of his arguments, and the boldness of his patriotism. It is to be hoped that historical justice may be done by others, better furnished with the means of doing it. With friendly respects

James Madison

RC (MBBS); draft (DLC). Minor differences between the copies have not been noted.

1. In the draft, JM placed an asterisk here and wrote in the left margin "*John Adams."

From Thomas B. Parker

Sir Boston Jany 18th. 1821

Permit me, though personally a stranger to you, respectfully to solicit your opinion, if I am not too intrusive, on two important political questions, which, at present, agitate the publick mind in massachusetts.

You, doubtless, have heard, Sir, that the people of this Commonwealth, deemed it necessary, on the seperation of Maine, to amend their state constitution. Accordingly delegates were chosen from every town, and have met in convention, and have made alterations and amendments in the constitution, which are to be submitted to the people the ensuing spring, for their acceptance or non-acceptance.

The convention, after much opposition, have concluded not to make any alteration in the manner of apportioning the Senate, that is the Senate are to be apportioned *on valuation* and not *on population.* It is held by those who are in favor of this method that it is the best method they can devise to secure in the Senate a sufficient negative on the popular branch, and by those, who are in favor of the senate's being based on population and chosen in districts, it is held that to apportion the senate on property or valuation is contrary to the principles of republicanism and equal rights and has an aspect too aristocratical to be relished by them. The convention have also concluded that the people should be compelled to support publick teachers of morality and religion. This question has been strenuously opposed by able divines, as well as laymen, on the ground, that civil government has no right to interfere with religious concerns and that religion needs not the aid of government to support it, and that to compel men to aid in support of religious teachers, is infringing on the sacred rights of conscience.

Now Sir, if I am not too presuming, I respectfully solicit your opinion on those two questions; as I am in doubt, and seek information, being anxious to decide correctly, and not give my humble support, however small, to measures that are not con[s]istent with genuine republican principles and equal rights. Pray Sir excuse the liberty I have taken. With sentiments of great Respect I am Sir Your obt. Humb. Servt.

Thomas B Parker[1]

RC (DLC). Docketed by JM.

1. Thomas B. Parker (ca. 1796–1822) was an assistant in the Boston post office (*Independent Chronicle and Boston Patriot*, 9 Feb. 1822).

To William S. Cardell

Sir Montpr. Jany 19. 1821

I have recd your letter of the 12th. inclosing a copy of your Circular one, on the subject of the "American Academy of Language & Belles Lettres." It informs me at the same time that the Society has been pleased to put [me] on the list of its honorary members.

I request Sir, that they may be assured of the respectful impressions with which I receive this mark of distinction.

Having heretofore made known my good wishes for the Institution now developed under the above title, I have only to renew my tender of them; and to express the confidence inspired by the names enlisted in the cause, that the Academy will be the means as well of illustrating the present advance, as of extending the future improvement of useful & ornamental literature in our Country.

Draft (DLC). RC cover sheet addressed by JM to Cardell at New York, and franked. Marked "Orange C H 23 January 1821" (offered for sale in Paul C. Richards Autographs, Catalogue No. 232, item 169).

From James Monroe

Dear Sir Washington Jany. 19. 1821

Mr Lawrance[1] & Mr Jones[2] of New York, young gentlemen of merit, well connected there, expressing a wish to visit you & Mr Jefferson, I have felt it due to the introduction they have presented me, to make them known to you. They intend to visit Europe in the Spring, & will I am satisfied, take much interest in bearing any letters from you, or being in any respect useful to you. With great respect & sincere regard your friend

James Monroe

RC (DLC). Docketed by JM.

1. William Beach Lawrence (1800–1881), a graduate of Columbia College (1818), was reading law immediately before his visit to JM in the winter of 1821. He served as secretary of legation in London in 1826 and U.S. chargé d'affaires there, 1827–28. Lawrence practiced law in New York City and wrote widely on issues of public and international law. On moving to Rhode Island in 1850, he was elected lieutenant governor of that state in 1851 (*New York Times*, 26 Mar. 1881).

2. John Quentin Jones (ca. 1804–1878) studied at Columbia College before leaving for a position in the countinghouse of Lawrence and Trimble. He was president of the Chemical Bank in New York City, 1844–78 (ibid., 3 Jan. 1878).

From Nathan Sanford

Sir Washington 19th. January 1821.

William Beach Lawrence and John Q. Jones Esquires of New York, are about to travel through Virginia; and if they should pass near your residence, they will do themselves the honor to visit you. I beg leave to introduce them to you, in this manner. They are young gentlemen of great personal merit, and of the most amiable dispositions. Their parents and friends, are among the most respectable citizens of New York.

I pray you Sir, to present my respectful compliments to Mrs. Madison, and to accept for yourself, the assurance of my highest respect. May you, in your retreat from public cares, long enjoy health and happiness. I have the honor to be With the highest consideration Sir Your most obedient servant

NATHAN SANFORD[1]

RC (DLC). Docketed by JM.

1. Nathan Sanford (1777–1838) was a New York City lawyer and U.S. attorney for the district of New York, 1803–15. He served in the U.S. Senate, 1815–21, and 1826–31 (*PJM-SS*, 7:347 n. 2).

From William Thornton

DEAR SIR CITY OF WASHINGTON Jany. 20th: 1821.

I have just heard that Mr. Charles Todd, of Kentucky, is returning from the Republic of Columbia, & as another Agent will most probably be appointed, I am exceedingly desirous of succeeding him. I had been very highly recommended to the President before Mr: Todd was appointed, by the honorable Colonel Johnson,[1] & some other respectable Senators, & the Colonel & many other Friends are desirous of aiding me in obtaining the appointment now: but as this is a popular Government, & the voice of the people is always attended to, it has been thought proper to convince the President that it would be a popular appointment before I could expect to receive this honor.

I have served this Government above twenty six years, & have been so happy as to obtain the approbation of the successive Presidents. I have been invited by the Officers of the highest grade in the Republic of Colombia to accept of Commissions from them: but I have very explicitly refused every offer, though very tempting. The Secretary of State & Finance of Colombia, Señor Don José R: Revenga,[2] being my very intimate Friend, the celebrated Roscio,[3] Vice President of the Republic, being also my Friend; & having been intimate with the famous Orator Don Pedro Gual[4] L.L.D. formerly Govr: of Carthagena, I am confident I should be well received as an Agent to that Country. One of my Objects is to write the natural History of, & describe by drawings &c, that very extensive, rich & interesting, but almost unknown Country: and I am now so far advanced in life that I have not a moment to lose. The celebrated Franklin offered if I would travel in the Service of the United States, keep a Journal of what I though[t] worthy of record, without subjection to any restraint whatever, & deliver my writings to the United States, he would obtain for me a Salary that should be worthy of any Gentleman, & as his individual Subscription to aid in carrying into Effect what he wished, he would give his Salary as Governor of Pennsylva: for one Year, which was a thousand pounds Pennsylva: Curry: but my delicate State of Health solely prevented me from accepting one of the most honorable Appointments that perhaps was ever offered from one so justly renowned, & so high in Science, to one so young as I then was. I have written to the late President Jefferson that great patron of the Sciences & Arts, to favor me with a few lines if he think me worthy, & I solicit from you whatever you can with good conscience say in my behalf on this Occasion. I shall never forget the Obligation, & shall consider your Opinions, if in my favor, as the Summum of all that can be desired. Be assured, also, that I shall never cease to endeavour to prove myself worthy of your patronage.

Govr: Barbour of Virginia mentioned to some of my Friends a few Days ago, an Expression of Mr: Jefferson's in my favor, which I shall never forget, but cherish in the most grateful remembrance.

My wife & her mother would not perhaps go with me at first; but if I should be appointed & agreeably established I am in hopes they would not refuse to go afterwards. Please to give our best regards & most respectful compliments to your amiable Lady. Her name is mentioned very often, with uncommon kindness, & her kind & condescending deportment & friendly attentions to the Citizens will never be forgotten. I am dear Sir, with the highest respect, most sincere regard & consideration Yrs &c

William Thornton

An Answer as soon as your time will permit will very much oblige me, as there is not a moment to be lost. Yrs. W.T.

RC (DLC). Docketed by JM.

1. Richard Mentor Johnson (1781–1850) was a Kentucky lawyer who served in the U.S. House of Representatives, 1807–1819, and 1829–36, in the U.S. Senate, 1819–1829, and as vice president of the United States, 1836–40. He supported the Madison administration, and raised two regiments of mounted volunteers, commanding troops in several engagements during the War of 1812, including the Battle of the Thames, where he is said to have killed Tecumseh (*Biographical Encyclopaedia of Kentucky* [1980 reprint], 297–98).

2. José Rafael Revenga (1781–1852) was sent to the United States in 1810 to gain recognition of the revolutionary government of Venezuela. He dined with JM in Washington in November 1811. An associate of Simón Bolívar, Revenga was sent on diplomatic missions to the United States (again in 1815), Spain (1821), and Great Britain (1822), and was several times, secretary of state for foreign relations (Donna Keyse Rudolph and G. A. Rudolph, *Historical Dictionary of Venezuela*, 2 ed., [Lanham, Md., 1996], 593; *PJM-PS*, 4:11 and n. 1).

3. Juan Germán Roscio (1769–1821), a doctor of canon and of civil law from the University of Caracas, was a key participant in the independence movement in Venezuela in 1810 and thereafter. In 1812 he was imprisoned in North Africa for his revolutionary activities.

In 1818 he visited the United States, where he published *El Triunfo de la Libertad Sobre el Despotismo*. He was briefly president of the department of Venezuela in the Republic of Colombia before his death (Rudolph and Rudolph, *Historical Dictionary of Venezuela*, 2d ed., 614–15).

4. Pedro Gual (1784–1862) was a Venezuelan revolutionary and diplomat who served as provincial governor, minister of foreign affairs, and organizer of and delegate to the Congress of Panama in 1826. He represented Ecuador in Spain and Great Britain and was briefly president of Venezuela in 1861. He visited the United States in 1812 (ibid., 320–21).

To Thomas B. Parker

SIR MONTPR. Jany. 24. 1821

I have recd. your letter of Jany. 18. & thank you for the 2 papers containing very interesting parts of the debates & proceedings of your Convention.

I am very sensible Sir of what I owe to the respect & confidence marked by your request of my opinions on 2 great points in the articles of amendment proposed to the State Constitution. But I must appeal to the same friendly dispositions for an excuse from a compliance with it. Naked opinions could have no claim to attention. And if it were less inconvenient than it is at present, to explain the grounds of them, I could not but feel the delicacy of the task; at the same time that I have every reason for presuming that I could throw no new light on subjects wch. have been publickly discussed, & doubtless with so much ability & information. With friendly respects

J. MADISON

Draft (owned by David S. Light, Bay Harbor Islands, Fla., 1988).

To Lynde Walter and Others

GENTLEMEN MONTPELLIER (VIRGA.) Jany. 24. 1821

I have just recd. your letter of the 15th. instant; and I cannot be insensible to the marks of respect & confidence contained in it. But besides that it attaches a very undue weight to my opinion on the subject of a Bankrupt act, I am not sure that the interference you suggest would be received in the light you anticipate. Candor requires also an acknowlegement, that though sincerely anxious for the relief of the prevailing distresses every where, and not opposed altogether to the resource of a Bankrupt system, my reflections would call for modifications which I have no reason to believe coincide with the views of the subject likely to be taken at Washington. I tender you, Gentlemen my respect & good wishes

J. M

Draft (DLC).

To Reynolds Chapman

Dr Sir Jany 25 1821

I recd. yours of the 16th.[1] some days ago. Particular engagements have prevented an earlier answer.

Different plans for reading history have been recommended. What occurs as most simple & suitable, where the object is such as you point out, is to begin with some abridgement of Genl. History. I am not sure that I am acquainted with the best; late ones having been published wch. I have not seen. Millots history ancient & modern translated from the French[2] would answer well enough. The work is not large, and might be preceded or accompanied by Colvins historical letters now publishing at George Town, in a single volume.[3] After this outline, Humes History of England[4] & Robertsons Hist: of Scotland[5] might follow: Then Ramsay's history of the U.S. & of the American Revolution;[6] and Burkes Histy. of Virga. continued by Jones, & Gerardin's.[7] This course being ended, particular histories of different Countries according to leisure & curiosity might be taken up: such as Goldsmith's history of Greece, do. of Rome[8] preceded or accompanied by Tooks Pantheon.[9] Robertsons history of America[10] would also deserve attention. This fund of information, with a competent knowledge of Geography, would prepare the mind for reading with advantage, the Voyages round the world and the most intelligent travels into the most interesting countries. Geography is a preliminary in all cases to a pleasing & instructive course of historical reading. That & Chronology, have been called the two eyes of History. Geography might be called the right one.

No studies seem so well calculated to give a proper expansion to the mind as Geography & history; and when not absorbing an undue portion of time, are as beneficial & becoming to the one sex as to the other.

Draft (DLC).

1. Letter not found.

2. Claude François Xavier Millot, *Elements of General History. . . . Part First. Ancient History* (2 vols.; Worcester, Mass., 1789; Evans 21965) and Millot, *Elements of General History. . . . Part Second. Modern History* (3 vols.; Worcester, Mass., 1789; Evans 21966).

3. See Joseph Milligan to JM, 4 May 1821, and n. 1.

4. See *PJM-RS*, 1:355 n. 3.

5. William Robertson, *The History of Scotland, during the Reigns of Queen Mary and of King James VI. until His Accession to the Crown of England* . . . (2 vols.; Philadelphia, 1811; Shaw and Shoemaker 23824). This was the first American edition, taken from the sixteenth London.

6. See *PJM-RS*, 1:183 n. 1.

7. See ibid., 355 n. 4.

8. Oliver Goldsmith, *The Grecian History, from the Earliest State to the Death of Alexander the Great* (2 vols. in 1; Washington, [Pa.], 1800; Evans 37531), and *Dr. Goldsmith's Roman History* . . . (Philadelphia, 1795; Evans 28755).

9. François Pomey and Andrew Tooke, *The Pantheon, Representing the Fabulous Histories of the Heathen Gods and Most Illustrious Heroes* . . . , 6th ed. (London, 1713).

10. See *PJM-RS*, 1:284 n. 3.

From Ethan A. Brown

COLUMBUS, OHIO, January 26th. 1821

To Mr. Madison, long considered the ablest expositor of the principles of the federal Constitution, the accompanying report[1] is transmitted, by his obedient Servant

ETHAN A. BROWN[2]

RC (DLC). Docketed by JM.

1. The enclosed report (not found) was probably a copy of the *Report of the Joint Committee of Both Houses of the General Assembly, on the Communication of the Auditor of State, Upon the Subject of the Proceedings of the Bank of the United States, Against the Officers of State, in the United States Circuit Court* (Columbus, Ohio, 1820; Shoemaker 2592). For the conflict between the state of Ohio and the Second Bank of the United States, see Edmond Kelly to JM, 26 Sept. 1820, and n. 8.

2. Ethan Allen Brown (1776–1852) was born in Connecticut, read law with Alexander Hamilton in New York City, and moved to to Cincinnati, Ohio, in 1804, where he opened a law practice. He served as governor of Ohio, 1818–22, and in the U.S. Senate, 1822–25. President Andrew Jackson appointed Brown chargé d'affaires to Brazil in 1830, a post he held until 1834. Brown also served as commissioner of the General Land Office, 1835–36 (Sobel and Raimo, *Biographical Directory of the Governors*, 3:1196).

From Thomas Jefferson

DEAR SIR MONTICELLO Jan. 28. 21.

My neighbor, friend and physician, Doctr. Watkins, being called to Philadelphia, is desirous to pay his respects to you en passant, and asks me, by a line to you, to lessen his scruples on doing so. You will find my justification in his character when known to you. His understanding is excellent, well informed, of pleasant conversation and of great worth. As a Physician

I should trust myself in his hands with more confidence than any one I have ever known in this state, and am indebted to his experience and cautious practice for the restoration of my health. Receive him therefore with your wonted kindness and accept the assurance of my affectionate respect.

TH: JEFFERSON

RC (DLC); FC (DLC: Jefferson Papers).

To Henry Wheaton

MONTPELLIER Jany. 29. 1821

J. Madison presents his respects to Mr. Wheaton,[1] with thanks for the copy of his "Anniversary Discourse," which is well calculated to attract attention to a subject deeply interesting to the U.S. by the views under which it is presented, and the lights thrown on it by his valuable researches & investigations.

RC (NNPM).

1. Henry Wheaton (1785–1848) was a graduate of the College of Rhode Island and practiced law in Providence. He edited the pro-administration newspaper, the *National Advocate*, in New York City from 1812 until 1815. Wheaton was United States Supreme Court reporter, 1816–27, publishing an annual volume of the *Reports* as well as writing on a variety of law and political topics. In 1826 he published *Some Account of the Life, Writings, and Speeches of William Pinkney*, a project that had been encouraged and supported by JM, who provided Wheaton with extracts of his correspondence with Pinkney. In 1827 Wheaton was appointed chargé d'affaires at Copenhagen; in 1835 he took the same position at Berlin, only to become U.S. minister to Prussia the following year. He resigned that post in 1846. Wheaton is best known for his volumes on international law, especially *Elements of International Law* (1836), which went through four editions in his lifetime and was translated into many languages. The "Anniversary Discourse" to which JM referred was Wheaton's *A Discourse on the History of the Science of Public or International Law* (New York, 1821), delivered to a meeting of the New-York Historical Society on its anniversary, 28 Dec. 1820 (Elizabeth Feaster Baker, *Henry Wheaton, 1785–1848* [Philadelphia, 1937], 3, 7, 10, 15, 18–20, 25, 27, 29, 33, 68–70, 76–77, 132–33, 146, 151–52, 295–96, 301, 307, 312, 314).

To Peter Stephen Chazotte

SIR MONTPELLIER Jany. 30. 21

I have recd & thank you for your little tract on the culture of vines Olives &c. Its practical views of the several articles derived from long personal experience, with the apparent aptitude for them of soils & climates in a certain portion of the U. States justly claim the attention of those particularly living within its limits. Experiments for introducing these valuable productions are strongly recommended by the success which attended the culture of Rice & Cotton, the importance of which was at one time as little understood as that of the articles whose merits you discuss. With friendly respects

(Signd) JAMES MADISON

FC (DLC). In an unidentified hand. Marked by JM "Peter Stephen Chazotte."

From Thomas Jefferson

DEAR SIR MONTICELLO Jan. 30. 21.

The inclosed letter to mr. Cabell[1] so fully explains it's object, and the grounds on which your signature to the paper is proposed if approved, that I will spare my stiffening & aching wrist the pain of adding more than the assurance of my constant & affectte. friendship.

TH: JEFFERSON

[Enclosure]

We the subscribers, visitors of the University of Virginia being of opinion that it will be to the interest of that institution to have an occasional meeting of the visitors, by special call, on the 1st. day of April next, do therefore appoint that day for such meeting, and request the attendance of the sd. Visitors accordingly; personal notice being to be given to them respectively one week at least before the said day. Witness our hands on the several days affixed to our respective signatures.

TH: JEFFERSON rector. Jan. 30. 1821.
JAMES MADISON Feby. 3. 1821
C. JOHNSON 10th. Feby. 1821
JOSEPH C. CABELL 10 Feb: 1821
JAMES BRECKINRIDGE 10 Feb. 1821
ROBERT TAYLOR Feby 13th. 1821

RC (ViU: Special Collections; on loan from the National Trust for Historic Preservation, Montpelier, 1985) and enclosure (ViU: Jefferson Papers, Special Collections). Enclosure in Thomas Jefferson's hand.

1. Jefferson's letter to Joseph C. Cabell, 30 Jan. 1821 (DLC: Jefferson Papers), sought concurrence from the board of visitors to schedule a special meeting in order that Chapman Johnson, who had yet to attend a meeting of the board, should not fall victim to the law requiring a visitor's commission to be vacated for *"failure to act for the space of one year."* The action of signing the call for a special meeting, in Jefferson's opinion, was a *"visitorial act,"* thus satisfying the law in question.

From George Alexander Otis

SIR, PHILADELPHIA January 31st. 1821.

I feel very sincerely obliged by your letter of 17th instant, and by the general benignity with which you have deigned to view my undertaking. I now have the honor of transmitting you the last volume of the Translation, which if honored with your approbation will reward me for all my toils in a task, which if it does not yield me reputation I fear will yield me nothing.

The venerable J. Adams, after having finished reading the 1st and 2d volume of the translation, has waived his objections entirely; and compliments me in high terms. He agrees with many other gentlemen ["]that the Translation has great merit, has raised a monument to my name, and performed a valuable Service to my Country." &c. &c.[1] I have the honor to be, with the most Sincere veneration, Your obliged humble Servant

GEORGE ALEXANDER OTIS

RC (DLC). Docketed by JM.

1. Adams to Otis, 16 Jan. 1821 (printed in the *Daily National Intelligencer*, 14 Feb. 1821).

From Lynde Walter and Others

SIR BOSTON 3 Feby 1821

Accept our particular thanks, for the kind expressions contained in your esteemed favor 24 Jany, & for the candor with which you have given us a frank exposition of your views. Whatever Bankrupt system may at first be adopted will, we fondly hope, receive such beneficial amendments, as experience may show to be necessary, to render it worthy of your support. Receive the renewed assurance of our high regard & esteem.

LYNDE WALTER
JOHN MACKAY
P.P.F.
DEGRAND
N.G. CARNES
Committee

RC (DLC). In Degrand's hand. Docketed by JM.

From George W. Featherstonhaugh

SIR DUANESBURGH Feb 6. 1821

I had the honour to receive your very obliging Letter of December last,[1] and now request your acceptance of the Volume accompanying this:[2] being with the most unfeigned respect Sir Your very faithful humble St.

GW FEATHERSTONHAUGH

RC (ICN). Docketed by JM.

1. JM to Featherstonhaugh, 23 Dec. 1820.

2. *Memoirs of the Board of Agriculture of the State of New-York* (Albany, N.Y., 1821; Shoemaker 6251). This volume included JM's *Address to the Agricultural Society of Albemarle* (*PJM-RS*, 1:260–83).

From Edmond Kelly

SIR COLUMBIA TEN 6th feby 1821

I have just read the 2 last acts of Congress for the future protection of the US Bank[1] which I consider insufficient—there is no clause to anull any fraudulent or collusive Conveyances from delinquent bank officers or agents and their securities—nor is the vesting of the property of such persons in the Bank Corporation on their admission to office required—as summary a remedy against disguised City sharpers as could properly be given would prevent fraud & Embezzlement—tho such frauds would in the first instance be most severely felt by the bank Corporation—future experience will shew them to be very pernicious & Injurious to the Genl Govt & the Comy—that Institution well and honestly conducted would Equalise the national Currency—prevent losses by discount or exchange—and so accumulate & concentrate Capital as to supply & support the Genl Govt on any Emergency as the national Bank of England has done that Govt during the long french war.

I have read a letter from Mr. Cobbett to Mr Gallatin[2] in which he condemns the United States Bank on the principle that it will give the Genl Govt. the same Controul over the american Mercantile Interest which the Bank of England gives the british Govt over the british Mercantile Interest who he says would otherwise oppose that Govt. Mr. C is evidently mistaken in his application of the name or Term of Merchant to those of the Mercantile Interest in England who are Zealous in their hostility to the b Govt. The B Merchant is generally well educated & adheres steadily to his Interest, and that is not to engage in any Imprudent opposition or hostility to that Govt which protects and secures to him advantages not enjoyed by any Mercantile man or men in the world—he is the Merchant of every Country & of every Climate on the globe—his exclusive or universal monopoly supports him in affluence & secures to him Opulence—in fact he supports the Govt and the Govt supports him and if his duties are high they are charged on the goods to the Consumer & therefore he looses nothing by them—his gains by the late french war & his reading & Experience have taught him that civil commotions and revolutionary warfare are fatal to the Mercantile pursuits of every country they happen in and he is not the man Mr Cobbett represents him to be. If he aided to overthrow the B Govt (which he refused on a former Occn) what would become of his national debt of at lest five hundred Millions—he might as well sign a Bankrupt Certificate for it.

But there are other Mercantile characters of a different cast & such as Mr C described—poor young men taken into Merchants Counting houses as clerks whose Erudition is limitted to Arithmetic & Bookkeeping and who after some years of faithfull and diligent services obtain goods from their principals on credit and become respectable retailers—these men are frequently met with at Taverns, porter houses and places of public resort, and after having gained a perfect Knowledge of all the arcana of Exporting Importing storeing Invoiceing &ca. &ca. Know every thing and Exceed Mr C himself in Volubility. The lower orders of the people in England and London are decidedly democratic and he whose passions and Expressions are most violently democratic secures to himself most Custom. Many of these men would vote to hang or Decapitate with as little hesitation as they would Cut the pack thread that tyed a Customers Bundle or parcel—and su[r]ely no friend to humanity would give such men the Controuling power Mr C appears to Contend for on their behalf in any Country—nor can there be a doubt that a Controuling power to be created or given by the American Govt to the Ud Sts Bank over such American Merchants as memorialed against the Tariff would not be a wise a prudent & a necessary precaution. These and the following Considns. led me to suspect his motives for writing that Letter.

Mr Cobbetts public letter to the Duke of Bedford is another very suspicious document[3]—untill that Letter appeared that nobleman was foremost among the most patriotic & public spirited of the british Nobility and as Chairman of the new Market Club had gone so far as to expell the prince of Wales (the prest King) for Misconduct. Mr C.s letter alarmed him—he erroneously considered Mr C the Oracle of the Republican party and that on accot. of his property or conduct he had been secretly proscribed by it and sought safety by Joining Cromwells hereditery Banditi under whose Influence that letter seems to have been written & he has since made Common Cause with them & laments the Whigs as they call themselves being out of Office—that part of the Bedford family property Cobbetts letter aluded to & for which he became alarmed was taken from the Monks and other Clergy by Henry the 8th. and given by him to his favorite Lord Russell—and unless the Monks should be restored or the wealthy siners who gave these Lands to the Clergy for passports to heaven shall return and reappear here to demand them on the ground of their being refused admittance or admission into heaven I do not see what so patriotic a man had to dread from any patriotic party—but the Case of the descendants of Cromwells officers is very different. Cromwell found it necessary to secure these officers in his interest—this could only be done by bribing and Enriching them—he did so—he robbed and destroyed not only the Royal party but also the most peaceable the most antient & wealthy & respectable families in England & Ireland and thereby secured the army in his Interest with which he destroyed that Liberty he was specially appointed to protect. History attests these facts. He dissolved the Republican parliament assumed all legislative and Executive authority—became Tyrant Dictator & as he called himself Lord protector and was as fatal to british Liberty as Robertspierre was to that of France—all this Cromwell effectd sword in hand at the head of these Bloodhounds. Mr Cobbett appears to be whipper in to this party—he can abuse the King and the Ministry with Impunity provided he promotes this Cromwell party Interest for they nominate & return so large a portion of the Members of the House of Commons and the Ministerial Majority that it is not prudent to displease them and yet these descendants of the armed Ruffians who destroyed the liberty of England and thereby have since held Europe in chains (for Europe would have gradually followed the Example of England) these paricidal Ruffians & robbers of the british and Irish nations are the heads of the Orange Lodge party in America and the facts I stated are a certain Criterion whereby to Judge of their principles. These are the men that have voted hundreds of millions and sacrificed hundreds of thousands of men in the late wars to secure their ill gotten possessions and whose accumulat[ed] Villianies far exceed their properties accumulated by rapine murder treason and paricide—these are the Men that have a party in America organised and sworn to destroy their Own Govt and to replace it with the british Govt. A correct Estimate of the Criminality of the Amn Orangemen could only be made by glanceing at the privations pauperism sufferings & distresses of the british people—and he that would do so and say that Cromwells paricidal Robbers & assassins ought not to be deprived of the power to do more mischief to the human species or restore the property they plundered from the Community is a Misantrophist and an Enemy to Mankind. I have often when harassed Cursed the Memory of Charles the 2d for Confirming Cromwells grants to these men as dishonest and ungratefull but on reflecting that by rewarding the Exterminators of Freedom he served the cause of Kings I perceived his conduct was consistent with his station but I do hope that these properties will some time or other be restored or if not applyed to pay the british national debt & I do seriously believe that untill some such event takes place the world will remain convulsed by their Intrigues and never Enjoy peace. These matters have so direct an Influence and bearing on the peace of America that any Correct Elucidation of them cannot be unacceptable and shew that Bonaparte was deemed a usefull man untill his Invasion of Spain and that the fame of his Victories was not the sole cause of his popularity.

The queens success is a greater triumph to the british people than I at first or most superficial people imagined—indeed she deserved it for it appears she was put away because she outlived the Kings likeing (Mrs Fitzherbert being the favorite) in which case as Lord Kenyon properly observed she was Justifiable even if the charge had been proved—he thereby Violated every duty and obligation he was under and she did not marry to become a nun or a Vestal and was therefore perfectly Justifiable—but there is a debt of gratitude due by her to the nation & if she will consent to discharge it no queen Eliza or other Queen will be deemed so great a Benefactress. If they will but patronise the british patriotic Minority so far as to sanction a reform in the House of Commons by abolishing all Boroughs & nominations to seats in parlt. by apportioning the Representation the equalised districts & proportions of the population—by abolishing all unnecessary places and pensions & sinecures and by disqualifying any placeman from siting to Legislate—the british taxes would be reduced one thousand per Cent—the Kings prerogative and the undue Influence of Cromwells oligarchs would be more limitted. Pauperism would disappear and be succeeded by peace & plenty Expectants for places from Scotland Ireland Wales & the Colonies would quit England & relinquish to the farmers the Lands they monopolise or reserve to themselves in prejudice of the laborious poor—such a Change would regenerate England and the queen would very deservedly become the Titular Divinity of that nation—such a change would effectually Check the Overbearing arrogance of the royal family as they are called—prevent exorbitant oppressive taxatn. and effectually relieve the poor & tho last not lest the odious & Cloven Limbs and features of the diabolical Oligarchy would forever disappear. Its Intrigues would decline and the Internal peace and repose of America would be secured by it. If the King resists such an Amelioration that he may end his days in Hanover or on the borders of Gothland the Region of Despotism secure from the disagreeable Importunity of Freemen is the wish of Your Most obt. H Servt

Edmond Kelly

As I am accused of Belying Mr John Bull Donnellan I shall attempt a description of Irish parties their Views & policy from which an Estimate Can be made of his political Importance matters that can scarcely be guessed at by any persons here except Comnr. Emmett[4] & Doctor McNevin of New York[5] to whom a reference as to its Verity will be conclusive. The Impression on my mind when I began the within letter that british Agents Knowing the Importance of a well managed Natl Bank would as they had done cause it to be plundered if not sufficiently protected by law & that to create such an Institution without affording it adequate protection was erroneous in policy & Legislation—that it is tempting swindlers & sharpers & leaving the public in their care & at their discretion & that it requires severer laws to restrain them than plain Farmers.

RC (NN). Addressed by Kelly to JM "at his residence state of Virginia Washington City or elsewhere," and franked. "Washington City" has been crossed out and "Orange C:H: V" written below it in an unidentified hand.

1. Kelly referred to the law that incorporated the Second Bank of the United States, "An Act to incorporate the subscribers to the Bank of the United States," 10 Apr. 1816, and "An Act to enforce those provisions of the act, entitled 'An act to incorporate the subscribers to the Bank of the United States,' which relate to the right of voting for directors, and for other purposes," 3 Mar. 1819 (*U.S. Statutes at Large*, 3:266–77, 508–9).

2. Kelly referred here to a letter from William Cobbett to then secretary of the Treasury Alexander James Dallas, 13 Jan. 1816, published in *Cobbett's American Political Register* 30 (25 May 1816): 33–48.

3. For Cobbett's letter to the Duke of Bedford on parliamentary reform, 28 Jan. 1819, see *Cobbett's Weekly Political Register* 34 (24 Apr. 1819): 955–86.

4. Thomas Addis Emmet (1764–1827), a graduate of Trinity College, Dublin, was trained as a physician at the University of Edinburgh and practiced in Dublin but on the death of his older brother, Temple, decided to become a lawyer. He was admitted to the Irish bar in 1790. As a leader and outspoken defender of the United Irishmen and an advocate of Catholic emancipation, Emmet was arrested in 1798 and imprisoned until 1802, when he was released and expelled from Great Britain. After his brother Robert's execution by the British in 1803, Emmet emigrated from Paris to the United States in 1804, settling in New York City, where he carried on a celebrated law career. One of his sons, John Patten Emmet, was the first professor of chemistry at the University of Virginia (Thomas Addis Emmet, *Memoir of Thomas Addis and Robert Emmet with Their Ancestors and Immediate Family* [2 vols.; New York, 1915], 1:202, 203, 206, 211, 213, 228, 248, 330, 372, 389, 391, 406, 458–60, 468, 472; see also a letter introducing Emmet to JM from DeWitt Clinton, 25 Nov. 1804, *PJM-SS*, 8:322).

5. William James MacNeven (1763–1841) was born in Ireland and educated in Prague and Vienna. A United Irishman, he practiced medicine in Dublin until his arrest and imprisonment by the British in 1798. Released four years later, he immigrated to New York in 1804, where he continued his practice and served as professor of various subjects, including chemistry and materia medica, at the College of Physicians and Surgeons of Columbia University from 1807 to 1826. The following four years MacNeven taught materia medica at the Rutgers Medical College. He wrote a number of treatises on chemistry, as well as *Pieces of Irish History* (1807) (Samuel D. Gross, ed., *Lives of Eminent American Physicians and Surgeons of the Nineteenth Century* [Philadelphia, 1861], 479–87).

From Richard S. Hackley

Sir Washington 9th Feby. 1821.

Presuming, on the letter of Introduction, from Governor Randolph, which I had the honor to deliver to you, some short time since,[1] The friendly dispositions, expressed towards me, and evinced, in your recommendation of me, to the President,[2] I beg permission to State, That I yesterday, solicited the appointment of Collector of the Port of St. A[u]gustine, in East Florida, whenever the Executive shall deem it proper to make such an appointment.

The president, sugested the propriety of directing my recommendations, for that office, to the Secretary of the Treasury, Mr. Crawford, as the channel through which this appointment will properly come, and that of addressing yourself & Governor Randolph, for a line of recommendation to that Gentleman.

Unprovided with recommendations to that Gentleman, I can only calculate upon the goodness of such acquaintance as I have in Congress, to name me to him. And I shall feel most grateful, for whatever recommendation of me, you may deem it proper to add. With Sentiments of the highest respect, I have the honor to be Sir Yr: Most Obt. Hble sert.

Richd: S: Hackley

RC (DLC). Docketed by JM.

1. See Thomas Mann Randolph to JM, 28 Dec. 1820, and n.
2. See JM to James Monroe, 6 Jan. 1821.

From George Joy

Dear sir, London 9th febry 1821.

You shall have no cause to complain of a tardy rejoinder to your favour of the 25th Novr. last, altho' in that war of recrimination I was long since offered the Alliance of my friend Jeremy Bentham; and it was literally the fact that at the hour of receiving your Letter last Evening and from that to the present, I have had more of Correspondence to attend to than for any week together in the current year. However we sometimes manage best when put to our shifts;[1] and the Receipt of your Letter determined me to divert to Montpellier a Newspaper I was about sending to Washington, and even to add to it the Copy of a Letter I wrote a few Days before, and which you will see I had retained for some such purpose. I have a young Myrmidon here, the only Servant I can afford to keep, who writes a hand so like my own (albeit he can write much better) that I am afraid Physiologists will mistake him for one of my Bastards, for I have seen a deal of family Conformation in handwriting—(tho' by the way there are no two of my own family that write at all alike)—but what I dread much more is that his Orthography should be mistaken for mine, especially when he writes from dictation or from the reading to him from a Stenographic Copy—for the enclosed he had the original before him; but I am afraid to trust it, without this Notice. It is a Letter to my Sister,[2] who had bored me more than once for an opinion on the Speech of our Nephew at the Wiltshire Meeting; and I have not time to clip it. I have however marked the Scripture phrases in quotations as a New Englander should always do in writing to a Virginian. I shall also eke out my despatch by an Extract from a Letter just received from my Brother,[3] on a Work of Wm Tudor (Letters on the Eastern States published in New York) and another from my own Letter to Tudor of this date.[4] I am reminded by his Letter on Politics of the Efforts I made to remove the Notion entertained here that the Members of the opposition to our Government could be counted on as friendly to this; particularly in my Conciliator Nr 5.[5] The importance of inculcating this opinion—(now, I trust, confirmed at home)—is one of the strongest motives for getting the Work into Circulation here. I have little apprehension of a Collision; but it is well to take Time by the Forelock; and reference to a Work written *now* may be more satisfactory than any Statement drawn up *pro re nata*.[6]

By the way I have tried in various ways to get Copies of my Conciliator, printed in the National Intelligencer, of which Mr: Gales sent me the first three Numbers with his Exordium; and he wrote that he had printed the whole. I have particular reasons for wishing to have them in that form. I am afraid the wish is hopeless; but if you could put me in the way to procure them, it would oblige me greatly. If I had covered the Wiltshire Paper to Mr. Gales, I should have repeated a requisition of this kind; but besides the Intervention of your Letter to give it another direction, here is now the Speaker himself saying, to send it to the Nat. Int. would be too like the Puff direct. This however is not to prevent your making any use you please of it or of the *learned* Comments upon it; and as I cannot lay hold of the preceding County Paper to compleat the Series; I cover the Times of the 19th Ult. containing with the Wiltshire an Account of the Kent County Meeting.[7] With respect to the distresses arising from superabundance, I cannot help thinking if the Moonites have sufficiently good Telescopes what a miserable set of Lunarians they must take us for. But Ministers shall not have my project of redress, till I have a better Guarantee than they can give me, that in "waxing fat, like Jessurun," they will not also "kick."[8] I have held it back for years under this apprehension, and I should not wonder if it never came forward.

In respect to the Changes taking place in Europe, I note your distinction between the precise dangers from within and the *probable* dangers from without—it is not in the nature of things that Monarchs should be pleased with those Changes; and however prudent, and wise it may be to yield with a good Grace where the insurrectionary movement is already made; if those to whom it is only approaching should make no Effort to keep it off, it will only be because "their Poverty and not their Will consents."[9]

I see no reason to alter the opinion I have uniformly held on the subject of Manufactures. I wish not for an isolated Independence; but rather, if it could be had, the freest possible interchange of all the Commodities of Life—but this, depending on a general acquiescence, is rather possible than at once practicable. All the world must be Quakers before we can have universal peace—and to this sect I beg you to tell Mrs. M. with my Compliments, tho' I have not made up my mind on the subject, I think I approach the nearest—and if such general acquiescence cannot be had; it behoves every nation to take care of herself. Hamilton reported long since on the policy of encouraging such manufactures as would make the Country independent on foreign Nations for the Munitions of War,[10] and these include many Articles ancipiti usus[11]—what would an Army do in our Climate without Blankets? Laisser faire is a good general rule; but there are occasions on which the Government may lend a hand. If there were none other than offensive wars; I should never desire the means to be of easy acquirement; but where to be defenceless is to invite insult, I must say, Si vis pacem, para Bellum.[12] But even the Doctrine of Laisser aller must bring about Manufactures in the Case you mention, and they should have *some* encouragement. "If you cannot sell you cannot buy"—then as Dr: Franklin said 50 years ago, you must use the Loom more and the Plough less.

Now you will think I have made out a Dispatch of sufficient Bulk; and I see my Boy has shown his predilection for Legitimacy, by copying the Extracts in a hand less resembling mine than the Letter to Miss Joy. He is one of the nova progenies;[13] and not a bad example of the benefit of giving education to the poorer Classes. I know only the outline of the Missouri Question, and am sorry to say it presents itself to me as a thing of some difficulty—a sort of Collision between Justice and Humanity. I trust there is sufficient Virtue, and sufficient good temper, in the U.S. to render these objects compatible with each other; and shall rejoice to hear that it is settled on satisfactory terms.

The Bag of the regular Boston Ship goes tomorrow; and I shall avail myself of your monstrous Sinecure[14] to give this a long Sweep of postage by that route.

I am always gratified in receiving a Letter from you; and hope you will indulge me at your leisure, addressing as this last to No 13 Finsbury Square. Always, very faithfully, Dear sir, Your most obedt Servt

G. Joy

RC and enclosures (DLC: Rives Collection, Madison Papers). Docketed by JM. For enclosures, see nn. 2–4.

1. Put to our shifts: "to bring to extremity" (*OED Online*).

2. Joy enclosed a copy of a letter to his sister, Betsy, 5 Feb. 1821 (4 pp.), that included criticism of his nephew's speech and comments on the purging of Queen Caroline's name from the liturgy. As Joy explained, "as to any Spiritual advantage or disadvantage from her name being retained, omitted, or restored to the Liturgy, I would not give 18*d* one way or the other. The Prayers of the whole Kingdom would not pray away or restore the Life of a worm."

3. The enclosure is an extract of a letter from Michael Joy to George Joy, 7 Feb. 1821 (2 pp.), praising *Letters on the Eastern States* by William Tudor and urging that it be brought to the notice of the *Quarterly Review* or *Edinburgh Review*. Of the former he wrote that "if their commendation cannot be obtained, the next best thing is to secure their enmity; for this goes almost as far towards selling a book, as their praise."

4. Joy enclosed an undated extract of his letter to William Tudor (1 p.), commenting on Tudor's book and "the Amalga[ma]tion of the Ancient Nobility with the modern Meritists" in England.

5. Joy referred here to his essays under the signature of "Conciliator," some of which he enclosed in manuscript in his letter to JM, 23 Feb. 1815, DLC. In his Conciliator essay No. 5, Joy described the Henry affair, in which the Irish adventurer, John Henry, was employed by the British government to assess the degree of antiadministration feeling in New England during and immediately after the Embargo. For the background of this story and the sale of Henry's letters to the Madison administration in February 1812, see Elbridge Gerry to JM, 2 Jan. 1812, and nn. 1–2 (*PJM-PS*, 4:116–17).

6. Pro re nata: "as required, or as needed" (*OED Online*).

7. The County of Wilts meeting, at which Henry Joy spoke, was called "to consider the propriety of declaring the 'unabated and unalterable attachment of the county to the constitution and government of this country, as by law established; to express their deep regret at the late unjustifiable and unconstitutional proceedings instituted against the Queen; and to petition both Houses of Parliament to take the most effectual steps for the removal of every obstacle to a satisfactory and final arrangement, as well as to prevent a recurrence to measures of a similar tendency, and the revival of discussions equally mischievous to the public morals, and dangerous to the peace of the country'" (*Times* [London], 19 Jan. 1821).

8. Joy paraphrased the verse "But Jeshurun waxed fat, and kicked" (Deut. 32:15 [AV]).

9. Joy paraphrased the line "My poverty, but not my will, consents," Shakespeare, *Romeo and Juliet*, 5.1.75 (*Riverside*).

10. One rationale for Alexander Hamilton's *Report on the Subject of Manufactures*, 5 Dec. 1791, was to identify "the means of promoting such [manufactures] as will tend to render the United States, independent on [*sic*] foreign nations, for military and other essential supplies" (Syrett and Cooke, *Papers of Alexander Hamilton*, 10:230).

11. *Ancipitis usus:* in international law, "goods susceptible of being used for warlike and peaceful purposes" (*Black's Law Dictionary* [9th ed.], 101, 365).

12. *Si vis pacem, para Bellum:* if you want peace, prepare for war.

13. *Nova progenies:* new offspring.

14. On 1 Mar. 1817 Congress had passed "An Act freeing from postage all letters and packets to and from James Madison," *U.S. Statutes at Large*, 3:350.

To Robert H. Rose

Sɪʀ Mᴏɴᴛᴘʀ. Feby. 10. 1821

I have recd your letter of Jany. 21.[1] with a Copy of your address to the Agricultl. Socy. of Susquehanna County,[2] for which I return my thanks. I offer but a just tribute to the Address, in saying that it contains very judicious observations presented in the best form, & apparently very appropriate to the rural circumstances of the new County.

The multiplication of these Societies is among the many proofs of the spirit & progress of improvement in our Country. And the establishment of them in districts unimpoverished by a vicious cultivation may prevent those wasteful errors which it is found so difficult & expensive to repair. With friendly respects

J. M.

Draft (DLC). With JM's note in top margin: "R.H. Rose. Silver Lake Pena." Robert Hutchinson Rose (1776–1842) was born in Chester County, Pennsylvania, and educated in Philadelphia. He was trained as a doctor but never practiced. In 1809 he purchased an enormous tract of land in northern Pennsylvania, built a home on the shores of Silver Lake, and for the rest of his life worked to develop the area (Rhamanthus M. Stocker, *Centennial History of Susquehanna County, Pennsylvania* [1887; reprint, Baltimore, 1974], 500).

1. Letter not found.
2. Robert H. Rose, *An Address Delivered before the Agricultural Society of Susquehanna County, at Its Organization, December 6, 1820* (Montrose, Pa., 1820).

To Thomas Todd

Mʏ ᴅᴇᴀʀ Sɪʀ Mᴏɴᴛᴘᴇʟʟɪᴇʀ Feby. 11. 1821

We learn by a letter from Mrs. Cutts[1] with much pleasure that you had ended your journey to Washington in good health; and we flatter ourselves that you will give us the opportunity of being eye witnesses to its continuance, on your return to Frankfort. I need not say how truly glad we shall be to see you; how much we shall expect it; and what a disappointment we shall feel, if you should take a different route. The disappointment will be the greater as Mrs. Todd has been so good (God bless her) as to let us know that she had laid the proper injunctions on you. I would not bespeak the visit from you if I were not perfectfully [*sic*] confident that it would expose you to no danger from a fever which has lately found its way into our family, & been fatal to some of the black part of it. Besides that we hope the last of the cases has occurred, there is every reason to believe, that no danger whatever attends a transient intercourse even with the sick in the most tainted atmosphere; much less, with the well, in that which is the purest. Favor us therefore with an assurance that we shall be able in due time to embrace you at our fireside.

I have been very sensible of your kindness in forwarding the several portions of our Legislative Journals, and have to thank you particularly for those of 1783. lately recd.

In a letter to Judge Washington,[2] I inclosed some time ago, certain letters which he was so obliging as to send me with a permission to copy. I promised to return them & wish to know that they got safe to hand. Be so good as to take an occasion for asking him whether this was the case. Mrs M. & Payne are at my elbow with all the affectionate wishes of which I pray you to accept assurances from yours tru⟨ly⟩

James Madison

RC (NjMoHP).

1. Letter not found.
2. See JM to Bushrod Washington, 14 Oct. 1820.

¶ To an Unidentified Correspondent. Letter not found. *11 February 1821.* Described as a two-page autograph letter, signed, from Montpelier, in Stan. V. Henkels Catalogue No. 1425 (14 Feb. 1929), item 41.

From John A. Wharton

Sir — Nashville February 12th. 1821

I am unacquainted with you; yet an unmeaning ceremony, I believe, to be as disagreeable to you, as it is foreign to the purpose. It will not therefore, I hope, be thought presumption in me to address you at present, on a subject of the first importance. But to the purpose. I am a young man in pursuit of an education, and desirous of enjoying the benefits offered by the establishment of The University of my native state. My object at present is to solicit any information which you possess relative to the seminary at Charlottesville Viz: When it will go into operation, and as economy is by no means to be disregarded by me I wish to ascertain what will be the probable annual expense of a student at the University. And lastly what are the qualifications necessary to ensure an entrance into each class. I entertain doubts, whether it will be in your power [to] answer the last of my enquiries. However as information on that head would obviate many difficulties, I thought it necessary to insert it. As my residence in Tennessee is only temporary, I have to request you to direct your answer to Davis' store, Bedford Virginia, the place of my residence. I have now to beg pardon for intruding on your patience & to pray you to accept the assurance of my profound respect and esteem.

JNO. A. WHARTON[1]

RC (DLC). Docketed by JM.

1. John Austin Wharton (1803–1888), born in Bedford County, Virginia, was a lawyer and banker until 1847, when he was ordained a deacon in the Episcopal Church. He served as rector in Bedford, Virginia, until his death (Joanne Spiers Moche, *Families of Grace through 1900: Remembering Radford* [1 vol. to date; Westminster, Md., 2008—], 1:142).

¶ To Henry Baldwin. Letter not found. *Ca. 13 February 1821.* Printed facsimile of RC cover sheet, addressed and franked by JM; postmarked 13 Feb. 1821 at Orange Court House. Offered for sale in Robert F. Batchelder Catalog 64 [1988], item 32. Henry Baldwin (1780–1844), a Connecticut-born, Yale-educated, Pittsburgh lawyer, was half-brother to Abraham Baldwin and Ruth Baldwin Barlow. Baldwin served in the U.S. House of Representatives, 1817–22, where he was chairman of the committee on manufactures, 1819–22. From 1830 until his death he was an associate justice of the U.S. Supreme Court (M. Flavia Taylor, "The Political and Civic Career of Henry Baldwin, 1799–1830," *Western Pennsylvania Historical Magazine* 24 [1941]: 37–50).

From Robert S. Garnett

WASHINGTON CITY Feb. 14. 1821.

Mr Garnett[1] presents his compliments to Mr Madison and begs that he will accept of the Report of the Committee on Agriculture herewith enclosed.[2]

RC (DLC). Docketed by JM. Below Garnett's letter is the draft of JM to Garnett, 20 Feb. 1821.

1. Robert Selden Garnett (1789–1840) of Essex County, Virginia, was a U.S. congressman, 1817–27 (Tyler, *Encyclopedia of Virginia Biography*, 2:109).

2. *Report of the Committee on Agriculture, on the Memorial of the Delegates of the United Agricultural Societies of Sundry Counties in the State of Virginia. Feb. 2, 1821* ([Washington], 1821; Shoemaker 7427).

¶ To Robert H. Rose. Letter not found. *14 February 1821.* Calendared as a one-page letter in the lists probably made by Peter Force (DLC, series 7, box 2).

To Ethan Allen Brown

Montpellier (Virga.) Feby. 15. 1821

J. Madison presents his respects to Governour Brown with many thanks for the "Report" accompanying his Note of Jany. 26. It is a very able paper, on a subject well meriting the consideration and discussion, to which the views taken of it by the Committee are calculated to lead.

RC (ViU: Madison Papers, Special Collections); draft (DLC). RC docketed by Brown.

To William Harris Crawford

Dr. Sir Feby. 15. 1821.

Mr Hackley heretofore in the Consular service of the U.S. in Spain, is desirous of an appt. in E. Florida, which it seems to be understood, is soon to come within their jurisdiction.

My personal acquaintance with Mr. H. is very limited. I can say with truth & with pleasure, nevertheless, that I have been led by it to a very favorable opinion not only of his agreeable manners but of his general intelligence and his capacity for pub: service. And I find that he is held in very particular estimation by his highly respectable friends & connections; all of whom taking a warm interest in his behalf will be much gratified, should no superior pretensions be an insuperable obstacle, at seei[n]g him in an improved way of making provision for a most deserving & amiable family. Begging pardon for this intrusion, I tender you, Sir assurances of my high consideration & cordial regards

J. M.

Draft (DLC). Below JM's initials is the draft of JM to Richard S. Hackley of the same date.

To Richard S. Hackley

Dr. Sir. Feby. 15. 1821

In consequence of your letter just recd.[1] I have dropped a few lines on the subject of it to the Secy. of the Treasy: which are enclosed. With friendly respects

J. M.

Draft (DLC). Written below the draft of JM to William Harris Crawford, 15 Feb. 1821.

1. Hackley to JM, 9 Feb. 1821.

From Thomas L. McKenney

Sir, Weston—Heights of Geo Town—Feby, 17. 1821.

I hope I may be excused for troubling you with the enclosed pamphlet.[1] I am prompted to enclose it to you, Sir, by other considerations than those which relate to its merits.

I avail myself of the occasion to make a tender of my remembrance to Mrs. Madison, in which I am join'd by Mrs. McKenney; and to assure you of my Sincere & respectful regards.

Tho: L: McKenney

RC (DLC). Docketed by JM.

1. This was probably *Letter from the Superintendent of Indian Trade, to the Chairman of the Committee on Indian Affairs, Communicating a Report in Relation to Indian Trade. December 13, 1820* (Washington, 1820; Shoemaker 3860).

From James Monroe

Dear Sir Washington Feby 17. 1821

I regret to have to inform you of the death of Mr Wm. Burwell[1] which took place on yesterday, after a long illness. He was a virtuous man & good member.

The treaty with spain has been ratified unconditionally by her govt., & the grants annulld in the instrument of ratification.[2] It is now before the Senate on the question whether it shall be accepted, the time stipulated for the ratification having previously expird. No serious opposition is anticipated.

There is some hope that Missouri will be admitted, on a mov'ment on the part of Pennsyla., by her Senators in concert with some members in the H. of R. Mr Biddle[3] who is here, has renderd some service in this important occurrence.

There is also some hope that our commercial difference with France will be adjusted. Your friend

James Monroe

RC (DLC: Rives Collection, Madison Papers). Docketed by JM.

1. William Armistead Burwell (1780–1821), a Franklin County, Virginia, planter, served as President Thomas Jefferson's private secretary, 1804–6, and as a member of the U.S. House of Representatives, 1806–21 (Kneebone et al., *Dictionary of Virginia Biography*, 2:439–40).

2. Article 8 of the Transcontinental Treaty between the United States and Spain confirmed all Spanish land grants in the Floridas made before 24 Jan. 1818 (Miller, *Treaties*, 3:9). That date was meant to annul three immense land grants that had been recently made by the king of Spain, but since there was some question about the timing of the grants, royal orders, and other decrees, there was great anxiety on the part of American officials to clarify this point. For a discussion of the annulled grants, see ibid., 42–49.

3. Nicholas Biddle (1786–1844), a graduate of the College of New Jersey, was secretary to John Armstrong, U.S. minister to France, 1804–7, and for a short time secretary to James Monroe when the latter was U.S. minister to Great Britain. On his return to Philadelphia, Biddle read and then practiced law, and contributed to, and then became editor of, the Philadelphia literary magazine the *Port Folio*. In 1819 President Monroe appointed Biddle a director of the Second Bank of the United States, and in 1822 he became its president. Biddle led the unsuccessful fight to recharter the bank in 1832; on the charter's expiration in 1836, he carried on as president of the newly named United States Bank of Pennsylvania until his retirement in 1839 (Thomas Payne Govan, *Nicholas Biddle: Nationalist and Public Banker, 1786–1844* [Chicago, 1959], 1, 8–9, 11, 13, 19, 20–21, 22, 39, 50, 59, 77 and n. 24, 172, 201, 283, 350, 411). During the Missouri crisis, Biddle reported political developments in Pennsylvania to Monroe and in the final stages of the debate helped persuade several Pennsylvania representatives to support measures designed to end the restriction on Missouri's admission as a state (Forbes, *The Missouri Compromise and Its Aftermath*, 71, 118).

From John Laval

Sir, Philadelphia Feby. 19th 1821

I have the honor to inform you that the fourth Edition of Nature Displayed[1] is just published: the Cause of the delay of the publication, until this period, is the long absence of Mr. Dufief from the U.S. I forward you, by this day's Mail, the first Volume, & Shall transmit, by the next, the Second of the Copy for Which you paid four Years Since. I am With Consideration & respect Sir, Your very humble Servant

John Laval[2]

RC (DLC). Docketed by JM.

1. For *Nature Displayed*, see Nicholas Gouin Dufief to JM, 17 Mar. 1817, *PJM-RS*, 1:12, 13 n. 1.

2. John Laval (ca. 1769–1839), an emigré from Saint-Domingue, was a Philadelphia merchant who in 1802 occupied 44 Lombard Street. A longtime friend of Nicholas Gouin Dufief, Laval took over management of the latter's Universal Book Store in 1817 (Stern, *Nicholas Gouin Dufief of Philadelphia*, 61–63, 67).

To Robert S. Garnett

Feby. 20. 1821

J.M. presents his re[s]pects to Mr. Garnet with thanks for the Report of the Come. on agriculture which well merits the perusal for which an opportunity was politely afforded.

Draft (DLC). Written below Garnett to JM, 14 Feb. 1821.

To Robert Mackay

Dr. Sir Feby. 20. 1821

I duly recd. yours of .[1] The Mill saw was safely brought by the Waggoner. I am sorry to observe that it was not only without the usual holes for fixing it in the wooden frame; but had a *flaw* inward from the teeth near the middle of the saw, *visible* at the slightest glance. This defect is particularly unfortunate, as it requires a slackness in working the Saw, that loses both time & water, the latter a very scarce article. If it will be taken back; I request the favor of you, to send me another and a better, by the first oppy. you can confide in. Before I was informed of the defect in the Saw, orders had been given for punching the necessary holes. These however are now an advantage to it. Be so obliging as to forward the inclosed as soon as may be to Liverpool.[2]

Draft (DLC).

1. Left blank in ms. Letter not found.
2. The enclosed letter was JM to James Maury, 20 Feb. 1821.

To James Maury

Dr. Sir Feby. 20. 1821

Your favor enclosing Act. Sales & invoice came safe to hand.[1] The articles sent are liable to no objection except that some of them are rather of a superior sort & of course, price, than was in view. I have arranged with Mr. Mackay, the balance due from me so as [to] stand debited in his books for it.

The sales of the Tobo. did not fully meet expectation. That of the best quality it was thought wd. have equalled the price of the James River, and the difference in the prices of the different Hhds was less than the *supposed* difference in their qualities. I am afraid that a distinction is made in England, between Tobo. going from Rappahannock & from James River, to the disadvantage of the former; tho' of the same quality, from the same soil, and such as would sell at Richd at the same price. If this be the case, I must send my future Crops to the latter place whether to be there shipped or sold. One of the motives for sending the last Crop to Fredg. was that it saves nearly half the expense of transportation; and it was presumed that its *quality alone* wd. determine its price in the foreign market. Be so good as to favor me with an early line of information on this subject. My late crop of Tobo. is of the best quality the year on the whole having been favorable, and the soil such as you know.

Draft (DLC).

1. See Maury & Latham to JM, 24 Oct. 1820. For JM's shipment of tobacco and his request for articles to be purchased, see JM to James Maury, ca. July 1820.

From Edmond Kelly

SIR COLUMBIA TEN [post–20] Feby 1821

On the debate of the Misouri question in the last session Mr Barbour in Senate asserted that the restriction would drive that country into insurrection & that an Ignited spark might sever it from the Union.[1] A poor white population is always opposed to Negroes—the slaveholders in Misouri do not exceed 3 out of 12 of the white people & the Idea of an attempt at Insurrection by one fourth slave Owners against the other 3 4ths. and the general Govt. would cause as Little Terror as Mr Bs speech. The sentiment of this would be father Conscript betrays more timidity & artifice than firmness and wisdom and if it was not an attempt at imposition was at best erroneous. I suspect he Identifies me with his Ignited spark. If so he wrongs me & whatever were my Errors when a boy age & Experience taught me to correct them. I am neither a Demagogue nor an Incendiary but opposed to them—since I came to America my efforts have been zealously & invariably used to check expoze and defeat faction & treason. The Injury and Injustice done me by the british Govt. Interrested me to resist its secret machinations to destroy Amn Indepce. That I contributed to check its progress is evident for which I consider the abuse of Orangemen, Traitors to their Country as Dr Wolcot says exalted praise.[2] Mr B is not one of them but a temporising Coward who wishes to Influence adverse parties to agree to his elevation as president—no honourable man wd descend to such meaness—in the same speech aludeing to the Orange Lodge Sistem he remarks—It was lately but as a speck above the horizon—but that then it obscured the heavens, and hoped the day of its success might be his last—the B King finds himself disappointed through Orangemen. His aristocratic Orange Lodge partizan and Incendiary was unsuccessfull and therefore he sends a democratic Incendiary who he expects will be more acceptable & successfull—the Kings object being to robb and destroy me & to extend british Govt Influence he cares not whether the Incendiary is an Orangeman or a Jacobin if he effects his purpose. The most capable & successfull is the most favoured—and when men in the highest stations extend patronage to these freebooters and Incendiaries they in effect disseminate very pernicious prejudices among the people at large who are thus divided into parties and arrayed in hostil[it]y to each other in favour of one or other of the Dogs of a british party Itinerants on a british court prostitute Expedn. British patriots would hold such a Conduct in Contempt—neither do the assertions of such adventurers supported only by party Malice & the vindictive passions of the Monarch sanction any Interference with the Jurisprudence of the Country where the property is situate[d] out of which rent was transmitted here—no man was Ever deemed entitled to rent untill he proved Title to the Estate it was recd from—no such proof was ever attempted there or could be made here & unless a court of Justic[e] there certifies such proof to have been made it would be an act of the foulest Injustice to pay away the property of any unfortunate person to such adventurers & sharpers—it would be giving it to them as a quantum meruit[3] for their services to a british court bawd instead of protecting that Just right to it which the Constin. enjoyns. Mr Barbour in one of his late speeches reasserts John Bulls Claims—that is he condemns *the narrow and selfish policy by which he insinuates I am actuated* to protect my rights and recommends *a broad principle*—this led me to reflect what Jacks broad principle is or means which I find to be neither more nor less than a Complimt to his superior broad size & stature—had he or his senatorial advocate contended that my property ought to be divided equally among all the satelites or british Intrigue who could prove relationship or Affinity it might be more consistent with the broad principle of Jacobinism & the Guillotine but neither Mr Bull or his advocate means any such thing. Jack wants this property exclusively for himself & is actuated by that selfish principle he disapproves of in me—it is saying in effect, my opponent is of spare & narrow stature blind & useless & so selfish that he wants to preserve his family property. I am of broad & huge stature & superior strength—a sistem Monger or teacher of Jacobinical Doctrines On a representative Sistem—a despiser of superstition & priestcraft believing Nature the only true god & that her grace intended the narrow and the weak should labour for the benefit of the broad and the strong against whom all social Compact is an unjust & unnatural Combination of the weaker & more envious part of mankind. I can be usefull. I can bully a british Ct Prostitute or be bully for her as the public safety or the good of the poor requires it (for every thing a demagogue does tho it be to cram & fill his pockets full as a Bishop from the treasury is for the good of the poor & to enable him to do the more good). The public good required that I should aid the King in the Contest between him & the Oligarchs (Cromwells) about the property of my narrow selfish Opponent & as his ruin is determined on I ought to be the gainer—such are the sentiments & claims of John Bull—that they are execrable Cannot be disputed. I did not suppose the most superficial pretender to philosophy could Sanction them—this broad principle of rapacity which Mr Bull and his advocate rely on Decapitated the proprietors of property in France and struck a Terror into wealthy Men in the british Isles that prevents their risking the most expensive state of security for the prospect of amelioration from a populace Enfuriated by poor Ambitious & avaricious men—like Cain the Jacobin murders his brother & is more ferocious and Cruel than the barbarous African or arabian robber who do not murder their brethren or prey on their Own societies—the divine law which enjoyns fraternal love and Justice Jack calls a falsehood o[r] cheat because it is a Veto to his rapacious and murderous designs—if Mr B had that Knowlege of the Sciences which a legislator and a Senator Ought to have he would not have advocated such principles—for altho every rational man Condemns the Conduct of the Christian Church from the usurpation of the popedom to the period of modern reformations Yet Science deduced from Celestial observations corroborates & supports the Divine laws and proves that there is no such thing as chance which Atheists assert Created and governs this world and that there is a cause for every thing & that nothing is without a Cause—the retiring of Presidts. Madison & Jefferson from public life I suppose could alone leave Mr B room to hope for the Presidentcy but I hope while there is such a man as Mr Pinkney to offer that Mr P will be the person elected.

Having said so much of the person who enjoys the british Kings patronage a similar description of the King himself will not be uninterresting.

A rigid Adherence to that Interest that transferred the Crown to the house of Orange & subsequently to the Elector of Hanover was Visible during the reign of Geo the 3d. Legal disabilities & disqualifications of all sects & of the papists continued & the Govt. was administered with so much party Illiberality that good patriotic men were displeased with it. A dread that France wd afford the Irish papists protection & aid similar to what she gave to the US made it politic to relax the penal Code against them and to give them hopes of its progressive removal conditioned for their future loyalty & fidelity but in other respects it continued a Govt. of sistematic exclusion Very disagreeable to liberal men—the borough Majority on all occasions Voted enormous taxes so equalised in their Collection between the Opulent Landlord and the poor renter that they became oppressive to the poor Farmer or Tenant on whom the Landlord subsequently shifted the payment of them exacting his rent without deduction for there was no back country to move to & Compliance could not be avoided—in fact the *borough* Majority supported the Crown & protected the Oligarchs (Cromwells men) in their usurpations—this state of Oligarchic oppression gave so much disgust that discontent became general—the lower Orders were anxious to change their Govt for a democratic one but Experience of what happened in France and the Accumulation of property rendered such a Change Dangerous—it also involved the safety of the Colonies & of all the british possessions nor could the national Debt be secured and Messrs. Fox Sheridan[4] and others who had the Confidence of the nation expected that when their favourite the Prince of Wales the prest King Came into power he would authorise them to reform the Legislature & the Govt & abolish the boroughs—the Influence of the leaders of the opposition & their friendship & partiality for the prest King appears to have had much weight in preventing any attempt to Overthrow the Govt. These national hopes were disappointed. When this favourite of the people came into power he proved himself worthless ungratefull and unprincipled—he reformed no abuse & tho without any necessity for extra Expence did nothing to relieve the people from a load of taxation so oppressive that it Converted the Labouring poor into paupers totally unable by their Labour in a Land of plenty & the most productive soil in Europe to ear[n] or rather to reserve a sufficiency of Bread—of Food and of Raiment. Besoted and callous to every tender Simpathy and humane feeling he neither sees nor cares for their sufferings. He does not consider himself a King for the good of the people but like a remorseless slave Owner the people for his benefit and his thoughts are so exclusively occupyed by sordid selfish and sensual pursuits that one may say of him with the poet

> There goes a man in Vice and folly bred
> to sense of honour as to Virtue Dead[5]

In short he has continued every tax & every burden which Mr Pitt found it necessary to create to subsidise foreign princes & pay their armies to anihilate democratic France—he has thereby converted the labouring poor into half famished paupers which was the Condition of France previous to the Revolution—he has Violated every humane & honourable principle & every obligation which gratitude for public Indulgence & unmerited national partiality Imposed on him. Dissipation Immoral habits & Dishonourable pursuits are the peculiar traits of his character—the popular sentiment & feeling renders it necessary for him to Continue his Expensive Majorities—but to Continue their expences is a Wanton Injury which will Exasperate the people—& to loose these Majorities risks the loss or at lest the reduceing of his Authority—& there is no friend to humanity that would not wish the last. The british are a great & a magnanimous people & except the love of Conquest have fewer faults & more excellence than other nations—when they do wrong it is by Order of their King or of Cromwells Oligarchs & an ameliorated Change in their Govt wd benefit the world—put their govt Intrigues to rest—confirm & uphold the Improved changes on the European Continent and ultimately restrict the Infamous Francis Emperor of the Goths the Champion of European Despotism & the Orange Lodge Bully—but alas while british Monopoly continues uninterrupted such a change is scarcely to be expected without Convulsion—if the Amn Govt wd do its duty—establish D Manufs. the british King would loose much of his means to pay those Majorities that Oppress & Enchain England & a radical Change of Govt. wd relieve the british people for if England exported less she would & ought to reduce her taxes one thousand per cent by it—on this principle every friend to despotism & oligarchic oppression every disaffected American will oppose Domc Manufactures & side with Mr Floyd[6] who dislikes Taleyrand for attempting to overthrow the oligarchs—but every patriotic man will vote for them.

I shall conclude these remarks on the King with a few words relative to his attacks on my family property for however worthless myself & undeserving the distinguished Character of my Ancestors for Sevl Ages procured me the patronage of those antient families that were most opulent & respectable—the patriotic and Virtuous Minority of the british Legislature was always opposed to the rapacious conduct and attacks of the younger branches of the royal family on this property—the supposed influence of this Minority on the Prince of Wales so alarmed Cromwells oligarchs (who expected that his Govt would be unprejudiced liberal & Just & that he wd protect the Just rights of all men without distinction or regard to party feeling[)] that they restricted him in his qualification oath for Regent from calling any one to the peerage without their Consent—they did not stop here. They represented to him the advantage of Adding my family property to his royal funds—& converted him into the Staunchest hound of their pack—poisons were & are since incessant but as he was unable to slay or under that pretence they denied him the reward & his patronage of John Bull was but the effect of disappointment—the King erroneously considered Jack in confidence of & supported by the United Irishmen and by the wealthier patriotic Interest—& thought him an Acquisition to gratify his revenge. My next letter will shew he was mistaken & that European patriots equally despise a disguised Ruffian whether King Demagogue Incendiary or prostitute Bully. Even Men of honour sometimes find a foil necessary not to destroy but to protect property & unfortunately the rage of Cromwells party to destroy this property subjected it to the attacks of the rapacious & unprincipled.

About twenty thousand pounds of it thus scattered was collected & saved by the royal Canal Company Ireland[7]—patriotic men—revenge was resolved on—their Canal carried through a rich Country would when finished be very productive but some Misconduct of bad Agents similar to what happened to the US. Bank Embarrassed the Company—they solicited royal aid but prince Shylock or Waterlock would have it to himself & at a Fete given by him on that Occasion at Carlton house Wine was Conveyed from one end of the Table to the other through a silver Canal. Overcome with Immoderate Joy Geo Brute paid mor⟨e⟩ attention to the present Queen of France than was agreeable to her & the french King deemed the friends of Ireland—it was either offensive or displeasing as not being reciprocated—but his Ministers shortly after told him it was inconsistent with his dignity to become a waterman however profitable so the Canal speculation droped—sevl such anecdotes could be related to shew him as addicted to acts of unprincipled Speculative avarice as he was in youth to wastefull & boundless profligacy.

In feby last he issued a proclamation enjoyning an observance of piety & ordering all adulterous Siners to quit the precincts of St Jamess his holy residence.[8] It was so little expected that few Knew the reason of it—in March afterwards a very improper british dose deprived a Married Lady here of her senses—her husband untill then a friendly man dreaded Elopement & Dishonour. I was at some trouble to undeceive him. The King gained the husband but was disappointed in the wife for there was neither Elopement nor faux pas—in truth these dishonourable acts are Characteristic of Cowardice and Villiany—his flight to Brighton caused by the first alarm on the queens Trial[9] reminds one of the flight of his grandfather Sir Cymon Luttrell[10] Commander of the Irish Horse at Aughrim from the pass he guarded on the flank of the Irish Army—to the british Camp. I would sacrifice all the Estates my ancestors ever possessed rather than I would descend to be the Tool of such a worthless cross bombastard and if he perseveres in harrassing me I will address to him a public letter in some good newspaper to that Effect which I think will travel to England and shall quote Junius[11] as my authority—the human Countenance does not appear to me a surer Index of the mind than base conduct is indicative of a base Origin.

The necessity to defeat british Govt Intrigue in every Stage and form it may assume and to expoze the falsehoods misrepresentation and Sophistrys of its agents will excuse my long Explanation of the Doctrine & principles advanced by John Bull & his Senatorial advocate who I have no doubt if Elected president will contest the race for royal favour and patronage with our worthy Governor McMin—they are both of anti Orange Interest tho not less ambitious for Legitimate Dignity. It appears Your Lordship would sound like Magic to either of them. Jacks only Title to a small remnant of my property he Occupies was a Lease for 31 years that Expired & alas there are many others Occupants of the rest whom the bloodhound Beresfords deem Equally Entitled—from which it is evident I gave the true Explanation. This Doctrine reverses the received Maxim Doctrina promovet Vim[12]—with Jack it is mea Vis promovet meam Doctrinam[13] which in plain Language means give me up your cash or my broad and brawny strength shall wrest it from you. Honour & Justice I hope forbid it. Mr Barbour is no statesman—the threats of the british Oligarchs through the Scotch Review[14] appear to have terrified him Into temporising subservience to avert Imaginary Danger—untill America Interferes as a Belligerent Bully in the affairs of Europe british artifice cannot effect a coalition against her—the Emperor Francis who apppears possessed of a high sense of honour & Justice is already Disgusted & the other Monarchs of the Holy Aliance will have some thing to mind at home more Important than Crusadeing against the Inoffensive American population & if France & Spain have not Assimilated their Governmts to that of America having nothing oligarchic they are more approximated so that America has nothing to fear—therefore the man that such threats could terrify wants capacity resolution & penetration—& might be terrified (if presidt) into Concessions not less Dishonourable than fatal. I am with the utmost respect Your Obedient H Servant

EDMOND KELLY

RC (NN). Day of month not indicated; conjectural day assigned based on the postmark "Columbia Ten. Feb. 20." Addressed by Kelly to JM "at his residence—state of Virginia City of Washington or elsewhere," and franked. "City of Washington" is crossed out and "Orange C.H. V" written below it in an unidentified hand.

1. *Speech of Mr. J. Barbour, of Virginia, on the Restriction of Slavery in Missouri. Delivered in the Senate . . . January 31, 1820* (Washington, 1820; Shoemaker 317). JM's copy is in the Madison Collection, Special Collections, University of Virginia Library.

2. "Thus, Reader, ends the Prologue to my Ode. / The true-bred Courtiers wonder while I preach; / And, with grave vizards, and stretch'd eyes to God, / Pronounce my Sermon a *most impious* speech.— / With all my spirit: let them damn my lays; / A Courtier's Curses are exalted Praise," John Wolcot, "Ode upon Ode . . . ," in *The Works of Peter Pindar, Esq. to Which Are Prefixed Memoirs of the Author's Life*, rev. ed. (5 vols.; London, 1812), 1:389.

3. *Quantum meruit:* "the reasonable value of services" (*Black's Law Dictionary* [9th ed.], 1361).

4. Richard Brinsley Sheridan (1751–1816), playwright and politician, whose close associates were Charles James Fox and the Prince of Wales, was a Whig member of Parliament, 1780–1812 (Linda Kelly, *Richard Brinsley Sheridan: A Life* [London, 1997], 1, 59, 69, 76–77, 96, 98–100, 102, 291, 294–95, 308).

5. "Is there a man, in vice and folly bred, / To sense of honour as to virtue dead;" Charles Churchill, "The Apology," in *The Poetical Works of Charles Churchill*, ed. Douglas Grant (Oxford, England, 1956), 45.298–99.

6. John Floyd (1783–1837) of Jefferson County, Virginia (now West Virginia), was educated at Dickinson College and studied medicine at the University of Pennsylvania. A veteran of the War of 1812, Floyd served in the U.S. House of Representatives, 1817–29, and as governor of Virginia, 1830–34 (Sobel and Raimo, *Biographical Directory of the Governors*, 4:1636).

7. The building of the Royal Canal to link Dublin with the River Shannon began in 1789, and its first section opened in 1798. It came under public management before its completion and finally ceased operations in 1960, but its passenger service ended in 1849 (Siobhán Kilfeather, *Dublin: A Cultural History* [New York, 2005], 18–19).

8. "A Proclamation, For the Encouragement of Piety and Virtue, and for the preventing and punishing of Vice, Profaneness, and Immorality," 22 Feb. 1820 (*Times* [London], 23 Feb. 1820).

9. In a report dated "Brighton, Feb. 29": "His Majesty [George IV], attended by Sir W. Knighton only, arrived in Marlborough-row at half-past 5 o'clock this evening. His Majesty came in the most private manner, not in his usual carriage, but in one equally plain, and followed by one servant merely" (ibid., 3 Mar. 1820).

10. Kelly confused Simon Luttrell (ca. 1643–1698) with his brother Henry (ca. 1655–1717). Both were colonels of cavalry in the service of James II, but it was Henry Luttrell whose refusal to engage his cavalry against the Williamite troops at Aughrim contributed to the Jacobite defeat there in 1691 (John Childs, *The Williamite Wars in Ireland, 1688–91* [London, 2007], 336–37).

11. In 1769–72 a series of more than sixty anonymous letters, signed "Junius," were published in the London *Public Advertiser*, attacking the ministers of the Grafton administration and defending the British constitution. The letters caused great excitement and intense speculation as to the author (John Cannon, ed., *The Letters of Junius* [Oxford, England, 1978], xiii–xix).

12. *Doctrina vim promovet:* the doctrine promotes the force.

13. *Mea vis promovet meam doctrinam:* my force promotes my doctrine.

14. For the reference to the *Edinburgh Review*, see Kelly to JM, 6 Dec. 1820, and n. 13.

From Robert Mackay

Dr Sir. Fredericksburg Feby 23. 1821.

Yr favour 20th. is before me. I regret exceedingly that the Saw does not meet your expectations. Being no judge myself, I requested others to choose, and at Same time agreed that it should be returned if it did not answer. I have mentioned the Subject to Mr. Richards[1] from whom it was purchased, who Says he is willing to take it back, although holes are punched, provided it has not been used so as to be perceived & thereby prevent a Sale. I however imagine this is the case.

The letter for Mr. Maury is already forwarded. Yours with esteem,

Robert Mackay

RC (DLC). Docketed by JM.

1. This was probably George Bird Richards (1786–1847), a Fredericksburg merchant in partnership with John Scott of the firm Scott and Richards (*Lineage Book: National Society of the Daughters of the American Revolution* [Washington, 1934], 141: 257; ViU: Special Collections, A Guide to the Scott and Richards Mercantile Firm Papers).

¶ To George Alexander Otis. Letter not found. *25 February 1821.* Offered for sale in Kenneth W. Rendell, Inc., Catalogue No. 88 (1973), item 100, where it is described as a one-page autograph letter, signed, with the following text: "I have received the favor of your last volume of Botta for which I make you my acknowledgments. On running it over, my opinion is not lessened either as to the value of the work itself or the public patronage due to your laudable task in translating it. And I join in every wish which has been expressed that you may be disappointed of no part of the reward to which you are entitled." For the letter JM refers to, see Otis to JM, 31 Jan. 1821.

From Francis Corbin

My dear Sir The Reeds. Wh: Ch: Po: Off: March 3d. 1821.

Gout in the Head and Stomach, occasioned more, I believe, by uneasiness than by abstinence, have been my almost constant companions ever since I had the pleasure to receive your last very obliging letter.[1] These, together with a fear of intruding upon you, during the Session of Congress, when, I presume, your correspondents must be numerous, and the Subjects of your correspondence important, have prevented me from thanking you for your kind Efforts to console me in these disastrous times. My numerous and solicitudinous cares for the welfare of *nine* Children require consolation. A Family increasing with a Fortune decreasing are enough to shake the fortitude of better Stoicians than I am. In our Country of wretched Slavery, where the Expenses of our Estates are certain as death, and the profits uncertain as life; the "lucrum cessens" and the "damnum emergens" are convertible terms, because here—"non progredi est regredi."[2] With me, paradoxical as it may seem, my chief profits are my chief expenses, or vicê versâ. Wherever Indian Corn is made in plenty—and Tobacco is cultivated, Negroes, being well fed, well clothed & humanely treated, will be obedient to the *first great Law*, however disobedient they may be to all others. Thus it is that we become the victims of our own virtue, for, as they multiply, our plagues are multiplied also. If it be true that virtue is it's own reward, as I devoutly believe it is, it is no less true that vice, especially the vice of Slavery, is it's own punishment, and punished we shall be most severely before we have done with it, or it with us. The settlement of the Missouri question, as it has been technically termed, a question which, I believe, I predicted in one of my letters to you, 18 months ago[3] would cause great fermentation, is only a postponement of our Evil days. This great bone of Contention must grow with our growth, till it works thro' *the Skin* of our present Confederation, and completely divides one part of us from another. Such is the decree of Fate, the "ΔΙΟΣ ΒΓΛΥ"! It is remarked by Cicero somewhere, perhaps in his "Paradoxa," that the characteristic distinction between a wise man and a fool is this—"a wise man changes his opinions *often*, a Fool *never*."[4] I confess then to *you*, My dear Sir, that my opinions are changed as to our present *form* of Federal Government. When Individuals holding high offices of Trust can, without blushing, without punishment, and even without having the finger of Scorn pointed at them, rob States, (as here,) and States, under the roguish pretext of "State Rights," (the Grecian Horse of these times!) can rob Individuals, (as in Ohio) without being put under "the Ban of the Empire" who can say that we are not "gone astray?"[5] In the year 1787 the Arch Deacon Paley[6] tickled my youthful fancy with our Chimerical Project, and induced me to think that new States might be comprehended within it "ad infi[ni]tum." But, I am now convinced that a Representative Republic extending from the St. Lawrence to the Gulf of Mexico, and from the Atlantic to the Pacific "haud unquam evenire potest."[7] With *biennial* Elections it is impossible, nor could it be of long duration even with Septennial. But, it may be said—"Sufficient for the day is the Evil thereof,"—"let us hold together as long as we can."[8] To this, like our old friend Patrick Henry, I shake my Head. The longer we continue together the more violent will be the concussion when we do seperate, as seperate we must, and the longer will it take for the wounded parts, at the points of seperation, to heal. I question much whether our present Federal compact will survive *our* Dynasty. If it does—it will only be by continuing the present Chief Magistrate for another term, and another to that, if he lives, and so on for life. Then will come the "wreck and crush."[9] But—the Legs of the Tripos upon which I am now seated may give way! The Oracle may fail in his predictions!

Four and a half Millions more, you observe, Sir; are to be borrowed—and this is not by one half enough. The Land Fund will not be available for years—if ever. The larger it grows the more certain will be it's loss. The Custom house taxes, those cunning contrivances of profligate Princes, will fall far short of Mr. Crawford's calculation, & if the Bankrupt Law should indeed pass—three fourths of the Duty Bonds will become Waste Paper. We Country people too, whose property the Merchants have in their Hands, will be swindled out of it. We shall hear of one hundred Bankruptcies a day. In *our* Towns *here* they will be numerous and almost immediate. Our Banks, I fear, will suffer severely. If the Northern Merchants have their hands full of Southern Produce—then they will become Bankrupt by dozens—instantor. If not—then they will wait till their Hands are full. The Bankrupt Law will always be their Assylum. I have ever believed the clause in the Constitution relative to it insidious and dangerous. The Bankrupt System is questionable, you know, even in England, where Commerce rules almost every thing. I knew a man in London who made a *trade* of becoming Bankrupt. He became so three times within my recollection, and never *failed* to set up his Carriage *after* he *had failed.* By "hook or by Crook" our Northern *Brethren* will contrive to get all our produce, as they have already contrived to get all our Public or funded Debt. To pay the Interest on this—we luxurious Southern *Consumers* pay ultimately, and in reality, two thirds of the Custom House Taxes. In opposing the Current of Slavery to the South and South West—their right hand—(or left—or both,) for the first time, within my recollection, seems to have forgot it's Cunning.

Pardon me, My dear Sir, for obtruding upon you these my philosophical and political—perhaps pseudo-philosophical and pseudo-political lucubrations.

I am glad to hear that you made a good crop of Tobacco this year. I have just recd. an Acct. of Sales for mine shipped to London in Augt. last which, including the advance of 5 pr. ct. on the Exchange *netts* me something more than $10 pr. hundred. In these times—this is not amiss.

Be pleased to present my respectful Esteem to Mrs. Madison and my friendly regards to Mr. Todd. I wish he could be prevailed on to visit us. My Son Robert, who has been all the winter in Philada., bound in silken fetters, as I hear, and not weather bound, will be at home shortly and will be as happy to see him as I shall be. I am very sincerely, My Dr. Sir, Your much obliged, most faithful & devoted Friend & Servt.

FRANCIS CORBIN

RC (DLC). Docketed by JM.

1. JM to Corbin, 26 Nov. 1820.

2. For *lucrum cessens* and *damnum emergens*, see ibid., nn. 3–4. *Non progredi est regredi:* not to go forward is to go backward.

3. See Corbin to JM, 10 Oct. 1819, *PJM-RS*, 1:525–30.

4. *Nemo doctus umquam . . . mutationem consilii inconstantiam dixit esse:* no philosopher ever called a change of plan inconsistency (Cic., *Letters to Atticus* 16.7, trans. E. O. Winstedt, Loeb Classical Library [3 vols.; London, 1918], 3:396–97).

5. For the embezzlement by John Preston of the Virginia state treasury, see Francis Preston to JM, 30 Jan. 1820, *PJM-RS*, 1:596–97 and n. 1. For the tax imposed on the Second Bank of the United States in Ohio, see Edmond Kelly to JM, 26 Sept. 1820, and n. 8.

6. William Paley (1743–1805) was archdeacon of Carlisle, England, and author of *The Principles of Morals and Political Philosophy* (1785) and *A View of the Evidences of Christianity* (1794), among other titles.

7. *Haud unquam evenire potest:* can hardly happen.

8. "Sufficient unto the day *is* the Evil thereof," Matt. 6:34 (AV).

9. "Wreck and crush" probably is a reference to Joseph Addison's phrase "the wrecks of matter, and the crush of worlds" in *Cato: A Tragedy* 5.1.31 (Joseph Addison, *Cato: A Tragedy, and Selected Essays*, ed. Christine Dunn Henderson and Mark E. Yellin [Indianapolis, 2004], 89).

From Francis Glass

LEBANON, OHIO,
VIR EXCELLENTISSIME. Tertio die Martii. [3 March] A.D. 1821.

Quamvis non sim de numero eorum, qui Tui notitiam habent, tamen, quia compertum jamdiù habebam, te literarum omnis generis patronum insignem semper fuisse: ideò ausus sum, Vir inclyte, hasce epistolas ad te mittere, sperans Te eodem, quo mittitur animo accepturum hanc epistolam. Scripsi, et in lucem jamjam daturus sum libellum, cui titulus, "Vita Georgii Washingtonii, ducis nuperi harum Civitatum Foederatarum Americae septentrionalis copiarum omnium, earundemque primi præsidis." In animo est mihi, istum librum tibi, Vir clare, *dicare dummodò* id Tibi bonum gratumque videbitur. Ideòque, valdè scire laboro, utrùm ausim illum Tibi dicare, necne; Liber, de quo agitur, in usum scholarum à me exaratus est. Pauca de me ipso dicenda videntur: Oriundus de Republicâ Pennsylvaniensi sum, haud procùl ab urbe Philadelphiâ. Duobus annis abhinc, migravi in hanc regionem, ubi in pueros erudiendo operam navavi; sed ingravescente valetudine, coactus fui, istud munus relinquere, et ad extremam pauperiem redactus sum, propterea quòd, cum uxore, et sex parvulis liberis, nequaquam par fui, qui eos, in afflictâ valetudine, (*praesertim his temporibus*,) sustineam. Proinde inductus inopiâ, dirâque necessitate, Vitam, *Latinè*, illustrissimi Washingtonii, ad scribendum me contuli. Semper in votis meis fuit, assignationem *aliquam* in exercitu patriae adipisci; sed, nescio quomodo, propter *humilitatem amicorum*, ab isto conatu depulsus fui. Sed, (ut vetus adagium prae se fert, "*dum spiro, spero*"); *aliquem gradum* in exercitu obtinendi spes me tenet.

Nonnumquam aveo nonnihil *agri* coëmere; at pecunia mihi deest; et, vereor, ut semper deerit in hâc regione, cum omnia collegia referta sunt *clericis*; nam, quod ad me spectat, *laïcus* sum; disciplinae *ecclesiae anglicanae obnoxius. Linguas*, et *artes mathematicas*, per decem ferè annos, docui; sed docti et indocti praeceptores hâc in regione, eodem in numero habentur.

Sed, quia juvenis sum, spero me aliquando ex hâc aerumnâ miseriâque emersurum esse. Volo interdum reverti ad Philadelphiam, meum natale solum, sed paupertas, (durum telum, ut Erasmus facetè ait,) me prohibet. Sed, quoniam valetudo mea habet sese meliùs nemo, quam dudùm, spero me posse adhuc visere meliores regiones nostrae felicis Reipublicae; hanc licentiam mihi, Vir excellentissime, condonare et ignoscere Te precor, bonique consulere, supplicite peto, humillïmequè rogo. Sum, Vir Clarissime, Tuae Celsitudinis Observantissimus, Humillïmusque Tuus Servus,

Franciscus Glass[1]

CONDENSED TRANSLATION

Is not among those who have JM's notice, nevertheless, experience has shown for a long time now, that JM has been a leading patron of letters of all kinds, has taken the liberty to send this letter to JM, hoping that it will be received in the same spirit in which it has been sent. Has written, and is now about to give forth, a little book whose title is "The Life of George Washington, formerly the leader of all the armies of these United States of North America, and the first president of the same." Has in mind to dedicate this book to JM, on condition that it will please him. Is trying to ascertain, whether he ought to take the liberty to dedicate it to JM, or not. Has written it for the use of schools. Is originally from Pennsylvania, not far from Philadelphia. Moved to this area two years ago and taught school; was forced to give it up through sickness and has been reduced to extreme poverty. Has not been able to support his wife and six little children while suffering this sickness (especially in these times). Induced by want and dire necessity, has written the life of the most illustrious Washington in Latin. Had always wished to obtain some employment in the army of our country, but doesn't know how. His connections are humble men and he was discouraged from making the attempt. But, as the old adage plainly says, "While I live, I hope"; has still the hope of obtaining *some rank* in the army.

Sometimes wishes to buy some little field to plow but lacks money. Fears that it will always be lacking in this area. Since all the schools are entrusted to clergymen, is a layman and at the mercy of the Anglican church. Has taught languages and mathematical arts for nearly ten years; but, in this area, learned, and unlearned, teachers are considered the same. Is young and hopes that some day he will emerge from this trouble and misery. In the meantime, desires to return to Philadelphia, his native soil, but poverty, (a harsh weapon, as Erasmus jokingly says) holds him back. Since his sickness has somewhat abated, hopes to visit more prosperous regions of our fortunate Republic. Prays JM to pardon this liberty, and beseeches and most humbly begs him to think well of Glass.

RC (DLC). Docketed by JM. The editors are indebted to Ms. Racquel Yerbury and the senior Latin class of St. Andrew's Episcopal School, Potomac, Maryland, for the transcription and translation of this letter, from which the condensed translation was made.

1. Francis Glass (1790–1824), an Ohio schoolteacher originally from Philadelphia, wrote his biography of Washington in Latin in the winter of 1824; it was published posthumously

in 1835 (Francis Glass, *A Life of George Washington, in Latin Prose*, ed. J. N. Reynolds [New York, 1835], i–ii, vii–xii).

To George W. Featherstonhaugh

SIR MONTPELLIER Mar. 6. 1821

I offer you many thanks for the 1st. vol: of Memoirs published by your Agricultural Board.[1] It contains a very valuable mass of instruction both Theoretical & Practical. If it had not the benefit of the materials expected from the subordinate Societies, it must be of great use in stimulating and guiding their reports which may succeed it.

I am very glad to find that it fell within the scope of your disquisitions, to unfold the present Chemical doctrine with regard to the elements of matter; particularly the organized parts of it. It will answer well the purpose of counteracting any general imputations from unfriendly quarters; should pretexts for such be taken from the defective views of the subject, in the paper, which I see has been honored with a place in your Volume.

On the supposition, as authorized by facts, that a combination of two elements may produce a third substance different from both; that a combination of a greater number may proportionally diversify such new results; and that a change even in the proportions of the same elements combined may have like effects; a field seems to be opened for a possible multiplication, from a few elements, of the forms and qualities of matter such as the face of our globe now presents. It does not necessarily follow however from this possibility, that all the varieties now beheld in the productions of nature, could be converted into a single or few classes of them. It is more than probable that there are laws, in the economy of nature, which would not admit so entire a metamorphosis of her original System; that there may be certain relations between different classes of her productions, which require for their preservation and increase, the existence & influence of each other. And it seems certain that such a revolution would have the consequence, not easily to be admitted, of rendering a portion of elementary matter, supernumerary & useless for the laboratory of nature.

Whatever be the number of distinct elements or gases, as these must be inconvertible one into another, the existing mass of each element must be of fixt amount, and bear of course a fixt proportion each to the others, in the existing order of things. Taking then any particular class or classes of plants, (those for example of human use) which happen not to comprize *every* distinct element, or tho' comprizing every element, yet in proportions not[2] corresponding with the proportions now existing in the whole vegitable creation, a destruction of every other class of plants would necessarily leave unemployed all the elements not required for the new modelled Systems.

Perceiving how far I have wandered from my proper object, I hasten a return to it, by repeating my acknowledgments for your valuable Book, with assurances of my esteem and cordial respects.

JAMES MADISON

RC (NIC); draft (DLC). Minor differences between the copies have not been noted.

1. See Featherstonhaugh to JM, 6 Feb. 1821, and n. 2.
2. "Not" omitted from draft.

From Peter Minor

DEAR SIR RIDGEWAY Mar 7th. 1821

A special meeting of the Agricultural society of Albemarle, was held yesterday upon a business, the nature of which you will understand from a perusal of the enclosed papers under cover to Mr. Skinner.[1]

As the paper appointing Mr Skinner the Societys agent, will necessarily be exhibited in Spain, it was thought it would go forth better authenticated with the addition of your Signature as President of the Society; & I now comply with their wishes & resolution, in asking you to affix it. I further ask the favor of you to inform me if this comes to hand, and request you to forward the packet by mail to Mr Skinner.

The committee ask your indulgence for having opened the letter of Matro de la Serna, addressed to you.[2] A well grounded belief that it related to the business in question, & your absense & distance from this place they thought would excuse the liberty. With very great respect Yr. obt. Sert.

P. MINOR Secy.
Agl. Soc: of Albemarle

RC (DLC). Docketed by JM.

1. The correspondence referred to was between a committee of the Agricultural Society of Albemarle and Luis de Onís, the Spanish minister to the United States, and Matro de la Serna, Spanish chargé des affaires, asking permission "to purchase in Spain and transport to the United States a Horse of the best race in that country with a view to improve the breed in our own." The consent of the king of Spain being given, the society had appointed John S. Skinner of Baltimore, editor of the *American Farmer*, to be "the agent of the Society in effecting the object contemplated." The correspondence and the accompanying resolution was sent to JM to be signed and forwarded to Skinner (True, "Minute Book of the Albemarle Agricultural Society," printed in *Annual Report of the American Historical Association for . . . 1918*, 1:292).
2. Letter not found.

From William Maury

Dear Sir, New Orleans 8 March 1821

Ere this I intended to have thanked you for the letters of introduction which you were kind enough to send to Tom Maury for me,[1] not only as such, but for the very flattering attention I have met with from them.

Luckily I arrived at Lexington before Mr Clays departure for the Seat of Government, other wise I should have missed the opportunity he gave me of enjoying a Society, more improved & polished than many I have seen in larger Towns—this will surprize many of my English friends, as you may suppose from Mr Clays ironical observation to me. What; said he, did you come alone? Yes. And did you meet with no Buffaloes or Bears? No. But with Wild Indians certainly you had an encounter.

This tho is really an idea entertained by many, otherwise well informed in the Old Country.

At Frankfort I only staid a couple of days, where I found Judge Todd on the point of starting. I could not see him, but left your letter.

I attended the Legislature, the first Body I had seen in this Country. They were rough & unpolished, but seemed to possess a great deal of shrewdness for their own interest.

Thence I proceeded to Louisville, still pleased with my tour & mode of travelling, but the prospect for the Roads & Weather was so bad that I came down the River in a Steam Boat; the passage was agreeable enough but I prefer Horse back so much, that I shall return by Land, in about a Month.

I am glad tho that I had an opportunity of witnessing the grandeur of the River, & Resources of this City, in a few years to become one of the greatest in the United States & one day to vie with all the former splendor & magnificence of Alexandria!

'Tis not with the general society & manners of the City that I have been as much pleased, as the contrast with other Cities in the United States for this is the first specimen I have seen of French manners, & I cannot *speak French.*

The Governor[2] has been very attentive to me; in him I find a well informed & polite Gentleman, tho he will laugh a little at John Bulls expense.

Last week I was in Natchez, but Governor Poindexter[3] was at his Seat 40 miles from there & Mr. Holmes[4] gone to Washington. That is also a very thriving place, containing about 4000 people, the Society formed by the neighbouring planters very good.

The American inhabitants now beginning to predominate in this City its improvement is commencing, first by paving it, which must considerably add to its health, to say nothing of beauty or convenience.

This Season will I think be very unhealthy from the immense quantity of provisions &c, that must for want of sale be warehoused. Even now when the heat is only 70 a 75 they are beginning to putrify.

The poor Kentuckian is only getting 2.50 for Flour, 30 for Corn & 2 a 4½ for his Tobacco.

The best thing to be done is to turn Cotton planter, getting 12 a 18 for what will produce 11 a 17 in Europe! Certainly a few copies of Adam Smiths Wealth of Nations ought to be sent here.

Pray present my respects to Mrs Madison & accept the assurance with which I have the honor to be Your obliged servant

William Maury

RC (DLC). Docketed by JM.

1. For Thomas W. Maury's request of JM to furnish letters of recommendation for William Maury, see Maury to JM, 23 Oct. 1820. The letters have not been found.

2. Thomas Bolling Robertson (1779–1828) was born in Virginia and graduated from the College of William and Mary. He practiced law in Petersburg, Virginia, but moved to Orleans Territory in 1807, where he was territorial secretary, 1807–11, U.S. congressman, 1812–18, and governor of Louisiana, 1820–24. He was judge of the U.S. court for the District of Louisiana, 1825–27 (Sobel and Raimo, *Biographical Directory of the Governors*, 2:557).

3. George Poindexter (1779–1853) was born in Louisa County, Virginia, read law privately, and practiced in Richmond until he moved to the Mississippi Territory in 1802. He was a delegate from the territory to the U.S. Congress, 1807–13, U.S. district judge of the territory, 1813–17, member of the U.S. House of Representatives, 1817–19, and governor of Mississippi, 1820–22. He served in the U.S. Senate, 1830–35 (ibid., 801–2).

4. David Holmes (1770–1832), a Pennsylvania-born lawyer, served as a U.S. representative from Virginia, 1797–1809. JM appointed him territorial governor of Mississippi in 1809, and he served until 1817, when he became governor of the newly admitted state. Holmes was governor of Mississippi twice, 1817–20, and 1826. He also served as U.S. senator, 1820–25 (ibid., 801).

From Joseph C. Cabell

Dear Sir, Richmond 10 March 1821.

It would have given me great pleasure to write you from time to time the state of our business in the Assembly, and I should have done so, but that my constitution was scarcely able to support the pressure of my regular duties. In the interview which I shall have the pleasure to have with you at Monticello in April, I will give you any details you may desire respecting past transactions & future prospects. But I must ask leave to say a few words to you in anticipation. You see our Bill has passed, but in a shape very different from what we desired.[1] "Two or three more such victories & we are undone."[2] The Academies have joined the Primary Schools, & we are hemmed in between the $45,000, & the surplus over $60,000, with a debt the interest of which amounts to nearly half of our annuity. It is really strange: no body in the country seems to care for this poor school system: and yet in the House of Delegates it remains popular. My present impression is that to get rid of our debt, we must look beyond the Literary Fund, and the Assembly will always be difficult on that head. Many respectable men in the Assembly are becoming impatient about the Academies, and are pressing the opinion that the University should go forward by degrees. Our leading friends about Richmond discover great anxiety as to the future. The enemies of the Institution are gaining ground with the Bulk of the people generally thro' the State. The Appointment of Doctor Cooper has enlisted all the religious orders of Society against the Institution.[3] You have not an idea how excessively unpopular Doctor Cooper now is in Virginia. I verily believe that 99/100s of the people of Virginia would now vote against him. Even all the free thinkers of my acquaintance about Richmond protest against his being made a Professor of the University; all on the ground of policy, & some on the ground of principle. I sincerely believe that if Doctor Cooper should be made President, it will cause the entire overthrow of the institution. Possibly he may be sustained as a Professor, if he comes in with others, after a time. I doubt whether he would get any votes except yours, Mr. Jefferson's & mine. If he should, the further support would be reluctant homage to yourself and Mr. Jefferson. This state of things vexes & distresses me: and I apprize you of it, to prevent you and Mr. Jefferson from being taken unawares, & from committing yourselves to Doct: Cooper. For further information on this head I refer you to the Visitors in full meeting. It is the Universal opinion of all our friends that we should never come here again for money to erect buildings. This is the last donation for that object. Our friends tell me—"For God's sake, beg Mr. Jefferson & Mr. Madison, to finish the buildings with this $60,000. and if it should not be enough, not to commence any building which cannot be finished." Many think we had better not spend any more of the $60,000, than is indispensably necessary to put the institution into operation, & to keep as much as possible of the Annuity for the annual support of the establishment. They think it would be a great recommendation to report a balance unexpended next winter. The two Houses parted on very bad terms; the House of Delegates in a state of great excitement, because the Senate would not consent to an unconditional surrender of the back quotas. The Senate only insisted on a few very reasonable amendments calculated to prevent waste & misapplication. We are falling into days of ignorance & bigotry where local & petty interests, take captive the general good, as the Liliputians did Gulliver. Looking to the future, with better hopes, at the begining of our session, I had made up my mind to offer no more for the Senate but I have at the request of Mr. Jefferson & some other friends consented to come again, & render any service in my power. I have written in various directions to my friends with the hope of bringing in auxiliaries. I hope to succeed with Mr. Taylor of Chesterfield,[4] the gentleman who acted so great a part on the subject of the site. Mr. Archer of Powhatan[5] will also join us. He is a man of considerable energy of character, & very zealous in whatever he undertakes. Col: Mallory of your county,[6] is of the same class, is very enthusiastic on this subject & ought to return. Mr. Morton[7] appears to me a most amiable & enlightened young gentleman, & would go any lengths for the University. Doddridge[8] joined us heartily at the close of the session: he will not return. Blackburn[9] united cordially with us, & was a valuable friend. He will probably return & run with us. But he was much offended about the failure of the Primary School-bill. Mr. Morris of Hanover,[10] one of our best friends will come again. So I hope will Mr. Crump, Mr. Bowyer, Mr. Watson & Mr. Gordon.[11] But I greatly fear that our principal friend, Genl. Breckenridge will not consent to serve again. This is a point of infinite importance, for he is the only man that can keep the western delegation correct. He promised me not to commit himself till our meeting in April, but I am credibly informed that when he left town, he declared he could not consent to serve again. Botetourt Court is on monday next, and I fear he will then publicly decline, and another candidate be declared in his place. Yet I have reasons to believe that if such should be the fact, the person will be the late Speaker Watts,[12] son in law to the Genl. who could be prevailed on to give place to his father in law. I now write you, as I have this day written Mr. Jefferson, chiefly for the purpose of conjuring you to write immediately to the Genl. and to use all your influence with him to serve one more term. He is our Bulwark in the House of Delegates, & if we lose him, without a great change in the public mind, I shall be in utter despair for years to come. His address is Fincastle. We shall lose our valuable friend Mr. Stevenson, who will go to Congress. I am, Dr. Sir, with great respect & sincere regard yr. obt. servt.

JOSEPH C. CABELL

RC (DLC). Docketed by JM.

1. The act, passed on 24 Feb. 1821, authorized the president and directors of the Literary Fund to make a second loan of $60,000 to the board of visitors of the University of Virginia in order to complete its buildings (Bruce, *History of the University of Virginia*, 1:297).

2. Cabell was referring to Pyrrhus's comment upon being congratulated on his victory over the Romans at Asculum that "such another victory and we are undone" (John Langhorne and William Langhorne, trans., *Plutarch's Lives, Translated from the Original Greek; With Notes . . . and a New Life of Plutarch* [6 vols.; London, 1794], 3:26).

3. Though Thomas Cooper had been teaching at South Carolina College in Columbia for the past year, both he and Jefferson hoped that by some arrangement Cooper would find a permanent home at the University of Virginia. For the attacks by John H. Rice, a

Presbyterian divine, and others on Cooper, see Malone, *Public Life of Thomas Cooper* (1961 reprint), 239–47.

4. Samuel Taylor (ca. 1781–1853), a lawyer from Chesterfield County, served in the Virginia House of Delegates, 1816–19, and 1825–26, and in the Virginia Senate, 1826–30 (John Redd, "Reminiscences of Western Virginia," *VMHB* 7 [1899]: 126; Swem and Williams, *Register*, 436).

5. Branch T. Archer (1790–1856), attended the College of William and Mary, practiced medicine, and represented Powhatan County in the Virginia House of Delegates, 1819–20. In 1831 he moved to Texas, where he held a number of political posts in the Texas republic (Tyler, *Encyclopedia of Virginia Biography*, 2:209–10).

6. For Robert Mallory, see his letter to JM, 7 Feb. 1818, *PJM-RS*, 1:215–16 and n. 2.

7. William Morton represented Orange County in the Virginia House of Delegates, 1818–22 and 1824–26 (Swem and Williams, *Register*, 410).

8. Philip Doddridge (1773–1832) was a Bedford County, Virginia, lawyer who served in the Virginia Senate, 1804–9, the Virginia House of Delegates, 1815–16, 1820–21, 1822–23, and 1828–29, and in the U.S. House of Representatives, 1829–32 (Tyler, *Encyclopedia of Virginia Biography*, 2:106; Swem and Williams, *Register*, 368).

9. Samuel Blackburn (1761–1835), a lawyer and planter in Bath County, Virginia, served multiple terms in the Virginia House of Delegates, including the sessions, 1820–22, 1823–24, and 1825–26. Vociferous Federalist though he was, "Gen. Blackburn took the floor most zealously in favor of the measure [see n. 1 above], and is now fairly enlisted" (Kneebone et al., *Dictionary of Virginia Biography*, 1:518–19; Joseph C. Cabell to Thomas Jefferson, 25 Feb. 1821, Cabell, *Early History of the University of Virginia*, 208).

10. Richard Morris of Hanover County served in the Virginia House of Delegates, 1819–22, 1823–25, and 1830–31 (Swem and Williams, *Register*, 409).

11. George William Crump (1786–1850), a physician and graduate of the College of New Jersey, represented Cumberland County in the Virginia House of Delegates, 1817–22, 1825–26, and 1827–28, and served in the U.S. House of Representatives, 1826–27. He was chief clerk of the U.S. Pension Bureau, 1832–50 (Tyler, *Encyclopedia of Virginia Biography*, 2:105; Swem and Williams, *Register*, 364). John Bowyer of Rockbridge and David Watson of Louisa counties were delegates to the Virginia General Assembly in the 1820–21 session. William Fitzhugh Gordon (1787–1858), a Charlottesville lawyer, served in the Virginia House of Delegates, 1818–21 and 1822–29; in the Virginia Senate, 1829–30; and in the U.S. House of Representatives, 1830–35 (Tyler, *Encyclopedia of Virginia Biography*, 2:110–11; Swem and Williams, *Register*, 380). All four delegates supported the loan bill for the University of Virginia (Swem and Williams, *Register*, 103–4; Cabell to Thomas Jefferson, 25 Feb. 1821, Cabell, *Early History of the University of Virginia*, 208).

12. Edward Watts (1779–1859), a graduate of the College of New Jersey, was a planter and lawyer in Campbell County, Virginia. He served in the Virginia House of Delegates, 1808–9, and in the Senate, 1809–21. Watts was speaker of the Virginia Senate, 1817–21 (Philip Alexander Bruce et al., *History of Virginia* [6 vols.; Chicago, 1924], 6:226; Swem and Williams, *Register*, 443).

From George W. Featherstonhaugh

SIR DUANESBURGH March 10. 1821.

But for the satisfaction I have received from the interesting Letters you have taken the trouble to write to me,[1] I should sincerely regret having offered[2] those Observations in a previous Letter, which have led to a Correspondence so advantageous and agreeable to myself. It required all your friendly Assurances to Satisfy me upon reflection, that I had not Seriously trespassed upon propriety, even when my motives were understood.

I am particularly pleased that you approve of the introduction, in the Essay, of the chemical relations of the Elements of matter; being well aware that it is to intelligent minds alone, I must look for some Countenance, to justify its appearance in a discourse upon Agriculture: but I must say with all sincerity, I cannot admit, that any opinions of mine to be found there, can have the Effect of counteracting what you call "defective views" in your address.[3] I apprehend that but one opinion will be entertained of it, and that it will be greatly to your honor.

In regard to your remarks in your Letter of the 6th instant: I certainly mean to go no further than to say, that the theory I incline to, is sustained quite satisfactorily to me, by all the facts of which I have any Knowledge. The probability, that there are undiscovered Laws in Nature, the Knowledge of which would reveal a Scheme and intention different from what I now perceive, is not to be denied in a few words. The progress of Knowledge is like the ascent of a mountain. At every stage the view becomes more extended. You reach the Top, and with the more enlarged horizon, perceive and are satisfied that there is a great deal beyond that, not to be seen from that place. So in attempting to look at the Scheme of Providence for this Globe; from the base of human reason we discern the natural Condition of Man; higher up, how Agriculture affects that: from the heights we perceive how Chemistry affects this. From thence we spring into the Balloon of Metaphysics, to See what we are not able to See, and therefore that which is not to be Seen. Some come down safe in a parachute, some do not. I should not dislike to have a favourable Opportunity of making an argument out, for the intention of Providence, as a man may discern it from what is around us. It would be somewhat metaphysical, but if it were conceded that the welfare of Man were the great Object of the Scheme; I should not despair of shewing, that the whole Concern *might be* Carried on by the Economical principles already Known to us.

My Essay which is very imperfect, and I could not avoid it, has been favourably received; but as it is distributed by Law gratis, amongst the County Societies, those who desire to purchase, cannot be gratified. I think of enlarging it into a thick Octavo, making it more practical, and general; adding Engravings &c. and publishing it. My Object is not profit, nor do I wish to lose money by it. I have been strongly solicited to do so, and the Booksellers here would gladly publish it, provided I would permit them to receive subscriptions, which I cannot Consent to. I must therefore publish it at my own risk. Pray do you imagine that a work of this Character would be favourably recd in the Southern States?

I hope you will Excuse the great length of this Letter, and receive the Assurances I can very sincerely give you, of my being Sir Your faithful hble St

G W Featherstonhaugh.

RC (NN). Docketed by JM.

1. JM wrote Featherstonhaugh on 7 Mar. and 23 Dec. 1820, and 6 Mar. 1821.
2. "Offered" interlined by JM.
3. See JM to Featherstonhaugh, 6 Mar. 1821.

From Alexander Scott

Dear Sir, George Town March 10th 1821

In addition to the favors heretofore received from you,[1] (which I shall ever hold in grateful recollection) I feel a reluctance at making any other request, and must premise a wish that you will not comply with it unless perfectly agreeable to your feelings.

I should wish to fill a situation created under the Spanish treaty[2] (Secretary to the Board of Commissioners,) and consider myself qualified for it by a knowledge of the French and Spanish Languages, which the law requires. The former I learned in early youth, and by a subsequent residence in France attained a more perfect knowledge of it. The latter I can translate, not with the same facility but with correctness. I am recommended strongly by my friends Genl Mason,[3] Mr. Wirt, & Chancellor Kilty,[4] also Col Lloyd[5] of the Senate. The present Pressure of the times has much augmented the competition for office, and the number of applicants is further encreased by the diminution of the army. A few lines from you to Col Monroe would, I am persuaded turn the scale in my favor. I do assure you Sir, it shall be the last time I will ever ask your interference, and do it now with much unwillingness.

Mrs. Scott, who is in very bad health and under great mental depression from the recent loss of our two promising sons, desires her best respects and wishes to Mrs Madison. With great respect and Esteem I am Dr Sir Yr mo: obedt. Servt

Alexander Scott

RC (DLC). Docketed by JM.

1. For Alexander Scott and his previous requests for letters of recommendation, see Scott to JM, 7 Apr. and 11 Aug. 1819, and 2 Jan. 1820, *PJM-RS*, 1:446, 447 nn., 496, 579–80 and n. 1.

2. "An Act for carrying into execution the treaty between the United States and Spain, concluded at Washington on the twenty-second day of February, one thousand eight hundred and nineteen," 3 Mar. 1821, *U.S. Statutes at Large*, 3:637–39.

3. John Mason (1766–1849), son of George Mason of Gunston Hall, the owner of Analostan Island in the Potomac River, and one of the leaders of Washington society, was a wealthy merchant and president of the Bank of Columbia. He had been brigadier general of the District of Columbia militia, 1802–11 (*PJM-PS*, 1:236 n. 3; *PJM-SS*, 1:448 n. 1; Van Horne, *Papers of Benjamin Henry Latrobe*, 2:208 n. 1).

4. William Kilty (1757–1821), a lawyer and veteran of the Revolutionary War, was chancellor of Maryland, 1806–21 (William L. Marbury, "The High Court of Chancery and the Chancellors of Maryland," *Report of the Tenth Annual Meeting of the Maryland State Bar Association* [1905]: 132–35).

5. Edward Lloyd (1779–1834) was a Maryland planter who served in the U.S. House of Representatives, 1805–9; as governor of Maryland, 1809–11; in the Maryland Senate, 1811–19 and 1826–31; and in the U.S. Senate, 1819–26. He was a strong supporter of the Madison and Monroe administrations (Sobel and Raimo, *Biographical Directory of the Governors*, 2:652–53).

From Thomas Cooper

Dear Sir Columbia S. Carolina March 12. 1821

When I first engaged to act as chemical Professor at the south Carolina College, I refused to contract for a longer period than a twelve month, expressly on account of my engagement in Virginia.[1]

At my departure from this place last autumn, I refused making any promise to return here on a permanent engagement, untill I had an opportunity of ascertaining the prospects of the Charlottesville University. In meantime, a Dr. Porter[2] came here, on invitation of some of the Trustees, recommended by Professor Silliman of Yale College to take the chair of Chemistry should I decline it.

When I returned here, I passed thro' Virginia, & staid a week at Monticello. Mr Jefferson told me, he was quite uncertain whether the Virginia legislature would afford sufficient aid to the Charlottesville institution to enable it to go on: that it was a very unpropitious time to make the application owing to the losses the state had lately incurred: that if they should refuse the necessary aid, the Buildings might remain unoccupied for seven years to come.

I found Governor Randolph also in great doubt wher. any thing wd. be done by the Legislature or not. I returned with this hopeless kind of information to Columbia.

I there found the Trustees desirous of retaining me, but hesitating about my election for another limited period: Dr. Porter meanwhile ready for the Chair, as my Suppleant, should I relinquish it.

I was not able to waste any more time indefinitely. My family were anxious to join me some where. I had no encouragement to go to your state, and I was compelled to accept of the chemical Chair on the conditions of permanent residence, and removing my family here. I have done so, and I consider myself as fixed in this place.

Since I have been here, the Trustees have influenced the Legislature to add 1000 Dlrs to my Salary as mineralogical Professor, and have since elected me President of the College for a period, which will end I presume at my option or my demise.

Under these circumstances, I feel myself bound in honour to recommend if I can an efficient Professor of Chemistry & Mineralogy to your Institution; and under that obligation I write now.

Mr Lardner Vanuxem,[3] now with me here as an assistant, was formerly a student of mineralogy and Chemistry for two years in Philadelphia, and since that time for 3 years with exemplary industry at Paris, where he received the public compliment of approbation in the introductory lecture of the Mineralogical professor in the school of Mines. His good character, talents, & merit are well known to Mr Gallatin who will confirm this report.

I think I know every man in the United States who has pretensions to Chemical and mineralogical Knowledge: I speak with the utmost confidence, & without scruple, when I say, that Mr Vanuxem has no equal among them. You *cannot* procure a person so well qualified in point of Knowledge. How he would perform as a public lecturer I know not, but the necessary fluency is easily acquired, where there is the necessary knowledge, as there is here.

Mr Vanuxem is about 30 Years of age: of a well known family in Philadelphia, his father, a merchant of very long standing there, attached to the Virginia politics, having a very large family natives of the United States.

It is true I wish to render Mr Vanuxem a service, but I have not the slightest motive to interest myself in his behalf, but his merit: and it is because I feel personally and anxiously concerned for the interest of the Virginia Institution, that you are now troubled with this detail from Dear Sir Your obliged & faithful friend and Servant

THOMAS COOPER

RC (DLC). Docketed by JM.

1. For Thomas Cooper's appointment as professor of chemistry and law for the University of Virginia, see Minutes of the Board of Visitors of the University of Virginia, 29 Mar. 1819, *PJM-RS*, 1:444.

2. Arthur L. Porter (1794–1845) of Portsmouth, New Hampshire, was educated as a physician at Dartmouth College and in Edinburgh before becoming professor of chemistry and pharmacy at the University of Vermont. From 1825 to 1829 he worked for the Dover Manufacturing Company in New Hampshire, after which he moved to Detroit, Michigan

(Frank Blaisdell, "President's Address," *Transactions of the New Hampshire Medical Society* [1910]: 60; "Members of First Church. 1718–1850," *Collections of the Dover, N.H., Historical Society* [Dover, N.H., 1894], 225; Caroline Sloat, "The Dover Manufacturing Company and the Integration of English and American Calico Printing Techniques, 1825–29," *Winterthur Portfolio* 10 [1975]: 54).

3. Lardner Vanuxem (1792–1848), the son of Philadelphia merchant James Vanuxem, formerly of Dunkirk, France, graduated from the École des Mines in Paris in 1819. Shortly thereafter he became professor of chemistry and mineralogy at Columbia College in South Carolina, remaining there until 1826, when he traveled to Mexico, New York, Virginia, and other states to report on their geological features and collect specimens for his private collection. In 1836 he undertook the geological survey of the state of New York, which he finished in 1842 (William Jay Youmans, ed., *Pioneers of Science in America: Sketches of Their Lives and Scientific Work* [New York, 1896], 270–78).

From Alexander Scott

SIR GEO TOWN March 12th 1821

I took the liberty to write you a few lines by mail,[1] but understanding that the direct mail to Orange Court House does not leave this place until thursday, I write a few lines by way of Fredericksburg.

The object of my former letter was to ask the favor of a few lines to Col Monroe in my favor, in relation to an office now in his gift. I mean the secretary to the board of Commissioners under the Spanish treaty; Of my qualifications to fill, and discharge the duties of that office Col Monroe is able to Judge. If any candidate is better qualified in the requisites specified by the law, I willingly resign my pretensions. I have been strongly recommended by Genl Mason Mr Wirt Col Lloyd (of the Senate) Chancellor Kilty &ca. The present pressure of the times, with the reduction of the army, produces an unprecedented competition for office, but I am persuaded that a few lines from you would greatly promote my success, and most probably turn the scale in my favor; After your former acts of kindness, which never shall be forgotten, I with great reluctance make another request, and I beg leave to add a proviso, that you do not comply with it, unless perfectly agreeable to your feelings, and also my assurance that it shall be the last time I shall importune you in this way. With great respect & Esteem I am Sir Yr obedt Sert

ALEXANDER SCOTT

PS As the appointments are to be made soon I have no time to lose.

AS

RC (DLC). Docketed by JM.

1. Scott to JM, 10 Mar. 1821.

To James Breckinridge

Dear Sir — Mar. 15. 1821

An alarm has been communicated from Richmond that you think of refusing to return thither at the next Session of the Legislature.[1] I trust it has proceeded more from the anxiety of those who feel the necessity of your co-operation, than from any real danger. I well know the sacrifice you have already made, and readily conceive the just repugnance you may feel to a renewal, perhaps increase of it. I cannot but flatter myself however that you will not leave unfinished the work so much indebted to your efforts for its progress, & which I under⟨stand⟩ is likely to need them more than ever. I pray you then, my de⟨ar Sir,⟩ not to risk the effect of your absence at the critical & final ⟨struggle⟩ which awaits the University in Decr. next. I know the ⟨impor⟩tance you attach to this Institution, & I believe you do not overrate it as a source of the light & improvement so much wanted in our State. Make one more sacrifice then, & seal its triumph over the opposing difficulties. Let me add the personal hope that you will be accompanied by Mrs. Breckinridge to Richmond, & that you may be able to take Montpellier in your way. Mrs. M. & myself wd. be truly gratified by such a visit, & wd. not fail to make you both sensible of it by the warmth of our welcome. Yrs. with friendly respects & best wishes

James Madison

RC (NUtM); draft (DLC). RC addressed by JM to Breckinridge at Fincastle, Virginia. RC damaged by removal of seal; words and parts of words in angle brackets have been supplied from the draft. Minor differences between the copies have not been noted.

1. See Joseph C. Cabell to JM, 10 Mar. 1821.

To James Monroe

Dr. Sir — Mar. 15. 1821

I congratulate you most heartily on the happy close to the first period of your public trust, and on the very conspicuous result which introduces you to the second.

One of your successful measures is of course bringing on you the irksome task of making selections from a crowd of candidates. On this list is I find Mr. A. Scott, who has again appealed to the motives which on other occasions drew from me the mention of his name to you. His particular object appears the Secretaryship to the Commission[e]rs for claims under the Florida treaty for which he thinks himself qualified by his knowledge of the Spanish as well as French languages. It appears also that he has a very respectable patronage in gentlemen near you, more intimately acquainted with his personal qualities than myself. All that I can say in the case is, that I have always be⟨en⟩ led to think favorably of them, as was implied by the appt. he recd when I was in the Administration, and that such a mark of public confiden⟨ce⟩ as he solicits cd. not but be agreeable to me, the more so as he has an amiable family to share its benefits: provided always that pu⟨b⟩lic considerations of which you are the only as well as best judge do not preclude gratification of his wishes.

Draft (DLC).

From Richard Rush

Dear Sir, London March 15. 1821.

Your favor of the fourth of December came safely to hand, and with it the letter for Mr Joy, and one for Miss Wright, both of which have been delivered. Mr Smith[1] into whose hands I put the latter, informs me that there was no difficulty in forwarding it to its destination. I have to beg, dear Sir, that you will without scruple commit to my care whatever letters you may have occasion to write to this country, and I would add indeed, that if you should ever wish any forwarded to any other part of Europe, opportunities by the way of England being the most frequent, I shall be at all times happy if you will entrust them to my charge. I beg you also to command me in all other ways whilst I stay here, in which it may ever occur to you that I can be useful. The friendship with which you have honored me, stands forward as among the first pleasures and gratifications of my life, and to be still kept in your recollection whilst I am away, keeps alive feelings in me that I shall ever greatly prize.

Knowing that it was your wish to see a good answer to Malthus on population, I had great pleasure in sending you, about a month ago, Godwins work on this express subject.[2] It was at a moment when I was not able to accompany it by a line, as I had wished, nor indeed had I then had the leisure to look into the book. I have since read it through, and with extraordinary interest. What is thought of it here, I do not yet know, as nobody in the circles where I chiefly move seems to be acquainted with it, and the Reviews have not yet that I have seen taken it in hand. But the book will probably make some noise in the world. Whatever Godwin writes, is calculated to set people to thinking, whether he be in the right or not; and it is understood that he is chiefly desirous that his fame should rest upon this work. It makes some startling appeals to the legislator and the political economist. I see that he has fallen into some extravagant mis[s]tatements respecting our country; but the general current of his facts and reasoning, taking the work throughout, has something in it curious and awakening. He writes too much in a passion; yet, if passion does blunder sometimes it is also its characteristick to be energetick, and so is he in this work. He battles his cause fiercely, and with frequent if not constant success. It seems difficult to rise from his pages without looking upon a man in some new lights. We begin to regard him as an animal more rare and valuable than we had supposed; as no incumbrance to the earth in England, or even in China itself, and as proper to be brought into being in all countries by bounties, rather than kept away by prohibitions. I am afraid to say all that I think of his theory, not being able at present to carry my investigations enough into it to satisfy my own conclusions, and being too much under the influence of first impressions. I have for some years inclined to an opinion that the true policy of the United States would consist in extending the rights of citizenship to all new-comers upon terms far easier and more alluring than we do now; as Holland did in the best days of her history, and as Russia does at this moment. How then must this book have affected me? I shall wait with impatience for Malthus's rejoinder. Rejoin I presume he will, after all the hard blows this formidable adversary has given him.

The agricultural address with which you were so kind as to favor me a couple of years ago, contained sentiments, as nearly as I can recollect, in accordance with some of Godwins leading views.[3] But perhaps I am wrong. Having been forced to part, as I formerly mentioned, with both my copies of the pamphlet, I regretted that I could not turn to it.

Events of the highest moment are daily expected to take place in Italy. You will have seen the official letter of Lord Castlereagh respecting the merits of the dispute between Naples and Austria.[4] That the troops of the latter may be discomfited in their unjustifiable invasion, is, I should say, the ardent wish of a majority of the people of this country; but not, I believe, of the ministry.

Begging to join Mrs Rush in affectionate remembrances to Mrs Madison, I tender to you, dear Sir, the assurances of my perpetual respect and attachment.

RICHARD RUSH

RC (PHi).

1. For John Adams Smith, see *PJM-RS*, 1:251 n. 2.

2. William Godwin, *Of Population: An Enquiry concerning the Power of Increase in the Numbers of Mankind* . . . (London, 1820).

3. For population growth as the result of progressive agriculture, see JM's Address to the Agricultural Society of Albemarle, 12 May 1818, *PJM-RS*, 1:260–83.

4. Lord Castlereagh to His Majesty's Missions at Foreign Courts, 19 Jan. 1821 (*The Annual Register, or A View of the History, Politics, and Literature, of the Year 1820* [2 vols.; London,

1822], 2:737–39). For the Neapolitan revolution of 1820–21, see Acton, *Cambridge Modern History* (1969 reprint), 10:111–14.

From John Rhea

SIR, WASHINGTON 19th. March 1821

Please to accept the within copy of a circular Letter[1]—and be so good as to present my respects to your Lady. I have the honor to be Your obt servt

JOHN RHEA

RC (DLC). Docketed by JM.

1. For John Rhea's circular letter to his constituents, 5 Mar. 1821, see Cunningham, *Circular Letters of Congressmen*, 3:1140–47. JM's copy is in the Madison Collection, Rare Book and Special Collections Division, Library of Congress.

From Peter S. Du Ponceau

DEAR SIR PHILADELPHIA 23d. March 1821.

Understanding that the new Virginia University at Charlotte[s]ville is to be opened in December next, & that a Professor of Chemistry & Mineralogy is to be elected, I take the liberty of recommending for that station, Mr Lardner Clark Vanuxem, now of Columbia S.C. He is a native of this City, from respectable parents, who from his infancy Shewed such a disposition to the studies connected with natural Philosophy, that his whole mind was employed in them until he came to the age of chusing a profession when his father finding that the bent of his genius was not to be conquered, Sent him to Paris, where he pursued for three Years his favorite studies under the best teachers, & returned home fraught with knowledge. He is now an assistant to Dr Cooper who thinks highly of his acquirements & most probably will recommend him to you. For my part I am free to certify to his excellent Moral Character, & to his unconquerable attachment to the studies he has pursued, which I have for many Years witnessed. I have the honor to be With the greatest veneration & respect Dear Sir Your most obedt humble Servant

PETER S. DU PONCEAU

RC (DLC). Addressed by Du Ponceau to JM, and franked. Docketed by JM.

From Jonathan Elwell

Respected Sir March 26th 1821 State of Main

I Write to Inform You of my Lemantable Sitewation & if Your Exelincey recolects in 1811 and 1812 I Was on to se You and made an Aplication Concerning the Schoner Hero and Cargo that Was robed from me and My regester forged in Wilmington North Carlonia. You Advised me to wait Untill Congress met and lay my Greviance befour the House Which I did take Your Advise and petioned for releif. The petion was dispenced With reading befour the House and refered to a Comitee Of Comerce and Manefactors Which I think was the Wrong Comitee to have layed the business befour as I think the Comitee of the Judicary Would have been more proper. Then the Whole business of the Courts would have been examined into and the Matter fully explained—by Some Means the business was delayed so that I Could Not Obtain no Information nor redress Whatever. Neither have I had a full knoledge of the whole business since I left Washington on the Account of having to render the same fate in this state for the proceedings has been Just alike in Both states by the Influence of that Combination of swindlers of the Laws of our Cuntry. When Ariving into the state of Massachusetts their I found a power put on reccord perporting to be a General power. I then Advertised the Whole proceedings a forgery in the Argis paper printed in portland a forgery in order to back all their fallce proceedings Under that stolen power. They sold reail and personal property to a Large an Amount and received the money and gave deeds Contrary to law Which the Combination of theives and swindlers Cannot deny because those deeds was put on reccord in the County of Hancock—and Now they Come forrawd and say it was to try to save my property So like the Theif When he is de[te]cted Must and will have some excuse. They Own they Ment to steel but the Whole business Neads no further proof than the records where the deeds Are recorded and the Stattitute violated by their artfull proceedings. I Humbly if they meant to serve me Which they pretended Why did they place my Whife and Children in a state of starvation in my absence from Them So that they were Obliged to Cawl on the town For relief. So the thing speaks for it self. They not ondly Set out to destroy me but the Whole famely Which has been a Grevious thing as my Children has had but a Slim Chanc to get their edication. I have tryed to learn them What has been Cause of such a delay of Justice that if Death should take me away from them by Copys from the deferant Courts and Notery publicks protest of their Protentions they would be able to look up their fradulent Transactions Except that the Covenant was broken and our bill of rights violated and taken from us. I Want Your Exelincys Opinion Wuther a man Can be Debard from the laws of his Cuntry except he has been Outlawed by some Open violation that he has been Guilty of or be debard from a Jury of our Cuntry—but it seems as tho it Now is the Cace in this Odious trancaction for they never dare to let this Cace go to a Jury even for the damages on account of the Crimanality. Now sir if This is the Case on the account of such a Large Combination has been Guilty of violating the Laws of God and man that The Law Cant Give redress do they not place the Individual Over their heads to Make the Law to sute himself. I very Well know their has been a rumer spread by that Combinatn Of swindlers that I was a Crazey man but I Will apeal to Your Exelenceys Judgement if their was not more of a Crazey turn in their brains than Your H Servant. If Ever such an Open violation of permidated piece of treachery would ever taken place Under this Goverment to Robe One of their own sitzans and family out of some Where about Twenty thousand dollars Worth of real and personal property Besides placeing me out of my business for twelve years. They have tryed to excuse themselves Under ever transaction that Man was able to invent but all proved fruitless. You may think it very strange that the mater has been Delayed by me not makeing a more perservering atempt for this length of time as it was a business of such a Magenitud. I have been expecting that Congress would do something for me and my family as I hope and trust they will by the ⟨action?⟩ Of You and some of my good friends as I and my family are determined to look up the proceedings as soon as may be for I Now have a Whife and four sons Men grown that have with myself been a wating with a great deal pacience. If they will Not Come forrowd to Grant me No releif What are we to do in such a Case? Why we Must Cawl on the diferant Legislatures of the states and from them to the people Which are all Liable under our elective Goverment. But I pray that will not be the Case for I have a better opinion of our Rulers and I trust that they have more regard for their oathe of office than to Neglect One Indvidual and his family by haveing the Constitution and the Laws of our Cuntry trampled upon in such a manner by a sett of Swindlers. I Expect if I had let that Combination Of the violaters of the Law have my vesell sail under a forged register the same as tho I had it sold to a British Merchant the business would have been setled with And My money paid over to me. Then Where was my Oath in such a Case besides my own Conscience by being Gilty of such anormis Crime? Would Not such a proceeding have been High treason by asisting a foreigner With our sertificates of register to help their trade. You now se the begining of this business. A Foreigner one George Cameron set out To Rob me out of my vesell and Cargo and sertifcte. of Registery to help their trade. You now se the beginning of this business. A Foreigner one George Cameron Of the town of Wilmington North Carolina had Been a resident for a Number of Years but Never Would take the Oath of Alegance to this

Goverment Set out to rob me out of My vesell and Cargo and a Sartificat of the Government Because as he afterwards Said that I Was a Dambd Yankee the Ofspring of those Rebels that rebeled against his Goverment. He With som Others More friendly to his Goverment than they Ware to their own Especialy one Samuel R. Goselin a Lawyer then set out to take pertentions as a proctur of the Laws of the General Goverment Which was a pretended Libell befour the district Court for the United States in Wilmington N Carolina. After the proceedings was dismissed by the District Judge Potter he then Obtained an other pretence from the County of Hanover in the state afoursaid and Caused the Whole Vesell and Cargo to be sold befour my face and at the sail I Loudly Exclamed Who ever bought that property bought Stolen Goods. The Sheriff William Nut did sell the Whole property to William Camell. He finding the sail fradulent sold herr again to get herr of his hands for says he to the Cheif Judge of the County I have ruined my self for I have bought Stolen Goods for the Owner was Present and Loudly Exclaimed that whoever bought that property bought Stolen Goods and Where Liable to the provisions of the Law. His Advice was You Must sell herr again for to get herr of Your hands. He then sold herr to one Whiple as he said belon[g]ing to New York. After Geting ready for sea I asked him how he was a going to saile that vesell. His reply was You will Grant request papers for herr will You Knot. My reply was she sould lay their and rott first—he then aplyed to the Collector for the papers but he refused by saying You Nor No Other Shall have them papers Untill Jonathan Elwell is paid and Setled with. The vesell Layed about Tenn days and then a Clearance Was Granted by the Collector Rober Cochran of Wilmington and the said Schooner did sail a Number of Voy[ag]es under some Clande[s]tine head I supose to serve that Scotch foreigner In order for to earn Money for to pay the damages Still keeping me their Without furnishing me with any Suport What ever. I made a number of Atempts to Scivill Authorities for to Obtain Warrants to aprehend them Robers to bring them to Justice but they all refused. If I had Money I Should have sued them for their Denying their duties Injoined Uppon by Law. The Courts seeing such a Comitment they delayed the Matter, thinking to Weare me out or that I should be so Much dissatisfyed to seek some other Cuntry for redress but they found out their Mistake for Wher evver I am robed out of my property their I am determined to seek Redress to the Last end of life. Sir pardon me for this Naritive as it is very Lengthy and Meanly Wrote as You must expect from the sitiwation I am placed in To Work hard and fare the same with My property and damages in the hands of them swindlers and their Accomplices. Now sir this is sent to you by the desire of My second son that is on his Death beed. He repeats the request over and again Never to quit Writeing to You and the heads of the Nation Untill redress is Granted for my Greivanc as he Lays his death to the Cause of Workeing hard and faring the same with the perplexity of Mind that has Caused a Consumption of his vitals To se such high Crimes and Misdominors in ofice that Justice Could Not Be obtained Intirely a dead Letter of the Law, Laws against Us but None in our favour for us. He has been expecting to get better for to Come on to se You if the Covenant was broken or What steps was Necsary for my relief but alass he is no More but Intirely Resigned himself Up to the hands of his Gracious God by saying he was Glad to retire from this theifing Combination and their Accomplicies. He alltho my son he has allways been admired for his tallents and virtues. Seeing and hearing of My Constant adhearing to the Constitution and the Laws of the Land With the perticuler favour for the Administration he has Made it [h]is studdy to find out such a delay of Justice Which I in som degree have sati[s]fyed by My papers and doctuments in my possesin With the pub[l]ick News papers in my possion in the State Where the robery took place. Sir their is no doubt that forgery with Lys has taken place that My property has been restored with damages by some and Others that My property never was Robed from me. Then what mus be my feeling taking Such a solemn Oat[h] befour My god besides the proof by their pretended Athorities of the General Goverment and state Goverments. Allso if I Could Not prove those Asertions should I dare to Cawl On the diferant tribunals with this asurance. No the diferant tribunals Up to Congres knows the facts. The Courts have tried the Causse and the precidents have pardoned alltho kept in secret from the publick but Not from me as I think I know Every proceeding from the County court up to Congress. I Humbly ax You What must be your feelings Was You to be placed in such a situwation Humbly Beging for your own property that was Robed from You that You had spent the principle part of You[r] days by brousing the seas and that the Chief Magistrate for the Nation would give you No sati[s]faction so that the Loer tribunals would Not adheare to Your suplications as they expect that the Large Weale must be set a going then of Course the small Weale would of Course follow to do Justice. Sir You stated to me that I Could do More than You Could. I Expect in Case of Impeacment Agreable to the Constitution of the Judges that the president shall Not pardon but the plaintiff Shall have his triall by a Jury of the Country and if they are Condemned their is their State the Gallos. This I know to be the Case. But What steps Upon the Humane side of the Law. Death is a tereable terror but if It was Not for this terror Where would be the security for any personal property for every thinking person is shure that the Majestry of the Law is the Next step from the father of all. Good Sir I Humbly axk ten thousand Pardons For waring Your paticen with this awfull ⟨Moras?⟩, but I hope You will forgive me as we desire the Great and Gracious God will forgive Us all by our Hum station This from Your Most obd Humble Servant

JONATHAN ELWELL[1]

RC (DLC). Docketed by JM.

1. Jonathan Elwell (ca. 1769–1834) was a merchant sea captain from Belfast, and later Northport, Massachusetts (both now Maine) (Portland, Maine, *Eastern Argus*, 28 Oct. 1813 and 1 Dec. 1834). For the details of the *Hero* case, see Elwell's letter published in the Raleigh, North Carolina, *Star*, 24 May 1810. Elwell's petition for redress in this case was presented to Congress and submitted to the Committee of Commerce and Manufactures on 7 May 1812; it was discharged from consideration by that committee two weeks later (*Journal of the House of Representatives*, 8:331, 346).

From Charles H. Philips

SIR BALTIMORE March 30th 1821

In writing to a person who has filled one of the greatest offices in our country, that of chief magistrate of our republic, I am sensible of the many disadvantages I labour under in introducing myself to your notice; not only from my own inferiority, in talents and knowledge; but from the obscurity of my life, which is little known beyond my own private circle: but Sir, I am far from being discouraged in my attempt, particularly when a few days ago, I see you were toasted at a public dinner as the friend of Man.[1] Now Sir to whom else could I better apply than to the friend of man and I assure you Sir I should be far from applying to any one if I did not really stand in need of a friend and though it may appear strange, that I should address a person on this subject at so great a distance, and with whom I have no acquaintance; yet it is from the conviction that the Philanthropist has his friends every where and that he is a friend to them any where. You must know sir that after receiving a first rate education I commenced business in this city and from unforeseen events was so unfortunate as to lose a great part of my capital and consequently became involved in debt: the property coming to me from my fathers estate I can not get yet and I have applied to several of my friends here to let me have some money on mortgage but their reply is they can not spare any &ce.

Now Sir you are fully sensible of the many failures and calamities that has befallen our city and pervaded every rank, age and desc[r]iption of People and being a young man just commencing business I felt very loathe to cheat any one or take the benifit of the insolvent act: in fine Sir I stand very much in need of a friend and if you are disposed to assist me I will give you all the information necessary as to my character &ce from some of the most respectable people in this city; at least sir if you can not let me have any money be so good as to return me a little of your salutary advice which will be thankfully received by your very humble Servant

CHAS H PHILIPS

RC (DLC). Docketed by JM.

1. At a public dinner given for Henry Clay in Washington on 14 Mar. 1821, John Law gave the toast: "James Madison—the friend of man" (*Daily National Intelligencer*, 17 Mar. 1821).

From James Monroe

DEAR SIR WASHINGTON March 31. 1821

Since I have been in this office many newspapers have been sent to me, from every part of the union, unsought, which, having neither time nor curiosity to read, are in effect thrown away. I should have stopped the practice, but from delicacy to the Editors, & expecting also, that they would subject me to no charge. Lately I have been informed that the same practice took place in your time, & had been tolerated till you retird, when the editors sent you bills for the amount of the subscription, to their papers, for the eight years, making an enormous sum. Be so kind as to inform me whether this was the fact, as in case it was, I may write to the Editors (a few excepted, & very few) not to send them.

The law for executing the Florida treaty has subjected me to great trouble & embarrassm[e]nt. The organizing a govt. in Florida, & appointment of officers there, is in itself a serious duty. I have as yet appointed the Govr. only, who is Genl. Jackson. The institution of a board of commissrs., for the settlement of claims on Spain, is attended with still greater difficulty. In general, the persons best qualified live in the great towns, especially to the Eastward. In those towns also the claimants live. If I appoint a Commissr. in one only, and not in the others, all the latter will complain; and it is impossible to appoint them in all, the number not admitting of it. I have therefore thought it best to avoid the great towns, & propose to appoint Govr. King of Maine, Judge Green of Fredericksbg, & Judge White[1] of Knoxville Tenn:, two Lawyers & one Merchant. They are all able & upright men unconnected with the claims & claimants. I may make some changes, the commn. not having issued, & therefore wish you not to mention it.

From Europe we have nothing interesting since the accounts lately publishd of the menacd movment on Naples, by Austria & perhaps Russia & Prussia, tho it is intimated, that the two latter, will only place armies of observation, near the scene of action, to be governd by events; & also of the decision of the British govt., not to interfere in the contest.

Mrs Monroe's health continues to be very delicate. The rest of my family including our youngest daughter, & her daughter, are in good health, & all desire to be affectionately rememberd to you & mrs Madison. Very sincerely your friend

James Monroe

RC (DLC). Docketed by JM.

1. William King, Littleton Waller Tazewell, and Hugh Lawson White were appointed claims commissioners by President Monroe. White (1773–1840) was a Tennessee lawyer and successively judge of the superior court of that state, 1801–7, and judge of the Tennessee Supreme Court of Errors and Appeals, 1809–15. He served on the claims commission, 1821–24, and was a U.S. senator, 1825–40 (Nancy N. Scott, ed., *A Memoir of Hugh Lawson White . . . with Selections from His Speeches and Correspondence* [Philadelphia, 1856], 8, 15, 16, 17, 33, 34–35, 36, 420).

From Eyrien Frères & Cie.

Monsieur. Havre 2 avril 1821.

Messieurs les administrateurs du jardin du Roi a Paris, nous ont fait Passer une caisse de grains pour vous. Nous l'avons jointe a quelques autres caisses du même Envoy & avons embarqué le tout abord du navire americain *Cadmus* Capn. Witelok,[1] a l'adresse de Monsieur Hosack[2] Directeur du jardin de Botanique de l'Etat de New-york, de qui vous voudrez Bien la reclamer.

Nous Prenons La liberté de Vous offrir nos Services pour Votre Correspondance avec Messieurs les administrateurs du jardin du Roi, ou pour tout autre objet qui pourrait vous interesser en france. Nous avons l'honneur d'être, avec La plus parfaite Consideration Monsieur, Vos tres Humbles & obeissants Serviteurs

Eyrien Freres & Cie

CONDENSED TRANSLATION

The administrators of the King's Garden at Paris have forwarded to us a package of seeds for you. We added it with some other packages for the same shipment and sent it all on board the American ship Cadmus, Capt. Whitlock, addressed to Mr. Hosack, director of the Botanical Garden of the State of New York, from whom you will please request it.

We take the liberty of offering you our services for your correspondence with the administrators of the King's Garden, or for any other object in France which might interest you.

RC (DLC). Docketed by JM.

1. The *Cadmus*, S. B. Whitlock, master, owned by William Whitlock Jr., a merchant at 71 South St., New York, arrived in New York on 26 May 1821 from Le Havre, France (*New-York Evening Post*, 26 May and 8 and 27 June 1821).

2. David Hosack (1769–1835), a graduate of the College of New Jersey, was a physician and botanist, who at various times, in addition to maintaining a large private practice, was professor of botany at Columbia College, the College of Physicians and Surgeons, and Rutgers College. He used his own funds to establish the Elgin Botanic Garden in 1801 and persuaded the state of New York to purchase it in 1810 (Ruth L. Woodward and Wesley Frank Craven, *Princetonians, 1784–1790: A Biographical Dictionary* [Princeton, N.J., 1991], 402–12).

Minutes of the Board of Visitors of the University of Virginia

[2 April 1821]

At a meeting of the Visitors of the University of Virginia at the said University on Monday the 2d. of April 1821. present Th: Jefferson Rector, James Breckenridge, Chapman Johnson & James Madison.

A letter having been recieved by the Rector from Thomas Appleton of Leghorn[1] stating the prices at which the Ionic & Corinthian capitels wanting for the Pavilions of the University may be furnished there in marble, and these prices appearing to be much lower than they would cost if made here in stone, Resolved that it be an instruction to the Committee of superintendance to procure the sd. Capitels in marble from Italy.

Resolved as the opinion of this board, that it is expedient to procure the loan of 60,000.D or so much thereof as may be necessary, as authorised by the late act of the General Assembly concerning the University of Virginia, and that the Committee of superintendance be instructed to negociate the same with the President & Directors the literary fund of preference, or if not to be obtained from them, then with others according to the authorities of the sd. act.

Resolved that it is expedient to proceed with the building of the Library on the plan submitted to the board: provided the funds of the University be adequate to the completion of the buildings already begun, and to the building the Western range of hotels & dormitories, & be also adequate to the completion of the Library so far as to render the building secure & fit for use: & that it be an instruction to the Commee. of superintendance to ascertain as accurately as may be the state of accounts under the contracts already made, the expences of compleating the buildings begun & contemplated, and not to enter into any contracts for the Library until they are fully satisfied that, without interfering with the finishing of all the pavilions, hotels & dormitories, begun and to be begun, they have funds sufficient to put the library in the condition above described.

And the board adjourns without day.

TH: JEFFERSON. rector.

Ms (ViU: Jefferson Papers, Special Collections). In Jefferson's hand.

1. Thomas Appleton to Thomas Jefferson, 10 Oct. 1820 (DLC: Jefferson Papers). Appleton (d. 1840) was U.S. consul at Leghorn, Italy, 1798–1840 (*PJM-SS*, 8:496 n. 1).

To George W. Featherstonhaugh

SIR MONTPELLEIR Apl. 5. 1821.

I have received your favour of March 19.[1] & am glad to find that you think of giveing still more value to your Agricultural work, by extending in a new Edition, your practical veiws of the subject. I retain at the same time my opinion in favour of the Chemical instruction which your original plan combined with them.

I know not well what to answer to your enquiry relative to the reception such a Volume would meet with in the Southern States. As to the state in which I live I dare not speak with confidence; so difficult is a deffusion of literary productions thro' its dispersed readers, and so universal is the present dearth of means even for the minuter articles of cost. I can scarcely doubt however that the attention which has been excited to the practice & the science of rural economy would produce a demand sufficient at least to give a right turn to the scale, if it should need such a weight, which I should not easily suppose would be the case. For myself I sincerely wish that your calculations may justify the experiment: & that, without a pecuniary loss, which would be very unreasonable, it may reward you with the satisfaction of contributing more extensively to enlighten & animate a persuit so deeply interesting to the public prosperity. I renew to you Sir assurances of my esteem & good wishes

JS MADISON

FC (DLC). In Dolley Madison's hand, with JM's note: "G.W. Featherstonhaugh." RC cover sheet (NjP: Crane Collection) addressed and franked by JM to Featherstonhaugh at Duanesburgh, New York. Marked "Orange CH Va April 10." Docketed by Featherstonhaugh.

1. Featherstonhaugh to JM, 10 Mar. 1821.

To Richard Rush

Dear Sir Montpellier apl. 5. 1821

This will be presented by John P. Wilson Esqr.[1] of this State. I cannot speak of his worth from personal knowlege, but it is well vouched to me by a friend on whom I can entirely rely. He avails himself of resources & a leisure which enable him to indulge his curiosity in a trip to Europe; and he will be so much gratified by being made known to you that I can not refuse him a line of introduction. Yours with the highest esteem

James Madison

RC (NjP). Addressed by JM to Rush in London and marked "Mr. Wilson." Docketed by Rush.

1. John P. Wilson (d. 1865), a graduate of Washington College in 1810, was a lawyer and planter who represented Campbell County in the Virginia House of Delegates, 1823–25, and Cumberland County, 1829–31. Wilson was also a trustee of Hampden-Sydney College from 1819 to 1848 (Wilmer L. Kerns, *Waltons of Old Virginia and Sketches of Families in Central Virginia* . . . [Westminster, Md., 2005], 68 n. 54; *Catalogue of the Officers and Alumni of Washington and Lee University, Lexington, Virginia, 1749–1888* [Baltimore, 1888], 63; Swem and Williams, *Register*, 446; *General Catalogue of the Officers and Students of Hampden-Sidney College. Virginia. 1776–1906* [Richmond, Va., 1908], 17).

To Thomas Cooper

Dear Sir Montpr apl. 6. 1821

I recd. some days ago your letter of Mar. 12. recommending Mr. L. Vanuxem for the Chemical Chair in our University, which we can no longer hope to fill as we had wished. He could not certainly be presented under better auspices; but it is not yet known who may be brought into comparison with him, and it is ascertained moreover that the University cannot be opened for a year or two; and must be unopened for a number of years, unless the Legislature of the State should, exchange into a Gift, the loans it has afforded.

Deeply as I regret the loss we have sustained, I cannot but congratulate you on the footing you at length find yourself; with a tender of my best wishes, that it may prove in every r⟨egard⟩ as beneficial to yourself, as I am sure it will to the institution which has had the good fortune, of which the course of circumstances deprived ours.

I duly recd. the copy of your introductory Lecture,[1] which you were so good as to send me. I did not thank you for it at the time, because it was uncertain whether you were in Pena. or S. Cara. Permit me now to supply the omission. I read the discourse with real pleasure; the views taken of the subject, appearing to have been happily selected, and presented in lights peculiarly adapted to make the desirable impressions. Be assured always of my great esteem & cordial regards

J. M

Draft (DLC).

1. Thomas Cooper, *Introductory Lecture, on Chemistry, Delivered at the College of South-Carolina, in Columbia, January, 1820* (Columbia, S.C., 1820; Shoemaker 868). JM's copy is in the Madison Collection, Rare Book and Special Collections Division, Library of Congress.

From William Maury

DEAR SIR, NEW ORLEANS 6 April 1821

I addressed you some weeks since[1] from this place, & now submit for your inspection & opinion the annexed copy of a letter which I have to day received from my Fathers partner.[2]

It is a subject upon which I would not have taken the liberty of addressing you, did I not know the strong friendship you have always manifested towards my Father. Pardon me therefore in doing this for his sake.

Might I ask the favor of you to consult Mr Monroe at your convenience, whether an application from my Father for the Office of Consul, in the event of his resignation for myself, would be successful.

His delicacy upon such a subject would be such, that unless there was a strong probability of success he would not apply; & even then, he could not, except taking into consideration that for the first 20 years the Office cost him from 1 a $400 ℔ annum & that now, he should be reimbursed, his Family will from the usual course of Nature with persons at his advanced stage of life lose their only chance.

Indeed my Dear Sir, tis but from these considerations alone that I thus address you, & again I pray you pardon the liberty.

The weather is becoming very warm thermometer 80 & this is so great a warning for a Stranger that I shall take it next week.

The Governor was married last evening to Mr Skipwiths eldest daughter[3]—she is 18.

I hope to find Mrs Madison & yourself in good health when I call for *quarters* in May. Meantime I have the honor to be Dear Sir Your most obedient servant

WILLIAM MAURY

RC and enclosure (DLC). RC docketed by JM. For enclosure, see n. 2.

1. William Maury to JM, 8 Mar. 1821.

2. The enclosure (2 pp.) was a copy of William Latham to William Maury, 25 Jan. 1821, in which Latham wrote: "Your Father never appears to have looked to the possibility of one of his Sons succeeding him in his situation as Consul, altho a matter that would be very desirable for his family—as the situation is now becoming valuable & ought from this time to Nett £700 c £800 ℔ annum—at least to any one who would succeed him, as you[r] Father is at an expence for Clerks &c. which certainly might be considerably lessened—he appears to dislike taking it into consideration & therefore your Mother is unwilling to say anything to him of it, but she authorizes me to tell you that in the event of anything happening to your Father, & which at his time of life ought to be taken into view; for the sake of his family, she would be most anxious that you should succeed him, provided that there was any prospect of an application being successful. The point is—to ascertain that prospect."

3. Thomas Bolling Robertson married Lelia Skipwith, the eldest daughter of Fulwar Skipwith, former U.S. commercial agent and consul general at Paris, and governor of the West Florida Republic (Conrad, *Dictionary of Louisiana Biography*, 2:689; *PJM-PS*, 2:333 n. 2).

To James Monroe

Dear Sir Montpellier Apl. 7. 1821

I have recd. your favor of the 31. ult. The retrospective claim for Newspapers has been made on me, in one instance only, since I was out of office. A printer in Vermont sent me a charge for a weekly paper during my term of 8 years, several years after I was out of office.[1] I answered that I had never subscribed for the paper, and had always supposed it to have been forwarded without pecuniary views. The reply was that the original Editor had died, & that the paper had been continued by his successor, on the ground that my name was on the list, and in expectation of payment. The correspondence ended with a suggestion on my part, that the original printer, whose Books had passed into the new hands, had probably never meant to make a charge; but that I would pay for the period subsequent to his death, as it was alledged that the paper had been continued with that expectation. No further answer has been recd. and the lapse of time makes it probable that the claim is abandoned. I may add that at the expiration of the first four years, an acct. was presented by Poulson, whose paper had been regularly sent without a sanction. I declined paying it, as it was not legally due and had certainly no plea of any other sort. He stated that it had been sent to every President from the commencement of the Govt. and had been understood that its continuance was a matter of course. I then paid for it. It was sent afterwards, as long as I remained at Washington. But no charge has ever been made for it. Since I have been out of office, several papers gratuitously sent before have been continued, and several others from other presses have been sent me, some regularly some occasionly, for which no charge has been made, as yet at least. I shd. have put a stop to most of them, but from the delicacy which has swayed you.

I attended the meeting of the University Visitors the first of the month. It appears that the buildings will be compleated for opening it next year, or at farthest the Spring following: But unless the loan from the State can be changed into a gift, the annuity of 15.000 Dolrs will not be liberated for a long period, & in the meantime professors cannot be engaged. The hope of this liberality from the Genl. Assembly, depends a good deal on the payment of the State claims on the Genl. Govt. We are much interested therefore in this payment both as to the amount and the *time* of it. As far as it can be accelerated, with propriety, a very essential service will be rendered to the Institution. Mr. Jefferson will probably write to you on the subject.[2] I left him quite well & several years younger in Constitution & appearance, than he was in April last. We have I fear lost all our fruit, the peaches & cherries certainly. When do you mean to leave the City? & give us the pleasure of seeing you. We hope you will be accompanied as heretofore. With our best wishes for you all Yrs. truly & respectfully.

JAMES MADISON

RC (DLC: Monroe Papers).

1. See JM to Nicholas Van Zandt, ca. 1 Mar. 1820, and n. 2.

2. As Thomas Jefferson explained to Monroe in his letter of 8 Apr. 1821, DLC: Jefferson Papers: "You doubtless know that our legislature constituted the debt due to them from the US. into a Literary fund, for the purposes of education, & that on this fund the University is established, and dependant. At their late session they authorised the Literary board to advance to the University 60,000. D. of the monies still to be recieved from the US. I am told that the liquidation of that account has proceeded so far as to shew that that amount may be safely paid as admitted to be due. Our request is for as speedy a payment of that sum to our Literary board as circumstances and forms admit."

From James Maury

MY DEAR SIR LIVERPOOL 7 April 1821.

I regret to find, by your letter of the 20th Feby that some of the goods sent were higher priced than you contemplated: & I can readily account for your remark so far as relates to the glasswares, the silk hose, & furniture calico: each of these being entitled to a drawback on exportation, but the expences at the excise office & custom house in *stamps* bonds & entry would, on such small quantities, greatly exceed the amount of those Drawbacks; as to the other articles most of them being designated *fine*, the orders to our trades men were in conformity: on future occasions of the sort we shall be obliged by your giving us your directions as to price.

In regard of your tobo., it having been shipped at Norfolk, a general port for taking in cargoes from all the rivers, I verily believe the idea of Rappahannock was out of the question, because the samples were exhibited with those we had on sale at the same time from Richmond; & indeed the average price of your consignment is almost, if not quite, equal to most of those we had from our correspondents in Upper James river: yet, had your's been landed out of a vessell direct from Rappahannock, it possibly might have been somewhat unfavorable, & therefore, permit me to suggest, whether it might not on the whole, be better to submit to the extra expence of carriage to Richmond, be it your intention to sell in the country or ship to a British market; & was I a Planter situated as near to James River inspections as Montpellier is, I think I should pursue the course I suggest.

Indeed, Sir, I am at a loss what to recommend under the present aspect of things for our *antient staple;* prices now are as annexed which I consider equal to a reduction of 1d. @ 2d. from those of last year. This is written in behalf of my partner & of your old obliged friend.

JAMES MAURY

James River leaf tobo
Faded 2¼ @ 2½
Ordinary sound 2¾ @ 2½
Middling 3¼ @ 4½
Good & fine 4¾ @ 7

Stemd. Tobo
Top Stemd 4 @ 6
Short do 3 @ 4

RC (DLC). In a clerk's hand, signed by Maury. Marked "Duplicate." Docketed by JM.

¶ From William Shepherd. Letter not found. 7 *April 1821.* Referred to in JM to James Francis Madison Shepherd, 8 Dec. [1825] (DLC), where JM quotes from William Shepherd's letter: "A family of the negroes that belonged to my brothers Estate have been taken back for the benefit of Betsy Shepherd: if you think proper to subscribe $500 towards paying for them, it will be thankfully recd. The money is now due." Dr. William Shepherd (d. 1825) was the brother of Alexander Shepherd, who married Elizabeth (Betsy) Conway Madison Shepherd, the daughter of JM's deceased brother Francis (*Southeastern Reporter* [200 vols; St. Paul, Minn., 1887–1939], 2:273; Chapman, "Who was Buried in James Madison's Grave?," 253).

To Francis Glass

Sir Montpr. Apl. 8. 1821

I have recd. your letter of Mar. 3. on the subject of your "Life of Washington written in Latin for the use of Schools."

If it were less foreign to my inclination to be distinguished by a Dedication, I should recommend as more expedient, that you should bestow that mark of respect, on some one who would find it more practicable to give value to his acceptance of it by a previous examination of the work, and whose known critical knowledge of the Language would satisfy the public of the merit of its execution. This precaution is rendered particularly worthy of attention, by the difficulty of giving to Modern Latinity, the classical purity requisite for a School Book, & by the fewness of Examples, in which the undertaking has been regarded as successful.

I regret the failure of your laudable efforts to make your acquirements a resource for the maintenance of your family; and wish that your future ones may be more fortunate. With respect

J. M

Draft (DLC). Written on the cover sheet verso of Glass to JM, 3 Mar. 1821.

From C. J. Brand

Sir, London April 10th. 1821.

I have the honor to offer to You, a copy of a treatise on the Rights of Colonies,[1] which I beg You will condescend to accept, as a mark of the highest respect and esteem, which I entertain for the Honorable Colleague, of the ever memorable Washington. Believe me Sir! that in offering the said copy, I am only actuated by a sense of admiration for a Country, which from a colony elevated itself to the rank of a free and independant Nation, and which was the native Country of a man, whose memory shall be always dear to me, who has the honor to be a colonist, (for I feel it a honor since Washington was such:) and who, when returned in his dear Country the Cape of Good Hope, shall never cease to look up to Washington, as a guide in his future life, and consecrate in his own heart, the Memory of that great civil Reformist.

Allow me Sir, wishing You all happiness and prosperity, and independence to the American Nation, to Subscribe myself with the highest consideration and regard; Sir, Your most obedt: humble and devoted Servant.

C. J. Brand[2]

RC (DLC). Docketed by JM.

1. C. J. Brand, *Dissertatio politico-juridica de jure coloniarum* (Leiden, 1820).

2. Christoffel Joseph Brand (1797–1875), a graduate of the University of Leiden, returned to Cape Colony, South Africa, in 1821, where he practiced law. He was elected a member from Stellenbosch of the first Cape parliament in 1854 and was chosen as speaker for that and subsequent parliaments until his resignation owing to ill health in 1874 (Ralph Kilpin, *The Old Cape House: Being Pages from the History of a Legislative Assembly* [Cape Town, South Africa, 1918], 97–112).

From Solomon Southwick

DR. SIR, ALBANY, April 12, 1821.

I take the liberty of begging your acceptance of my Address, &c. herewith Sent.[1]

I have only to add, that I went to Washington several years ago,[2] having previously imbibed prejudi[c]es against you as a political character, but I had not conversed wit[h] you fifteen minutes, before I was convinced that I had been duped into a wrong view of your character by designing men in whom I had placed confidence. I left Washington your friend & admirer; & I felt mortified that I had yielded myself to such erroneous impressions. In the address I am send[ing] you, I have laboured to guard the inexperienced against similar errors.

I sincerely pray, that you & your good Lady, to whom please tender my respectful compliments, may long live to enjoy the pleasures of dignified retirement, & the fruits of that public liberty you have so eminently contributed to establish. Your most obed't Serv't

S SOUTHWICK[3]

RC (DLC). Docketed by JM.

1. Solomon Southwick, *An Address, Delivered by Appointment, in the Episcopal Church, at the Opening of the Apprentices' Library, in the City of Albany, January 1, 1821* (Albany, N.Y., 1821; Shoemaker 6833). JM's copy is in the Madison Collection, Special Collections, University of Virginia Library.

2. Southwick visited Washington in the winter of 1815–16 (Southwick to JM, 30 May 1816, DLC).

3. Solomon Southwick (1773–1839), a prominent Clintonian Republican, edited and published the *Albany Register*, 1792–1800, and 1808–17. He served as clerk of the New York Assembly, 1803–7, clerk of the New York Senate, 1807, Albany county sheriff, 1809–10, and postmaster of Albany, 1815–22. By the time of this letter, Southwick was in political and economic straits, although he ran, unsuccessfully, for governor of New York twice, in 1822 and 1828. He edited the agricultural paper, the *Plough Boy*, 1819–23, and the Albany *National Democrat*, 1823–26 (Brigham, *American Newspapers*, 1:539; *ASP, Post Office*, 247–48; Albany *New-York Statesman*, 14 July 1820).

From Spencer Roane

Dear Sir, Richmond Apl. 17. 1821.

Flattered as I was by a very interesting letter from you on a former occasion,[1] I have, yet, forborn to break in upon your well-merited retirement from the public Service. Although highly valuing, and often needing, your Counsel, touching the public affairs of our Country, I have respected your repose too much, even to ask your opinions concerning them. Yet, Sir, a Crisis has arrived, when I hope I shall be pardoned for addressing you. It is firmly believed, and deeply lamented, that the *late* decision of the Supreme Court of the United States,[2] has sapped the foundations of our Constitution: of that Constitution, which, in its' original form, and its' subsequent amendments, you were so instrumental in establishing; and which you supported, by the celebrated report,[3] that produced the glorious revolution of 1799. In fact it is beleived, that this decision has entirely subverted the principles of that revolution.

From my residence at this place, from my age, the ardour of my character, and the partiality of the republicans towards me, I have opportunities to know, and I am authorized to say, that this is their strong and universal sentiment; and that, in their opinion, the crisis is truly dangerous, and most alarming. In this exigency their Eyes are turned upon you, as one of our most virtuous, most distinguished, and most efficient citizens. They see in your pen, which has so often charmed them, and saved the liberties of our Country, the only certain antidote, to the ingenious and fatal Sophistries of Marshall. Other, and inferior, pens, may, no doubt, take up the Subject; but to *yours*, an universal homage would be paid.

We cannot, therefore, avoid indulging a glimmering of hope, that your aid will not be entirely withheld, on this last and greatest occasion. We hope that you may add, yet another Claim, to the lasting gratitude of your Country. If, however, this aid ought not to be expected, under the present circumstances, it would be highly gratifying to *me*, to be favoured with your counsel, and opinions, on the subject. With very great respect, Esteem, and regard, I am, Dear sir, your friend, & obedt. Servant,

Spencer Roane

RC (DLC: Rives Collection, Madison Papers). Addressed by Roane to JM, with the direction: "by mail to orange C:H:," and franked. Docketed by JM.

1. See JM to Roane, 2 Sept. 1819, *PJM-RS*, 1:500–503.

2. The unanimous decision of the Supreme Court in *Cohens v. Virginia*, 3 Mar. 1821, written by Chief Justice John Marshall, established for the Supreme Court "broad jurisdiction to decide cases involving the conflicting powers of the general and state governments"

(Johnson et al., *Papers of John Marshall*, 9:106). The decision was met with outrage by states' rights proponents in Virginia and elsewhere, including Spencer Roane, who wrote a series of essays under the pseudonym "Algernon Sidney," attacking Marshall. For Marshall's opinion and a detailed analysis of the case, see ibid., 9:106–41.

3. For JM's Report of 1800, see *PJM*, 17:307–50.

To Anthony Charles Cazenove

DEAR SIR MONTPELLIER Apl. 18. 182⟨1⟩

If you have any remains of the Lisbon Wine I had from you a year ago,[1] or any of similar quality & price viz 125 Cents per Gallon, be so good as to send me a pipe or Hhd. *well cased* by the first opportunity to Fredericksburg addressed to the care of Messrs. Mackay & Campbell: also a twenty Gallon Keg of best Cognac brandy, and a like keg of best West India Spirits, both cased also. If I do not step out of your line I ask the further favor of you to send a Barrel of good brown Sugar, and another of good White do. with a Bag of Java Coffee, or of nex[t] best quality, the whole addressed as above. With friendly respects

JAMES MADISON

RC (owned by William Reese Company, New Haven, Conn., 1999). Year illegible on document; conjectural year assigned based on comparison with Cazenove to JM, 25 Apr. 1821, where Cazenove thanks JM for his "very obliging favor of 18th instt." Docketed by Cazenove as received 21 Apr.

1. For the shipment of Lisbon wine Cazenove sent JM in September 1819, see Cazenove to JM, 7, 20, and 23 Sept. 1819, *PJM-RS*, 1:507–8, 514, 515.

To Richard Rush

DEAR SIR MONTPELLIER April 21. 1821.

Your favor of Novr. 15. came safe to hand, with Mr. R's farming Pamphlet,[1] for which I return my thanks.

The inflexibility of G.B. on the points in question with the U.S. is a bad omen for the future relations of the parties. The present commercial dispute, tho' productive of ill humour, will shed no blood. The same cannot be said of Impressments and Blockades.

I have lately recd. also Mr. Godwins attack on Malthus, which you were so good as to forward.[2] The work derives some interest from the name of the Author, and from the singular views he takes of the subject.

But it excites a more serious attention by its tendency to disparage abroad, the prospective importance of the U.S. who must owe their rapid growth to the principle combated.

In this country the fallacies of the Author will be smiled at only; unless other emotions should be excited by the frequent disregard of the probable meaning of his opponent, and by the harshness of the comments on the moral scope of his doctrine. Mr. G. charges him also with being dogmatical. Is he less so himself? And is not Mr. G. one of the last men who ought to throw Stones at Theorists? At the moment too of doing it he introduces one of the boldest of speculations, in anticipating from the progress of Chemistry, an artificial conversion of the air, the water, and the Earth into food for man of the natural flavor & colour.

My memory does not retain all the features of Mr. Malthus's System. He may have been unguarded in his expressions, and pushed some of his notions too far. He is certainly vulnerable in assigning for the increase of human food, an arithmetical ratio. In a Country thoroughly cultivated, as China is said to be, there can be *no* increase, and in one as partially cultivated, and as fertile as the U.S. the increase may *exceed* the geometrical ratio. A surplus beyond it, for which the foreign demand has failed, is a primary cause of the present embarrassments of this Country.

The two cardinal points on which the two authors are at issue are 1. the prolific principle in the human race. 2. its actual operation, particularly in the U. States. Mr. G. combats the extent of both.

If the principle could not be proved by direct facts, its capacity is so analogous to what is seen throughout other parts of the animal, as well as vegitable domain, that it would be a fair inference. It is true indeed that in the case of vegitables on which animals feed, and of animals the food of other animals, a more extensive capacity of increase might be requisite than in the human race. But in this case also it is required, over & above the ordinary wastes of life, by two considerations peculiar to man; one that his reason can add to the natural means of subsistence, for an increasing number, which the instinct of other animals can not; the other that he is the only animal that destroys his own species.

Waving however the sanction of analogy, let the principle be tested by facts either stated by Mr. G. or which he can not controvert.

He admits that Sweeden has doubled her numbers in the last hundred years, without the aid of emigrants. Here then there must have been a prolific capacity equal to an increase, in ten Centuries, from *two* Millions to a *thousand* Millions. If Sweeden were as populous ten Centuries ago, as now, or should not in ten Centuries to come arrive at a thousand Millions, must not 998 Millions of births have been prevented, or that number of infants have perished? and from what causes?

The two late enumerations in England which shew a rate of increase there much greater than in Sweeden, are rejected by Mr. G. as erroneous. They probably are so, tho' not in the degree necessary for his purpose. He denies that the population increases at all. He even appeals with confidence to a comparison of what it has been, with what it is at present, as proving a decrease.

There being no positive evidence of former numbers, and none admitted by him of the present, resort must be had to circumstantial lights; and these will decide the question with sufficient certainty.

As a general rule, it is obvious, that the quantity of food produced in a Country determines the actual extent of its population. The number of people cannot exceed the quantity of food; and this will not be produced beyond the consumption. There are exceptions to the rule, as in the U.S. which export food, and in the West Indies, which import it. Both these exceptions however favor the supposition that there has been an increase of the English population; England adding latterly imported food to her domestic Stock, which at some periods was diminished by exportation. The question to be decided is whether the quantity of food produced, the true measure of the population, consuming it, be greater or less now than heretofore.

In the Savage State where wild animals are the chief food, the population must be the thinnest. Where reared ones are the chief food, as among the Tartars, in a pastoral State, the number may be much increased. In proportion as Grain is substituted for animal food, a far greater increase may take place. And as cultivated vegitables, and particularly roots enter into the consumption, the mass of subsistence being augmented, a greater number of consumers, is necessarily implied.

Now it will not be pretended, that there is at present in England more of forest and less of cultivated ground, than in the feudal or even much later periods. On the contrary it seems to be well understood, that the opened lands have been both enlarged & fertilized; that bread has been substituted for flesh; and that vegitables, particularly roots have been more & more substituted for both. It follows that the aggregate food raised & consumed now, being greater than formerly, the number who consume it is greater also.

The Report to the Board of Agriculture quoted by Mr. G. coincides with this inference. The animal food of an individual, which is the smaller part of it, requires, according to this authority, two acres of ground; all the other articles 1¾ of an acre only. The report states that a Horse requires four acres. It is probable that an ox requires more; being fed less on grain & more on grass.

It may be said that Horses which are not eaten, are now used instead of oxen which were. But the Horse, as noted, is supported by fewer acres than the ox; and the oxen superseded by the horses, form but a small part of the eatable Stock to which they belong. The inference, therefore can be at most, but slightly qualified by this innovation.

The single case of Ireland ought to have warned Mr. G. of the error he was maintaining. It seems to be agreed that the population there has greatly increased of late years; altho' it receives very few if any emigrants; and has sent out numbers, very great numbers as Mr. G. must suppose, to the U.S.

In denying the increase of the American population from its own stock, he is driven to the most incredible suppositions, to a rejection of the best established facts, and to the most preposterous estimates & calculations.

He ascribes the rapid increase attested by our periodical lists, wholly to emigrations from Europe; which obliges him to suppose, that from the year 1790 to 1810, 150,000 persons were annually transported; an extravagance which is made worse by his mode of reducing the number necessary, to one half; and he catches at little notices, of remarkable numbers landed at particular ports in particular seasons; as if these could be regarded as proofs of the average arrivals for a long series of years, many of them very unfavorable for such transmigrations. In the year 1817, in which the emigrants were most numerous according to Docr. Seybert,[3] they did not, in the ten principal ports, where with few if any exceptions they are introduced, exceed 22,240. little more than 1/7 of the average number assumed.

Were it even admitted that our population is the result altogether of emigrations from Europe, what would Mr. G. gain by it.

The Census for 1820, is not yet compleated. There is no reason however, to doubt, that it will swell our numbers to about ten Millions. In 1790. the population was not quite four millions. Here then has been an increase of six millions. Of these Six, not less than five millions will have been drawn from the population of G.B. & Ireland. Have the numbers there been reduced accordingly? Then they must have been, thirty years ago, greater by five millions than at this time. Has the loss been replaced? Then, as it has not been by emigrants, it must have been by an effect of the great principle in question. Mr. G. may take his choice of the alternatives.

It is worth remarking that New England, which has sent out such continued swarms to other parts of the Union for a number of years, has continued at the same time, as the Census shews, to increase in population; altho' it is well known that it has received comparatively very few emigrants from any quarter; these preferring places less inhabited for the same reason, that determines the course of migrations from N. England.

The appeal to the case of the black population in the U.S. was particularly unfortunate for the reasoning of Mr. G; to which it gives the most striking falsification.

Between the years 1790 & 1810, the number of slaves increased from 694,280. to 1,165,441. This increase, at a rate nearly equal to that of the

Whites, surely was not by *emigrants* from Africa. Nor could any part of it have been imported (*except thirty or forty thousand into S. Carolina & Geo); the prohibition being every where else strictly enforced throughout that period. Louisiana indeed brought an addition amounting in 1810 to 37,671; This number however (to be reduced by the slaves carried thither from other States prior to the census of 1810) may be regarded as overbalanced by emancipated blacks and their subsequent offspring. The whole number of this description in the Census of 1810 amounts [to] 186,446.

The evidence of a natural & rapid increase of the Blacks, in the State of Virginia alone is conclusive on the subject. Since the Epoch of Independence the importation of slaves has been uniformly prohibited, and the spirit of the people concurring with the policy of the law, it has been carried into full execution. Yet the number of slaves increased from 292,627. in 1790 to 392,518 in 1810, altho' it is notorious that very many have been carried from the State by external purchasers, and migrating Masters. In the State of Maryland to the North of Virginia whence alone, it could be surmised that any part of them could be replaced, there has also been an increase.

Mr. G. exults not a little (p 420–2) in the detection of error in a paper read by Mr. W. Barton in 1791 to the Philosophical Society at Philada.[5] I have not looked for the paper; but from Mr. G's account of it, a strange error was committed by Mr. B: not however in the false arithmetic blazoned by Mr. G. but by adding the number of deaths to that of births in deducing the productiveness of marriages in a certain parish in Massts. But what is not less strange than the lapsus of Mr. B. is that his critic should overlook the fact on the face of the paper as inserted in his own page, "that the population had doubled in 54 years," in spite of the probable removals from an old parish to newer settlements. And what is strangest of all, that he should not have attended to the precise Statement in the record, that the number of births within the period exceeded the number of deaths by the difference between 2247 and 1113. Here is the most demonstrable of all proofs of an increasing population; unless a Theoretic zeal should suppose that the pregnant women of the neighbourhood made lying in visits to Hingham, or that its sick inhabitants chose to have their dying eyes closed elsewhere.

Mr. G. has not respected other evidence in his hands which ought to have opened his eyes to the reality of an increasing population in the U.S. In the population list of Sweeden, in the authenticity of which he fully acquiesces, as well as in the Census of the U.S., the authenticity of which he does not controvert, there is a particular column for those under 10

*The precise no. from official returns from the Custom Houses where a poll tax was paid was laid before the Senate of the U.S. at the last Session; but I cannot lay my hand on it. It made part of a Speech by Mr. Smith a Senator from S. Carolina.[4]

years of age. In that of Sweeden the number is to the whole population as 2,484 to 10,000 which is less than ¼. In that of the U.S. the number is as 2,016,704 to 5,862,096. which is more than ⅓. Now Mr. G. (p. 442) refers to the proportion of the ungrown to the whole population, as testing the question of its increase. He admits and specifies the rate at which the population of Sweeden increases. And yet with this evidence of a greater increase of the population of the U.S., he contends that it does not increase at all. An attempt to extricate himself by a disproportion of children or of more productive parents emigrating from Europe, would only plunge him the deeper into contradictions & absurdities.

Mr. G. dwells on the Indian Establishment at Paraguay by the Jesuits, which is said not to have increased its numbers, as a tr[i]umphant disproof of the prolific principle. He places more faith in the picture of the Establishment given by Reynal[6] than is due to the vivid imagination of that author, or than the author appears to have had in it himself. For he rejects the inference of Mr. G. and reconciles the failure to increase with the power to increase, by assigning two causes for it—the small pox—and the exclusion of individual property, and he might have found other causes in the natural love of indolence till overcome by avarice and vanity, motives repressed by their religious discipline; in the pride of the men retaining a disdain of agricultural labour; and in the female habit of prolonging for several years, the period of keeping children to the breast. In no point of view can a case marked by so many peculiar circumstances, & these so imperfectly known, be allowed the weight of a precedent.

Mr. G. could not have given a stronger proof of the estrangement of his ideas from the Indian character & modes of life than by his referring to the Missouri Tribes; which do not multiply "altho' they cultivate Corn." His fancy may have painted to him fields of Wheat cultivated by the plough, and gathered into Barns as a provision for the year. How would he be startled at the sight of little patches of maize & squashes, stirred by a piece of wood, & that by Squaws only; the hunters & warriors spurning such an occupation, and relying on the fruits of the chase for the support of their Wigwams. *Corn-eaters*, is a name of reproach given by some tribes, to others beginning, under the influence of the Whites, to enlarge their cultivated Spots.

In going over Mr. G's volume, these are some of the remarks which occurred, and in thanking you for it, I have made them some supply the want of more interesting materials for a letter. If the heretical work should attract conversations in which you may be involved, some of the facts, which you are saved the trouble of hunting up, may rebut mistatements from uninformed friends, or illiberal opponents of our Country.

You have not mentioned the cost of Godwin's book, or the pamphlet of Rigby. I suspect they overgo the remmant [*sic*] of the little fund in your hand. If so let me provide for it. You will oblige me also by forwarding with its price, the Book entitled "The Apocryphal New Testament translated from the original Tongues" printed for Wm. Hone, Ludgate Hill.[7] Always with affectionate esteem Yours

James Madison

RC (ICN: Ayer Collection); draft (DLC). Minor differences between the copies have not been noted.

1. Edward Rigby, *Framingham, Its Agriculture, &c. Including the Economy of a Small Farm* (Norwich, 1820). JM's copy, including his signature on the title page, is in the Madison Collection, Special Collections, University of Virginia Library.

2. See Rush to JM, 15 Mar. 1821, and n. 2.

3. Adam Seybert (1773–1825), a Philadelphia physician and a pioneering chemist and mineralogist, served in the U.S. House of Representatives, 1809–15, and 1817–19. Among his many publications was *Statistical Annals . . . of the United States . . . [1789–1818]* (Philadelphia, 1818; Shaw and Shoemaker 45692).

4. The speech on the Missouri question by Sen. William Smith of South Carolina, 8 Dec. 1820, contained a recapitulation of the African trade between 1804 and 1807, during which time 39,075 slaves were imported into Charleston (*Annals of Congress*, 16th Cong., 2d sess., 50, 51–77).

5. William Barton, *Observations on the Progress of Population . . .* ([Philadelphia], 1791; Evans 23158).

6. Guillaume Thomas François Raynal, *L'Histoire philosophique et politique, des établissemens & du commerce des Européens dans les deux Indes* (6 vols.; Amsterdam, 1770).

7. *The Apocryphal New Testament, Being All the Gospels, Epistles, and Other Pieces Now Extant, Attributed in the First Four Centuries to Jesus Christ . . .* (London, 1820).

To Solomon Southwick

Sir Montpellier April 21. 1821

I have recd. your letter of the 12th. with a copy of your address at the opening of the Apprentices' Library.

This class of our youth is a valuable one; and its proportional numbers must increase as our population thickens. It is a class too which particularly claims the guardianship of benevolence. Their age, their separation from their parents, and their residence for the most part in towns or villages, where groups are readily formed in which the example of a few may attaint many, create snares into which their relaxations from labour too often betray them. Among the provisions against the danger the establishment of special Libraries was a happy thought to the author of which your eulogy was a just tribute.[1] A proper assortment of books always at hand will enable the apprentices to put their morals and their understandings both to a good school, for their own happiness; at the same time that they are acquiring the professional arts so useful to the community of which they are members. Your Address is an eloquent & persuasive recommendation of the opportunity. I hope it may have all the success which your laudable zeal merits. Mrs. Madison joins in a return of the good wishes you have expressed for us both. With friendly respects

JAMES MADISON

RC (owned by Herman Blum, Philadelphia, Pa., 1959); draft (DLC). Minor differences between the copies have not been noted.

1. Benjamin Franklin.

From George Hay

SIR, WASHINGTON. April 23. 1821.

You were good enough when I had the pleasure of being at your house, during the last Summer, to offer me the use of Valen's commentary on the "Ordonnances de la Marine."[1] The possession of that work at this time, would be a great accommodation to me. Will you pardon me for asking, that it may be forwarded by the mail to this City?

I have devoted some time lately to an investigation of the decision and reasoning of the S. Court in the Case of Anderson vs. Dunn;[2] involving the question concerning the power of the H.R. to punish for a Contempt. If you have not attended to this decision, published in the Nat: Intr. you will be amused by looking into it. The decision is erroneous, and the doctrines ultra-federal. Yet they seem to have made no impression here, or indeed any where else.

I beg leave to offer to Mrs. Madison my most respectful Salutations: and am with the highest respect for yourself Yr. mo: ob. Sr.

GEO: HAY

RC (DLC). Docketed by JM, with his note: "The Books sent."

1. See George Hay to JM, 18 Sept. 1820, and n. 8.

2. The case *Anderson v. Dunn*, turned on the issue of whether Congress had the right to punish a private citizen for contempt. John Anderson was accused of attempting to bribe a U.S. congressman, whereupon the Speaker of the House, Henry Clay, ordered Thomas Dunn, the sergeant at arms, to bring Anderson before the House to answer the charge. Anderson was reprimanded and discharged from arrest but sued for assault and battery and false imprisonment. In his decision, Justice William Johnson upheld Congress's action, writing that, although "there is no power given by the constitution to either House to punish for contempts, except when committed by their own members," there are implied powers, and further, "there is not in the whole of that admirable instrument [U.S. Constitution], a grant of powers which does not draw after it others, not expressed, but vital to their exercise, not substantive and independent, indeed, but auxiliary and subordi-

nate" (6 Wheaton 204–35). Justice Johnson's opinion was printed in the *Daily National Intelligencer*, 23 Mar. 1821.

From Anthony Charles Cazenove

DEAR SIR ALEXANDRIA April 25th. 1821.

I improve the first moment that I can write after a trifling accident to one of my eyes, to answer your very obliging favor of 18th. instt.

I have no more Lisbon Wine on hand, nor do I know of any as good in town at present, but if you wish it will make the best purchase I can, or order some from Baltimore or Philada. When inquiring for some have found some very superior Sicily Madeira @ $1.40/100. What Java Coffee there is in town is of so inferior quality & so full of fatty grains, that I will substitute some other quality. Please let me know as early as convenient what you have concluded about the wine, that it might be sent with the other articles offerd per first opportunity for Fredericksburg; & whenever you may feel disposed to resume your former orders for Murdoch's Madeira, to be imported for you, or supplied from the Stock on hand, shall be pleased to be favor'd with your commands. I beg leave to assure you I shall be happy to attend to any others you may have in this place & neighborhood & remain with highest regard very respectfully Your Obedt. Servt.

ANT. CHS. CAZENOVE

P.S. Should you feel disposed to order here in the Spring your Linens & in the fall your Woollens for the people on your estate, it is likely you would make a saving worth the trouble, on what you can get them at in your neighborhood.

RC (DLC). Cover sheet docketed by JM.

To Anthony Charles Cazenove

DEAR SIR Apl. 30. 1821

I have recd. your favor of the 25th.

As the injury to your eye was slight, I hope it has been of short continuance. My want of Lisbon wine not being urgent, I prefer waiting till you can supply such as I formerly recd.; if the prospect of it be not remote or uncertain. In either of these cases be so good as to give the order you suggest on Baltimore or Philada. enjoining particularly the precaution of having it well cased. I prefer the Lisbon to the Sicily Madeira. Of the true

Madeira, my Stock on hand renders an addition unnecessary. I thank you for your advice & offer as to Woolens & Linnens for my people; But am endeavoring to have both manufactured in the household way; from my own materials. Whilst the present prohibitions on prices of our produce in foreign Markets continue, our labour must be transferred from agriculture to the objects which agriculture can no longer purchase.

Draft (DLC).

To Peter S. Du Ponceau

DEAR SIR MONTPELLIER May 1821

I cannot return my thanks for your "Address" on the subject of a Central Seminary of Jurisprudence,[1] without offering my best wishes for the success of such an Institution.

The Citizens of the U. States, not only form one people governed by the same code of laws, in all cases falling within the range of the Federal Authority; but[2] are connected by a daily intercourse and by multiplying transactions, which give to all an interest in the character, and in a reciprical knowledge of the State laws also.

It is not only desireable therefore that the national Code should receive whatever improvements, the cultivation of a law as a Science may impart, but that the local codes should be improved in like manner, and a general knowledge of each facilitated by an infusion of every practicable identity through the whole.

All these objects must be promoted by an Institution concentrating the talents of the most enlightened of the legal profession, and attracting from every quarter, the pupils most devoted to the studies leading to it.

Such an assemblage in such a position would have particular advantages for taking a comprehensive view of the local codes, for examining their coincidences and their differences, and for pointing out whatever in each might deserve to be adopted into the others: and it cannot be doubted that something would be found in each worthy of a place in all.

This would be a species of consolidation having the happy tendency to diminish local prejudices, to cherish mutual confidence, and to accommodate the intercourses of business between citizens of different States, without impairing the constitutional separation & Independence of the States themselves, which are deemed essential to the security of individual liberty as well as to the preservation of Republican Government.

Uniformity in the laws of the States might have another effect not without its value. These laws furnish in many cases, the very principles &

rules on which the decisions of the National Tribunal are to be hinged. A knowledge of them in such cases is indispensable. The difficulty of acquiring it, whilst the several codes vary so much, is obvious; and is a motive for imposing on the Judges of the Supreme Court of the Nation those itinerary duties which may neither suit their years; nor can long be practicable within the expanding field of them; and which moreover preclude those enriching "lucubrationes" by which they might do fuller justice to themselves, fulfill the better expectations at home, and contribute the more to the national character abroad.

I received some time ago your recommendation of Mr. Vanuxem for the Chemical Chair in the University of Virginia.[3] President Cooper has borne his testimony also in favor of Mr. V.[4] Nothing can be said of the prospect of his success, the other Candidates not being yet known; and the time even of opening the University being uncertain. Be assured always of my great esteem & cordial respects.

RC (PHi); draft (DLC); letterbook copy (PHi: Peter S. Du Ponceau Letterbook, 1777–1839). Minor differences between the copies have not been noted.

1. Peter S. Du Ponceau, *An Address Delivered at the Opening of the Law Academy of Philadelphia, before the Trustees and Members of the Society for the Promotion of Legal Knowledge, in the Hall of the Supreme Court, on Wednesday, the 21st of February 1821* (Philadelphia, 1821). JM's copy is in the Madison Collection, Rare Book and Special Collections Division, Library of Congress.
2. The draft has "as Citizens of the different States" here.
3. Du Ponceau to JM, 23 Mar. 1821.
4. Thomas Cooper to JM, 12 Mar. 1821.

To David Hoffman

MONTPELLEIR May. 1821.

J Madison presents his respects to Mr Hoffman,[1] with thanks for the copy of his "Syllabus."[2]

It has not been convenient for him to bestow on it the critical attention necessary, if he were better qualified, to remark defects, if there be any, or to do justice to its merits. To the view he has taken of the plan, it appears to embrace the subject in its due extent and to designate and arrange the particular topics in a manner well adapted to a highly instructive course of Law Lectures.

FC (DLC). In Dolley Madison's hand; verso marked by JM "Hoffman May 1821."

1. David Hoffman (1784–1854) was a lawyer and professor of law at the University of Maryland, 1816–36 (Eugene Fauntleroy Cordell, *University of Maryland, 1807–1907 . . . With Biographical Sketches . . . of Its Founders, Benefactors, Regents, Faculty, and Alumni* [2 vols.; New York, 1907], 1:344–48).

2. David Hoffman, *Syllabus of a Course of Lectures on Law: Proposed to Be Delivered in the University of Maryland; Addressed to the Students of Law in the United States* (Baltimore, 1821; Shoemaker 5608).

From George M. Dallas

My Dear Sir, 1 May 1821.

I cannot hope, by any expressions in a letter, to convey to you my deep sense of your Kindness in having indulged me with the loan of the inclosed correspondence.[1] Although my professional business, by which only I am able to keep a small family from want, has prevented, and must still, for some time, prevent, the publication of my father's biography and writings, delay appears to increase, rather than diminish, the interest of the subject: and upon a rapid revisal, I perceive but very few passages in the inclosed letters, which need, or can, with propriety, be omitted.

For my own part, I am desirous of communicating to the world, the portrait of my father such precisely as he was: nothing extenuating: fully convinced that the virtuous and meritorious features of his character, are the bold and obvious ones; and that if he had passions and foibles, they rather ministered to the efficacy of his nobler qualities, than interfered with them. Even his personal hostilities—if they can bear so harsh a name—sprung from the same source with his friendships, a zealous love of virtue and honor. The picture must have its shades: yet I am certain that every moral connoisseur will pronounce them to be beautiful and becoming.

My father is but little known, except as a public man. Even his hospitality was so unbounded that he may be said to have lived, for many years, constantly in a crowd: And strangers, those not immediately connected with his domestic circle, enjoyed but few opportunities of perceiving his great worth as a private instructor, example, monitor, parent. No one could easily detect how sincerely he was adored by his children, and how entirely and devotedly he possessed the confidence of his friends. I wish him known in this light. It is a scene altogether of his own creating: and it is one beyond the influence of any changes in public opinion.

With these views, will you pardon me if I suggest that there may probably be in your possession some letters entirely unconnected with his official relation to you, that may assist in pourtraying his disposition of heart, and his patriotic feelings? I have been told, that shortly after the burning of the Capital by the British, he wrote to you, volunteering his services, in any way in which they might be useful. Such a letter, resembling one which, in a similar case, he addressed to the Governor of Pennsylvania, is an invaluable illustration of character: and would be *proof* to those, naturally inclined to suspect the impartiality of my delineations.

I renew, Sir, my grateful acknowledgments for the indulgence you have shewn: and respectfully desire to be remembered to Mrs. Madison. Very sincerely, Your friend and faithful Serv.

G. M. Dallas

RC (DLC: Rives Collection, Madison Papers). Docketed by JM.

1. For the loan of JM's correspondence with Alexander James Dallas, see George M. Dallas to JM, 19 May 1817, and JM to Dallas, 28 May 1817, *PJM-RS*, 1:48–49, 53.

From Gilbert J. Hunt

Respected Sir, New York May 1, 1821

I have the honor of inclosing you the prospectus of another work,[1] similar to the last I sent you.[2] By returning the Prospectus with your Signature you will confer a particular obligation on a friend and native inhabitant of this Republic. The book, handsomely bound, will be forwarded on to you, as soon as finished. The other work was particularly patronized by Mr. Jefferson. Yours most respectfully

G. J. Hunt[3]
care of G & R Waite[4]

RC (DLC). Addressed by Hunt to JM at Washington, and franked. Postmarked 14 May at New York. Docketed on cover by JM.

1. The enclosed prospectus was *Proposals for Publishing by Subscription, the History of America, from Its Discovery by Christopher Columbus to the Year 1812: To Be Comprised in One Volume. Written in the Ancient Historical Style, by G. J. Hunt*... ([New York?; 1821]; Shoemaker 5660). JM's copy is in the Madison Collection, Rare Book and Special Collections Division, Library of Congress.

2. Not found.

3. Gilbert J. Hunt was the author of *The Late War, between the United States and Great Britain, from June 1812, to February 1815, Written in the Ancient Historical Style* (1816), and he chose to tell the story in chapter and verse, as if he were writing a book of the Bible.

4. G. & R. Waite was a printing and bookselling establishment at 64 Maiden Lane in New York City (Rita Susswein Gottesman, comp., *The Arts and Crafts in New York*... *1800–1804*, Collections of the New-York Historical Society (1949), The John Watts DePeyster Publication Fund Series, 82:314–16 [New York, 1965]).

From William S. Cardell

Orange C. House 2nd. May [1821]

Mr. Cardell of New York has the honor to present his respects to Mr. Madison and will call on him this morning. The circumstances and prospects of the American Academy of Language & Belles Lettres are becoming interesting and on that subject a personal interview with Mr. M. is particularly desired.

RC (DLC). Year not indicated; assigned based on JM's docket "Cardell May 2. 1821."

To James Monroe

Dear Sir — Montpellier May 4. 1821

I observe that Genl. A. Moore[1] has resigned the office of Marshall for Virga. I know not who may be candidates for the vacancy. I beg leave to name for your consideration Mr. Robert Taylor of this County, formerly a Speaker of our Senate, & of a character well established for intelligence, proberty [*sic*], and habits of punctuality in business. I am particularly induced to bring him into view by the circumstance, of my having postponed him to Genl. Moore, when they were competitors for the office, which he may possibly suppose was occasioned less by the inferiority of his pretensions, than by a delicacy, a false one as it might appear to him, suggested by his kindred to me.[2] I have had no communication with him; nor does he know that I am writing to you on the subject. With the highest esteem & consideration, yours always,

James Madison

RC (DLC: Monroe Papers).

1. Andrew Moore (1752–1821), a Revolutionary War veteran and Republican from Rockbridge County, Virginia, served in the U.S. House of Representatives, 1789–97 and 1803–4, and in the U.S. Senate, 1804–9. JM appointed him marshal for Virginia in 1810, and he held that post until shortly before his death (*PJM-SS*, 8:540 n. 1; Monroe to JM, 19 May 1821).

2. Robert Taylor was JM's second cousin (*PJM-PS*, 2:50 n.2).

From Joseph Milligan

Georgetown May 4th 1821

By this days mail I have sent two parcels which contain five copies of Historical Letters for Mrs Madison.[1] There is in one [of] the parcels a book for your neighbour the Hnbl. P. P. Barbour. He requested me to send it together with the copies that I was to send to Mrs M. With respect I am yours

Joseph Milligan

RC (DLC). Docketed by JM.

1. John B. Colvin, *Historical Letters, Including a Brief but General View of the History of the World, Civil, Military, and Religious, from the Earliest Times to the Year of Our Lord 1820*, 2d ed. (Georgetown, D.C., 1821; Shoemaker 5039). The book was dedicated to Dolley Madison "as a proof of the estimation in which I hold your intellectual endowments" (second iii).

To Spencer Roane

Dear Sir — Montpellr. May 6. 1821.

I recd. more than two weeks ago your letter of April 17th. A visit to a sick friend at some distance, with a series of unavoidable attentions, have prevented an earlier acknowlegement of it.

Under any circumstances I should be disposed rather to put such a subject as that to which it relates, into your hands, than to take it out of them. Apart from this consideration, a variety of demands on my time would restrain me from the task of unravelling fully the arguments applied by the Supreme Court of the U.S. to their late decision. I am particularly aware moreover that they are made to rest not a little on technical points of law which are as foreign to my studies, as they are familiar to yours.

It is to be regretted that the Court is so much in the practice of mingling with the Judgments pronounced, comments & reasonings of a scope beyond them; and that in these there is often an apparent disposition to amplify the authorities of the Union, at the expence of those of the States. It is of great importance, as well as of indispensable obligation, that the constitutional boundary between them should be impartially maintained. Every deviation in practice detracts from the superiority of a chartered over a traditional Government, and marrs the experiment which is to determine the interesting problem, whether the organization of the political System of the U.S. establishes a just equilibrium, or tends to a preponderance of the national or of the local powers; and in the latter case, whether of the National or of the local.

A candid review of the vicissitudes which have marked the progress of the General Government, does not preclude doubts as to the ultimate and fixed character of a political Establishment distinguished by so novel & complex a mechanism. On some occasions, the advantage taken of favorable circumstances, gave an impetus & direction to it which seemed to threaten subversive encroachments on the rights & authorities of the States. At a certain period we witnessed a spirit of usurpation by some of these, on the necessary & legitimate functions of the former. At the present date, theoretic innovations at least, are putting new weights into the scale of federal authority[1] and make it highly proper to bring them to the bar of the Constitution.

In looking to the probable course and eventual bearing of the compound Government of our Country, I can not but think that much will depend not only on the moral changes incident to the progress of society, but on the increasing number of the members of the Union. Were the members very few, and each very powerful, a feeling of self-sufficiency would have a relaxing effect on the bands holding them together. Were they numerous & weak, the Govt. over the whole would find less difficulty in maintaining and increasing subordination. It happens that whilst the power of some is swelling to so great a size, the entire number is swelling also. In this respect, a corresponding increase of centripetal and centrifugal forces, may be equivalent to no increase of either.

In the existing posture of things my reflections lead me to infer that whatever may be the latitude of jurisdiction assumed by the Judicial power of the U.S. it is less formidable to the reserved sovereignty of the States, than the latitude of power which it has assigned to the Legislature; and that encroachments of the latter are more to be apprehended from impulses given to it by a majority of the States seduced by expected advantages, than from a love of power in the Body itself controuled as it now is by its responsibility to the Constituent Body.

Such is the plastic faculty of Legislation, that notwithstanding the firm tenure which the Judges have on their offices, they can by various regulations, be kept or reduced within the paths of duty; more especially with the aid of their amenability to the Legislative Tribunal in the form of impeachment. It is not probable that the Supreme Court would be long indulged in a career of usurpation opposed to the decided opinions & policy of the Legislature.

Nor do I think that Congress, even seconded by the Judicial power, can without some great change in the character of the nation, succeed in durable violations of the rights & authorities of the States. The responsibility of one branch to the people, and of the other to the Legislatures of the States, seem to be, in the present stage at least of our political history, an adequate barrier. In the case of the Alien & Sedition laws, which violated the sense as well as the rights of the States, the usurping experiment was crushed at once, notwithstanding the co-operation of the federal Judges with the federal laws.

But what is to controul Congress when backed and even pushed on by a majority of their Constituents; as was the case in the late contest relating to Missouri; and as may again happen, on the constructive power relating to Roads & Canals? Nothing, within the pale of the Constitution, but sound arguments, & conciliatory expostulations, addressed both to Congress & their Constituents.

On the questions brought before the public by the late doctrines of the Supreme Court of the U.S. concerning the extent of their own powers & that of the exclusive jurisdiction of Congress over the ten miles square & other specified places, there is as yet no evidence that they express either the opinions of Congress, or those of their Constituents. There is nothing therefore to discourage a development of the flaws the doctrines may contain, or tendencies they may threaten. Congress if convinced of these, may not only abstain from the exercise of powers claimed for them by the Court; but may find the means of controuling those claimed by the Court for itself. And should Congress not be convinced, their Constituents, if so, can certainly under the forms of the Constitution, effectuate a compliance with their deliberate judgment & settled determination.

In expounding the Constitution, the Court seems not insensible that the intention of the parties to it ought to be kept in view; and that as far as the language of the Instrument will permit, this intention ought to be traced in the contemporaneous expositions. But is the Court as prompt and as careful in citing & following this evidence when against the federal authority, as when agst. that of the States?[2]

The exclusive jurisdiction over the ten miles square is, itself an anomaly in our representative System. And its object being manifest and attested by the views taken of it, at its date, there seems a peculiar impropriety in making it the fulcrum for a Lever stretching into the most distant parts of the Union, and overruling the municipal policy of the States. The remark is still more striking when applied to the smaller places over which an exclusive jurisdiction was suggested by a regard to the defence & property of the nation.

Some difficulty, it must be admitted, may result in particular cases, from the impossibility of executing some of these powers within the defined spaces, according to the principles & rules enjoined by the Constitution, and from the want of a Constitutional provision for the surrender of malefactors, whose escape must be so easy, on the demand of the U.S. as well as of the individual States. It is true also that these exclusive jurisdictions, are in the class of enumerated powers, to which is subjoined a power in Congress to pass all laws necessary & proper for their execution. All that could be exacted however by these considerations would be, that the means of execution should be of the most obvious & essential kind, and exerted in the ways as little intrusive as possible on the powers & police of the States. And after all the question would remain whether, the better course would not be to regard the case as an omitted one, to be provided for by an amendment of the Constitution. In resorting to legal precedents, as sanctions to power, the distinction should ever be strictly attended to, between such as take place under transitory impressions, or without full examination & deliberation, and such as pass with solemnities & repetitions, sufficient to imply a concurrence of the judgment & the will of those who having granted the power have the ultimate right to explain the grant. Altho' I can not join in the protest of some agst. the validity of all precedents, however uniform & multiplied, in expounding a Constitution, yet I am persuaded that Legislative precedents are frequently of a character entitled to little respect; and that those of Congress, are sometimes liable to peculiar distrust. They not only follow the example of other Legislative Assemblies in first procrastinating, and then precipitating their acts; but owing to the termination of their session every other year at a fixed day & hour, a mass of business is struck off as it were at short hand & in a moment. Those midnight precedents of every sort ought to have little weight in any case.

On the question relating to involuntary submissions of the States to the Tribunal of the supreme Court, the Court seems not to have adverted at all to the expository language held when the Constitution was adopted; nor to that of the 11th. amendment which may as well import that it was declaratory, as that it was restrictive of the meaning of the original text. It seems to be a strange reasoning also which would imply that a State in controversies with its own Citizens, might have[3] less of sovereignty, than in controversies with foreign individuals, by which the national relations might be affected. Nor is it less to be wondered that it should have appeared to the Court that the dignity of a State was not more compromitted, by its being made a party against a private person, than against a co-ordinate party.

The Judicial power of the U.S. over cases arising under the Constitution, must be admitted to be a vital part of the System. But that there are limitations and exceptions[4] to its efficient character is among the admissions of the Court itself. The Eleventh amendment introduces exceptions if there were none before. A liberal and steady course of practice can alone reconcile the several provisions of the Constitution literally at variance with each other; of which there is an example in the Treaty power, and the Legislative power, on subjects to which both are extended by the words of the Constitution. It is particularly incumbent, in taking cognizance of cases arising under the Constitution, and in which the laws or rights of the States may be involved, to let the proceedings touch individuals only.

Prudence enjoins this, if there were no other motive, in consideration of the impracticability of applying coercion to States.

I am sensible Sir that these ideas are too vague to be of value, and that they may not even hint for consideration any thing not occurring to yourself. Be so good as to see in them at least an unwillingness to disregard altogether your request. Should any of the ideas be erroneous as well as vague, I have the satisfaction to know that they will be viewed by a friendly as well as candid eye. With very great esteem & cordial respects Yours

James Madison

RC (ViU: Madison Papers, Special Collections); FC (DLC). Cover addressed by JM to Roane at Richmond "via Frederi⟨c⟩k⟨s⟩b⟨ur⟩g," and franked. Redirected in an unidentified hand: "*Forwarded* Hanover Town." Marked "Orange CH may 12." Docketed by Roane. Minor differences between the copies have not been noted, nor have the numerous pencil underlinings of words and phrases in the RC, probably made by Roane.

1. "Sovereignty" in the FC.

2. In the FC, JM wrote after this sentence: "(see the partial reference of the Court to 'The Federalist')." In his opinion in the case of *Cohens v. Virginia*, Chief Justice John Marshall quoted from Federalist No. 82, in which Alexander Hamilton had discussed the extent of federal judicial power. In "instances of concurrent jurisdiction" between federal and state courts, Hamilton wrote and Marshall quoted approvingly, "an appeal would certainly lie from the latter, to the supreme court of the United States" (Johnson et al., *Papers of John Marshall*, 9:135, 142 n. 17).

3. In the RC, JM interlined "exempt from national" above a number of crossouts here; the phrase is not in the FC.

4. Someone, probably Roane, inserted in pencil an "(a)" here in the RC and in the left margin of the page wrote: "(a) In Mad's report, *an* exception is, where the Controvy. is (as here) between the *parties* to the Compact." Roane referred to JM's assertion in his Report of 1800 that "the federal powers are derived from the Constitution, and that the Constitution is a compact to which the states are parties," and his explanation of the latter clause (*PJM*, 17:308–9).

To Anthony Charles Cazenove

Dr. Sir May 13. [1821]

I have been favd. with yours of the 7.[1] and am giving orders for getting up the articles you have forwarded as soon as they arrive at Fredg. I am taking measures also for having the amt. due remitted. Should they not have immediate effect, others will be adopted.

Draft (DLC: Dolley Madison Papers). Year not indicated; conjectural year based on the fact that the letter is written at the foot of the second draft of JM to Mackay & Campbell, 14 May 1821.

1. Letter not found.

From Francis Corbin

My dear Sir The Reeds. May 13th. 1821. Wh: Ch: Po: Off:

A few days ago I had the pleasure to meet with your Nephew Major Madison, of whom I made, as I always do, of ev'ry body who comes from your part of the Country, the most anxious Inquiries about your health and Mrs. Madison's. He informed me that you were both well, but, to my great sorrow, confirmed some intelligence which my Relation Tayloe had given me, concerning your late loss of many valuable Servants by some contagious disorder. Such a loss—at all times distressing—is peculiarly so in *these* times, by far the most calamitous that I ever saw.

Yesterday my friend A. Stevenson told me that you were engaged in writing a political History of our Country, or some work of this description. I was glad to hear it. Such a work is a desideratum, and from your pen will be a valuable acquisition. If, between the years 1784 & 1796, during which periods I was a member of the Legislature, any thing should have escaped your memory which mine can supply—it will give me pleasure to fill up the "Hiatus."

On Sunday last I dined with Col: Taylor who is also writing another Book. The highly wrought panegyrick which Mr. Jefferson bestowed upon his "Construction Construed," (a work certainly very ingenious, and containing many sound remarks,) has encouraged him, I presume, again to exercise his Pen. I did not inquire what the subject was of his present lucubrations, but—I conjecture it to be the prevailing topic of *State Rights.* A topic which will always continue to agitate the few *large* States, which, in speaking *one* Word for the little States, speak *twenty* for themselves. But as the Votes of States "are counted not weighed,"[1] this favorite political Stalking Horse will answer no other purpose than to afford ground for a *constant* opposition to the *Government.* I use this Word in the sense in which my Lord Bolingbroke uses it—as contradistinguished from the *Constitution.*[2] *That* ground for a constant opposition to the existing Administration is, perhaps, as harmless as any other, for after all it is but playing at Battledore & Shuttle Cock, as the *Majority* will always make the Constitution, like the Cap of Fortunatus,[3] what they wish to make it. Language is so equivocal, as Lord Bacon said to James the first "that he could work Treason out of any half dozen Sentences that any man could write." "Construction construed" may, therefore, be itself construed.

The immediate object, however, of this letter, next to my condolence for the losses you have lately sustained, is to request that you will now water a tree which you planted some years ago. Mr. Edward Randolf,[4] that amiable and gallant youth to whom you were kind enough to give, at my instance, a Commission in the Army, and who acquitted himself so well at

Lundy's Lane and Chippewas as to have been distinguished by General Scott in his official communications, has solicited the Collectorship at Pensecola, where, under an expectation that Florida would be ceded to us sooner or later, he has established himself. The President, Col: Tayloe tells me, is well disposed towards him. This good disposition will be greatly promoted by a *single* word from you. May I then take the liberty of soliciting your patronage for him? If, in my humble endeavors to promote the prosperity of this promising and praise worthy young man, I feel great satisfaction, how much more will your benevolent Heart feel in *Effecting* it! To such a Heart—I am sure I need not say more.

Be pleased to present my most respectful Compliments and Esteem to Mrs. Madison and believe me to be, My Dear Sir, Your most faithful and much Obliged Friend & Sert.

FRANCIS CORBIN

RC (DLC). Docketed by JM.

1. "Votes go by number, not weight" (Pliny, *Letters* 2.12, trans. William Melmoth, Loeb Classical Library [2 vols.; London, 1915], 1:137).

2. "It may be asked, perhaps, how men who are friends to a government, can be enemies at the same time to the constitution upon which that government is founded. But the answer will be easy, if we consider these two things: first, the true distinction, so often confounded in writing, and almost always in conversation, between constitution and government. By constitution we mean, whenever we speak with propriety and exactness, that assemblage of laws, institutions and customs, derived from certain fixed principles of reason, directed to certain fixed objects of public good, that compose the general system, according to which the community hath agreed to be governed. By government we mean, whenever we speak in the same manner, that particular tenor of conduct which a chief magistrate, and inferior magistrates under his direction and influence, hold in the administration of public affairs" (David Armitage, ed., *Bolingbroke: Political Writings* [Cambridge, England, 1997], 88).

3. The German folk hero, Fortunatus, had a cap that could transport its wearer anywhere he desired (Cyrus Hoy, *Introductions, Notes, and Commentaries to Texts in "The Dramatic Works of Thomas Dekker,"* ed. Fredson Bowers [4 vols.; Cambridge, England, 1980], 1:74, 77).

4. Edward Brett Randolph (1792–1848) entered the U.S. Army with an ensign's commission in May 1812 and was brevetted first lieutenant in 1814 for distinguished service in the Niagara campaign. He resigned his commission on 31 Oct. 1817 and later settled at Goshen, a plantation in Lowndes County, Mississippi. After his conversion to Methodism in 1834, he freed his slaves and sent them to Liberia. Randolph moved to Columbus, Mississippi, where he was receiver of public moneys, 1843–48 (Heitman, *Historical Register*, 1:815; Elmo Howell, *Mississippi Scenes: Notes on Literature and History* [Memphis, 1992], 60–63; Randy J. Sparks, *On Jordan's Stormy Banks: Evangelicalism in Mississippi, 1773–1876* [Athens, Ga., 1994], 73–74; Haskell M. Monroe Jr. and James T. McIntosh et al., eds., *The Papers of Jefferson Davis* [12 vols. to date; Baton Rouge, La., 1971—], 2:433 n. 4).

To John Quincy Adams

DEAR SIR — MONTPELLIER May 14. 1821

I have received the Copy of your Report on weights and measures, which you were so good as to inclose to me.[1]

Not knowing how long it may be before I shall be able to give it a due perusal, I tender at once my best thanks, anticipating as I certainly do, both pleasure and instruction from your execution of the important task committed to you. Be pleased, Sir, to accept a repetition of my high esteem and cordial respects.

JAMES MADISON

RC (MHi: Adams Papers).

1. Letter not found. Adams, *Report of the Secretary of State, upon Weights and Measures, Prepared in Obedience to a Resolution of the Senate of the Third March, 1817. Feb. 22, 1821* (Washington, 1821; Shoemaker 7456).

To Mackay & Campbell

GENTN — May 14. 1821

I am to receive from Mr. Cazenove of Alexa several Bbles &ca which I took the liberty of requesting him to address to your care. Shd they have come to hand, the Waggoner Aleck[1] will bring them up. The cost of these articles is $243.36. If you can witht. inconvenience make Mr. C. this remittance you will oblige me: if not let me know. I have a little more flour to send down wch. will follow the Tob.[2] now occupying my Waggons; & wch I wish to hasten to Liverpool as much as I can. There will be abt. 14 Hhds. for which I must get to provide a freight. How soon may I expect to get it into a situation authorizing me to draw a Bill.

The Bearer will bring also a Garden Watering Pot if you can have one delivered to him.

Draft, two copies (DLC: Dolley Madison Papers). The first draft is written on the verso of the second draft, which JM struck through. Minor differences between the copies have not been noted.

1. The second draft has "the Bearer Aleck" here.

2. In the second draft the paragraph from this point reads: "which at present employ my Waggons, and as soon as I can get the Tobo on board for Liverpool, I shall be able to draw a bill. At what time may I expect an oppy. for the shipment? I shall have abt. 14 Hhds. and hope to have them in Fredg. in 2 weeks from this date."

¶ From Elizabeth (Betsy) Conway Madison Shepherd. Letter not found. *14 May 1821.* Acknowledged in JM to James Francis Madison Shepherd, 8 Dec. [1825] (DLC), in which JM quotes from the letter: "my object is that an arrangement may be made for those Negroes to be bought in & secured. The Docr. [William Shepherd] I am confident will only say, what he has already said to me, that they must be sold and that he could devise no plan by which they can be purchased. I flatter myself, my uncle, by what passed between us, that you will not let me lose them. The probability is that they wi⟨ll⟩ go low, as they will be sold by the Sheriff."

To James Monroe

Dear Sir Montpellier May 16. 1821

I am just informed by Mr. F. Corbin, that E. Randolph, who held a Commission in the late Army, is desirous of the Collectorship at Pensacola, at which place he had established himself, in anticipation of its becoming a port of the U.S. As his military appointment originated in my nomination, and it was so well justified by his distinguished gallantry on several important occasions, it seems to be expected that I should not withold an expression of my sense of his merit, and of the satisfaction I should feel in seeing it rewarded. His military merit needs no other testimony than is found in the official communications of the Commanding General; and if in other respects his character be as praiseworthy as is represented by those best acquainted with it, you will I am sure feel the same pleasure in gratifying his wishes and those of his friends, as I shall do in lear[n]ing that it has taken place; I well know however that these feelings must always be subject to the controul resulting from rival pretensions, of greater weight, in impartial scales, a controul which though unknown to me, may be insuperable to you. With the greatest esteem and attachment Yours

James Madison

RC (DLC: Monroe Papers).

From Mathew Carey

Sir Philada. May 16. 1821.

By this day's mail, I take the liberty of sending you a set of papers, intended to prove the pernicious effects of our present policy on the best interests of the agriculturists generally.[1] Hoping it may meet with your approbation, I remain, respectfully, Your obt. hble. Servt.

MATHEW CAREY

RC and enclosure (DLC). Addressed in an unidentified hand to JM, and franked. The RC, docketed by JM, is written on the front half of a folded folio sheet, the second half of which is a printed catalogue of books for sale by Carey. For enclosure, see n. 1.

1. Mathew Carey, *Address to the Farmers of the United States, on the Ruinous Consequences to Their Vital Interest, of the Existing Policy of This Country* (Philadelphia, 1821; Shoemaker 4913).

From Mackay & Campbell

SIR FREDERICKSBURG May 16. 1821.

Some days ago we received Bill of lading from Mr. Cazenove for the goods you mention, which have not got to hand. When they come shall retain them for your own waggon unless otherwise directed. In the course of the week shall remit $243.36 to Mr. Cazenove as you request, which will probably place us about that Sum in advance for you, & which will do to be replaced in the receipt of the remnant of yr flour & when you are enabled to Value on your Tobacco, for which we will look out a conveyance to Liverpool in Company with some of our own. We however do not expect it will leave the country before Middle of July, which is soon enough, for it does not answer to have it sampled in England before Septr. or, until the arrival of Cool Weather.

Alick has the watering pot with him. With esteem Your friends

MACKAY & CAMPBELL

RC (DLC). Docketed by JM.

From James Monroe

DEAR SIR WASHINGTON May 19. 1821

Had I receiv'd your letter respecting Mr. Robt. Taylor,[1] before the appointment of General Pegram[2] to the office of marshall was made, I would not have hesitated to appoint Mr Taylor. But I knew nothing of his wish on the subject, & being appriz'd by the person who sent forward the resignation of General Moore, that an immediate appointment of his successor, would be necessary, as judge Tucker intended to hold a court, as soon as the vacancy was filled, & not before, I acted without the usual delay. General Pegram occurr'd to me, as a person well qualified to discharge the duties of the office, & whose appointment promised to be satisfactory to the public. I had not heard from him, nor did I know that he would accept it. I thought if he declin'd it, that I should have done my duty in having, offer'd it to him, & gain'd time to receive & weigh the applications & pretentions of others. He accepted the office, as soon as he heard of his appointment, tho' the commission being directed to Petersburg did not immediately reach him. The census had not been fully taken under General Moore, which was another strong motive for dispatch. His health & mind had been severely shocked, as I heard, by disease, and on his own account, as well as that of the public, I was glad that he withdrew. It is said that he has sufferd much from that cause, by the misconduct of his deputies.

I have at length made the arrangments, and appointments, that were injoind on me, by the late law, for carrying into effect the treaty with Spain.[3] Judge White of Tennessee Govr King of Maine, & Mr Tazewell, are the Commissrs. for the settlement of claims on Spain. Dr. Watkins of Bal:[4] is secretary & Jos: Forrest[5] of this city, Clerk of the board. The territory from St Mary's to Cape Florida makes one collection district for the revenue; from the cape to Apalachicola, a second; & thence to the perdido, the third. At the last, I have appointed Mr Alexr Scott Collector, Steuben Smith[6] naval officer, who will appoint John Martin Baker Inspector. At St. Augustine Mr Hackley is appointed, Surveyor and Inspector. The salaries to these officers will be small, but I shall endeavour to send them to their stations in a public vessel, & to have them quarterd in the public buildings. The territory ceded, having been divided under Spain, into two provinces, & St Augustine being so very distant from Pensacola, & separated by a wilderness, it was thought adviseable to retain in some circumstances that form. The appointment of the governor extends of course over the whole; but as he will probably reside at Pensacola, a secretary is appointed for St Augustine, and another for Pensacola. Two judicial districts are also form'd, and one Judge appointed for each. Mr Fromentin to the one, and Mr. Duvall,[7] formerly member of Congress from Kentucky for the other. Judge Anderson's son[8] is appointed district attorney for Pensacola.

Mr, now Baron de Neuville, has been negotiating with Mr Adams a commercial treaty, without much prospect from the beginning of concluding one. The restrictive duties on both sides had cut up the commerce between the two countries, which on our part was making its way into France, thro England, nice, genoa &c, and had not Florida been surrender'd, would have been smuggled from France into the UStates through its ports. There is reason to think that this resource had been in part relied on in the early stages. The great inequality of the duties imposed by France, compar'd, with those of the UStates, was as you know the motive to our last law, which producd that of France, which cut up the commerce between us. He proposed a reduction of one third of the existing duties on both sides, which would still preserve the inequality. This was rejected. He has been offerd, a reduction of the duties on French wines & silks, or an augmentation on silks from China in lieu of the latter, simply, for the establishment of equality on ships, on the principle of our act of the 3d. of March 1815.[9] which he has refused. He has since been offerd a regulation on another principle, that of a nominal equality, on both sides, of one and half pr cent for example, on the articles ad valorem, which on a vessel of 250. tons if loaded with cotton would make a duty of 450. dolrs, a regulation, notwithstanding its nominal equality, which by the greater bulk & less value of our articles, would operate decidedly in favor of France, & he now has this proposition under consideration, but with little expec[ta]tion of his accepting it. In short I do not think that there is much, if any prospect, of an agreement.

The reduction of the army is now compleated. It has been a painful duty, as it will dismiss many good officers, who had relied on the profession as a support, & have no other resource at present.

The termination of the Neapolitan movment, has by its manner disgracd that country,[10] if it does not injure the cause in Spain & Portugal. The foundation is weak; the people are ignorant, depravd, & unequal to such a trial. Mrs Monroe & Mrs Hay have been sick since Congress left us, & recently, our gd. daughter, Hortensia has been dangerously ill, with a sore throat & fever which had nearly carried her off. The complaint is atmospheric, & has taken off several children in this part of the city. The fever has left her, & her throat getting well, but she is reducd to a skeleton. I shall move them to Loudoun (where Mrs Gouverneur was sent with her child for safety) as soon as she can travell. The Board of Commissrs. will meet the 1st. of June, and I wish to be here to confer with them generally on their business; and other concerns will necessarily bring me here occasionally, so that for the present my residence will be principally in Loudoun. Should we visit Albemarle, or I alone, we shall certainly call on you. Our best respects to Mrs Madison & family. Very sincerely I am your friend

JAMES MONROE

RC (DLC).

1. See JM to Monroe, 4 May 1821.

2. John Pegram (1773–1831) of Dinwiddie County, Virginia, served in the Virginia House of Delegates, 1797–1801 and 1813–15, and in the state Senate, 1804–8. He was a major general in the state militia during the War of 1812 and served briefly in the U.S. House of Representatives, 1818–19. He was appointed U.S. marshal for the eastern district of Virginia in April 1821. He died in a riverboat accident on the Ohio River.

3. Section 4 of "An Act for carrying into execution the treaty between the United States and Spain, concluded at Washington on the twenty-second day of February, one thousand eight hundred and nineteen," 3 Mar. 1821, provided for a board of commissioners to carry

out the provisions of the eleventh article of the treaty, which dealt with U.S. claims against Spain (*U.S. Statutes at Large*, 3:637–39).

4. Tobias Watkins (1780–1855) was a graduate of St. John's College, Annapolis, Maryland (1798), and the Medical College of Philadelphia (1802). He practiced medicine in Baltimore, where he was physician to the Marine Hospital. A veteran of the War of 1812, Watkins edited the *Portico*, a monthly literary magazine, 1816–18. In 1821 he translated a pamphlet written by the Spanish minister to the United States, Luis de Onís, defending his work in negotiating the Transcontinental Treaty. The pamphlet was entitled *Memoir upon the Negotiations between Spain and the United States of America Which Led to the Treaty of 1819* (Baltimore, 1821; Shoemaker 6348). Watkins served as fourth auditor of the Treasury, 1824–29, but was later tried and imprisoned for fraud (Howard A. Kelly and Walter L. Burrage, eds., *American Medical Biographies* [Baltimore, 1920], 1205; Mott, *History of American Magazines*, 293).

5. Joseph Forrest (1768–1845) was a Washington merchant and justice of the peace in the District of Columbia (Van Horne, *Papers of Benjamin Henry Latrobe*, 2:871 n. 3).

6. William Steuben Smith (1787–1850), grandson of former president John Adams, was secretary of legation at St. Petersburg under his uncle, John Quincy Adams, 1809–15. Smith was nominated naval officer for Pensacola, 7 Jan. 1822, but was not confirmed by the Senate. He later served as U.S. Army paymaster (Kline, *Papers of Aaron Burr*, 2:710 n. 2; *Senate Exec. Proceedings*, 3:261, 270, 365, 366).

7. William Pope Duval (1784–1854) was born in Virginia but moved to Kentucky, where he practiced law. He served as a Republican in the U.S. House of Representatives, 1813–15. Monroe appointed him judge of the East Florida district in May 1821, and soon thereafter territorial governor of Florida, in which position he served from 1822 to 1834. He moved to Texas in 1849.

8. Alexander Outlaw Anderson (1794–1869), the son of Joseph Inslee Anderson, a veteran of the War of 1812 and future senator from Tennessee, 1840–41, did not serve as district attorney for Pensacola. That post was taken by Tipton B. Harrison (*Senate Exec. Proceedings*, 3:293).

9. "An Act to repeal so much of the several acts imposing duties on the tonnage of ships and vessels, and on goods, wares and merchandise, imported into the United States, as imposes a discriminating duty on tonnage, between foreign vessels and vessels of the United States, and between goods imported into the United States in foreign vessels and vessels of the United States," 3 Mar. 1815 (*U.S. Statutes at Large*, 3:224). For a discussion of the commercial negotiations with France, see Bemis, *John Quincy Adams and the Foundations of American Foreign Policy*, 450–57.

10. For the revolt in Naples of the Carboneria and its sympathizers, its immediate success, and the means by which Austria crushed the revolutionaries and restored the Bourbon king, see Acton, *Cambridge Modern History* (1969 reprint), 10:111–14.

To Francis Corbin

Dr Sir, May 21, 1821.

On the receipt of yours of the 18th, post-marked 14th,[1] I dropped a few lines to the President, as you wished, reminding him of the views of your young friend, and the grounds on which his hopes rested. I just see that the office had been otherwise filled.

On looking over the papers and letters which I had preserved through a long course of public life, during a memorable period, I found so much matter relating to current events, and transactions which, in many particulars, may not so fully, if [at] all, be found elsewhere, that I have thought it incumbent on me to digest the most material parts, at least, into a form that may not be without future use. The task is a very tedious one. I thank you for the kind offer of your memory in case of any reference to occurrences within the range of your participations. I do not, however, foresee, at present, that I shall have occasion to avail myself of it. If you have preserved a copy of the Journals of the General Assembly for 1785, you will oblige me by a loan of it.

We have had, as you were informed, a severe visitation of a fever of the typhus character. The cases amounted to between 40 and 50; and the deaths to about one-fourth of the cases. We hope the disease has left us, or, at least, is doing so. The last cases have been so mild as to make their real character doubtful. A remarkable circumstance in this endemic is, that it seems to have preferred situations the most elevated and healthy. It attacked, I understand, the family living on the summit of Peter's mountain,[2] the Chimborazo of our Lilliputian Andes.

Your favor of March 3d came duly to hand. I hope you are freed from the gouty guest in your stomach. Come, and let the excursion and a bottle of the old Bachelor[3] aid in driving or keeping him out. It may dispose us, at the same time, to cast an eye at the reverse of the medal which has presented you with such a group of gloomy features in our national affairs.

Printed copy (Madison, *Letters* [Cong. ed.], 3:224–25).

1. See Corbin to JM, 13 May 1821.
2. At 1,500 feet, Peter's Mountain in Albemarle County, Virginia, is the highest point in the Southwest Mountains (Woods, *Albemarle County in Virginia*, 14).
3. JM probably referred here to the Madeira wine that he had "put away in the pediment of the portico" at Montpelier. According to Dolley Madison's niece, Mary E. E. Cutts, "this [wine] on his retirement from public life until his death was favored above all new importations, and will doubtless be remembered by many for whom he brought it forth and always called it his 'Batchelor Wine'" (DLC: Mary E. E. Cutts Memoir).

From C. William Brock

D Sir, Orange Ct He. 25th May '21

I still hold in my possession the few bills which I presented you last summer, & have to request the favor of you to send the amt. ($22:41) to this place on Monday next. The return day has past Several months ago & I have accounted for them to the Clerk. Mr. Eddins has promised numerous times to pay them, but has failed to do so. With great respect, I am Sir, Yr. Obt. Svt.

C. Wm. Brock,[1] Dy
M. F. C. D.

RC (DLC). Docketed by JM.

1. C. William Brock was deputy marshal for the Superior Court of Chancery at Fredricksburg (Fredericksburg *Virginia Herald*, 26 Jan. 1822).

To Mathew Carey

Sir Montpellier May 26. 1821

I have received your letter of the 16th. inst: which was followed by the printed Sheets to which it referred. Of these I can not say less than that they exhibit the same extent of statistic research, the same condensation of ideas, and the same tone of disinterested patriotism, which have been remarked in other publications from the same pen.

The subject which they discuss has been so ably presented under variant aspects, not only among ourselves, but by foreign authors of much celebrity, that it is not wonderful that different opinions should still exist on particular questions involved in it.

In a theoretic point of view I cannot but concur with those who maintain that the sagacity and interest of individuals will best guide the application of their industry and their capital, and that this principle ought to be the basis of the general policy of every Governmt. In free Governments, where the intelligence and activity of the people are entitled to most confidence, the greater ought to be the caution in controuling the spontaneous pursuits of the community.

On the other hand I think it equally certain, that there are exceptions to this general rule of policy; and that the wisdom of a Government is to be tested by its selection of the cases forming the exceptions, and by its apportionment of the patronage due to & needed by them.

Some of the exceptions are so obvious and pressing that all readily acquiesce in them. No nation ought to depend on another, for articles essential to its defence & safety. The implements of husbandry used in procuring the necessaries of life, ought in like manner to be secured by an internal economy. (In the policy of encouraging our navigation also, not only as a nursery for manning a defensive navy, but as a vehicle independent of foreign conveyances for our bulky & valuable exports to foreign markets, all opinions seem to be united).

But there are other exceptions, which though less striking, seem when fully understood to fall within the scope of a provident system of national policy.

As one example, we may take the case on which you dwell, of manufacturing emigrants attracted by a prospect of bettering their condition, and who will add to the stock of manufacturing labour, without diverting a single hand from agriculture, or any other useful occupation.

Another case may arise from the difficulties & casualties incident to new undertakings of a costly & complicated nature, especially when they are to encounter a wealthy and politic rivalship from abroad; although when once brought into adequate and regular operation, they may prosper by their inherent capacities. But for these obstacles to the introduction of manufacturing Establishments, there is probably scarce a nation in Europe, which would not long ago have substituted in no small degree their own workshops for the foreign ones which have supplied their wants. That there may be cases where manufactories once established will be stable & prosperous, under circumstances which would not have given birth to them, is proved by those which grew up under the forcing circumstances of the late war, and which have withstood the trials to which the effects of peace subjected them. It is altogether probable that not one of the manufactories now said to be in a flourishing condition would spontaneously originate in the state of things which gives them their present productive support.

The frequency & effect of foreign wars, to say nothing of the possible ones of our own, furnish another case well meriting Legislative attention. During the last hundred years, the manufacturing nations of Europe have been half the time at war, and the effect of a state of war on the price of labor, of freight, and of ensurance, has been too much felt not to be well understood. In calculating therefore the patronage that could be afforded to domestic fabrics, attention ought to be given not simply to the cost of foreign ones in times of peace, but to the average cost in peace and war taken together; and to the just presumption that manufacturing establishments at home will not be undertaken during a state of war which are likely to be broken down by a return of peace. In deciding on a given rate of impost for the encouragement of domestic manufactures, it is always a fair question whether the consumer will be most taxed by such a tariff in periods of peace, or by a dependence on supplies from abroad in periods of war.

The mention of these excepted cases, will not be understood as excluding others which may rest on equivalent considerations. Far less are they meant to espouse a frequency of legal interpositions, warping the course of private industry, which would convert the exceptions into a general rule of political economy.

Draft (DLC).

From John R. Triplett

Dear Sir Norfolk 26 May. 1821.

I received a few days Since the enclosed Invoice, from Messrs. Maury & Latham, and have since recd. the Salt & forwarded the Same to Messrs. Mackay & Campbell of Fredericksburg. I also sent to them the acct of charges duty &c. paid on it here. I shall feel great pleasure at all times, if by being located here, I can be made serviceable to you, and hope you will, whenever your convenience can be promoted by it, put my services in requisition.

Mr Stone & family are here & well. Very Respectfully I am Yr. Obt St.

John R. Triplett[1]

RC and enclosure (DLC). RC docketed by JM. The enclosure (1 p.; docketed by JM: "Maury & Latham Invoice of Salt"), dated 22 Mar. 1821, is an invoice for ten sacks of "fine stove salt," valued at £2 17*s* 7*d*, including freight, duty, and commission.

1. John Richards Triplett (1785–1843), a Norfolk merchant, married Louisa Richards Stone, the daughter of William S. Stone. By 1829 he had moved his business to Richmond, where he was also agent of the Farmers Fire Ensurance and Loan Company of New-York (Joanne L. Gatewood, ed., "Richmond During the Virginia Constitutional Convention of 1829–1830 . . . ," *VMHB* 84 [1976]: 296 n. 44; *American Beacon and Norfolk & Portsmouth Daily Advertiser*, 8 June 1819; *Richmond Enquirer*, 10 Dec. 1829).

From Robert B. Corbin

My dear Sir "The Reeds" May [June] 1st. 1821.

It is my painful duty to communicate to you, as the friend of my Father, the melancholy intelligence of his death. He expired on Wednesday the 23d. ulto. in the sixty second year of his age, after a short, but painful illness. The high place which you held in his confidence and esteem, together with your intimacy with him in early life, as well as in later years, induce me to give to you the first information of this sorrowful event. It is our wish that the office of delineating his enviable character, and of announcing to the world his decease, should be performed by some kindred mind: and we know of no one who is more able to do justice to the subject, or better entitled to undertake it, than yourself. You, my dear Sir, are the most prominent of that distinguished class of Virginians to which it was my Father's pride to belong—the task would, therefore, be performed by you with peculiar propriety and, I am confident, with equal pleasure.

As you are well acquainted with the history of my Father's political life, much of which passed under your own observation, it is unnecessary for me, at this time, to remind you of any of it's events. My worthy friend Mr. Kingman,[1] who will have the honor to deliver this letter, will give you the particulars of his illness and any information in relation to his family that you may desire.

My Mother, Brother and all the younger members of the family unite their affectionate regards with mine, for you and Mrs. Madison. With sincere respect and esteem, I am, My dear Sir, yours most truly,

ROBERT B. CORBIN

P.S. Mr. Kingman having lived in the family as Tutor for the last two years, and having had, during that time, much conversation with my Father, will be enabled to refresh your memory in regard to any facts, which you may deem it necessary to make use of.

RC (DLC). Docketed by JM.

1. Eliab Kingman (1797–1883) was born in Warren, Rhode Island, and graduated from Brown University in 1816. He traveled to Virginia and acted as tutor to the Foote, and later, Corbin families, after which, in 1824, he settled in Washington. Thereafter he worked as a journalist. In 1830 he moved to Boston and purchased the *New-England Palladium* but later sold it and returned to Washington, where he was a correspondent for a number of newspapers until he retired in 1861 (Increase N. Tarbox, "Necrology of the New-England Historic Genealogical Society," *New-England Historical and Genealogical Register* 38 [1884]: 93; Ben Perley Poore, "Washington News," *Harper's New Monthly Magazine* 48 [1874]: 227).

To Robert B. Corbin

DEAR SIR MONTPELLIER June 4. 1821.

Your letter of the 1st. inst: was duly handed to me by Mr. Kingman. Altho' unversed in such tasks, the motives to which the occasion appeals, would not permit me to decline at [*sic*] attempt to fulfil the one committed to me. I am aware at the same time that the haste in which the sketch I inclose was penned, and my deficient knowledge or recollection of many circumstances in your Father's history may have produced errors or omissions which ought to be avoided. Should this be the case, your letter itself is a proof that there is a pen on the spot which can well apply a remedy.

I need not express to you Sir, the very painful impressions with which I recd. the melancholy & unexpected event of which Mr. K. was the bearer; or the unfeigned sympathies of Mrs. Madison & myself with Mrs. Corbin & the whole family in the heavy affliction under which they are suffering. For yourself Sir, accept assurances of my cordial regards & best wishes.

JAMES MADISON

[Enclosure]

Departed this life on [1] at his seat "The Reeds" Francis Corbin Esqr. at the age of sixty two years. His death was occasioned by an attack of the gout to which he had been occasionally subject.

Mr. Corbin was the youngest son of Col: Richard Corbin,[2] a gentleman of[3] a highly cultivated mind, and who held a distinguished Rank in the Government of Virga. in its Colonial State.

The son was sent to England at an early age,[4] for his education; which was commenced at Canterbury[5] School, and finished at the University of Cambridge. He afterwards read law at the Temple in London.[6]

Immediately after the peace in 1783, he returned to his native State; bringing with him a mind well stored with classical studies; and what was far more meritorious, an ardent love of Country, and principles of liberty congenial with its new rank as an Independent Nation, and with its new form as a Republican Government.

His superior talents and engaging manners[7] attracted at once the notice & confidence of his fellow Citizens, whose suffrages gave him a seat in the Legislature of the State. As a member of this Body, tho' young and under the disadvantage of his long absence, he was able to bear an important part in the Legislative business. In debate, he gave constant proof of his enlarged information, of his reasoning powers, and of an elocution uncommonly graceful & persuasive.

He continued a representative of his County, untill the great crisis, which ended in the change of the Original Confederation of the States into the present Govt. of the U.S. Mr. C. was among the first to espouse & promote the efforts for bringing about the appointment of the General Convention which had that for its object; and he was not overlooked in the choice of worthies for the Convention of Virginia, when the plan proposed by the General Convention was submitted to the several States for their sanction.

In this select assembly, Mr. C.'s name is on the list of those who bore a conspicuous part in the discussions. His Speeches in the published proceedings shew that his mind embraced the whole subject in its true principles, and various aspects; and that he was able to give to his arguments all the advantages depending on a suavity of manner, and a polish of language.

After the new Constitution had been organized & put into operation he was annually re-elected for a number of years as a delegate to the Legislature of the State, where he always sustained the reputation which his talents had acquired.

For some years previous to his death, he had withdrawn himself from public life; and devoted much of his time to the indulgence of his taste for literature & philosophy, & to the guidance of the education of children, of whom as a parent he had every reason to be proud. The other portions of his time were given to the care of his ample estate, and to the Society of his numerous friends, who could no where enjoy more of the sweets of hospitality, and the repast of elegant & interesting conversation, than under his roof: nor could any one enjoy more fully those social scenes, than Mr. C. himself. But, alas! Death, with his unsparing hand, has translated[8] him for ever from all sublunary enjoyments; leaving in sorrow the friends who admired him; and in tears an amiable family; in the bitterest of them, her who was bound to him by the most tender of the ties that have been severed.

This[9] hasty tribute to his memory is offered by one who having partaken largely of his friendly sentiments whilst living, wished to lay on his tomb some token of what was felt in return.

RC and enclosure (owned by The Scriptorium, Beverly Hills, Calif., 1988); draft and draft of enclosure (DLC). RC addressed by JM to Corbin at "The Reeds" and marked "Mr. Kingman." In the left margin of the draft JM wrote: "This hasty [t]ribute to his memory is offered by a friend who long had a share in his esteem." Draft of enclosure filed after 30 June 1821. The eulogy was printed in the *Richmond Enquirer*, 15 June 1821, where it is ascribed to "his great and good friend Mr.____." Minor differences between the copies have not been noted.

1. Left blank in enclosure and draft of enclosure.

2. Richard Corbin (1713 or 1714–1790) was a planter and politician from Middlesex County, Virginia, which he represented in the House of Burgesses, 1748–50. He subsequently moved to Laneville, his plantation in King and Queen County. Corbin was appointed a member of the governor's council in 1750 and served in that capacity throughout the colonial period, as well as deputy receiver general, 1762–76 (Kneebone et al., *Dictionary of Virginia Biography*, 3:466–68).

3. The draft of enclosure has "great wealth and of" here.

4. The draft of enclosure has "some years before the Amr. Revloution [*sic*] to Grt B." in place of "to England at an early age."

5. JM wrote "Eaton" here and in the draft of enclosure; "Eaton" was crossed out in the enclosure and "Canterbury" interlined in an unidentified hand.

6. This sentence does not appear in the draft of enclosure. JM wrote: "He returned to his native state in the year [left blank]."

7. The draft of enclosure has "very soon attracted" in place of "attracted at once."

8. The draft of enclosure has "snatched" in place of "translated."

9. This paragraph is omitted from the draft of enclosure.

From William F. Gray

SIR, FREDBG June 6. 1821

I take the liberty of handing your acct. since the last settlement. Having a pressing occasion for money, if it be perfectly convenient to you—you would oblige me by remitting the amt. due—$46.37½.

W. F. GRAY

[Enclosure]

James Madison Esq. To Wm: F. Gray Dr.

1820					
Mar. 13	For	1 Mosheims Ecclesiastical Hist.[1]			18.
Apl. 27	"	1 Quarterly Review No. 43			1.25
May 16	"	No. 64 Edinburgh Review			1.25
June 29	"	No. 65 Ditto Ditto		1.25	
	"	No. 44 Quarterly Ditto		1.25	2.50
Sept. 23	"	No. 66 Edinburgh Ditto		1.25	
	"	No. 45 Quarterly Ditto		1.25	2.50
Octo: 27	"	1 Abbott 2 Vols.[2]			1.75
Nov. 9	"	2 Horace Delphini[3]	3.	6.	
	"	6 qrs. Letter paper	.25	1.50	
	"	1 Bunch of Quills		.62½	8.12½
Decr. 13	"	No. 67 Edinburgh Review			1.25
31	"	Sub. to Analectic Mag. 1820[4]			6.
1821					
Apl. 30	"	46 & 47 Quarterly Review		2.50	
	"	68 Edinburgh Do		1.25	3.75
					$46.37½

RC and enclosure (DLC). Fragment of cover, addressed by Gray to JM, and franked; docketed by JM. Below Gray's signature on RC is JM's note: "$40. sent by mail."

1. John Lawrence Mosheim, *An Ecclesiastical History, Ancient and Modern, from the Birth of Christ, to the Beginning of the Present Century: In Which the Rise, Progress, and Variations of Church Power Are Considered in Their Connexion with the State of Learning and Philosophy, and the Political History of Europe during That Period* (6 vols.; Philadelphia, 1797–98; Evans 32513, 34154). This is the first American edition.

2. Sir Walter Scott, *The Abbot; Being the Sequel of The Monastery* . . . (2 vols.; New York, 1820; Shoemaker 3132).

3. This was one of the many editions of the works of Horace, originally edited and expurgated for the use of the French dauphin, son of Louis XIV (John Devoe Belton, comp., *A Literary Manual of Foreign Quotations; Ancient and Modern, With Illustrations from American and English Authors and Explanatory Notes* [New York, 1891], 5).

4. For JM's subscription to the *Analectic Magazine*, see Gray to JM, 7 Sept. 1818, *PJM-RS*, 1:354 and n. 1.

¶ To William F. Gray. Letter not found. *11 June 1821*. Offered for sale in Stan. V. Henkels Catalogue No. 1405 (24 June 1927), item 41, where it appears as the following extract: "J.

Madison presents his respects to Mr. Gray and encloses $40—which balances his account within 37½ cents (which cannot be well sent in a letter) after deducting $6.—for two copies of Horace paid for by J. P. Todd."

To Joseph Gales Jr.

Dr. Sir. June 12 1821

I recd. lately a letter from Mr. Geo. Joy in London,[1] in wch. he expresses a particular desire to possess in the Newspaper form a series of papers published by him during the war of 1812, under the title of Conciliator. He remarks that they were republished in the Intelligencer, and that you sent him the 3 first numbers, with your exordium. From what he says I infer that he will be very glad to receive the whole from you, & that he calculates on my giving the intimation; shd. I be unable to furnish a copy myself, which happens to be the case. I beleive also that I do not err from his intention, in handing over to you the 2 Newspapers enclosed in his letter, and put under this cover. Mr. J. is an old acquaintance of mine & an occasional correspondent which may explain his application to me and must be the apology for my agency in extending it to you. With much esteem & friendly wishes

J.M.

Draft (DLC).

1. See George Joy to JM, 9 Feb. 1821.

From Jonathan Thompson

Customhouse N York Collectors Office

Sir June 14. 1821.

There is in the public Store of this Port a small box directed to you said to contain garden seeds from the Royal Garden near Paris rec'd per Ship Cadmus from Havre.[1] Please direct how it shall be forwarded to you. I am with the greatest respect your Obt. Servt.

Jonathan Thompson[2]
Collector

RC (DLC). Docketed by JM, with his note: "requested to send the Box to Messrs. M. & C. direct or via Norfolk."

1. See Eyrien Frères & Cie. to JM, 2 Apr. 1821.

2. Jonathan Thompson (1773–1846) was a New York merchant and Republican party leader whom JM appointed collector of direct taxes and internal duties for the second district of New York in 1814. Thompson was collector of the port of New York, 1820–29 (Frederick Diodati-Thompson, "The Family of Thompson, of the County of Suffolk, New York," *New York Genealogical and Biographical Record* 22 [1891]: 41–42; *PJM-PS*, 6:519 n. 1; *Senate Exec. Proceedings*, 3:218, 220).

To John B. Sartori

Sir [ca. 18 June 1821]

Several years ago, I recd from Mr. Edwd. Caffarana of Genoa, a small equestrian Statue of Napoleon Bonaparte, executed by a young artist.[1] Not being disposed to accept it as a present, I signified as much to him, with a request to be informed of its price. Of three answers to my letter which it appears he wrote, the last only came to hand, & that very lately.[2] In this he tells me the original cost of the statue was $90. observing that he does not ask that sum, and leaving the decision with myself, in communication with you as his particular friend. I do not doubt the polite intention of Mr. C. in sending me this article; but it seems to be one too strongly marked with defects to be very valuable as a specimen of the art; and consequently one on account of which it could not be my wish under any circumstances to be at much expence. Be so good as to let me know your estimate of the article, that I may form my decision. Perhaps you may find some who wd set a higher value on the Statue than I sd. do, in which case it will [be] due to Mr C. to take advantage of that circumstance. The Statue has suffered no injury since it reached me. On its way to Washington, the reins of the bridle & a finger of the right hand were broken. With friendly respects

J. M.

Draft (DLC). Undated; conjectural date assigned based on comparison with Sartori to JM, 21 June 1821.

1. See Edward Caffarena to JM, 12 July 1817, *PJM-RS*, 1:85 and n. 1.
2. See JM to Caffarena, 1 Nov. 1817, ibid., 148–49, and Caffarena to JM, December 1820.

From Spencer Roane

Dear Sir Richmond, June 20th. 1821

I had the honor to receive, some short time since, your interesting favour,[1] on the subject which is discussed in the Enclosed Numbers. I found it extreemly able, and satisfactory, and I return you my thanks for the favour.

The Enclosed No's were written by me, just before, and have been published in the Enquirer.[2] I had hoped to have had a few Copies struck in a more Eligible form, to be presented to my particular, and my distinguished friends, but have been disappointed. I now doubt whether I ought to venture to send them to you, as taken from the Columns of a news paper. Yet the *subject* is important; and I am desirous of placing them before the Eyes of the distinguished citizen, who, more than any other, contributed to found our excellent constitution. With great consideration, respect, and Esteem, I am, dear sir, Yr: obt: Servant

SPENCER ROANE

RC (DLC: Rives Collection, Madison Papers). Docketed by JM.

1. See JM to Roane, 6 May 1821.

2. The five essays written by Roane under the pseudonym "Algernon Sidney," attacking the Supreme Court decision in *Cohens v. Virginia*, appeared in the *Richmond Enquirer* on 25 and 29 May, and 1, 5, and 8 June 1821. They are reprinted in "Virginia Opposition to Chief Justice Marshall," *John P. Branch Historical Papers of Randolph-Macon College* 2 (1906): 78–183. For a discussion of the case, see Roane to JM, 17 Apr. 1821, and n. 2.

From John B. Sartori

SIR TRENTON 21st June 1821.

I have just received your esteemed favr. of [*illegible*] Inst. Mr. Caffarena never wrote to me the particulars of his Letter to you, But if you desire from me an opinion as his Friend on the Subject of your Letter, I think if the Statue is not of use to you, the best way will be to have it packed up and Send it to me in Philad, where I will Keep it Subject to his order. Please to present my best respects to Mrs. Maddison, and to accept the sentiments of my Sincere respects and Consideration with which I have the honor to remain Your Most Obed & Huml sert.

JOHN B. SARTORI

RC (DLC). Docketed by JM.

From Joseph Gales Jr.

RESPECTED SIR: WASHINGTON, June 22. 1821.

I am honored by your favor of the 12th instant. I much regret, that it is wholly out of our power to oblige Mr. Joy. Admiral Cockburn, when he paid his respects to us,[1] took care to leave us no spare copies of the National Intelligencer—having burnt them, with the few books I had at that time collected.

I have been uneasy to perceive that a paragraph from the Enquirer, remarked on by us, has made an erroneous impression on the public mind respecting your present occupations, as though you were preparing a Work for the Press—which I understand is not the fact.[2] Should you think this worth contradicting, we shall be happy to hear from you. Begging to be most respectfully remembered to Mrs. Madison, I am, with profound respect, Your faithful servt.

J: Gales Jr

RC (DLC). Addressed by Gales to JM, and franked. Docketed by JM.

1. For the burning of Washington, and for Admiral George Cockburn's personal supervision of the destruction of the offices of the *National Intelligencer*, see Robert S. Quimby, *The U.S. Army in the War of 1812: An Operational and Command Study* (2 vols.; East Lansing, Mich., 1997), 2:693–94.

2. Gales referred here to the article entitled "Debates of the Convention, &c." printed in the *Daily National Intelligencer*, 4 May 1821: "In noticing the volume of debates of the Federal Convention, reported by Chief Justice Yates of New York, and about to be published, the Richmond Enquirer subjoins the following interesting note. 'We have for a long time, (says the Enquirer) understood that a distinguished member of the Federal Convention from Virginia has a plan of this sort before him, and that he has probably prepared a large portion of it for the press. No one who is acquainted with the gentleman we refer to, (and who is not acquainted with his transcendant abilities?) will deny, that of all other men he is best qualified for the task which he has undertaken. He was conversant with the scheme of the Constitution from its very egg-shell. 'He may indeed literally say, "*quorum magna pars fui* [in which I played a great part]." He has had his eye steadily fixed upon it from the time it was submitted to the people, and adopted by the State Conventions, down to the present moment. He has every advantage of his own notes, and those of other members, to assist him in the sketch which he has prepared. "In elucidating the principles of the Constitution, and the views of the sages who formed it, it will be an invaluable acquisition to the statesman and the politician." It will clear up many of the dark passages which are to be found in the Journals of that Convention, (recently issued from the press.) It will show us, whether, when any power was proposed to be given, and not finally engrafted into the Constitution, the omission arose from the idea that it was *already* given, or that it was not proper to be given *at all.* Could this valuable present also exhibit the present views of its author respecting the Constitution; could *it give* us the results of his experience since he saw the machine in operation; wherein it seemed to him defective, and how it was to be improved, the author would render a still more acceptable service to his grateful countrymen.'

"No one can mistake the allusion of the Enquirer. There is but one man left in Virginia who signed the constitution; and if that were not the case, there is scarcely a surviving member of the Convention, whose name would justify the language of the Enquirer, save that of James Madison. We had understood that this venerable patriot occupied much of his time, since his retirement from public life, not only on the work mentioned by the Enquirer, but also in reviewing and arranging his correspondence with the numerous distinguished men with whom he interchanged sentiments on public concerns during his long connection with public affairs. Such works from such a source, should their illustrious author give them to his countrymen, will possess a value and an interest not equalled by any publication since the era of the formation of the constitution."

To George M. Dallas

Dear Sir Montpellier June 23. 1821

I recd. lately by the return of J. P. Todd, your letter of May 1, accompanying the correspondence of your father. I am sorry to be obliged to say that altho' I have made a pretty thorough search among my papers, I cannot find such a letter as the one supposed to have been written by him after the British visit to Washington in 1814: nor do I recollect that such a one was recd. It is possible that the letter may have miscarried, or may have been mislaid & lost after reaching me, and its patriotic language was confounded with oral evidence of the same tenor, which I have heard from & of him. I send herewith all the letters from him of whatever description, not heretofore sent; and should I find any others, particularly that to which you have alluded, they will be added. Be so good as to return them at the proper season.

In glancing at the correspondence which has been in your hands, I observe that your marginal lines embrace passages in several letters; which if marked for publication, & not merely for your attention or preservation, may be displeasing to individuals, & deserve reconsideration. I refer to the letter of Aug. 1. 1815.[1] in which "the character of the man" as applied to Genl. Jackson may admit a construction at least equivocal: to that of May 20. 1815,[2] in which Mr. E. Livingston is brought into unfavorable view: to that of June 1816.[3] which speaks of Mr Adams "Metaphysical" letter &c. & to that of Octr. 5. 1816.[4] which in giving the character of Mr. Lowndes, distrusts his nerves &c. a term liable to an unjust tho' susceptable of an innocent construction. Unless the remarks on Mr Lee be deemed sufficiently qualified by "it is said," perhaps he also may be touched by them.[5]

I wish sincerely Sir that you may find time to do justi⟨ce⟩ both to yourself & to the memory of your father in pourtraying to the world his shining talents, his pub: services & his exemplary virtues.

Draft (DLC); Tr (ViU: Special Collections). Minor differences between the copies have not been noted.

1. JM interlined a "(2)" above the date. In his letter to JM of 1 Aug. 1815, Alexander James Dallas wrote that he had drafted a letter to Andrew Jackson. "The nature of the subject, and the character of the man, have made it difficult to address him" (DLC). None of the letters mentioned by JM in this letter were included in George Mifflin Dallas, *Life and Writings of Alexander James Dallas* (Philadelphia, 1871).

2. JM interlined a "(1)" above the date. "Genl. Jackson has placed his defence, upon the only tenable ground, an imperious, evident, provable, necessity; but I wish he had abstained from indulging Mr. Livingstone as a Lawyer, in technical objections," Alexander J. Dallas to JM, 20 May 1815, DLC.

3. "Mr. Adams's metaphysical letter, to establish the prosperity of England, against every public fact, and morbid symptom, surprizes, but does not satisfy me," Alexander J. Dallas to JM, 26 June 1816, ibid.

4. "Your selection of Mr. Lowndes for the Treasury will give general satisfaction. He is intelligent; and his acquirements in politics and literature have been occasionally displayed. He certainly appears to possess the respect and confidence of the House of Representatives; and the tone of his mind is so placid, his dispositions so amiable, his manners so unassuming, that I question, whether any other public man is better qualified to please, and to be pleased, in a station calculated to try the temper, as well as the talents, of the Occupant. This view of Mr Lowndes's character, however, has suggested some apprehension, that he may shrink from the task; doubtful whether his Constitution can bear incessant labors, and his nerves maintain the warfare for official independence, with Banks and Brokers &c.," Alexander J. Dallas to JM, 5 Oct. 1816, DLC: Rives Collection, Madison Papers.

5. "I feel some uneasiness, at the course pursued by Mr. [Richard Bland] Lee; and beg you to consider, when you arrive at Washington, whether the latitude which he gives to the powers of his office, will not lead to an expenditure, far exceeding the legislative intention. It is said, that he thinks himself authorised to pay for all the Houses and property destroyed upon the Niagara frontier! Without impugning the principle, the real principle, of the Act of Congress, I cannot conceive a more improvident measure, than that of laying the Treasury open to the awards of an individual, without checks, and without appeal. If some restraint be not imposed, our treasure will be absorbed almost imperceptibly," ibid.

From Richard Rush

Dear Sir London June 25. 1821.

Your favor of the 21st of April reached me a few days ago, and I have great pleasure in sending you herewith, a copy of Hones new testament, which I hope will be in time for the return of the packet. I have no account of the price, it having been just left at my house without a bill. It is but a trifle, and can be thought of at a future day. There is no other account between us. I have also to acknowledge on behalf of Mrs Rush, a letter received with yours, which Mrs Madison has been so kind as to write her.[1]

The views which you have taken the trouble to throw together on Godwin's work, are many of them very striking, and will be valuable to me. Though impressed favorably with parts of his theory, I saw the extravagance of his errors of fact respecting our country, as also his errors of reasoning. Both became more perceptible as the subject was more looked into, and I accordingly sought an opportunity of conversing with Mr Malthus, with a view to suggest to him a few such remarks as obviously occurred in opposition to Mr Godwins statements. I do not as yet know positively that Malthus contemplates a reply; but must take it for granted that he does, after so very fierce an attack. I am in the habit of meeting with him in some of my intercourse here, and shall not fail to seek a further conversation with him, armed as I now am with the fresh matter of your acceptable communication. In case he intends an answer, I shall intimate to him the expediency of waiting for the complete returns of our census now going on. I remain dear Sir, for the present, with my constant attachment and respect

RICHARD RUSH

RC (PHi).

1. Letter not found.

To Joseph Gales Jr.

DEAR SIR MONTPELLIER June 26. 1821

I have received yours of the 22d. I know not why Mr. Joy should be desirous of his political essays in a Newspaper form. As he has them in the more convenient form of a pamphlet, his disappointment cannot be an afflicting one.

On looking into the Mass of my papers having relation to the long & interesting period through w[h]ich my public life extended, I have thought that I ought not to leave in a useless state, such of them as have preserved a more authentic, or a more exact account of certain important transactions and events than may exist elsewhere. My enquiries in particular quarters for a few explanatory documents probably led to the conjectures which found their way to the press. I have no reason to believe that taking them together they have made any public impression that requires a special notice: and it not being my wish that the subject should be prolonged or revived, especially where it would be most likely to excite attention, I do not avail myself of the offer you so kindly make of the Intelligencer for contradicting any erroneous suggestions which may have been published. With much esteem and friendly wishes

JAMES MADISON

RC (NN: Ford Collection); draft (DLC). RC addressed and franked by JM to Gales in Washington. Docketed by Gales as received 30 June. Minor differences between the copies have not been noted.

From Mathew Carey

SIR June 26. 1821

I have duly recd your kind favour of the 26th ult. which want of leisure has prevented me from answering earlier.

Next to the delightful & cheering testimony of a man's own Conscience, in favour of any course of conduct, is the approbation of gentlemen of high standing, of full capacity to judge, & free from the suspicion of another bias. It is not therefore extraordinary that I prize very highly the strong & unequivocal approbation you express of my feeble efforts to promote the prosperity of a Country in which I have been so fortunate as to realize a comfortable independence, & in whose welfare I am interested by all those ties which duty towards a large family can create.

To the course I have pursued & the exertions I have made, I have been impelled by high considerations, which, unfortunately, have not due weight with our statesmen & politicians. Our present policy impoverishes the Country, & blights & blasts the industry & happiness of our citizens, in the grain growing states, particularly those in the western Country, who are writhing under the deepest distress & embarrassments in all their various forms, notwithstanding that they almost universally own the soil they cultivate, which is blest with the most exuberant fertility, & notwithstanding the mildness of the climate, & the variety of other advantages they possess. Discontent, be assured, is spreading rapidly among them. They openly weigh the advantages they enjoy, & the disadvantages they suffer, from the union, & many of them incline to believe that the balance is greatly against them. An embarrassed & discontented people are the appropriate materials for demagogues to work upon. The public mind in such a state of things becomes highly combustible—& it only requires a slight spark to excite an explosion. The maxim "obsta principiis"[1] is as sound in government as in medicine. There is an immense disproportion between the means adequate to prevent moral & political evils, & those necessary to cure them.

It is of deep importance to apply a radical remedy to their distresses, before they produce the effects which distress & embarrassment have so frequently produced in every part of the world. Our own brief history is not without its admonitions on this subject. A little more talent & good fortune might have rendered Shays[2] a Cæsar, a Cromwell, or a Bonaparte. And the conflagration of Baltimore, Philadelphia, & New York, which the imbecility of the British ministry, & the death of Ross prevented,[3] might have disolved the Legislation of the eastern section of the Union or a Hartford or Boston Convention.

There never was a nation without its Shayses. They lie dormant in times of peace & prosperity. But the hotbed of faction & public distress brings them into activity, & it is the paramount duty of governmts to adopt every measure necessary to guard against that state of things of which they so adroitly avail themselves.

But the misery of human affairs, is, that experience is almost wholly thrown aw⟨ay⟩ on us. We proceed blindly in the same career of error & folly as our predecessors, & pay the proper forfeit for such outrageous absurdity. Charles I lost his head for his despotic system. In the twenty eight years that succeeded the restoration, his two sons pursued the same career that led him to the block—& the one endangered & the other lost his crown, through an utter disregard of the lessons taught by their father's fate. Respectfully your obt. hble. Servt.

MATHEW CAREY

RC (DLC). Docketed by JM.

1. *Obsta principiis:* oppose at the beginning.

2. Daniel Shays (1747–1825), a Revolutionary War veteran and Western Massachusetts farmer, was one of several leaders of armed insurgents who closed courts and intimidated state officials in the summer and fall of 1786, and attacked the Springfield, Massachusetts, armory in January 1787. Shays became the figurehead for the uprising that was suppressed by an army of volunteers led by Maj. Gen. Benjamin Lincoln in the winter of 1787. Shays fled the state and eventually settled in Western New York (Leonard L. Richards, *Shays's Rebellion: The American Revolution's Final Battle* [Philadelphia, 2002], 5–6, 9–12, 23, 26, 28–29, 30–32, 163).

3. Maj. Gen. Robert Ross, a veteran of the Peninsular War, commanded the British expeditionary forces during the Chesapeake campaign of 1814. He was killed in the Battle of North Point near Baltimore on 12 Sept. 1814 (Quimby, *U.S. Army in the War of 1812*, 2:653, 655, 717–19).

To Peter S. Du Ponceau

MONTPR. June 29 1821

J. Madison presents his friendly respects to Mr. Duponceau with thanks for his "Discourse on the early history of Pennsa."[1] He has found it one of those fine morsels which can not be tasted without a Wish that there was more of it.

Draft (DLC); letterbook copy (PHi: Peter S. Du Ponceau Letterbook, 1777–1839).

1. Peter S. Du Ponceau, *A Discourse on the Early History of Pennsylvania: Being an Annual Oration Delivered before the American Philosophical Society, Held at Philadelphia, for Promoting Useful Knowledge; Pursuant to Their Appointment, in the Hall of the University of Pennsylvania, on Wednesday, the 6th of June, 1821* (Philadelphia, 1821; Shoemaker 5213). JM's copy, which is inscribed to him by Du Ponceau on the title page, is in the Madison Collection, Special Collections, University of Virginia Library.

To Spencer Roane

DEAR SIR MONTPELLIER June 29. 1821

I have received and return my thanks for your obliging communication of the 20th. instant. The papers of "Algernoon Sydney" [*sic*] have given their full lustre to the arguments against the suability of States by individuals; and against the projectile capacity of the power of Congress within the "ten miles square." The publication is well worthy of a pamphlet form, but must attract public attention in any form.

The Gordian Knot of the Constitution seems to lie in the problem of collisions between the federal & State powers, especially as eventually exercised by their respective Tribunals. If the knot cannot be untied by the text of the Constitution, it ought not certainly, to be cut by any political Alexander.

I have always thought that a construction of the Instrument ought to be favored, as far as the text would warrant which would obviate the dilemma of a Judicial rencounter, or a mutual paralysis; and that, on the abstract question whether the federal, or the State decisions ought to prevail, the sounder policy would yield to the claims of the former.

Our Governmental System is established by a compact, not between the Government of the U. States, and the State Governments; but between the States as sovereign communities, stipulating each with the others, a surrender of certain portions of their respective authorities to be exercised by a common Government, and a reservation, for their own exercize, of all their other authorities. The possibility of disagreements concerning the line of division between these portions could not escape attention, and the existence of some provision for terminating regularly & authoritatively such disagreements, but be regarded as a material desideratum.

Were this trust to be vested in the States in their individual characters, the Constitution of the U. States might become different in every State, and would be pretty sure to do so in some; the State Governments would not stand all in the same relation to the General Government, some retaining more, others less of sovereignty; and the vital principle of equality which cements their Union, might thus gradually be deprived of its virtue. Such a trust vested in the Government representing the whole and exercised by its tribunals, would not be exposed to these consequences: whilst the Trust itself would be controulable by the States who directly or indirectly appoint the Trustees; whereas in the hands of the States no federal controul direct or indirect would exist, the functionaries holding their appointments by tenures independent of the General Government.

Is it not a reasonable calculation also that the room for jarring opinions between the national & State Tribunals will be narrowed by successive decisions sanctioned by the public concurrence; and that the weight of the State Tribunals will be increased by improved organizations, by selections of abler judges; and consequently by more steady and enlightened proceedings? Much of the distrust of these Departments in the States, which prevailed when the National Constitution was formed has already been removed. Were they filled every where as they are in some of the States, one of which I need not name, their decisions, at once indicating & influencing the sense of their Constituents, and founded on united interpretations of constitutional points, could scarcely fail to frustrate an assumption of unconstitutional powers by the Federal Tribunals.

Is it too much to anticipate even that the federal & State Judges, as they become more & more of co-ordinate talents, with equal integrity, & feeling alike the impartiality enjoined by their oaths, will vary less & less also in their reasonings & opinions on all Judicial subjects; and thereby mutually contribute to the clearer and firmer establishment of the true boundaries of power, on which must depend the success and permanency of a Federal Republic, the best guardian ⟨as⟩ we believe, of the liberty safety & happiness of men.

In these hypothetical views I may permit my wishes to sway too much my hopes. I submit the whole nevertheless to your perusal, well assured that you will approve the former, if you can not join fully in the latter. Under all circumstances I beg you to be assured of my distinguished esteem & sincere regard.

James Madison

RC (Forbes Magazine Collection, New York, N.Y.); FC (DLC). Minor differences between the copies have not been noted.

From Jonathan Thompson

Custom House New York Collectors Office

Dear sir June 30. 1821.

I rec'd your letter of the 21st. inst.[1] in relation to the Box of Seeds—there being no opportunity to Fredericksburg, have forwarded it as per enclosed Bill of Lading to Norfolk to be forwarded from thence to the care of Messrs. Mackay & Campbell, Fredericksburg Va. No charge has been made to me for it. I am sir with respect Your Obt. Servt.

Jonathan Thompson
Collector

RC and enclosure (DLC). RC in a clerk's hand, signed by Thompson. Addressed by Thompson to JM, and franked. Cover docketed by JM. The enclosure (1 p.; filed with

Thompson to JM, 14 June 1821) is a printed bill of lading with manuscript additions, dated 21 June 1821, directing the box of seeds to be shipped to Norfolk on the schooner *Tell-Tale*, R. Churchward, master, and forwarded to Mackay & Campbell at Fredericksburg.

1. Letter not found.

From Edmond Kelly

Sir, Columbia Ten [ca. 30] June 1821

In my postscript to my last letter[1] I mentioned what appears to me to be the fact that the improper conduct of Mr Monroe and of men in Congress whom the fallacious and Insidious misrepresentations of the british Govt. & its agents influenced to promote the success of british Intrigue had agitated the union and I do suppose that except Ohio & a few other states whose Legislative Councils were guided by factious men such improper Cooperation of Leading Characters in the different departments of the genl Govt. with british govt Agents alarmed other Legislatures and caused that spirit of resistance to the authority of the Genl Govt which threatened a dissolution of the union—such appear to me to be the bad effects of an unwarrantable interference in matters foreign to american legislation & Jurisprudence and of subservience to the requisitions of the british Govt. & no wonder it alarmed good republicans—that the b Govt is anxious & alert to deceive & divide americans from a hope that discord & disunion would facilitate a reconquest which concord and union would render Impracticable is evident but that to prevent such a state of things is the duty of the next congress is equally so, to effect which excluding all matters foreign to its legislative & Constitutional duties would contribute—if Mr Barber & Mr Monroe would but reflect that the suggestions of the b Govt are as deceptious as the assertions of Interrested adventurers influenced by cupidity and avarice are false as contrary to truth as to Justice much factious declamation & inflamatory harangues would cease to agitate congress from the first citizen and attempts to form alliances with the satelites of the british Govt. (as done by Genl Hull) would not distinguish Mr Monroes presidential Carreer from all others that preceded him. I would willingly remind those Gentn. that where authority & proof are wanted any Legislative Decisions of or in One Country are what is solely cognizable by the Legislature of an other Country & on suffict. proof is as unjust as it wd. be for me to go on my neighbours plantation and order things as I pleased on it & it is hoped that this principle recognised by every law national & International human & divine the next congress will not suffer Individuals to Violate, in which case to conciliate the different states to confirm the authority of the genl Govt. and the Jurisdiction of the federal court are indispensably necessary towards preserving the union for if the Doctrine asserted by Al[g]ernon Sidney be acquesced in the union of the states is at and end[2]—it is like John Bulls broad principle who in effect says recognise my broad principle & the strength of my Arm shall do the rest. So with the states. If Congress will once recognise their Legislatures uncontroulable irresponsible & insubordinate to the Genl Govt. I have no doubt but that the Harford Convention for Connecticut and the Legislatures of Ohio &ca. will soon form foreign Alliances, dispense with the protection of the Genl Govt. & contrive to pocket the states quota of the taxes to defray the expences of the Genl Govt and make a foreign Govt. to supply the states with Manufactures as the Genl Govt does the Indians and also follow the grand example of the Citizens of St Lou[i]s otherwise Missouriopolis who have already Commenced a foreign trade and scorn to touch at Orleans outward or homeward bound but as that happened before her admission & perhaps when in an ill humour it is hoped she will now dismiss her resentments become a worthy sister of the union & as she is legally married into it substitute for Miss. Mistress Ouriopolis which I suppose will be more suitable tho perhaps less agreeable to her Ladyship. In saying her Ladyship I do not mean any of those aristocratic Titles of Baroness Countess Marshioness or Duchess sounds as odious as discordant to the presidential family as they are to democratic virtue but I Mean that plain Title which befits the wife of any plain country squire and that is Lady Mistress Ouriopolis. Long may it remain so.

What appears to me would be the most effectual Check on factious men who gain an ascendancy in the different states Legislatures wd be the creating of a power in the Judiciary of each state to peruse and revise all acts of the states Legislatures after they pass them and then to certify them as constitutional to the Governors (if so) for their signatures—but if not to certify them as unconstitutional which last should operate as a Veto and prevent what wd violate the Constitn. becoming a law tho I do not say that this is the proper time to attempt it.

After the submission of the neapolitans I submitted my Opinion as to the cause of that submission—Vizt. that it is not attributable to any want of manhood if it manhood could be in the first Onset exerted by a people long habituated by passive submission to slavery but to the pontifical superstition & the secret influence precepts & preaching of the priesthood who are Interrested to stop the progress of mental Improvement rational Knowledge & Legislation which is always hostile to superstition & Imposture but for a more particular Knowlege of that superstition to such as cannot have local Knowledge of its effects on the Illiterate & unfortunately the most enervateing & Effeminateing of any that prevails in Europe I referr to the work of a man of considerable Genius and Talent Don Antonio [3] a spanish Bishop who escaped the Vengeance of the spanish Inquisition &

fled to England where he published it—it is called a master Key to Popery and the title is but expressive of the merit of the work in fact it Justifies it.

My motive for writing so fully on that event arose from the necessity there appeared to be to Justify what spain had done—she had published no Justificatory declaration manifesto or address to the holy aliance which if newspapers are correct is disposed to anihilate her constitutional freedom—she has published no Justificatory address to demonstrate her Inherent right or her obvious necessity for the change—prudence & policy required it & I did hope that some philantrophic Individual gifted with sufficient ability wd vindicate her conduct particularly as I am apprehensive that if spain is invaded by Austrian & Rusian Armies the same cause which operated On the neapolitan peasantry will occasion a similar defection & submission of the spanish peasantry—it appears the spanish clergy have under protection of Almighty God (occasionally the british King & the Duke of York whose sneers are become habitual to the spanish priesthood) already prejudiced & Irritated the Spanish peasantry against Constitutional freedom—have denounced it as so heretical & impious as to excite that Infatuated bigoted people to hostility against the Constituted Authorities—to Civil War—& such is the paralising effects of popery that neither Naples portugal or spain ever entered into any aliance to aid each other against the combined attacks of the Combined armies of the holy Aliance—it is however satisfactory to reflect that if Despotism is reestablished the Duke of York & the british princes who secretly sanctioned their political Changes & anticipated from them civil wars—royal abdications—Regicide—partitionment & desolation will be disappointed at lest as to Spain but I am doubtfull as to France where british Intrigue & influence has made rapid progress and may have or cause fatal effects—but altho I am satisfied of the necessity & the right of Spain to supercede the operation of arbitrary power & to substitute for it Constl Freedom I am not equally satisfied that the constitution[4] is faultless. It appears from newspapers that her legislature is comprised in one house consequently more like a roman Senate or a Convention than a british or American Legislature composed of two distinct and seperate chambers—every days experience shews that it is not untill after a difficult question is discussed & decided in one house that it is perfectly understood and may necessarily undergo special alterations and modifications in the other such as to render it efficient & unobjectionable—besides the Individuals of most wealth will under such Circumstances always secure their Election and appointment in total exclusion of the persons of the middleing & poorer classes—such a state of things is always sure to cause Civil war anarchy & ultimately some national Calamity and by no means calculated for permanence in so old & populous a Country as Spain. I consider a senate whether elective as the American—whether appointed for Life or some special Term or whether hereditary as the british but in which no man under 30 years of Age should have a vote as representing the wisest most eminent and Experienced of the Elders of the Community deciding with sage and cautious Deliberation on all national questions & I consider the representatives of the people as selected for their superior Intelligence diligence and activity and invested with the two very Important duties of public Agents and Legislators for the public good & security regulating the rects. & Expenditure—an Institution Indispensably necessary.

The roman Senate or nobility whom I revere for unequaled Magnanimity and Virtue was guilty of this error—it monopolised legislation and by that means incurred the hatred & envy of the turbulent tribunes & of the roman population which being inflamed & prejudiced by the tribunes permitted the ruin of the republic & of roman freedom—had these men shifted even the drudgery of Legislation to the tribunes & the people with a due proportion of its Emoluments Cesar would not have dared to attempt subverting roman freedom. If he did he & his few Veteran Legions would have been sacrificed. But as the people hated the nobles he met with no Such opposition as he Otherwise would have done. Dean Swift remarks that such was the apathy & so neutral were the people that the numbers of those Imbattled under Cesar & Pompey were not mised out of the aggregate of the population which ought to be a memento to future law givers.

But it may be sayed and I su[s]pect is so but Know it not that the Spanish Constin or the greater part of it is taken from the code of Joseph Buonaparte & was hastily adop[t]ed from necessity—a bad excuse for men so learned as the Spaniards—the Original french democratic Code from which most of their Subsequent legislation is deduced was formed or pened whe⟨n⟩ France had to contend with the Coalesced Armies & with a host of domestic enemies—no country ever had greater difficulties to encounter—it became necessary to elevate the poor so as to Interrest the mass of the population to repell the Coalesced armies & Crush domestic enemies—thus then that equality which superficial people affect to deride that is equality of rank and of rights & a total abolition of aristocratic privilege produced the desired or expected Effect & Caused an Enthusiasm in the french people which was never before equaled & which caused the defeat of the Successive Coalitions—to create public property to benefit the lower Orders & defray the expences of larger fleets and Armies than the revenue was equal to was also not less politic than necessary. In fact such of their first efforts as were unjust were necessary towards self defence & preservation & were caused by the flight of Louis the 16th. Spain had no such difficulties to Encounter & ought to have legislated better. My Opinion of the necessity of a decent provision for the Spanish Clergy of the state of France & England shall be the subject of the next letter from Your obt H Servt

EDMD KELLY

RC (NN). Day of month not indicated; conjectural day assigned based on comparison with the postmark "Columbia Ten July 3." Addressed by Kelly to JM: "late presidt. US at his residence in the state of Virginia Washington City or elswhere."

1. The letter has not been found, but for Kelly's unfavorable opinion of James Monroe, see Kelly to JM, 30 Sept. 1820.

2. Spencer Roane, writing as "Algernon Sidney," attacked not only the U.S. Supreme Court decision in *Cohens v. Virginia*, but the court itself, asserting that, as the United States was a confederation of states, each of which had freely entered into a compact, the Supreme Court had no jurisdiction in the case (Johnson et al., *Papers of John Marshall*, 9:111).

3. Left blank in RC. Kelly referred to Antonio Gavin, *A Master-Key to Popery . . .* (Dublin, Ireland, 1724). The first American edition was published in Newport, Rhode Island, in 1773 (Evans 12784).

4. Kelly referred here to the Spanish Constitution of 1812, written by the Cortes in Cádiz when the rest of Spain was under French occupation. The liberal and reformist constitution was declared null and void by Ferdinand VII on his return to Spain in 1814, but it remained a rallying point for liberals and the army, leading to a period of unrest and attempted military coups during the period, 1814–23 (Raymond Carr, *Spain, 1808–1975* [Oxford, 1982], 94, 118–19, 124–42).

From Edmond Kelly

Sir — Columbia Ten [ca. 30] June 1821

I hope you will find from this letter that the Vanity of giving an opinion on the spanish Constitution was not the cause of the Conclusion of my last long letter. I Conjecture it to be the Code given by Joseph Buonaparte and to be of french & not of spanish Manufacture, & to acct for the unity of the legislative departments in one body. If I am correct in the opinion that a senate & house of Representatives is an actual delegation from the older & younger Classes of a large & populous Community where the deliberative wisdom of the first Operates correctively on the Zeal ardour & activity of the 2d. the result of their Councils is best calculat[ed] to ensure public security & protection & is therefore the best sistem—for these reasons I Deem the spanish Constn. as defective & erroneous in Theory as it is in practice a partial Exclusion of the Intelligent middling classes who ought to represent the people—that as the opulent land Owners can always secure their Election it will cause envy discontent & discord which are the sure Effects of such a partial Exclusion & must finally lead either to a necessary amendment or a worse Change—the spaniards are deemed the proudest people in Europe, & wd agree much better as to what Mr Adams properly calls equal rights to acquire property than Equal rank[1] & probably Joseph who was a zealous candidate for popularity wished to Captivate the people by that Equality of rank when he established it—subsequently the Govt was arbitrary. Any Constitution was preferable to it—to delay deliberate divide or oppose it might be unsafe & particularly as the popular feeling & Excitement made it prudent for the spanish Gentry & Nobility to acquiesce in the Inovation.

The brilliant display of genius in the french Convention and its effects on France appears to have contributed not a little to the opinion that a Convention is the Chief de: Ouvre of or in Constitution making & hence the preferrence of it but there is as great a diversity in the human character and in mental Endowment as there is difference between frenchmen & spaniards whose Conduct would differ from the former on a similar Occasion—that the french Convention answered the sanguine hopes entertained & Expected from it and created an enthusiasm in frenchmen to defend their Country never before surpassed I admitt—but that it was the chief de Ouvre of necessity alone and not of Choice is what I have not a doubt of and that if France had not then been Menaced by the most appaling dangers Caused by the flight of Louis the 16th. and been as free to chuse a Constitution as Naples Spain and Portugal were her Code would have been a different One and the Just rights and properties of all descriptions of Frenchmen secured by it as Illimitably as Justice & equal rights required it there cannot be a doubt of (I do not include special aristocratic privileges Among Just rights—neither do I defend Robertspieres Govt). But those who think that every Convention ought to be like that of France and every people under such Conventions equally unanimous enthusiastic brave & successfull would be disappointed by the result of Experiments. I therefore adopt the Opinion that the french Conventional Constitutn. was the chief de ouvre not of Choice but of Imperious necessity which alone obliged the french democratic Govt. to Violate the rights of Individuals in any Instances where Justice necessity & expediency did not require it is what there cannot be a rational doubt of.

I made the foregoing remarks chiefly to explain & elucidate my Opinion of the Injustice done to the spanish Clergy—of the treatment they have Experienced from men who appear to have claims to Infallibility in constitution making similar to what the pontiffs exercise Jure divino[2] & of the treatment they ought to experience which opinion is that the indiscriminate sequestration of ecclesiastical property is unjustifiable—the priest who devoted his youth to the study of Divinity and the subsequent part of his life to the faithfull discharge of the duties of a profession he had no doubt would be permanent is as unjustly Injured by the suppression of it & the loss of its emoluments without Compensation or equivalent as the artizan the trader or Lawyar would be in the event of a similar suppression of the trade calling or profession of either without Compensation—for the time & application of the priest is as much his capital & his property as the time and application of the other persons creates their capital & property—to suppress either without making such Compensation is equally unjust—but

I would not have the Compn. to the clergy to exceed a decent support & not more than would be needed by genteel professional men who devoted themselves to a life of Celibacy. I therefore consider that indiscriminate sequestration of Ecclesiastical property as unjust an exercise of power & as wanton a Injury as the arbitrary mandate of the sultan could Inflict.

It is true that the Doctrine of the popish priesthood has the worst possible Effects on the Ignorant & Iliterate and that it envelops the human mind in a despotic Bastile which as effectually reconciles the Captive to his chain as training does the horse to the bridle—but however pernicious the Doctrine the profession has been deemed not only respectable but sanctified & includes in Spain thousands against whom there is no other objection than that of their being priests and Monks & possessing more property than they needed. Where the public safety & necessity require it the sequestration of any unnecessary property from them is perhaps Justifiable—but to leave them without support is doing what cannot be excused or defended on any Known principle of Justice or humanity.

As I sayed that their doctrine has a pern[i]cious & bad effect on the Ignorant it is fit I should support it by Explanation lest it might seem to be an assertion without proof & consequently false—the doctrine is to this effect—that man is prone to disobey the divine law, that God is a severe and a Jealous God who punishes to the 3d and 4th Generation the guilty with eternal torments to which there are no limitt—that the poor should not envy the rich who are always punished in the other world for their Indulgence & neglect of duty in this world for that as the possession of wealth without distributing it (doubtless some to the Church) in Charitable Donations is a mortal sin it is as easy to draw a Campbell through the Eye of a Needle as it is for a rich man to go to Heaven—that God will reward the poor the humble & the faithfull with everlasting happyness and punish the rich with everlasting misery and torments (I now quoted their own words)—that the King and the Clergy are appointed by God on his divine authority & that any disobedience to either is punished as severely as the transgressions of the rebel Angels—and thus is the poor papist made a Victim to Imposture & the passive Instrument of despotism rejoicing that his misery patience & humility secure his salvation & eternal happyness in the next world—where the proud and the rich are doomed to eternal torments & believing that Heretics & Infidels are damned to all Eternity & also that to resist the King & the pope &ca. Eternal Damnation—such is popery or as Sterne sayed slavery[3]—a bitter draught, seemingly a disease without a remedy but which like all other shallow Enquiries I cannot refrain Suggesting the following simple remedy for—

To Expunge from the Doctrine of Jesus Christ and his apostles all the Inovations of the popes—to reduce that doctrine to what it was when preached recommended & written by J. Christ & his apostles & the

Converts to it, to take the name of Apostolic Christians—and to permitt the Conforming Clergy to marry and for additional Compensation to superintend the Education of Youth & thereby Convert them into usefull and Meritorious members of society—and also to provide an Agreeable retreat Assylum & fit support for the superannuated Clergymen who would preferr a life of solitude seclusion & piety to conformity & its active & laborious duties—this is what would quiet Spain—extinguish priestcraft and superstition, & Convert her peasantry into rational beings & thereby qualify them to become good Citizens and good subjects—the sure road to Industry & that Improvemt and happyness they appear to want.

Catholics or papists believe (being so taught) that every other Religion is an Herecy which sends the reformed sects to Hell without redemption & that there is no Salvation but through their own religion—it is for these reasons they have an insuperable aversion to conform to any other that is more rational—it is also for that reason that an Adherence to their own Religion purified from all pontifical Inovation would most effectually reconcile the multitude to a necessary recision of its errors unauthorised additions or Inovations but its Immediate & General adoption wd much depend on the Conformity & Exertions of the young and active part of their clergy to whom considerable Encouragement ought to be given to preach & recommend it.

Had Mr Grattan[4] the political Champion of the Irish Catholics applied his gigant⟨ic⟩ Talents to this object he would with the aid and cooperation of Lord Donoughmore[5] their most strenuous advocate in the house of Lords have perswaded the learned and liberal part of the Irish Catholics to adopt accept & profess the religion thus corrected and purified or restored to its original purity & however few or limitted at first Such a society might be as to members its adoption would soon cause it to progress extensively and produce incalculable good—for it is that fatal superstition & priestcraft that Keeps the people divided—that is catholics, protestants & dissenters & in such a state of rancorous hostility to each other as no sense of national poverty misfortune or calamity can reconcile into any real or even political friendship. The Priest tells his Congregation that the protestants not Content with robbing and murdering their Fathers, Continue to oppress themselves & Keep them in bondage & degradation for not abjuring their holy religion out of which there is no redemptio⟨n⟩ but that as Herecy leads to eternal damnation in the next world their sufferings in this Short life and adherence to the only true faith ensures them eternal happyness and Immortality in the next world—therefore to bear it with patience that the day of retribution is at hand when their sufferings will end—the protestant on the other hand says these people perseverd in an Irreconcileable hatred & preserve vindictive Intentions, and their sanguinary threats prove that if we put power into their hands (so formidable for their numbers) that it will be ascerted to destroy us—such is the real Cause of their divisions & unhappyness for which I see no remedy but the one I suggest of restoring religion to its pristine apostolic purity & Converting the Conforming priesthood into benevolent Christian preachers preaching forgetfullness & forgiveness of wrongs & Injuries and love and good will to mankind.

Small as the space aloted to my remarks on the pernicious operation of bigotry in Ireland is in this letter I Own my concern for the state of that Island & had much greater influence on me to write them than the Vanity of giving a speculative opinion on the affairs of Spain and regrett that Mr Emmett is not at the seat of Govt or I would have transmitted them for his Opinion of their Correctness. I am confident his local Knowledge experience & Judgment qualify him to give a correct opinion of their practical appl⟨ic⟩ability, & am perswaded he feels sufficiently Interrested in the fate of that ill fated Island to do so. In that respect I should seek no confidence whatsoever for I am not only descended from but actually the Heir of one of the 5 families between whom that Island was at a remote period divided[6] and consequently retain those partialities for an Aristocracy but not a fewdal one or their special privileges or Cromwells which a democratic Republican wd correctly consider a weakness. Very respectfully &ca.

EDMD KELLY

RC (NN). Day of month not indicated; conjectural day assigned based on comparison with the postmark "Columbia Ten July 7." A second postmark reads: "Washn. City Jul 23." Addressed by Kelly to JM: "late presidt US at his residence state of Virginia City of Washington or elswhere," and franked. "City of Washington" has been crossed out and "Orange C.H. V" written below it. Damaged by removal of seal.

1. On 14 Dec. 1820, former president John Adams, as a representative from Quincy, entered into debate at the Massachusetts Constitutional Convention: "The Constitution declares, that all men are born free and equal. But how are they born free and equal? Has the child of a North American Indian, when born, the same right, which his father has, to his father's bow and arrows? No—no man pretends that all are born with equal property, but with equal rights to acquire property" (*Journal of Debates and Proceedings in the Convention of Delegates, Chosen to Revise the Constitution of Massachusetts, Begun and Holden at Boston, November 15, 1820, and Continued by Adjournment to January 9, 1821* [Boston, 1821; Shoemaker 5972], 7, 134).

2. *Jure divino:* by divine right.

3. "So that in many countries where Popery reigns,—but especially in that part of Italy where she has raised her throne, though, by the happiness of its soil and climate, it is capable of producing as great variety and abundance as any country upon earth; yet so successful have its spiritual directors been in the management and retail of these blessings, that they have found means to allay, if not entirely to defeat, them all, by one pretence or other. . . . It is not surprising . . . that many thousands . . . should fly from the rigours of such a government, and seek shelter rather amongst rocks and deserts, than lie at the mercy of so many unreasonable task-makers, under whom they can hope for no other reward of their

industry, but rigorous slavery, made still worse by the tortures of unnecessary mortifications" (Laurence Sterne, "Sermon XXXVII. Penances," in *The Works of Laurence Sterne* [10 vols.; London, 1783], 8:134–36).

4. Henry Grattan (1746–1820) was an Anglo-Irish lawyer and politician who led the fight for an independent Irish parliament and for Catholic emancipation (James Kelly, *Henry Grattan* [Dundalk, Ireland, 1993], 5, 7, 8, 17, 18, 27, 31, 38, 45).

5. Richard Hely-Hutchinson, first Earl of Donoughmore (1756–1825), was an Irish lawyer and politician who represented Sligo in the Irish House of Commons, 1777–83, and served thereafter in the House of Lords. He was a leader in support of Catholic emancipation.

6. Kelly referred here to the five kingdoms that dominated Ireland from the fourth to the twelfth centuries. Each kingdom was led by one or two families (John O'Beirne Ranelagh, *A Short History of Ireland* [Cambridge, England, 1983], 11–12).

From Elisha Callender

HOND SIR BOSTON July 4th 1821

I feel most sencible how incorrect it may appear, to address a Gentleman, who I have no personal acquaintance with; but am fully persuaided, when I shall hereafter, introduce the Subject, for your perusal, grant me a ready forgiveness, for further apology.

I am fully convinced, the Cultivation of the Olive Tree, is practible in our climate, and do not hesitate to say, it can be brought to full perfection—how desirable, would it be to see an Olive Plantation, rising to Individual, and Public utility; what Patriotic Breast, would not expand, or what Heart, that would not glow, for a signal service, rendered to his common and Parent Country—your position of Lands, having large possessions, with there variety of Soil, being in a climate simular in Latitude & Longitude, of Triest, & Gallipo, where the finest Olives, are produced, incourages me to hope, and view the subject, in the fairest light. I see no obsticle in the way, of introducing them, in our Country, attented with every advantage; they are nearly, as easy raised, as the common Plumb Tree, but of much greater durability, they have been known to reach the great age of 60 to 70 Years—after arriving to age of maturity, which will require five years & upwards, for producing fruite; each Tree then, will on an average, give from fourteen to Twenty Gallons, first years product, and as the health & Strength of the Trees increase, so will the quantity of Oil augment in proportion—this Oil, in general fill [*sic*] demand, owing to the great consumation for Table use, Woolen Manufacturers, Machinry & &ca. viewing quality, for each purpose, it has seldom or ever known to be sold, less by quantity, than \$1.33 pr Gallon, and of late years, \$1.50 to \$1.75. You will see by this statement, Sir; the value of each Tree. This is not the only p[r]operty, attached to the Olive, is its Oil, for after pressing, put the remains in hot water and suine[1] as, will answer well for Soap, but still more preferable, for an excellent manure for the Earth. In order to effect, this most desirable plan of promoting, & cultivating this Tree, will be to send a suitable Person, to either of the before mentioned Places, there let him wait, the Olive Harvest, and attend the pressing of them; that he may select the best Kernals or stones, and place them in a Cask, and at evry row of Stones, let him place a Layer of moist Earth, to keep them as much seperated as possible; and in Order to prevent all casualties, I should advise to procure, two hundred or more Scions or suckers, from the best and largest Trees. Let the roots or bottom be Beded with moist Clay, or Earth, and well secured with Matts. This mode will prevent injury, and keep them in health, untill they can be convey'd to our Shores—when ready for planting and you have on your Lands, or Estates, an elevated position to keep the north Winds from injurying them, it would be desirable—let each kernal be inserted in the Earth, from twelve to fourteen feet distant on Every angle, in order that each Tree when arrived at maturity, should not be crouded. Plant, nine Inches deep, with a Small quantity of Horse manure in the hole; when arrived above the Earth, take care for two or three following falls of the year, they may have a warm Covering of manure around the Stem, at least Six Inches in height; after that they will have health & Strength to take care of them Selves, on a second reflection I would plant two Kernals in one hole, fear full that one may not take, and should they both Vegitate, it will be very easy to transplant the other. May Health & every blessing attend you & Family is the wish of a friend, to

AGRICULTURE

RC (NN). Unsigned; identified as Elisha Callender based on comparison of handwriting in his letters to JM of 16 Feb. 1823, 12 June 1825, and 3 Oct. 1830. Addressed by Callender to JM at "Monticello Virginia," and franked. Docketed by JM, "Anonymous . . . on the Olive Tree." Elisha Callender (1776–1838?) was the son of Joseph Callender, a Boston baker, and Elizabeth Russell. He worked for his brother-in-law, J. P. Bradlee, a Boston merchant, at his store in Butlers Row. Given Callender's scientific interests, it is possible that he was also the man who gained a patent for an improved lightning rod on 3 Oct. 1808 (Esther Littleford Woodworth-Barnes, "Descendants of Ellis Callender of Boston," *New England Historical and Genealogical Register* 145 (1991): 33–34, 37–38; Callender to JM, 12 June 1825, DLC; ASP, Miscellaneous, 2:135).

1. Suine: "A fatty substance made from pig's lard" (*OED Online*).

From Robert Briggs

DEAR SIR MADISON July 5. 1821

I received yours of the 12 Ultimo[1] several days since but my time has been so occupied as to prevent me from noticing its contents sooner. It affords me pleasure to lern that you are at length likely to be freed from so unpleasant a visitant as the disease with which your family has been long disturbed. Agreeably to your request I enclose a statement of my account. Accompa[n]ying this are the several numbers of the Journal you were so good as to loan me which I hope you will receive safe.

Please present my thanks to Mr Todd for his kindness in procurings [*sic*] the work which I receivd with your friendly letter. With sentiments of high respect & sincere esteem I am Dear Sir Yours &c

Robert Briggs[2]

RC (DLC). Docketed by JM.

1. Letter not found.

2. Robert Briggs (1785–1838) of Madison County, Virginia, was JM's physician for at least two years after the death of Charles Taylor in 1821 (see Briggs to JM, 26 July 1823, DLC). Briggs served as the corresponding secretary of the American Bible Society for Madison County and after his removal to Richmond, Virginia, as an officer of the Virginia Historical and Philosophical Society (William Armstrong Crozier, ed., *The Buckners of Virginia and the Allied Families of Strother and Ashby* [New York, 1907], 116; *Annual Reports of the American Bible Society . . .* [169 vols.; New York, 1838–1995], 1:221; "Virginia Historical and Philosophical Society," *Southern Literary Messenger* 1 [1835]: 257).

From William Maury

My Dear Sir Richmond 9 July 1821

I returned from Fredericksburg yesterday, where I was much pleased with the view of your Crop of Tobacco. It really looks well, & is such, that from the late advices from Liverpool it cannot fail of doing well. Under these circumstances you can draw for £250.

The Tobacco will be on board the Glide this week & bills of lading sent to Mr Mackay as you directed.

Insurance has been ordered already.

My Father writes to me upon the subject I wrote to you from New Orleans[1]—at present I shall take your advice & say nothing of it.

I shall leave this for New York in 2 days to embark by the 10 August & bid adieu to a Country from whose inhabitants I have received every attention a Stranger could expect.

Be assured my Dear Sir I shall ever remember with gratitude the kindness of yourself & Mrs Madison to whom I pray you to present my respects. I am Dear Sir Your most obedient servant

William Maury

My Trunk is in the River, if in time I will send on to Mrs M. my promised present of Natchitoches Snuff.

RC (DLC). Docketed by JM.

1. See William Maury to JM, 6 Apr. 1821, and n. 2.

To John Quincy Adams

Montpellier July 16. 1821.

J. Madison presents his respects to Mr. Adams with many thanks for his "Address" on the 4th. of July,[1] which is not less rich in excellent thoughts, than eloquent in the enunciation of them.

RC (MHi: Adams Papers).

1. John Quincy Adams, *An Address Delivered at the Request of a Committee of the Citizens of Washington; On the Occasion of Reading the Declaration of Independence, on the Fourth of July, 1821* (Washington, 1821; Shoemaker 4400). JM's copy, inscribed by Fontaine Maury, is in the Madison Collection, Special Collections, University of Virginia Library.

From Edmond Kelly

Sir Columbia Ten [ca. 17] July 1821

A dull or stupid attack prevents me from continuing my remarks on the urgent necessity & great advantage of restoring the roman Catholic Religion to its original apostolic purity which appears to me not less needed by Spain than by Ireland—the only thing that would lead to unanimity & rationality, & guarantee & secure the Internal repose & welfare of their Countries. I consider Bigotry as the sole cause of that discord & animosity that convulses Spain and divides the people of Ireland. I consider the Divisions in Ireland as prolonging the disqualifications they Complain of, but which a cordial unanimity of the people would remove & I am perswaded that such unanimity would Induce the Irish nation to Cooperate with the british in procuring that most Important of all other laws—parliamentary reform—that such Cooperation of the people of both Countries would abolish all nomination & concede or restore to the people the right of Election which however it might reduce the power of the oligarchs & the domineering arrogance of their Leader the Duke of York & of the King would be an Incalculable benefit to the nation as it would so reduce exorbitant taxes as to proportion the national Expences to the Expenditure really necessary & the ability of the poor to defray its quota in which case it is presumeable a sense of public distress would Induce the King & the Royal family to relinquish two thirds of the Income they now squander to relieve public distress & thus at once remove the necessity for exorbitant oppressive taxation which deprives the poorer classes not only of the Comforts but of the necessaries of life & Converts them into paupers—such a Retrenchment would regenerate both Countries.

In saying so I wish not to be misunderstood as Canvassing for any share of that popularity which properly belongs to the old and tried friends and Leaders of the people. They have earned it by their Exertions & their sufferings. If I did I would deserve the Chastisment which Sir Francis Burdetts Letter to the friends of parliamentary Reform[1] Inflicts but which I cannot presume was dictated by any such suspicion or sceptical apprehensions on that head. I have heretofore Considered him as one of the most Virtuous of the british patriots & if either Irritation or Injury causes an alteration in his conduct his mind will not be more at ease nor his exertions promote the public Interest so well as by preserving his former moderation. If any one has mistaken the Simpathy of men of honour & patriotism towards me caused by the persecutions of the royal family & oligarchs that is if such Simpathy has Shielded or saved me my conduct was but a helpless attempt at Cooperation to defend myself & not a Canvass for popularity. At all events it verifies the truth of Lord Mansfields assertion (if I gained any) that popularity gained without Merit is lost without a crime[2]—in truth I am Indebted to patriotic men & honourable men too not only for existence but for what I have or Ought to have—it has shielded & saved me from the effects of royal & oligarchic hatred & Villiany—& conscious of these obligations I feel an Interest in reducing & limitting their oppressive power but not by transferring more of it to the people than the british Constitution Originally Intended so as to preserve the Constitutional Equilibrium and untill that is effected I believe the people of both Countries will be discontented & unhappy—after this & a further Explanation of my sentiments I hope no one will consider me a Demagogue that reads it—that part of Sir F Burdetts Letter which Identifies me with the Ass who Knew his Masters Crib is untrue as Applied to me. I had no Master & paid the man he aludes to for what Corn I bought from him. I found him an Obliging Neighbour & friendly man untill Royal Influence & artifice & an Infamous prescription Converted him into an Othello—his dread of dishonour tho groundless afterwards Influenced his conduct or rather made him subservient to british Intrigue & probably he has sayed what he Ought not to say but my Conduct here & since I came to Manhood & sense defies Scrutiny. I am so harassed & so accustomed to such Conspiracies against Character that I of late treat them with Indifference. I find the most Iliterate men in society are now aware that abuse and aspersion do not Justify nor Create in the King the Duke of York or Moll any Title to my property which I would sooner Scatter to the winds if my wishes could do so rather than any of them shd have it—however I can no more Controul their attacks & Conspiracies than I can the power & Influence of the Crown or Sir Francis Burdetts pen—or passions but I hope I can safely say that my Conduct will be what it has been firm & Consistent & that it shall neither Veer for Despot or Dictator however patriotic. In truth I preferr the Esteem of Learned Virtuous and patriotic men to the shouts & Applauses of a Capricious Iliterate multitude.

I am aware that the Insidious suggestions of british Govt. Agents have rendered me suspected—that is that I am in principle a Monarchist if the b King & Oligarchs had not persecuted me. I can sincerely assure such persons that I am an Enemy to Arbitrary power in any hands & equally so to a crowned Despot or a Robertspiere who abuse it but do not deny that I consider a virtuous aristocracy subsisting on its own private property & such as that of Rome was as the most magnanimous body that ever did or can Ornament human life but I deem A house of Representatives as more necessary to public freedom & security & that my Opposition to Federalists is not for their aristocratic principles but for their hostility to american Independence and secret Alegiance to a foreign Enemy. I perceive the ablest & best statesmen America has produced & that for 6 years last past appeared in Congress have resigned their seats in disgust because they could not in honour and in Justice conform to and adopt the prejudices of a factious Constituency prejudiced by british Govt agents & demagogues which I consider a probable Indication that before the end of the present Century America will shelter herself or seek Intestine security and repose under a sistem which as the roman poet says is not to be affected by the Capricious veering of popular air[3]—such are my sentiments & Opinions whether Correct Or not I do not dissemble them.

Americans are more in the habit of Censuring Europeans for not being in principle exclusively democratic than is correct or warranted by experience or local knowledge of the british dominions—it is deciding on matters like a parisian Citizen who thinks nothing is right anywhere otherwise than it is at Paris—the fact is that European Gentn are learned liberal and patriotic—but Democracy there is Jacobinism which affords no safe and sufficient security for Life and property—property has accumulated there more than in any other Country & was acquired by the wealthier classes (Cromwells Oligarchs & queen Annes favourites excepted) by the most meritorious & progressive Industry, Manufactures and Commercial and it cannot be consigned to the discretionary protection of a crouded population & their favourites which population Irritated and inflamed by their sufferings & privations and by Demagogical Declamation would abuse its power—this is what obliges the wealthier classes to give a reluctant preferrence to that Govt which bad as it is protects them tho at an exorbitant Expence and proves the correctness of Doctor Wolcots remark on french Jacobins that they had demolished one Edifice without leaving or building up one pebble to supply its place[4]—finally the opulent classes there consider

Jacobinism or Jacobins as Conspirators against their Lives and properties—this is not mere assertion or conjecture but the Information of persons of Grade who deserted that cause & untill Inovators substitute a Just & Economic Sistem of Govt. which gives compleat security to life & property and as effectually protects the wealthier classes from the avarice & rapacity of mobs & Demagogues as the present Govt. does—they cannot succeed—but if they can do so they will have my vote and aid & I think the votes & aid of more efficient persons to supercede the Operation & functions of spurious Royalty. If they (Inovators) do not afford such Effectual security they cannot succeed & will only disturb the public peace—Injure Commerce and Industry and sacrifice an Industrious & manly populace so enthusiastically devoted to Republicanism & so easily deceived by appearances that any demagogues can drive it into hopeless Insurrection wherein Success is as probable as the Conjectures of John C Symes.[5]

I am aware it is unbecoming in a person of humble grade to abuse or asperse the british Reigning family without a Just cause & necessity for it therefore consider the following explanation of a Villianous Conspiracy by them against myself which is bottomed on falsehood prostitution & Intrigue Justifies Retaliation supported by truth. I was but 15 years of age when the Princess Marys Intrigues but which I was then as blind to as to futurity seperated my Father from his wife and got me a very severe whiping. I then erroneously attributed my Fathers severity to a fixed hatred of me and not to the secret Instructions of a british strumpet—& Concluded to leave him. I did so—came to Dublin and got into an office where after a little time I was Entrusted with the rect. and payment of money—among others—A female had frequent Orders on me for Money which I paid—from this we became acquainted—& the british strumpet mad with disappointment had her usual dose administered by which I became Infatuated with my new acquaintance and Kept her Company tho forbid it & nothing but the d⟨read?⟩ of poverty and want & a gradual decline of the Infatuation prevented us from realising the fate of Voltaires Candid and Cunnegund[6]—but our acquaintanc⟨e⟩ shortly after ceased. I believe she is now a married woman & altho she had not a Licence to sanction a previous attachment she had more Continence than many that had—about this time the princess Mary distributed £60.000 pounds of my money among her Gallants & I never heard the female I mentioned allude to her in any other way than by calling her the whore of Destruction or any other person in low life at the time but I did not then Know or enquire who the Infamous strumpet was—this disappointed Court prostitute became enraged by neglect & the public Contempt & from thenceforth became a factious enemy and that spurious royal family Created a Conspiracy to rob me & to Justify it aledged that my female acquaintance kept a house of Ill fame & that I was privy to her assignations—this is evidently as Villianous a

Conspiracy as ever was formed against any one & the story to this day goes the rounds of the newspapers to Justify the robberies of the Crown & is also repeated by every shallow hotheaded demagogue who expects that a Guillotine & a Convention will secure his fortune—to reply to Such slanders would be to give them more Importance than they deserve since it must be evident to any man of Common sense that any Company I may have blindly or Imprudently Kept when I was not 17 years of age with any person of Inferior grade can no more divest me of my rights or create a Title in the crown or Influence the operation of the laws against me any more than the cloths I wore—the marbles I played or the lessons I previously sayed at school all which is Misrepresented by spurious Royalty—the King I perceive is now in Ireland offering as he did as Regent Catholic Emancipation as a bribe to the chiefs of the roman Catholics Lord Fingal & the Plunkets[7] for their Influence with the body not to Oppose his Intended Robbery of me & the seisure of my family estates. I have Just heard that my uncle is Dead which vests in me the Legal Estate which before was in him & Shall return as soon as Convenient to Assert it in which Case the King and the Duke of York the spurious Descendant of Lord Bute will find me a firm & Inflexible Opponent. I have no Objection the King should have the Estates of his deceased brother Earl Carhampton (Luttrell)[8] but mine he shall not have—it is notorious that George the 3d was the cross born bastard of Lord Bute by a german whore so that it is no wonder an hereditary baseness of Disposition should distinguish these spurious being[s] from honourable men. The late King Knew the present King not to be his son and hated him—he Knew the Duke of York to be his son and Carressed him but altho there is more avarice & malignity in the scotchmans bastard progeny than in the Irishmans & their national traits of Character Visible any submission or reliance on either would prove fatal to your Obt. St

Edmd Kelly

RC (NN). Day of month not indicated; conjectural day assigned based on postmark: "Columbia Ten July 17." Addressed by Kelly to JM: "late presidt U States at his residence state of Virginia City of Washington," and franked. Damaged by removal of seal.

1. Sir Francis Burdett's 4 Apr. 1821 letter to the friends of parliamentary reform was published in the *Washington Gazette*, 24 May 1821.

2. For Lord Mansfield's speech, see Kelly to JM, 26 Sept. 1820, and n. 1.

3. Hor., *Odes* 3.2.19–20 (*Horace: Odes and Epodes*, Loeb Classical Library [1978 reprint], 174–75). The exact wording, "capricious veering of popular air," comes from a 1783 Edinburgh edition.

4. "Mad fools! And can we deem the French *profound*, / And pleased their infant politics embrace, / Who drag a noble Pyramid to ground, / Without one Pebble to supply its place?," John Wolcot, "The Remonstrance," in *Works of Peter Pindar* (1812 ed.), 2:457.

5. John Cleves Symmes Jr. (1780–1829), a former U.S. Army captain and veteran of the War of 1812, proposed in 1818 the idea that the earth was "hollow, and habitable within," and promoted his theory vigorously until his death (Duane A. Griffin, "Hollow and Habitable

Within: Symmes's Theory of Earth's Internal Structure and Polar Geography," *Physical Geography* 25 [2004]: 382–84).

6. The fate of Candide and Cunégonde, the lovers of Voltaire's *Candide*, was to marry out of spite.

7. The earldom of Fingall was created and given to Lucas Plunkett in 1628. Kelly referred here to Arthur James Plunkett, the eighth Earl of Fingall (Sir Egerton Brydges, *A Biographical Peerage of the Empire of Great Britain: In Which Are Memoirs and Characters of the Most Celebrated Persons of Each Family* [4 vols.; London, 1808–17], 4:40, 41).

8. Henry Lawes Luttrell, second Earl Carhampton (1743–1821), was a member of Parliament and after the death of his father, Simon Luttrell, in 1787, member of the House of Lords. He had an army career, beginning as an ensign in 1757, and rising to the rank of general in 1798.

From Mackay & Campbell

DEAR SIR FREDBG 19th July 1821

Your favour of 17th Inst. to our R. Mackay[1] was received this morning, he is at present from home, and is expected to be absent ten or fifteen days.

Enclosed you will please find blank Bills of Exchange as requested. Our last advice from New York Quotes Exchange at 9 pr Cent Premm. but we think it probable that not more than 8½ prct. could now be obtained. Your's however shall be disposed of to the best advantage. We are very Respectfully Dear sir Your Mo Obt servts.

MACKAY & CAMPBELL

RC (DLC). Cover sheet addressed by Mackay & Campbell to JM, and franked. Docketed by JM.

1. Letter not found.

From an Unidentified Correspondent

SIR BOSTON July 20th. 1821

Excuse me of taking the liberty to send you one of the papers inclosed within concerning the African Abolition of Slave Trade.[1]

RC (DLC). Addressed to JM at Washington, and franked. Docketed by JM: "Africans in Boston, Celebration by."

1. JM's copy of this broadside, entitled *Celebration of Freedom* (Boston, 1821; Shoemaker 4931), with text that begins: "Monday the Africans and descendants of Africans in this town, held their annual commemoration of the commencement of measures for the abolition of the slave trade . . ." is in the Madison Collection, Rare Book and Special Collections Division, Library of Congress.

To Mackay & Campbell

DEAR SIR July 21. 1821

I have just recd. your favor of the 19th. and inclose the Blank bills filled with a draft on Maury & Latham for $250 Stirling [*sic*]. I lose no time in sending them; because I understand there is an advantage in having bills in the market in time for the Monthly Packet from N. York. I wish as much of the proceeds to be applied to the Bank in Fredg. as will cancel the discount and reduce my debt from $1200 to $800. and the balance to be remitted by a safe oppy. With friendly respects

J. M.

Draft (DLC).

To Samuel Wyllys Pomeroy

DEAR SIR MONTPELLIER July 21. 1821

I return my thanks for the Agricultural Journal[1] for which I observe I am indebted to your politeness.

Several of the Articles have well rewarded the perusal. Those on the culture of flax are particularly interesting, being calculated to gratify curiosity at the same time that they instruct the husbandman.

I send herewith samples of flax in the several Stages of its preparation by a machine of modern invention, adopted by the Linnen Board in Ireland, & protected by a special act of Parliament. They came to my hands whilst I was in public life at Washington, accompanied by a letter from a person who wished his name to be concealed;[2] in which the machine is represented as very cheap & simple, and capable of being worked by hand, horse, or steam. It is said to be adapted to a similar preparation of hemp, which must add much to its value, hemp being produced from much greater quantity than flax from equal ground, having a stronger fibre, and exhausting much less the soil.

It is not improbable that this information may not be new to you, it being said that a person had arrived several years ago in the Northern quarter, with the knowlege of the machine & its uses; and that you may have even seen samples such as are now sent. In that case the communication I make will answer no purpose but that of confirming the respect of which I offer you assurances with my good wishes.

JAMES MADISON

RC and enclosures (NHi); draft (DLC). Addressed and franked by JM to Pomeroy at Brighton, Massachusetts. The enclosures are four flax samples, each folded in a sheet of paper and labeled in JM's hand: "No. 1. in its green state from the field and one end passed thro' the first machine"; "No. 2. worked thro' the entire machinery, except the fining & not bleached."; "No. 3. Same as No. 2. only being perfectly dried before passing thro' the machine"; and "No. 4. in a finished State, to which it can be brought in a few hours from its being pulled from the field." Minor differences between the copies have not been noted.

1. *Massachusetts Agricultural Repository and Journal* 6 (1821). Pomeroy published three essays on the cultivation of flax in this issue.

2. JM referred here to a letter from John Walsh, 10 Sept. 1815 (owned by Charles M. Storey, Boston, Mass., 1961).

From Mackay & Campbell

DEAR SIR FREDBG 23d July 1821

Your favour of the 21st enclosing a Sett of Exchange on Messrs. Maury & Latham for £250 Sterling was received this morning. Our best exertions shall be used for your interest in the disposition.

In Order to meet your views respecting the Bank debt, you'l find enclosed, a note which please have executed & returned to us by the 1st. next Month.

We forward a small Box to your address by this opportunity, which was recd. by us last week. Yours Very Respectfully

MACKAY & CAMPBELL

RC (DLC). Docketed by JM.

From Mackay & Campbell

DEAR SIR FREDERICKSBURG 30th July 1821

Your respects of the 27th.[1] with your Note for $800 received this morning—we could make it answer every purpose, but as there is plenty of time, perhaps it would be better to execute the one enclosed & get Mr. Eddins to endorse. You will perceive we have dated the Note 3d Augt. when your $1200 Note is due. Yours Very Respectfully

MACKAY & CAMPBELL

If we get the Note by 9 OClock Friday Morning it will be on time. M. & C.

RC (DLC). Docketed by JM.

1. Letter not found.

Bond by Rector and Visitors of the University of Virginia

[3 August 1821]

Know all men by these presents that we Thomas Jefferson, rector and James Breckenridge, James Madison, Joseph C. Cabell, John H. Cocke, Chapman Johnson and Robert B. Taylor, visitors of the University of Virginia, are held & firmly bound to the President & Directors of the Literary fund in the sum of 56,200 to the payment whereof well and truly to be made, we bind ourselves and our successors to the sd. President & Directors and their successors firmly by these presents, sealed with the common seal of the sd. Rector & Visitors and dated this 3d day of Aug. in the year one thousand eight hundred and twenty one.

The Condition of this obligation is such that, Whereas the President and Directors of the ⟨Literary Fund?⟩, under authority of the Act of the General Assembly of the 24th day of February last past, intituled "An act concerning the University of Virginia," have this day loaned to the Rector and Visitors of the sd. University, the sum of 29. thousand 100 Dollars, for the purpose of compleating the buildings, and making the necessary preparations for putting the said University into operation, on the conditions that the lawful interest on the sd. sum of 29,100 Dollars shall be annually paid, and the principal be redeemed according to the provisions of the sd. act, and that the annual appropriation made by law to the sd. University be legally pledged to the sd. President and Directors for the punctual payment of the annnual interest and redemption of the principal as aforesaid: Now therefore, if the sd. Rector & Visitors & their successors shall faithfully pay to the sd. President and Directors of the Literary fund and their successors annually on the   day of   [1] the lawful interest on the sd. sum of 29,100. Dollars, or on so much of the sd. sums as shall be bearing interest, until the whole of the principal shall have been paid and shall also faithfully pay the sd. principal sum of 29,100 Dollars according to the provisions of the sd. act of assembly, applying for that purpose the sums of money appropriated annually by law to the use, or for the benefit of the sd. University, or so much thereof as may be requisite, which sums of money so appropriated in each year, so far as requisite for the purpose, are hereby pledged and set apart by the sd. Rector & Visitors to be applied by the President and Directors of the Literary fund to the payment of the sd. interest & principal sum of 29,100 Dollars, borrowed as aforesaid, and to no other uses or objects until the sd. payment shall have been made, then the above obligation shall be void, otherwise shall remain in full force and virtue.

Th: Jefferson
(seal)

signed sealed and delivered in presence of

NICHS P TRIST
WILLIAM BANKHEAD

Ms (ViU: Jefferson Papers, Special Collections). In Thomas Jefferson's hand, signed by Jefferson, Nicholas Trist, and William Bankhead. Endorsed at top margin by Jefferson: "Copy of bond of Aug. 3. 21. for 29,100."; and in the bottom margin "1822. Jan. gave a bond for 30,900.D. verbatim as this except as to the sum." Damaged by removal of seal.

1. Left blank in ms.

From Thomas Gibson

RESPECTED SIR, FAUQUIER August 6th 1821

Not having the Honor of being personally acquainted with you, I must beg leave to be excused for troubling you upon a subject, that may prove highly beneficial to me. From the best information that I can collect, there is a considerable estate in England that the family of Gibsons are entitled to and probably can be obtained provided the necessary testimony can be exhibited to satisfy that this family is of that line—and presuming that Mrs Madison (your mother) (if still living) has some recollection of them, I must beg leave to request of you to make the requisite enquiry, and should she have any recollection of them, to take her deposition, authenticated in such form as you may deem sufficient to obtain the same. The property alluded to was in possession of Edmund Gibson of England; and William Gibson of Scotland Brothers to Jonathan Gibson my great Grandfather who had but one Son, (named Jonathan) who was father, to my father also named Jonathan—the said Edmund & William having died without issue.

Your compliance will singularly oblidge Dr sir Your Mo respectful & obdt Humble Servt.

THOMAS GIBSON[1]

My address
Elk Run Church
Fauquier County

RC (DLC). Docketed by JM.

1. Thomas Gibson, a cornet then captain in the Fauquier County, Virginia, militia in 1781 and 1785, respectively, was the son of Jonathan Gibson (d. 1791), one of JM's godfathers. His mother, Mary Catlett Gibson, was an aunt of JM's mother, Nelly Conway Madison. Upon his father's death, Thomas inherited the family plantation near Elk Run Church in Fauquier County (*PJM*, 1:3 and n. 2; John P. Alcock, *Fauquier Families, 1759–1799* [2 vols.; Athens, Ga., 1994–2001], 1:136, 137).

From Samuel Wyllys Pomeroy

SIR BRIGHTON 12 August 1821.

I have to acknowledge the rect of your highly valued favor of 21 Ult. with the samples of flax in the several Stages of preparation by the late invented machines. They were exhibited to the Trustees of the Massct. Agril. Society at their meeting yesterday, & afforded much gratification as nothing of the kind had been seen by any member of the board—a lively interest was excited, which resulted in a vote authorising a comme. to offer premiums for *models* of the machines; deeming it impracticable to obtain them at present, compleat, owing to the jealousy of foreign governments, and presuming that the ingenuity of our mechanics would overcome all obstacles could they but possess an accurate model.

As it is possible, Sir, that you may not have met with an elaborate report of a Comme. of the House of Commons on the subject of two flax machines invented in England—or with an accot of one contained in "Les Archives Philosophiques &c" invented in France, published in our journal for Jany. 1819, I herewith transmit that number.[1]

It appears by late accounts from England and by the French account, that boiling in an alkaline lye or immer[s]ing in sulphuric acid is necessary to finish the article after being dressed by the machines. I am inclined to think that if the flax was subjected to the operation of *Steam* for a few hours, those deleterious substances might be dispensed with, and the facility of dressing so much increased as to compensate for the extra expence—with the mills now in use in this country, it probably is the best mode of preparation—and our board are about to offer premiums for specimens of flax prepared by *Steam* the present season, & it is probable that our next Jany. Journal may contain the results.

I have packed with the journal some seed of the *Yellow Aberdeen Turnip* sent me by Mr Young[2] the Secretary to the Nova Scotia board of Agre., who recd it last year from Scotland: he states that it is a new & Superior variety for the Table, retaining its sweetness & keeping good nearly as long as the Rutabaga. I hope it may arrive in time to produce a crop the present season, should you not have been possess'd of the same kind. I remain Sir with high respect & consideration your obt &c

S W POMEROY

RC (DLC). Docketed by JM.

1. Pomeroy referred to the "Report of the Committee of the House of Commons on Petitions relating to Machinery for Manufacturing Flax, May 23d, 1817," an "English Account of Mr. Lee's Invention of a New Mode of Manufacturing Hemp and Flax, published in 1815," "On the Preparation of Flax and Hemp without Steeping," and "Same Subject

Continued, from Les Archives Philosophiques Politiques et Literaires, No. 2," in *Massachusetts Agricultural Repository and Journal* 5 (1819): 268–81.

2. John Young (1773–1837), a Scottish-born Nova Scotia merchant, published a series of letters on agriculture in the Halifax *Acadian Recorder* under the the pseudonym "Agricola" between July 1818 and the spring of 1821. The letters helped spark the creation, in 1819, of a Central Board of Agriculture, of which Young became secretary and treasurer, but the legislature failed to renew its charter in 1826. Young was elected to the Nova Scotia House of Assembly in 1824 and served as a member until his death (Francess G. Halpenny, ed., *Dictionary of Canadian Biography* [15 vols. to date; Toronto, 1966–], 7:930–34).

From Thomas Jefferson

Circular.

Dear Sir. Monticello Aug 15. 21.

In obedience to the resolution of the visitors of the university at their last session, the Proctor has been constantly employed in "ascertaining the state of accounts under contracts already made, and the expence of compleating the buildings begun and contemplated": and we have consequently suspended, according to instructions, "the entering into any contracts for the Library until we see that it may be done without interfering with the finishing of all the pavilions, hotels and dormitories begun and to be begun." The Proctor will require yet considerable time to compleat his settlements; insomuch that it is very doubtful whether there will be any thing ready for us to act on at our stated meeting in october, should that take place. But by deferring our meeting to the approach of that of the Genl Assembly, it is believed we shall be able to report to them that nearly the whole of the buildings of accomodation are finished, and the sum they will have cost; that the few remaining will be finished by the spring, and what their probable cost will be, as ascertained by experience, and further to show the balance of the funds still at our command, & how far they will be competent to the erection of the library. On this view of the unreadiness of matter for our next stated meeting, & of the prospect that a deferred one will enable us to make a clear & satisfactory report, I venture to propose the omission of our october meeting, & the special call of an occasional one on the thursday preceding the meeting of the legislature. That day is fixed on for the convenience of the gentlemen who are members of the legislature; as it brings them so far on their way to Richmond, with time to get to the 1st day of the session. Not having an opportunity of personal consultation with my colleague of the committee of advice, I pass the letters thro' his hands. If he approves the proposition he will subjoin his approbation & forward them to their several addresses; otherwise, not. If approved, it will be proper you should subscribe the enclosed notice and return it to me to be placed among our records.

I have just received an order of the Literary board for 29.100 D in part of the loan of 60.000 D lately authorised; and following the practise of the Legislature, I have thought it just and safest to have the deposit made by moieties in the Virginia & Farmer's banks. I salute you with great friendship & respect.

TH: JEFFERSON
approved JOHN H. COCKE

[Enclosure]

We the subscribers visitors of the University of Virginia being of opinion that it will be to the interest of that institution to have an occasional meeting of the visitors by special call on the thursday preceding the next meeting of the General assembly do therefore appoint that day for such meeting, and request the attendance of sd visitors accordingly. Witness our hands on the several days affixed to our respective Signatures.

TH: JEFFERSON Aug. 15. 21.
JOHN H. COCKE Aug: 20.
JAMES MADISON Aug. 29.

RC (DLC); enclosure, four copies (ViU: Jefferson Papers, Special Collections). RC in Joseph C. Cabell's hand, signed by Jefferson, with his designation "James Madison." to the left of his signature, and by John Hartwell Cocke, with his note: "Approved"; docketed by JM. The enclosure received by JM, in Cabell's hand, is signed and dated by Jefferson, Cocke, and JM.

From Edmond Kelly

SIR, COLUMBIA TENNESEE [ca. 18] Augt. 1821

Much sickness has prevented me from resuming the Subject of my last letters on the state of Spain and Ireland,[1] particularly on the necessity for abolishing the papal Inovations in Religion—on the good effects of rendering that R Catholic Religion rational edifying and salutary which unfortunately in its practical Operation & effect is Irrational demoralising pernicious & hostile to mental Improvement—recent events demonstrate that the Italian Clergy secretly influenced the neapolitan peasantry to submitt without a struggle—and it is evident had Spain been Invaded the same Influence would prove fatal to the spanish Constitution—popery is indisputably the worst Enemy to European Liberty—no wonder we find the british Govt the restorer & protector of it—if the Irish papists are refused Emancipation or admission into the british parliament it is because Cromwells Nobility & Annes party who possess the properties the papists were robbed of in Violation of the Articles of Limerick[2] dread a party of papists in parliament and perhaps in power shareing the royal patronage might claim some restitution—in fact it is the dread of restitution that Excludes them—but the Illiterate herd of Lazy Idle papists of Spain Portugal & Italy being neither Competitors in Manufacturing Industry or monopoly but on the Contrary good Customers and Consumers have the good fortune to enjoy the patronage of the british Govt. All experience proves that however Learni[n]g and reading qualify Individuals of the wealthier classes professing popery for good Republicans—it is such Improvement alone that causes a departure in them from spirit effect and operation of popery and that therefore such instances can only be Considered (if they can be deemed so) as partial exceptions to its general principle and operation—a Knowledge of the classics does not appear to me more necessary to qualify a person for coledge than a rational sistem of Religion & Education to qualify men to be good Republicans—however I am at present unequal to the subject but shall resume it as soon as my health permitts accompanied with such remarks on the state of Ireland and on the *Erroneous conduct of men whose Influence on the peasantry has converted Land lords & Tenants into Enemies—so as to Terrify & Urge the former into Vindictive & precautionary severity—and thereby reduce the later to privation and its attendant Miseries.* I am no Misantrophist—no party man—no Enemy to either class or I would not disclose such errors—in truth the Innocent and the Ignorant are the most Injured & the Victims to these Errors—errors as repugnant to humanity as to good policy and public good—it is evident those who caused such Errors not being Intentionally Enemies to their Country were destitute of Judgment rationality & Experience & if the disclosure of them could only produce future Amendment & Conscientious reparation all parties would be mutually benefited by a measure that would promote the public good & welfare of all classes.

In one hour after I threw my last letter into the post office I recollected a blunder in it Vizt. that the text—the Ox Knoweth his owner & the Ass his Masters crib &ca. was prefixed to one of Sternes Sermons[3] I read 20 years ago—reproving us for censuring faults in others while we have greater faults ourselves which we do not correct but indulge—supposing it however to be what I heard a Gentn who resided in France call a double Entendre—I Cannot perceive How any faults of mine could warrant sanction or Justify the british King—the Duke of York and the princess Mary (who is sayed to be occasionally with Mrs. Clarke the Dukes Mistress), and their satelite John Bull in their attempts to robb me. If any faults or weaknesses of mine can Justify or sanction their Interference in my affairs or their Intrigues to abuse me out of my property I own my sense of Justice is very erroneous—but if not the reproof is as to me the effect of prejudice—& how any such prejudice could Influence the honourable Bart not to treat with abhorrence british court prostitute satelite Intrigues to rob any one obnoxious to the british court & Cromwells Oligarchs is what I am surprised at—perhaps it was but the result of some momentary Irritation—he ought to have reflected that what is at this day my fate might at no remote period be the fate of some of his own descendants if obnoxious to the Crown & the Oligarchs—and that a power once recognised & vested in the Crown & the Oligarchs to subject Imprudent but obnoxious Individuals to a party Inquisition (which is but a conspiracy to take property by fraud) & composed of the most abandoned unprincipled dependants of party appointed soley to abuse asperse and Intimidate with intent to disqualify or operate as a disqualification is a usurpation no good patriot ought to sanction. If such a power is once Conceded to & recognised in the Crown I am not the only person that will be pelted and abused out of his property—such a power acqu[i]esed in would quickly enrich the reigning family & the favourites—nor would there be in respect to wresting property from the subject and vesting it in the Crown any difference between such an Inquisition & that of Spain which was dissolved—such an Inquisition once recognised would enrich its nefarious principals at the expence of the patriotic part of the Community whom it would Impoverish and ruin.

What induced me at all to notice the honourable Baronets letter[4] was a boast made by John Bull when I ridiculed his Vapouring about patriotism & representative Govt. Vizt. that by a referrence to Irish democratic patriots the high Esteem Confidence and patronage he enjoyed would appear—& the only thing like a response I could perceive was the honourable Barts letter which was not I admitt very flattering or Complimentary & disappointed the Bulls Vanity. I am perswaded the Irish Jacobins are persons Individually or collectively the Bart is unconnected with whose principles Except as to their being antimonarchical he is a stranger to—and whose sistem of Govt if disclosed would be condemned by the most Zealous advocates for reform in Westminster as affording no adequate protection to life and property—and as the Barts Conduct has hitherto been not only Very respectable but dignified and patriotic it is to be wished he may not be Influenced by Injury or Irritation to lend his name or sanction to men whose principles & designs he is a total stranger to at lest untill he is satisfied they are not unjust. On this principle he declined to support Mr Cobbett & perhaps a little reflection will suggest a similar Consistency. Jacobinism is not the legitimate of[f]spring of any Just well regulated & rational sistem of Republicanism antient or modern—it resembles implacable wicked & sanguinary slaves or Helots murdering the paternal proprietors of the soil & possessing themselves of the properties of the Victims Extirpated much more than it does good Govt of any denomn. Robertspiere and Christophe were Identified in their Carreer & what good or patriotic man would support either. I alude not to Louis the 16. & the French

Nobility who followed him to England Mr Thos Paines Escape & the decapitation of all the patriotic & Opulent Characters of France is a melancholy proof that Jacobinism is but a Conspiracy against life and property. I mention these Circumstances because I expect the Conspiracy Organised in France under the sanction & patronage of the Duke of York and the Oligarchs to drive the French into Insurrection for the purpose of Enslaving France and causing it to be partitioned by the holy aliance—will bring the british Army to France & it is only in the absence of the british Army that the King & the Oligarch⟨s⟩ can be coerced into concessions of parliamentary reform and a reduction of the Civil List or should Circumstances render it necessary a radical Change of Govt. but not indeed by substituting Jacobinism—the opulent reflecting & respectable part of the british people could not consent to the last form of Govt with safety & security—that such a change is not possible is what I believe but that if proposed such proposition would be rejected I have no doubt of could an opportunity to make it Occurr—these I think are the reflections that should engage the thoughts of the political leader of the London & Westminster Citizens but to patronise this or that faction to abuse the Members of the house of Commons because they did not what they could not do effect a reform which the King & the house of Lords can withhold or not is both illiberal Impolitic & unjust—the Members of the House of Coms appear to me to have acted magnanimously—to have sacrificed personal obligations to the public interest however unavailingly the motives were so meritorious that I Cannot avoid Considering the Baronets letter Impolitic illiberal and unjust. I am respectfully yr obt H Servant

EDMD KELLY

RC (NN). Day of month not indicated; conjectural day assigned based on the postmark "Columbia. Ten. Augst. 18." Addressed by Kelly to JM "at his residence state of Virginia City of Washington." A second postmark reads: "Wash City Sep 6."

1. Kelly to JM, ca. 30 June (second letter) and ca. 17 July 1821.

2. The Treaty of Limerick, negotiated in 1691 and ratified in 1692, ended the war between the Jacobites and the supporters of William and Mary, king and queen of England. The civil articles of that treaty ensured property rights and the exercise of the Roman Catholic faith, under terms Catholics had enjoyed during the reign of Charles II, to Jacobites who swore a loyalty oath to the English crown and chose to remain in Ireland. The articles were heavily abridged by the penal laws passed by the Irish parliament soon thereafter (Childs, *Williamite Wars in Ireland*, 385–87).

3. "The ox knoweth his owner, and the ass his master's crib: *but* Israel doth not know, my people doth not consider," Isa. 1:3 (AV). Kelly referred here to Laurence Sterne's Sermon XIV on "Self-Examination" (Sterne, *Works of Laurence Sterne* [10 vols.; 1783 ed.], 6:269–84).

4. The reference here is to Sir Francis Burdett, a staunch advocate of parliamentary reform. For Burdett's letter to the friends of parliamentary reform, see Kelly to JM, ca. 17 July 1821, and n. 1.

From Joseph Gales Jr.

Honored Sir: Washington, Augt. 20, 1821.

The enclosed is cut out from the New York Commercial Advertiser received this day, and is enclosed to you only because it is supposed it may be interesting to you to see it.[1] If the whole work be of the same texture, it must be of little value, & less authority. With the highest respect Your faithful Servt

Jo: Gales Jr

RC (DLC). Docketed by JM.

1. The enclosure was an extract of Robert Yates's convention notes of a JM speech and an announcement of the published book, New York *Commercial Advertiser*, 18 Aug. 1821. The newspaper clipping is in series 7, box 2, of the Madison Papers, Library of Congress.

From Thomas John Gantt

Dear Sir, Charleston 23rd. August 1821

By a resolve of the 76 Association, made in consequence of their high regard for your republican principles, and gratitude for the services you have rendered the nation I send you a copy of Mr. Elliotts oration, delivered before that Society on the last 4th. of July.[1] I also send you a copy of Mr. Ramsays delivered the year previous.[2] I am aware that you should have recd. the latter long since, and can only say (in excuse for its not being sent) that I had not at that time the honor of being on the committee. I am with sentiments of great respect your Huml. Servt.

Thomas John Gantt[3]
Chairman comee. arrangets.
76. Association

RC (DLC). Docketed by JM.

1. Thomas Odingsell Elliott, *An Oration, Delivered in St. Philip's Church, Charleston, South-Carolina, on the Fourth of July, 1821; Before the '76 Association* (Charleston, 1821; Shoemaker 5244).

2. David Ramsay, *An Address Delivered on the Fourth of July, 1820, by Appointment of the '76 Association, and Published at Their Request* (Charleston, 1820; Shoemaker 2937). JM's copy is in the Madison Collection, Special Collections, University of Virginia Library.

3. Thomas John Gantt (b. 1795) was the son of Richard Gantt, who had been clerk of the South Carolina General Assembly, 1804–15, and was associate judge of the Court of General Sessions and Common Pleas, 1815–41 (Robert deTreville Lawrence, ed., "Family Bibles of Lawrence Brothers of Charleston," *South Carolina Historical Magazine* 53 [1952]: 79; Edgar et al., *Biographical Directory of the South Carolina House of Representatives*, 4:222–23).

To Joseph Gales Jr.

Dear Sir Montpr. Aug. 26. 1821

I thank you for your friendly letter of the 20th. enclosing an extract from notes by Judge Yates, of debates in the Convention of 1787, as published in a N.Y. paper.* The letter did not come to hand till yesterday.

If the extract be a fair sample, the work about to be published will not have the value claimed for it. Who can believe that so palpable a mistatement was made on the floor of the Convention, as that the several States were political Societies, *varying* from the *lowest* Corporation to the highest Sovereign; or that the States had vested *all* the essential rights of sovereignty in the Old Congress? This intrinsic evidence alone ought to satisfy every candid reader of the extreme incorrectness of the passage in question. As to the remark that the States ought to be under the controul of the Genl. Govt. at least as much as they formerly were under the King & B. Parliament, it amounts as it stands when taken in its presumable meaning, to nothing more than what actually makes a part of the Constitution; the powers of Congs. being much greater, especially on the great points of taxation & trade than the B. Legislature were ever permitted to exercise.

Whatever may have been the personal worth of the 2 delegates from whom the materials in this case were derived, it cannot be unknown that they represented the strong prejudices in N.Y. agst. the object of the Convention which was among other things to take from that State the important power over its commerce to which it was peculiarly attached, and that they manifested, untill they withdrew from the Convention, the strongest feelings of dissatisfaction agst. the contemplated change in the federal system and as may be supposed, agst. those most active in promoting it. Besides misapprehensions of the ear therefore, the attention of the notetaker wd. naturally be warped, as far at least as an upright mind could be warped, to an unfavorable understanding of what was said in opposition to the prejudices felt.

I have thought it not improper due to the kind motives of your communication to say thus much; but, I do it in the well founded confidence, that your delicacy will be a safeguard agst. my being introduced into the Newspapers. Were there no other objection to it, there would be an insuperable one in the alternative of following up the task, or acquiescing in like errors as they may come before the public. With esteem & friendly respects

J.M.

Draft (DLC).

* Commercial Advertizer Aug: 18. 1821

From John Drayton

Sir SOUTH CAROLINA CHARLESTON September 3d: 1821.

I have the honor to present you, Memoirs of the American Revolution, lately written and published by me here:[1] hoping they may bring to your notice, some events, which have not been publickly known of a Revolution, in which you bore so honorable a part.

Hoping that you may live many years, to enjoy the honors you have received, and the good wishes of your fellow Citizens, I am Sir With gratefull respect and consideration Yr: most ob Sert.

JOHN DRAYTON[2]

RC (DLC). Docketed by JM.

1. John Drayton, *Memoirs of the American Revolution, from Its Commencement to the Year 1776, Inclusive; As Relating to the State of South-Carolina* (Charleston, 1821; Shoemaker 5206).

2. John Drayton (1776–1822) of Drayton Hall, near Charleston, South Carolina, was a state politician and writer who served as governor, 1800–1802 and 1808–10. JM appointed Drayton judge of the U.S. court for the district of South Carolina in 1812, and he served in that position until his death (Sobel and Raimo, *Biographical Directory of the Governors*, 4:1390–91; John Drayton to JM, 21 May 1812, *PJM-PS*, 4:406, 407 n. 1).

From Thomas Ritchie

DEAR SIR, RICHMOND, Sepr. 8, 1821.

I know not whether I can take the liberty of writing you on the subject of this letter; but I have had so many proofs of your goodness towards me, that I am tempted to address you. Whatever be your reply, I pledge myself not to abuse your confidence. If you wish me not to speak of it, I pledge myself not to do so.

I have long understood—and within the last 12 months from a mutual friend—that you have a design to give to the world a Sketch of the Proceeding of the Federal Convention. I know not whether you have abandoned this design, or whether and when you mean to execute it. But the appearance of the Albany Volume[1] has brought it to my Recollection, and suggests the idea, that perhaps it may hasten the publication of your Book.

Should this be the case, should you have made no other arrangements for the printing of the Volume, will you excuse me for asking whether it is not possible for me to obtain the printing of it? I will spare no pains to bring it out in a manner worthy of its great importance. I have communicated the contents of this letter to no one. I ought to add on my own account, that my own convenience would prefer the commencement of the Book not before the next spring. With the (———) & sentiment of respect, I am Sir, Your friend & obt. servant.

Ths. Ritchie

Printed copy (Charles H. Ambler, ed., "Unpublished Letters of Thomas Ritchie," *John P. Branch Historical Papers of Randolph-Macon College* 3 [1911]: 201–2).

1. For Robert Yates's notes on the Constitutional Convention, see Joseph Gales Jr. to JM, 20 Aug. 1821, and n. 1.

From Albert Picket and Others

Sir, Baltimore, M.d. Sept. 10, 1821

We address you on a subject of vital importance; we mean the subject of Female education, which has been, hitherto, much neglected, & yet, seems not to have received that attention which it deserves. It has not been conducted on a scale, in our opinion, commensurate to its importance. If it be worthy of national concern, to educate young men well, in all that pertains to their morals & intellect, it is no less necessary to educate females in an equally solid, if not splendid degree.

Under the impression, that the interests of Female Education should, and can, be placed on a more permanent basis, we intend to apply at the next session of the Legislature of Maryland, for means to erect a Female College, to be conducted on an extensive scale. The importance of such an Institution, properly managed, is seen and felt; & would, perhaps, be a means of bringing into existence, more of a similar nature, in the various states.

Having been engaged nearly 25 years in the instruction of Females, & having formed our opinion of the advantages of such an establishment, we solicit your attention to the following—

Your opinion of such an Institution

—— ——— of the course of Instruction to be adopted

An Answer as soon as convenient, would be very thankfully received. With the highest sentiments of regard, We remain Yrs

Albert Picket, Senr.[1]
John W. Picket,
Albert Picket, Jr.

RC (DLC). Docketed by JM.

1. Albert Picket Sr. (1771–1850), a New York City schoolteacher, conducted the Manhattan School for Girls, 1804–20, and wrote, sometimes in partnership with his son John W. Picket, a number of English-language primers, including the *Union Spelling Book.* Picket also published a semimonthly journal for teachers, the *Academician*, from 1818 to 1820. In

1826 Picket moved to Cincinnati, where he opened a school for girls. In addition to teaching and publishing, Picket organized teacher associations in both New York and Ohio (H. G. Good, "Albert Picket, Educational Journalist and Organizer," *Peabody Journal of Education* 19 [1942]: 318–22).

To Thomas Ritchie

(CONFIDENTIAL)

DEAR SIR MONTPELR. Sepr 15 1821

I have recd. yours of the 8th. instant on the subject of the proceedings of the convention of 1787.

It[1] is true as the public has been led to understand, that I possess materials for a pretty ample view of what passed in that Assembly. It is true also that it has not been my intention that they should for ever remain under the veil of secrecy. Of the time when it might be not improper for them to see the light, I had formed no particular determination. In general it had appeared to me that it might be best to let the work be a posthumous one, or at least that its publication should be delayed till the Constitution should be well settled by practice, & till a knowlege of the controversial part of the proceedings of its framers could be turned to no improper account. Delicacy also seemed to require some respect to the rule by which the Convention "prohibited a promulgation without leave of what was spoken in it";[2] so long as the policy of that rule could be regarded as in any degree unexpired. As a guide in expounding and applying the provisions of the Constitution, the debates and incidental decisions of the Convention can have no authoritative character. However desirable it be that they should be preserved as a gratification to the laudable curiosity felt by every people to trace the origin and progress of their political Institutions, & as a source perhaps of some lights on the Science of Govt. the legitimate meaning of the Instrument must be derived from the text itself; or if a key is to be sought elsewhere, it must be not in the opinions or intentions of the Body which planned & proposed the Constitution, but in the sense attached to it by the people in their respective State Conventions where it recd. all the authority which it possesses.

Such being the course of my reflections I have suffered a concurrence & continuance of particular inconveniences for the time past, to prevent me from giving to my notes the fair & full preparation due to the subject of them. Of late, being aware of the growing hazards of postponements, I have taken the incipient steps for executing the task; and the expediency of not risking an ultimate failure is suggested by the Albany publication from the notes of a N. York member of the Convention. I have not seen more of the volume than has been extracted into the newspapers, but it may be inferred from these samples, that it is not only a very mutilated but a very erroneous edition of the matter to which it relates. There must be an entire omission also of the proceedings of the latter period of the Session from which Mr. Yates & Mr. Lansing withdrew in the temper manifested by their report to their Constituents:[3] the period during which the variant & variable opinions, converged & centered in the modifications seen in the final act of the Body.

It is my purpose now to devote a portion of my time to an exact digest of the voluminous materials in my hands. How long a time it will require, under the interruptions & avocations which are probable I can not easily conjecture. Not a little will be necessary for the mere labour of making fair transcripts. By the time I get the whole into a due form for preservation I shall be better able to decide on the question of publication.[4] As to the particular place or press, shd. this be the result, I have not as must be presumed, turned a thought to either: nor can I say more now than that your letter will be kept in recollection, & that should any other arrangement prevail over its object, it will not proceed from any want of confidence esteem or friendly dispositions; of all which I tender you sincere assurances.

Draft (DLC); extract (Ct). Extract (2 pp.; in an unidentified hand, except for JM's date and note "Confidential" at top), copied at JM's direction and enclosed in JM to John G. Jackson, 28 Dec. 1821.

1. The extract begins with this sentence.

2. Among the rules adopted in the Federal Convention on 29 May 1787 was "that nothing spoken in the House be printed, or otherwise published or communicated without leave" (Madison, *Notes of Debates in the Federal Convention*, 28).

3. "Letter from the Hon. Robert Yates and the Hon. John Lansing, Jun., Esquires, to the Governor of New York; Containing Their Reasons for Not Subscribing to the Federal Constitution," Jonathan Elliot, ed., *The Debates in the Several State Conventions, on the Adoption of the Federal Constitution* . . . , 2d ed. [4 vols.; Washington, 1836], 1:480–82). For a discussion of this letter, see Pauline Maier, *Ratification: The People Debate the Constitution, 1787–1788* (New York, 2010), 91–92.

4. The extract ends here.

From Thomas Jefferson

Dear Sir Monticello Sep. 16. 21.

I have no doubt you have occasionally been led to reflect on the character of the duty imposed by Congress on the importation of books. Some few years ago, when the tariff was before Congress, I engaged some of our members of Congress to endeavor to get the duty repealed, and wrote on the subject to some other acquaintances in Congress, and pressingly to the

Secretary of the treasury.[1] The effort was made by some members with zeal and earnestness, but it failed. The Northern colleges are now proposing to make a combined effort for that purpose, as you will see by the inclosed extract of a letter from mr. Ticknor,[2] asking the cooperation of the Southern and Western institutions, & of our university particularly. Mr. Ticknor goes so ably into all the considerations justifying this step, that nothing need be added here, & especially to you: and we have only to answer his questions, Whether we think with them on the subject of the tax? What should be the extent of the relaxation sollicited? What mode of proceeding we think best? And whether we will cooperate in our visitatorial character? I must earnestly request your thoughts on these questions, fearful of answering them unadvisedly, and on my own opinions alone.

I think that another measure, auxiliary to that of petitioning might be employed with great effect. That is for the several institutions, in their corporate capacities, to address letters to their representatives in both houses of Congress, recommending the proposition to their advocation. Such a recommendation would certainly be respected, and might excite to activity those who might otherwise be indifferent and inactive. And in this way a great vote, perhaps a majority might be obtained. There is a consideration going to the injustice of the tax which might be added to those noticed by mr. Ticknor. Books constitute capital. A library book lasts as long as a house, for hundreds of years. It is not then an article of mere consumption, but fairly of capital, and often in the case of professional men, setting out in life, it is their only capital. Now there is no other form of capital which is first taxed 18. per cent on the gross, and the proprietor then left to pay the same taxes in detail with others whose capital has paid no tax on the gross. Nor is there a description of men less proper to be singled out for extra-taxation. Mr. Ticknor, you observe asks a prompt answer; and I must ask it from you for the additional reason that within about a week I set out for Bedford to remain there till the approach of winter. Be so good as to return me also the inclosed extract and to be assured of my constant & affectionate friendship.

TH: JEFFERSON

RC (DLC); FC (DLC: Jefferson Papers).

1. Letters not found. Jefferson did write Treasury secretary Alexander James Dallas on 26 Feb. 1816 on the subject of the impending tariff law, but it was to suggest changes to the duties on wine. On 10 Nov. 1818 Jefferson wrote a similar letter to then Treasury secretary William Harris Crawford (DLC: Jefferson Papers).

2. The enclosed extract has not been found, but it was surely a copy of George Ticknor to Jefferson, 1 Sept. 1821 (4 pp.; DLC: Jefferson Papers), which follows the full letter in the collection.

From James Leander Cathcart

Venerable, and respected Sir Washington Septr. 18th. 1821

After a lapse of more than five years,[1] permit me most respectfully to enquire, how do you enjoy your health, and to hope that it may long be preserved in a state as perfect as I have ever wish'd it to be in. Vicissitude, my good Sir, marks all human events, and how many of them have I experienced since I first had the honour of your personal acquaintance in 1796 then just return'd from a cruel state of captivity of eleven years continuance, in which I arrived at the highest station a Christian could attain, which enabled me to render essential service to my country, in laying the basis of our first treaty with Algiers,[2] at the risk of my life, and on very favorable terms, considering that at that period we had more than one hundred of our fellow citizens in Chains, and not one Vessel of War afloat to protect our Commerce, and that Portugal at the same time offered, through the mediation of Spain, assisted by Great Britain, a larger sum than was promised by the United States for Peace, which by my influence and Agency was rejected altho' that power had a Squadron station'd at Gibralter sufficient to confine the whole Navy of Algiers in their Ports, and it is well known to Capt: Richard OBrien, who is the only survivor of all those who were in any way connected with our first negotiations with that Regency; that I was offered by those Powers a gratuity, and employment which would have render'd me independant for life, if I would use my influence with the Dey and Ministry, so as to effect a peace for Portugal on the same terms that I procured it for the United States, which before our treaty was sign'd I rejected with disdain. It is likewise established by documents on file in the Dept. of State, in addition to the preceeding that I Procured a Truce with Tunis, for eight months by my own personal influence, without instructions, and without putting the United States to any expense whatever—that my life was for many months in jeopardy in consequence of my exertions to repress the Dey's impatience under the unavoidable delays which took place in fulfilling the stipulations of the Treaty after it was enter'd into, and, that to prevent a rupture, which besides the capture of our Vessels, and the enslaving of our fellow Citizens, would have involved in its consequences, the loss of all the presents which had already been made to that regency to a very considerable amount. I purchased a Polacre at Algiers man'd her with Moors, and Navigated her at my own expense, with dispatches to Alicant, Lisbon & Philada., & a letter from the Dey to Gen: Washington, then President of the United States, which ensured a further respite of nine Months, and enabled the United States to comply with their agreement & preserved the Peace of the Nation, and let it be remember'd that services render'd in 1794, 5, & 6 were of importance in proportion to our total want of means to repel the insult & indignity offer'd to us by the States of Barbary, and ought not to be forgotten in 1821, when we have a fleet of sufficient force to annihilate the whole Naval force of the Ottoman Empire.

My conduct while one of the Commissioners to effect an alteration in our Treaty with Tunis, and the arrangements which I made with the Bashaw of Tripoli without instructions in 1799 was highly approved, and was of much importance, for, in lieu of a vessel of War of 14 Guns & a cargo of Maritime stores, worth at least 60,000$ besides the risk of taking them out during the disturbance with France, which had been promised as the price of Peace, and which I was authorised by my instructions to assure the Bashaw, should be sent out as soon as possible. Notwithstanding his great impatience, two years having elapsed since our treaty was concluded with him, I prevaild upon him to receive 18,000$ in cash and Bills, and recd. his receipt under the Seal of the Regency in full of all demands from the United States forever, and altho' this perfidious Chief in little more than two years afterwards declared War against us—I temporized with him a sufficient length of time, to alarm our Commerce, and, a thing unprecedented in the Annals of Barbary, not one of our Vessels was captured by his Cruisers, altho' the Mediterranean was crowded with them, but on the contrary his Admiral & Vice Admiral,* were blockaded by our Squadron in the Bay of Gibralter, and had Com: Dale arrived only four days sooner he would have captured the whole of the Tripolitan squadron.

The appointments which I received afterwards, only subjected me to trouble, vexation and expense. The price of my acceptance at Tunis[3] was a promise, that I would use my influence with the Government, to present the Bashaw of Tunis with the Frigate Adams, or another of equal force: this I peremptorily refused to do, & destroy'd his expectations of ever receiving a Frigate from us. Had I temporized in order to promote my own interests, a promise to recommend the measure at some future period, would have been construed by the Bashaw into a promise of the Frigate, and would have subjected me to the merited censure of my own government; to which I preferred the enmity of the Bashaw, great personal inconvenience and expense, and the ruin of all my prospects.

It was besides known, that before I left the United States, that I had recommended to our Government to prohibit their Consuls in the Barbary States from evry description of Commerce, and that I had acted upon that principle, when the Bashaw of Tripoli offer'd, indeed requested me to take the choice of fourteen Swedish Prizes, or all of them, which were then in

* The Franklin the only Vessel captured during the War, was taken many Months after the arrival of our Squadron.

his Port, on credit, and very advantageous terms, which I politely declined, and that during the whole time I was Consul in Barbary, I kept myself independent of the Jews and their Colleagues by having no commercial dealings with them whatever: this produced a coalition between the Jew Brokers, in the three Barbary States, and those concern'd with them in trade, who were dependent on them for loans, & who represented me as a Person inimical to the interests of those States, which was certainly true, so far as they operated against our own, & prevented me from being received, because they knew that I would neither trade with them, nor employ them to transact the business of the United States, which I was competent to transact myself, without paying them heavy Brokerage, for their imaginary influence, which would only subject me to their impositions. A proof of this was evinced, by the release of the Brig Catharine of New-York, which was brought into Tripoli with a Cargo worth 50.000$ which I procured without putting the United States to any expense. A reference to the accounts of our Consuls at Algiers who were always dependent on the Jews, will prove that hardly any Vessel that was sent in by the cruizers of that Regency, was ever released without a considerable expense: indeed my accounts speak a very plain language; their whole amount from 1797 to 1805 including my compensation and ev'ry other expense does not amount to the value, of the Vessel of War, and cargo of Maratime and Military stores, which I was authorised to promise to that Regency by my instructions, or rather to confirm the promise already made when Peace was concluded—to which may be added the embecility of our commanding Officer, for which he was dismissed the Service immediately after his return to the U States.[4]

These Sir are the true causes of my returning home in 1805, in much worse circumstances than when I went out, while others who neither possessd the Knowledge of the manners, customs or language of the country, or had the same opportunity that I had, return'd home in independent circumstances, and altho' I do not assert that they were enriched by the spoils of their Country, I do not hesitate to say without fear of contradiction, that the privileges they enjoy'd could not be obtaind by any Consul, without sacrificing the interests and in Some instances the honor of the Nation they represented. My next tour of duty was to Madeira for more than 8 years,[5] during which period it was found necessary to resort to restrictive Measures, and War, which destroyed all my prospects of a commercial nature, and I suffered severely. Except the duties of the Consulate and the procuring flags of truce for four Cartels, in which I restored a great number of my fellow citizens to their country, and the strong language I was frequently obliged to make use of, to induce the Governor of Madeira, to insist that the neutrality of the Port should not be violated by

British Vessels of War, which in most instances was attended with success, I had it not in my power to be of any great Service, and I returnd to the United States to make some Commercial arrangements some Months after the Peace in 1815. On my arrival I found, that you had been so kind, before your departure from the seat of Government during the recess as to order a Commission to be made out for me as Consul at Cadiz.[6] As this was unsolicited on my part, and evidently given me as a reward for former services, it was too flattering a mark of approbation for me to refuse accepting, tho' the State of Commerce was such as not to authorize very flattering expectations. I therefore left a certainty, of small importance indeed, for an uncertainty, which might, or might not ameliorate my situation. I went to Cadiz in the Winter, without my family, and took possession of the Consulate, return'd in the same season, & in the Spring took my family to Spain, where we remain'd until the Summer of 1817, when I was obliged to return home to prevent myself from being involved in debt, as the trade between the U. States and Cadiz was so inconsiderable and had so many competitors, that it did not furnish means sufficient to pay house rent, much less to maintain a large family, and to pay the impositions of the Officers of the Spanish Government, levied annually under the names of presents without the payment of which, it was impossible to transact business in any of the public offices, and we would be subjected daily to the most vexatious acts of injustice! Thus what was intended as a reward for my services, only precipitated my ruin, and by circumstances which were not under the control of any human being. Four years have since elapsed, during which, except for some months in which I was employed in an Agency in Louisiana and the Territory, now State of Alabama, exposed a great part of the time to the inclemency of the weather in an open boat in the Gulf of Mexico, the Lakes, Mississippi—Tombeckbee & Alabama rivers. I have been soliciting employ from Government without success. The Money which I received from Congress in 1820, arrears of old accounts, is all expended in paying debts contracted for the maintenance and education of my family before I received it, & I am now in the fifty fifth year of my age, after so many years faithful service, in difficult, responsible, expensive and unprofitable situations, in which my conduct has met the approbation of evry successive administration of our Government since it commenced: reduced to indigence, afflicted with Rheumatism which renders great bodily exertion impossible, and with a family of ten children to Maintain & to educate, the eldest of six of whom is only fourteen years, and the youngest fourteen Months old, whose chief dependence is on the precarious hire of a Carriage and horses for Support.

Until 1818 I had not the most distant idea that it was necessary for a Person who had been so long in service as I have, to solicit recommendations from any one, but my friends inform'd me that it was customary & procured for me those of which the enclosed are Copies,[7] and are from influential characters.

The appointment then solicited has not been made, others which I have applied for, have been given to more fortunate candidates, and I find myself neglected and my services and recommendations forgotten, while the very circumstance of having been employed abroad for so many years, renders me less capable to provide for my family than those who have been stationary, and have taken advantage of circumstances, & made connexions either Political or Commercial which have ensured them permanent employ. Under these Mortifying and distressing circumstances, Knowing the goodness of your heart, I have ventured most respectfully to solicit your Kind aid and Patronage. A letter of recommmendation from you my good Sir, would have more weight, than all I have or may be able to procure, and would induce the President to take my situation into consideration, and to grant my request, but should any insurmountable impediment prevent the success of my application in so direct a manner, may I flatter myself that you will have the goodness to express your opinion (either to me, or in any other way most eligible to you) of my former services & how far you think they merit; and give me a claim to future employment in Common with my fellow Citizens.

I am very sensible both of the nature and Magnitude of the request, and fear that I may be accused of presuming too much on your Philanthropy in making it, but when I look around me, & see my little Children in danger of being in want of food, and what is worse, education, for I would sooner attend them to their graves than see them grow up in ignorance, a secret monitor emboldens me to make the request, and induces me to believe, that when you on reflection, perceive that a few lines from you, will raise the drooping Spirits, and form the fortunes of a large family, and their descendants, that strong must be the reasons indeed which will induce you to withold them.

I have conversed with many of the Senators who have expressed some surprise that amongst the many appointments which have been made in the last four years that I have not been able to procure a situation: they would recommend me themselves, but say, as it is their duty to confirm, or reject, it would have the appearance of interfereing with the executive authority, and several of them have assured me, that any appointment which the President would confer on me, would be confirm'd by the Senate, and I believe unanimously.

My necessities are of such a nature that I would accept of any appointment either at home or abroad which would furnish me with the means to educate my children. To this (to me) all important point, all my energies are directed, to sacrifice my own ease and Comfort to their benefit is a duty to which I would submit most cheerfully, but as I never intend to remove my family from the U States again, having already expended a small fortune in passages, and the loss on sales of Furniture, I would certainly prefer a situation of less importance, at home, to any abroad which would be offer'd me. Yet I would gladly have accepted the appointment to Buenos Ayres which was conferred on a person, who had not a large family born in Public service in Barbary, Italy, Portugal, Spain, and the United States, to support as I have, whose services have not been so important as mine, and with whose talents, and Knowledge of the Spanish language I have the ambition to think, mine (poor as they may be supposed to be) might have been held in competition.

Should I be so fortunate as to succeed in this my appeal to your Philanthropy, Gratitude and the prayers of a large family is the only tribute we have to offer, which with the consciousness of having done a gen'rous act, I am persuaded is to a noble mind, the most acceptable, and inspires feelings the most enviable.

Should disappointment and misfortune still be our portion, I respectfully request you not to lessen the personal esteem I have experienced on many occasions, nor the good opinion you formerly entertaind of my conduct and ability, for I am not conscious to have merited it, but to attribute my presumption to the great anxiety I feel for the welfare of an almost helpless family, who are generally esteem'd amiable, and whatever may be their fate, you may be assured that as they ever have, they will still continue to implore the Omnipotent ruler of the Universe to prolong your valuable life, & to bless you with temporal and Eternal happiness. With the highest respect and veneration, and with the most cordial Esteem permit me the honor to subscribe myself, Good and Respected Sir, Your often obliged, & Most devoted & Obt. Servt.

James Leander Cathcart

+The direction was omited in it's proper place by inadvertency.

P.S. Before my sons had finished the copies, I was hond. with a letter from the venerable Mr. Jefferson a copy of which is herewith submited.[8] This letter emboldens me to hope that you will grant my request, either in the same way, or in any other which you may think proper, which I hope will have sufficient weight with the President to induce him to compare my claims on the public for employment, with the pretensions of others, & will ultimately insure the success of my application. Mrs. Cathcart has been twenty five days confined with the billious fever, she is to day a little better, but still very low, hearing that I was writing to you, she desires me with her daughters, to request you to make their respects acceptable to Mrs. Madison, and to assure her of the continuance of their affectionate esteem.

RC and enclosures (DLC). RC docketed by JM. For enclosures, see nn. 7–8.

1. Cathcart had last written JM on 22 Mar. 1816 (DNA: RG 59, ML; 1 p.) as a prelude to a visit to the president.

2. For the 1795 U.S. treaty with Algiers, which ransomed American captives, authorized a U.S. consul, and guaranteed U.S. ships freedom from capture by Algerine corsairs in exchange for an annual tribute, see William Spencer, *Algiers in the Age of the Corsairs* (Norman, Okla., 1976), 136–37.

3. For JM's letter informing Cathcart of his appointment as U.S. consul at Tunis, see JM to Cathcart, 9 Apr. 1803, *PJM-SS*, 4:494–95. The bey of Tunis refused to accept Cathcart, ibid., 496 n. 3.

4. For Cathcart's opinion of Commodore Richard V. Morris, see Cathcart to JM, 5 May 1803, ibid., 575–76. For Morris's 14 May 1804 dismissal, see Callahan, *List of Officers of the Navy*, 393.

5. Thomas Jefferson appointed Cathcart U.S. consul at Madeira on 23 Dec. 1806. The Senate concurred six days later (*Senate Exec. Proceedings*, 2:46).

6. JM made a recess appointment of Cathcart to be U.S. consul at Cádiz; he later nominated Cathcart for that office on 8 Jan. 1816. The Senate approved the nomination the next day (ibid., 3:20, 21).

7. Cathcart enclosed copies (filed after Anthony Cazenove to JM, 28 July 1818) of the following letters of recommendation in support of his application for an appointment as naval purser: Isaac Chauncey to Benjamin W. Crowninshield, 20 July 1818 (1 p.), and an undated memoir (3 pp.), signed by William Jones and forty naval officers and merchants of Philadelphia and Baltimore. Also enclosed (filed after William Plumer to JM, 8 June 1819) was John Rodgers to Cathcart, 9 June and 6 Aug. 1819 (each 1 p.), thanking Cathcart on behalf of the Navy commissioners for the "valuable information" contained in a journal and summary he had submitted to them; and an extract from Secretary of State John Quincy Adams's report to Congress of 14 Dec. 1819 (1 p.), praising Cathcart's "long, faithful, and important services" to the United States, to which is appended a statement from Cathcart, dated 18 Sept. 1821 (2 pp.): "Thus ends a series of eleven years captivity, in which I rendered our country services the value of which were incalculable at that period, and twenty five years faithful service since, which have been acknowledged by every successive administration of our government since it commenced for since the duties of the above mentioned Agency terminated I have not been employed in public service; they were performed to the satisfaction, and met the approbation of the Department to which I was accountable: and as a further proof of the opinion which the present Administration entertains of my former services, I have subjoined an extract from the Secretary of States report to Congress of the 14th. of December 1819 yet; although I have been told that the administration is well disposed towards me, I am neglected, & left with my wandering tribe of Africans, Italians, Spaniards, Portuguese, & Americans [his children] to pine in anxious expectation, and want, without any provision being made for me, this unfortunate circumstance brings to my remembrance the following anecdote of James the 2nd. of England. That Monarch being in conversation with a Mr. Floyd, one of the gentlemen in waiting, who had render'd some service to his Country, observed 'That he never knew a modest man to get forward in a court.' Mr. Floyd laconically replied '*Whose fault is that Sire.*' The King stood corrected, and Mr. Floyd was provided for!!!"

8. The enclosure (1 p.; filed after John Drayton to JM, 3 Sept. 1821) is a copy of Thomas Jefferson to Cathcart, 10 Sept. 1821, praising Cathcart's past government services, commiserating with his current situation, and noting that "there cannot fail to arise occasions

whereon they [the administration] will be glad to avail the public of your integrity and experience in business."

To Thomas Jefferson

DEAR SIR MONTPELLIER Sepr. 20. 1821.

I recd. yesterday yours of the 16th. inclosing the paper from Mr. Ticknor, on the tax imposed on Books imported. He has taken a very comprehensive and judicious view of the subject. The remark you add to it is a proper one also; that books being a permanent property ought not to be taxed whilst other permanent property is exempt, both in the acquisition and possession.

I have always considered the tax in question as an impolitic and disreputable measure; as of little account in point of revenue, and as a sacrifice of intellectual improvement to mechanical profits. These two considerations however produced the tax and will be the obstacles to its removal. Of the precise amount it yields to the revenue I have no knowlege. It cannot I presume be such as to weigh, even in the present difficulties of the Treasury, against the arguments for its discontinuance. If the fiscal consideration is to prevail, a better course would be to substitute an equivalent advance on some other articles imported. As to the encouragement of the Book printers their interest might be saved in the mode suggested by Mr. T. by a continuance of the tax on Books republished within a specified time. And perhaps the encouragement is recommended by the interests of literature[1] as well as by the advantage of conciliating an active & valuable profession; reprinted books being likely to obtain a greater number of purchasers & readers, especially when founded on previous subscriptions, than would seek for or purchase imported originals. As I approve therefore of the general object of the Northern Literati, I should prefer at the same time a modification of it in favor of Republishers. I see no adequate reason for distinguishing between English & other books whether in modern or ancient languages. If it were possible to define such as would fall under the head of luxurious or demoralizing amusements, there might be a specious plea for their exception from the repeal; but besides the impracticability of the discrimination, it would involve a principle of censorship which puts at once a veto on it.

The proposed concert among the Learned Institutions in presenting the grievance to Congress would seem to afford the best hope of success in drawing their favorable attention to it. A captious or fastidious adversary may perhaps, insinuate that the proper petitioners for redress are those who feel the grievance, not those who are exempt from it; that the latter assume the office of Counsellors, under the name of petitioners; and that from Corporate bodies, above all a combination of them, the precedent ought to be regarded with a jealous eye. The motives & modesty which would doubtless be stamped on the face of the interposition in this case, will be the best answer to such objections: or if there should be any serious apprehension of danger from them; the auxiliary expedient you suggest of addressing the respective representatives instead of Congress, might be made a substitute instead of an auxiliary. I should suppose that our University would not withold their concurrence in either or both modes. In that of addressing[2] to the particular representatives in Congress, there could be no room for hesitation. Mr. Ticknors wishes for information as to the other Institutions in Virga. & to the South & West proper to be invited into the plan, you can satisfy as well without as with my attempt to enumerate them. The members of Congress most proper to be engaged in the cause could be best selected on the spot, where I presume some well chosen agent or agents, none better than Mr. T. himself, will be provided in the quarter giving birth to the experiment.

These are hasty thoughts, but I send them in compliance with your request of an immediate answer. Take them for what they are worth only. Affectionately yours

James Madison

RC (DLC); draft (DLC: Rives Collection, Madison Papers). RC docketed by Jefferson "recd Sep. 25." Minor differences between the copies have not been noted.

1. In the draft, this part of the sentence reads: "And perhaps this encouragement to republication is recommended by public considerations."

2. In the draft, "letters" follows "addressing" here.

To James Leander Cathcart

Dear Sir Montpellier Sepr. 23. 1821

I received yesterday your letter and communications of the 18th. instant. I have read them with a sincere sympathy for the situation in which you find yourself; and with regret that a more fortunate one has not followed your long continuance in the public service. I shall of course feel much pleasure at any occurrence which would brighten your prospects for the time to come. I know not however that I can in any way contribute to it; all the recommenda[to]ry circumstances in your career & character being already within the knowledge of those who dispense the public employments: nor have I any reason to doubt the favorableness of their personal dispositions towards you. If my testimony nevertheless can be of any value or satisfaction to you; I cheerfully bear it to the zeal fidelity and ca⟨p⟩acity for business, evinced in the discharge of your public trusts as it became known to me; and to the reputation you always en⟨jo⟩yed for the virtues of private life.

I thank you Sir for the kind wishes you express in my behalf. Mrs. M. is equally thankful for those of Mrs. Cathcart, to whom she offers her best in return. Be assured yourself of mine, as well as of my esteem & friendly respects.

James Madison

RC (DNA: RG 45, Misc. Letters Received); draft (DLC); Tr (THer); Tr (MHi: Adams Papers); Tr (DNA: RG 59, LAR, 1817–25, filed under "Cathcart"). RC addressed and franked by JM to Cathcart at Washington. Minor differences between the copies have not been noted.

To John Drayton

Dear Sir Montpellier Sepr. 23. 1821

I have duly received the copy of your Memoirs which you were so good as to send me.[1] Be pleased to accept my thanks for it. I have looked sufficiently into the work to be sensible of its value not only to those who take a more immediate interest in local details; but as a contribution also to the fund of materials for a general history of the American Revolution. Every incident connected with this great & pregnant event is already an object of patriotic curiosity; and will be rendered by the lapse of time more & more so. It is much to be desired that the example you have given may be followed in all the States by individuals who unite with industry & opportunities the requisite judgment & impartiality. Besides the more general obligation to engage in the task, a special one will be found in the occasions for doing justice to individual merits which might otherwise escape the historical tribute due to them. Be pleased to accept Sir assurances of my esteem and best respects.

James Madison

RC (PWacD: Feinstone Collection, on deposit PPAmP); draft (DLC). Minor differences between the copies have not been noted.

1. See Drayton to JM, 3 Sept. 1821.

To Albert Picket and Others

GENTLEMEN MONTPELLIER Sept. 23. 1821

I have recd. your letter of the 10th. instant, asking my opinion as to th⟨e establishment of a female college,⟩ and a proper course of instruction in it.

The importance of both these questions, an⟨d the⟩ novelty of the first, would require more consideration than is allowed by other demands on my time, if I were better qualified for the task, or than is permitted indeed by the tenor of your request which has for its object an early answer.

The capacity of the female mind for studies of the highest order can not be doubted; having been sufficiently illu⟨s⟩trated by its works of genius, of erudition and of Science. Th⟨at⟩ it merits an improved System of education, comprizing a due reference to the condition & duties of female life, as distinguished from those of the other sex, must be as readily admitted. How far a collection of female Students into a public Seminary would be the best of plans for educating them is a point on which different opinions may be expected to arise. Yours as the result of much observation on the youthful minds of females, and of long engagement in tutoring them, is entitled to great ⟨respect; and as experiment⟩ alone can fully decide ⟨the interesting problem, it is a⟩ justifiable wish that it ⟨may be⟩ made; and it could not as would appear be made under ⟨better⟩ auspices than such as yours. With fr⟨iendl⟩y respects

JAMES MADISON

RC (owned by Debra Collins and John Pickett, Overland Park, Kan., 2000); draft (DLC). RC docketed by Albert Picket Sr. Extensively damaged; words and parts of words in angle brackets have been supplied from the draft. RC addressed and franked by JM to Albert Picket Sr. Postmarked 29 Sept. at Orange Court House.

From Littell & Henry

SIR PHILADELPHIA 24 September 1821.

The enclosed prospectus of an edition of Blackstone's Commentaries, is respectfully submitted to your examination by the publishers.[1]

As it is of much importance to attract to it as early as possible the attention of the public, and as nothing would so certainly secure this as an expression of the favourable opinion of those who are most competent to judge of its utility, we have been induced to trouble you with this letter, and to take the further liberty of requesting from you an answer containing your opinion of the plan which is proposed.

We are aware, Sir, that the time of men who are distinguished in public life, is often unwarrantably encroached upon by the eagerness of publishers to procure recommendations that will guide the public opinion, but we beg leave to assure you that we should not have ventured thus to intrude ourselves upon you for the purpose of promoting our own interest, had we not believed that it is, in this instance, connected with the public good. With the highest respect, We are Sir, Your Most Obedt. servts.

Littell & Henry[2]

RC (DLC). Cover addressed by Littell & Henry to JM, and franked. Docketed by JM.

1. Sir William Blackstone, *Blackstone's Commentaries: Proposals by Littell & Henry . . . for Publishing by Subscription, a New Edition of Blackstone's Commentaries on the Laws of England, with Notes and Additions; Exhibiting a General View of the Principal Diversities between the Laws of England, and . . . the United States . . .* (Philadelphia, 1821; Shoemaker 5832). JM's copy is in the Madison Collection, Rare Book and Special Collections Division, Library of Congress.

2. The partners Eliakim Littell and R. Norris Henry conducted business as booksellers and publishers at 74 South Second Street, Philadelphia (H. Glenn Brown and Maude O. Brown, "A Directory of the Book-Arts and Book Trade in Philadelphia to 1820 Including Painters and Engravers," *Bulletin of the New York Public Library* 53 [1949]: 568).

From James M. Bell

Dear sir Orange Ct House 25th. Sep: 1821.

I regret much that my personal acquaintance with you is so limited; However, from the long and intimate one that has prevailed between our families you will no doubt pardon me for breaking in upon your time by requesting you to use your influence (consistent with your feelings) to obtain a berth for my son William Bell[1] at West Point. He is between eighteen & nineteen years old and I trust from his general moral deportment and his susceptibility of improvement would not prove an ill timed patronage. A grateful acknowledgment will be rememberd by your attention. I am Sir Yr Most Obt. H Servt.

James M. Bell[2]

PS. My place of residence is near Culpeper Ct House J. M. Bell

RC (DLC). Docketed by JM.

1. William Bell (1803–1874) entered the United States Military Academy at West Point, New York, on 1 July 1822. For many years, he was a clerk in the U.S. Post Office in Washington (*Register of the Officers and Cadets of the U.S. Military Academy, June, 1823* [1823; reprint,

West Point, N.Y., 1884], 15; John W. Bell, *Memoirs of Governor William Smith, of Virginia. His Political, Military, and Personal History* [New York, 1891], 4, 128).

2. James Madison Bell (d. 1840) was a Culpeper County, Virginia, planter and the father of Peter Hansborough Bell, governor of Texas, 1849–53 (Chapman's Adm'rs v. Shepherd's Adm'r & als., 24 Gratt. 377, 380 [Peachy R. Grattan, comp., *Reports of Cases Decided in the Supreme Court of Appeals of Virginia* (33 vols.; Richmond, Va., 1845–81)]; Sobel and Raimo, *Biographical Directory of the Governors*, 4:1516–17).

From James Maury

My dear Sir, Liverpool 25 Sept 1821.

In June last Mr Wilson presented your letter of the 5th of April,[1] and I had much pleasure in attending to one so worthy.

My son William has been with us about three weeks & feels greatly obliged by your kindnesses to him, as do all of us & pray you and the ladies to accept our grateful acknowlegements.

My three sons, who have visited the land of their father, are so attached to it that I predict they are to return to it for good at a future & not distant period.

The farmers in this country have long been complaining of inability to pay their rents from the low price of wheat, and the prospect of an increased abundance & still lower prices this crop continued, until about four weeks ago; ever since which there has been so much rain that it once was expected the ports would be opened to foreign wheat in November; but that opinion has now ceased: however it is probable the advices hence during the prevalence of that opinion may have occasioned an advance where you are, with a view to this market: and I shall be glad to hear of your having availed of the circumstance by selling at home instead of shipping, which last I cannot recommend.

I have been looking at the samples of the Tobaccoe you have been so good as to consign M. & L. and beg leave to refer to their report on it:[2] I wish it was better.

My son has communicated to me the conversation with you respecting the office I have so long had the honor of holding under our government[3] & I pray you to accept my particular thanks for your friendship on the occasion. I have no intention of resigning so long as the president may please to continue me & while I am blessed with that good health for which I have so much reason to be thankful to the giver of good things. We all unite in best respects and wishes to you, the ladies & Mr Todd. I am your old & obliged friend

James Maury

RC (DLC).

1. The letter has not been found, but see JM's letter to Richard Rush, 5 Apr. 1821, introducing John P. Wilson.

2. See Maury & Latham to JM, 2 Oct. 1821, and enclosure.

3. For that conversation, see William Maury to JM, 6 Apr. 1821, and n. 2.

From Richard Rush

Dear sir. London September 25. 1821.

The last number of the Edinburgh Review[1] having just come out, I have great pleasure, whilst making up my despatches for the October packet, in sending it to you. It may probably be the means of putting you in possession of it rather sooner than you would otherwise see it, and I know the interest you will take in casting your eye over the article on Godwin's work. These great northern criticks, it will be perceived, treat it with as little ceremony, as he treated Malthus, and certainly whatever leaning I may have had towards some parts of Godwins theories, is rebuked sharply enough in this Review. I have had a partiality for Godwins pen so long, that its very errors perhaps (and whose has had more with all its genius?) make more impression upon me than they should. I think that the Reviewers, with all their ability, handle his book somewhat too succinctly in their known devotion to the doctrines of Malthus. There are some other articles in this number of the Review, that may perhaps attract your attention, especially that on capital punishments, and the one on degrading the standard of money.

Mrs Rush has lately added another son to our flock.[2] This has enabled me to gratify a wish which both she and I have long cherished, of giving to one of our boys the name of Madison. On this occasion I cannot help concluding with the remark, that however I may have faltered between some parts of the theory of Godwin and Malthus, the practice in my own family looks so wholly to the support of the latter, that, in the course of a few years more, (matters going on as they have gone,) I must needs become his ardent disciple!

Asking our kind compliments to Mrs Madison, I remain, dear sir, with my constant attachment and respect most faithfully yours

Richard Rush

RC (PHi).

1. *Edinburgh Review* 70 (July 1821).

2. J. Madison Rush (1821–1856) entered the U.S. Navy in 1836 as a midshipman, was promoted to first lieutenant in 1849, and resigned in 1856. He drowned that same year in

Red Lake River in Minnesota Territory (*Proceedings of the Academy of Natural Sciences of Philadelphia* 8 [1856]: 143; Callahan, *List of Officers of the Navy*, 477).

From Thomas Jefferson

DEAR SIR MONTICELLO Sep. 30. 21.

Mr Brockenbrough[1] has been closely engaged, since our last meeting in settling the cost of the buildings finished at the University, that we might obtain a more correct view of the state of our funds, and see whether a competency will remain for the Library. He has settled for 6. pavilions, 1. hotel, and 35. dormitories and will proceed with the rest; so that I hope, by our next meeting, the whole of the 4. rows will be nearly settled. From what is done he has formed an estimate of the cost of what is yet to be done; and guided in it by actual experience, it is probably nearly correct. The result is that our actual receipts heretofore, with what is still to be received of the loan of this year, after paying for the lands and all incidental and current expenses, will exactly compleat the 4. rows of buildings for the accommodation of the Professors and students, amounting in the whole to 195.000. Dollars, and leave us without either debt or contract.

In the conjectural estimate laid before the visitors at their last meeting it was supposed that the 3. annuities of 1822. 23. & 24. would suffice for the Library and current charges, without the aid of the *unpaid subscriptions*, which were reserved therefore as a contingent fund. By this more actual estimate it appears that the unpaid subscriptions, valued at 18.000 D. will be *necessary* to compleat that building. So that the conjectural estimate fell short by 18.000. D. of the real cost of the 4. rows; which in a total of 195.000. D. & is perhaps not over-considerable. I call it the *real* cost because that of the unfinished buildings is reckoned by the real cost of those finished. The season being now too far advanced to begin the Library, and the afflicting sickness in Genl. Cocke's family having deprived me of the benefit of consultation with him, I think it a duty to leave that undertaking entirely open and undecided, for the opinion of the visitors at their meeting in November, when it is believed the actual settlements will have reached every thing, except 1. pavilion and 3. hotels, which alone will be unfinished until the spring. The considerations which urge the building the hall, at least, of the Library, seemed to impress the board strongly at their last meeting; and it is put in our power to undertake it with perfect safety, by the indefinite suspension by the Legislature of the commencement of our instalments. This leaves us free to take another year's annuity, to wit, that of 25. before we begin instalments, should the funds fall short which are here counted on for that building. The undertakers are disposed to accept and collect themselves the outstanding subscriptions in part of payment. You will distinguish in this statement, by their enormous cost, the pavilions No. 3 & 7. and 16. dormitories contracted for in 1817 & 18 at the inflated prices prevailing then while we acted as a central college only. In 1819. & the following years, prices were reduced from 25. to 50. per cent. The enlarged cost of the latter dormitories has been occasioned by the unevenness of the ground, which required cellars under many of them.

I shall hope to have the pleasure of receiving you at Monticello a day, at least, before that of our meeting, as we can prepare our business here so much more at leisure than at the University. I salute you with constant and affectionate Friendship & respect

Th: Jefferson

[Enclosure]

A view of the whole expences & of the Funds of the University	Actual cost	estimated do.	Averages
	D	D	D
Pavilions. No. 3. & 7. undertaken in 1817.18	19,149.81		9,574.90
No. 2. 4. 5. 9.	33,563.15		8,390.78
17. marble capitels for No. 2. 3. 5. 8. from Italy	1,784.		
No. 1. 6. 8. 10. not finished		33,563.15	
Hotel. B.B.	4,609.58		
5. other Hotels not finished		20,000.	4,000.
6			
Dormitories. 16. undertaken in 1817.	13,898.34		868.64
19.	11,083.63		583.34
74. not finished, but contracted for		38,462.60	519.76
109.			
Lands, wages, and contingencies (suppose for round numbers)		18,885.74	
	84,088.51	110,911.49	
		195,000	

Funds. Glebe lands	3,104.09	
Annuities of 1819. 20. 21	45,000.	
loan of 1820	60,000.	
loan of 1821	60,000.	
Subscriptions received to Sep. 1821 about	25,000.	
balance to be carried forward	1,895.91	195,000.

Expences still to be incurred.		
Walls of backyards, gardens etc about 100,000. Bricks		1,500.
wages and contingencies for 1822.23.		6,000.
Library Hull 30,200. D + Interior 13,476 D		43,675.
Interest for 1821. 22. 23		13,700
		64,875.

Funds. Balance brought forward	1,895.91	
Subscriptions. 19,133.33 of which are Sperate	18,000.	
Annuities of 1822. 23. 24.	45,000.	64,895.91

A more summary view of the cost of the 4. rows of buildings & Library

10. Pavilions	88,060.11
6. Hotels	24,609.58
109. Dormitories	63.445.57
Library	43,675.
	219,790.26

RC and enclosure (DLC); RC and enclosure (ViU: Special Collections); FC (DLC: Jefferson Papers). Both RCs in Virginia Jefferson Randolph's hand, except for Jefferson's date at head, complimentary close, and signature. First RC marked "Mr Madison."; postmarked 4 Oct. at Charlottesville, and franked. Second RC marked "Mr Cabell"; postmarked 7 Oct. at Charlottesville, and franked by Jefferson; docketed by Cabell. Both enclosures in Jefferson's hand. A copy of this letter was sent to each member of the board of visitors of the University of Virginia.

1. Arthur S. Brockenbrough (1780–1832) was proctor of the University of Virginia, 1819–31, and supervised its building (*Genealogies of Virginia Families: From the William and Mary College Quarterly Historical Magazine* [5 vols.; Baltimore, 1982], 5:282; *A Sketch of the History of the University of Virginia . . .* [Washington, 1859], 13; Bruce, *History of the University of Virginia*, 1:275–78).

From Maury & Latham

SIR, LIVERPOOL 2 Octor 1821

Enclosed we beg to hand you the valuations of your Tobacco ℔ Glide—also the account of some which have been sold—to which we may add No. 14 @ 4¾ d.

The Tobacco is certainly good, but our manufacturers run now entirely upon long leafed perfect in the points &c; for such we are getting 7½ & the writer knows that your land will produce as fine as Mr Rives[1] in Nelson.

We would recommend your planting in future the Big Frederick or some large description for really this parcel sells below its intrinsic value from prejudice.

Your Bill for £250 has appeared & met due honor.

We are now holding your Tobacco for ¼ d advance owing to the loss of a Cargo off our Port.

We think there is no prospect for our Ports opening to Flour now & would advise your selling in preference to holding.

We have sent you the annexed circular merely supposing that the view of our operations in your great Staples might afford you some amusement. We have the honor to be Sir Your most obedient servant[s]

MAURY & LATHAM
℔WILLIAM MAURY

4 Octr. Tobacco has rather advanced & we sold 1 Hhd No. 13 @ 4¾. We hold the remaind[e]r at that price.

[Enclosure]

28 Sept. 1821

Weights & Valuations of JM 14 Hhds of Tobacco P Glide on a/c of Mr. Madison.

Value	No.	Cwt	yrs	℔s	
3¾ d	1	11	3	26	ordinary quality, rough & strong
"	6	11	1	22	
"	10	11	3	7	
	12	12	2	1	
"	13	11		"	
4¼	11	11	3	16	rather better
4¼ to 4½	4	12	3	6	strong useful leaf, rather soft
4¾	8	12	"	12	ditto, & a little better
"	9	13	"	16	
	3	12	1	21	
	2	11	3	2	sold at 5d
	5	10	1	26	sold at 4¾
	7	11	2	"	sold at 4¼
4¾ d	14	10	3	7	good planter's stem'd

165.2.25 Total Landing weight or	18,561 lb.
Shrinkage 17 lb.p hhd	238 "
Nett Sale weight	18,323 "

RC and enclosure (DLC). RC addressed by William Maury to JM, and franked. Postmarked 19 Nov. at New York. Docketed by JM. Filed after James M. Bell to JM, 25 Sept. 1821. JM made figure calculations in the lower left margin of the enclosure.

1. This was probably Robert Rives (1764–1845), a Revolutionary War veteran, proprietor of the plantation Oak Ridge in Nelson County, Virginia, and the father of William Cabell Rives (Alexander Brown, *The Cabells and Their Kin: A Memorial Volume of History, Biography, and Genealogy*, 2d ed. (Richmond, Va., 1939), 236–44).

From Mackay & Campbell

Sir Fredericksburg 4. October 1821.

There is $400. of your $800. note due on tomorrow, which we will have to pay, having no note of yours to renew it. We enclose a note dated 12th. inst for $400. which please sign & return so that we may replace the money to be advanced tomorrow.

There is some furniture here marked R. Cutts respecting which we have recd. no directions. Can you give us any? Yours Very Respectfully,

MACKAY & CAMPBELL

Wheat 100 a 104¢
Flour 5¼ a 5⅜$.

RC (DLC). Addressed by Mackay & Campbell to JM at Orange, and franked. Docketed by JM.

From Maury & Latham

SIR, LIVERPOOL. 6th. October 1821

Tobacco has been in good demand this week, particularly for the last three days & the sales are not far from 400 Hhds, chiefly Virginias, & at an advance of full ½ upon strips & ¼ upon leaf—holders are looking for a further advance of ¼ perhaps ½. & will probably be sparing sellers until then. The rise is owing to the continued accounts of short supplies this season, the expected arrival of the Mary & Susan without a *full* cargo, in corroboration, the partial loss of the Dariens cargo, & the recent accounts of the growing crops in Virga. not being very favourable. These circumstances have had much effect upon both holders & buyers, & should the London market become equally good, we may expect that the present prices will be fully maintained, & probably advanced upon ½ should the supplies prove really short—we quote strips @ 3½ a 6½–& 6¾–leaf 2¾ a 7½.

The average price of wheat for the week ending the 29th ulto is 70/7 ℔ Qr. Should it equal 67/ for the next six weeks, (not improbable) the ports will open to British America. They are not likely to open to the United States this year. Old Wheat is steady @ 12/ @ 13/6. Flour in bond is quite nominal @ 35/–38/ but 30/ has been refused. Sour[1] in bond would not bring 25/— but in fact, no enquiry. We are, respectfully yours

MAURY & LATHAM

RC (DLC).

1. Among other industrial uses, sour flour, "flour which has been fermented for several weeks," was used in the finishing of cloth (F. Crace Calvert, "On Improvements and Progress in Dyeing and Calico Printing since 1851," *Journal of the Society of Arts, and of the Institutions in Union* 10 [7 Feb. 1862]: 177).

To Lafayette

[ca. 7 October 1821]

I did not receive, my dr. frd. your favor of July 1.[1] till a few weeks ago. It came thro' the post office from N. York. Of Dr. Barba[2] I have not heard a word. I shall keep in mind the title your recommendation gives to any marks of my attention, for which opportunities may be afforded.

I have read with great pleasure your opinion occasioned by the Budget. Sentiments so noble, in language so piercing, can not be without effect. The deafness to them within doors, will not prevent their being heard & felt without, and the present atmosphere of Europe, is favorable to an echo of them everywhere. The toleration of such bold & severe truths, is a proof that altho' the time may not be arrived for their compleat triumph, it is approaching, and will be accelerated by such appeals to honest hearts and reflecting minds. Go on my friend in your consistent & magnanimous career; and may you live to witness and enjoy the success of a cause the most truly glorious that can animate the breast of man, that of elevating & meliorating the condition of his race. Representative & responsible Governments are so congenial with the rights and the feelings of all nations, that their progress cannot be arrested. Sooner or later they must expel despotism from the civilized world. Their forms will improve as experiments shall be multiplied. The experiment here cannot fail to add new lights on the Science of Constitutions.

We have seen with regret, and not without some disappointment, Emperor Alexander throwing himself into the breach in defence of Arbitrary power agst. national reforms. His language at Laybach, his conduct towards Naples, and his unparallelled armaments furnishing to some the motives, to others the pretexts to follow the oppressive example, forfeit his pretensions to be regarded as a patron of the liberal ideas of the age, as a guardian of the independence of nations, and as a friend to the relief which peace ought to give the people from military burdens. How account too for his having no scruples to interfere in the domestic struggles of Naples in favor of a vitiated monarchy, and his pleading them agst. an interference in behalf of the Christian Greeks, struggling agst. the compound & horrible despotism at Constantinople? His apostasy if he was ever sincere, is a conspicuous proof of the necessity of Constitutional barriers agst. the corrupting influence of unbridled power.

I have lately been looking over Dupradt's Europe in 1819. He has taken many instructive views of its nations with their mutual relations & prospects. His prophetic conjectures seem however to ascribe too much permanency to the gigantic growth of Russia on the land, and to the ascendancy of G. Britain on the ocean. Without a civilization of the miscellaneous hordes, spread over so many latitudes & Longitudes, at present nominal rather than real subjects, the Russian power can not be measured by the extent of her territory; and in the event of a civilization & consequent multiplication of these barbarians, her empire like that of all overgrown ones must fall to pieces. Those of Alexander, of Rome, of Charlemagne, of Chs. V. all experienced this fate, after the personal talents or temporary causes which held the parts together had ceased. Napoleon would have furnished another example if his fortune had equalled his ambition. His successors would have found a physical & moral impossibility of wielding either a sceptre or sword of more than a given length. The vast power of G. Britain rests on a basis, too artificial to be permanent. She owes it not to the extent of her natural resources, but to the prosperity of her manufactures her commerce & her navigations. As other nations infuse salutary principles into their forms of Govt. and extend the policy they are adopting of doing for themselves what G.B. has been permitted to do for them, her power like that of the Dutch who once enjoyed an artificial ascendancy on the same element, will be reduced to the limits prescribed by nature. These are undoubtedly consistent with the rank of a great and important member of the Society of Nations. Nor will Russia fail to continue a great power, tho' without the overwhelming accumulation of means assigned to her destiny.

Will you indulge my partiality as an American in remarking, that in looking forward to the comparative resources for naval ascendency, the trident will ultimately belong not to the Eastern but to the Western Hemisphere. Naval power depends on ships & seamen; and these on the materials for constructing the former, and the bulky & coveted products for loading them. On which side will there be the greatest & most Durable abundance for both purposes? And can it be supposed that there will be less disposition on this than there has been on the other side of the atlantic to take at least a *fair* advantage of the fortunate lot. I hope and pray that the transatlantic example may not be followed beyond that limit.

The Negro slavery is as you justly complain a sad blot on our free Country tho' a very ungracious subject of reproaches from the quarter wch. has been most lavish of them. No satisfactory plan has yet been devised for taking out the stain. If an adequate asylum cd. be found in africa that wd. be the appropriate destination for the unhappy race among us. Some are sanguine that the efforts of an existing Colonization Society will accomplish such a provision; but a very partial success seems the most that can be expected. Some other region must therefore be found for them as they become free and willing to emigrate. The repugnance of the Whites to their continuance among them is founded on prejudices themselves founded on physical distinctions, which are not likely soon if ever to be eradicated.

Even in States, Massachussetts for example, which displayed most sympathy with the people of colour on the Missouri question, prohibitions are taking place agst. their becoming residents. They are every where regarded as a nuisance, and must really be such as long as they are under the degradation which the public sentiment inflicts on them. They are at the same time rapidly increasing from manumissions and from offsprings, and of course lessening the general disproportion between the slaves & the Whites. This tendency is favorable to the cause of a universal emancipation.

The State of our Country is in other respects highly flattering. There have been pecuniary difficulties in the Govt. & still more among the people; but they are curing themselves. Little eddies also occasionally arise, which for a moment ruffle the political surface, but they gradually sink into the general calm. Every thing as yet favors the principle of self Govt. on which our destinies are staked.

I am glad to find you retain so feelingly all your American recollections, even the itinerant scenes in which we were associated; and that you cherish the idea of giving your friends here an oppy. of once more embracing you. God forbid that your visit shd. result from one of the causes you glance at. Happen it how it may, you will find that they have forgotten nothing of what always endeared you to their best feelings, and that this is more true of no one than of your cordial & stedfast friend.

J.M.

Mrs. M. and our son Todd are gratified by your kind expressions & those of your family; and join in returning every assurance of regard and good wishes.

Draft (DLC). Undated; conjectural date assigned based on the fact that Thomas Jefferson received Lafayette's 1 July 1821 letter on 17 Sept. (DLC: Jefferson Papers). If JM received his letter from Lafayette on or about 17 Sept., on the supposition that Barba posted them at the same time (see n. 2 below), this reply would be dated several weeks later.

1. Letter not found.

2. "This Letter goes by Dr. Barba, Son to a celebrated book Seller and printer in paris, who goes to the U.S. with a view to fix himself on that Happy Land and to Exercise His profession as a physician" (Lafayette to Thomas Jefferson, 1 July 1821, DLC: Jefferson Papers). Barba did not deliver these letters but posted them.

James Barbour to Dolley Madison

BARBOURSVILLE Octr. 13. 21

James Barbour presents his respects to Mrs. Madison with a view to express his regret at the indisposition of Mr Madison and to enquire how he does. JB would have been to have visited Mr Madison but from an apprehension that company is but ill adapted to a sick man. Should Dr. Watkins be at Mr M's if proper he would confer a favor by immediately visiting Mrs. Barbour who has been indisposed for a few days. And which will not yield to the remedies she has applied.

RC (DLC).

To Mackay & Campbell

GENTLEMAN [*sic*] [ca. 15 October 1821]

I returned the note covered by yours of the 4th duly signed. I forwarded some days ago one to meet the object of it, which I hope reached you on Friday morning. Should it have miscarried that now sent will replace the advance which you will have been good enough to make.

The Articles of furniture marked R. Cutts were intended for me & early measures will be taken to have them brought up. With friendly respects

JAMES MADISON

FC (DLC). Undated; conjectural date assigned based on internal evidence, Mackay & Campbell to JM, 4 Oct. 1821, and JM's illness at this time. In John Payne Todd's hand, except for JM's complimentary close and signature.

To Littell & Henry

GENT: Ocr. 18. 1821

I duly recd. your letter of Sepr 24. The answer it requests has been delayed by an indisposition from which I am just recovering.

I very cheerfully express my approbation of the proposed Edition of Blackstones Commentaries accompanied by a comparative view of the laws of the U.S. & of the several States.

Such a work executed with the ability to be presumed in its authors must be very useful in several respects. It will be so not only to the Bench & the Bar; but to the Citizens generally, by facilitating to those of each State a knowlege of the laws of the others, in which the intercourses of business give them an interest. Nor will a Comparison of the different Codes be without value to the Legislator also who will be able to extract whatever improvements may be found in the examples before him, and it may well be supposed that there are few of the different codes which do not contain something worthy of adoption as well as something requiring amendment. Finally such a work will have a tendency to assimilate gradually the codes of all the States, on subjects not merely local; to assimilate them too according to a model formed by a selection of the best parts and features of each.

The Citizens of the U.S. in their federal association, have now the same Constitution and the same code of laws. A uniformity among the State Codes would extend the advantage without violating the Constl: separation, jurisdiction & independence of the States themselves.

Should it be an object with the Compilers to include in their review of the State laws, observations on the practical advantages & inconveniences of such as differ in different States, it will not a little enrich the instruction they are about to give to their Country; and indeed to all who make the Science of legislation their Study.

Draft (DLC).

From Maury & Latham

Sir, Liverpool 19 Octo 1821

Since we had this pleasure we have disposed of your remaining Tobacco at prices which we hope will be satisfactory & now beg to hand you Account Sales of the same leaving to your Cr. £278. 13. 5.

The business done in Tobacco this month has been extensive & at ¼ a ½ advance upon prices of August—supposing however that these advices would bring forward heavy supplies we have availed ourselves of the demand.

We would recommend your planting the larger description of Tobacco in future as such is so much preferred here that our manufacturers will give for equal quality of a larger description fully 1 d ℔ lbs more.

Our Ports will not open to Flour from the United States in Feby even—possibly they may in May, for the Crop is certainly materially injured. However the low price at which inferior Wheat must be sold will keep down the average.

We quote Tobacco @ 3 a 7 d & 7½–Flour 30/. We have the honor to be Sir With high respect Your most obedient servants

Maury & Latham
℔ William Maury

RC and enclosure (DLC). Enclosure docketed by JM.

[Enclosure]

Account sales of 14 hhds tobacco recd. ℔ Glide Wm Adams from Virginia on account of James Madison Esq.

1821																
Sep	21	Wm Stewart 2 hhds IM	7.	11.	2.	"	..	17	or	1271	lbs	at	4¼	22	10	1
			2.	11.	3.	2	..	17	"	1301	"		5	27	2	1
Oct	1	T. Brown & Son 1	5.	10.	1.	26	..	17	"	1157	"		4¾	22	17	11
"	2	Thos Roberts & Co 1	14.	10.	3.	7	..	17	"	1194	"		4¾	23	12	7
"	3	Rayner & Co 1	13.	11.	"	3	..	17	"	1218	"		4¾	24.	2.	1
"	4	Moulsons & Co. 9	8.	12.	"	2	..	17	"	1339	"		4¾	26	9	11

3.	12.	1.	21	..	17
4.	12.	3.	6	..	17
6.	11.	1.	22	..	17
9.	13.	-.	16		17
1	11.	3.	26.		17
12	12.	2	1.		17
11.	11.	3.	16.		17
11.	11.	3.	7.		17
	98.	3.	136.		10843 " 4¼ 192 2

338 14 10

——Charges——

			£	s	d	£	s	d
Augt	2.	To insurance £336 at 25/ ℘cent & Policy	5.	8.	—			
Sep	22	freight at 46/6 ℘ hhd & primage 5 ℘ct	34.	3.	7			
		landing charges 10/ ℘ hhd	7.	—.	—			
		fire insurce. 6/ postage of remces., & abated 2/10	—.	8.	10			
		commission including brokerage & risk of debt on £338.14.10 at 4 ℘ cent	13.	11.	—	60	11	5
		Nett proceeds due in cash 3. March 1822.				£278	3	5

Errors excepted

Liverpool 10 October 1821

Maury & Latham

℘ William Maury

From Joseph Wheaton

SIR CITY OF WASHINGTON Octr. 20. 1821.

Last autumn I had the honor to enclose to your address, my pamphlet, "an appeal to Congress from the decision of the accounting officers of the War Department for compensation while detained by their orders in the Settlement of my public accounts, and for Extra Service,["][1] Which so far as respected myself could have been Settled much earlier, but was prolonged unnecessarily, by the accounting officers, from year to year, and operated greatly to my disadvantage and injury. Acting as I did through the war, under a positive order of the Secretary (never revoked) charging me "*not to withhold myself from any good work*" which though Couched in terms the most positive, is at the Same time the most delicate, and calculated to inspire a Soldier with confidence, and to expect of him the filling up of every deficiency in the department committed to his charge, not interfering directly with the commanding General, or the order meant nothing, the order was obeyed as Such, the Services's were faithfully performed, the nation injoys the benefit, but no compensation therefor, has been awarded me, altho it has ever been the rule, and Still is the practice of office[r]s and of the government to allow compensation for Extra Service, and for Such time as one officer (having the power) detains another in Service. As those Services Sir, refefered [*sic*] to in my appeal were performed during your Presidency, and while you were commander in Chief (therefore your own order through your Secretary at War) and "much of them came under your notice." I need not draw any inference as to what would have been the issue, or the result of the campains had I wavered for a moment with the artillery ammunition and the Supplies, or State by what means the affairs in the NW eventuated, or on the protection of Norfolk, the labor of the ordnance Department, and that of Marching the quotas of troops by your requisitions, on the State of virginia, with the cares of the Hospital, and the relief to your fellow Citizens at Richmond. May I then be permitted to ask of you to give to these objects your reflection, and to make an expression to the Honle. Mr. Barber of the Senate, and to his brother of the House of Representatives (both of whom I understand reside near you) your Sense of the amt. of Compensation that ought to be allowed to me. My appeal was refered to Committee's in each House, and altho reported upon unfavorably, was not finally acted on, in Consequence of more pressing business being before Congress and therefore among the unfinished business. I wish Such a compensation as Justice & practice will approve—and which would rescue me from the vile mire of dependance, and a virtuous family from that poverty which overwhelms *them*, in consequence of my having neglected *them* to Serve my Country. I have the honor to be with the most profound respect your most Obedient humble Servant

JOSEPH WHEATON

RC (DLC). Docketed by JM.

1. This letter has not been found, but the pamphlet was *Appeal of Joseph Wheaton, Late Deputy Quarter Master General and Major of Cavalry, to the Senate and House of Representatives of the United States of America* (Washington, 1820; Shoemaker 4256).

To Joseph Wheaton

DEAR SIR MONTPR. [ca. 30] Ocr. 1821

I have recd. yours of the 20th. instant. You will be sensible that I cd. not know sufficiently the value of the particular extra services rendered by you during the late war, to decide on the amount of compensation equitably due for them. I can therefore only mention to the gentlemen you have named, my general impression of the zeal & activity with which you promoted the public service as far as was in your power; and this I shall do, if not disappd. of an opportunity, with pleasure and with a sincere wish that you may succeed in establishing satisfactorily every just claim you may have on the public.

Draft (DLC). Day of month not indicated; conjectural day assigned based on Wheaton to JM, 20 Oct. 1821.

From Thomas Jefferson

DEAR SIR MONTICELLO Oct. 30. 21.

I heard in Bedford that you were attaked with the prevailing fever, and with great joy on my return that you were recovered from it. In the strange state of the health of our country every fever gives alarm.

I got home from Bedford on the 27th. and am obliged to return there within 3. or 4. days, having an appointment at the Natural bridge on the 11th. prox. As our proposed petition to Congress will of course be in collation with those from other ceminaries, I availed myself of my leisure at Poplar Forest to sketch it, and I now inclose it to you[1] to be made what it should be which I pray you to do with severity.

Knowing my time would be crouded thro' the month of November, I took the same opportunity to sketch our November report on the basis of mr. Brockenbrough's settlement as far as he has gone,[2] which I had communicated to you, with some subsequent corrections. His further advance in the settlements, will by the time of our meeting enable us to put into the class of settled accounts 7. pavilions, instead of 6. 3 hotels instead of 1. 65. dormitories instead of 30. leaving in the estimated class 3. Pavilions, 3. Hotels, and 44. dormitories, & these estimated from experience. He has corrected too the article of the cost of lands, hire of laborers Etc. The cost of the Library must be thrown on the 3. ensuing years of the annuity which had always been included in our estimates: and I am decidedly of opinion we should undertake it on that ground. If we stop short of the compleat establishment, it will never be compleated. On the other hand the stronger we make the mass, the more certainly will it force itself into action. The world will never bear to see the doors of such an establishment locked up. And if the legislature shall become disposed to remit the debt, they will swallow a pill of 165.M.D. with the same effort as one of 120.M.D. Be so good as to return me these papers with your amendments by the middle of November. With my respectful souvenirs to mrs. Madison accept assurances of my constant affections and respect.

TH: JEFFERSON

RC (DLC); FC (DLC: Jefferson Papers).

1. The enclosure has not been found, but for the petition to Congress, see From the Rector and Visitors of the University of Virginia, 30 Nov. 1821.

2. The enclosure has not been found, but for the report, see Minutes of the Board of Visitors of the University of Virginia, 30 Nov. 1821.

From Mackay & Campbell

DR SIR FREDERICKSBURG 1 Novem 1821.

Yr esteemed favour 30 Ulto. is recd.[1] Alick has taken the furniture.

Our accounts from England the Same as yours. These accounts have been the cause of more speculation than probably ever took place in the articles of wheat, flour, Corn & Whiskey. Flour got up to $8 in the different towns north of us, & even here it was $8 on the day before yesterday—it is now $7⅓ here & will Very likely be $7 tomorrow, & until another arrival from England, which will no doubt, either reduce or enhance prices Very considerably. Here, wheat has been 150 cts—is now 142 to 145 cts.

We are anxious to give employment at our Orange Mill & receive wheat there at a deduction of 15 cts from the Fredg price with liberty to fix when the owner chooses, prior to 1 Jan & also to have the amount in flour at 4/6

℔ Barrel. We also buy wheat Delivered a[t] Dades Mill at a Deduction of 1/– ℔ Bushel from the Fredg Price. Your friends

MACKAY & CAMPBELL

RC (DLC). Docketed by JM.

1. Letter not found.

From Maury & Latham

SIR, LIVERPOOL 1 Novr 1821

Annexed we beg to hand you your Account Current[1] shewing a balance in your favor of £21.15.2 which we hope will be found correct.

Since our last letter no material alteration has taken place in our Tobacco market—holders of it continue firm at the late advance. We have the honor to be Sir Your most obedient servants

MAURY & LATHAM
℔ WILLIAM MAURY

RC and enclosure (DLC). RC docketed by JM.

[Enclosure]

Dr Jas Madison Esq in acct currt & intst to 3d March 1822 with Maury & Latham Cr 1821

				£	s	d								£	s	d	
1821													1821				
Mar	22		To invoice of 10 sacks salt	2	17	7	May	25	282		24		Oct 10 By nett proceeds of 14 hhds tobo ꝑ Glide	278	3	5	Mar 3
Sep	28	"	your dft on us favor Mackay & Campbell	250			Nov	30	93	3	38						
Octo	31	"	postages		4	8											
	"	"	interest ꝑ account	3	6												
	"	"	balance carried down	21	15	2	Mar	3									
				£278	3	5				3	6 .			£278	3	5	" "
													" 31 " balance brought down	21	15	2	" "

Errors excepted

Liverpool 31st October 1821
Maury & Latham
ꝑ William Maury

From Benjamin Drake

Sir, Cincinnati Nov. 6. 1821.

Having recently embarked in the collection of materials for a Biographical Sketch of the celebrated *Tecumseh*,[1] I am induced to take the liberty of addressing you upon the Subject.

I am solicitous to ascertain the nature of Tecumseh's alliance with the Brittish army and the tenor of his Commission as a Brigadier General in the service of England during the late war; and I have supposed that during your Presidency, official information touching these subjects might have come to your Knowledge.

Any information Sir which you may be enabled to communicate concerning the points alluded to, or connected in any manner with the "King of the Woods" as he was emphatically styled by Genl. Proctor,[2] will be highly acceptable and tend materially to the advancement of a feeble effort of mine, to rescue from oblivion the history of one of our distinguished aboriginal chiefs.

Excuse Sir, the freedom which I have taken in addressing you and accept the assurance of my high consideration and esteem.

Benjamin Drake[3]

RC (DLC). Addressed by Drake to JM, and franked. Docketed by JM.

1. Tecumseh (1768–1813), of Creek and Shawnee heritage, fought U.S. forces in the Ohio country during the 1790s. During the War of 1812, Tecumseh and his brother, the Prophet, projected an Indian confederacy, allied their forces with the British, and participated in a number of battles. Tecumseh was killed at the Battle of the Thames (*PJM-PS*, 2:523 n. 1; John Sugden, *Tecumseh: A Life* [New York, 1997], 15, 22, 63, 79–93, 203–14, 280–93, 329–38, 368, 372–75).

2. Henry Procter (1763–1822), an Irish-born career British army officer, commanded British forces on the Detroit and Niagara frontiers until after the Battle of the Thames in 1813, for which defeat he was publicly reprimanded and suspended from command (Halpenny, *Dictionary of Canadian Biography*, 6:616–18).

3. Benjamin Drake (1794–1841), editor of the literary weekly *Cincinnati Chronicle*, wrote *Life of Tecumseh, and of His Brother the Prophet; With a Historical Sketch of the Shawanoe Indians* (1841), as well as biographies of Black Hawk and William Henry Harrison (Evert A. Duyckinck and George L. Duyckinck, *Cyclopaedia of American Literature* . . . [2 vols.; New York, 1856], 2:79). Drake's "collection of materials" on Tecumseh are now in the Draper Collection at the Wisconsin State Historical Society.

From William Plumer

Dear Sir, Epping (N.H.) Novr 6. 1821

Permit me to request you would accept the enclosed copy of an address delivered by my son[1] to the Rockingham Agricultural Society.[2] The interest you take in Agriculture induces me to think it will not be unacceptable to you. I am with much respect & esteem, Dear Sir, Your friend & servant

William Plumer

RC (DLC). Docketed by JM.

1. William Plumer Jr. (1789–1854), a Harvard-educated lawyer, served several terms in the New Hampshire legislature. In 1817 JM appointed him commissioner of loans for New Hampshire. He served in the U.S. House of Representatives, 1819–25 (Sidney Perley, "The Plumer Genealogy," *Essex Institute Historical Collections* 52 [1916]: 22; *Senate Exec. Proceedings*, 3:70, 72).

2. William Plumer Jr., *An Address Delivered before the Rockingham Agricultural Society, October 18th, 1821* (Exeter, N.H., 1821; Shoemaker 6492).

To Thomas Jefferson

Dear Sir Montpellier Novr. 10. 1821

I return the several papers which accompanied yours of the 30th. ult. I have interlined with a pencil for your consideration a very slight change in the petition to Congress, and another in the Report to the P. & D. of the Lit: Fund. The first is intended to parry objections from the reprinters of foreign books, by a phraseology not precluding exceptions in their favor. The exceptions can be made without injury to the main object; and altho not necessary for the protection of the American Editions, the greater cheapness here being a sufficient one, will probably be called for by the patrons of domestic industry. I find that besides the few Classics for schools, and popular works others of solid value continue to be republished in the Northern Cities. The other interlineation suggests the objects other than the Library to be provided for in the Pantheon. It will aid in accounting for the estimated cost, and may otherwise mitigate difficulties.

The view you take of the question of commencing the Library and trusting to the alternative with the Legislature will claim for it a fair consideration with the Visitors. I shall endeavor to be with you at time you have fixed for their meeting. Yours always & affectionately

James Madison

RC (DLC); draft (DLC: Rives Collection, Madison Papers). RC docketed by Jefferson "recd Nov. 20." Minor differences between the copies have not been noted.

To William Plumer

Dear Sir Montpellier Novr. 17. 1821

I have received the Agricultural Address of your son which you politely inclosed to me. It has handled a very beaten subject in a manner instructive to many and persuasive to all; and is well entitled to the thanks which I tender, with assurances of my great esteem and cordial respects.

James Madison

RC (MB).

From Frederick C. Schaeffer

Sir, Newyork, Nov. 19th 1821.

On a former occasion I took the liberty of submitting to your inspection, a little publication, which I had prepared for the Managers of the Society for the Prevention of Pauperism in NewYork.[1] I was actuated by a desire, which I believe is common to all authors, however trifling their performances, the desire of making known their works to the Great and Good.

I am emboldened to trouble you again, by the kind manner in which you received the "Report to the Managers" &c.—and by the common law of our land, to send a copy of all new publications to the Honorable and distinguished Gentlemen, who, after having presided over a great Republic, enjoy a peculiar degree of happiness, which is confined to them alone, and which must be enhanced by the continual evidences of public veneration and gratitude.

Though your repose may often be disturbed by such of my fellow-citizens, who, like myself, are instrumental in ushering a pamphlet into the world, still, the activity which it intimates cannot be displeasing; and whatever marks the tendency of the times, or may be likely, though even in a small degree, to become subservient to the advantage of any portion of the community and country whose interests you have eminently promoted, is unquestionably acceptable.

These arguments may apologize for the boldness with which I approach you at the present time, in offering you an exemplar of my "Address, pronounced at the laying of the Corner Stone of St. Matthew's Church, NewYork, Oct. 22. 1821; with the Ceremonial on the occasion."[2]

I have always thought, that the view which is generally taken of "the merit of Luther's deeds," is too limited. In the inclosed Address, you will find, I trust, that while I endeavor to give him full credit for what he has performed, I do not subject myself to the accusation of selfish or sectarian principles. With the highest regard, and with the best wishes for your welfare, I am Your friend and servant

F. C. SCHAEFFER

RC (DLC). Docketed by JM.

1. See Schaeffer to JM, 30 Dec. 1819, *PJM-RS*, 1:576–77 and n. 1.

2. Frederick C. Schaeffer, *An Address, Pronounced at the Laying of the Corner Stone of St. Matthew's Church, New-York, October 22, 1821; With the Ceremonial on the Occasion* (New York, 1821; Shoemaker 6723). JM's copy is in the Madison Collection, Rare Book and Special Collections Division, Library of Congress.

To Richard Rush

DEAR SIR MONTPELLIER Novr. 20. 1821

I have been for some time a debtor for your favor of June 21.[1] which was accompanied by the "Apochryphal New Testament." Accept my thanks for both.

I have not yet seen any notice in this Country of Godwin's last work; nor has it been reviewed by any of the English critics which have fallen under my eye. I think with you however that it can scarcely fail to attract public attention. It merits a solid answer; and Malthus himself challenged as he is, will be expected to give one. Our Census is now compleated, tho' I have not seen the precise result. The number it adds to our population, that is, according to Mr. Godwin, the number of emigrants from Europe, of Constitutions more than ordinarily robust, will put this ingenious Author to new difficulties in finding transports & prolific pairs to account for the phenomenon. The increase of the blacks also, where neither emigration nor importation can be pretended, is another hard nut for him to crack.

I observe in the quarterly list of new publications[2] (Decr. 1820) "Classical excursions from Rome to Arpino, by Charles Keilsall" for whom I troubled you with a letter returned with a non est inventus.[3] The absence which produced this volume accounts for his not being then discoverable. As I wish to make him the acknowledgments contained in the letter, and presume he will have got back to England, I take the liberty of replacing it in your hands, in the hope that it may now reach him. I must ask the favor of you also to procure for me a Copy of his recent publication.

We have seen not without some little disappointment the latter developments of character in the Emperor Alexander. He is no longer the patron of the liberal ideas of the age, of the independence of nations, and of their relief from the burdens of[4] warlike Establishments. What is the object of those gigantic armaments which furnish motives or pretexts for imitation throughout Europe? Whether for conquest, or for interference agst. the people in their struggles for political reforms, they equally belye the professions which gave a lustre to his name. What too must be thought of his having no scruples at stepping into the domestic quarrels of Naples agst. the people contending for their rights, and his scrupling to intermeddle in the domestic affairs of Turkey agst. the most atrocious of despotisms wreaking its worst cruelties on a people having peculiar claims to the sympathy of the Christian as well as the civilized world.

Russia seems at present the great Bug-Bear of the European politicians on the land, as the British Leviathan is on the water. They are certainly both formidable powers at this time, and must always hold a high rank among the nations of Europe. I cannot but think however that the future growth of Russia, and the stability of British ascendancy, are not a little overrated. Without a civilization of the Hordes nominally extending the Russian dominion over so many latitudes & longitudes, they will add little to her real force, if they do not detract from it: and in the event of their civilization and consequent increase, the overgrown empire, as in so many preceding instances, must fall into separate & independent States. With respect to G. Britain her overbearing power is derived from the vast extent of her manufactures and of her commerce, which furnish her naval resources. But as other nations infuse free principles into their Governments, and extend the policy they are adopting of doing for themselves, what G.B. has been allowed to do for them, she will, like the Dutch who once enjoyed a like ascendancy on the same element, be reduced within her natural sphere.

If my partiality, as an American, does not misguide my judgment, the Trident will ultimately belong not to the Eastern, but the western Hemisphere. It is in the latter, not the former, that the greater and more lasting fund of materials is found for constructing ships, and for bulky cargoes; and consequently for the employment of mariners. With dispositions therefore on this side the Atlantic to take advantage of the gifts of nature, corresponding with those on the other to make the most of factitious resources, the inference drawn seems an obvious one. I pray & hope at the same time that the Trident may not[5] be the symbol of lawless power in the New, as it has been in the Old world.

The year past has been distinguished by much sickness throughout a great portion of the U.S: tho' the mortality has not been very considerable, except in particular spots. Virginia has had a large share of the calamity; and this part of the State more than an equal one. In my own family the fever has been very severe. At present we are happily freed from it. It was of the typhoid character, and seemed to select for its visitations the more elevated & healthy, rather than the situations most subject to annual complaints. Its type has been most malignant also in the cold season.

The year has been unfavorable also to the productions of our soil. In the States North of Maryland, the Wheat Crops are said to be below the average; and in Maryland & Virginia the failure has been beyond example, occasioned by a very wet spring, and continued rains during the harvest. The Crops of Maize, on the other hand, tho' not universally are generally good; and in this particular quarter, uncommonly abundant. The crops of Tobacco are somewhat deficient I believe every where, tho' better in the result than they were in the promise. Complaints are made I observe, from the Cotton Country of scanty crops there also. But I can not speak with certainty on that point. There is probably both truth and exaggeration in the reports. Tho' you are not on the list of either farmers or planters, the interest you feel as a good citizen in whatever concerns so great a portion of them, will render such agricultural notices not unobtrusive.

Mrs. Madison charges me, as she does on all such occasions, with her affectionate salutations for Mrs. Rush, to which I add mine with equal sincerity; with assurances to yourself of my high esteem and my stedfast attachment.

James Madison

Will you let me trouble you with a letter which I have occasion to write to Mr. Joy?[6]

RC (PHi: Richard Rush Collection); draft (DLC). Minor differences between the copies have not been noted.

1. Rush to JM, 25 June 1821.
2. In the draft JM added here "in England for."
3. *Non est inventus:* he has not been found. For JM's letter to Charles Kelsall, October 1817, and Rush's attempt to deliver it, see *PJM-RS,* 1:136, 249–50, 251 nn. 1–2.
4. The draft has "imposed by" in place of "of" here.
5. The draft has "never" in place of "not" here.
6. JM to George Joy, 21 Nov. 1821.

To George Joy

Dear Sir Montpellier Novr. 21. 1821

I have not forgotten your favor of Feby. last,[1] tho' I am so tardy in acknowledging it. The truth is, I find as generally happens, that age is daily increasing my disinclination to use the pen, as it possibly may, tho' I am less sensible of it, an inclination for the other mode of communicating our thoughts. I might find an apology also, in a very afflicting fever of the typhoid character which has been constantly in my family for a year past, and from which I did not escape myself. I should nevertheless have not failed to answer that part of your letter which called for my aid in procuring (for I did not possess) a Newspaper Copy of your "Conciliator,["] if I could have procured one. I give you the answer of Mr. Gales to my application on the subject in his own words. "I much regret that it is wholly out of my power to oblige Mr Joy. Admiral Cockburn, when he paid his respects to us, took care to leave us no spare copies of the National Intelligencer, having burnt them with the few books I had at that time collected."[2] In writing to Mr. Gales I took occasion to hand over to him the newspapers you were so good as to send me. Whether he republished any thing from them, I can not say. If he did not, it was probably owing to the crowd of matte⟨r⟩ which his paper experiences, and to the decreasing interest taken by his readers in what occurs abroad, as the importance increases in their eyes of what occurs at home. Heretofore every incident in the great nations of Europe, especially in G.B. awakened a lively curiosity in the public here: and this tendency still exists in a considerable degree. It is however becoming less & less; as on the other hand, what passes here is understood to be more & more an object of attention abroad. This is a natural consequence of the change going on in the relative growth of this Country. If it should continue to prosper till it reaches a population, which self love predicts, of 60 or 70 millions, the scene will be reversed; and the eyes of England will be as much turned toward the U.S. as the eyes of the latter have been towards her and their eyes as little towards her, as hers have been towards them. This is a light in which the people of G.B. are too proud to view the future; and the people of this country too—vain—if that be the epithet, not to regard it.

I did not send Mr. Gales the newspapers without looking over the speech of your nephew in one of them. I will not say that your criticisms might not have improved it; but it is a specimen of talents which promise to do well without your or any other aid. I can say nothing of the work of Mr. Tudor, not having had an oppy. of looking into it. From the general commendations bestowed on it, and the literary reputation of the Author, I can not doubt that it merits all you say of it.

We had a very wet harvest, throughout a great portion of our Wheat Country, as appears to have been the case in G.B. There is a surplus here however which would gladly supply the deficiency there; and the supply would be as welcome there I presume as here if the question were to be decided by the manufacturers, instead agriculturists. Whilst the prohibitory laws continue, the effect must be an increase of ploughs on that side, and of looms on this. With a tender of my respects and my best wishes I remain your friend & servt.

J.M

Draft (DLC).

1. George Joy to JM, 9 Feb. 1821.
2. Joseph Gales Jr. to JM, 22 June 1821.

To Dolley Madison

My dearest Monticello Friday Morning [30 November 1821]

I snatch a moment and a very bad pen to tell you that we ended our journey in good time that is before it was dark. The roads, with a little exception, were better than was expected. We found every body well, much regretting that you could not join in the visit. It was well that I did not decline it, for there would not have been a Quorum without me, Gen'l Taylor & Mr. Breckinridge, not being heard from & Mr. Cabell sick in Williamsburg. Genl. Cocke arrived just before me, himself imperfectly recd. from his late illness. To-day we shall make a Quorum with the aid of Mr. Johnson who is in the neighbourhood on his way to Richmond & will be sent for to meet us at the University. It seems that yesterday was the day requiring me to be *there*, instead of at Monticello; so that if others had attended I should have been a day after the fair. I hope the business will be over today & that tomorrow evening I may be again with you or the morning after at farthest, unless I shd. be obliged to stop at Col: Lindsay, or the weather shd. embargo us. Yrs most affectly.

James Madison

Typescript of RC (obtained from ICU in 1967). RC owned by Harry J. Sonneborn, Theodore, Ala., 1968. Undated; conjectural date established on the basis of internal evidence, the meeting of the visitors of the University of Virginia, 29–30 Nov. 1821, and Jefferson to James Breckinridge, 9 Dec. 1821 (DLC: Jefferson Papers).

Minutes of the Board of Visitors of the University of Virginia

Nov. 30. 1821.

November 30. Present Thomas Jefferson, Chapman Johnson, James Madison & John Hartwell Cocke.

The board being informed that of the 60,000.D. permitted to be borrowed from the Literary fund by the act of the last General assembly, the sum of 29.100.D. only has as yet been obtained, and that there is uncertainty as to the time when the balance may be obtained they deem it expedient that the Annuity of 15,000.D. recievable on the 1st. of January next be applied to the accomplishment of the buildings, & other current purposes, in the first place, and that, should further sums be wanted before the reciept of the balance of the sd. loan, the Committee of Superintendance be authorised to borrow from the banks to the amount of that balance, to be replaced by the sd. balance when recieved.

Resolved that the Superintending committee be authorised to have an engraving made of the ground-plat of the buildings of the University including the Library, and so many copies struck off for sale as they shall think proper, and also to engage a good painter to draw a Perspective view of the upper level of buildings, to be engraved, yielding to him, for his trouble, the patent right, and paying his reasonable expences coming, staying and returning, should it be required.

A proposition having been recieved to join with other seminaries in a petition to Congress for a repeal of the duty on imported books, Resolved that this board will concur in such a petition, and a form being prepared and approved, and a form also of a letter to our Senators and representatives in Congress requesting them to present & advocate the sd. petition, the Rector is desired to authenticate & forward the same.

A form of a Report, as annually required to be made to the President and Directors of the Literary fund, on the funds and condition of the University, was then proposed, amended & agreed to in the following words.

To the President & Directors of the Literary fund.

In obedience to the act of the General assembly of Virginia, requiring that the Rector and Visitors of the University of Virginia should make report annually to the President and Directors of the Literary fund (to be laid before the legislature at their next succeeding session) embracing a full account of the disbursements, the funds on hand, and a general statement of the condition of the sd. University, the sd Rector & Visitors make the following Report.

At their meeting in April last the attention of the Visitors was first drawn to the consideration of the act of the late General assembly which authorised the Literary board to lend, for the use of the University a further sum of 60,000.D. from such monies as should thereafter come to their hands, and taking such view as could then be obtained of the expences already incurred for the lands, buildings, and accessory purposes for the accomodation of the Professors and Students of the University, so far as already compleated, or in a state of advancement, and the further expences still to be incurred necessarily to compleat those accomodations, they concluded it to be for the benefit of the institution to obtain the said loan. Application was accordingly made to the Literary board, a sum of 29,100.D. was obtained, and the further sum of 30,900.D. is expected so soon as the reciepts of that board shall enable them to furnish it.

In the mean time the board deemed it incumbent to obtain as early as possible a correct statement of the actual cost of what was already done, and a probable one of that still to be done, estimated according to the experience now obtained. They therefore instructed their Proctor to apply himself assiduously to the completion of the buildings generally, to a settlement of all accounts of the actual cost of those finished, and an estimate, according to that, of what would be the cost of those still to be finished. The completion of the buildings of accomodation, which are in 4. rows of about 600. feet in length each, as may be seen by the plan accompanying this Report, has been pressed with as much effect as could be expected; insomuch that there are now compleat, and in readiness for occupation, 6. Pavilions for the accomodation of the Professors, 82. dormitories for that of the Students, and 2. Hotels for their dieting; and the others will all be compleated in the ensuing summer. The accounts for the construction of those already finished have been actually settled; and the probable cost of the unfinished has been estimated according to the rates which the others have been found to cost.

The following is a summary view of the actual expenditures of the institution from the beginning, of those yet to be incurred to it's completion, & of the funds recieved & still recievable, as nearly as can at present be stated.

6. Pavilions finished have cost	52,713.76	
17. capitels for them expected from Italy are to cost by contract	2,052.	
2. Hotels finished have cost	8,215.82	
82. Dormitories finished have cost	52,997.74	
	113,927.	[*sic*]

The following are nearly finished,
& are estimated at the rates the others have cost, or at prices actually contracted for.

4. Pavilions	33,563.15	
4 Hotels	16,000.	
27. Dormitories	11,982.21	61,515.
Back yards and gardens		1,500.
making the whole cost of the 4. rows of buildings of accomodation		176,942
The purchase of 245½ acres of land & the buildings on them, past compensations to the Bursar and Proctor, hire & maintenance of laborers, & all other accessory and contingent expences		24,607
making a total for the lands, buildings Etc. compleat		201,550 [*sic*]
to which add for interest on the loans, calculated to Dec. 31. 1821.		6,160
		207,710 [*sic*]
The funds applied and applicable to these expenditures are	D	
The sale of Glebe lands	3,104.09	
A state certificate No. 32. bearing interest	176.77	
Annuities of 1819. 20. 21.	45,000.	
loan of 1820.	60,000.	
loan of 1821.	60,000.	
Subscriptions recieved to Nov. 27. 21.	24,676.37½	
Balance of subscriptions (due 19,668.91 of which suppose 3000. lost)	16,668.95	209,626.18
from this would result a small Surplus of		1,915.48
		207,710.70

According to the Proctor's Accounts for the present year (which, with the Bursar's are herewith inclosed, and) which contain minuter specifications of the expenditures

To finish and pay for the whole of the buildings of accommodation not yet finished and paid for will require a further sum to be placed at his command of		53.494.79
The resources for this are		
the balance of the loan of 21. still to be recieved	30,900.	
the balance still due of subscription monies, sperate	16,668.95	

Cash in the banks undrawn as per Bursar's account	2,301.23	
do. in the Bursar's hands, as per his account	447.84	
State certificate No. 32	176.77	
from which would result a deficit to be supplied from the annuity of	3.000.	53,494.79

So far then as can at present be seen (and we are now so near the end of this work that there is room for little error) the funds recieved and recievable, will, within a small fraction, pay for the lands purchased, for the whole system of buildings of accomodation, and all accessory expences.

The building for the library, comprehending Halls indispensably necessary for other public purposes, and estimated by the Proctor, according to past experience, to cost 46,847.D. will remain to be erected from the same fund of the Annuity. The anticipations of this by loans, for expediting the other buildings, will have weakened it by nearly one half it's amount by the sums of interest to which it is subject; and will consequently retard the commencement of it's applications to the discharge of the sums borrowed by annual instalments; if such should continue to be the will of the Legislature.

The buildings of accommodation will be finished, as before observed, in the ensuing summer, and will constitute the whole establishment, except that of the library. With the close of these works, the accounts of their costs will also be closed. These will be first examined by a committee of the Visitors that nothing may enter into them not sanctioned by the board. They will then be finally submitted to the Accountant of the Literary board, for the assurance of the public that the monies have been correctly and faithfully applied.

In the course of these works, as is unavoidable perhaps generally in those of considerable magnitude, there have occurred instances of monies paid, not in direct furtherance of the legitimate object. The first was the case of a contract by the Visitors of the Central College, for a Professor, while acting for that as a private establishment, and under an expectation of it's immediate commencement. But that institution being afterwards merged in this of the University, and the enlargement of the plan occasioning that of the time of it's commencement also, it became important that that contract should be rescinded. This was done on a just and reasonable compromise and indemnification of 1500. Dollars. Another instance was the importation of a foreign Artist, for carving the capitels of the more difficult orders of the buildings. The few persons in this country, capable of that work, were able to obtain elsewhere such high prices for their skill and labor that we believed it would be economy to procure an Artist from some country where skill is more abundant, & labor cheaper. We did so. But on trial the stone we had counted on in the neighborhood of the University was found totally insusceptible of delicate work; and some from a very distant, but the nearest other quarry known, besides a heavy expence attending it's transportation, was extremely tedious to work, and believed not proof against the influences of the weather. In the mean time we had enquired and learned that the same capitels could be furnished in Italy, and delivered in our own ports for a half, or third, of the price, in marble, which they would have cost us here in doubtful stone. We arrested the work here therefore, and compromised with our Artist at the expence of his past wages, his board and passage hither, amounting to 1390 D. 56C. These are the only instances of false expence which have occurred within our knolege.

The two Pavilions and their adjacent Dormitories, begun & considerably advanced by the authorities of the Central College, were contracted for by them, when all things were at their most inflated paper-prices, and therefore have been of extraordinary cost. But all the buildings since done on the more enlarged scale of the University have been at prices of from 25. to 50. per cent reduction; and it is confidently believed that, with that exception, no considerable system of building, within the US. has been done on cheaper terms, nor more correctly, faithfully, or solidly executed, according to the nature of the materials used.

That the style or scale of the buildings should have met the approbation of every individual judgment was impossible from the various structure of various minds. Whether it has satisfied the general judgment, is not known to us. No previous expression of that was manifested but in the injunctions of the law to provide for the accommodation of ten Professors, and a competent number of students; and by the subsequent enactments, implying an approbation of the plan reported by the original Commissioners, on the requisition of the law constituting them; which plan was exactly that now carried into execution. We had therefore no supplementary guide but our own judgments, which we have exercised conscientiously, in adopting a scale and style of building believed to be proportioned to the respectability, the means & the wants of our country, and such as will be approved in any future condition it may attain. We owed to it to do, not what was to perish with ourselves, but what would remain, be respected and preserved thro' other ages. And we fondly hope that the instruction which may flow from this institution, kindly cherished, by advancing the minds of our youth with the growing science of the times, and elevating the views of our citizens generally to the practice of the social duties, and the functions of self-government, may ensure to our country the reputation, the safety and prosperity, and all the other blessings which experience proves to result from the cultivation and improvement of the general mind. And, without going into the monitory history of the antient world, in all it's quarters, and at all it's periods, that of the soil on which we live, and of it's occupants, indigenous & immigrant, teaches the awful lesson, that no nation is permitted to live in ignorance with impunity.

And the board adjourned without day.

TH: JEFFERSON Rector
Nov. 29. 1821. [*sic*]

Ms (ViU: Jefferson Papers, Special Collections). In Jefferson's hand.

From the Rector and Visitors of the University of Virginia

THE RECTOR AND VISITORS OF THE UNIVERSITY OF VIRGINIA TO THE SENATORS AND REPRESENTATIVES OF THE SD. STATE IN CONGRESS.

GENTLEMEN UNIVERSITY Nov. 30. 1821

We learn that it is in contemplation with other seminaries of science in the US. to petition Congress at their ensuing session for a repeal of the duty on books imported from abroad. This tax, so injurious to the progress of literature, concerning nearly the interests of those for whose benefit our state has established the institution committed to our charge, we think it our duty to cooperate with our sister institutions in obtaining the relief so desirable for all. We have therefore prepared the petition now inclosed, in which the grounds of our application are so particularly detailed, that they need not be here repeated. Persuading ourselves that you will consider this measure for the benefit of our youth claiming equally with the University itself the patronage of the state, we have to sollicit your advocation of it in both houses of Congress. As similar applications are proposed from other quarters of the Union, your own judgment and discretion will decide on the degree of concert, in the time and mode of proceeding which will be most advisable. Committing the subject therefore to your enlightened sense of it's importance to our common country we salute you with assurances of our esteem and high consideration.

TH: JEFFERSON Rector

[Enclosure]

To the Senate and House of Representatives of the United States of America in Congress assembled.

The Petition of the Rector and Visitors of the University of Virginia On behalf of those for whom they are in the office of preparing the means of instruction, as well as of others seeking it elsewhere,

Respectfully representeth:

That the Commonwealth of Virginia has thought proper lately to establish an University for instruction generally in all the useful branches of science, of which your petitioners are appointed Rector and Visitors, and as such are charged with attention to the interests of those who shall be committed to their care:

That they observe in the Tariff of duties imposed by the laws of Congress on importations into the US. an article peculiarly inauspicious to the objects of their own, and of all other literary institutions throughout the US.

That at an early period of the present government, when our country was burthened with a heavy debt contracted in the war of Independance, and it's resources for revenue were untried and uncertain, the national legislature thought it as yet inexpedient to indulge in scruples as to the subjects of taxation, and among others imposed a duty on books imported from abroad, which has been continued, and now is of 15. percent on their prime cost, raised by ordinary Custom house charges to 18. percent, and by the importers profits to perhaps 25. percent, & more:

That, after many years experience, it is certainly found that the reprinting of books in the US. is confined chiefly to those in our native language, and of popular characters, and to cheap editions of a few of the Classics, for the use of schools; while the valuable editions of the Classical authors, even learned works in the English language, and books in all foreign living languages (vehicles of the important discoveries and improvements in science and the arts, which are daily advancing the interests and happiness of other nations) are unprinted here & unobtainable from abroad but under the burthen of a heavy duty.

That of many important books in different branches of science, it is believed that there is not a single copy in the US. of others but a few, and these too distant and difficult of access for students and writers generally:

That the difficulty resulting from this of procuring books of the first order in the sciences, and in foreign languages, antient and modern, is an unfair impediment to the American student, who, for want of these aids, already possessed or easily procurable in all countries, except our own, enters on his course with very unequal means, with wants unknown to his foreign competitors, and often with that imperfect result which subjects us to reproaches not unfelt by minds alive to the honor, and mortified sensibilities of their country:

That to obstruct the acquisition of books from abroad, as an encoragement of the progress of literature at home, is burying the fountain to increase the flow of it's waters.

That books, and especially those of the rare and valuable character thus burthened, are not articles of consumption, but of permanent preservation and value, lasting often as many centuries as the houses we live in, of which examples are to be found in every library of note:

That books therefore are Capital, often the only Capital of professional men on their outset in life, and of students destined for professions, as most of our scholars are, and who are barely able too for the most part, to meet the expences of tuition, and less so to pay an extra tax on the books necessary for their instruction: that they are consequently less instructed than they would be, and that our citizens at large do not derive from their employment all the benefits which higher qualifications would procure them:

That this is the only form of Capital on which a tax of from 18. to 25. per cent is first levied on the gross, and the proprietor then subject to all other taxes in detail as those holding capital in other forms, on which no such extra tax has been previously levied:

That it is true that no duty is required on books imported for seminaries of learning: but these, locked up in libraries, can be of no avail to the practical man, when he wishes a recurrence to them for the uses of life:

That more than 30 years experience of the resources of our country prove them equal to all it's debts and wants, and permit it's legislature now to favor such objects as the public interests recommend to favor:

That the value of science to a republican people, the security it gives to liberty by enlightening the minds of it's citizens, the protection it affords against foreign power, the virtues it inculcates, the just emulation of the distinction it confers on nations foremost in it, in short it's identification with power, morals, order and happiness, (which merits to it premiums of encoragement rather than repressive taxes) are topics which your petitioners do not permit themselves to urge on the wisdom of Congress, before whose minds these considerations are always present & bearing with their just weight:

And they conclude therefore with praying that Congress will be pleased to bestow on this important subject the attention it merits, and give the proper relief to the candidates of science among ourselves devoting themselves to the laudable object of qualifying themselves to become the Instructors and benefactors of their fellow-citizens:

and your petitioners as in duty bound will ever pray Etc.

Th: Jefferson Rector of the
University of Virginia
Nov. 30. 1821.

FC and draft of enclosure (ViU: Special Collections). In Jefferson's hand.

From Mathew Carey

Dear sir   Philada Decr 1. 1821

I am writing some essays on the situation & policy of this Country, previous to the revolution—and am desirous of obtaining information on the following points.

Was the balance of trade between Great Britain & the southern Colonies, particularly Va. against the latter?

Was there a heavy balance due from the Colonies to Great Britain?

Can you form any idea of the amount? Your obt. hble. servt.

Mathew Carey

RC (DLC). Addressed in an unidentified hand to JM, and franked. Docketed by JM.

To Frederick C. Schaeffer

Revd. Sir   Montpr. Decr. 3. 1821

I have recd. with your letter of Novr. 19: the copy of your address at the ceremonial of laying the Corner Stone of St. Mathews Church in N. York.

It is a pleasing & persuasive example of pious zeal, united with pure benevolence; and of cordial attachment to a particular creed, untinctured with Sectarian illiberality. It illustrates the excellence of a system which, by a due distinction to which the genius & courage of Luther led the way, between what is due to Cæsar & what is due to God, best promotes the discharge of both obligations. The experience of the U.S. is a happy disproof of the error so long rooted in the unenlightened minds of well meaning Christians, as well as in the corrupt hearts of persecuting Usurpers, that without a legal incorporation of religious & civil polity, neither could be supported. A mutual independence is found most friendly to practical Religion, to social harmony, & to political prosperity. In return for your kind sentiments I tender assurances of my esteem & my best wishes.

J. M.

Draft (DLC).

To Benjamin Drake

Sir Decr. 8. 1821

I recd. a few days ago your letter of Novr. 6. on the subject of materials for a "Biographical sketch of the Celebrated Tecumseh."

I cannot better answer it, than by referring you to the Dept. of War, the files of which contain the official correspondence and communications from the military Commanders & Indian Agents most likely to furnish interesting particulars relating to that Chief as well as to his brother the prophet. It is probable that some of the Officers, particularly Genl. Harrison,[1] may be consulted with advantage, on points not included in their official letters & transactions.

I wish you may be successful in collecting adequate materials for your proposed work: I wish it the more, as your attention will of course be drawn to general views of the Indian Character in tracing the particular features of that of the distinguished individual in question.

Draft (DLC). RC offered for sale in Stan. V. Henkels Catalogue No. 694 (6–7 Dec. 1892), item 80.

1. William Henry Harrison (1773–1841) served in the U.S. Army, 1791–98, as secretary of the Northwest Territory, 1798–1800, and as governor of the Indiana Territory, 1800–1813. During the War of 1812 Harrison was commissioned a brigadier general and given command of the army of the Northwest. He was promoted to major general in March 1813. In October of that year Harrison's troops secured a victory at the Battle of the Thames in which the great Indian leader Tecumseh was killed. Harrison later served as an Ohio representative to Congress, 1816–19, as a U.S. senator, 1825–28, as U.S. minister to Colombia, 1828–29, and as ninth president of the United States, a term that lasted about a month before his death from pneumonia.

From John G. Jackson

Dear Sir, Clarksburg December 9th. 1821

Ever since your retirement from the chief executive magistracy of the Union, I have indulged a constant desire to commence a correspondence with you. At first for a season I thought it prudent to defer the expression of this desire, because I imagined it would be a work of much labor to you to give in your retreat a final arrangement to the voluminous papers, connected with your great, & arduous official functions. And since the time has elapsed, which a due allowance for that employment would seem to indicate as sufficient, I have felt further restraint in the fear that I might be exacting a favor from your kindness, to which, as nothing I could communicate would furnish the least equivalent, you must necessarily feel some reluctance. I now only venture to address you because I believe that the period has arrived when a publication of the debates &c of the federal Convention, which you are known to possess in manuscript, is demanded by a regard to justice & expediency. May I therefore respectfully solicit you to give them to the public? It is not a mere inordinate curiosity that excites me to desire it—nor yet the belief that your reputation as a politician requires any vindication. The meagre journal of the Convention, & the notes of Chief Justice Yates which have been printed; have excited a laudable curiosity, & interest, common to all your friends, to know the real facts. If however I err in the opinion I entertain, & any thing may exist of which I am ignorant, rendering their publicity clearly improper, I would not be understood as desiring that the considerations they suggest should be disregarded. If indeed you did propose to infuse more vigor, & strength into the national Government than it possesses, I will frankly own that an attentive observation of its progress for more than twenty years, has convinced me, (contrary to my first impressions) that the Union has more to fear from inadequacy of power in the head, & anarchy in the members, than from every other danger combined. I appeal to the history of the late War, for proofs of the correctness of this opinion. They are too recent, & striking to require enumeration. The paralysis of the operations of the government—the enormous expenditure of public treasure—& the extent of individual, & national misfortune produced by the infamous practices of a faction in some of the States; have taught a lesson never to be forgotten.

It is some time since I heard of you & Mrs. Madison. I hope you both enjoy good health. In my family we have been visited in the past six months with great & distressing sickness. Our most lovely child Madisonia six years old, & an infant son nine months old fell victims to it. We have surviving a Daughter Sophia eight years old, & a Son James four years old. Mary is now at home, she is well, & is quite large. Mrs. Jackson & her unite in sending their affectionate regards to Mrs. Madison. Please present me to her respectfully, & believe me to be with great Regard your mo. obt. Servt.

JG Jackson[1]

RC (DLC: Rives Collection, Madison Papers); draft (InU: Jackson Collection). RC addressed by Jackson to JM, and franked; docketed by JM.

1. John George Jackson (1777–1825) of Clarksburg, Virginia (now West Virginia), was a surveyor and lawyer who was married to Dolley Madison's sister, Mary Payne, by early 1801. After Mary's death in 1808, he married Mary Sophia Meigs, the daughter of Return Jonathan Meigs Jr. Jackson represented Harrison County in the Virginia House of Delegates, 1798–1801, 1811–12, and was a member of the U.S. House of Representatives, 1803–10 and 1813–17. He was appointed U.S. judge for the western district of Virginia in 1819 and held that office until his death (Stephen W. Brown, *Voice of the New West: John G. Jackson, His Life and Times* [Macon, Ga., 1985], 1, 8, 9, 10–11, 15, 27, 45, 47, 59, 69, 81, 92, 96, 100, 103, 141, 168, 185, 225–26, 242).

To Mathew Carey

Dear Sir Montpellier Decr. 12th. 1821.

I have received your letter of the 1st. inst. and am sorry that neither my memory, nor my knowledge goes far enough back to furnish the desirable answers to your questions, whether and to what amount, the balance in the trade with G. Britain was against the colonies, particularly Virginia previous to the Revolution. That the ordinary balance was unfavorable cannot be doubted, and the limit to its amount was probably determined pretty much by the limit beyond which credit would not be extended.

The general fact of an unfavorable balance might be inferred from the mode in which the trade was carried on, in the Southern states at least, and particularly Virga. G. Britain had then a monopoly both as a buyer of Colonial commodities, and as a seller of her own; and her factors in the colonies, were in the practice of giving long credits, with little discriminations among customers; the responsible part of whom were made, by high prices, to afford indemnities for defaulters. Long credits are always snares to the inconsiderate, and often to those who are not so.

It is well known accordingly, that at the commencement of the Revolution, there were heavy debts due to G.B. from some of the Colonies, if not all, and particularly from Virginia. The amount was such as to make an important Article in the Treaty of peace,[1] and to occasion difficulties in carrying it into execution. These debts must have been accumulations of unfavorable balances for a series of preceding years.

The successive emissions of paper money by the Colonies[2] are another indication of the general fact. These emissions were founded on petitions and pleas growing out of a scarcity of coin, to be best accounted for by its remittance to G.B. towards discharging the commercial balance in her favor. Were the immediate cause of the emissions to be sought in the interest of the authors as debtors, in providing a depreciated currency, the conclusion would not be different; the debts being for the most part due to British factors, for British merchandize consumed beyond the products of the consumers; and consequently due to G.B. beyond the ordinary means of paying for them.

I am aware that these views of the subject are too vague to be of avail to your particular researches. They will not probably suggest any general Ideas which will not of themselves occur to you. They can only be regarded therefore as a testimony of the respect of which I take occasion to repeat my assurances.

FC (DLC). In John Payne Todd's hand, with JM's note "Mathew Carey" at the top of the first page.

1. Article 4 of the 1783 Treaty of Paris between the United States and Great Britain provided that "creditors on either Side shall meet with no lawful Impediment to the Recovery of the full Value in Sterling Money of all bona fide Debts heretofore contracted" (Miller, *Treaties*, 2:154).

2. "By the Colonies" interlined by JM.

From Benjamin H. Rand

SIR PHILADELPHIA 16th. Decr 1821.

I have just Published an elegant Edition of the Farewell Address of the late President Washington.[1] If you will condescend to give a Copy of it a place in your Library, you will confer a particular favour on Your Obedient & Very Humble Servant

B. H. RAND[2]

The Work alluded to I have forwarded to the care of Mr Wm Browne of Georgetown D.C.

RC (DLC). Docketed by JM.

1. Rand's engraved broadside of *Washington's Farewell Address to the People of the United States* is one of many of his printed works described in Ray Nash, *American Penmanship, 1800–1850: A History of Writing and a Bibliography of Copybooks from Jenkins to Spencer* (Worcester, Mass., 1969), 103.

2. Benjamin Howard Rand (1792–1862) was a professional teacher of penmanship who published twenty-six copybooks and manuals on the subject (ibid., 20–21).

To Mackay & Campbell

GENTLEMEN Decr 18 1821

The bills on M. & L. lately sent you expressed the balance due to me as stated in the Acct. Sales. The Acct current just come to hand, contains a few items of which I was not aware, reducing the balance from £28.3.5. to £21.15.2. Should the Bills not be out of your reach be so good as to let me replace them with a correct set. Should the oppy. be past, I must ask the favor of you to adjust the difference in your Acct. with Messrs. M. & L. and retain as much of the proceeds of the Bills as will reimburse you.

Draft (DLC).

From Thomas Munroe

SIR WASHINGTON 20th. December 1821

My Son, Thomas,[1] now in the 24th year of his age, who was educated at Yale College, and afterwards studied law, having always evinced, and still continuing to have so decided a preference of the military, to all other professions, that his mother and myself have yielded to his wishes; and he will shortly proceed to St. Petersburg to offer his services to the Emperor of Russia; with the explicit understanding that his object is to obtain a Military Education, at his own expense, that he may be useful to his own Country, to which he is to be at liberty to return at pleasure, unrestrained by any allegiance or other obligations, except an Oath of fidelity whi[l]st he may be employed in the Russian service. This Mr Politica, who has entered warmly into my Sons views, says is all that will be expected by his Government.

The testimonials and kind interest in favor of my Son by the Executive, Mr Adams & Mr Pinkney, former ministers to Russia, and some other distinguished American Characters, now at the Seat of Government, together with all the Foreign ministers and Charge des Affaires, are very flattering, do him much honor, and will, it is believed, put him on a favorable and advantageous footing in a foreign Country; but we are told by Mr. Politica and others what indeed, both my Son & myself, are very confident of, that nothing would be so useful to him as something that you, Sir, might be pleased to say of a young American on such an occasion, addressed either to the Emperor himself (which Mr. Politica says would be received with great deference from you, Sir, or from Mr Jefferson) or if preferred by you, to Count Nesselrode,[2] Mr. Middleton,[3] our minister at St. Petersburg, or to him, Mr Politica.

If I have been too presuming in thus addressing you, Sir, I trust that the interesting nature of the subject to a parents feelings, and the high value I should place on any thing that you might be pleased to say on it will plead my excuse. I have the honor to be with the highest respect & veneration Sir Yr mo Obt Servt

THOMAS MUNROE[4]

P.S. I take the liberty of enclosing a Copy of Mr Adams's Letter.[5] All the others are nearly like it in substance.

RC and enclosure (DLC). Addressed by Munroe to JM, and franked. Cover docketed by JM. For enclosure, see n. 5.

1. Thomas Munroe Jr. had been a clerk in the Washington post office headed by his father. A notice in the *Richmond Enquirer*, 17 May 1822, stated that Munroe had arrived in Liverpool on 6 Apr. (Madison Davis, "A History of the City Post-Office," *Records of the Columbia Historical Society* 6 [1903]: 169).

2. Karl Robert Nesselrode (1780–1862) was a Russian diplomat and statesman who headed the Russian delegation at the congresses of Vienna, Aix-la-Chapelle, Troppau, Laibach, and Verona. Between 1815 and 1822 Nesselrode shared responsibilities in the foreign ministry with Ioannis Capodistrias (Joseph L. Wieczynski, ed., *The Modern Encyclopedia of Russian and Soviet History* [60 vols.; Gulf Breeze, Fla., 1976–2000], 24:162–64).

3. Henry Middleton (1770–1846) was born in England, the son of a South Carolina planter. He served in the state's legislature, 1802–10, and as governor of South Carolina, 1810–12. Middleton was a member of the U.S. House of Representatives, 1815–19, and served as U.S. minister to Russia, 1820–30 (Sobel and Raimo, *Biographical Directory of the Governors*, 4:1392–93).

4. Thomas Munroe (1771–1852) served as postmaster of Washington from 1799 to 1829. He was also involved in a number of civic endeavors, which included serving as an officer of the Bank of Columbia, an incorporator of the Washington Bridge Company, and as one of the founders of the Bank of the Metropolis (Davis, "History of the City Post-Office," *Records of the Columbia Historical Society* 6 [1903]: 157–59).

5. The enclosure (1 p.) is a copy of a letter of recommendation from John Quincy Adams to Petr Ivanovich Poletika, 15 Dec. 1821, in favor of Thomas Munroe Jr.

To Henry Middleton

Sir Decr. 24. 1821

Mr. Ths. Munroe son of Ths. Mu[n]roe Esqr. of the City of Washington, having compleated his academic Studies, has fixed his thoughts so earnestly on the profession of arms, that he is about to offer his services in the Military estabt. of Russia, as a school favorable to his proficiency. It is understood that he is to serve at his own expence; that as his services are to be entirely voluntary, so will be the time of his retiring from them; and that the nature of his engagement is in no respect to impair his character of Citizen of the U.S. to which he hopes to return with capacities to be a more useful one.

So much evidence is before me from the most respectable sources, of the promising qualities and laudable views of this young gentleman, that he necessarily carrys with him my wishes that he may be successful in his pursuit; and I cannot better manifest them than by the liberty I take of recommending him to whatever patronage, you may find most proper and most likely to introduce his object with advantage. I avail myself Sir, of this occasion to tender you assurances of my high consideration & particular respect

J.M.

Draft (DLC). RC enclosed in JM to Thomas Munroe, ca. 24 Dec. 1821.

To Thomas Munroe

DR SIR [ca. 24] Decr 1821

I have just recd. your letter of the 20th. and inclose a few lines, on the subject of it to our E. Exy. & M. Plenipo: at St. Petersburg.[1] I am not sure that I could properly take the liberty of addressing them to the Emperor himself.

I sincerely wish Sir that your son may find in the course he has chosen, all the success, which he enjoys in prospect: and that he may return with all the acquirements suited to gain him distinction in his own Country and gratify the feelings & expectations of his parents. Be pleased Sir to accept my esteem and my good wishes.

Draft (DLC). Day of month not indicated; conjectural day assigned based on comparison with Munroe to JM, 20 Dec. 1821, and JM to Middleton, 24 Dec. 1821.

1. JM to Henry Middleton, 24 Dec. 1821.

From John A. Wharton

SIR NEAR DAVIS' STORE Dec. 27th 1[8]21

Some five or six months since, I addressed a letter to you, from Nashville Tennessee:[1] requesting any information which you might possess relative to the University established near Charlottesville. From the circumstance of your not having acknowledged the receipt of it, I am persauded [*sic*] you did not receive it: I therefore take the liberty of addressing a second letter, the object of which is precisely the same as that of the first, to wit:

When the institution will be opened for the reception of students?

What qualifications are necessary to insure an entrance into either class?

What will be the expenses of board and tuition per annum?

You will pardon the last enquiry, as econimy in my financial calculations, is indispensably necessary: and as I entertain fears that I will be compelled, with an eminent degree of reluctance, to abandon the pursuit of a favorite object. Any other information which you can communicate, will be thankfully received. I tender you the assurance of my profound respect and very high esteem.

JN: A: WHARTON

RC (DLC). Docketed by JM.

1. Wharton to JM, 12 Feb. 1821.

To John G. Jackson

Dear Sir — Montpellier Decr. 28. 1821

Your favor of the 9th. came to hand a few days ago only; and the usages of the season, with some additional incidents, have not allowed me time for more promptly acknowledging its friendly contents.

You were right in supposing that some arrangement of the mass of papers accumulated thro' a long course of public life would require a tedious attention after my final return to a private Station. I regret to say that concurring circumstances have essentially interfered with the execution of the task. Becoming every day more & more aware of the danger of an ultimate failure from delay, I have at length set about it in earnest; and shall continue the application as far as health and indispensable avocations will permit.

With respect to that portion of the mass which contains the voluminous proceedings of the Convention, it has always been my intention that they should some day or other see the light. I have always felt at the same time the delicacy attending such a use of them; especially at an early season. In general I have leaned to the expediency of letting the publication be a posthumous one. The result of my latest reflections on the subject, I can not more conveniently explain than by the inclosed extract from a letter[1] *confidentially* written since the appearance of the proceedings of the Convention as taken from the notes of Ch: Justice Yates.

Of this work I have not yet seen a copy. From the scraps thrown into the newspapers, I cannot doubt that his prejudices guided his pen; and that he has committed egregious errors at least, in relation to others as well as to myself.

That most of us carried into the Convention profound impressions, produced by the experienced inadequacy of the old Confederation, & by the monitory examples of all similar ones antient and modern, as to the necessity of binding the States together by a strong Constitution, is certain. The necessity of such a Constitution was enforced by the gross and disreputable irregularities which had been prominent in the internal administrations of most of the States. Nor was the recent and alarming insurrection headed by Shays in Massachusetts, without a very sensible influence on the public mind. Such indeed was the aspect of things, that in the eyes of the best friends of liberty, a crisis had arrived which was to decide whether the American experiment was to be a blessing to the world, or to blast for ever the hopes which the republican cause had inspired. And, what is not to be overlooked, the disposition to give to a new System all the vigour consistent with republican principles, was not a little stimulated by a backwardness in some quarters towards a Convention for the purpose, which was ascribed to a secret dislike to popular Government, and a hope that delay would bring it more into disgrace, and pave the way for a form of Government more congenial with Monarchical or aristocratical predilections.

This view of the crisis made it natural for many in the Convention to lean to a higher toned system than was perhaps in strictness warranted by a proper distinction between causes temporary as some of them doubtless were, and causes permanently inherent in popular frames of Government. It is true, also, as has been sometimes suggested, that in the course of discussions, where so much depended on compromise, the patrons of different opinions, often set out on negociating grounds more remote from each other, than the real opinions of either were, from the point at which they finally met.

For myself, having from the first moment of maturing a political opinion, down to the present one, never ceased to be a votary of the principle of self-Government, I was among those most anxious to rescue it from the danger which seemed to threaten it; and with that view was willing to give to a Government, resting on that foundation, as much energy as would ensure the requisite stability and efficacy. It is possible that in some instances that consideration may have been allowed a weight greater than subsequent reflection within the Convention, or the actual operation of the Government would sanction. It may be remarked also that it sometimes happened, that opinions as to a particular modification or a particular power of the Government, had a conditional reference to others, which, combined therewith, would vary the character of the whole.

But whatever might have been the opinions entertained in forming the Constitution, it was the duty of all to support it in its true meaning as understood *by the Nation* at the time of its ratification. No one felt this obligation more that[2] I have done; and there are few perhaps whose ultimate and deliberate opinions of the merits of the Constitution, accord in a greater degree with that obligation.

The departures from the true & fair construction of the Instrument have always given me pain; and always experienced my opposition when called for. The attempts, in the outset of the Govt. to defeat those safe if not necessary, and those politic if not obligatory amendments introduced in conformity to the known desires of the Body of the people, & to the pledges of many, particularly myself, when vindicating and recommending the Constitution, was an occurrence not a little ominous. And it was soon followed by indications of political tenets, and by rules, or rather the abandonment of all rules, of expounding it, which were capable of transforming it into something very different from its legitimate character as the offspring of the national Will. I wish I could say that constructive innovations had altogether ceased.

Whether the Constitution, as it has divided the powers of Govt. between the States in their separate and in their united capacities, tends to an oppressive aggrandizement of the General Govt. or to an anarchical Independence of the State Govts., is a problem which time alone can absolutely determine. It is much to be wished that the division as it exists, or as it may be made with the regular sanction of the people, may effectually guard against both extremes: For it can not be doubted that an accumulation of all power in the General Govt. would as naturally lead to a dangerous accumulation in the Executive hands, as that the resumption of all power by the several States, would end in the calamities incident to contiguous & rival Sovereigns: to say nothing of its effect in lessening the security for sound principles of administration within each of them.

There have been epochs when the Genl. Govt. was evidently drawing a disproportion of power into its vortex. There have been others when States threatened to do the same. At the present moment, it wd. seem that both are aiming at encroachments, each on the other. One thing however is certain, that in the present condition and temper of the Community, the Genl. Govt. can not long succeed in encroachments contravening the will of a majority of the States, and of the people. Its responsibility to these, would, as was proved on a conspicuous occasion, quickly arrest its career. If, at this time, the powers of the Genl. Govt. be carried to unconstitutional lengths, it will be the result of a majority of the States & people, actuated by some impetuous feeling, or some real, or supposed interest, overruling the minority, and not of successful attempts by the General Govt. to overpower both.

In estimating the greater tendency in the political system of the Union to a subversion or a separation of the States composing it, there are some considerations to be taken into the account, which have been little adverted to by the most oracular Authors on the Science of Govt. and which are but imperfectly developed as yet by our own experience. Such are the size of the States; the number of them; the territorial extent of the whole; and the degree of external danger. Each of these I am persuaded will be found to contribute its impulse to the practical direction which our great political Machine is to take.

We learn for the first time the second loss sustained by your parental affections. You will not doubt the sincerity with which we partake the grief produced by both. I wish we could offer better consolations, than the condoling expression of it. These must be derived from other sources. Afflictions of every kind are the onerous conditions charged on the tenure of life; and it is a silencing if not a satisfactory vindication of the ways of Heaven to Man, that there are but few who do not prefer an acquiescence in them, to a surrender of the tenure itself.

We have had for a great part of the last & present years, much sickness in our own family; and among the black members of it not a little mortality. Mrs. Madison & Payne were so fortunate as to escape altogether. I was one of the last attacked, and that not dangerously. The disease was a typhoid fever. At present we are all well and unite in every good wish to Mrs. Jackson & yourself, and to Mary and the rest of your family. Very sincerely yours

James Madison

RC (ViU: Madison Papers, Special Collections); draft (DLC). Draft dated "27 Dcr." Minor differences between the copies have not been noted.

1. In the draft, JM placed an asterisk here and wrote in the left margin: "*see letter of the [left blank] of Sepr. 1821. to Thos. Ritchie." For the extract and the letter, see JM to Thomas Ritchie, 15 Sept. 1821, and n. and nn. 1 and 4.

2. In the draft, this word is "than."

Madison and the Allegory of Jonathan and Mary Bull

Editorial Note

Sometime during the Missouri Crisis of 1819–21, most probably during the winter of 1821, James Madison wrote this allegory on slavery. Using a form that dated from the American Revolution, but which owed its popularity to one of Madison's friends, James Kirke Paulding, Madison created a dialogue on slavery between Jonathan Bull, representing the northern states, and Mary Bull, representing those of the south. After drafting it, Madison put it aside (R. W. Van Alstyne, *The Rising American Empire* [New York, 1960], 53; Robert J. Allison, "'From the Covenant of Peace, A Simile of Sorrow': James Madison's American Allegory," *VMHB* 99 [1991]: 330–31).

In late February 1835, Thomas Willis White, the editor of the *Southern Literary Messenger*, wrote Madison to ask if "you might have by you some manuscripts which you would have no objection to seeing transferred to the columns of the Literary Messenger" (White to JM, 27 Feb. 1835, DLC). There is no known response by Madison to this letter, perhaps because, as Dolley Madison wrote, "he is still feeble, and confined to his rooms," and she was acting as his amanuensis (Dolley Madison to John Vaughan, 26 Feb. 1835, *DMDE;* draft of Dolley Madison to George A. Miller, 1 Mar. 1835, DLC). Two weeks later, however, Dolley Madison wrote White, enclosing "a Copy of a Manuscript paper for his Magazine if he thinks it worthy of a place there," and enjoining White "that the communication is meant to be strictly anonymous." "Should it be printed," she continued, "it may be destroyed instead of being returned" (Dolley Madison to White, 10

Mar. 1835, *DMDE*). The manuscript Dolley Madison enclosed was most likely Madison's allegory.

White lost no time: the story appeared in the March 1835 issue of the *Southern Literary Messenger*, where White commented that while he was sorry that he was "not permitted to announce the source" from which the story was derived, "its own merit however, and its obvious application to events of the time at which it was written, will attract a due share of attention" (*Southern Literary Messenger* 1 [1835]: 387). The fair copy that was sent to him by the Madisons and that White used for his text has not been found.

The allegory was reprinted in the *Richmond Enquirer*, 24 Apr. 1835, under the heading "Miscellaneous. Conciliation—Between the North and South." The editor called the article "a very superior production . . . worthy of the pen of Addison himself." Another notice in the same paper on 1 May 1835, reporting on the contents of the March issue of the *Southern Literary Messenger*, "just published," called Madison's essay "a beautiful allegory, enforced by powers of reasoning, which betoken a master mind." Noting that while "the conciliatory spirit in which the question" of slavery is treated, "cannot offend the warmest partisan upon the subject, the argument used by Mary Bull, cannot but arrest attention."

The allegory was again reprinted, acknowledging Madison for the first time as its author, in *De Bow's Review* 21 (1856): 369–74, courtesy of J. C. McGuire, who owned the draft as well as many other Madison manuscripts. Two comments by the *Review*'s editor attached to this new printing are worth noting. The first concerns Mary Bull's exclamation that she is as anxious as Jonathan Bull to get rid of slavery. Here the editor wrote: "This is the old fashioned mode of speech. Men have been better enlightened at the South since the Slave discussions have taken place." The second comment occurs where Madison wrote that Jonathan had "a good heart as well as a sound head and steady temper"; here the editor wrote "that might have been the case with 'Jonathan' in times long past, but in his later course it is impossible to find any evidences of either."

J. C. McGuire republished the allegory as a fourteen-page limited edition pamphlet in 1856, *Jonathan Bull and Mary Bull: By James Madison. An Inedited Manuscript. Printed for Presentation by J. C. M'Guire.* Two copies are in the Papers of William C. Rives at the Library of Congress. It has been reprinted several times since.

(Secondary source used for this note: Robert J. Allison, "'From the Covenant of Peace, A Simile of Sorrow': James Madison's American Allegory," *VMHB* 99 [1991]: 327–50).

Jonathan Bull & Mary Bull

[1821]

Jonathan Bull & Mary Bull, who were descendants of old Jno. Bull, the head of the family, had inherited contiguous estates in large tracts of land. As they grew up & became well acquainted, a partiality was mutually felt, and advances on several occasions made towards a matrimonial connection. This was particularly recommended by the advantages of putting their two estates under a common superintendance. Old B. however, as guardian of both, and having long[1] been allowed certain valuable privileges within the Estates, with wch. he was not long content, had always found the means of breaking off the match, which he regarded as a fatal obstacle to his secret design of getting the whole property into his own hands.

At a moment favorable as he thought for the attempt, he brought suit agst. both, but with a view of carrying it on in a way that would make the process bear on the parties in such different modes times and degrees, as might create a jealousy & discord between them. J. & M.[2] had too much sagacity to be duped. They understood well old Bull's character and situation. They knew that he was deeply versed in all the subtleties of the law, that he was of a stubborn & persevering temper, and that he had moreover a very long purse. They were sensible therefore that the more he endeavoured to divide their interests, & their defence of their[3] suit, the more they ought to make a common cause and proceed in a concert of measures. As this could best be done by giving effect to the feelings long entertained for each other, an intermarriage was determined on & solemnized, with a deed of settlement as usual in such opulent matches, duly executed, and no event certainly of the sort was ever celebrated by a greater fervor or variety of rejoicings among the respective tenants of the parties. They had a great horror of falling into the hands of Old B. and regarded the marriage of their proprietors under whom they held their freeholds, as the surest mode of warding off the danger. They were not disappointed. United purses and good advocates compelled Old B. after a hard struggle to withdraw the suit, and relinquish forever not only the new pretensions he had set up, but the old privileges he had been allowed.

The marriage of J. & M. was not a barren one. On the contrary every year or two added a new member to the family and on such occasions[4] the practice was to set off a portion of land sufficient for a good farm to be put under the authority of the Child on its attaining the age of Manhood. And these lands were settled very rapidly by tenants going as the case might be from the Estates, sometimes of J. sometimes of M. and sometimes partly from one & partly from the other.

It happened that at the expiration of the non-age of the 10th or llth fruit of the marriage some difficulties were started concerning the rules & conditions, of declaring the young party of age, and of giving him as a member of the family, the management of his patrimony. Jonathan became possessed with a notion, that an arrangement ought to be made that would prevent the new farm from being settled and cultivated, as in all the latter instances, indiscriminately by persons removing from his and M's estate and confine this privilege to those going from his own; and in the perverse humour which had seized him, he listened moreover to suggestions that M. had some undue advantage from the selections of the Head Stewards which happened to have been made much oftener out of her tenants than his.

Now the prejudice suddenly taken up by J. agst. the equal right of M's tenants to remove with their property to new farms, was connected with a peculiarity in Mary's person not as yet noticed. Strange as it may appear, the circumstance is not the less true, that M. when a Child had unfortunately recd. from a certain African dye, a stain on her left arm which had made it perfectly black, and withal somewhat weaker than the other arm. The misfortune arose from her being prevailed on to let a Ship from Africa loaded with the article whic⟨h⟩ had been permitted to[5] enter a river running thro' her estate, and dispose of a part of the noxious Cargo. The fact was well known to J. at the time of their marriage and if felt as an objection, it was in a manner reduced to nothing by the comely form and pleasing features of M. in every other respect; by her good sense and amiable manners; and in part perhaps by the large and valuable estate she brought with her.

In the unlucky fit however which was upon him, he looked at the black arm, and forgot all the rest. To such a pitch of feeling was he wrought up that he broke out into the grossest taunts on M. for her misfortune; not omitting at the same time to remind her of his long forbearance to exert his superior voice in the appointment of the Head Steward. He had now he said got his eyes fully opened, he saw every thing in a new light, and was resolved to act accordingly. As to the Head Steward he wd. let her see that the appointment was virtually in his power; and she might take her leave of all chance of ever having another of her tenants advanced[6] to that Station. And as to the black arm, she should, if the color could not be taken out, either tear off the skin from the flesh or cutt [*sic*] off the limb; For it was his fixed determination, that one or other should be done, or he wd. sue out a divorce, & there should be an end of all connection between them and their Estates. I have he said examined well the Marriage settlement, and flaws have been pointed out to me, that never occurred before, by which I shall be able to set the whole aside. White as I am all over, I can no longer consort with one marked with such a deformity as the blot on your person.

Mary was so stunned with the language she heard that it was some time before she could speak at all; and as the surprize abated, she was almost choked with the anger & indignation swelling in her bosom. Generous and placable as her temper was, she had a proud sensibility to what she thought an unjust & degrading treatment which did not permit her to suppress the violence of her first emotions. Her language accordingly for a moment was such as these emotions prompted. But her good sense, and her regard for J. whose qualities as a good husband she had long experienced, soon gained an ascendancy, and changed her tone to that of sober reasoning & affectionate expostulation. Well my dear husband you see what a passion you have[7] put me into. But it is now over,[8] and I will endeavor to express my thoughts with the calmness and good feelings which become the relation of wife & husband.

As to the case of providing for our child just coming of age, I shall say but little. We both have such a tender regard for him and such a desire to see him on a level with his brethren as to the chance of making his fortune in the world, that I am sure the difficulties which have occurred will in some way or other be got over.

But I cannot pass so lightly over the reproaches you cast on the colour of my left arm, and on the more frequent appointment of my tenants than of yours, to the head-Stewardship of our joint estates.

Now as to the first point, you seem to have forgotten, my worthy partner, that this infirmity was fully known to you before our marriage, and is proved to be so by the deed of settlement itself. At that time you made it[9] no objection whatever to our Union; and indeed how could you urge such an objection, when you were conscious that you yourself was [*sic*] not entirely free from a like stain on your own[10] person. The fatal African dye, as you well know, had found its way into your abode as well as mine; and at the time of our marriage had spots & specks scattered over your body as black as the skin on my arm. And altho' you have by certain abrasions and other applications, taken them in some measure out, there are visible remains which ought to soften at least your language when reflecting on my situation. You ought surely when you have so slowly and imperfectly relieved yourself from the mortifying stain altho the task was comparatively so easy, to have some forbearance and sympathy with me who have a task so much more difficult to perform. Instead of that you abuse me as if I had brought the misfortune on myself, and could remove it at will; or as if you had pointed out a ready way to do it, and I had slighted your advice. Yet so far is this from being the case that you know as well as I do, that I am not to be blamed for the origin of the sad mishap; that I am as anxious as you can be to get rid of it; that you are as unable as I am to find out a safe & feasible plan for the purpose; and moreover that I have done every thing I could, in the mean time, to mitigate an evil that can not as yet be removed. When you talk of tearing off the skin or cutting off the unfortunate limb, must I remind you of what you can not be ignorant, that the most skilful surgeons have given their opinions that if so cruel an operation were to be tried, it could hardly fail to be followed by a mortification or a bleeding to death. Let me ask too whether, should neither of the fatal effects ensue, you would like me better in my mangled or mutilated condition than you do now![11] And when you threaten a divorce and an annulment of the Marriage settlement, may I not ask whether your estate wd. not suffer as much as mine, by dissolving the partnership between them? I am far from denying that I feel the advantage of having the pledge of your arm, your stronger arm if you please, for the protection of me & mine; and that my interests in general have been, and must continue to be the better for your aid & counsel in the management of them. But on the other hand you must be equally sensible that the aid of my purse will have its value, in case Old B. or any other rich litigious fellow should put us to the expence of another tedious lawsuit. And now that we are on the subject of loss & gain, you will not be offended if I take notice of a report that you sometimes insinuate that my estate according to the rates of assessment, does not pay its due share into the common purse. I think my dear J. that if you ever entertained this opinion you must have been led into it, by a very wrong view of the subject. As to the direct income from rents, there can be no deficiency on my part there;[12] the rule of apportionment being clear & founded on a calculation by numbers. And as to what is raised from the articles bought & used by my tenants, it is difficult to conceive that my tenants buy or use less than yours, considering that they carry a greater amount of crops to market the whole of which it is well known they lay out in articles from the use of which the bailiff regularly collects the sum due. It wd. seem then that my tenants selling more, buy more; buying more use more, and using more pay more. Meaning however, not to put you in the wrong, but myself in the right, I do not push the argument to that length, because I readily agree that in paying for articles bought & used, you have, beyond the fruits of the soil on which I depend, ways & means which I have not. You draw chiefly the interest we jointly pay for the funds we were obliged to borrow for the fees & costs the suit of[13] Old Bull put us to. Your tenants also turn their hands so ingeniously to a variety of handicraft & other mechanical productions, that they make not a little money from that source. Besides all this, you gain much by the fish you catch & carry to market; by the use of your teams and boats,[14] in transporting and trading on, the crops of my tenants; and indeed in doing that sort of business for strangers also. This is a fair statement on your side of the account, with the drawback however, that as your tenants are supplied with a greater proportion of articles, made by themselves, than is the case with mine, the use of which articles does not contribute to the common purse, they avoid in the same proportion, the payments collected from my tenants. If I were to look still farther[15] into this matter and refer you to every advantage you draw from the union of our persons & property, I might remark that the profits you make from your teams & boats & which enable you to pay your quota, are in great part drawn from the preference they have in conveying & disposing of the products of my soil; a business that might fall into other hands in the event of our separation. I mention this as I have already sd. not by way of complaint, for I am well satisfied that your gain is not altogether my loss in this more than in many other instances; and that what profits you immediately may profit me also in the long run. But I will not dwell on these calculations & comparisons of interest which you ought to weigh as well as myself as reasons agst. the measure to which you threaten a resort. For when I consult my own heart & call to mind all the endearing proofs you have given of your's[16] being in sympathy with it, I must needs hope that there are other ties than mere interest, to prevent us from ever suffering a transient resentment on either side, with or without cause, to bring on both all the consequences of a divorce; consequences too which wd. be a sad inheritance indeed, for our numerous and beloved offspring.

As to the other point relative to the Head Stewards, I must own, my worthy husband, that I am altogether at a loss for any cause of dissatisfaction on your part or blame on mine. It is true as you say that they have been oftener taken from among my tenants than yours; but under other circumstances the reverse might as well have happened. If the individls. appointed had made their way to the important trust, by corrupt or fallacious means; if they had been preferred merely because they dwelt on my estate, or had succeeded by any interposition of mine, contrary to your inclination; or finally if they had administered the trust unfaithfully, sacrificing your interests to mine, or the interests of both, to selfish or to unworthy purposes, in either of these cases, you wd. have ground for your complaints. But I know, J. that you are too just and too candid not to admit that no such ground exists. The head Stewards in question cd. not have been appointed without your own participation as well as mine. They were recommended to our joint choice by the reputed fairness of their characters, by their tried fidelity & competency in previous trusts; and by their exemption from all charges of impure & grasping designs. And so far were they from being partial to my interest at the expence of yours, that they were rather considered by my tenants as leaning to a management more favorable to yours than to mine. I need not say that I allude to the bounties, direct or indirect, to your teams & boats, to the hands employed in your fisheries, and to the looms and other machineries, which witht. such encouragements wd. not be able to meet the threatened rivalships of interfering neighbors. I say only that these ideas were in the heads of some of my tenants. For myself I shd. not have mentioned them but as a defence agst. what I must regard as so unfounded[17] that it ought not to be permitted to make a lasting impression.

But laying aside all these considerations, I repeat, my dear J. that the appt. of the Head Steward lies as much if not more with you than with me. Let the choice fall where it may, you will find me faithfully abiding by it, whether it be thought the best possible one or not; and sincerely wishing that he may equally improve better opportunities of serving us both than was the lot of any of those who have gone before him.

J. who had a good heart as well as a sound head & steady temper, was touched with this tender & considerate[18] language of M. and the bickering wch. had sprung up ended as the quarrels of lovers always,[19] & of married folks sometimes[20] do, in an increased affection & confidence between the parties.

Draft (DLC). At the top of the first page of the draft is JM's note: "written but not published at the period of the Missouri question (1821)." A version of this essay, differing only slightly in spelling and punctuation, was published in the *Southern Literary Messenger* 1 (1835): 342–45 (hereinafter *SLM*). For differences between the two texts, see nn. Minor differences between the text and published version have not been noted.

1. "Long" was omitted from the text published in the *SLM*.
2. In the *SLM* text, "J" and "M" are always written out as "Jonathan" and "Mary," respectively.
3. "Their" is "the" in the *SLM* text.
4. In the draft JM had written "events" here and interlined "occasions"; the *SLM* text has "occasions."
5. "Whic⟨h⟩ had been permitted to" is omitted from the *SLM* text.
6. "Advanced" is "advance" in the *SLM* text.
7. "Have" is "had" in the *SLM* text.
8. The *SLM* text has "over now" here.
9. "It" is omitted from the *SLM* text.
10. "Own" is omitted from the *SLM* text.
11. In the *SLM* text, there is a question mark here.
12. "There" is omitted from the *SLM* text.
13. "Of" is omitted from the *SLM* text.
14. Here JM first wrote, then crossed out, "of which you own such a number."
15. "Farther" is "further" in the *SLM* text.
16. "Your's" is "yours" in the *SLM* text.
17. "A charge," is added here in the *SLM* text.
18. "Considerate" is "conciliatory" in the *SLM* text.
19. "Always" is italicized in the *SLM* text.
20. "Sometimes" is italicized in the *SLM* text.

From George Joy

Dear sir, London 2nd Janry 1822

If a man were to note the Coincidencies of his day, he might find a bookful of amusement in the evening of Life. Poring yesterday over an old Correspondence, I had just reached the following Viz ·

"Had the Dollars arrived, I dare say they would have fallen to 3/ an ounce, and if I were to send an expedition to Pandæmonium to bring away the Roof in a Hurricane, Gold would fall to the same price. Nay, I expect that before the Tallow arrive, if that should ever happen, the use of it will be superseded by some mode of igniting, and at the same time confining inflammable air; and I should not wonder to see an artificial Sun of this kind suspended over London, and giving to every part of it as much light in the night at least as it has in the day." This I had hardly finished when the Chronicle was laid before me, with the anecdote of Caporali, that if he were to turn Hatter, men would be born without Heads.[1] Some have appeared since with little of that Article; but they are for the most part among the most Thrifty—non omnia possumus omnes.[2] In pursuit of the same object which brot. me to the letter above quoted, and to which I have been called by the late arrangement for settling the Claims under the Florida Treaty I had this day taken up my Letter to you of the 16th April 1804,[3] and your answer of the 10th with PS. of the 23rd Novr. of that year;[4] when I received from Mr: Rush your favor of the 21st Novr. last, and the post brot: me a letter from my brother,[5] which, if it contains more than is to the purpose, my Boy has more leisure to copy than I to abridge. The Coincidence here is twofold—1st. in the disinclination to use the pen—(tho' it is the first letter I have had from him since he broke his Arm)—2nd. in the topic of both the progress and prosperity of the Country. I might add a third instance in the evidence that what passes with us is more and more an object of attention here, and this is not less evident in his Comments on the publications I had sent him than in the last paragraph but one (after his remark on the North American Review) with certain corollaries in my recollection. Matthews[6] is not now unfriendly to us. I have heard him run hard on writing profoundly upon subjects of which he knew nothing—but he has been assiduous of late in collecting an American Library; and he commended highly the Article on England and America in the N.A.R. which he told me he had read at the Traveller's Club, where the work is subscribed for and will get into the hands of the most respectable men in the kingdom. In my Brother's Book Club, which consists, among others of three Poets,* and several members of Parliament, and where the best publications circulate and are afterwards sold at auction to the Members, the two American works he mentions are the first that ever brought their cost. While things are taking this turn, I hold it unfortunate that my friend Adams should be canningising in his Oration of the 4th July.[8] God knows I have said some hard things (Sinner that I am) under the peacemaking Title of Conciliator;[9] and would again if the occasion called for it. To relax a fibre in preparing adequately for the defence

* Bowles, Crabbe, and Little Moore[7]—this last has become a great American of late, in atonement for his former offences.

of the Country would be unpardonable; but with this the spirit of the nation may be safely trusted without exciting hostility beforehand. "What you see amiss in others amend in yourselves"—a Maxim of my good mother which Mrs Rush has promised to treasure up for her Boys—the Girls of course will not want it. Mr: Gales is out in his Chronology; but I will write him about it; he has probably confounded Conciliator with Anticipation of Marginal Notes or possibly with the Cosmopolite.[10]

I cannot flatter myself that you have preserved any part of my Correspondence—our Government does not allow sufficient help for the subsidiary Arrangement even of official Documents—but if you have any part; I should look confidently for the Letters abovementioned—for I observe my Letter to you announces itself as on "real business;" and on your answer which is before me I observe I have endorsed in short hand "of this there is a Duplicate"—it appears too to have awaited the Presidents sanction, and has so far the Air of officiality, that I should expect it's Copy to be found in the Archives, were it not for information received thro' Mr B. Joy at Boston, from his Agent at Washington, that nothing of the kind was among "the Papers transmitted to the Commissioners by the Department of state." He mentions of my Correspondence only a letter of recent date to Mr Adams. I shall be cautious of disturbing your repose by raking up these old Concerns, albeit the present question is of serious Amount, and to judge impartially by the Letters before me, as a man must necessarily do of what he wrote seventeen years ago, I think I should have made a very pretty Commissioner myself, had I been invited; but if, without personal labour or worriment you can advert to Documents, which will ipso facto be satisfactory to the Commissioners; I shall look confidently to your friendship for such assistance; and such I should presume would be the Character of my original Letter referred to, and of any Copy you may have of your Answer; and possibly of other papers, which a further scrutiny may enable me to point out. This is after packet day; but I dispatch it to L'pool in full faith of it's reaching her—as the wind that has been blowing a head for six weeks will hardly chop round in 36 hours. I hope it may find you quite well and rest always very faithfully Dear sir, Your friend & Servt.,

G. Joy

RC, two copies, and enclosure (DLC). First RC docketed by JM. Second RC marked "(Copy) 1st via Lpool." Cover addressed by Joy to JM and marked "℔ Robt. Edwards via New York"; postmarked 10 Mar. at New York, and franked. For enclosure, see n. 5.

1. The anecdote of one "Caporali, a native of Modena," who "was unfortunate in every thing he undertook, and not more unfortunate than discontented," was published in the Bridgeton, New Jersey, *Washington Whig*, 6 May 1822.

2. *Non omnia possumus omnes:* we can't all do everything.

3. *PJM-SS*, 7:70–72.

4. Letter not found (calendared in PJM-SS, 8:280).

5. The enclosure is M. Joy to George Joy, 1 Jan. 1822 (3 pp.), commenting on a book about the construction of the Erie Canal and on a volume of the *North American Review*.

6. Joy may have referred to John Matthews (1755–1826), a British physician and writer, who composed many anonymous fugitive works in verse and prose.

7. William Lisle Bowles, George Crabbe, and Thomas Moore were well-known British poets of the time. For Moore's 1804 visit to Washington and his poetic libel of Thomas Jefferson, see Malone, *Jefferson and His Time*, 4:391.

8. In his Fourth of July address delivered in Washington, John Quincy Adams began, as a prelude to celebrating the American Revolution, with the long, dark, and bloody struggle of the British people against king and church to achieve a grant of human rights. As he noted, "from the impenetrable gloom of this intellectual darkness, and the deep degradation of this servitude, the British nation had partially emerged." The address was published in, among other papers, the *Baltimore Patriot & Mercantile Advertiser*, 12 July 1821. For JM's copy, see JM to Adams, 16 July 1821, and n. 1.

9. For Joy's "Conciliator" essays, see Joy to JM, 9 Feb. 1821, and n. 5.

10. Joy referred here to his essays: *Anticipation of Marginal Notes on the Declaration of Government of the 9th of January, 1813. In the American National Intelligencer* (London, 1813), and *The Dispute with America, Considered in a Series of Letters from a Cosmopolite to a Clergyman* (London, 1812). For a discussion of these essays, see Bradford Perkins, "George Joy, American Propagandist at London, 1805–1815," *New England Quarterly* 34 (1961): 199–202, 207–8.

From Maury & Latham

SIR LIVERPOOL 2 January 1822

We beg to refer you to the annexed annual report upon Tobacco &c.[1] The Sales of last month have been limitted, amounting only to about 400 Hhds. of which, 182 were Virginia leaf & 140 Strips—60 Hhds Kentucky leaf & 7 Strips—2 Hhds. Maryland, fair quality @ 7½. Holders have been pretty steady during the month; but by the last advices from Virginia received by the packet, it does appear to us that too much Tobacco will come forward soon, to allow the present prices to be fully maintained. The London market is very flat, & further arrivals there will tend to damp it. Should this be the case it must affect us here also.

There has been little doing for some days past, but that is usually the case at the Season of Christmas. The Tobacco Plant is arrived—the Comet looked for shortly.

The Stock of Tar in the hands of importers & speculators is 5700 barrels—we quote Carolina 14/ @ 15/ ℔ bbl. & Virginia 16/ @ 17/. No decline apprehended, & may advance 6d @ 1/. The Stock of Turpentine 2300 bls. & steady @ 10/6 @ 13/ ℔ Cwt.

For new Flaxseed, 65/ ℔ Hhd. would be given. We remain Yours very respectfully

MAURY LATHAM & CO

RC (DLC). Addressed to JM and marked "℔ Albion via N York"; postmarked 4 Feb. at New York. Docketed by JM.

1. Enclosure not found.

From Henry R. Schoolcraft

ALBANY January 5th. 1822.

Henry R. Schoolcraft[1] has the honor of presenting to James Madison Esqr., the inclosed geological memoir,[2] which he begs will be accepted with the respectful compliments of the author.

RC (DLC). Docketed by JM.

1. Henry Rowe Schoolcraft (1793–1864) was a geologist and later an ethnologist who wrote voluminously about his travels in Missouri, Arkansas, and the Great Lakes region and the Indians he met there. In 1822 he was appointed agent for the Indian tribes around Lake Superior; he was superintendent of Indian affairs for Michigan, 1836–41.

2. Henry R. Schoolcraft, *A Memoir, on the Geological Position of a Fossil Tree, Discovered in the Secondary Rocks of the River Des Plaines.* (Albany, N.Y., 1822; Shoemaker 10187). JM's copy is in the Madison Collection, Special Collections, University of Virginia Library.

To Hezekiah Niles

MONTPELLIER Jany. 8. 1822

In Ramsay's History of the American Revolution[1] Vol: 2. pa. 300–301 is the following passage.

"Mr. Jay was instructed to contend for the right of the U. States to the free navigation of the river Mississippi, and if an express acknowlegement of it could not be obtained, he was restrained from acceding to any stipulation by which it should be relinquished. But in February 1781, when Lord Cornwallis was making rapid progress in overrunning the Southern States, and when the mutiny of the Pennsylvania line and other unfavorable circumstances depressed the spirits of the Americans, Congress, on *the recommendation* of Virginia, directed him to recede from his instructions so far as they insist on the free navigation of that part of the Mississippi, which lies below the thirty first degree of North Latitude; provided such cession should be unalterably insisted on by Spain, and provided the free navigation of the said river above the said degree of North Latitude should be acknowledged and guaranteed by his Catholic Majesty, in common with his own subjects."

In this account of the instruction to Mr. Jay to relinquish the navigation of the Mississippi below the Southern boundary of the U. States, the measure would seem to have had its origin with the State of Virginia.

This was not the case: And the very worthy historian, who was not at that period a member of Congress, was led into his error by the silence of the journals as to what had passed on the subject previous to Feby. 15. 1781. when they agreed to the instruction to make the relinquishment, as moved by the Delegates of Virginia in pursuance of instructions from the Legislature. It was not unusual with the Secretary of Congress, to commence his entries in the Journal, with the Stage in which the proceedings assumed a definitive character; omitting, or noting on separate & informal sheets only, the preliminary steps.

The Delegates from Virga. had been long under instructions from their State to insist on the right to the navigation of the Mississippi; and Congress had always included it in their ultimatum for peace. As late as the 4th. of Ocr. 1781 (see the Secret Journals of that date)[2] they had renewed their adherence to this point, by unanimously agreeing to the report of a Committee to whom had been referred "certain instructions to the delegates of Virga. by their constituents and a letter of May 29 from Mr. Jay at Madrid," which report* prohibited him from relinquishing the right of the U. States to the free navigation of the River Mississippi into and from the sea, as asserted in his former instructions. And on the 17th. of the same month, October (see the secret Journals of that date)[4] Congress agreed to the report of a Committee explaining the reasons & principles on which the instructions of October the 4th. were founded.

Shortly after this last measure of Congress, the Delegates of S. Carolina & Georgia, seriously affected by the progress and views of the Enemy in the Southern States, and by the possibility that the interference of the Great neutral powers might force a peace on the principle of *Uti possidetis*,[5] whilst those States or parts of them might be in the military occupancy of G. Britain, urged with great zeal, within & without doors, the expediency of giving fresh vigour to the means of driving the enemy out of their country, by drawing Spain into an Alliance, and into pecuniary succours, believed to be unattainable, without yielding our claim to the navigation of the Mississippi. The efforts of those Delegates did not fail to make proselytes till at length it was ascertained that a number was disposed to vote

* drawn by J.M.[3]

for the measure, sufficient without the vote of Virginia, and it happened that one of the two delegates from that State,[6] concurred in the policy of what was proposed. (see the annexed letter of Novr. 25. & extract of Decr. 5. 1781. from J. Madison to Jos. Jones).[7]

In this posture of the business, Congress was prevailed on to postpone any final decision, untill the Legislature of Virginia could be consulted; it being regarded by all, as very desirable, when the powers of Congress depended so much on the individual wills of the States, that an important member of the Union, on a point particularly interesting to it, should receive every conciliatory mark of respect; and it being calculated also, that a change in the councils of that State, might have been produced by the causes producing it in others.

A joint letter bearing date Decr. 13. 1780 (which see annexed)[8] was accordingly written by the Delegates of Virginia to Governor Jefferson, to be laid before the Legislature then in Session simply stating the case and asking instructions on the subject; without any expression of their own opinions, which being at variance, could not be expressed in a letter to be signed by both.[9]

The result of these communications from the Delegates was a repeal of the former instructions, and a transmission of different ones, the receipt of which, according to an understanding when the decision of Congress was postponed, made it incumbent on the two Delegates to bring the subject before Congress. This they did by offering the instruction to Mr. Jay agreed to on the 15th. of Feby. 1781, and referred to in the historical passage above cited.

It is proper to add that the instant the menacing crisis was over, the Legislature of Virginia revoked the instruction to her Delegates to cede the navigation of the Mississippi, and that Congress seized the first moment also for revoking theirs to Mr. Jay.

I have thought a statement of these circumstances due to truth: and that its accuracy may be seen to depend not on memory alone the copies of cotemporary documents verifying it are annexed.

In the hope that this explanation may find its way to the notice of some future Historian of our Revolutionary transactions, I request for it a place, if one can be afforded, in your Register, where it may more readily offer itself to his researches than in publications of more transient or diffusive contents. With friendly respects

J.M.

Draft (DLC). In the dateline, JM crossed out "Dcr. 29. 1821" and interlined "Jany. 8. 1822." In the top margin, probably at a later date, he wrote: "For this letter see Appendix to volume of Debates." JM's letter was printed under the title "Navigation of the Mississippi" in *Niles' Weekly Register* 21 (26 Jan. 1822): 347. Minor differences between the copies have not been noted.

1. David Ramsay, *The History of the American Revolution* (2 vols.; Philadelphia, 1789; Evans 22090).

2. JM referred here to the 4 Oct. 1780 committee report on John Jay's instructions (*Secret Journals of the Acts and Proceedings of Congress* [Shoemaker 4058], 2:323–25).

3. "*Drawn by J.M." was not included in the letter printed in *Niles' Weekly Register.*

4. For the committee report of 17 Oct. 1780 to which JM referred, see *Secret Journals of the Acts and Proceedings of Congress* (Shoemaker 4058), 2:326–39, or *PJM*, 2:127–35.

5. *Uti possidetis:* "personal property captured during wartime and still held by the captor when the war ends becomes the captor's legal property" (*Black's Law Dictionary* [9th ed.], 1686).

6. Here JM wrote and then crossed out "Col. Theodorick Bland."

7. JM referred here to his letters to Joseph Jones of 25 Nov. and 5 Dec. 1780, which were published along with his letter in *Niles' Weekly Register* 21 (26 Jan. 1822): 347–49. For these letters, see *PJM*, 2:202–4, 223–25.

8. JM referred here to JM and Theodorick Bland to Virginia governor Thomas Jefferson, 13 Dec. 1780, which was published along with JM's 8 Jan. 1822 letter in *Niles' Weekly Register* 21 (26 Jan. 1822): 349. For this letter, see *PJM*, 2:241–42.

9. At this point JM wrote and then crossed out: "Col. Bland had prepared a letter bearing date Novr. 22 to be jointly signed; which being objected to by his Collegue, was turned into one from himself. It was addressed to the Speaker of the House of Delegates and of course laid before the Legislature. (see these letters)."

From George Joy

DEAR SIR, LONDON 9th Janry 1822

The wind did chop round and blew a Hurricane; but the Albion sailed from L'pool, & how my Letter of the 2nd. will be transmitted thence I know not. I have put a Copy on board this ship; and now, on further reflection, I take the liberty to trouble you with Copies of the Letters referred to therein. In the Letter of Mr. B. Joy's Agent at Washington (a Mr: Alexr. Bliss, partner of Mr Webster of Boston)[1] I find as follows under date 19th Septr: 1821–vizt. "I am informed here by good authority that the dispersion and loss of papers, once deposited in the Department of State, is to be attributed to their having been forwarded to Mr: Young[2] when Consul at Madrid, whose papers were all destroyed upon the occupation of Spain by the French;" and in a Letter from Mr: Pinckney to the Secretary of State (Madrid 22nd Septr: 1805)[3] I find him proposing to "leave Mr: Young charged with our affairs &ca." In my enclosed Letter 16th April 1804[4] you will find me speaking "confidently that Mr Pinckney has had regular advice &ca."

Now if the Documents sent to our ordinary Minister should be thus lost, and we must have recourse to Copies; it may be important that you were thus advised; and if my said Letter should have been sent to the Trunkmaker's, the recognition will surely have weight with such "impartial men" as you will find me referring to in the 3rd page of this Copy 19 lines from the bottom.[5]

It is with a view to the better recollection of the subject that I hand you the whole Letter—otherwise the last half-sheet might be spared.

I am afraid this does not quite comport with my promise not to disturb your repose. I mean however to adhere to it. When I look back to the tedious length of my Communications to you, which this business has brought me into contact with; I think I gave you my full share of trouble in the bustle of active Life. This subject, I trust will give you but little. It is ex abundanti Cautela[6] that I bring it before you. I hope it may not discourage you from allowing me to hear from you occasionally in the assurance that I am always in great truth, very respectfully yours

G. Joy

There is in the Times of this morning and the Courier of this Evening, an address to the french Legislature signed Loveday.[7] I saw them late in the Day; and have in vain sought a Copy to send you. This ship's bag will leave town early in the morning; but if it can be got in time; it will accompany this under another cover.

RC (DLC).

1. Letter not found. Alexander Bliss (1792–1827), an 1812 graduate of Yale College, was an associate in Daniel Webster's law office (Charles M. Wiltse et al., eds., *The Papers of Daniel Webster: Correspondence* [7 vols.; Hanover, N.H., 1974–86], 2:37 n. 1).

2. Moses Young (1752–1822), who was born in Ireland and emigrated to the United States in 1771, was a veteran of the American Revolution. He served in various diplomatic posts, including that of U.S. consul at Madrid, and clerked in the State Department (*PJM-SS*, 8:565 and n. 1).

3. Charles Pinckney to JM, 22 Sept. 1805, DNA: RG 59, DD, Spain, vol. 6A.

4. *PJM-SS*, 7:70–72.

5. Joy was probably referring to that portion of a sentence in his copied letter to JM of 2 Jan. 1822: "to judge impartially by the Letters before me, as a man must necessarily do of what he wrote seventeen years ago."

6. *Ex abundante cautela:* from an abundance of caution.

7. The *Pétition ampliative à la Chambre des Députés, par M. Douglas Loveday, Anglais et Protestant; Avec les pièces justificatives de son contenu, et des observations additionelles* (Paris, 1822) followed an earlier petition to the French legislature in 1821 to intervene in the case of Loveday, whose two daughters and a niece had converted to Catholicism and been hidden away by a religious society in Paris. A translation of the petition, taken from the London *Morning Chronicle* of 10 Jan. 1822, was published in the Bridgeton, N.J., *Washington Whig*, 25 Mar. and 1 Apr. 1822.

From Samuel Miller

Sir, Princeton, Jany. 11 1822.

Having lately made a small publication, in support of what I deem to be truth, I do myself the honour most respectfully to request your acceptance of a copy of it[1]—and am, Sir, with the highest consideration, your obedient servant

SAML: MILLER[2]

RC (DLC). Docketed by JM "Miller S. (Revd)."

1. Samuel Miller, *A Letter to the Editor of the Unitarian Miscellany: In Reply to an Attack, by an Anonymous Writer in That Work, on a Late Ordination Sermon Delivered in Baltimore* (Baltimore, 1821; Shoemaker 6052).

2. Samuel Miller (1769–1850) was a 1789 graduate of the University of Pennsylvania and served as professor of Ecclesiastical History and Church Government at the Theological Seminary at Princeton, 1813–49 (H. A. Boardman, *A Discourse Commemorative of the Character and Life of the Late Rev. Samuel Miller, D.D. of Princeton, New Jersey. . . .* [Philadelphia, 1850], 38–40).

From Benjamin Romaine

DEAR SIR, NEWYORK 11th. January 1822.

I take the freedom to send to you (by mail) two Pamphlets containing an exhibition of reasons opposed to the adoption of the New Constitution of the State of New York, by an "old Citizen."[1] Accept, Sir, my grateful acknowledgments to yourself, and best wishes for the happiness of Mrs. Madison.

BJN. ROMAINE[2]

Permit me, Sir, to add the following Note—

You may not recollect that the Subscriber obtained from you, during the late War, the Nomination to the Senate of Deputy Q. M. General of the third Military District, which duties I continued to discharge until after the close of the War.

It does appear to me that, the assumption of yielded rights to the General Government by the States, ought to be *indignantly frowned at* in every instance. If such course is permited to progress—the central force, now existing in the United States Government, will shortly be frittered away thro' the contracted medium of "State Sovereignties." The above pamphlet was written by me. I now discover some errors, too late to be altered.

BJN. ROMAINE

RC (DLC). Docketed by JM.

1. [Benjamin Romaine], *A Comparative View and Exhibition of Reasons, Opposed to the Adoption of the New Constitution, of the State of New-York* (New York, 1822; Shoemaker 8413). JM's copy is in the Madison Collection, Special Collections, University of Virginia Library.

2. Benjamin Romaine (1762–1844), a Revolutionary War veteran, was grand sachem of Tammany Hall, 1808 and 1813, and frequently sachem. JM appointed Romaine deputy quartermaster general for the Third Military District in 1814 (*Pittsfield Sun*, 29 Feb. 1844; Gustavus Myers, *The History of Tammany Hall*, 2d ed. [1917; reprint, New York, 1968], 25; *PJM-PS*, 5:438 n. 1).

From John O. Lay

SIR RICHMOND 12th. Jan. 1822

Understanding from my friend Col. Dade[1] that you would probably make trial of this market with your present crop of Tobacco and having heretofore effected satisfactory Sales for several of your neighbors I beg leave to offer you my services as a Commission Merchant. The Tobacco from your neighborhood so far as it has come under my observation is in high repute with us and I think generally commands a preference.

Sales of very indifferent quality are now made at $5 @ $6. and for 2 Hhds. of Mr. C. Macons I this morning obtained $9¼ which latter price however is more than any other of the new crop has been sold for this season. I am Sir Very Respy Your Obt. Servt.

JNO. O. LAY[2]

RC (DLC). Docketed by JM.

1. Lawrence Taliaferro Dade (1785–1842), a veteran of the War of 1812, represented Orange County, Virginia, in the Virginia House of Delegates, 1808–19, and in the state senate, 1819–32. He later moved to Owensboro, Kentucky, where he died (Hayden, *Virginia Genealogies* [1973 reprint], 733).

2. John Olmsted Lay was a Richmond merchant and agent for the Aetna Fire Insurance Company. He handled JM's tobacco sales in 1824 and 1825 (*Richmond Enquirer*, 19 June 1829 and 29 Dec. 1838; Lay to JM, 11 May 1824 and 2 Aug. 1825, DLC).

From Peter Minor

DEAR SIR, RIDGEWAY Jan. 12. 1822

I have had the pleasure to receive your letter, enclosing one from Monsr. Thouin[1] at Paris. The Box you mention I have not yet sent for, but can get it at any time from Monticello. This is quite a flattering present to our Society—but I am at a great loss to know what we shall do with the seeds. The intention of this letter is, to request some instructions & suggestions from you on the subject.[2]

As our society does not regularly convene untill may, it will be necessary to have an early extra meeting to dispose of these seeds, before the proper time of sowing them passes by—& as the power of convening such meetings is vested exclusively in the Prest. or 1st Vice President, I ask the favour of you to authorise such a call. Say the 1st. Monday in Feb. If I may be excused for expressing the opinion, I doubt much the propriety of making a general distribution of these seeds among our members, particularly among those who will be most likely to attend a meeting at this season of the year. With the exception of a very few, who live dispersedly, there are none who have an inclination, or who think they have leisure for experiment, or innovation upon the beaten tract. I am inclined to think that a more useful disposition of them could be made by yourself among the intelligent amatuers of this & the other States, than to commit them to the society at large. Or suppose a part of them are placed in the hands of Mr Skinner[3] the Editor of the Am. Farmer for distribution? He is zealous in this sort of business—besides he is a member of our Society & might be considered in the light of a committee for turning them to the most useful account.

I presume the packages of seeds are labeled in their Botanical names. This will be a difficulty with us who know nothing of that science, & this with other considerations renders it desirable that you would attend our meeting, if yr. health & leisure will permit. If not, I hope you will forward us some plan or proposition for disposing of them.

If it is your wish & intention to reciprocate the present of Monsr. Thouin according to his request, it will give me great pleasure to assist you as far as I am able during the ensuing Summer. I presume it would be most acceptable to him, to receive not only the seed, but a sample of the plant in flower, in a Herbarium. I could merely make the collection, as my knowledge of Botany is neither sufficient to class or name them. With very great respect yr. Frd. & Sert.

P Minor

RC (DLC). Addressed by Minor to JM, and franked; postmarked 15 Jan. at Charlottesville. Docketed by JM.

1. The letter has not been found, but for the box of seeds, see Eyrien Frères & Cie. to JM, 2 Apr. 1821, and Jonathan Thompson to JM, 14 June 1821. The noted botanist André Thoüin (1747–1824) was head gardener of the Jardin des Plantes (after 1792, the Muséum d'Histoire Naturelle) in Paris from 1764 until his death (Looney et al., *Papers of Thomas Jefferson: Retirement Series*, 1:202 n.).

2. A special meeting of the Agricultural Society of Albemarle was held on 4 Feb. 1822 in which "a letter was received and read from Mr. Madison [not found] . . . enclosing one addressed to him from Monsr. Thouin of The Museum of natural History at Paris, and accompanied by a box of seeds presented by the said Museum to this Society." A committee was then formed to investigate the seeds, provide them with their common names, separate useful from ornamental plants, and to disseminate the seeds to the members of the society (True, "Minute Book of the Albemarle Agricultural Society," in *Annual Report of the American Historical Association for . . . 1918*, 1:296).

3. John Stuart Skinner (1788–1851) was a Maryland lawyer who JM appointed U.S. agent at Annapolis for dealing with the British mail-packets under flags of truce, and also agent for the exchange of prisoners, soon after the War of 1812 began. In 1813 JM appointed him U.S. Navy purser at Baltimore, and in 1816, postmaster of that city, a position he held for twenty-three years. Skinner was editor and publisher of several magazines that promoted agricultural improvements, including the *American Farmer*, which he founded in 1819 (Benjamin Perley Poore, "Biographical Notice of John S. Skinner," the *Plough, the Loom, and the Anvil* 7 [1854]: 1–20).

From David Easton

SIR, WASHINGTON CITY 14th January 1822.

Accompanying this are Copies of a letter from Major Genl. Lafayette[1] and of the Document therein alluded to, as also a printed sheet containing copies of a Certificate from Mr. Monroe, now our present chief Magistrate and of a few letters from General Washington to the late Colo. Harrison,[2] the whole of which I take the liberty of sending you at the recommendation of the President of the U. States.

The object in view is to obtain if practicable positive evidence that Colo. Harrison when he retired from the Army in ill health in 1781. actually did so on furlough, for although he did not rejoin the army again, it is well known that the foundation of his ill health was laid in Camp which Phisically incapacitated him from further labours in the field, and which finally terminated his life in 1790.

His Daughters were left young at their fathers death, and his valuable papers which were preserved with great care until the decease of his widow, which followed Colo. Hs about two years thereafter, suddenly disappeared, with the trunk which contained them: and but for this loss I feel confident it would not have become necessary to resort to any other source to establish the fact of their fathers having a Commission, tho' not in active service, until the close of the war. Should you know, Sir, any thing of this matter, which, from your high official station at the time is not improbable [...] declaration of the fact, would probably be attended with beneficial [...] to his daughters in enabling them to establish their just claim to the gratitude of their Country, for their fathers long, faithful and important services, which remain unrequited by the UStates until this day. I would therefore in their behalf respectfully solicit from you any information you may be in possession of, either personally, or from general impressions as the case may be, as early as your convenience will permit. With sentiments of the highest respect & Esteem, I have the honor to be, Sir, Your Mo hum & obedt. Servt.

DAVID EASTON[3]

Mrs. E desires a tender of her affectionate regards to Mrs Madison.

RC and enclosure (DLC). RC docketed by JM. RC and enclosure extensively damaged at foot of pages. For surviving enclosure, see n. 1.

1. The enclosure (3 pp.; marked "(Copy)") is Lafayette to Easton, 28 Oct. 1821, certified as authentic by James Monroe, 4 Jan. 1822, enclosing testimonials by Lafayette and Monroe of Robert H. Harrison's Revolutionary War service.

2. Originally from Charles County, Maryland, Robert Hanson Harrison (1745–1790) was an Alexandria, Virginia, lawyer who served as George Washington's private secretary with the rank of lieutenant colonel, 1775–81. He was chief justice of the Maryland General Court, 1781 (Jackson and Twohig, *Diaries of George Washington*, 2:181 n.).

3. David Easton (ca. 1765–1835) was a Scottish-born merchant in Alexandria, Virginia, who married Sarah Harrison, a daughter of Robert Hanson Harrison (*PJM-SS*, 8:499 n. 1; 4:317 n. 1).

From Jesse Torrey Jr.

(Confidential)

Sir, Chambersburg, (Penna) Jan. 15, 1822.

In addressing you I deem it my duty to commence with a humble petition to you and Mrs. Madison to pardon the enthusiasm and eccentricities which I *displayed*, when at your residence, and in Washington; particularly in troubling her with my crude and incoherent rhapsodies on the subject of African Slavery, *et cetera*. Not unconscious, at the time, of my ardent zeal, I exculpated myself, by the purity of my intentions. I do not know that I can offer any sufficient apology; but I claim a little lenity on account of being at that time, a victim of a slow incessant fever, which probably extended its effects to the brain, and consequently the mind. Besides this, it is probable that I inherited a sensitive sympathy and a spirit of enthusiasm from my ancestors; of whom I am informed that my *grand-mother* was a very pious and zealous Connecticut presbyterian, who, in addition to her acquired resources, (as she was a lady of great reading and knowledge) possessed the sympathetic faculty of combining the eloquence of *tears* with her fervent religious exhortations. I was almost in a state of desperation from extreme poverty joined with debility.* I was at the same time elated with the belief (of which I am still not entirely exempt) that I had made discoveries, both in morals and physics, of the highest importance to the welfare of mankind. On this subject I will only add that I trust,

* My situation is now far more tolerable in both respects. By a rigid adherence to a regimen of milk and bread, as my only food, and pure water as my only drink, for five years past, I have attained a comfortable degree of health, compared with what it was for nine years previous.

with confidence, that you are so much my friend, as to be disposed to forgive my past harmless aberrations.

Sir, I forward you herewith, a copy of the Moral Instructor,[1] of which I am the Compiler, and in part, the Author. As it is designed to advance the progress of knowledge and virtue in our Republic, I hope you will consider it sufficiently worthy of your notice to oblige me with a careful examination of it, and a perusal of the original parts, which I will designate.

You would oblige me particularly, by the communication of your sentiments, (through the Post Office in this village) respecting my project of gratuitous circulating Libraries, as well as your opinion of the probable tendency of the Moral Instructor, if generally circulated, to promote the general welfare of our country. The commanding example of Boston, in establishing a free Library for the exclusive benefit of Apprentices, (which I suppose resulted from the previous circulation of one of my tracts in Boston, which contained the second, and other sections of the first part of the Moral Instructor) has given popularity to Apprentices' Libraries, and been imitated in several other populous towns. Besides the effect of example, the title of *Apprentices'* added to Library, is calculated to excite the sympathy of the humane. But this distinctive appellation is not adapted to the country at large, nor ought to exclude all other classes of youth in cities from a participation in the benefit of free Libraries.

I have lately formed a resolution to recommence *practical* efforts for the accomplishment of my original Project of National Instruction by means of the universal institution of Free Circulating Libraries. And as the success of all new institutions depending on popular encouragement, is greatly assisted by the favorable opinions and influence of individuals in whom public confidence has been long concentrated, I should value your sentiments on the subject as an essential benefit to the Republic as well as to myself.

I recollect that you expressed your approbation of my views respecting the diffusion of knowledge when I was at your residence: I hope therefore, if you should conclude to comply with my solicitation, that you will add to your opinion of the plan in view, such suggestions, as may occur, of the best measures to be pursued for facilitating its execution and the extension of its utility. I am, Sir, with sentiments of great respect, your sincere Friend &c.

Jesse Torrey Junr.[2]

P.S. My residence is at New Lebanon, (N.Y.) but I expect to remain in this vicinity several months; having come into this country, as an agent for Jethro Wood for the purpose of introducing the manufacture of his cast iron plough; an occupation which requires much travelling, and hence is favorable to my health, and my design of promoting the institution of free Libraries.

RC (DLC). Addressed by Torrey to JM, and franked. Cover docketed by JM.

1. Jesse Torrey Jr., *The Moral Instructor, and Guide to Virtue and Happiness* (Ballston Spa, N.Y., 1819; Shaw and Shoemaker 49613).

2. Jesse Torrey Jr. (b. 1787) of New Lebanon, New York, was trained as a physician but became a prominent antislavery advocate who wrote frequently and traveled often in support of that cause, and those of free libraries, universal education, and prohibition (Jesse Torrey Jr., *The Intellectual Torch: Developing a Plan for the Universal Dissemination of Knowledge and Virtue by Means of Free Public Libraries*, ed. Edward Harmon Virgin [Woodstock, Vt., 1912], v, viii, xiii–xiv).

From Mackay & Campbell

DEAR SIR, FREDERICKSBURG Jany 16 1822.

We now return herewith your Sett of Exchange on Mess. Maury & Latham for £28. 3/5. which was in New York when your last favour was received. Yr note is due in Va. Br. Bank on 8th. proximo, and should you wish it renewed, or any part of it, it may be as well to Send us a note for that purpose. Wheat 6/9. Flour 5¾ dollars. With much Respect,

MACKAY & CAMPBELL

RC (DLC). Docketed by JM.

¶ To Peter Minor. Letter not found. *18 January 1822*. Described as a two-page autograph letter, signed and franked by JM, in *American Book-Prices Current* (1905), 11:589.

To Samuel Miller

DR SIR MONTPR. Jany 19 1822

I have just recd. the volume from your pen which you politely forwarded. Not being sure that I shall very soon be able to give it the due perusal, I think it proper not to postpone my acknowledgements for the favor. I can not doubt that I shall find the subject discussed with the ability, the erudition and the candour of which you have heretofore given pledges to the public.

Draft (DLC).

From Hezekiah Niles

Sir, Baltimore, Jan. 19, 1822

I am honored with the receipt of your communication in relation to certain proceedings during the revolution as to the navigation of the Mississippi river, which are laid off for ensertion, and shall appear in the next weeks Register, unless something important & of a more *immediately* interesting character should intervene. With thanks that you have been pleased to select my work on this occasion, I am with great respect, Yours &c

H Niles

RC (DLC). Docketed by JM.

From John Williams

D Sir Senate Chamber Jany. 21st 1822.

Enclosed I send you an argument in support of the claim of Massachusetts depending before Congress.[1] This claim will be much pressed during the present Session. Present my respects to Mrs. Madison and accept for yourself assurances of my sinsere regard.

John Williams[2]

RC (DLC). Docketed by JM.

1. This was probably the *Report on the Merits of the Claim of the State of Massachusetts, on the National Government for Expenses of the Militia, during the Late War, to the Governor and Council of the Commonwealth. January, 1821.* (Boston, 1822; Shoemaker 9414).

2. John Williams (1778–1837) was born in North Carolina but moved to Knoxville, Tennessee, where he began to practice law in 1803. He served in the U.S. Army as a captain, 1799–1800, and as colonel of the U.S. Thirty-Ninth Infantry during the War of 1812, when he took part in the Battle of Horseshoe Bend. He was attorney general of Tennessee, 1807–8, and represented his state in the U.S. Senate, 1815–23. President Adams appointed him chargé d'affaires to the Central American Federation in 1825, and he lived in Guatemala until December 1826 (McBride and Robison, *Biographical Directory of the Tennessee General Assembly*, 1:794–95).

To Henry R. Schoolcraft

Sir Montpellier Jany. 22. 1822

I have received the copy of your Memoir on the fossil Tree, which you politely forwarded. Of the decisive bearing of this phenomenon on important questions in Geology, I rely more on your judgment than my own.

The present is a very inquisitive age, and its researches of late have been ardently directed to the primitive composition and structure of our Globe, as far as it has been penetrated, and to the processes by which succeeding changes have been produced. The discoveries already made are encouraging; but vast room is left for the industry & sagacity of Geologists. This is sufficiently shewn by the opposite Theories which have been espoused; one of them regarding water, the other fire, as the great Agent employed by nature in her work.

It may well be expected that this hemisphere, which has been least explored, will yield its full proportion of materials towards a satisfactory system. Your zealous efforts to share in the contributions do credit to your love of truth & devotion to the cause of Science. And I wish they may be rewarded with the success they promise, and with all the personal gratifications to which they entitle you. With friendly respects,

James Madison

RC (CLjC); draft (DLC). RC addressed and franked by JM to Schoolcraft in Albany; postmarked 26 Jan. at Orange Court House. Docketed by Schoolcraft as received 31 Jan. Minor differences between the copies have not been noted.

To John A. Wharton

Sir Montpr. Jany 22. 1822

Your enquiries with respect to the University do not admit an answer until what is now contingent shall be reduced to certainty. The time of opening it depends on further aids from the legislature, and on obtaining eligible professors, after provision for them shall be authorized. The qualifications for the admission of Students, will doubtless be made public as soon as they shall be regularly settled. In the mean time, the rules of other Universities may be some guide to conjecture. The expences of Education, the boarding particularly which must be a principal part, will of course depend on the prices of food of which no exact estimate can be made at so early a day.

Your anxiety to partake the advantages to be expected from this Institution, is very laudable and I wish I could have given you information of a more satisfactory nature.

J. M

Draft (DLC).

From Joseph Delaplaine

DEAR SIR, PHILADELPHIA January 23d. 1822.

I take the liberty of sending to you at the request of my friend Mr. Charles Mead, a book for the use of schools[1] which he has been at considerable pains in preparing, & for which he has received unqualified approbation. He would feel highly honoured by receiving a testimonial in its favour & if it may be agreeable it would give me pleasure to receive it from you. With very high respect & regard I am D sir Your obed. & huml st.

JOSEPH DELAPLAINE

P.S. I beg leave to be presented most respectfully to Mrs. Madison & Mr Todd.

RC (DLC). Docketed by JM.

1. For this book, see Delaplaine to JM, 11 Oct. 1820, and n. 3.

From Mackay & Campbell

DR SIR, FREDERICKSBURG Jany 24. 1822.

Your favour 21st.[1] is before us covering your Note for $800. to renew one for a Similar Amount due on 8th. of next month. It also covered a Sett of Exchange on Mess Maury & Latham for £21.15/2 Which we return for your Signature. Very Respectfully

MACKAY & CAMPBELL

Flour 5.75 to 5.80.
Wheat 112½ cts.
Exch: in England 11 @ 12 above.

RC (DLC). Docketed by JM.

1. Letter not found.

To Benjamin Romaine

DR. SIR MONTPR. Jany 26. 1822

I have duly recd. the two pamphlets which followed your favor of the 11th inst. Not having critically examined, as you have done, the Constitution on foot with an eye to a comparison with the existing one, or to its connection with the Constitution of the U. States, I cannot presume to speak of its merits or defects in either respect. I have indulged the reflection only, that it is propitious to the cause of self-Government, that the trying task of revising an established Constitution should have been so deliberately conducted, & so tranquilly concluded, by a Body elected and acting in conformity to the freedom & forms of the popular System.

J. M.

Draft (DLC).

To Jesse Torrey Jr.

Sir Montpr. Jany. 30. 1822.

I have recd. your letter of the 15th. with a copy of "The Moral Instructor." Neither Mrs. M. nor myself have recollections which called for your apology. If there had been occasion for one, that offered would be more than sufficient.

I have looked eno' into your little volume to be satisfied that both the original & selected parts contain information & instruction which may be useful not only to juvenile but most other readers. I must suggest for your consideration, however, whether, contrary to what you suppose, the labor of part of the community especially with the aids of machinery, may not be sufficient to provide the necessaries & plainest comforts of life for the whole, and consequently that the remaining part must either be supported in idleness, or employed in producing superfluities, from the sale of which they may derive their own necessaries and comforts. It may deserve consideration also whether, by classing among noxious luxuries, some articles of general, and it would seem, innocent use, prejudices may not be excited unfavorable to the reception & circulation of the book itself.

Your plan of free libraries, to be spread thro' the community, does credit to your benevolent zeal. The trial of them in behalf of apprentices, seems to have been justly approved, and to have had an encouraging success: As apprentices are generally found more together in particular spots, than youths of other descriptions, such a provision can the more easily & effectually be made for them. For the same reason these establishments may without difficulty be made accessible to others dwellg. in Towns who need them. In the Country, the difficulties will be greater or less as the population is more or less sparse. Where it is the most so, the best efforts may fail. It is not to be forgotten however that every day is multiplying situations in which the obstacles will not be insuperable, and which consequently invite the philanthropic attention of which you have given examples. A Tree of useful knowledge planted in every neighbourhood, would help to make a paradise, as that of forbidden use occasioned the loss of one. And I wish you success in propagating the fruitful blessing. With friendly respects

J. M.

Draft (DLC).

From Thomas P. McMahon

SIR PHILADA. Jany. 30: 1822

On the 22nd. of June 1818[1] I done myself the pleasure of transmitting to you an account due for seeds sent you per order of the late Mr. Latrobe, to the Estate of Mr. B. McMahon deceased, amounting to twenty one dollars and 12½ cents; and since then not having heard from you, am desirous of requesting your attention to the Subject as speedily as possible, as the Executrix to the Estate is at present very much pressed for funds; and unless She is able to collect in the outstanding debts due the Estate of her late husband, she will be obliged to sacrafice the principal part of the property left for her Support. She earnestly desires me to request your immidiate attention and trusts that her Situation will be an excuse for tenor of this communication. I have the honor to be sir With great respect Your Obt. Servt.

THOMAS P. MCMAHON[2]

RC (DLC). Docketed by JM.

1. Letter not found.

2. Thomas P. McMahon (ca. 1791–1831), a veteran of the War of 1812, who resigned from the U.S. Army in 1818, was a son of Irish-born horticulturalist, Bernard McMahon (d. 1816), who had established a nursery and seed business in Philadelphia and who nurtured and sold seeds from the plant specimens sent back by Lewis and Clark from their western expedition. When he was president, JM had purchased seeds for a vegetable garden through Benjamin Henry Latrobe (McMahon to Latrobe, 27 June 1809, DLC). Bernard McMahon was also the author of the popular *American Gardener's Calendar; Adapted to the Climates and Seasons of the United States. . . .* (1806). After Bernard's death, his wife, Ann, and his son, Thomas, continued the business, though Thomas was admitted to the bar in 1825 and had become a notary public by 1827 (Heitman, *Historical Register*, 1:676; José Corrèa de Serra to JM, 12 Feb. 1819, *PJM-RS*, 1:414 n. 2; Robert S. Cox, "'I Never Yet Parted': Bernard McMahon and the Seeds of the Corps of Discovery," in Robert S. Cox, ed., *The Shortest and Most Convenient Route: Lewis and Clark in Context* [Philadelphia, 2004], 109–29; "Notices of Marriages and Deaths in Poulson's American Daily Advertiser, 1831–1833," *Collections of the Genealogical Society of Pennsylvania* 177 [1907]: 277).

From Adam Cooke

Dear Sir Fredericksburg 31 January 1822

The two Boxes Sent by R Cutts Esqr I forwarded to you yesterday by Mr Barbours Wagon. Enclosed you have your account up to this time. With Due Respect I am Sir your Hu[m]ble St

A. Cooke[1]

[Enclosure]

James Madison Esqr

In account With Jas Cooke[2] Dr.

Octor	16		To Cash paid for 2 u Snuff 13/6	$2.50
		"	6 Bottles Porter	1.20
	30		For 2 Bottles Oil at 83 cts.	.83
		"	To Cash paid for Candlemoulds 3/9	.67
Novr.	19	"	For 1 Barrell Sugar 250 u. at 13 cts Bll 25¢	32.75
		"	Cash for 3 Bushels Oysters 150¢	1.50
		"	6 u. Cheese 6/–	1.00
	27	"	51 u. 5 oz piece Sugar at 26¢	13.24
		"	Cash for 2 Bushels Oysters 6/	1.00
Decr	6	"	33¼ Gals Whiskey at 44¢ Bll 75¢	15.38
		"	3 Bushels potatoes 3/–	1.50
	14	"	6 u. Rice @ 4d.½ 6 u. Cheese 6/	13.7½
		"	Cash for Canister snuff 3/9	.62½
Januy	4	"	2 Bottles Oil at 5/3 1 u. Chocolate 2/	1.99
		"	Cash for 10 Galls Beer @ ⅔ Keg 4/6	4.50
				$80.76
	25	"	To Cash paid Stage for 2 Boxes	2.00
				$82.76

Settled in account with
Mackay & Campbell.

for James Cooke
A. Cooke

RC and enclosure (DLC). RC addressed by Cooke to JM, and franked. Docketed by JM "Cooke Js."

1. Adam Cooke (ca. 1771–1839) was born in Ireland and came to the United States about 1792. He was surveyor and inspector of the revenue at Fredericksburg, from 1816 until his death (Harry Warren, "Col. William G. Cooke," *Quarterly of the Texas State Historical Association* 9 [1906]: 210–11; *Daily National Intelligencer*, 14 Nov. 1816; Baltimore *Sun*, 13 May 1839 and 1 Feb. 1840).

2. James Cooke (ca. 1795–1873), the son of Adam Cooke, was educated as a physician at the University of Pennsylvania and practiced medicine in Fredericksburg. He was the author of *A Sketch of the Autumnal Fever, as It Prevailed in the Town of Fredericksburg, Virginia, 1821* (Philadelphia, 1822). For a time he ran a grocery business in Fredericksburg with his father (Warren, "Col. William G. Cooke," *Quarterly of the Texas State Historical Association* 9 [1906]: 211; Fredericksburg *Virginia Herald*, 2 Jan. 1822).

From Maury & Latham

Sir, Liverpool 1 February 1822

Referring you to our annexed monthly report upon Tobacco &c.,[1] we may remark that there appears rather more disposition to purchase in London, by which market ours must now be regulated; about 200 Hhds. had been sold to a Dealer, 128 of which were rather under middling & brought 4½d.; there, as well as here, the want of desirable quality for Ireland & the Home demand is felt, & our highest quotations could be obtained.

About 100 hhds. Kentucky leaf were purchased yesterday for Rotterdam p 2¼ @ 2½, a few @ 2d. & some Virginia @ 2¼ d—such will have the good effect of clearing our market for the new crop; we cannot however conclude this letter without once more repeating our former opinion, that our prices, as well as sustaining a decline in the fall, from an overstocked market, will be still further affected by the absence of any speculativ[e] demand; for what reasonable man is there, who would invest his money in an article, (on speculation) the cultivation of which he knows will continue as great as the last year, until either the Planter is not reimbursed, or a demand for Bread Stuff exists in this Country?

Then, & not until one of these events takes place, may you with safety calculate upon any other prices than what the demand for consumption will afford. We are, Sir, Very respectfully yours,

Maury Latham & Co.

RC and enclosure (DLC). RC addressed to JM, and franked; postmarked 2 Apr. at New York; docketed by JM. For enclosure, see n. 1.

1. The enclosure (1 p.) is a printed monthly report, dated 31 Jan. 1822, giving prices in Liverpool for a number of commodities, including cotton, tobacco, grains, potash, tar, beeswax, gold, copper, tin, and lead, as well as stock shares.

From George Joy

Dear sir, London 2nd febry. 1822.

I purchased, some three years ago, the first volume of the Histoire de l'Esprit revolutionaire des nobles en France,[1] and left an Order with my french Bookseller here to send me the second as soon as it should arrive; intending after perusal to pass them to you. To various enquiries since, I have received various answers—the last of which was that they did not believe it would be published at all. However they have now sent it to me, in time to be bound and go by this ship. It embraces only those points of french history that apply to the subject, but will be found a good refresher, and may be read rapidly. I must apprize you however that, when the Author tells you in his preface that it is peu chargé de reflexions,[2] you are not to understand a paucity of number—on the contrary there is a sprinkling of Attic throughout the work that hath not "lost it's savour;"[3] from which a set of short, to be sure, but very pithy apophthegms may be collected. I should think it was a work that would entertain Mr: Jefferson. I was going to say amuse, but the scenery is too barbarous. Having written you too copiously of late, this is all I shall trouble you with on this occasion; save assuring you that I am always very faithfully yours

G. Joy

RC and enclosure (DLC). RC cover addressed by Joy to JM, and marked "℔ Henry Clay / Captn Potts"; postmarked 14 Apr. at Baltimore, and franked. The enclosure (1 p.) is a letter from Joy to Capt. Potts, 2 Feb. 1822, instructing him as to the disposition of the parcel of books to be sent to JM.

1. *Histoire de l'esprit revolutionnaire des nobles en France, sous les soixante-huit rois de la monarchie* (2 vols.; Paris, 1818).

2. "Son récit est simple et uni, peu chargé de réflexions" (ibid., 1:xv): His [the author's] story is simple and plain, little burdened by reflection.

3. "Attic": Attic salt, refined wit like that of the Athenians. Here Joy is playing off Matt. 5:13 (AV): "Ye are the salt of the earth: but if the salt have lost his savour, wherewith shall it be salted? it is thenceforth good for nothing, but to be cast out, and to be trodden under foot of men."

From Mackay & Campbell

Dear Sir Fredericksburg Feby 7. 1822.

Today we received your favour 4th. inst.[1] covering James Cooke's Account against you for $82.76/100 which had been previously Settled by us & which We now return under cover. The dividend on your Turnpike

Stock is at your Credit in $37.50/100. The proceeds of your Bill on Maury & Latham ℔ £21.15/2 Sterlg. at 11 ℔ cent advance, is also at your Credit in $107.33. With great Respect,

Mackay & Campbell

RC (DLC). Docketed by JM.

1. Letter not found.

From Joshua Gilpin

Sir Kentmere Feby 8th. 1822

Since I had the honor of receiving your kind attention at Washington no opportunity has occurred of expressing the respect and attachment I have ever felt for you, till now when the publication of a little work induces me to beg your acceptance of a copy of it.[1] It is upon the old subject of the Chesapeake & Delaware Canal and may amuse an idle hour and claim a part of that interest for the improvement of our country which I am sure you never cease to feel.

I have never had an opportunity Sir of thanking you for the favorable sentiments you were pleased to express towards me on my application for the London Consulate in 1811 which Mr Bayard had the goodness to convey to me; that I did not press the subject further arose from my unpleasant situation in England arising from the extreme personal hostility exercised towards every American especially among the country gentry; on my arrival there I became immediately impressed that if ever war was necessary to redeem the insulted honor and interests of a country it was imperiously demanded by our situation—in the conduct of it I felt nothing to regret but the divided sentiments of our countrymen at home which were certainly a great if not the only cause of its protraction and the peace which closed it I consider in common I believe with all Europe as one of great glory which fixed our rank in the scale of Nations beyond all other circumstances. With sentiments like these which tho' I did not obtrude I could not dissemble my situation was not a pleasant one even surrounded as I was by friends and I compounded against further molestation by remaining within ten miles of my own house during the war at the close of which I returned with my family and reside partly in the city but principally here occupied by some attention to my manufacturing establishments but chiefly by farming and objects of political economy particularly that one which I now present to your notice. If ever Mrs Madison or yourself should pass thro' Wilmington Mrs Gilpin and myself shall deem ourselves highly honored by a visit at our house which is within sight of the town and hope you will not omit it. In the meantime we both beg leave to present our respects and best wishes for her happiness and your own and I remain truly Sir Your Obt Hle Servt

JOSA. GILPIN[2]

A slight paralytic affection of my right hand compels me to use ⟨an⟩ amanuensis.

RC (DLC). In an unidentified hand, signed by Gilpin. Addressed partially by Gilpin to JM, and franked; postmarked ⟨8?⟩ Mar. at Washington. Docketed by JM. Damaged by removal of seal.

1. Joshua Gilpin, *A Memoir on the Rise, Progress, and Present State of the Chesapeake and Delaware Canal, Accompanied with Original Documents and Maps* (Wilmington, Del., 1821; Shoemaker 5461).

2. Joshua Gilpin (1765–1841) was a member of a prominent Philadelphia family of merchants and entrepreneurs. In 1811 he solicited from JM "the appointment to a Consular Office, Agency, or some similar object in England" (Gilpin to JM, 19 June 1811, *PJM-PS*, 3:344 and n. 1). One of Gilpin's sons, Henry D. Gilpin (1801–60), served as U.S. attorney general under President Martin Van Buren. It was under Henry Gilpin's direction that the 1840 edition of the *Papers of James Madison* was published (*PJM*, 1:xviii).

From Nicholas Biddle

DEAR SIR, ANDALUSIA BUCKS CY. PENNA. Feby 9. 1822

I have so often derived pleasure from your writings, that I should deem it an act of gratitude to present to you the paper which accompanies this note,[1] were I not sensible how little it enables me to repay my obligations. I can therefore only request that you will place it in your library as a mark of my great respect for one who is realizing the best hopes of all statesmen by closing a distinguished career of public service in the pursuits of letters and agriculture. With sentiments of great consideration I am very respectfully Yrs.

NICHOLAS BIDDLE

RC (DLC); draft (DLC: Nicholas Biddle Papers). RC docketed by JM.

1. Nicholas Biddle, *Address Delivered before the Philadelphia Society for Promoting Agriculture, at Its Annual Meeting, on the Fifteenth of January, 1822* (Philadelphia, 1822; Shoemaker 8059).

To Joseph Delaplaine

DEAR SIR MONTPELLIER Feby 12. 1822

I have recd. your letter of Jany. 23. and with it the little volume of Mr. Mead entitled "School Exercise."

A plan which brings into a small compas[s] the several branches of youthful instruction, which places them in the proper order of succession, and conducts the Student, by easy gradations in each, from an early to an advanced Stage of education, speaks sufficiently its own commendation. That this merit is due to Mr. Mead I readily admit, on the sanction given to it by those who must be well qualified to form a just estimate. To make myself in any measure a critical judge, would require a more attentive examination of the work than other engagements would permit. If the glance I have been able to take of its contents, would justify me in hazarding any remark on the subject it would be to suggest for consideration, whether in a future edition, it would not be an improvement to annex to some of the descriptions, such as those in the chapter on Architecture, plates, however cheaply engraved, presenting to the eye the figures described. The parts of a column or an entablature can scarcely be made intelligible without that aid; and with it the perception is instant and durable. Perhaps more frequent illustrations by example, might also be advantageously applied to the technical & scientific definitions.

When the pamphlets &c which had been put into your hands, were returned, you desired that in case of any omission, you might be reminded of it. I do not find among the articles, the chronological memoranda in manuscript;[1] which for the reason given when the return was requested, I wish to have an opportunity of revising. You will oblige me therefore by sending me the omitted paper. With friendly respects

JAMES MADISON

RC (PHi); draft (DLC); FC (ViU: Special Collections). FC in an unidentified hand. An extract of this letter was printed in the "recommendations" section of the second edition of Charles Mead's *School Exercise* (Shoemaker 13275). Minor differences between the copies have not been noted.

1. For the "pamphlets &c" and the "chronological memoranda," see JM to Delaplaine, ca. 31 Oct. 1820, and nn.

From Jesse Torrey Jr.

Sir, Washington City Feb. 12, 1822.

Having received information, a few days after the date of my letter to you, from Mr. Word, that he expected shortly to be in this place, and having some other business here besides with him, I came to this city about a fortnight ago, and expect to remain here 2 or 3 weeks longer, before I return to Chambersburg.

Not knowing, therefore, whether you have sent any letter for me to Chambersburg or not, I have thought proper to give you notice of my arrival here; wishing also, to inform you that I have nearly finished an Address to the citizens of the United States on the subject of education and free libraries, which I shall endeavor to publish before I leave this city, for gratuitous distribution among the post offices generally in the United States, and otherwise. And whether you have already written or not, I should feel gratefully obliged, by receiving while I am here, a brief expression of your sentiments on the particular subject of free libraries; provided you should be disposed so to favor me without the least reluctance or objection.

Permit me, also, to use this occasion to mention to you, that as the printing of my Address, (making probably 20 pages) will probably cost upwards of one hundred dollars; for which I am compelled to depend entirely on subscription or contribution, if you should be cheerfully disposed to aid my design, by enclosing me a small sum for that purpose, its value would be trebled or more by the example. I am sir, with sentiments of great respect, your sincere friend, &c.

Jesse Torrey, Jun

RC (DLC). Docketed by JM, with his note: "Answered by referring him to the answer to his last forwarded to Chambersburg."

To Benjamin H. Rand

Sir Feby. 15. 1822

I duly recd. your letter of Decr. 16. 1821. offering for my acceptance a copy of your Edition of President Washington's address. The intrinsic value of the Document may well have invited the elegance of form, I doubt not, you have given to it; and I am very sensible of your politeness in forwarding me a copy. I have postponed this expression of it, in the hope of being able to say at the same time that I had obtained the little volume from

George Town. I have not yet done so, but shall probably find an opportunity shortly.

J M.

Draft (DLC).

To James Monroe

Dear Sir Montpellier Feby. 16. 1822

A letter from Mrs. Dallas has just come under my eye,[1] by which I find she is subsisting on very scanty resources, and is under impressions that two of her sons particularly, are not as well off as the public services of their father, and their own personal worth had promised. The elder one belonging to the Navy has, it seems, been a considerabl⟨e⟩ time without a ship. The other, George, tho' holding a place of some little value in the business of the Bank, has lost by the vicissitudes of party, his office under the State and is struggling in a crowd of forensic competitors for the principal support of a growing family. I know so well your respect for the character of Mr. Dallas and for his meritorious labours as a member of the Executive during a very trying period, and your good will towards his family, that I am afraid in saying any thing on the subject, I say more than I ought. I can not decline, however, bearing my testimony to the fine talents, excellent principles & amiable dispositions of the younger brother as I have always regarded them, and acknowledging the pleasure I should feel in seeing his situation improved by any patronage from the Government, for which a proper opportunity might be afforded. With respect to the other brother Alexander, I must necessarily presume that his being unemployed is the effect of rules in the Navy Department not to be dispensed with, and that there can be no disposition there which would not be more tempted to waive them in his favor than to turn them against him. Excuse this addition to the intrusions which circumstances have occasionally exacted from me, and be assured always of my high consideration, and my affectionate respects.

James Madison

RC (NjP); draft (DLC). RC docketed by Monroe. Minor differences between the copies have not been noted.

1. This was almost certainly a letter [not found] from Arabella Maria Smith Dallas to Dolley Madison, whose reply [not found] was acknowledged in a letter from Mrs. Dallas to Mrs. Madison on 14 Mar. 1822: "I have delay'd thanking you, in the hope that I shou'd have been enabled to tell you, that your good Husbands kind attention had been noticed by

Mr. Monroe, sufficiently to have moved him to some exertion . . . it still however remains undetermined" (*DMDE*).

From Jedidiah Morse

SIR, WASHINGTON CITY Feb. 16th. 1822.

I have the honor, in fulfilment of my official duty, to transmit to you a copy of the Constitution of a Society,[1] just established, which recognizes the general System of measures, or rather the spirit of them, which were pursued during your Administration in reference to Indians. From this consideration, I am permitted to indulge a confident hope, sir, that this Constitution, & the office under it to which you are appointed by the Society,[2] will meet your approbation and acceptance. With high consideration & respect, I have the honor, to be, sir, your most obdt. Servt

JEDH. MORSE[3] Cor. Secy

RC (DLC). Docketed by JM.

1. *American Society for Promoting the Civilization and General Improvement of the Indian Tribes within the United States* (Washington, 1822; Shoemaker 7806).

2. "The successive Presidents of the United States, who shall have retired from office, shall be, ex-officio, Patrons of this Society. . . ." (*The First Annual Report of the American Society for Promoting the Civilization and General Improvement of the Indian Tribes in the United States* . . . [New Haven, Conn., 1824], 4).

3. Jedidiah Morse (1761–1826), a 1783 graduate of Yale College, was minister of the First Congregational Church of Charlestown, Massachusetts, 1789–1819, and a powerful voice of Calvinist orthodoxy against the rising tide of Unitarianism. He was an outspoken Federalist in politics. Morse is best known for his works of geography, beginning with *Geography Made Easy* (1784) to the larger work, *The American Geography* (1789), which passed through many editions and later was published as *The American Universal Geography* (1793). After he resigned the pulpit in 1819, he took up the cause of Indian improvement, though his plans for a proposed organization (see n. 1 above) were unsuccessful (Joseph W. Phillips, *Jedidiah Morse and New England Congregationalism* [New Brunswick, N.J., 1983], 13, 17, 18, 25, 26, 27, 71, 129–30, 157, 176, 198–99, 212–13, 219).

To Mathew Carey

DEAR SIR MONTPELLIER Feby 21. 1822

I have recd. the copy of the "Appeal to common sense and common Justice" which you were so good as to send me.[1] And I have since received one of your letters inviting observations on it.[2]

It would be impossible for me to do justice, even to my own view of the subject within the time limited, were the attempt permitted by engagements of other sorts. It is I believe not unknown to you that I accede to the general policy of leaving the industrious pursuits of individuals to their own sagacity & interest; guides to which perhaps the people of this country, may be as safely trusted, as those of any Country whatever. I concur, nevertheless, in the practical wisdom of certain important exceptions to this Theory, which may justly claim a legislative interposition. A correct enumeration of these excepted cases, with the reasons in support of them would, I think, be a very valuable service rendered to this branch of political Economy. It would be a work however requiring talents, information, and leisure, too seldom united in the same individuals.

Whilst the pen is in my hand, I will glance at a general argument in favor of legislative encouragement, to a certain extent, of domestic manufactories. It is the argument drawn from the frequency of wars, & their effect on the cost of imported articles. The calculations which favor these, on account of their greater cheapness, seem to have been founded too much on peace-prices, and a supposition that peace is never to be interrupted; when, to be conclusive, they ought to be founded on the medium prices, taking the probable periods of peace and of war together, and keeping always in mind that to have the command of domestic supplies when foreign ones are the dearer the domestic must be protected against a destructive interference of the foreign when these are the cheaper. Reflection suggests what experience has shewn, that manufacturing establishments which are to be put down by a state of peace, will be a precarious resource in the emergency of war. They will either not be undertaken, or be defectively carried on with disproportionate prices for their products. I can not but think that an illustration of this point, by a comparative view of the probable periods of war and of peace, which for the last century have been nearly equal, and by the estimated increase of the cost charges & freight of imported articles during a state of war among the great manufacturing and commercial nations of Europe, to say nothing of wars involving our own country, would find a proper place in the discussions of the Tariff question which has engaged so much of the public attention. It would present a naked question whether the consumer would be most taxed by a given tariff, or by war, for the want of it. With friendly respects

James Madison

RC (NjMoHP); draft (DLC). RC addressed and franked by JM to Carey in Philadelphia. Cover docketed by Carey. Minor differences between the copies have not been noted.

1. Mathew Carey, *An Appeal to Common Sense and Common Justice; or, Irrefragable Facts Opposed to Plausible Theories . . .* (Philadelphia, 1822; Shoemaker 8259).

2. JM's copy of the broadside announcement of a new edition of *An Appeal to Common Sense*, dated 13 Feb. 1822 (Shoemaker 8256), is in the Madison Collection, Rare Book and Special Collections Division, Library of Congress. Carey wrote that he would "regard, as a very particular favor, the suggestion of any errors or deficiencies . . . or any improvements."

To Nicholas Biddle

Dear Sir Montpellier Feby. 23. 1822

I duly recd. your favour of the 9th. accompanied by a copy of your agricultural address, which I have read with much pleasure, and I can add with instruction also. It is made particularly interesting by the views taken of the ancient and modern husbandry, where unless parts of China be exceptions, the earth has made the greatest returns to human labour. The advantage of contracting and fertilizing the area on which our farmers exert their faculties, seems every where to be more & more understood; but the reform does not keep pace with the change of circumstances requiring it. The error, as a radical one, can not therefore be too clearly exposed, or the remedy too strongly inculcated.

You have very properly, under that impression, noticed the minuteness of the farms allotted to proprietors by the early laws of Rome, and it seems certain that they were not a little remarkable in that respect. I must own however that the limitation of them to about 1¼ of our acres, from which must be deducted the site of the houses; or even the extension of them to a little more than 4 of our acres, has always appeared to me so extraordinary as to be scarcely credible. The fact, nevertheless, as far as I have seen, has been neither disproved, nor denied. Dickson in his elaborate work on the husbandry of the Ancients[1] cites the usual authorities witht. calling them in question. And Wallace another Author distinguished for his learned researches, in his treatise on the numbers of mankind,[2] makes these subdivisions of the Roman soil, one of his arguments for the superiority of the ancient populousness of the earth over the modern. Nor do I recollect that the sagacious & sceptical Hume, who maintains an opposite opinion,[3] has critized [*sic*] the alledged size of the Roman farms. Still it is difficult, more for Americans, perhaps, than for a more compact people, to conceive in what manner a family averaged at six only (and the number was probably greater in the early rate of increase) could be fed & otherwise provided for, by the product of such specks of ground. The puzzle is the greater, if it be understood that half of the farm only was annually in cultivation, the other being fallow. And the fact would be altogether incredible, if, according to Columella,[4] the increase of the seed was not more than fourfold. This however must refer to a later period of the Republic, or rather to his own time, when the soil had been deprived of its primitive fertility, or its productiveness impaired by a degenerate husbandry: For so small a space as even 4 acres, could not possibly, at that rate of increase, suffice for a family; without supposing a quantity of seed given to the earth, beyond all measure, when it was more probably reduced in its proportion by peculiar care in sowing it, and harvesting the crop. In the dibbling mode sometimes practised in England, which produces the greatest of crops, the quantity of seed, if I rightly remember, is somewhere about a peck to the Acre.

If we are not at liberty to contest the fact as to the diminutive size of the early Roman farms, the attempt to account for the phænomenon, must take for granted, and make the most of, the circumstances, that none of the usual quadrupeds were kept on the farm, that the ground was tilled by the hand alone of the farmer himself, and with more than a garden attention to every inch: and that all the cloathing was wrought within the family. Even on this last supposition, the question arises, whence the materials for the fabrics? The wool, & the lint, if produced on the farm must have subtracted so much from the crop of food: if purchased, they must have been paid for out of the crop. And purchased from whom? It could not, of course, be by such farmers from one another. Questions of a like cast are presented by the materials necessary for household utensils, farming implements &c &c. which the farm itself could not supply. Do we know of any population where less than an acre supports the individuals? The Agrarian regulations of earliest date among the Romans must have reduced the quantity to 1/5 of an Acre.

We seem to be driven to the necessity of some subsidiary resources, for the support of a family confined to such scanty portions of soil. The military policy may have been a partial one. As the nation was almost constantly at war, at small distances from Rome, and the farmers were all soldiers, they may have drawn their subsistance, whilst in the field, from the farms of their neighbours; and have carried home, among the spoils of successful expeditions, an additional stock of provisions for the use of their families.

The entire subject is curious. It involves three questions. 1. whether the fact be rightly stated that the Roman farms were of no greater size. 2. if rightly stated, and there were no resources beyond the farms, in what way did the family subsist on them. 3. if there were extraneous resources, what were they?

I hope you will not understand that in putting these questions I wish to impose on you the task of searching for answers, & that you will be assured of my sincere esteem and friendly respects.

James Madison

RC (owned by Charles J. Biddle, Philadelphia, Pa., 1961); draft (DLC). RC docketed by Biddle. Minor differences between the copies have not been noted.

1. Adam Dickson, *The Husbandry of the Ancients* (2 vols; Edinburgh, 1788). The size of Roman farms is discussed in 1:6–15.

2. Robert Wallace, *A Dissertation on the Numbers of Mankind, in Ancient and Modern Times*, 2d ed. (Edinburgh, 1809). The argument to which JM referred is at 119–21.

3. David Hume, "Of the Populousness of Ancient Nations," in *Essays and Treatises on Several Subjects*, new ed. (2 vols.; London, 1788), 1:389–91.

4. Columella, *De Re Rustica (On Agriculture)* (Loeb Classical Library; 1941 ed.).

To Richard Peters

Dear Sir Montpellier Feby. 23. 1822

I have recd. the copy of Mr. Biddle's address so obligingly forwarded by you.

I knew before that Mr. B. was a fine writer; but I did not know that he was so accomplished a farmer. His address shews that he is both. I have read it not only with pleasure but with instruction: and I return you my thanks for the opportunity of doing so. Accept in addition to them my cordial regards and my best wishes

James Madison

RC (NjMoHP); Tr (owned by Charles J. Biddle, Philadelphia, Pa., 1961). Tr included in Richard Peters to Nicholas Biddle, 28 Mar. 1822.

From Thomas Jefferson

Dear Sir Monticello Feb. 25. 22.

I have no doubt you have recieved, as I have done, a letter from Dr. Morse with a printed pamphlet, proposing to us a place in a self constituted society for the civilisation of the Indians &c. I am anxious to know your thoughts on the subject because they would affect my confidence in my own. I disapprove the proposition altogether. I acknolege the right of voluntary associations for laudable purposes and in moderate numbers. I acknolege too the expediency, for revolutionary purposes, of general associations, coextensive with the nation. But where, as in our case, no abuses call for revolution voluntary associations so extensive as to grapple with & controul the government, should such be or become their purpose, are dangerous machines, and should be frowned down in every regulated government. Here is one proposed to comprehend all the functionaries of the government executive, legislative & Judiciary, all officers of the army or navy, governors of the states, learned institutions, the whole body of the clergy who will be 19/20 of the whole association, and as many other individuals as can be enlisted for 5.D. apiece. For what object? One which the government is pursuing with superior means, superior wisdom, and under limits of legal prescription. And by whom? A half dozen or dozen private individuals, of whom we know neither the number nor names, except of Elias B. Caldwell[1] their foreman, Jedediah Morse of Ocean memory their present Secretary & in petto[2] their future Agent, &c. These clubbists of Washington, who from their residence there will be the real society, have undertaken to embody even the government itself into an instrument to be wielded by themselves and for purposes directed by themselves. Observe that they omit the President's name, and for reasons too flimsy to be the true ones. No doubt they have proposed it to him, and his prudence has refused his name. And shall we suffer ourselves to be constituted into tools by such an authority? Who, after this example, may not impress us into their purposes? Feeling that the association is unnecessary, presumptuous & of dangerous example, my present impression is to decline membership, to give my reasons for it, in terms of respect, but with frankness. But as the answer is not pressing, I suspend it until I can hear from you in the hope you will exchange thoughts with me, that I may shape my answer as much in conformity with yours as coincidence in our views of the subject may admit: and I will pray to hear from you by the first mail. Ever and affectionately yours

TH: JEFFERSON

RC (DLC: Rives Collection, Madison Papers); FC (DLC: Jefferson Papers).

1. Elias Boudinot Caldwell (1776–1825), a graduate of the College of New Jersey, was a lawyer, a sometime preacher at the First Presbyterian Church in Washington, clerk of the U.S. Supreme Court, 1800–25, and a founder and secretary of the American Colonization Society in 1816 (Hallie L. Wright, "Sketch of Elias Boudinot Caldwell," *Records of the Columbia Historical Society* 24 (1922): 204–13).

2. *In petto:* in secret.

From Samuel Wyllys Pomeroy

SIR BRIGHTON 25 Feby. 1822.

In the Agricultural Journal, which I have now the pleasure to forward, you will observe that Mr Dey[1] of N York has in operation a machine for dressing flax & hemp, in an unrotted [*sic*] state, that bids fair to rival those invented in Europe. The samples of flax dressed by his machine, I find, on comparison, to equal those you were so kind as to send me: and in a letter, recently received, Mr Dey states that he has "been able to bring hemp into as fine, white & beautiful State, as flax, & much finer quality." The value of this discovery will appear to be enhanced, by the information I rec'd. a few days since, from a gentleman of respectability, lately arrived from Leeds in Yorkshire, who has been extensively, & profitably engaged in the manufacture of linen by machinery. He states that it is considered as yet, by no means certain, that Hill & Bundys machines[2] will ever become of extensive utility. That at present, the expence of dressing by them, including the cleansing & bleaching, amounts to 6d. Sterling ℔ pound; Mr. Dey estimates his to cost two cents ℔ pound when completely bleached.

This gentleman confirms the position taken in my "Essay on flax husbandry," as respects the manufacture of flax by machinery. He says that in those parts of Great Britain where the manufacture is considerable, Spinning by hand is mostly abandoned. That machines containing twenty thousand spindles, are now employed in *Leeds:* where two thousand tons of flax, prepared by the common method, was spun the last year: and he does not hesitate to assert, that linen can be manufactured as cheap *yard* for *yard* as cotton! including the bleaching (by a careful process with *muriate of lime*). He has brought his family, & contemplates engaging in the linen manufacture, having ordered out improved machinery for that purpose.

Whether flax or hemp, can be profitably prepared for the *heckle*, without being subject to the present tedious process, will probably soon be demonstrated. I trust the fact now established, beyond question, that the material can be manufactured with the same facility as Cotton, (should no advantage be derived from the machinery for dressing) will rank it among our most important Staples, tending to place our farmers, especially those in the interior, upon more independent ground than they have heretofore had reason to expect. Of this prospect, Sir, I take leave to offer sincere congratulations, with the assurance that I am with the highest respect Your obt St

S W Pomeroy

RC (DLC). Docketed by JM.

1. For Anthony Dey's letter to Pomeroy, 1 Dec. 1821, on the subject of flax, see the *Massachusetts Agricultural Repository and Journal* 7 (1822): 61–72. Anthony Dey (1776–1859) was a New York City lawyer who made and lost a fortune in real estate in northern New Jersey. He also was a director of the New Jersey Railroad. Sometime in the early 1840s, Dey filed for bankruptcy (George H. Farrier, ed., *Memorial of the Centennial Celebration of the Battle of Paulus Hook, August 19, 1879* [Jersey City, N.J., 1879], 155; Edward J. Balleisen, *Navigating Failure: Bankruptcy and Commercial Society in Antebellum America* [Chapel Hill, N.C., 2001], 278 n. 33).

2. Samuel Hill and William Bundy of Camden Town, London, had invented and obtained a patent for a machine for "breaking and preparing raw flax and hemp" ("Report of the Select Committee of the House of Commons on Petitions relating to Machinery for Manufacturing of Flax," *Quarterly Journal of Science and the Arts* 5 [1818]: 30–44; Alexander Jamieson, *A Dictionary of Mechanical Science, Arts, Manufactures, and Miscellaneous Knowledge* . . . [2 vols.; London, 1829], 1:451).

To Jedidiah Morse

Sir Montpellier Feby. 26. 1822

I have received your letter of the 16th. with the printed constitution of a Society for the benefit of the Indians.

Esteeming as I do the objects of the Institution, I can not decline the honorary relation to it which has been conferred on me; though good wishes be the only returns I shall be able to make.

Beside the general motive of benevolence, the remnants of the Tribes within our limits have special claims on our endeavors, to save them from the extinction to which they are hastening, and from the vices which have been doubled by our intercourse with them. This can not be done without substituting for the torpid indolence of the Wigwam, and the precarious supplies of the chase, the comforts & habits of civilized life. With the progress of these may be sown those elements of moral and intellectual improvement, which will either not be received into the savage mind, or be soon stifled by savage manners.

The Constitution of the Society very properly embraces the object of gathering whatever information may relate to the opinions, the Government, the social conditions &c. of this untutored race. Materials may thus be obtained for a just picture of the human character, as fashioned by circumstances which are yielding to others which must efface all the peculiar features of the Original. Be pleased to accept Sir, the expression of my esteem & friendly wishes

James Madison

RC (NjP); draft and FC (DLC). RC addressed and franked by JM to Morse at Washington. Cover docketed by Morse. Draft and FC dated incorrectly 16 Feb. 1822. FC in Dolley Madison's hand. Minor differences between the copies have not been noted.

From Thomas Cramer

Extract from the proceedings of the Agricultural Society of the Valley, Winchester 4th. March 1822

Resolved that our illustrious citizen & dignifyed Farmer Jas. Maddison Esqr. in consideration of his love for the "peacefull triumphs of the plow" and the Valuable aid, and assistance which he has rendered, and is still rendering to the Agricultu[r]e of his Native State, be & he is hereby elected an honorary Member of this Society, and that the Secretary is hereby ordered to notify him of the same.

a true copy Thos. Cramer,[1] Secy
of the A: S: of the Valley

Sir

I think myself peculiarly fortunate ('tho entirely unknown to you) in having the honor to communicate the above resolve of the Agricultural

Society of the Valley, to a gentleman distinguished for his active exertions in the cause of agriculture, as well as all the usefull and valuable Virtues which serve to embellish the human character. I have the honor to be, with the highest respect your Obt. Hbe. St.

Thos. Cramer

RC (DLC). Docketed by JM.

1. In 1814 Thomas Cramer served as a captain in the Virginia militia recruited from Frederick County (Stuart Lee Butler, *A Guide to Virginia Militia Units in the War of 1812* [Athens, Ga., 1988], 87).

To Thomas Jefferson

Dear Sir Mar. 5. 1822

This is the first mail since I recd. yours of the 25 Ult: which did not come to hand in time for an earlier answer; having lain a day or two at Or: Ct. House.

Regarding the New Socy. for the benefit of the Indians, as limited to their civilization, an object laudable in itself; and taking for granted, perhaps too hastily, that the plan had not been formed & published without the sanction of the most respectable names on the spot; finding moreover that no Act of Incorporation from the Govt. was contemplated, I thought it not amiss to give the inclosed answer to Mr. Morse.[1] In its principle, the Association, tho' a great amplification, is analogous to that of the Academy of Languages & Belles lettres.

The project appears to me to be rather ostentatious than dangerous. Those embraced by it are too numerous, too heterogeneous, and too much dispersed to concentrate their views in any covert or illicit object; nor is the immediate object a sufficient cement to hold them long together for active purposes. The Clergy who may prove a great majority of the whole, and might be most naturally distrusted are themselves made up of such repulsive Sects, that they are not likely to form a noxious confederacy, especially with ecclesiastical views.

On a closer attention than I had given to the matter before I recd. your letter I perceive that the organization of the Board of Directors is a just subject of animadversion. The powers vested in it may devolve on too few to be charged with the collection & application of the funds. As the proceedings however will be at the seat of Govt. and under the eye of so many of every description of observers there will be no little controul agst. abuses. It is pretty remarkable that Docr. Morse and one of his own name[2] may be ⅔ of a majority of a Board. This person has I believe lately returned from some Agency under the Govt. along with Govr. Cass,[3] among the Northern Tribes of Indians; which makes it the more probable that his present plans are in accord with the ideas of the War Department at least.

Had I not written my answer, I should be led by my present view of the subject to suspend it till more should be known of this project, and particularly how far the high characters named, on the spot or elsewhere had embarked in it.

I find by a Gazette just recd. that a member of the Senate has denounced the project in very harsh terms.[4] He is from a State however not distant from the Indians, and may have opinions & feelings on topics relating to them not common to the members of the Body. Always & affecy. yours

James Madison

RC (DLC); FC (DLC: Rives Collection, Madison Papers). RC docketed by Jefferson "recd Mar. 7." FC in Dolley Madison's hand. Minor differences between the copies have not been noted.

1. The enclosure (not found) was a copy of JM to Morse, 26 Feb. 1822.

2. According to the society's constitution, Jedidiah Morse's son, Sidney Edwards Morse, was second assistant secretary of the organization but not one of the thirteen members of the board of directors, five of whom constituted a quorum for business purposes (*First Annual Report of the American Society for Promoting the Civilization and General Improvement of the Indian Tribes*, 5, 8).

3. Lewis Cass (1782–1866) was born and educated in Exeter, New Hampshire, moved to Ohio and practiced law in Zanesville, and was appointed state marshal by Thomas Jefferson in 1806. He served as a colonel in the Ohio militia, and was later made a brigadier general in the U.S. Army during the War of 1812. In 1813 JM appointed him governor of Michigan Territory, a post he held until 1831, when he became secretary of war. He was U.S. minister to France, 1836–42, U.S. senator from Michigan, 1845–57, and secretary of state, 1857–60. Cass also ran unsuccessfully for president as the Democratic nominee in 1848 (Frank B. Woodford, *Lewis Cass: The Last Jeffersonian* [New Brunswick, N.J., 1950], 3, 10, 11–12, 24, 25, 28–29, 40, 52–53, 80, 88, 90, 169–70, 172, 193, 212–13, 228, 313, 315, 324, 326, 342).

4. JM may have been referring to an article signed "Caution" in the 4 Mar. 1822 *Daily National Intelligencer*.

From Richard Rush

Dear Sir, London March 6. 1822

Your favor of the 20th of November got to hand in January. The letters which it enclosed for Mr Keilsall and Mr Joy, were both delivered, no difficulty having occurred this time in finding the former. I had equal pleasure in procuring his book, which was sent to Liverpool in January with directions to be forwarded in the regular packet from that port on the 1st of February. I hope it will have reached you safely.

I have seen, with the greatest satisfaction, in looking over my last file of the National Intelligencer, that the final returns of the census, give us a population of 9.625.734.[1]

The ancients used to say, that there were two subjects over which even the immortal gods themselves had no power, viz, past events and figures. Mr Godwin's book so far as his extraordinary errors respecting the United states are concerned, is now certainly silenced forever in the eyes of all who will merely look at figures. It is thus. In 1790 our population, (Pitkin 256)[2] was 3.929.326. and in 1800 it was 5.309.758. Divide this increase into two, and it places our numbers in 1795 at 4.619.542, the double of which in 1820 (the twenty five years) would be 9.239.084, whereas we have in 1820 an excess over this number of 386.650. Now, if we allow 8.000 emigrants to have come to us annually since 1795, (and this I think a large allowance for we know that during many of the years they were greatly below 8.000 and I can find accounts of but two or at most three years when from very peculiar causes they were higher,) and admit an increase among these emigrants also at the rate of 100 per cent in the 25 years during the successive years that they dropped in upon us, and then add the extraneous numbers which we got with Louisiana, it will still be found, from a calculation I have hastily made, insufficient by a few thousands to absorb this excess. This simple calculation must put at rest the question of our capacity to double by natural increase in twenty five years.

Affairs between Turkey and Russia, continue unsettled. I take the predominant opinion of this cabinet still to be, as it has been from the beginning, that a rupture will be avoided. Its endeavours have been unceasing both at Constantinoble [*sic*] and St Petersburgh, to stave off a rupture. England satisfied, for the present, with her already enormous and disproportionate power, is for keeping things as they are. She is for keeping Turkey as she is, lest Russia should come any nearer to the Mediterranean, which would be to encroach upon British maritime rights! She is for keeping the Greeks as they are, or perhaps a little lower, they being essentially maritime, and likely, if freed from the yoke of the Mahometans, to start into commercial importance. As to the Emperor Alexander, Mr Bentham, whom it is my good fortune to see often, and who as a man is as estimable as he is great and profound as a political philosopher, Mr Bentham says, that Alexander, unhappily for the power which he wields, is both a fop and a hypocrite, the most so that Europe has seen for ages. He anticipates nothing advantageous, but much of harm, to human liberty, from his reign.

Your notices of the internal state of our country were, as they are always, interesting to me. They are often topicks in circles where I mix, and if they were not, there are none others that I can ever hold so dear. Nothing is so grateful to me, under the separation from my country, as accounts from it, and I reckon them when they come in the shape of letters, as constituting the chiefest pleasures that I know here. My children are growing up fast about me, and there are moments when the thoughts of their being so long in a foreign land, almost get the better of the gratifications I have a right to experience at the continued manifestations of confidence from the government towards me in this post. To correct as much as I can this feeling, I do not trust one of them from under my own roof, having the greatest possible objections to the publick schools, and boarding schools, of England, and wishing to keep the Americanism of my boys as their minds open, free from all taint.

With my wife's kindest remembrance for Mrs Madison, I beg to tender to you, dear sir, the constant offerings of my affectionate respect and friendship.

RICHARD RUSH

P.S. I enclose an English pamphlet, which, having read, I have no further use for. Though anonymous, it is agreed to be, in effect, a ministerial production, and large allowances are therefore to be made for its ministerial colourings.

Permit me to offer through your medium, whenever the opportunity may occur, my respectful remembrances to Mr Jefferson. I have said to him what I beg to repeat to you, that if my agency whilst I remain here can ever be of any service to the University of Virginia, I shall be happy to be commanded in any line.

R. R.

RC (PHi: Richard Rush Papers).

1. This information was given under the headline "Fourth Census of the People of the United States" in the *Daily National Intelligencer*, 3 Jan. 1822.

2. Timothy Pitkin, *A Statistical View of the Commerce of the United States of America . . .* (Hartford, Conn., 1816; Shaw and Shoemaker 38648), 256.

To Edward Everett

DEAR SIR MONTPELLIER Mar. 9. 1822

I have recd. with your letter of Feby. 14.[1] the volume on "Europe"[2] for which I am indebted to the politeness of your brother and yourself. I have run thro' it with pleasure, and return my thanks to you both.

The interior view which the writer takes of the Institutions and situations of the several Nations of Europe furnishes more information of the valuable sort than I have any where found. Looking at every thing with an American eye he has selected the facts & features most acceptable to

American curiosity, and which are in truth most worthy of reflection there also. Some of his political speculations will not obtain the concurrence of all. Others can not fail to do so. And no one can reject the evidence given of a capacity & spirit of observation on an enlarged scale. If there be not in some of the pages that condensation of ideas which often renders them the more lucid, as it always gives them more force, there is enough in others to claim the apology offered by Pascal for the length of one of his Provençal letters—that he had not time to make it shorter.[3] Be pleased to accept, Sir, the assurance of my esteem with my cordial respects.

James Madison

RC (MHi); draft (DLC).

1. Letter not found.

2. [Alexander Hill Everett], *Europe: or A General Survey of the Present Situation of the Principal Powers; With Conjectures on Their Future Prospects* (Boston, 1822; Shoemaker 8646).

3. This explanation is given toward the end of the sixteenth letter in Blaise Pascal's *Provincial Letters.*

From James Monroe

Dear Sir Washington March 9. 1822

I have had the pleasure to recieve your letter[1] with one from Mr Lee, and regret that you should say one word, as to the necessity you are under to send it, or such papers on to me. I need not assure you that I am always happy to hear from you, and am glad of any occurrence which draws from you a letter. My situation, as you well know, renders it impossible for me to write you often or regularly. At this time, it was my intention, to have written you, fully, on the subject of a message sent in yesterday which you will see in the Intelligencer,[2] but I have been so much interrupted all the morning that I have but one moment, to refer you to it, and assure of the sincere regard with which I am yr. friend

James Monroe

Mrs Monroe has been dangerously ill, but is now free from fever. We hope that you & Mrs Madison are in good health.

RC (DLC). Docketed by JM.

1. Monroe may be referring here to JM's letter to him of 16 Feb. 1822. The letter from "Mr Lee" has not been found.

2. Monroe's message of 8 Mar. 1822 recommended to Congress that the South American "Provinces which have declared their Independence, and are in the enjoyment of it, ought to be recognized." The provinces named were Buenos Aires, Colombia, Chile, Peru, and Mexico (*Daily National Intelligencer*, 9 Mar. 1822).

To Joshua Gilpin

Dear Sir Mar. 11. 1822

Your favour of Feby 8. with the little volume on the Delaware and Chesapeake Canal, were so long on the way that they did not come to hand till a few days ago.

I have not done more than look over the introductory Memoir, which has been drawn up with great jud[g]ment and in a manner well suited to its object.

I am a great friend to canals as a leading branch of those internal improvements, which are a measure of the wisdom, and a source of the prosperity of every country. Where the authority to make them is possessed I wish it to be exercised; and to be given where it is not possessed and can be usefully exercised.

The great Canals which are going forward and contemplated in the U.S. will do them great credit: and I hope will have a salutary effect by shewing the practicability as well as value of works of discouraging magnitude; and particularly by demonstrating how much good can be done at an expence so inconsiderable when compared with the sums wasted for unprofitable or perverted to injurious purposes. This reflection will express the praise I regard as due to yourself and your Associates, for your persevering efforts in the undertaking so well explained & enforced in your Memoir.

Mrs. M. and myself are very sensible of your & Mrs. Gilpin's kindness in the invitation to your present residence. Whether we shall be able to express[1] it on the spot or not we shall not forget the mark of regard, and shall be happy in returning it by a cordial welcome at our farm, if your excursions should ever afford the opportunity. With much esteem & friendly respects

James Madison

RC (NjMoHP); draft (DLC). RC addressed and franked by JM to Gilpin at Wilmington, Delaware. Postmarked 16 Mar. at Orange Court House.

1. In place of "shall be able to express" in RC, JM wrote "have the pleasure of expressing" in draft.

From William T. Barry and Others

Sir, March 13, 1822.

We take the liberty of addressing you on one of the most important interests of society, the cause of Education. The Legislature of Kentucky, at their last session, made liberal appropriations of money for the benefit of Schools, Academies, Colleges and the University. We were appointed a Committee to collect information and to arrange a plan for carrying into effect, in the best manner possible, the benevolent purposes of the state. We are aware of the difficulty of the task, of the extent of our responsibility, and of the value of the aids which we may derive from the experience of our elder sisters in the Union. We wish to avoid, if possible, the evils attending upon a bad beginning, and to secure to ourselves and to our children, the advantages of a good system from the commencement of our labors. Believing you to be friendly to an object intimately connected with the prosperity and happiness of our common country, and willing to contribute whatever may be in your power to its accomplishment, we beg leave to trouble you with this circular, and to call your attention to the questions subjoined. Any information or suggestions which you may give in aid of our plan, will be gratefully received and faithfully employed. We shall be much obliged to you for as early an attention to our communication as your convenience will permit. Letters can be directed to our Chairman, at Lexington. With great regard, we are, sir, yours,

W. T. Barry, *Chairman.*
D. R. Murray,
John Pope,
D. White,
J. R. Witherspoon,
W. P. Roper.

Questions.

1. Has any system of common schools been established by law in your state?

2. If so, are they supported by a public fund, by taxation, or by a charge upon parents and guardians—whose children and wards are sent to school?

3. Are your counties or townships divided into school districts, with one school in each, or otherwise?

4. What officers are employed in carrying into effect your system of schools, how are they appointed, what are their several duties and what their compensation?

5. Are your teachers employed by the month, or at a certain price for each scholar?

6. What is the average price given per month, or per scholar?

7. In what manner is the teacher boarded?

8. Is any particular qualification required in teachers?

9. Can they be removed, and by what authority?

10. Are females ever employed as teachers?

11. If so, what is the difference in cost between male and female teachers?

12. How many months in the year, and at what seasons are your schools kept?

13. How many children usually attend one school?

14. To what kind of superintendance are they subjected?

15. Are they free to all children, or only the children of the poor?

16. Are they attended by children of every class of the community?

17. What portion of children in your community receive the rudiments of education at these schools?

18. What is the probable average expense per month or per year, of educating a child at one of your common schools?

19. What branches of knowledge are taught therein?

20. Of what improvements does your system seem to be susceptible?

21. Do the people of your state appear to be satisfied with the present plan?

22. If you can give a brief detail of the origin and progress of your system, it might afford many useful hints for the guidance of the Commissioners in avoiding those errors which have been discovered in your state only by experience.

Printed circular (William T. Barry, *Circular Letter from a Committee Appointed by the Legislature of Kentucky to Collect Information and to Arrange a Plan for Carrying into Effect in the Best Manner Possible, the Benevolent Purposes of the State regarding Education* [Lexington, Ky.], 1822; Shoemaker 7962). This copy, addressed by Barry to JM, and postmarked "Lexn. K Jun 27," is in the Madison Collection, Rare Book and Special Collections Division, Library of Congress.

To Stephen Van Rensselaer

Dear Sir Mar. 14. 1822

I recd. some time ago the copy of the geological & agricultural Survey[1] which you were so obliging as to send me; but I have not till within a few days been able to look into it.

I can not bestow more commendation than is due to the liberal patronage to which the public owe the work. Such surveys will not only contribute handfuls of valuable facts towards a Geological Theory, but will more & more unveil the subterraneous treasures of the Country. And as far as Agricultural & statistical researches may be embraced, will be useful in those views also. Be pleased Sir to accept my esteem & friendly wishes

J.M

Draft (DLC). Stephen Van Rensselaer (1764–1839), heir to the Van Rensselaer fortune, served many terms in the New York legislature, was lieutenant governor of New York,

1795–1801, and served in the U.S. House of Representatives, 1822–29. He was a veteran of the War of 1812, commanding the American troops at the Battle of Queenston in 1812. He was known for his devotion to agricultural, educational, and philanthropic causes in New York, including the founding of the Rensselaer Polytechnical Institute (*PJM-PS*, 6:194 n. 2).

1. Amos Eaton, *A Geological and Agricultural Survey of Rensselaer County, in the State of New-York: To Which is Annexed a Geological Profile, Extending from Onondaga Salt Springs, across Said County, to Williams College in Massachusetts* (Albany, N.Y., 1822; Shoemaker 8587).

From Horatio Gates Spafford

ESTEEMED FRIEND, BALLSTON SPA, 3 MO. 15, 1822.

I present a copy of my Proposals for a second edition of the Gazetteer of this State,[1] & am in hopes I shall soon have the pleasure of sending the Book to thee. If it give thee no information, it will enable me to recall thy recollections of the poor old dandy of an Author, & to renew assurances of high regard.

I do not recollect whether I have informed thee that I am preparing a sort of American Plutarch, for the youth of the Republic, the youth of the two Americas.

My History of this State is held in reserve for the era of the completion of our Canals. With great esteem & regard, thy friend,

H. G. SPAFFORD

☞ I wish your Booksellers would encourage me to write a Gazetteer of Virginia. I could travel all over the State, collect my materials, & prepare the Work for the press, in about two years, on a salary of 1000 dollars a year, & a few copies of the Work.

RC (DLC). Addressed by Spafford to JM, and franked. Postmarked 18 Mar. at Ballston Spa, New York. Docketed by JM.

1. The proposal has not been found, but Spafford published in 1824, not a second edition, but as he called it, "a new Work," entitled *A Gazetteer of the State of New-York: Embracing an Ample Survey and Description of its Counties, Towns, Cities, Villages, Canals, Mountains, Lakes, Rivers, Creeks, and Natural Topography . . .* (Albany, N.Y., 1824; Shoemaker 18063), 4.

To Samuel Wyllys Pomeroy

DEAR SIR MONTPELLIER Mar. 16. 1822

I thank you for the communication made in your favour of the 25 Feby. and the Agricultural Journal sent with it.

If flax can be prepared by the new Machinery for 2 cents per ℔s and spun with a facility resembling that of Cotton, you are well warranted in your anticipations of advantage to the Farmers. If Hemp can be carried with equal success through like processes, the advantage will be more than doubled.

I was not surprized at the improvement made here on the European Model. It accords with the inventive genius and practical turn of our Citizens. And augurs still further improvements of the Machine in question; as well as continued fruits of the labour-saving ingenuity, of which so many examples have been already given. Be pleased to accept Sir my esteem & friendly respects

James Madison

RC (NHi). Addressed by JM to Pomeroy at "Brighton near Boston," and franked. Postmarked 19 Mar. at Orange Court House.

To Benjamin Joy

Dear Sir Mar. 18. 1822

I have recd. a letter from your brother George of the 2d. & another of the 9th. of Jany. in which he wished me to search among my papers for a letter from him to me of Apl. 16. 1804, and my answer to it dated Novr. 10th. I have found the former, but not the latter.

As you are connected with the business & are referred to by your brother I have thought it proper to send you his copy of his letter of Apl. 1804 that from a view of its contents you may the better decide on the disposition to be made of the original. This, to which your brother attaches value, it seemed best not to commit it without your approbation to the hazards of the mail. If the original of my letter of Novr. 10. be of any use, it can be obtained from your brother if not already furnished by him. I can not from memory authenticate the copy, altho' I can not doubt its fidelity. With great esteem & respect

J. M.

Draft (DLC).

From Frances Taylor Rose and Robert H. Rose

Dear Brother   Near Fincastle March 19th 1822

When we arrived within two miles of Keazle town we learnt with certainty that the Waggon with our Family had proceeded on five days before; in this dilema we were compelled to keep Harry untill we could overtake the waggon, to effect which we sent Ambrose on in the stage from Stanton on friday morning to overtake and stop the waggon until we could get up with it, and send our gig back to assist us on. Hugh met us this morning with it and we now dispactch Harry back by way of Lynchburg as a nearer and better way that [*sic*] the one we have come. I regret extremely the imperious circumstances which have compelled us to detain so long your servant and horse, but hope you will excuse the liberty I have taken as I assure nothing but absolute necessity would have induced me to have done so. We are all well and have gotten this far in perfect safety, & without fatigue on my part. We are now at Mr Wm. Preston's,[1] and shall remain here until tomorrow morning. The waggon is about thirty five miles in advance of us. I trust this Letter will find our dear Mother and all of you in good health, and assure her I shall write as often as possible to her, during my journey. The family all join in affectionate regards to all with you and ever beleive me you[r] truly affectionate Sister

F. T. Rose[2]

P. S. I have consulted with Mr Cabell and he will act under the Power of Attorney if it should be necessary and he will attend to the paying the Taxes and the Advertiseing the Land immediately in the Enquirer and Lynchburg Press to be sold on the first day of August next at Public Auction in Lynchburg;[3] at which time I shall certainly attend, and when your Brothers Bond shall be paid and the other Bond to Ambrose Madison I will pay as soon as I can get to Huntsville, by remitting the amount to you by the Mail.

Robert H. Rose

RC (NN: Arents Tobacco Collection).

1. This was probably Smithfield, built by William Preston (1729–1783), and home to his widow, Susanna Smith Preston (1740–1823) in Montgomery County, Virginia (Dorman, *Prestons of Smithfield and Greenfield in Virginia*, 12–13).

2. JM's sister, Frances (Fanny) Taylor Madison Rose (1774–1823), married physician Robert H. Rose (d. 1833) in 1801. They had eleven children, among them Hugh Francis Rose and Ambrose James Rose, mentioned in this letter. Another son, James Madison Rose, died in the fighting at the Alamo in 1836. The Rose family moved to Huntsville, Alabama, in 1822 (Chapman, "Descendants of Ambrose Madison," 38–39; Frances Rose to Dolley Madison, 19 Mar. 1822, *DMDE*).

3. The land referred to, 563 acres "in Amherst, on Harris's creek, a considerable branch of James river, and within four miles from Lynchburg," was advertised by Landon Cabell and William Madison in the *Richmond Enquirer*, 16 July 1822. This land sale was almost certainly part of the settlement of James Madison Sr.'s will, with which the Roses were unhappy. For the estate and its settlement, see *PJM-SS*, 2:125 n. 1, 197 n. 2, 268 n. 3, 4:72–73 and n. 4, 387, 5:332–33; *PJM-PS*, 6:137–38 and nn. 1–2. For the Roses' antipathy toward William Madison, see *PJM-SS*, 2:268 n. 3.

¶ To Thomas Jefferson. Letter not found. *29 March 1822*. Listed as a one-page autograph letter, signed, in Parke-Bernet Galleries Sale No. 451 (5–6 Apr. 1943), item 389, with the following extract: "I am sorry that the approaching meeting of the Visitors will furnish an exception to the punctuality of my attendance . . . I presume that my failure, even if it prevents a quorum, is rendered of little consequence by the obduracy of the Assembly to the pleas in behalf of the University, whose interests are certainly the best interests of their constituents. . . ." Docketed by Jefferson: "Madison, James. Montpelier, Mar. 29, 22. recd Apr. 4." Acknowledged in Jefferson to JM, 7 Apr. 1822.

From William Smith

Dr. Sir, 31st. March 1822

The day I was at your House I saw Reuben Smith[1] And requested him in your name as well as my own to attend at the mouth of Blue Run on Monday to assist in Settling a line betwean us he observed he did not wish to have any thing to do with it that he was particularly Situated & would give no Reason why he was so situated—being anctious to put up my fence to prevent the depredation of Hogs in my field I Rode over yesterday to George Scotts to Know of him if he knew where the River ran before it made a Breach through your land he told me he did. I requested him to attend betwean the Hours of Ten & Eleven oclock tomorrow, he promised me he would, I also saw Capt. Hord watts yesterday he promised to attend stating that he recollects where the River ran before it broke through your land I also rode to Augustin Webbs[2] yesterday to get him & was informed he was in Albermarle. Brother Samuel told me some time ago he well recollects where the river ran when he was a boy & before it changed its Course, but shall dispence with his testimony. Will thank you to get any person you can think of to attend that can strike any light on the Business. I shall not attend myself But hope you will If you do not attend in person will thank you to send Capt Eddins as I am really anctious to put up my fence. Yrs with Great respect.

William Smith[3]

RC (DLC). Docketed by JM, with his note at the bottom of the letter: "NB tomorrow is the day the 1st. Apl."

1. Reuben Smith owned land to the southwest of Montpelier (Miller, *Antebellum Orange*, 8–9, 61).

2. Augustine Webb (1763–1827), a Revolutionary War veteran, was the son of William Crittenden Webb of Orange County. He owned property to the southwest of Montpelier (*PJM*, 15:315 n. 3; Miller, *Antebellum Orange*, 8–9, 67).

3. William Smith (d. 1856), a captain in the Virginia militia and a veteran of the War of 1812, amassed a plantation that at his death comprised 1,500 acres and fifty-eight slaves. In 1843 he built a brick mansion on the plantation, which was situated to the northwest of Montpelier (Calder Loth, ed., *The Virginia Landmarks Register*, 4th ed. [Charlottesville, Va., 1999], 367; W. W. Scott, *A History of Orange County, Virginia* [Richmond, Va., 1907], 244; Miller, *Antebellum Orange*, 8–9, 106).

To William Smith

Dear Sir [31 March 1822]

I have just recd yours of this date. I am sorry Mr. R Smith who probably remembers with much certainty & accuracy the original course of the river as the true boundary between us, finds a difficulty in giveg us his aid.

The question is not where the river ran before it left the S. Side of what is called the Island and got into its present bed. It doubtless had successive temporary channels after quiting the original course, as the boundary between us before it got into its present channel which is admitted not to be the boundary. The original course may have been where I contend: notwithstanding its be[i]ng at one time where you contend, being then in its progress of change. Some may have noticed, or may recollect only this midway course. The knowledge & recollection of others may go back to the right period. The testimony of both therefore may be correct: but the older one only bears on the question. Perhaps under present circumstances, yr brother S. & my bro: Wm. are likely to have the oldest memories, among those whose situations led them to attend particularly to the course of the river. I am content to let them decide this point, & I presume they will neither of them decline the trouble of doing so. If you concur be so good as to name a day for their meeting, and I will endeavor to procure the attendance of my brother.

Draft (DLC). Undated; conjectural date assigned based on internal evidence and by comparison with Smith to JM, 31 Mar. 1822.

To Robert Mackay

Dr. Sir Apl. 1. 1822

I must again avail myself of your aid in prolonging the loan to me from the Bank. The note per the purpose is inclosed.

I must also again refer to your judgment the time for disposing of the flour & Wheat you have recd on my acct. I had inferred from the character of the last crop of Grain in parts of Europe, particularly G.B. and from other circumstances, that the prices wd. be likely to rise here, as the defect in quality equivalent to one in quantity shd. begin to be felt abroad. Whether this will now be the case and what may be the probable effects of incidental causes, I leave to your better information & foresight, & I shall cheerfully abide by the decision these may suggest. As soon as it shall be made be so obliging as to let me know it, together with a State of the balance between us. Friendly respects.

Draft (DLC).

From Thomas Jefferson

Dear Sir Monticello Apr. 7. 22.

Your favor of Mar. 29. did not come to hand until the 4th. instant. Only mr. Cabell, Genl. Cocke and myself attended. Messrs. Johnson and Taylor were retained in Richmond on Lithgow's case,[1] and Genl. Breckenridge hindered by business. It was not material as there was not a single thing requisite to act on. We have to finish the 4. rows and appendages this summer which will be done and then to rest on our oars. The question of the removal of the seat of government[2] has unhappily come athwart us, and is the real thing now entangling us. Staunton & Richmond are both friendly to us as an University, but the latter fears that our Rotunda will induce the legislature to quit them, & Staunton fears it will stop them here. You will recollect that our brother Johnson has opposed constantly every proposition in the board to begin that building, and moved himself in the late session to suspend interest with an express Proviso that no money should be applied to that building; and mr. Harvie[3] one of the zealous friends to the University, in a Philippic against the Rotunda declared he would never vote another Dollar to the University but on condition that it should not be applied to that building. Our opinion, and a very sound one, has been from the beginning never to open the institution until the buildings shall be compleat; because as soon as opened, all the funds will be absorbed by salaries Etc. and the buildings remain for ever incompleat. We have thought it better to open it fully, altho' a few years later, than let it go on for ever in an imperfect state. I learn from those who were present at the last proceedings of the legislature, that there was a general regret even with the opposition itself, when they found that they had done absolutely nothing at all for the institution. Our course is a plain one, to pursue what is best, and the public will come right and approve us in the end. This bugbear of the seat of government will be understood at the next session, and we shall be enabled to proceed. The establishment is now at that stage at which it will force itself on. We must manage our dissenting brother softly; he is of too much weight to be given up. I inclose you his letter and two from mr. Cabell[4] which will inform you more particularly of the state of things. Be so good as to return them when perused. Ever & affectionately your's

TH: JEFFERSON

RC (DLC); FC (DLC: Jefferson Papers). RC docketed by JM.

1. The case in question, *Alexander Lithgow v. The Commonwealth*, was an appeal of a case in which Lithgow was tried for embezzlement, found guilty, and sent to prison for one year. The appeal rested on Lithgow's claim that one of the jury should have been rejected by the court because he had already expressed a decided opinion of Lithgow's guilt. Lithgow's challenge was ignored by the court. The General Court upheld Lithgow's appeal and ordered a retrial (William Brockenbrough, *Virginia Cases, or Decisions of the General Court of Virginia . . . Commencing . . . 1815, and Ending . . . 1826* [Richmond, Va., 1826], 297–313).

2. Joseph C. Cabell had written Jefferson on 3 Jan. 1822 that there had been discussion on the question of moving the state capital from Richmond: "Blackburn is said by some, to take to heart the removal of the seat of government to Staunton. I am not sure of this, but I suspect he seeks it with deep anxiety. Is it not possible that calculations may be made on our anxiety to endow the University? May they not say—these men would not oppose us, least we may retaliate? I feel the dilemma—I regret it—but I cannot vote to carry the seat of government to Staunton. We are committed against Charlottesville; because of the University being there. And I presume our best course is to keep it here [Richmond]" (Cabell, *Early History of the University of Virginia*, 226).

3. Jacqueline Burwell Harvie (1788–1856) of Richmond subscribed $500 to the Central College, which subsequently became the University of Virginia. Harvie entered the U.S. Navy in 1804 as a midshipman, was promoted lieutenant in 1809, and resigned his commission in 1812. He served in the Virginia House of Delegates, 1821–30, and in the Senate, 1830–39. Harvie married Mary Marshall, daughter of Chief Justice John Marshall, in 1813 (Johnson et al., *Papers of John Marshall*, 2:321 n. 5; Cabell, *Early History of the University of Virginia*, 411; Callahan, *List of Officers of the Navy*, 251; Swem and Williams, *Register*, 385).

4. The letter from Chapman Johnson has not been found, but Jefferson noted in his Epistolary Record (DLC: Jefferson Papers) that he received on 31 Mar. 1822 a letter from Johnson written two days earlier from Richmond. For Joseph C. Cabell's letters to Jefferson of 6 and 10 Mar. 1822, both of which contained detailed descriptions of political infighting in support of the university during the General Assembly session, see Cabell, *Early History of the University of Virginia*, 245–54.

From William Lambert

SIR, CITY OF WASHINGTON, April 8th. 1822.

I have the honor to inclose two printed copies of a report relative to the latitude and longitude of the Capitol in this City;[1] one of which is intended for your own use, the other for the use of the University or Seminary of learning near Charlottesville. With great respect, I have the honor to be, Your most Obedt. servant,

WILLIAM LAMBERT[2]

RC (DLC). Addressed by Lambert to JM, and franked. Docketed by JM.

1. *Message from the President of the United States, Transmitting a Report of William Lambert, on the Subject of the Longitude of the Capitol of the United States. January 9, 1822. Read, and Such Part Thereof as Relates to Compensation, Referred to the Committee of Ways and Means; the Residue to Lie upon the Table* (Washington, 1822; Shoemaker 11027).

2. William Lambert (d. 1834) was a native Virginian who early sought work in the federal government and clerked variously in the State Department, War Department, and the U.S. House of Representatives. He was a passionate astronomer who worked for years to ascertain a prime meridian through Washington and to establish a national observatory (*Daily National Intelligencer*, 21 and 23 Oct. 1834; John Pendleton to JM, 11 Feb. 1789, *PJM*, 11:440 and n. 1; James Monroe to JM, 12 Mar. 1801, *PJM-SS*, 1:13–14, 14 n. 1; Lambert to JM, 5 Dec. 1809, *PJM-PS*, 2:111 and n. 1).

From Horace C. Story

WASHINGTON CITY April 8th 1822.

Lieut. Story[1] of the U.S. Corps of Engineers presents his most respectful compliments to the Hon. Mr. Madison, & transmits from this place the accompanying pamphlet intrusted to his charge by the Salem East India Marine Society.[2] He regrets that no more appropriate mode of forwarding it to its place of destination is within his power.

RC (DLC). Docketed by JM.

1. Horace Cullen Story (1792–1823), the brother of associate Supreme Court Justice Joseph Story, was a graduate of Harvard College (1811) and a veteran of the War of 1812. A lieutenant in the U.S. Corps of Engineers, Story was superintending the construction of fortifications at Fort St. Philip at Plaquemine in Louisiana at the time of his death (Perley Derby, comp., "Elisha Story of Boston and Some of His Descendants," *Essex Institute Historical Collections* 51 [1915]: 50–51).

2. *The East-India Marine Society of Salem* (Salem, Mass., 1821; Shoemaker 6699). The society was established in 1799 for the relief of disabled seamen, widows, and families, and to promote the knowledge of navigation and trade to the East Indies. Membership was restricted to Salem residents or those sailing Salem vessels who had navigated the seas around

Cape Horn or the Cape of Good Hope. The society kept members' journals of observation of their voyages, and operated a museum, or "Cabinet of Curiosities," collected by the members ("Salem East India Marine Society," *North American Review* 6 [1818]: 283–85).

From William Smith

Dr. Sir, 9th. April. 1822

Mr. George Scott & Hord Watts attended on the River at the time you were Notifyed, Mr. Bradley only with them. Mr Watses recollection only goes Back to Thirty Six years or thereabouts. Mr. Scott recollects the River before the old Gentleman your Father purchased the Land he states it belonged to Roger Dixon & sold by Colo. James Barbour to Pritaman Merry[1] your Father Giving Merry 5£ for his Bargain having one Night to consider of it. I am told they both agree as to its Bend the Margin touching the Island. Mr. Scott is 68 years of age. I make no doubt on any fixed day he will Meet you at the Mouth of Blue Run & Give you any further Information he may Possess. My Brother Samuel will Meet yr Brother William on Wensday the 10th. Inst & if they can agree I have no objection for them to fix the Boundary betwean us, & to prevent a further altercation betwean our relatives. If you feel disposed to sell will give you 150$ for your Interest or 50$ ℔ Acre for the Iland & 25$ ℔ Acre for any aluvion land that May belong to it. I require no deed unless you prefer giving one a receipt will do—yrs. with respect

William Smith

RC (DLC). Docketed by JM.

1. Prettyman Merry (d. 1817) was a captain in the Orange County militia and owned land adjacent to the tract given by James Madison Sr. to JM in 1784. In 1795 JM considered purchasing that land from Merry, who eventually moved to Buckingham County, Virginia. JM sold a portion of the 1784 tract to his neighbor, James Newman, in 1830 (*PJM*, 13:304 n. 1, 8:99, 15:469; Indenture for the Sale of Land, 12 Feb. 1830, Tr [Vi: Orange County Courthouse Records]).

From Archibald W. Hamilton

Sir, Washington City 10th Apl 1822

I beg leave to enclose, copies of letters for your friendly consideration:[1] during the last four years, I held the appointment of Assistant Deputy Quarter Master General, in the Army of the United States: I have been, during that period, constantly occupied in the line of my duty: literally speaking "from Maine to Georgia." The law of the 2d March 1821.[2] reducing the army, having *excluded* all appointments of my grade, *not of the line*, I am consequently without employ—either in the army or otherwise—and as my pursuits in early life, mainly looked forward to preferment in the Military, or civil employment of my government—I respectfully ask your friendly aid, and influence, in furtherance of my application for an appointment, under the Treasury or State Departments. I have the honor to be very respectfully Sir Yr Obedt Srvt

A. W. Hamilton[3]

RC (DLC). Docketed by JM.

1. The enclosures have not been found, but see JM to Hamilton, 16 Apr. 1822.

2. "An Act to reduce and fix the military peace establishment of the United States," 2 Mar. 1821 (*U.S. Statutes at Large*, 3:615–16).

3. Archibald Wade Hamilton (ca. 1791–1842) of New York entered the British army around 1810 and by 1812 was a lieutenant serving in the West Indies. His refusal to fight against the United States during the New Orleans campaign resulted in an order for his arrest as a prisoner of war, but he escaped and returned to the United States, where he was commissioned in the U.S. Army in 1818. In 1823 he was appointed surveyor of the port of Pensacola, and in 1824 he was named collector of that port. He was removed by President John Quincy Adams (Brockholst Livingston to James Monroe, 8 Nov. 1815, DNA: RG 59, LAR, 1809–17, filed under "Hamilton, Archibald W."; *Brother Jonathan: A Weekly Compend of Belles Lettres and the Fine Arts, Standard Literature, and General Intelligence.* Advertising Cover. 1 [1842]: xxviii; Charleston *City Gazette and Commercial Daily Advertiser*, 7 Apr. 1823; *Senate Exec. Proceedings*, 3:120, 123, 354, 355, 360, 361, 364; Smith et al., *Papers of Andrew Jackson*, 7:695).

To Thomas Cramer

Sir: Apl. 13 1822

I recd. a few days ago your favor communicatg the resolution of the Agricultural Society of the Valley, placing my name on the list of its honorary members. I feel much indebted to the Society for this flattering mark of their attention, for which I beg that my acknowledgts. may be presented. I wish there were not necessarily mingled with them, a regret that no returns of more value are likely to be in my power. I thank you Sir for the kind expressions from yourself, which accompany the communication. With friendly respects

Draft (DLC).

To William Lambert

Dear Sir Montpellier April 15. 1822

I have duly received your favour of the 8th. inst: with the two copies of your Report relative to the Latitude & Longitude of the Capitol at Washington.

My confidence in the Ability with which the Observations & calculations have been made, justifies me in inferring that the result will be as honorable to yourself, as the object was worthy of the national Councils.

One of the Copies will be sent to the University of Virginia as you desire. For the other allotted for myself, I tender you my thanks with assurances of my esteem and my friendly wishes.

James Madison

RC (DNA: RG 59, LAR, 1817–25, filed under "Lambert"); draft (DLC). RC addressed and franked by JM to Lambert at Washington. Minor differences between the copies have not been noted.

To Archibald W. Hamilton

Sir Apl. 16. 1822

I have just recd. your letter of the 10th. inclosing copies of letters from Judge Livingston,[1] Mr. Brown,[2] & Docrs. Flood[3] & Cochrane.

Not being able to furnish any information relative to the peculiarities of your case; or to your personal worth not already authenticated to the Government from sources more directly & intimately acquainted with both, I perceive no grounds on which I could interpose a special recommendation in your behalf. All that I can say, and I say it very cheerfully, is that from the impression made on me by the marked proof given of your love for your Country, and by the testimony borne to the amiable & honorable features of your private character, I shd. learn with pleasure that it had been found practicable to substitute for the discontinued office, some equivalent respect for your sacrifices and qualifications.

Draft (DLC).

1. Henry Brockholst Livingston (1757–1823) of New York was a classmate of JM's at the College of New Jersey, from which he graduated in 1774. A Revolutionary War veteran and a lawyer, who served several terms in the New York legislature, Livingston also served as a justice of the New York Supreme Court. Thomas Jefferson appointed him to the U.S. Supreme Court in 1806, and he continued in that post until his death (Richard A. Harrison, *Princetonians, 1769–1775: A Biographical Dictionary* [Princeton, N.J., 1980], 397–406).

2. This may have been James Brown (1776–1835), a Virginia-born lawyer, who served as U.S. senator from Louisiana, 1813–17, and 1819–23, and as U.S. minister to France, 1823–29.

3. This may have been William Flood (ca. 1775–1823), a New Orleans physician, who held various offices in the Louisiana territorial government (Jared William Bradley, *Interim Appointment: W. C. C. Claiborne Letter Book, 1804–1805* [Baton Rouge, La., 2002], 557–59).

To Horatio Gates Spafford

DEAR SIR MONTPELLIER April 16. 1822

I have but just recd. your letter of March 15th. I wish you success in your new Edition of the Geographical Dictionary for N. York; as I do in the other literary tasks you have in hand, and in petto.[1]

I am not enough acquainted with our Booksellers and Printers to judge how far a Gazetteer for this State on the plan & terms you suggest would be espoused by them. A survey of the State is now on foot by a gentleman of Science;[2] but I know not the progress made, nor the details to which his attention extends. Mr. Ritchie Editor of the Enquirer at Richmond, would probably be the best source you could consult on the whole subject.[3]

Several years ago I recd. a letter from you whilst in the Western parts of Pena. which I answered.[4] As the answer may never have reached you, I take this occasion to mention that one was sent, & that your request was complied with.

You then alluded to an indigenous species or variety of the Potato not before known. What was the result of the experiments made of it? With friendly respects

JAMES MADISON

RC (NjP); draft (DLC). Minor differences between the copies have not been noted.

1. "*In petto*": in secret.

2. The "gentleman of science" was John Wood (d. 1822), a Scottish-born instructor at Petersburg Academy, who had been chosen to carry out an act of the Virginia General Assembly, 27 Feb. 1816, requiring "an accurate chart of each county and a general map of the Territory of this Commonwealth." After Wood's death, his work was completed by Herman Böyë, a Richmond engineer; the map of Virginia was published in 1826 (Walter W. Ristow, "Maps," *Quarterly Journal of the Library of Congress* 23 [1966]: 238–41).

3. Following this sentence, JM added in the draft "[see letter to Mr. Ritchie]."

4. Spafford to JM, 9 Aug. 1818, *PJM-RS*, 1:343–44. JM's reply to this letter has not been found.

To Horace C. Story

Sir Montpr. Apl. 16. 1822

I have recd. with your note of the 8th. the pamphlet commited to your charge by the East India marine Socy. of Salem, and I return thro' the same channel my thanks to the Socy. for their polite attention.

I cannot speak in terms too favorable of an Institution wch. unites with a benevolent object, the useful one of improving navigation, and another so interesting to all who have a taste for natural & artificial curiosities. This branch of the plan is the more to be commended as it will so readily extend itself to the acquisition from Countries visited by the Salem Mariners, of such new articles belonging to the vegetable & animal domain as may be acceptable to our husbandry. With friendly respects

J. M.

Draft (DLC).

To Mark Langdon Hill

Montpr. Apl. 18. 1822.

J. Madison, with his respects to Mr. Hill, returns his thanks for the copy of the Report of the Committee on Commerce.[1] The Report contains much important information on an important subject, and inculcates the true principles of reciprocity which ought to regulate the intercourse of Independent Nations. Whilst the U States contend for nothing beyond these, it ought not to be expected that they will be satisfied with any thing short of them.

Draft (DLC); Tr (NjP). The Tr is docketed "Mr. Hill sent to Mr. Madison the report I drew on the Commerce and Navigation of the U.S.—and this is a copy of Mr. Madison's letter to him—T.N." The author of the report was Thomas Newton Jr. Minor differences between the copies have not been noted.

1. *Report of the Committee on Commerce to Which was referred So Much of the President's Message as Concerns the Commercial Intercourse of the U.S. with Foreign Nations. March 15, 1822. Committed to a Committee of the Whole House To-morrow* (Washington, 1822; Shoemaker 11148).

From Richard Forrest

Dear Sir, Washington April 25th. 1822

The enclosed letter came by this day's Mail with those for the Dept of State, which I hasten to forward.[1]

My Son Julius, wrote me a few days ago, that he was desirous of collecting all the materials in his power, relative to the Society which has been established in Virginia commemorative of the first landing of our ancestors at James Town, as a similar one is about to be formed in Maryland, to celebrate the landing of those at St. Mary's. He has understood that two orations have been delivered on the occasion to which he alludes, one of which was by your late nephew, and thinks it probable that you may possess a copy of one or both[2]—in which case he begs you will have the goodness to loan them to him for a short time, when, if you wish it, they shall be safely returned.

The present weather is highly favorable to the growing crop of wheat, but there never was, in th⟨e⟩ recollection of the oldest inhabitant so miserable a prospect as at the present time. On this day three week⟨s⟩ I rode through Montgomery County, and not half the whea⟨t⟩ I saw, will pay the expense of reaping. Tobacco bears a good price. The Crops at Marlbro, and Queen Ann have been in brisk demand at 5 and 7 dollars for the second quality, and 8 and 10 for first.

Congress are about adjourning, an event most anxiously looked for by every Inhabitant of this place. Pray offer my best respects to Mrs. Madiso⟨n⟩ in which Mrs. Forrest, Sally and Mary join, and believe me dear [Sir], most sincerely your obt Serv

Richd. Forrest[3]

RC (ViU: Madison Papers, Special Collections). Docketed by JM.

1. This was probably Richard Rush to JM, 6 Mar. 1822.

2. One of these pamphlets was probably the *Report of the Proceedings of the Late Jubilee at James-Town, in Commemoration of the 13th May, the Second Centesimal Anniversary of the Settlement of Virginia . . .* (Petersburg, Va., 1807; Shaw and Shoemaker 13482). It contained the orations of Briscoe C. Baldwin and John Madison, two students at the College of William and Mary. John Madison (1787–1809) was the son of JM's brother, William Madison (Chapman, "Descendants of Ambrose Madison," 31).

3. Richard Forrest (ca. 1767–1828) married Sarah Craufurd of Maryland in 1787. They moved to Washington in 1800, where they were neighbors and friends of the Madisons. Forrest was a clerk in the State Department, 1801–28 (*Daily National Intelligencer*, 9 Oct. 1828; Kate Kearney Henry, "Richard Forrest and His Times, 1795–1830," *Records of the Columbia Historical Society* 5 [1902]: 87–95).

To Richard Rush

DEAR SIR MONTPELLIER May 1. 1822

I have duly recd. your letter of Mar. 6. accompanied by the English pamphlet on "The State of the Nation."[1] Keirsall's [*sic*] "Classical Excursion" had arrived some time before. For these several favours I give you many thanks.

Having not recd. at the date of my last, your favour of Sepr. 26. I take this occasion to thank you for that also, and for the accompanying Edinburgh Review. I owe particular attention to the paragraph which mentions the intended name for your new-born son. The friendly feelings from which alone the intention could spring, correspond too much with my own, not to give to such a mark of them its full value. The best wish I can form for the new comer is that he may inherit the virtues of his parents; and that if there has been any thing desirable in the lot of his namesake, he may enjoy it without its drawbacks.

I think with you that the Reviewer has handled too slightly the hollow theory of Mr. Godwin; and that the late census here must give the coup de grace to his Book, if it should not have previously died a natural death.

Mr. Keilsall's Book, like his "Phantasm of a University," shews learned research, some originality of thought, and a pregnant fancy. His details relating to Cicero, and his phantasm, as it may be called; of a Monument to the fame of that Orator & sage, will have an interest for his particular Admirers, and be amusing to all who indulge a relish for Roman antiquities.

I have run over the English pamphlet. There is in the workmanship of it, a political sleight which sufficiently discloses an official hand, or a hand furnished with official materials, and familiar with such a use of them. There is certainly in the publication much of the suppressio veri: I will not say how much of the suggestio falsi.[2] The notice taken of the U.S. is a proof that if the B. Govt. has not begun to love us, it feels the necessity of ceasing to disrespect us. It "calls cousin" as lavishly as we used to be stigmatised as the spawn of convicts and vagabonds. We can easily forgive them however, because we never injured them; and shall meet them in every friendly sentiment, as well as in all the beneficial intercourse which may be authorized by the principle of reciprocity.

I have not overlooked what you intimate in regard to Mr. Jefferson, who approaches his octogenary Climacteric with a mens sana in corpore sano.[3] The vigor of both is indeed very remarkable at his age. He bears the lamented failure of our Legislature to enable the University to go into immediate action, with a philosophic patience supported by a patriotic hope that a succeeding Representation of the people will better consult their interest & character. The University (the germ of which was the Central

College) or the Academic Village as it might be called, is prepared to receive ten professors & two hundred Students: but the funds having been exhausted in the Site & the Buildings, no professors even can be engaged without further aid from the public.

I take for granted you receive in official transmissions & in private correspondence what is most interesting in the occurences at Washington. The *length* & *sterility* of the session has attracted not a few animadversions on Congress. The remaining period however, limited as it is, may bring forth something in answer to the latter charge. Whether it will be of a nature to mitigate or invigorate the former is for the result to shew.

Our Country, the Western parts of it particularly, is still labouring under the fruits of pecuniary follies. The unfavorable exchange which carries off the coin is becoming also a fresh clog on the restorative policy. It has been made a question whether this evil be not the mere effect of a difference of value in the metals here & in G. Britain. But I suspect, notwithstanding the Custom-house returns, that there is an excess of our imports over our exported *products*, and I fear this is a course of things not easily to be got altogether right. Much reliance is put by some on a substitution of domestic for foreign manufactures, as a radical & permanent remedy. But however this might alleviate the malady of an unfavorable balance of trade, there would remain articles of luxury not provided at home for a consumption beyond the means of paying for it. And such are the habits of a great portion of our people, that they will not restrict their wants to their incomes as long as they can borrow from Banks, and obtain credit with the venders of merchandize. This indiscretion has, no doubt, a check within itself, & time may put an end to it; but whilst it continues it tends to keep the Country behind hand in its foreign dealings; and of course to produce the embarrassments incident to drains of the precious metals. Altho' a nation exchanging necessary & useful articles for the luxuries of another has a manifest advantage in a contest of prohibitions & restrictions, the advantage may be reversed in a trade entirely free; inasmuch as articles of the first description supply wants that are limited; whilst luxuries are of more indefinite consumption, and the want of some of them as boundless as the fancy itself.

The difficulties of the Country have had another cause in a scanty harvest and low prices. The Cotton planters have little ground for complaint. Nor have the Tobo. planters much on the score of prices which have made up in a good degree for the defect in the quantity & quality of the crop. But throughout the Wheat Country, South of Pena. at least, the harvest in point both of quantity & quality was never known to be so deficient, nor has the Market in any wise furnished a compensation. At this moment there is a re-animation of the demand for flour, occasioned by the expected renewal of the direct trade to the B. West Indies, but there is so small a part unsold that the farming class will scarely feel the benefit. It is too soon to speak positively of the prospects of the current year. In this quarter they are at present discouraging. The Winter was a bad one for the Wheat fields. And the fly has commenced its ravages with an activity that will be very fatal, if the weather should continue dry for 8 or 10 days. In Maryland I learn that the wheat fields wear a dismal aspect, in consequence of the unfavorable season. Whether & in what extent the ruin is augmented by the Insect, I have no information. Of the States further North, I can say nothing.

Mrs. M. offers an ample return to Mrs. Rush for her affectionate remembrances; to which I beg leave to add my respectful regards, with assurances to yourself of my constant friendship.

James Madison

RC (PHi: Gratz Collection); draft (DLC). Minor differences between the copies have not been noted.

1. *The State of the Nation, at the Commencement of the Year 1822 . . .* (London, 1822). JM's copy, with the inscription "R. Rush" on the title page crossed through and replaced by JM's name, is in the Madison Collection, Special Collections, University of Virginia Library.

2. *Suppressio veri:* suppression of the truth; *suggestio falsi:* suggestion of a falsehood.

3. *Mens sana in corpore sano:* a sound mind in a healthy body.

From Robert Mackay

Dr Sir, Fredericksburg 2 May 1822.

Your favour 24th. Ulto.[1] was duly recd. and I have since been making inquiry respecting Merino Wool and find only one person here disposed to purchase, at something like 35 to 40 cents for unwashed & 45 to 50 cts ℔ lb. for washed. I am however informed it will probably do much better in Boston, to which Port there are almost daily opportunities. Should you be disposed either to Sell or Ship I will with pleasure do the needful.

In consequence of a confident belief that the restrictions existing between the British W. India Islands & the U. States will soon be removed, our Staple articles have become in more demand, and I now quote flour at 6 to $6⅛. Wheat @ 115 @ 118 cts & Corn at 70 cents ℔ Bushel. I am Very Respectfly

Robert Mackay

RC (DLC). Docketed by JM.

1. Letter not found.

To Richard Forrest

Dear Sir Montpr. May 4. 1822

Your favor of the 25th. Ult: was duly recd, and I thank you for your attention to the letter enclosed in it.

I have searched among my pamphlets & without being able to find either of the Orations desired by your son Julius. A friend has been engaged to enquire elsewhere, and whatever he may procure will be forwarded. I am afraid the chance of success is but small: such is the rapid disappearance of such publications. Williamsburg is probably the place where all the information wanted by your son could be best obtained; and Mr. Bassett probably the best channel for seeking it. For so laudable a purpose, he wd doubtless lend his aid.

I take the liberty of enclosing a letter for Mr R.[1] which I hope may be forwarded from the Dept. of State without troubling Mr Adams with a direct application.

Our Wheat fields, in this quarter, tho of better aspect than those you describe, suffered a good deal from the winter. And the fly is making ravages that will be very fatal, in case of a dry & cool spell. The last Crop of Tobo. in Virga was rather a short one, and a very unusual proportion of it of the inferior descriptions. The prices however are not to be complained of. Tobo. of the first class, is in some instances above 10 drs.

Mrs. M. returns her kind remembrances to Mrs. F. and her daughters. Be pleased to add my particular respects, And to accept for yourself my regards & good wishes.

Draft (DLC).

1. JM to Richard Rush, 1 May 1822.

To Benjamin Joy

Dr. Sir May 6. 1822

Not having recd. an answer to the original I conclude it must have miscarried, and enclose a duplicate of it.[1] Should I not hear from you in time I will forward your brother's letter referred to the Scy of the Board of Commissioners, tho' I should prefer doing so to your Agent, were I acquainted with his name, and sure that it would find him at Washington.

Draft (DLC).

1. See JM to Benjamin Joy, 18 Mar. 1822.

To James Monroe

Dear Sir — Montpellier May 6. 1822

This will probably arrive at the Moment for congratulating you on the close of the scene in which your labours are blended with those of Congress. When will your recess from those which succeed, commence; and when & how much of it will be passed in Albemarle? We hope for the pleasure of halts with us, and that Mrs. M. and the others of your family will be with you.

Mr. Anduaga[1] I observe casts in our teeth the postponement of the recognition of Spanish America till the cession of Florida was secured, and taking that step immediately after. This insinuation will be so readily embraced by suspicious minds, and particularly by the wiley Cabinets of Europe, that I can not but think it might be well to take away that pretext against us, by an Exposé brought before the public in some due form, in which our Conduct would be seen in its true light. An historical view of the early sentiments expressed here in favor of our neighbours, the successive steps openly taken, manifesting our sympathy with their cause, and our anticipation of its success, more especially our declaration of neutrality towards the contending parties as engaged in a civil, not an insurrectionary, war, would shew to the world that we never concealed the principles that governed us, nor the policy which terminated in the decisive step last taken. And the time at which this was taken, is surely well explained, without reference to the Florida Treaty, by the greater maturity of the Independence of some of the new States, and particularly by the recent revolution in Mexico which is able not only to maintain its own Independence, but to turn the scale if it were doubtful, in favor of the others. Altho there may be no danger of hostile consequences from the Recognizing Act, it is desirable that our Republic should stand fair in the eyes of the world not only for its own sake, but for that of Republicanism itself. Nor would perhaps a conciliatory appeal to the candour & liberality of the better part of Europe be a superfluous precaution with a view to the possible collisions with Spain on the Ocean, and the backing she may receive from some of the great powers friendly to her or unfriendly to us. Russia has, if I mistake not, heretofore gone far in committing herself against a separation of the Colonies from Spain. And her enterprizing policy agst. revolutionary events every where makes it the more probable that she may resent the contrast to it in that of the U.S. I am aware that these ideas can not be new to you, and that you can appreciate them much better than I can. But having the pen in my hand I have permitted them to flow from it.

It appears that the Senate have been discussing the precedents relating to the appointment of public Ministers.[2] One question is, whether a public Minister be an officer in the strict constitutional sense. If he is, the appointment of him must be authorized by *law*, not by the President & Senate: If on the other hand the appointment creates the office, the office must expire with the appointment, as an office created by law expires with the law, and there can be no difference between Courts to which a public Minister had been sent, and those to which one was sent for the first time. According to my recollection this subject was on some occasion carefully searched into,[3] and it was found that the practice of the Govt. had from the beginning been regulated by the idea that the places or offices of pub: Ministers & Consuls existed under the law & usages of Nations, and were always open to receive appointments as they might be made by competent Authorities.

Other questions may be started as to Commissions for making Treaties; which when given to a public Minister employ him in a *distinct* capacity. But this is not the place, nor am I the person to pursue the subject.

We had a hard winter, and our Wheat fields exhibit the proofs of it. To make the matter worse, the fly has commenced its ravages in a very threatening manner. A dry & cold spell will render them very fatal. I know not the extent of the evil. There has been of late a reanimation of prices for the last crop, occasioned by the expected opening of the W. India Trade: but there is so little remaining in the hands of the Farmers, that the benefit will [be] scarcely felt by them. Health & all other blessings.

JAMES MADISON

RC (DLC: Monroe Papers); FC (DLC). RC docketed by Monroe. FC in Dolley Madison's hand; marked by JM at head of letter "President Monroe" and on the verso of last page: "Conc. appointment of ministers." Minor differences between the copies have not been noted.

1. Joaquín de Anduaga was Spanish minister to the United States, 1821–23 (*Washington Gazette*, 2 Nov. 1821; *Baltimore Patriot & Mercantile Advertiser*, 31 July 1823). For his 9 Mar. 1822 protest against U.S. recognition of the South American republics, see Jonathan Elliot, *The American Diplomatic Code, Embracing a Collection of Treaties and Conventions between the United States and Foreign Powers: From 1778 to 1834* . . . (2 vols.; Washington, 1834), 2:645–46. Anduaga's protest, and Secretary of State John Quincy Adams's reply, were printed in the *Daily National Intelligencer*, 29 Apr. 1822.

2. The question of appointments came up in the Senate on 29 Apr. during a discussion of the bill authorizing monies to support ministers to the newly recognized South American republics (*Daily National Intelligencer*, 30 Apr. 1822).

3. JM may have been referring to the controversy over Albert Gallatin's appointment as a member of the peace commission to treat with Great Britain under Russian mediation in 1813, for which see JM to Gallatin, 2 Aug. 1813, *PJM-PS*, 6:491–93, 494 n. 5. The controversy was revived in March 1814 when Christopher Gore reintroduced a series of resolutions in the Senate that called JM's recess appointments of the peace commissioners unauthorized by the Constitution (ibid., 7:393 n. 2).

Power of the President to Appoint Ministers and Consuls During a Recess of the Senate

[post–6 May 1822]

Power of the President to appoint publick ministers & Consuls, in the recess of the Senate.[1]

The place of a foreign Minister or Consul is not an *Office* in the constitutional sense of the term.

1. It is not created by the Constitution.

2. It is not created by a law authorized by the Constitution,

3 It cannot, as an office, be created by the mere appointment for it, made by the President & Senate, who are to fill, not create offices. These must be "established by law," & therefore by Congress only.

4. On the supposition even that the appointment could create an office, the office would expire with the expiration of the appointment, and every new appointment would create a new office, not fill an old one. A law reviving an expired law is a new law.

The place of a foreign minister or Consul is to be viewed, as created by the Law of Nations: to which the U.S. as an Independent nation is a party; and as always open for the proper functionaries, when sent by the constituted authority of one nation, and received by that of another. The Constitution in providing for the appointment of such functionaries, presupposes this mode of intercourse, as a branch of the Law of Nations.

The question to be decided is what are the cases in which the President can make appointments without the concurrence of the Senate; and it turns on the construction of the power "to fill up all vacancies which may happen during the recess of the Senate."

The term all embraces both foreign and municipal cases: and in examining the power in the foreign, however failing in exact analogy to the municipal, it is not improper to notice the extent of the power in the municipal.

If the text of the Constitution be taken literally no municipal officer could be appointed by the President alone, to a vacancy not *originating* in the recess of the Senate. It appears however, that under the sanction of the maxim, qui hæret in litera, hæret in cortice[2] and of the argumentum ab inconvenienti,[3] the power has been understood to extend, in cases of necessity or urgency, to vacancies, happening to exist, in the recess of the Senate, though not coming into existence in the recess. In the case, for example, of an appointment to a vacancy by the President & Senate, of a person dead at the time, but not known to be so till after the adjournment and dispersion of the Senate, it has been deemed within the reason of the constitutional provision, that the vacancy should be filled by the President alone;

the object of the provision being to prevent a failure in the execution of the laws, which without such a scope to the power, must very inconveniently happen, more especially in so extensive a country. Other cases of like urgency may occur; such as an appointment by the President & Senate rendered abortive by a refusal to accept it.

If it be admissible at all to make the power of the President without the Senate, applicable to vacancies happening unavoidably to exist, tho' not to originate, in the recess of the Senate, and which the publick good requires to be filled in the recess; the reasons are far more cogent for considering the sole power of the President as applicable to the appointment of foreign functionaries; inasmuch as the occasions demanding such appointments may not o⟨n⟩ly be far more important, but on the further consideration, that unlike appointments under the municipal law, the calls for them may depend on circumstances altogether under foreign controul, and sometimes on the most improbable & sudden emergencies; and requiring therefore that a competent authority to meet them should be always in existence. It would be a hard imputation on the Fram⟨e⟩rs & Ratifiers of the Constitution, that whilst providing for casualties of inferior magnitude, they should have intended to exclude from the provision, the means usually employed in obviating a threatened war; in putting an end to its calamities; in conciliating the friendship or neutrality of powerful nations, or even in seizing a favorable moment for commercial or other arrangements material to the public interest. And it would surely be a hard rule of construction, that would give to the text of the constitution an operation so injurious, in preference to a construction that would avoid it, and not be more liberal than would be applied to a remedial Statute. Nor ought the remark to be omitted that by rejecting such a construction this important function unlike some others, would be excluded altogether from our political System, there being no pretension to it in any ⟨o⟩ther department of the General Government or in any department of the State Govts. To regard the power of appointing the highest Functionaries employed in foreign missions, tho' a specific & substantive provision in the Constitution, as incidental merely, in any case, to a subordinate power, that of a provisional negociation by the President alone, would be a more strained construction of the text than that here given to it.

The view which has been taken of the subject overrules the distinction between missions to foreign Courts, to which there had before been appointments, and to which there had not been. Not to speak of diplomatic appointments destined not for Stations at foreign Courts, but for special negociations, no matter where, and to which the distinction would be inapplicable, it can not bear a rational or practical test, in the cases to which it has been applied. An appointment to a foreign Court, at one time, unlike an appointment to a municipal Office always requiring it, is no evidence of a need for the appointment at another time; whilst an appointment where there had been none before, may in the recess of the Senate, be of the greatest urgency. The distinction becomes almost ludicrous when it is asked for what length of time the circumstance of a former appointment is to have the effect assigned to it on the power of the President. Can it be seriously alledged that after the interval of a Century, & the political changes incident to such a lapse of time, the original appointment is to authorize a new one, without the concurrence of the Senate; whilst a like appointment to a new Court, or even a new Nation however immediately called for, is barred by the circumstance that no previous appointments to it had taken place. The case of diplomatic missions belongs to the Law of Nations, and the principles & usages on which that is founded are entitled to a certain influence in expounding the provisions of the Constitution which have relation to such Missions. The distinction between Courts to which there had, and to which there had not been previous missions, is believed to be recorded in none of the oracular works on international law, and to be unknown to the practice of Governments, where no question was involved as to the de facto establishment of a Government.

With this exposition, the practice of the Government of the U. States has corresponded,[4] and with every sanction of reason & public expediency. If in any particular instance the power has been misused, which it is not meant to suggest, that could not invalidate either its legitimacy or its general utility, any more than any other power would be invalidated, by a like fault in the use of it.

Ms (DLC). In JM's hand. Undated; conjectural date assigned based on the evidence in n. 1. On the verso of the last page, in an unidentified hand: "Note: It appears that Mr. Wirt had given officially the same construction to the term 'happen' tho' not known to Mr. M."

1. This issue was first raised in July 1813, when JM was under attack for making recess appointments to a peace commission that was to treat with Great Britain under the mediation of Russia (see JM to Monroe, 6 May 1822, and n. 3). The revival of this question in May 1822 may have provoked JM to write this formal answer to his critics and those of the president, James Monroe. There is no evidence the paper was ever published or even shared, but echoes of it appear in a letter to Edward Coles, 15 Oct. 1834 (NjP: Coles Papers). The editors have chosen to publish it here because JM's penmanship in this document resembles the clear and vigorous style of the 1820s, rather than his cramped and labored writing of the 1830s.

2. *Qui haeret in litera, haeret in cortice:* who clings to the letter, clings to the bark, i.e., in interpreting a legal instrument or law, one should not confine oneself to the literal meaning alone but search for the spirit and intention of the maker or lawgiver.

3. *Argumentum ab inconvenienti:* "an argument that emphasizes the harmful consequences of failing to follow the position advocated" (*Black's Law Dictionary* [9th ed.], 122).

4. Here JM first wrote then crossed out: "from its commencement to the latest date, thro' the whole series of Executive magistrates."

From Richard Forrest

DEAR SIR, WASHINGTON May 11h. 1822

I have duly received your much respected letter of the 6th inst[1] with its enclosure for Mr Rush, which I forward under cover to the Collector of the Customs at New York, with directions to place it with those of this Dept to go by the Packet which sails on the 16th.

I am truly thankful for the kindness which you have shown in searching for the Pamphlets respecting the first settlements in Virginia, and will avail myself of the suggestion to apply to Mr Bassett for any assistance he may be able to afford.

From the unfavorable appearance of the present crop of small grain in this Country, and recent accounts from Buenos Ayres and Montevideo, flour has already taken a rise, and will unquestionably continue to advance in price.

Mrs. Forrest and the family join me in sincere regards &c. to Mrs. Madison, yourself and our good friend Payne. Beleive me most truly yours &c

RICHD. FORREST

RC (ViU: Madison Papers, Special Collections). Docketed by JM.

1. JM's draft of his letter to Forrest is dated 4 May 1822.

From Thomas Jefferson

DEAR SIR MONTICELLO May 12. 22.

I thank you for the communication of mr. Rush's letter[1] which I now return. Mr. Bentham's character of Alexander is I believe just and that worse traits might still be added to it equally just. He is now certainly become the watchman of tyranny for Europe, as dear to it's oppressors as detestable to the oppressed. If however he should engage in war with the Turks, as I expect, his employment there may give opportunities for the friends of liberty to proceed in their work. I set out for Bedford tomorrow to be absent three weeks. I salute you with constant and affectionate friendship and respect.

TH: JEFFERSON

FC (DLC: Jefferson Papers).

1. Richard Rush to JM, 6 Mar. 1822.

From James Monroe

Dear Sir Washington May 12th. 1822

I have had the pleasure to receive your letter of the 6th, and entirely concur in the view which you have taken of both the subjects on which it treats. The uniform conduct of the government, towards the Spanish provinces, has manifested a friendly interest in their favor, without taking a single step, with which the Spanish government had a right to complain, from the commencement of their revolution, to the recognition, at the late Session. I will avail myself of your suggestion, to guard against the imputation endeavourd to be thrown on our character, by the Spanish minister. The time had certainly arrivd, when it became our duty to recognize, provided it was intended, to maintain friendly relations with them in future, & not to suffer them, under a feeling of resentment towards us, & the artful practices of the European powers, to become the dupes of their policy. I was aware, that the recognition, was not without its dangers, but as either course had its dangers, I thought it best to expose ourselves, after the accession of Mexico, & of Peru, to such as were incident to a generous & liberal policy.

Your view of the constitution, as to the powers of the Executive, in the appointment of public ministers, is in strict accord with my own, and is, as I understand, supported, by numerous precedents, under successive administrations. A foreign mission, is not an office, in the sense of the constitution which authorises the President to fill vacancies in the recess of the Senate. It is not an office created by law, nor subject to the rules applicable to such offices. It exists only when an appointment is made, and terminates when it ceases, whether by the recall, death, or resignation of the minister. It exists in the contemplation of the constitution, with every power, and may be filled with any, or terminated with either, as circumstances may require, according to the judgement of the Executive. If an appointment can be made by the Executive in the recess of the Senate, to a court, at which we have been represented, to fill a vacancy created by the death or resignation of the minister, I am of opinion, that it may be made to a court, at which we have never been represented. A different construction would embarrass the govt. much in its mov'ments & be productive of great mischief. I will search for the precedents which you have mentiond, as it is probable that I may have occasion for them.

I have never known such a state of things, as has existed here, during the late Session, nor have I personally ever experiencd so much embarrassment, & mortification. Where there is an open contest with a foreign enemy, or with an internal party, in which you are supported, by just principles, the course is plain & you have something to chear & animate you to action. But we are now blessed with peace, & the success of the late war, has overwhelmed, the federal party, so that there is no division of that kind, to rally any persons, together, in support of the admn. The approaching election, tho' distant, is a circumstance, that excites greatest interest in both houses, & whose effect, already sensibly felt, is still much to be dreaded. There being three avowed candidates in the admn.,[1] is a circumstance, which increases the embarrassment. The friends of each, endeavour to annoy the others, as you have doubtless seen by the public prints. In many cases, the attacks are personal, directed against the individual. They have been felt, principally, in their operation on public measures, by their effect, on the system of public defense adopted in 1815. 16. Under the pretext of Oeconomy, attempts have been made, and in some instances with success, to cut up that system, in many important parts, & in fact to reduce it to a nullity. Thus we should lose all the advantages, to be derivd, from the lessons of the late war, & get back to the state in which we were before it, after having expended, large sums under their admonition. They have been felt also, & personally by me, in the measures adopted, in execution of the law of last year, for the reduction of the army.[2] I appointed a board of Genl. officers, as was done by you in 1815, gave them the law, & precedents establishd in the former case, with my opinion, that original vacancies were open to selections from any grade, if indeed to be confind to the army. They made their report and I confirmd it without any change. The majority of the Senate rejected two nominations of great importance, affecting the construction of the law, & the principle on which it was executed, & compelling me, if acquiesced in, to transfer Col: Bissell,[3] from a regt. of infantry, to a regt. of artil[l]ery, filling by him an original vacancy, against the report of the bd. & my own opinion of the comparative merit of the parties. I withdrew the nominations on which the Senate had not acted, to explain my construction of the law; preparing a message to which effect, I renominated them, with the two (Towson & Gadsden)[4] who had been rejected. They were again rejected, the reasons, for which, are containd in a report of the committee, at the head of which, is Col: Williams of Tennessee. I then nominated Col Towson, to the office of paymaster genl., which has been confirmd, but have kept open the offices of adjt. genl. to which Col: Gadsden had been nominated, & of Colonelcy, to one of the new regts. of arty. to which Col: Towson, had been. These places will remain open till next Session. The reduction of the army, gives great discontent, to a numerous host of disbanded officers, notwithstanding every precaution to prevent it, by observing the strictest impartiality, as to the merits of the parties, their circumstances &ca. The door has been open'd to the discontented, & many unfounded reports from some of them, made the ground of charges on the admn., importing misconduct in the reduction of the army, of which that of interpolation, in some part of Genl. Scott's book,[5] containg rules & regulations for its govt., has perhaps attracted your attention. The fallacy of this charge has been completely refuted, in a correspondence between Doctr. Floyd & genl Scott,[6] & the evidence of its fallacy, had been more than a month before made known, to the Chairman of the Com: of the Senate, without being regarded. Under the experiences of the late war, the staff of the army is remarkably well organized, & its expence reducd, as it appears to me, to the minimum, for such an establishment, as indeed is the expence of the naval establishment, and of every branch of the admn., yet a different opinion is attempted to be propagated, throughout the union. The object is to raise up a new party founded on the assumd basis of Oeconomy, and with unjust imputations, against all those, who are friendly to the system of defense, in train, demolish the system, if in their power.

We have undoubtedly reachd a new epoch in our political career, which has been formd by the destruction of the federal party, so far at least not to be felt in the movment of the general govt., & especially in Congress; by the general peace, & the entire absence, of all cause, as to public measures, for great political excit'ment; & in truth, by the real prosperity of the union. In such a state of things, it might have been presumd, that the mov'ment would have been tranquil, marked by a common effort to promote the public good, in every line to which the powers of the general govt. extended. It is my fixd opinion, that this will be the result, after some short interval, & that the restless & disturbed state of the commonwealth, like the rolling of the waves after a storm, tho' worse than the storm itself, will subside, & leave the ship in perfect security. Public opinion will react on this body, & keep it right. Surely our govt. may get on, & prosper, without the existence of parties. I have always considerd their existence as the curse of the country, of which we had sufficient proof, more especially in the late war. Besides how ke[e]p them alive & in action? The causes which exist in other countries, do not, here. We have no distinct orders. No allurment has been offerd to the federalists, to calm them down, into a state of tranquility. None of them have been appointed to high offices, & very few to the lowest. Their misconduct in the late war, & the success of that war broke them as a party. It has been charg'd on me, to hav⟨e⟩ reard them up, & my trip to the Eastward, more particularly, has been alledged as the cause. But in what mode? Both parties, met me embodied together, & I receivd them with civility & kindness. Their addresses were republican, & my answers, as strongly marked, as were any of the acts of my public life. If therefore the existence of that party, might be considerd, as conducive to the public welfare, its destruction can not be charged on me. It was owing to a much higher cause. The attention shewn to me, was adopted by it as a propitiating circumstance, which I did not invite, nor expect, or wish. I took that trip, to draw the public attention, to the great object of public defense, and so far as I had a personal object, to improve my health, which had sufferd much by the fatigues to which I had been exposed in the late war. Altho' I have thought that it was consistent with the principles of our govt., & would promote the general welfare, to draw the people more closely together, & to leave the federal leaders without support, yet I have known that that object, without regarding other considerations of a more personal character, would be defeated, if the person in this station, went in advance of his own party: that he must rest exclusively on it, declining on his part persecution only, & extending to any of the opposite one, any portion of confidence, by appointing them even to the lowest offices, when invited, by his republican fellow citizens. On this principle I have invariably acted, so that the charge of amalgamation, is not correctly levelled at me; nor if a merit, do I claim the credit, of it, to a greater extent than is above stated. Parties have now calmd down, or rather have disappeard from this great theatre, and we are about to make the experiment, whether there is sufficient virtue in the people to support our free republican system of govt. My confidence is still as strong as ever in the result, but still that must be aided by all who can contribute to its support.

Has there been any case within your recollection, of a nomination of an officer of the army, to a particular office, to take rank from a certain date, in which the Senate have interposed, to give rank from another date? Do you recollect any instances, of filling original vacancies, in civil or military offices, in the recess of the Senate, when authority was not given by law? I think that I do, tho' I can not turn to the case.

Saml. Smith[7] was pressd on me, from many quarters, for Lisbon, but I gave the appointment to Genl. Dearborn, who did not think, much less ask for it.

Dr Eustis has been among the most steady & systematic assailants, that I have had to encounter, since his return to Congress. This circumstance has astonish'd and distressed me. With best regards to Mrs Madison I am dear Sir very sincerely yours

JAMES MONROE

Young Macon is appointed a member of the Legislative Council in Florida—intended to give him a commencment there.

RC (DLC: Rives Collection, Madison Papers). Docketed by JM. Partially printed, under date of 10 May 1822, in Hamilton, *Writings of James Monroe*, 6:284–91.

1. The three candidates in the administration jockeying for position before the presidential election of 1824 were Secretary of State John Quincy Adams, Secretary of the Treasury William H. Crawford, and Secretary of War John C. Calhoun.

2. For the law reducing the military establishment, see Archibald W. Hamilton to JM, 10 Apr. 1822, and n. 2.

3. Daniel Bissell (1769–1833) served as a fifer in the American Revolution and joined the First U.S. Infantry in 1788. He rose to the rank of brigadier general in the U.S. Army during the War of 1812 and was retained in the army on the peace establishment in 1816 as

colonel of the First Regiment of Infantry. In 1821, under the further reduction of the army, Bissell was found to be a supernumerary colonel and ordered to be discharged. The Senate disagreed, rejected his replacement, and Bissell remained in the army. In 1826 President Adams nominated Bissell colonel of the Second Regiment of Artillery, but after an argument between the president and the Senate over the appointment, Bissell's nomination was tabled (John C. Fredriksen, *American Military Leaders: From Colonial Times to the Present* [2 vols.; Santa Barbara, Calif., 1999], 1:52–53; Lawrence O. Christensen et al., eds., *Dictionary of Missouri Biography* [Columbia, Mo., 1999], 76; *Senate Exec. Proceedings*, 3:15, 32, 490, 491–92, 500–501, 529, 530–31, 542).

4. Nathan Towson (1784–1854) of Maryland entered the U.S. Army in 1812 as a captain of artillery and served with distinction throughout the war. He was retained as a colonel in the peace establishment and was paymaster general of the army, 1819–21 and 1822, until he retired (David S. Heidler and Jeanne T. Heidler, eds., *Encyclopedia of the War of 1812* [Santa Barbara, Calif., 1997], 519–20). James Gadsden (1788–1858) of Charleston, South Carolina, graduated from Yale College in 1806 and entered the U.S. Army shortly thereafter. He served in the War of 1812 and in the peacetime army, rising to the rank of colonel by the time he left the service in 1822. In 1840 he became president of the Louisville, Cincinnati & Charleston Railroad. Among his ambitions was to build a southern continental railroad that would link the south and west of the United States economically and politically. He served as U.S. minister to Mexico and was instrumental in obtaining from Mexico territory known as the Gadsden Purchase. For Monroe's original message of 21 Jan. 1822 nominating Towson and Gadsden, and his renomination message of 12 Apr. 1822, see the *Daily National Intelligencer*, 4 May 1822. For a discussion of the principles in question, see Ammon, *James Monroe*, 500–501.

5. [Winfield Scott], *General Regulations for the Army; or, Military Institutes* (Philadelphia, 1821; Shoemaker 7214).

6. After Scott's book (see n. 5 above) was published, John Floyd noted differences between it and the version that Congress had approved, and accused Scott of forgery. Scott demanded either an apology or a duel. Since the error was in the congressional committee, which had not incorporated some of Scott's final revisions, Floyd apologized (Johnson, *Winfield Scott*, 79). The correspondence between Floyd and Scott was published in *Niles' Weekly Register* 22 (11 May 1822): 176.

7. Samuel Smith (1752–1839), a Baltimore merchant who was a longtime power in state and national Republican party politics, was a veteran of the Revolutionary War and the War of 1812, served in the U.S. House of Representatives, 1792–1803, and 1816–22, and in the U.S. Senate, 1803–15, and 1822–33.

From George Tucker

SIR, LYNCHBURG. May 16. 1822.

I have requested Mr. Milligan, the bookseller to forward to you a copy of a work which I have lately published,[1] & of which I beg leave to ask your acceptance. With sentiments of profound respect, I am Sir, your obedt. Servt.

GEORGE TUCKER[2]

RC (DLC). Docketed by JM.

1. [George Tucker], *Essays on Various Subjects of Taste, Morals, and National Policy* (Georgetown, D.C., 1822; Shoemaker 10492).

2. George Tucker (1775–1861) was born in Bermuda and immigrated to the United States in 1787. He was brought up by a relative, St. George Tucker, the professor of law at the College of William and Mary. At the time of this letter he was practicing law in Lynchburg, Virginia. Tucker served in the U.S. House of Representatives, 1819–25. In 1825 he became professor of moral philosophy at the University of Virginia, a post he filled until 1845, when he moved to Philadelphia. He was an indefatigable writer, publishing books and essays on political economy, novels, histories, and biographies, including one of Thomas Jefferson.

To James Monroe

DEAR SIR MONTPELLIER May 18. 1822

I am just favored with yours of the 12th. in which you ask whether I recollect "any case of a nomination of an officer of the Army to a particular office to take rank from a certain date" in which the Senate have interposed to give rank from another date, and again whether I recollect "any instances of filling original vacances in civil or military offices in the recess of the Senate when an authority was not given by law."

On the first point I have no particular recollection; but it is possible that there may have been cases such as you mention. The Journals of the Senate will of course present them if they ever existed. Be the fact as it may, it would seem that such an interposition of the Senate would be a departure from the naked authority to decide on nominations of the Executive. The tenure of the officer in the interval between the two dates, where that of the Senate was the prior one, would be altogether of the Senate's creation: or if understood to be made valid by the commission of the President, would make the appointment *originate* with the Senate, not with the President: Nor would a posteriority of the date of the Senate, possibly be without some indirect operation not within the competency of that Body.

On the second point, altho' my memory can not refer to any particular appointments to original vacances in the recess of the Senate, I am confident that such have taken place, under a pressure of circumstances, where no legal provision had authorized them. There have been cases where offices were created by Congress, and appointments to them made with the sanction of the Senate, which were notwithstanding found to be vacant in consequence of refusals to accept them; or of the unknown death of the party at the time of the appointment, and thence filled by the President alone. I have a faint impression that instances of one or both, occurred within the Mississippi Territory. These however were cases of necessity. Whether others not having that basis have occurred, my present recollections do not enable me to say.

In the enclosed English Newspaper is sketched a debate in the House of Commons throwing light on the practice there of filling military vacances in certain cases. If I understand the sketch from a very slight perusal, the rule of promotion is not viewed as applicable to original vacances. In the abstract, it has always appeared to me desireable that the door to special merit should be widened as far as could possibly be reconciled with the general rule of promotion. The inconveniency of a rigid adherence to this rule gave birth to brevets; and favors every permitted mode of relaxing it, in order to do justice to superior capacities for the public service.

The aspect of things at Washington to which you allude could escape the notice of no one who ever looks into the newspapers. The only effect of a political rivalship among the members of the Cabinet which I anticipated, and which I believe I mentioned once in conversation with you, was an increased disposition in each to cultivate the good will of the President. The late effects of such a rivalship on & through the proceedings of Congress is to be ascribed, I hope, to a peculiarity and combination of circumstances not likely often to recur in our annals.

I am afraid you are too sanguine in your inferences from the absence here of causes which have most engendered and embittered the spirit of party in former times & in other Countries. There seems to be a propensity in free Govts. which will always find or make subjects, on which human opinions & passions may be thrown into conflict. The most perhaps that can be counted on, & that will be sufficient, is, that occasions for party contests in such a Country & Govt. as ours, will be either so slight or so transient, as not to threaten any permanent or dangerous consequences to the character and prosperity of the Republic. But I must not forget that I took up my pen merely to answer your two enquiries, and to remind you that you omitted to answer mine as to your intended movements after the release from your confinement at Washington. Health & success be with you.

James Madison

RC (DLC: Monroe Papers); draft (DLC). RC docketed by Monroe. Minor differences between the copies have not been noted.

From Edward Livingston

Sir, New Orleans 19th May 1822.

The Pamphlet which I have the honor to submit to your perusal[1] will disirve some Interest from the subject, altho' little from the manner I fear in which it is treated. The efforts making for the improvement of Criminal

Jurisprudence, in this part of the Union cannot but gratify those, who like you Sir, know how important that branch of Government is to the Liberties, as well as the happiness of the People. I cannot hope that you will either find leisure or Inclination to favor me with any Observations on the defects of the System I have proposed. If the perusal of the pamphlet should afford you either Interest or Satisfaction, the Object which induced me to take the Liberty of writing this Letter, will be attained. I have the honor to be with great Respect Your mo obt. Servt.

Edw. Livingston[2]

RC (DLC); draft (NjP: Edward Livingston Papers). RC in a clerk's hand signed by Livingston; docketed by JM. Minor differences between the copies have not been noted.

1. Edward Livingston, *Report Made to the General Assembly of the State of Louisiana, on the Plan of a Penal Code for the Said State* (New Orleans, 1822; Shoemaker 9283).

2. Edward Livingston (1764–1836), the younger brother of Robert R. Livingston, was graduated from the College of New Jersey in 1781, and admitted to the bar in New York in 1786. A fervent Republican, he served in the U.S. House of Representatives, 1795–1801, where he opposed the Jay Treaty and the Alien and Sedition Acts. He was appointed U.S. attorney for the New York district by Thomas Jefferson, but when in 1803 a large shortfall was found in federal money entrusted to his care, Livingston was forced to resign. He left New York for New Orleans, where he found success as a lawyer, speculator, and politician. He was again elected to the U.S. House of Representatives, 1822–28, then moved to the Senate, 1829–31. He served as secretary of state, 1831–33, and as U.S. minister to France, 1833–35 (Harrison, *Princetonians, 1776–1783*, 331–41).

From Benjamin Joy

Dear Sir Boston 23rd May 1822.

On my return, yesterday, from the interior of the state of NYork I had the Honor of receiving your letter of the 18th March and that of the 6th Inst. with copy of the former; for which be pleased to receive my thanks. I very much regret that by my absence you did not receive a reply to your favor of the 18th March which would have prevented you the trouble of again writing, tho' it lays me under a pleasing additional obligation to you. My Brother was, in my absence, informed of the contents of your letter. With sincere wishes for your happiness I beg you Sir to receive the unfain'd respects of your Obliged Hhble Servt

B: Joy

RC (DLC: Rives Collection, Madison Papers). Addressed by Joy to JM; postmarked "Boston 22 May." Docketed by JM.

To James Maury

Dr. Sir — Montpr. May 23. 1822

I have successively rcd. all the letters, I believe, with wch. I have been favd. by your Firm.

My last crop of Tobo. was not a very good [one]. The Grasshoppers compleatly destroyed the first planting, and in a very great degree the second also: so that the Tobo. was small, and was necessarily cut, from the approach of Frost before it got to be fully ripe. Another consequence was, as usually happens to Tobo got late into the House, that it did not cure of a good colour. I sent it however to Richd. with an intention to ship it, if a tolerable Market could not be had there. Beyond my expectation, it sold pretty well, averaging \$8½. 2 of the Hhds selling for \$11.60 per hundred, and 1 for \$11. The Mountain quality, notwithstandg. its defects, seemed to gain the particular attention of Purchasers.

The sale of the preceding crop at Liverpool has indeed discouraged me from shipments. The tobacco of that year was greatly superior to what I sold in Richd. in *size*, in substance, and in colour, and yet it did not nett me \$7 per hundred, which I was offered for it in Fredg. The rate of exchange only saved me from positive loss by not selling it there. Your son suggested that I should, enlarge the leaf of my Tobo. by planting the *Big* Frederick: but that is the very sort I have planted ever since I resumed the culture of Tobo. I can not help suspecting, that some prejudice sticks to the Rapk. Tobo. even when immediately shipped from James River.

It is too early in the season to speak of the planting prospects for the current year. Those of the Farmer in Virga & Maryd. are very unfavorable. The Winter was severe & with little snow & the Hessian fly has been very busy in our fields. I am not informed of the prospects in the ⟨W⟩heat States North of Maryd. With a continuance of my friend[ly] respects & good wishes to yourself & your Son

J.M.

Draft (DLC).

From James Monroe

Dear Sir, — Washington May 26, 1822.

Dr. Wm. Thornton who has long enjoyed your good opinion, has expressed a wish that I would also afford him a testimonial of mine, addressed to some friend, to be retained in his possession. To this request,

I have willingly acceded, and have presumed, that it might be agreeable to you, and particularly gratifying to him, that it should be addressed to you. I became acquainted with him, before the government was established in this city, and have since my residence here, had opportunities, of improving that acquaintance. He has long had the direction of the patent office, in the management of which, he has shown ability, and given satisfaction to the government; and before his appointment to this office, he held that of a Commissioner, of the public buildings of this city, in which I have always understood, that he was equally successful. I regard him as a man of strict integrity, possessing considerable literary attainments, patriotic, & of amiable disposition. He has always, in common with the general sentiment of our fellow citizens, taken a deep interest, in the success of our southern neighbors, in the great cause in which they are engaged. I am not aware that it is his intention, to withdraw from his present office, nor is this letter given on the presumption of such an event. In whatever line however he may embark, he will carry with him my best wishes for his welfare. I am dear Sir with the highest respect & esteem very sincerely yours

(Signed) James Monroe

FC (DNA: RG 59, Misc. Correspondence and Memoranda; Drafts of Letters and Memoranda of James Monroe, 1818–24). In a clerk's hand.

From George Joy

Dear sir, London 29th May 1822.

I left town before it was known what Letter Bags might float ashore from the Albion;[1] some having found their way at intervals to London. On my return Mr Rush has informed me that he has every reason to suppose there were Despatches on board her for him; and as two regular Ships have since arrived, I send this merely to apprize you that anything you may have favored me with by that Conveyance is irrevocable gone, and pray you in such case to repeat at your earliest leisure any advices you may have sent me by that Ship—remaining in haste, very truly and faithfully Dear sir, Your most obedt servt.

G. Joy

RC (DLC, series 7, box 1). Docketed by JM.

1. The *Albion*, a New York to Liverpool packet, was shipwrecked off the coast of Ireland on 23 Apr. 1822 with the loss of its cargo and all but nine of its fifty-two crew and passengers (*Boston Commercial Gazette*, 3 June 1822).

To Benjamin Joy

DR. SIR MONTPR. May 30. 1822

I have just recd. yours of the 23d. inst. in which you acknowledge the recet. of mine of Mar 18. & May. 16.[1] but say nothing as to the disposition to be made of your brothers letter to me therein referred to. Be so good as to drop me a line supplying the omission. In the mean time I will forward the letter to Mr. Cutts, who will comply with your instructions in that respect; which it may be well to address to him, as well as to communicate to me. I suggest this precaution, that if the letter is to be handed to the Board of Comrs. there may be less danger of being out of time, the limit to which I do not know.

Draft (DLC).

1. JM referred to his letter to Benjamin Joy of 6 May 1822.

To Richard Cutts

DEAR SIR MONTPELLIER June 3. 1822

I recd. some time ago a letter from Mr. Geo: Joy in London, requesting me to search my files for a letter from him to me of Apl. 16. 1804. which I inferred he meant to make some use of with the Board of Commissioners on Spanish Claims. I have apprized his brother Ben: Joy that I have found the letter, and that I should send it to you to dispose of it according to the instructions you might receive from him. The letter is accordingly enclosed. I understand [. . .] Washington an Agent of Mr. B. J. (Mr. Alexander Bliss) with whom it may be well to consult in case you should not hear from Mr. Joy himself in time for the proceedings of the Board.

I recd. your favor of May 23.[1] returning the letter from the Asserted Inventor of the fumigating bellows. In reply to what it contains on another subject, I cannot deny that a fulfilment of your wishes would have been convenient to me: but I can say with equal truth, it would not have given me so much pleasure as to find that the delay will have contributed to relieve you from the difficulties which have so much oppressed you, I know not what the law in the District is, with respect to the effect of a lapse of time on the validity of *unseal[e]d* obligations. If it be such as to bear on the case between us, you will be good eno' to send me a document in a form to guard agst. the consequence. Remember me affectionately to Mrs. C. and all around you, and be assured of my sincere regards & best wishes.

JAMES MADISON

RC (MHi).

1. Letter not found.

From Hiram Haines

Slate Mills

Honourable Sir, Culpeper County Va. June 4th. 1822.

A desire not only to see, but to possess and preserve relicts of those venerable Heroes an[d] Sages whose exertions won and whose counsells have preserved that Glorious Liberty which I in common with Millions of my happy fellow citizens enjoy, is the cause of my (at present) addressing you, in which I hope you will excuse the liberty An *intire stranger* has thus unceremoniously taken.

My wishes are to possess specimens of their hand writing and if possible correct copperplate engravings, or painted miniature likenesses of their persons. Should you, who has acted so important a part in the scenes referred to, be willing thus far to gratify me the favour will be received with pleasure and remembered with gratitude.

I am but a youth of Nineteen, to whom, neither Fortune nor Nature has been propitious or profuse, and should you please to favour me with a specimen of your hand writing, I wish it to embrace some maxim or moral lesson that may be useful to me as I Journey through life, and which would probably be better remembered and more strictly regarded as having emenated from so respectable a source.

On whatever subject you may please to write, affix your name in the style in which you have been in the habit of signing it. Address to Hiram Haines, Slate Mills Culpr. Cty. Va.

May the Great Architect of the Universe give you health and Peace for your remaining days.

H: Haines[1]

RC (DLC). Docketed by JM "(never answerd)."

1. Hiram Haines (ca. 1803–1841), a native of Culpeper County, Virginia, was editor of the Petersburg *American Constellation* and author of a volume of poetry, *Mountain Buds and Blossoms, Wove in a Rustic Garland* (Petersburg, Va., 1825) (Richard Beale Davis, *Intellectual Life in Jefferson's Virginia, 1790–1830* [Chapel Hill, N.C., 1964], 346). In the first poem of the volume, "The Virginiad," Haines devotes three stanzas to JM (40–41), the first of which is as follows:

In sweet seclusion 'mid Montpelier's shades,
Where Nature's face, Art's finest touch upbraids
Virginians look and learn with pride to prize,

Sage Madison—the polish'd, good and wise.
From pow'r retired—its loss, he can't deplore,
Its honors reap'd—he thinks of it no more;
But dwells on his sweet farm in classic ease,
His pride and pleasure, to instruct and please:
Admired—reverenc'd, and by all beloved,
Correct through life—his acts stand self-approved;
In one bright character we see him blend,
The Statesman,—Scholar,—Farmer—and the Friend.

From Benjamin Joy

SIR BOSTON 6th June 1822.

I have had the honor of rec[e]iving your favor of the 30th. Ulto. For your very friendly attention be pleased to accept my acknowledgement.

I had understood from Mr Webster who is agent for my Claim, that a Copy which I now have of my brothers letter to you might answer at Washington; and not wishing to cause you further trouble is the reason why I omitted to request you to forward the original. Be pleased to accept my thanks for forwarding the letter to Mr Cutts to whom I will write to deliver it to Mr Webster when he shall have occation for it. With the highest respect I am Sir your much obliged Hhble Servt.

B: JOY

RC (DLC: Rives Collection, Madison Papers). Docketed by JM.

From Benjamin Waterhouse

DEAR SIR, CAMBRIDGE 9th. June 1822

I here send for your acceptance a copy from a new edition of my Lecture on the pernicious effects of the too free use of Tobacco & ardent spirits on young persons.[1] How you in the South will approve my zeal in combatting this organ of "Virginia influence," I know not. I have felt a degree of regret as often as I reflected on the sums annually expended amongst ourselves for that which is neither meat—drink or clothing. With an high degree of respect I remain your obt. servt

BENJN: WATERHOUSE

RC (DLC). Docketed by JM.

1. Benjamin Waterhouse, *Cautions to Young Persons concerning Health, in a Public Lecture Delivered at the Close of the Medical Course in the Chapel at Cambridge, November 20, 1804: Containing the General Doctrine of Dyspepsia and Chronic Diseases; Shewing the Evil Tendency of the Use of Tobacco upon Young Persons; More especially the Pernicious Effects of Smoking Cigars. With Observations on the Use of Ardent and Vinous Spirits* . . . , 5th ed. (Cambridge, Mass., 1822; Shoemaker 11351).

From Thomas L. McKenney

SIR, WESTON. June 11. 1822

I beg leave respectfully to enclose you a prospectus of the Washington Republican, & Congressional examiner.[1] The first division of this title has been sanctioned, always, by the composition of our political parties; but for the last an apology must be sought in the extraordinary character which has marked the doings of the U.S. Congress during the last two or three years.

I avail myself of the occasion to assure you of my sincere attachment to you, & to your administr[a]tion, and to beg the favor of you to present my remembrance to Mrs. Madison.

THOS: L: MCKENNEY

RC (DLC). Docketed by JM.

1. Thomas L. McKenney, *Prospectus of the Washington Republican and Congressional Examiner* ([Washington], 1822; Shoemaker 9320). JM's copy of this broadside is in the Madison Collection, Rare Book and Special Collections Division, Library of Congress.

From Horatio Gates Spafford

ESTEEMED FRIEND, BALLSTON SPA, N.Y. 6 MO. 11, 1822.

By some delay of the Post Master at Ballston, to which thy favor of April 16 was directed, I did not receive it until yesterday.

My Geography & Gazetteer will soon be ready for the press, & greatly improved, by no small labor. Within the last 6 months, I have sent by Mail 1100 Letters, more than 300 of which were autographs, thinking, as indeed I have always found it, that less attention is paid to printed than M.S. Letters. Besides the United States' Census of 1820, a Census of this State in 1821, and all the public documents from the Offices of State at Albany of use in my labor, there now lie on my table upwards of 1200 original, M.S. Letters, from my Correspondents in relation to this Work, from which it is composed. I spare no pains, & indeed a man who performs such a task *must not.*

I am obliged by thy wish of success.

As to a Geography & Gazetteer of Virginia: may I ask of thee the favor to suggest the idea to Mr. Ritchie, of Richmond? As soon as I shall have completed the one of this State, say by next Winter, I should like well to engage in such a Work. Do me the favor to speak of it to thy friends.

I did receive thy favor, at my Cabin in the West, & read, with no small degree of interest & pleasure, thy Address, accompanying it, & which I have procured republished in this State. I thought I had acknowledged these favors.

The potato, is undoubtedly indigenous in W. Pa., & a valuable vegetable.[1] I have cultivated it, & it improves in size. Boiled, or roasted, it is a rich flavored vegetable for the table, mealy as the best common potato, but sweetish, a half way sweet potato. It grows abundantly in the rich little tracts of alluvion on the uplands, has a creeping vine, like the sweet potato, a sharp pointed beautiful leaf, & bears flowers of a bluish cast, in clusters. The fruit, is connected by a long slim root, growing to the size of a large walnut, & some 3 or 4 times that size, every 2 to 6 inches. I will send thee some of them, but how soon is uncertain. They seem to do best in a moist soil, composed of recent alluvion from clay or marle, intermixed with vegetable mold, good potato ground, in short. They grow so plentifully about my Cabin, that a man may dig as many as one could eat, in 1 or 2 minutes. Persons acquainted with the Yam of the W. Indies, told me this root tastes more like it than any other they know of.

I have none of them here, having distributed all I brought.

So far as I know, this has been overlooked, though somewhat like what the Voyageurs used to call the Mississippi Yam, a root found on the bottoms of the lower part of the Ohio, & that river.

I see, by the Gazettes, that John Wood, of Va., probably the person alluded to in thy Letter, as taking County Maps, preparatory to a Map of the State, is deceased. I wish Virginia would allow me to complete his design, have the aid of his Collections, & connect with its execution a Geography & Gazetteer of that State. Perhaps the gentleman at Richmond, named by thee, might be pleased to enter on such a business, & could get it from the State: I would like to engage in it with him. The Work on this State, has done it great service; far greater than can readily be imagined, by a person at the distance of Virginia. It has been the means of increasing our population a good many thousands, & such will be acknowledged as public opinion, when the Author shall be under the sod. But, excuse this, vanity, if it be such in thy opinion: parents love to talk of their children. I have made nothing, yet, by the Work; but the booksellers have, & the commity has been benefitted. A man can't be poor, whose passions & desires are so moderated as mine are: I am neither poor nor rich. With great esteem & regard, thy friend,

Horatio Gates Spafford

RC (DLC). Addressed by Spafford to JM, and franked. Docketed by JM.

1. From Spafford's description, this was probably a form of wild yam (*Dioscorea villosa*), native to North America (Steven Foster and James A. Duke, *A Field Guide to Medicinal Plants and Herbs of Eastern and Central North America*, 2d ed. [Boston, 2000], 230–32).

To Thomas L. McKenney

Dr Sir [ca. 14 June 1822]

I have been favored with yours of June 11. referring to the prospectus of an Evening paper you propose to publish.

Mrs. Madison & myself have a due sensibility to your kind expressions; and offer in return all the good wishes prompted by a recollection of the private virtues, & public principles which were always regarded as marking your character.

Having found it expedient to reduce rather than extend my receipt of Newspapers, I have for some time declined being a subscriber for new ones. I will thank you nevertheless to forward me with yours for the *first year* of its publication, & I will remit the price on the rect. of the first No. With esteem & friendly respects

J.M.

$5 sent see the rect.

Draft (PHi). Undated; conjectural date assigned based on comparison with McKenney to JM, 11 June 1822.

From Samuel B. H. Judah

Respected sir N⟨ew⟩ York June 14th 1822

I have the honor to present you a copy of a poem[1] that has obtained some considerable reputation in this country and is now republishing in England—but be assured I have not the vanity to think in sending to you that it is worthy of yr. notice but as a sincere tho' poor testimony of the reverance an unknown youth holds for the venerable patriot to whom his country owes so much. I should never have presumed to forward it faulty as I know it is but that being flattered by the favorable opinion expressed of it from several of our most distinguished critics I thought It might perhaps amuse you in an hour of Leisure. I beg of you not to judge of it by the strict rules of composition—it is the first work of the Kind from the pen of an youth of scarce sixteen years old—who if it should be his fate to try his pen again feels assured that another production will do himself more honor and perhaps add a laurel to his country. I have the honor to be Yr. Most obdt. serv.

SAML B H JUDAH[2]

RC (DLC: Rives Collection, Madison Papers). Addressed by Judah to JM at Washington, and franked; redirected to Orange Court House. Docketed by JM.

1. Samuel B. H. Judah, *Odofriede: The Outcast; A Dramatic Poem* (New York, 1822; Shoemaker 9173).

2. Samuel Benjamin Helbert Judah (1799–1876), was a New York City playwright, who in addition to writing the romantic dramatic poem, *Odofriede*, wrote a number of melodramas that were produced for the stage in the early 1820s. Judah is perhaps best known for *Gotham and the Gothamites* (1823), a scurrilous satire on prominent political and social New Yorkers for which he was imprisoned (Stephen H. Norwood and Eunice G. Pollack, eds., *Encyclopedia of American Jewish History* [2 vols.; Santa Barbara, Calif., 2008], 1:539).

To Benjamin Waterhouse

DEAR SIR MONTPELLIER June 22. 1822.

I have recd. your favor of the 9th. with a copy of your Lecture on Tobacco & ardent spirits. It is a powerful dissuasion from the pernicious use of such stimulants. I had read, formerly, the first Edition of the Lecture; but have read this last also, for the sake of the additions and Notes. Its foreign translations and its reaching a fifth Edition are encouraging evidences of its usefulness; however much it be feared that the listlessness of non-labourers, and the fatigues of hard labourers, will continue to plead for the relief of intoxicating liquors, or exhilarating plants; one or other of which seem to have been in use in every age & country. As far as the use of Tobo. is a mere fashion or habit, commencing not only without but agst. a natural relish, & continued without the need of such a resort, your reasonings & warnings might reasonably be expected to be an overmatch for the pernicious indulgence. In every view your remedial efforts are highly meritorious, since they may check if they can not cure the evil, and since a partial success may excite co-operating efforts which will gradually make it compleat: and I join heartily in every wish that such may be the result.

At present Virginia is not much threatened with a speedy loss of her staple, whatever be the character really belonging, or ridiculously ascribed to it. Its culture is rather on the increase, than the decline; owing to the disposition in Europe, particularly G. B. to chew our Tobo. rather than eat our Wheat. This is not the best state of things either for them or us. I beg you to accept a renewed assurance of my esteem & friendly respects

JAMES MADISON

RC (MBCo: Benjamin Waterhouse Papers); draft (DLC). RC addressed and franked by JM to Waterhouse at Boston. Postmarked 25 June at Orange Court House. Minor differences between the copies have not been noted.

From Robert C. Foster

Dear sir, Nashville June 22d 1822

It may be deemed a trespass for a stranger to address you and that too on business of a private nature, but trust your goodness will pardon the liberty, when I say to you, I am not personally acquainted with any man in your County, and that as Guardian for some amiable orphan Children, I want information on a subject relative to their interest. Some years ago perhaps Eight or nine, John S. Woods of the County of Orange Virginia died leaving a will (which is of record here) in which he gave all his estate real & personal to the Children of James Camp who married a sister of Said Woods. By virtue of that will I have received as guardian for the children Twenty odd negroes, and recently I am advised that the records of Orange County will shew that the said John S. Woods has a claim to a negro woman and her issue. Now Sir to this particular I beg your attention; who it was that made this deed or bill of Sale and who has the negroes in possession, and any other information that may shed light on the subject: to the intent that I as guardian may do my duty in obtaining said negro or negroes if they be the property of Said Children.

I assure you Sir I feel great delicacy in addressing you on this subject but beleiving the man who with so much dignity filled the first office in this great republic will not on returning to the peaceful abode of private life think himself exempt from assisting the *Fatherless children.*

Should it not be convenient for you to give this business personal attention, please hand this letter to some friend who would attend to the business. Respectfully Yr Mo Obt Servt

Robt. C. Foster[1]

RC (ViU: Madison Papers, Special Collections). Docketed by JM.

1. Robert Coleman Foster (1769–1844) was a prominent Nashville lawyer who also served terms in both houses of the Tennessee General Assembly (J. Wooldridge, ed., *History of Nashville, Tenn.* . . . [1890; reprint, Nashville, Tenn., [1970], 516; Smith et al., *Papers of Andrew Jackson,* 1:394 n. 2).

From Julius A. Bingham

Dr. Sir Rockville Md June 24th 1822

In presenting to the people of the United States, p[r]oposals for so important a work as the one which is here enclosed, I have thought it no less prudent than Respectful to make the objects known, in the commencement, to those who have born a conspicuous part in the fo[r]mation and administration of ower Goverment. Under this imp[r]ession, Sir, I have taken the liberty to address a prospectus to you,[1] and to State that an expression of your views Respecting it, will be *truly* gratifying, and may be beneficial to me. With Sentiments of high esteem, Sir, your friend

J. A. Bingham[2]

RC (DLC). Docketed by JM. Filed under 24 June 1811 in the *Index to the James Madison Papers*.

1. J. B. Colvin, *Prospectus of a New Work. Presidents' Speeches, &c. . . . To be Edited for the Publishers by J. B. Colvin . . .* (Rockville, Md., 1822; Shoemaker 8404). Advertised by J. A. Bingham in the *Baltimore Patriot & Mercantile Advertiser*, 10 July 1822. JM's copy is in the Madison Collection, Rare Book and Special Collections Division, Library of Congress.

2. Julius A. Bingham was the publisher of the Rockville, Md., *True American*, from 1820 until at least 1824. Thereafter he moved to Portsmouth, Ohio, where he published the *Western Times*, 1827–31, but left Portsmouth to found the village of Oak Hill, Ohio, in 1832, where he ran a country store (Brigham, *American Newspapers*, 1:269; Eugene B. Willard et al., eds., *A Standard History of the Hanging Rock Iron Region of Ohio . . .* [2 vols.; Marceline, Mo., 1916], 1:186–87, 486).

From James Maury

My dear Sir, Liverpool 24th June 1822

This is merely for the pleasure of inclosing a News paper, in which you will find that the bill for opening intercourse with the United States & the British Colonies has been passed in the Upper House also.[1] How many things have we lived to see come to pass, which, in this country have for ages been considered next to impossible! And this one of them. I rejoice with you on this thing being in a train of so soon terminating as (I have been told) you anticipated.

I do indeed Sir, beg pardon for so short a letter but it so happens that, at this juncture, I can only add my best respects & wishes to you & the ladies. Your old obliged friend

J. Maury

RC (DLC). Docketed by JM.

1. Great Britain's West Indian and American Trade Act, which became law on 24 July 1822, "permitted the importation of certain enumerated articles into certain enumerated ports in the British colonies in North America and the West Indies" (Benns, "Study No. 56: The American Struggle for the British West India Carrying-Trade," *Indiana University Studies* 10 [1923]: 83). For all the provisions of the act and reaction to its passage in the United States, see ibid., 83–86.

To Samuel B. H. Judah

SIR June 28. 1822

I have recd. & looked over the poem accompanying your favor of the 14th. Altho' candor will not permit me to bestow on it, unqualified praise, justice requires that I should not say less than that it exhibits a strength of thought & flights of genius, which time & taste may render worthy of the poetic rank to which the youthful author aspires. With respects & good wishes

J.M.

Draft (DLC).

From William T. Barry

DEAR SIR LEXINGTON KENTUCKY 30th. June 1822

A fiew days ago I sent you by the Mail a printed Circular;[1] the object of which is to gain information as to the best plan of establishing Schools & Acadamies for the education of the youth of Kentucky. The importance of the subject must be my apology for this liberty. I was reluctant to intrude upon your leisure or to tax your time; nor is it wished that our application to you for information should occasion you any particular trouble; if the subject of Education has heretofore engaged your attention, and you have fixed on any plan, your opinion would be highly useful; indeed any the smallest suggestion that you may think proper to make will have weight with the people of Kentucky, as comeing from one of the enlightened founders of our republic, who is loved & admired for his private and public virtues. Although a large majority of our citizens are friendly to the cause of education, yet there are many in our Legislative counsels who will oppose any general system—especially when it requires large appropriations of money out of the treasury. The sanction of your name will assist us in the effort that is now makeing in Kentucky. By uncommon exertions we have been enabled thus far to preserve & cherish our University at this place: if we can succeed in establishing common Schools & Acadamies, so as to display their advantages, there will be no danger of the peoples preserveing them ever after. We are a young people, and are fully sensible of the advantages that older states have over us in the means of education. It is hoped that when these advantages are enjoyed; and when our people combine Surperior intelligence, with their known zeal & ardent patriotism, that Kentucky will at no distant day attain what she aspires to, a character equal to that of her sister republics.

Allow me Sir to avail myself of this occasion to express the sentiments of friendship I have for you & the gratitude I feel in common with my countrymen, for the distinguished services you have rendered your country. I beg that you will present me respectfully to Mrs. Madison. That you may both continue to enjoy health & happiness is the sincere wish of your Obdt. Humbl. Sert.

W.T. Barry[2]

RC (DLC). Docketed by JM.

1. For the circular, see William T. Barry and others to JM, 13 Mar. 1822, and n.

2. William Taylor Barry (1784–1835), was born in Virginia, graduated from the College of William and Mary in 1803, and began the practice of law in Lexington, Kentucky, in 1805. He served numerous terms in the Kentucky legislature, beginning in 1807, as well as in the U.S. House of Representatives, 1810–11, and the U.S. Senate, 1814–16. He was lieutenant governor of Kentucky, 1820–24, and as such, headed a committee investigating the public school systems of other states. The Barry Report recommended a system of free public schooling for all the state's children. He was postmaster general in the administration of Andrew Jackson, 1829–35, and died in Liverpool, England, on his way to assume his post as U.S. minister to Spain (John E. Kleber et al., eds., *The Kentucky Encyclopedia* [Lexington, Ky., 1992], 55–56).

To Julius A. Bingham

Sir — Montpr. July 1. 1822

I have recd. your letter of the 24. Ul. with it a Copy of the prospectus to which it relates.

The collective form in which the proposed Documents are to be printed, will doubtless be a recommendation of the work. But most of them have been so often before the public in other forms that the success of the publication might be questionable without an interesting addition of original matter. This addition it appear[s] is to be made under the head of "illustrative notes;["] and if executed with the ability & information to be expected, may give a historical value to the work, rendering it extensively acceptable. Be pleased to forward the two copies of it whenever issued from the press.

Draft (DLC).

To Thomas Ritchie

Dr. Sir Montpr. July 2. 1822

I recd. some time ago a letter from Mr. H. G. Spafford at Ballston Spa N.Y. in which he says "I wish your Booksellers would encourage me to write a Gazetteer of Virga. I could travel all over the State, collect materials, & prepare the work for the press, in about 2 years on a salary of $1000 a year, & a few copies of the work."[1]

I answered that I could not undertake to judge how far a Gazetteer for the State on the plan & terms suggested would be espoused by our Printers & Booksellers: intimating at the same ⟨time?⟩ that a survey was on foot, the details & progress of which I could not tell him; & I took the liberty of referring him to you as the best source he could consult on the whole subject.

In his reply just recd. he says "As to a geography & Gazetteer of Virginia, may I ask of thee the favor to suggest the idea to Mr. Ritchie of Richmond? As soon as I shall have compleated the one of this State, say by next winter, I should like well to engage in such a work."[2]

Will you be so obliging as to drop me a line enabling me to say what may be proper to Mr. Spafford. He is I believe a worthy man, is very laborious in what he undertakes, and has executed works in N.Y. analogous to the one for which he offers himself here. He has been the author also of one if not more periodical publications. All these together would be a test of his qualifications.

I am sorry to be the occasion of any encroachment on your time especially as it may be a useless one; but apart from the introduction already made of your name, I should be at a loss for another resort equally capable of furnishing the desired information. With esteem & friendly respects

J.M.

Draft (DLC).

1. See Horatio Gates Spafford to JM, 15 Mar. 1822.
2. See Spafford to JM, 11 June 1822.

From John S. Skinner

Balt: July 3d: 1822.

A Sample of tobacco—such as has been sold recently in the Baltimore Market at $35. per Cwt: with the best respects of your obedt Sert.

The Editor of the American Farmer.

RC (DLC). Addressed by Skinner to JM "late President U.S. Orange Court House," and franked. Docketed by JM: "Skinner, J. S." On a slip of paper adhered to the middle of Skinner's letter is an undated draft of JM's reply, the RC of which is printed at 20 July 1822.

To Edward Livingston

Dear Sir Montpellier July 10. 1822.

I was favored some days ago with your letter of May 19. accompanied by a copy of your Report to the Legislature of the State on the subject of a Penal Code.

I should commit a tacit injustice if I did not say that the Report does great honor to the talents & sentiments of the Author. It abounds with Ideas of conspicuous value, and presents them in a manner equally elegant & persuasive.

The reduction of an entire code of Criminal Jurisprudence into Statutory provisions, excluding a recurrence to foreign or traditional codes, & substituting for technical terms, more familiar ones with or without explanatory notes, can not but be viewed as a very arduous task. I sincerely wish your execution of it may fulfil every expectation.

I can not deny at the same time, that I have been accustomed to doubt the practicability of giving the desired simplicity to so complex a subject, without involving a discretion, inadmissable in free govt; to those who are to expound and apply the law. The rules & usages which make part of the law tho' to be found only in elementary treatises, in respectable Commentaries, and in adjudged cases, seem to be too numerous & too various to be brought within the requisite compass; even if there were less risk of creating uncertainties by defective abridgments, or by the change of Phraseology.

This risk would seem to be particularly incident to a substitution of new words & definitions for a technical language, the meaning of which had been settled by long use, and authoritative expositions. Where a technical term may express a very simple idea, there might be no inconveniency or rather an advantage in exchanging it for a more familiar synonime [*sic*], if a precise one could be found. But where the technical terms & phrases have a complex import, not otherwise to be reduced to clearness and certainty than by practical applications of them, it might be unsafe to introduce new terms & phrases, though aided by brief explanations. The whole law expressed by single terms, such as "Trial, jury, evidence & &c." fill volumes when unfolded into the details which enter into their meaning.

I hope it will not be thought that by this intimation of my doubts, I wish to damp the enterprize from which you have not shrunk. On the contrary I not only wish that you may overcome all the difficulties which occur to me; but am persuaded that if compleat success should not reward your labours, there is ample room for improvements in the criminal jurisprudence of Louisiana, as elsewhere, which are well worthy the exertion of your best Powers, and which will furnish useful examples to other members of the Union. Among the advantages distinguishing our Compound Government, it is not the least, that it affords so many opportunities & chances in the local Legislatures, for salutary innovations by some which may be adopted by others; or for important experiments, which, if unsuccessful, will be of limited injury, and may even prove salutary as beacons to others. Our Political System is found also to have the happy merit of exciting a laudable emulation among the States composing it, instead of the enmity marking competitions among Powers wholly alien to each other.

I observe with particular pleasure the view you have taken of the immunity of Religion from Civil Jurisdiction, in every case where it does not trespass on private rights or the public peace. This has always been a favorite point with me: and it was not with my approbation, that the deviation from it took place in Congress when they appointed Chaplains to be paid from the national Treasury. It would have been a much better proof to their Constituents of their pious feelings, if the members had contributed for the purpose, a pittance from their own pockets. As the precedent is not likely to be rescinded, the best that ⟨can⟩ now be done may be, to apply to the Constitution, the maxim of the law, de minimis non curat.[1]

There has been another deviation from the strict principle, in the Executive Proclamations of fasts and festivals; so far at least as they have spoken the language of *injunction*, or have lost sight of the equality of *all* Religious Sects in the eye of the Constitution. Whilst I was honored with the Executive Trust, I found it necessary on more than one occasion to follow the example of predecessors. But I was always careful to make the Proclamations absolutely indiscriminate, and merely recommendatory; or rather mere *designations* of a day, on which all who thought proper might *unite* in consecrating it to religious purposes, according to their own faith & forms.[2] In this sense, I presume, you reserve to the Government a right to *appoint* particular days for religious worship throughout the State; without any particular[3] sanction *enforcing* the worship. I know not what may be the way of thinking on this subject in Louisiana. I should suppose the

Catholic portion of the people at least, as a small and even unpopular Sect in the U. S., would rally, as they did in Virginia, when religious liberty was a Legislative topic, to its broadest principle.

Notwithstanding the general progress made within the two last Centuries in favor of this branch of liberty, and the full establishment of it, in some parts of our Country, there remains in others, a strong bias towards the old error, that without some sort of alliance or coalition between Government & Religion, neither can be duly supported. Such indeed is the tendency to such a Coalition, and such its corrupting influence on both the parties, that the danger can not be too carefully guarded against. And in a Government of opinion, like ours, the only effectual guard must be found in the soundness & stability of the general opinion on the subject. Every new & successful example therefore of a perfect separation between ecclesiastical & Civil matters is of importance. And I have no doubt that every new example will succeed, as every past one has done, in shewing that Religion & Govt. will both exist in greater purity, the less they are mixed together. It was the belief of all Sects at one time that the establishment of Religion by law was right & necessary; that the true Religion ought to be established in exclusion of all others; and that the only question to be decided was, which was the true Religion. The example of Holland proved that a toleration of Sects dissenting from the established Sect, was safe and even useful. The example of the Colonies now States, which rejected Religious establishments altogether, proved that all Sects might be safely & advantageously put on a footing of equal & entire freedom. And a continuance of their example since the Declaration of Independence has shewn, that its success in Colonies was not to be ascribed to their connection with the parent Country. If a further confirmation of the truth could be wanted, it is to be found in the examples furnished by the States which have abolished their religious Establishments. I can not speak particularly of any of the cases excepting that of Virginia, where it is impossible to deny that Religion prevails with more zeal, and a more exemplary priesthood, than it ever did when established and patronized by Public authority. We are teaching the World the great truth, that Governments do better without Kings & Nobles than with them. The merit will be doubled by the other lesson, that Religion flourishes in greater purity, without than with the aid of Government.

My pen, I perceive, has rambled into reflections for which it was not taken up. I recall it to the proper object of thanking you for your very interesting pamphlet, and of tendering you my respects & good wishes.

James Madison

RC (NjP: Edward Livingston Papers); draft (DLC). Beneath his initials on the draft, JM drafted a letter to John R. Livingston, dated 11 July 1822: "J.M. presents his respects to

Mr. Livingston and requests the favor of him to forward the above enclosed letter to N. Orleans or to retain it as his brother may or not be expected at N. York." Minor differences between the copies have not been noted.

1. *De minimis non curat lex:* "the law does not concern itself with trifles" (*Black's Law Dictionary* [9th ed.], 496).

2. During his presidency, JM issued proclamations declaring particular days of public prayer on 9 July 1812, 23 July 1813, 16 Nov. 1814, and 4 Mar. 1815: each was in response to a congressional request (*PJM-PS*, 4:581–82, 6:458–59; *Annals of Congress*, 13th Cong., 3d sess., 1828–29; *Daily National Intelligencer*, 6 Mar. 1815). For a similar warning against religious proclamations by the executive branch, see JM's "Detatched Memoranda," ca. 31 Jan. 1820, *PJM-RS*, 1:615–17.

3. In draft, JM wrote "penal."

To George Tucker

Dr. Sir July 15. 1822.

I recd. some days ago your letter of May 16, accompanied by the volume of Essays which you caused to be forwarded by Mr. Milligan.

I have not been able to give the work more than a very hasty perusal. But I think myself warranted in saying that it contains much valuable matter: and that as a literary performance, it will be among the best answers to the charge of our national deficiency in that particular.

I thank you Sir for the opportunity you have given me of perusing the Essays, & pray you to be assured of my esteem & great respect.

Draft (DLC).

From Frederick D. Tschiffely

Respected Sir, Orange Court House, 15 July 1822.

Be pleased to receive my present application with the Kindness, that charact[er]ises you.

Put into Office by Mr. Gallatin at a salary of $310. per an. I rose gradually to one of $1,400, in the General Land Office.

On the 15 of March 1821, I was deprived of that situation, seven children & a wife, left albut without the means of subsistence.

I was Dismissed by the order of the Hon. Wm. H. Crawford— after nearly 12 years of service in the public Offices.

No reason, no cause ever alledged for my Dismissal!

I have been for too long a time travelling over the United States in pursuit of bread. I have not succeeded—& for six weeks past I am travelling, penny less, starving albut, & subsisting on the goodness of humane men. My shoes even won't carry me farther.

If possible, I want to reach Charlottesville, where I understand a Seminary is to be established, & where I wish to be employed as a teacher of the french, & german languages—Arithmetic, Geography &c.

If respected Sir, you would & with shame do I beg it (for never heretofore was I put to such an extremity) assist me with a trifle, to buy shoes, & to enable me to reach Charlottesville, I will thank you. Mr. Wirt has all my most important papers in his possession yet; I was not at home 8 days ago, as my son writes me, or else I could satisfactorily prove what I have advanced. Begging Your pardon for this intrusion, I have the honor to be, very respectfully, Sir, your most obdt serv

F. D. Tschiffely[1]

RC (DLC). Addressed by Tschiffely to JM "Present." Docketed by JM.

1. Frederick D. Tschiffely (ca. 1780–1839), a native of Switzerland and a government clerk, was granted naturalization in Washington in 1814. In 1821 he advertised his services as a French and German teacher and translator in Washington newspapers. By 1823 he and his wife had opened Minerva Academy, a school for boys and girls, in Charleston, South Carolina (Oak Hill Cemetery Burial Records, Georgetown, D.C., http://www.oakhillcemeterydc.org/Burials/226.pdf; *ASP, Miscellaneous*, 2:309; Michael Tepper, ed., *New World Immigrants: A Consolidation of Ship Passenger Lists . . .* [2 vols.; Baltimore, 1979], 2:260; *Washington Gazette*, 22 Mar. 1821; Charleston *City Gazette and Commercial Daily Advertiser*, 15 Mar. 1823).

From John O. Lay

Dear Sir Richmond July 17th. 1822

I have the pleasure to forward by your Brother's Waggon a Small Box of Seed which came to hand a few days since.

As I have frequent opportunities of sending to your neighborhood, it may perhaps facilitate the transportation of any articles you may wish forwarded through here, by directing them to my care, and, if so, I shall take pleasure in attending to them. I am Sir Very Respy. Your Obt. Servt

Jno. O. Lay

RC (DLC). Docketed by JM.

From William Taylor

My Dear sir City of Megico 19th. July 1822

You may have heard of the Consular Appointt. I recd. from the President of the United States to the Port of Vera Cruz.[1] I reached my Port of destination 17th April, remained there 2 days only, and then came on to this place, the Capitol of the Empire of Megico, where I have continued ever since, partly on account of the black vomit having made its appearance in Vera Cruz, and the Castle of San Juan de Ulua being still in possession of the Spaniards. As from a strong and almost irresistable desire to make myself some what acquainted with the situation of this Gouvernment, or more properly speaking—with those who are attempting to establish a Gouvernement &c.

I have now been in this City since the first day of May, have mixed a good-deal in society, and from information obtained, and my own Observations, have drawn the following Conclusions. That Iturbidie[2] had an oppy. to transmit his name to posterity as the Washington of his Country, by the establishment of a Republican form of Gouvernment, and the free exercise of Religious Opinions. This line of Conduct wch. was marked out to him by the voice of the People would, not only have secured to him their blessings, and benedictions, but have saved his Country from the worst of all evils—the Scourge of Civil War. But of the millions who have gone before us—who have appeared, flourish'd, and disappeared, how few, how very few have had their names recorded in History as the benefactors of mankind.

Self aggrandisement seems to have been [the] sole object of Iturbidie, and he has pursued, and obtained it, tho' at the expense of the dearest, and best interests of his Country. Yet his Course will have been that of a passing meteor. Already discontent and murmurings are heard in his very household. Two Regiments without their Officers, save one S [3] named Pio Marcha, made him Emperor. Two Other Regiments in the same tumultuous manner threaten to pull him down. The inteligent and wealthy, are opposed to him. The honorable part of the Army are opposed to him. The City Rabble support him. The Clergy, generally speaking, support him—'tis a common saying, that the Bishop of Peubla, made him. The plan of the Usurpation, is admitted to have Originated with the Bishop. There are however many of the Clergy Opposed to him. The Arch Bishop, would neither Crown him, nor sanction his being Crowned, & on this subject, it is said, wrote a Circular to the Bishops threatening them with the Popes displeasure, if they attempted to Crown Iturbidie. Nevertheless the day after to morrow, Sunday the 21st. inst, is fixed upon for the Coronation to take place. Many look forward to that day as the commencement of a strife that will again deluge this country with Blood. I could scarcely Credit the fact, did I not have it from the best authority, that upwards of 200,000 Mexicans have already lost their lives in the recent civil wares, in this Country, the Commencement of wch. they date as far back as 1810. I have recd. a written invitation to the Coronation, wch. I shall certainly accept, as I would not miss the Shew on any account whatever. At the same time, I trust in God, to see not only the base bauble itself, but the still baser wretch who dares to grasp it, dashed to the ground, and trampled under foot. And yet this man has his flatterers, his vile flatterers, and with shame be it spoken, that the foremost, should be a Citizen of the U.S. one who fought hard through the Revolutionary War, in defense of the liberties of his own Country, and has since been Conspicuous as the leader of her Armies, but he is now old, diseased, and infirm, and for his past services, reputed great, I forbear to name his name.[4]

Our latest advices are down to the 28 April only. Consequently we have yet to learn the decision of Congress respecting the Recognition Of the Independe. of this Country—as a Gouvernment separate & distinct from that of Spain.

Mr Ilysolda[5] the Gentleman first appointed as the minister from this Gouvernt. to the UStates, declined the Appointt. 7th June last. Mr Sosaya[6] has very recently been appointed in his Stead, and will probably leave here early in August for the U States. This Gentleman is said to be a Lawyer of some Talents but speaks neither English, nor French, has never been out of his Country, much through it, in her Counsels, or held any office of honor, or trust, under preceding Gouvernments. He has been further represented to me as possessing more intrigue than Talent, more cunning than principle.

Mr. Azcarate[7] the Minister to the Court of Saint James—is likewise a Lawyer, & said to be at the head of his profession here. He is a great Gambler, and firm friend to Despotism—speaks neither English, nor French.

This Country, this Kingdom of New Spain, which the good Citizens of the United States are prone to believe one solid mass of Gold, and silver, intersperced here, and there with beds of Jewels, and Other precious Stones—is miserably poor, and in a most deplorable Situation. The more respectable Citizens seldom walk the Streets, except to some neighbouring church to hear Mass. The multitude who usually throng & Croud the side walks, are so filthy and numerous withal, that not to come in contact with them occasionally, is morally impossible. On these occasions the Stranger, as a mere matter of course, puts his hand to that part of his dress touched, or rubbed against to, brush away the Vermin. In the whole course of my life I never saw so many beggars—witnessed so much real misery as since my arrival in this celebrated City of the Montezumas.

The people are idle, and averse to labour. The Army, and Officers of Gouvernment, are numerous as locusts; hungry as starved Wolves. The Treasury is void. The Key to the Empire on the Atlantic Side, (V.C.) in the hands of their enemies. The sources of commerce dried up. The mines not worked (enclosed is a statement of the money coined here since 1802).[8] No revenue, no regular System of Taxation. Forced loans resorted to, & the proceeds appropriated to the sole use of the Emperor & his satellites. Agents have been sent hence to Europe for the purpose of borrowing in France Ten millions of Dollars, in England Ten millions of Dollars. And they would fain borrow the sum of Ten millions of Dolls more in the UStates. The Secretary of State, Mr José Manuel Herrera[9] (A Priest who resided some time in Louisiana fitting out Expeditions against the then Gouvernmt. of Texas, and drawing on the Patriot Chief Genl. Gaudaloupe Victoria[10] for the expences attending the same, but which Bills were never paid. Such of our Citizens as were induced to embark in these expeditions, have been generally destroyed. The few who survive, are Shunned, neglected, and frowned upon. Genl. Long[11] their leader, formerly a Lieut. in the U.S.A. in attempting to visit some friends who dwelt in a House, at the Door of wch. a Sentinel was placed, (officers lodging within) and not Speaking the Language, was first Struck by the Sentinel and then pursued 15 a 20 steps & shot dead. The Sentinel has undergone no trial, no examination. I mention these facts, not to excite your Sympathy for these unfortunate men, but to shew the determination of this Gouvernment to destroy, or drive out of the Country men who, whatever vices they may possess, are nevertheless firm friends, warm advocates for a Republican form of Gouvernt.

The Individuals of N.O. who took Herrera's Bills—or in other words who advanced him money &c. have been nearly ruined by the total disregard of this Gouvernment to his Contracts. Among the Sufferers A. L. Duncan[12] Esqe with whose name you may be some what familiar, is most conspicuous—being a Creditor to the Amount of *200,000* Dollars.

The Advanc[e]s made to Mina[13] in Balto. And N.O. will nett a total loss, unless indeed, those concerned should consent to liquidate their Claims by Concessions or Grants of Land in the Province of Tegas—has already spoken to me on the proba[bi]lity of obtaining a Loan in the U. States. I replied that provided our merchants could have the necessary Confidence in the Stability of this Gouvernment, I did not believe there would be any difficulty in getting the Sum required—but gave him no encouragement to make the experiment.

Monday morning the 22nd.

The Coronation of their Majesties is over—it took place yesterday in the Cathedral, all *threats*, *menaces*, and evil *forebodings* to the contrary, notwithstanding. The Cathedral is a very Spacious building, capable of holding 8 a 9000 persons, nevertheless, on this occasion there were not more than *3,000* present, a pretty strong proof that the coronation was not much relished. The greatest order, however, prevailed during the whole ceremony, which commenced at 10. oClock in the morning, and lasted until 3 oClock in the afternoon. The President of Congress, if indeed, may so call a Body of cold *blooded*, miserable wretches, whose Servile, and Submissive Conduct cannot prevent their being soon Kicked out of Doors, & sent to their respective provinces in less than 6 weeks—Crowned the Emperor, who received the *precious gift* Kneeling—& Who then with his Own hands, placed another Crown on the head of his wife. It was to me a most tiresome pantomime, for altho' I was well situated to see yet I could not hear one word that was said; except the conclusion of the Bishop of Peubla's Sermon, wch. closed the Ceremony. Long live the Emperor—words that were repeated by 2 or 3 voices only—and these in so faint a tone of voice, as could not have been heard, but for the death like Silence that reigned throughout the Cathedral. I remarked that those who sat near me, after the first hour had gone by, seemed more intent with their own big thoughts, than the Coronation. Many fell into the Arms of old Morpheus, and our own General James Wilkinson who had accompanied me there in the full uniform Dress of a Major General of the United Army—enjoyed two very good naps. Notwithstanding this, I expect you will see published in Duane's paper, or some paper of N.O. a most pompous descriptions [*sic*] of the Coronation. I had permission to take with me such of my countrymen as were then in this City & mustered in all 16—add to these the Ministers Azcáraté, and Sosaya, with their Secretaries of Legation called for me at my Lodgings.

I scarce need inform you, my dear sir, that these pointed attentions were neither offered to, nor received by me as my right. As they were offered, I thought it my duty to accept them and did so, under the full beleif that I could not thereby in the smallest degree whatever, Commit the Gouvernment of the United States.

A Gouvernt. like this founded upon violence, will Catch at any thing that can give the least Countenance to its Usurpation, &c.

The coins of this country have undergone a total change. The head of Iturbidie has Supplanted that of Ferdinand the 7th. I regret this Change, as the hard dollars of old Spain, constituted the only solid part of her System. *Medals* to the Amount of *12000 Dollars* were thrown to the Crowd in front of the Cathedral. I enclose you one.

I understand that General Davila[14] commanding the Castle of San Juan de Ulua has recd from his master the King of Spain the Commission of Captain General of Mexico—& the famous Callava,[15] of Pensacola memory, is to take command of the Castle—there is no Jackson here to frighten him away.

Friday August 2nd.

All here has been confusion & alarm for the last several days. Genl Gaudeloupe has certainly raised the Republican Standard in the neighbourhood of Halapa, with what force, can't well be ascertained—3,000 horse left this City 4 days ago in pursuit of him—from what I can learn he is not in a situation to meet this force—& will therefore have to retreat to his inaccessable mountains. There is reports of risings in other Provinces. Certain it is that ere long this Country will be the Scene of a dreadful Civil War. On the night of the 31. ulto. Sérgeant—now Captain Marcha of Regiment No 1, of wch. Iturbidie always has been, & still is the Colonel—made an attempt to Close the Doors of Congress—and Disperse that Body—but was foiled—that it will take place ere long, and the Inquisition be reestablished, seems to be the general beleif, unless the present order of things be destroyed.

I have this day given a Letter of Introduction to you, to Mr Vt. Rocofuerte,[16] a Gentleman from Guyaquil near Lyma a great enthusiast in the Cause of Liberty, of liberal Education & great wealth, and able to give you much useful information respecting this Country.

I by no means wish any part of this Communication made publick—it would injure me not a little were it Known here that I had written such truths. If however, you should consider any of the facts worth communicating, you may make them Known to your neighbours Gouvernor—& P. P. Barbours Esquire. It is by no means a highly wrought picture of the State of this Country, but a fair statement of facts.

I beg you will make my respectful remembrance to Mrs Madison—to my much respected relative yr mother, & if not too troublesome, to my Other relatives in yr neighbourhood. I am Dr sir, with every wish for yr health & happiness Yr friend & obt. h. St.

William Taylor

RC and enclosure (DLC). RC docketed by JM. For enclosure, see n. 8.

1. Taylor was given a recess appointment as consul. He was nominated by the president in his message of 2 Jan. 1823 and was confirmed by the Senate on 28 Jan. 1823 (*Senate Exec. Proceedings*, 3:318, 319, 325, 328).

2. Agustín de Iturbide (1783–1824), born in Morelia, Mexico, was a leader of Spanish royalist forces in the War of Independence. But political events in Spain in 1820 led him to propose a plan for Mexican independence that united disparate elements of the populace, and he entered Mexico City on 27 Sept. 1821. Crowned emperor in 1822, he abdicated in March 1823 and was forced into exile in Europe. Returning to Mexico in 1824, he was executed for treason (Marvin Alisky, *Historical Dictionary of Mexico*, 2d ed. [Lanham, Md., 2008], 282; Michael C. Meyer and William H. Beezley, eds., *The Oxford History of Mexico* [New York, 2000], 301–5, 316).

3. Left blank in text; Taylor referred to the rank, "sergeant."

4. James Wilkinson.

5. The minister, Juan Manuel de Elizalda, had been appointed by October 1821 but resigned because of bad health (Joseph Carl McElhannon, "Relations between Imperial

Mexico and the United States, 1821–1823," in Thomas E. Cotner, ed., *Essays in Mexican History* [Austin, Tex., 1958], 131–32, 134).

6. José Manuel Bermúdez Zozaya was chosen Mexican minister to the United States in early 1822, but his nomination was not confirmed until September. He was officially received by President Monroe on 12 Dec. 1822. Zozaya left the United States in May 1823, after being informed of the fall of the Mexican imperial government (ibid., 134–39).

7. Juan Francisco Azcárate y Lezama (1767–1831) was a Mexico City lawyer and a leader in the movement for Mexican independence. He was named Mexican minister to Great Britain, but the emperor Iturbide was deposed before Azcárate could take up his duties (María del Carmen Rovira, comp., *Pensamiento filosófico mexicano del siglo XIX y primeros años del XX* [3 vols.; Mexico City, 1998–2001], 1:123).

8. The enclosure (1 p.) is an "Account of the coinage of the Mint of Mexico from the Year 1802 to the Year 1821 inclusive, furnished by Dn. José Mariana Pavia, July 1822." The coinage is broken down into gold, silver, and copper.

9. José Manuel Herrera (1776–1831), an early leader of the independence movement, was chosen to represent the Congress movement in Washington but seems never to have presented his credentials. He arrived in New Orleans in October 1815 and planned filibustering expeditions in association with José Álvarez de Toledo y Dubois. In 1816 he occupied Galveston Island, declaring it part of independent Mexico. He served as foreign minister in the reign of Iturbide and in other offices under President Vicente Guerrero in 1829 (José Rogelio Álvarez, ed., *Enciclopedia de México* [12 vols.; Mexico City, 1966–77], 6:833; Herrera to JM, 1 Mar. 1816, *Diplomatic Correspondence of the United States Concerning the Independence of the Latin-American Nations*, 3:1598–99; J. C. A. Stagg, *Borderlines in Borderlands: James Madison and the Spanish-American Frontier, 1776–1821* [New Haven, Conn., 2009], 179–80; Donald E. Chipman and Harriett Denise Joseph, *Spanish Texas, 1519–1821*, 2d ed. [Austin, Tex., 2010], 252).

10. Guadalupe Victoria (1786–1843), christened Juan Manuel Félix Fernández, was a general of insurgent forces, who fought for Mexican independence. He was president of Mexico, 1824–28 (Alisky, *Historical Dictionary of Mexico*, 2d ed., 543).

11. James Long (ca. 1793–1822), a veteran of the War of 1812, and a onetime merchant in Natchez, launched a filibustering expedition into Mexico from Nacogdoches, where he had declared an independent Texas republic with himself as president on 23 June 1819. In 1820 he joined forces with José Trespalacios, a Mexican revolutionary, and in March 1822 found himself in Mexico City, where he was killed by a sentry on 8 Apr. 1822.

12. Abner L. Duncan (d. 1823) was a prominent New Orleans lawyer. He had been a volunteer aide at the Battle of New Orleans (Smith et al., *Papers of Andrew Jackson*, 4:24 n.).

13. Francisco Javier Mina (1789–1817) was a Spanish guerilla leader during the Peninsular War in Spain. In 1816 he sailed from England to Baltimore, where he raised money, enlisted soldiers, and purchased supplies and ships for an expedition against the royalists in Mexico. He also visited Galveston, Texas, and New Orleans on his way. Mina landed in Mexico in April 1817 and soon thereafter launched his offensive. Taken captive in late October of that year, Mina was executed on 11 Nov. 1817 (*The History of Mexico*, vol. 4, [1885], in *The Works of Hubert Howe Bancroft*, [39 vols.; San Francisco, Calif., 1882–90], 659, 660 n. 2, 661 and n. 5, 662–82).

14. José Davila was the commander of the royalist fortress of San Juan de Ulúa in Veracruz, Mexico, which did not capitulate until 1825 (Meyer and Beezley, *Oxford History of Mexico*, 318–19).

15. José Maria Callava was the last governor of West Florida, 1819–21, and as such, presided over its transfer to the United States in 1821 (Smith et al., *Papers of Andrew Jackson*, 6:250 n. 8). For Callava's dispute with Andrew Jackson, which led to his imprisonment for one night, see Remini, *Andrew Jackson and the Course of American Empire, 1767–1821*, 410–17.

16. Vicente Rocafuerte (1783–1847), an advocate of South American independence, was president of Ecuador, 1835–39. Rocafuerte spent several months in New York City in 1823 (Albert William Bork and Georg Maier, *Historical Dictionary of Ecuador* [Metuchen, N.J., 1973], 128; Middletown, Conn., *Middlesex Gazette and General Advertiser*, 30 Oct. 1823).

To John S. Skinner

Dear Sir — Montpellier July 20. 1822

The sample of yellow Tobo. you were so good as to send came safe to hand. I have delayed my thanks in the hope that I might be able to return a leaf of the highest priced produced from the Virga. soil. In this I have been disappointed, all of that description in the Neighbourhood having been sent to Market. I regret it the less however, as you have probably been otherwise enabled to notice the contrast.

When you can snatch a moment to intimate my debt to the very valuable work you superintend[1] it shall be paid.With much esteem & friendly respects

James Madison

RC (owned by Butterfield & Butterfield, Los Angeles, Calif., 1997); draft (DLC). RC addressed and franked by JM to Skinner at Baltimore. Docketed by Skinner, with his note: "ansd.—Tobacco Sent." The undated draft is adhered to Skinner to JM, 3 July 1822.

1. Skinner was the editor of the Baltimore *American Farmer*.

From James Maury

Dear Sir, — Liverpool 20 July 1822

On the 24th Ulto I had the pleasure of presenting you a news paper, announcing the passage, in the Upper House, of a bill opening intercourse between the United States & the British Colonies in the vessells of each nation, which bill of course has become law.

On the 2d instant I had the honor to receive your letter of the 23d May; and it is indeed with pleasure that I see you had preferred the home, to a foreign, Market for your Tobaccoe, because I am pretty sure we could not have done as well for you here.

My eldest son,[1] who was in the United States several years ago, lately returned thither; and should he happen to be in your part of the country, I hope he will have the opportunity of paying his respects to you: this poor fellow, from a very early period of life & during a great portion of it had been so afflicted with nervous affections as to preclude the opportunities of improvement, of which he otherwise would have been availed: this, added to a certain timidity, makes him appear to great disadvantage; but he is amiable & good: if you meet with him, may I recommend him to your friendly notice?

My son William hopes for the pleasure of revisiting you before long.

I pray you, the ladies & Mr Todd to accept my best wishes & regards. I hope my antient friend your good venerable parent still is in the enjoyment of comfortable health. I am your obliged friend & faithful servant

JAMES MAURY

RC (DLC).

1. James Sifrein Maury (1797–1864) immigrated to Virginia in 1815 and returned to England in 1819. He went back to Virginia in 1822 and began farming a plantation called Ridgemont near Charlottesville, Virginia, which he sold in 1833. He died unmarried in New York (Maury, *Intimate Virginiana*, 53–55, 57, 59–60, 64, 69 n., 319).

¶ From Lewis Deblois. Letter not found. *23 July 1822*. Acknowledged in JM to Deblois, 19 Aug. 1822, and calendared as a two-page letter in the lists probably made by Peter Force (DLC, series 7, box 2).

From John S. Skinner

DEAR SIR BALTO 3d Augt 1822

I have had an oppy of making the contrast of Virga & Maryd Tobaccoes, thru the politeness of the Inspector at Lynchburg, who Stated that the enclosed dark sample was sold at 12 50/100 ℔ 100 lb. and the bright sample* at 8$ ℔ 100 lb. I exhibited both leaves to our Balto dealers at our chief ware House, and for the dark, under the impression that it was Maryland Tobo., they offered only 3½ to 4$—for the bright provided that in the Hhd was not bruised, as the leaf appd by the spots on it, to have been, they would give 18 to 20$ ℔ 100 lb: whether these spots were occasioned by bruises I cannot tell, but I doubt it.

In our Md Hhds of 48 inches by 35, we compress 700 to 1000 lbs of dark or heavy Tobacco, but only 500 to 600 lbs of bright, light quality; this, we fear to bruize. With great respect Truly Yours,

J S SKINNER

RC (DLC). Addressed by Skinner to JM, and franked. Docketed by JM.

* raised from Maryd. Seed

To William T. Barry

DR SIR Aug. 4 1822

I recd. some days ago your letter of June 30, and the printed Circular to which it refers.

The liberal appropriations made by the Legislature of Kentucky for a general System of Education can not be too much applauded. A popular Government, without popular information, or the means of acquiring it, is but a prologue to a Farce or a Tragedy; or perhaps both. Knowlege will for ever govern ignorance: and a people who mean to be their own Governours, must arm themselves with the power which knowledge gives.

I have always felt a more than ordinary interest in the destinies of Kentucky. Among her earliest settlers were some of my particular friends and neighbours. And I was myself among the foremost advocates for submitting to the will of the "District," the question and the time of its becoming a separate member of the American family.[1] Its rapid growth & signal prosperity in this character have aforded me much pleasure; which is not a little enhanced by the enlightened patriotism which is now providing for the State a plan of Education embracing every class of Citizens, and every grade & department of knowlege. No error is more certain than the one proceeding from a hasty & superficial view of the subject, that the people at large have no interest in the establishment of Academies, Colleges, and Universities, where a few only, and those not of the poorer classes can obtain for their sons the advantages of superior education. It is thought to be unjust that all should be taxed for the benefit of a part, and that too the part least needing it.

If provision were not made at the same time for every part, the objection would be a natural one. But, besides the consideration when the higher Seminaries belong to a plan of general education, that it is better for the poorer classes to have the aid of the richer by a general tax on property, than that every parent should provide at his own expence for the education of his children, it is certain that every Class is interested in establishments which give to the human mind its highest improvements, and to every Country its truest and most durable celebrity.

Learned Institutions ought to be favorite objects with every free people. They throw that light over the public mind which is the best security against crafty & dangerous encroachments on the public liberty. They are nurseries of skilful Teachers for the schools distributed throughout the Community. They are themselves Schools for the particular talents required for some of the public Trusts, on the able execution of which the welfare of the people depends. They multiply the educated individuals from among whom the people may elect a due portion of their public agents of every description; more especially of those who are to frame the laws; by the perspicuity, the consistency, and the stability, as well as by the just & equal spirit of which the great social purposes are to be answered.

Without such Institutions, the more costly of which can scarcely be provided by individual means, none but the few whose wealth enables them to support their sons abroad, can give them the fullest education; and in proportion as this is done, the influence is monopolized which superior information every where possesses. At cheaper & nearer seats of Learning parents with slender incomes may place their sons in a course of Education putting them on a level with the sons of the richest, Whilst those who are without property, or with but little, must be peculiarly interested in a System which unites with the more Learned Institutions, a provision for diffusing through the entire Society the education needed for the common purposes of life. A System comprizing the Learned Institutions may be still further recommended to the more indigent class of Citizens by such an arrangement as was reported to the General Assembly of Virginia in the year 1779, by a Committee* appointed to revise the laws in order to adapt them to the genius of Republican Government. It made a part of a "bill for the more general diffusion of knowledge"[2] that wherever a youth was ascertained to possess talents meriting an education which his parent could not afford, he should be carried forward at the public expence from Seminary to Seminary, to the completion of his studies at the highest.

But why should it be necessary in this case, to distinguish the Society into classes according to their property? When it is considered that the establishment and endowment of Academies, Colleges, and Universities are a provision not merely for the existing generation, but for succeeding ones also; that in Governments like ours a constant rotation of property results from the free scope to industry, and from the laws of inheritance, and when it is considered moreover, how much of the exertions and privations of all are meant not for themselves, but for their posterity, there can be little ground for objections from any class, to plans of which every class must have its turn of benefits. The rich man when contributing to a permanent plan for the education of the poor, ought to reflect that he is providing for that of his own descendants; and the poor man who concurs in a provision for those who are not poor that at no distant day it may be enjoyed by descendants from himself. It does not require a long life to witness these vicisitudes of fortune.

It is among the happy peculiar[it]ies of our Union, that the States composing it derive from their relations to each other and to the whole, a salutary emulation, without the enmity involved in competitions among States alien to each other. This emulation, we may perceive, is not without its

* the report was made by Mr. Jefferson, Mr. Pendleton & Mr. Wythe

influence in several important respects; and in none ought it to be more felt than in the merit of diffusing the light and the advantages of public Instruction. In the example therefore which Kentucky is presenting, she not only consults her own welfare, but is giving an impulse to any of her Sisters who may be behind her in the noble career.

Throughout the Civilized World, nations are courting the praise of fostering Science and the useful arts, and are opening their eyes to the principles and the blessings of Representative Government. The American people owe it to themselves, and to the cause of free Government, to prove by their establishments for the advancement and diffusion of Knowlege, that their political Institutions, which are attracting observation from every quarter, and are respected as Models, by the new-born States in our own Hemisphere, are as favorable to the intellectual and moral improvement of Man, as they are conformable to his individual & social Rights. What spectacle can be more edifying or more seasonable, than that of Liberty & Learning, each leaning on the other for their mutual & surest support?

The Committee, of which your name is the first, have taken a very judicious course in endeavouring to avail Kentucky of the experience of elder States, in modifying her Schools. I inclose extracts from the laws of Virginia on that subject;[3] though I presume they will give little aid; the less as they have as yet been imperfectly carried into execution. The States where such Systems have been long in operation will furnish much better answers to many of the enquiries stated in your Circular. But after all, such is the diversity of local circumstances, more particularly as the population varies in density & sparseness, that the details suited to some may be little so to others. As the population however, is becoming less & less sparse, and it will be well in laying the foundation of a good System, to have a view to this progressive change, much attention seems due to examples in the Eastern States, where the people are most compact, & where there has been the longest experience in plans of popular education.

I know not that I can offer on the occasion any suggestions not likely to occur to the Committee. Were I to hazard one, it would be in favour of adding to Reading—Writing—& Arithmetic—to which the instruction of the poor is commonly limited, some knowledge of Geography; such as can easily be conveyed by a Globe & Maps, and a concise Geographical Grammar. And how easily & quickly might a general idea even be conveyed of the Solar System, by the aid of a Planetarium of the Cheapest Construction. No information seems better calculated to expand the mind and gratify curiosity than what would thus be imparted. This is especially the case, with what relates to the Globe we inhabit, the Nations among which it is divided, and the characters and customs which distinguish them. An acquaintance with foreign Countries in this mode, has a kindred effect with that of seeing them as travellers, which never fails, in uncorrupted minds, to weaken local prejudices, and enlarge the sphere of benevolent feelings. A knowledge of the Globe & its various inhabitants, however slight, might moreover create a taste for Books of Travels and Voyages; out of which might grow a general taste for History, an inexhaustible fund of entertainment & instruction. Any reading, not of a vicious species, must be a good substitute for the amusements too apt to fill up the leisure of the labouring classes.

I feel myself much obliged Sir by your expressions of personal kindness, and pray you to accept a return of my good wishes, with assurances of my great esteem & respect

J.M.

P.S. On reflection I omit the extracts from the laws of Virga. which it is probable may be within your reach at home. Should it be otherwise, and you think them worth the transmission by mail, the omission shall be supplied.

Draft (DLC). Printed copy in *Niles' Weekly Register* 23 (15 Feb. 1823): 376–78.

1. For JM's part in the establishment of Kentucky as a state, see "Act Concerning Statehood for the Kentucky District," 22 Dec. 1785, *PJM*, 8:450–53 and nn. 1 and 3.

2. For the work of the committee of revisors and JM's part in presenting their draft bills before the Virginia General Assembly, see Bills for a Revised State Code of Laws, Editorial Note, ibid., 391–94. For a copy of the "Bill for the More General Diffusion of Knowledge," which would have established a system of public education in Virginia, see Boyd, *Papers of Thomas Jefferson*, 2:526–33.

3. JM referred here to a copy of *Sundry Documents on the Subject of a System of Public Education, for the State of Virginia, Published by the President and Directors of the Literary Fund, in Obedience to a Resolution of the General Assembly* (Richmond, 1817; Shaw and Shoemaker 51724).

From James Monroe

Dear Sir Highland augt 4th. 1822

I have been detain'd here longer than I had expected that I should be, but hope & presume that I shall, after attending the court to morrow get as far as Judge Nelson's in the evening, & be with you tolerably early the next day.

I wish you to examine the subject between the Senate & me, respecting military nominations,[1] that we may confer on it when we meet. I send you the material papers, the report of the Committee excepted,[2] which I fear I have left at Washington. You know however the nature of that document. Very sincerely your friend & servant

James Monroe

RC (DLC). Docketed by JM.

1. For Monroe's difficulties over military appointments in the context of the reduction of the U.S. Army, see Monroe to JM, 12 May 1822.

2. The documents have not been identified, but Senate proceedings relating to the dismissals or reassignments of Nathan Towson and James Gadsden, as well as Monroe's messages on that topic, were published in the *Daily National Intelligencer*, 4 May 1822.

From Thomas Ritchie

Dr. Sir Richmond, August 7, 1822.

My own indisposition, and the melancholy succession of calamities which has befallen the family of Dr. Foushee,[1] have prevented my earlier acknowledgment of your respected favor. My wish too to oblige an interesting stranger would have prompted me to attend sooner to his application, if these circumstances had not intervened.

It is my candid opinion, that Mr. Spafford's Gazetteer for Virginia will not succeed. Virginia is of less consequence than N. York in all the points which such a work would embrace. Our country is less thickly settled. Our towns are smaller. Our counties are less visited by strangers. Fewer wish for information about her topography. Our politics have made her of some consequence—but that is possibly a fleeting glory, and it does not illuminate the pages of a dry Gazetteer. In wealth, numbers, towns, commerce, routes for travel, in political power, N. York outstrips her. Even if the work for N York is called for, and obtains success, I should not expect a nearly equal demand for one which treats of Virginia.

At home, our citizens are not a very visiting people. A trip to a town, to the springs, or to our distant friends, is all that we seek—but there are always people enough to point out the roads to these, and give us the requisite information. Such a work would seldom be called for by our own citizens.

It is true the "Notes on Virginia" have run thro' several Editions. It will always be in demand. The charms of its style, the broad field of information which it covers, and the sound philosophy of its principles, will preserve it from oblivion, and give it a general circulation. I wish sincerely Mr. Jefferson could once more take it in hand, and engraft upon it all the new facts and discoveries which have been gleaned since it was written. But he has done enough to serve his Country, and to do honor to himself.

Admitting, however, that Mr Spafford could catch the bewitching style of Mr. Jefferson, his work would be stript of many of the topics which lend attraction to the "Notes on Virginia."

I have not rested content with my own opinio⟨n⟩ in this case. I have gone to the principal bookselle⟨r⟩ in our City. It is clearly his opinion that it would not justify the expence which it would require.

At all events, should Mr. Spafford eventually determine to undertake the work, he would have ⟨to⟩ wait till the new Map of Virginia is perfected. The death of John Wood has delayed it—and no ⟨one?⟩ has yet been appointed to take his place. It is probable that the whole Map will not be engraved, before the close of the next Year.

In laying this opinion before you, Sir, permit me to avail myself of the opportunity to say with how much pleasure I would execute any commission you might entrust to me—and to add the assurances of the great respect and attachment of Yours,

Thomas Ritchie

RC (ViU: Madison Papers, Special Collections). Docketed by JM.

1. William Foushee (1749–1824), a physician and the first mayor of Richmond, was postmaster in that city from 1808 until his death. He was also a member of the influential Richmond Junto. Ritchie was married to Isabella, one of Foushee's daughters. The "calamities" referred to were the deaths of two of Foushee's daughters, Mrs. Charlotte F. Carter, and Mrs. Margaret T. Parker (*PJM*, 10:543 n. 2; Harry Ammon, "The Richmond Junto, 1800–1824," *VMHB* 61 [1953]: 395–96, 399, 403; New York *Public Advertiser*, 27 June 1808; Charleston *City Gazette and Commercial Daily Advertiser*, 9 Sept. 1824; *Richmond Enquirer*, 30 July and 6 Aug. 1822).

¶ To Thomas Jefferson. Letter not found. *8 August 1822*. Enclosed in Dolley Madison to Lewis J. Cist, 4 July 1842 (DLC: Dolley Madison Papers). Acknowledged by Jefferson as received on 9 Aug. 1822 in his Epistolary Record (DLC: Jefferson Papers), with his note: "Hite & Baldwin."

To George Joy

Dr. Sir Aug. 10. 1822

On the rect of your letters of Jany. 2 & 9. last I searched for & found that of Apl. 16. 1804. and gave information thereof to yr brother B. I sent him at the same time your copy of that letter, with an intimation, that the original, wd. be disposed of as might best answer your purpose. Owing to his absence it was some time before I heard from him. Our correspondence resulted in his informing me that Mr. Webster your agent considered the copy as sufficient. The Original therefore is still on my files, subject to your order. This will answer the last favor from you of May 29. I was in no hurry to give you the information of what had taken place in consequence of your letters of Jany. because I took for granted that you wd. have recd it from your brother or your Agent.

It may be proper to note that the Book you mention in yours of Feby 2. if sent has miscarried.

I am glad to find that the [*sic*] G. Britain has at length taken juster views of her monopolizing attempts with regard to the navigation between her Cols. & the U.S. This country will not be behind her in a friendly policy of every sort. But it is too proud to acquiesce in inequalities; and sufficien[t] ly alive to its interests not to sacrifice them.

Draft (DLC).

To Thomas Ritchie

DR. SIR Aug. 13. 1822

Your favor of Aug 7 is so full & satisfactory an answer to my request of July 2. that I ought not to withold my thanks for it. The delay was immaterial. But I lament most sincerely the afflicting causes of it. With much esteem & friendly respects

Confidential

The Enquirer of the 6th. very properly animadverts on the attempts to pervert the historical circumstances relating to the Draught of the Declaration of Independence.[1] The fact, that Mr. Jefferson was the author and the nature of the alterations made in the Original, are too well known and the proofs are too well preserved, to admit of successful misrepresentation.

In one important particular, the truth, tho on record, seems to have escap⟨e⟩d attention: and justice to be so far left undone to Virga. It was in obedience to *her positive instruction* to her Delegates in Congs. that the motion for Independence was made. The instruction passed *unanimously* in her Convention on the 15. of May 1776 (see the Journal of that date): and the Mover was of course, the Mouth only of the Delegation, as the Delegation was of the Convention. Had P. Randolph the first named not been cut off by Death the motion wd have been made by him. The duty, in consequence of that event devolved on the next in order, R. H. Lee, who had political merits of a sort very different from that circumstantial distinction.[2]

Draft (DLC). The confidential enclosure was published in the *Richmond Enquirer*, 20 Aug. 1822.

1. The editorial in the *Richmond Enquirer*, 6 Aug. 1822, had reprinted a piece from the *Philadelphia Union* attacking Thomas Jefferson and his role in drafting the Declaration of Independence. The editorial had also reprinted a comment from the *Charleston Patriot*.

2. Here JM wrote and then crossed out: "Were such circumstances worth claiming for Revolutionary Patriots, the friends of Mr. Harrison might remind the public that he reported to Cong. the Decla. as agreed to in the Com. of which he was chairman."

¶ To Robert C. Foster. Letter not found. *17 August 1822*. Acknowledged in Foster to JM, 6 Jan. 1824, ViU: Madison Papers, Special Collections. In his letter JM provided a transcript from the Virginia Supreme Court: "Mrs. Mary Porter conveyed to John. S. Wood by deed dated, 12. of April 1809 and recorded in the supreme Court three Negroes Charity & her two Children, Eliza, & Levinia Signed, &c."

To Lewis Deblois

DEAR SIR MONTPELLIER Aug 19. 1822

Your letter of July 23. having taken a circuit thro' Montpellier in Vermont, has but just come to hand.

Mrs. Deblois's letter to Mrs. M. was not at once answered, because no advice that could be useful, presented itself; and she was persuaded that her sympathies & regrets would not be doubted.

I am truly sorry for the distress which has unexpectedly befallen you. But the course to be pursued, seems to be marked out by considerations not to be controuled. Whether the proceeding under the Insolvent law,[1] released you from the public claim, or whether the Act of Congress in 1820 reaches your case, are questions, on which the accounting Department and in the event of a suit, the Court, must decide according to its understanding of the law: and if you should obtain relief from neither, the only remaining resort must be to Congress by a representation of all the facts and considerations, which may be thoug⟨ht⟩ to have an equitable bearing on the case.

From this view of the subject, you will be sensible, that I can not do more than express a continuance of sincere wishes, in which Mrs. Madison joins me, in behalf of yourself, and your amiable family.

JAMES MADISON

Printed facsimile of RC (Paul C. Richards Autographs Catalogue No. 225 [1987], item 85); draft (DLC).

1. Deblois had been purser at the Charlestown, Massachusetts, navy yard from June 1815 to March 1821 (*Minutes of Proceedings of the Court of Enquiry, into the Official Conduct of Capt. Isaac Hull* . . . [Washington, 1822; Shoemaker 11057], 26). For his financial difficulties, see Deblois to JM, 3 Sept. 1817, *PJM-RS*, 1:121–22. JM's reference to the "Insolvent law" must have been to Massachusetts law, since no federal statute for bankruptcy existed at this time (David A. Skeel Jr., *Debt's Dominion: A History of Bankruptcy Law in America* [Princeton, N.J., 2001], 25).

From James Monroe

Dear Sir, Washington Augt. 25, 1822.

I enclose you a copy of a report of the Committee of the Senate on the nominations respecting which a difference of opinion took place between that body & me, in the manner shewn by its votes in the sequel of the document.[1]

The Senate confirmed the nominations in the rank, that is, the grades to which each officer was designated, but rejected the dates from which it was proposed that their ranks should commence. It is understood that by admitting the confirmation, & dating each commission from the day it was confirmed, the rank of neither of the officers will be affected relatively, either as to each other, or to any other officer in the army. The question therefore on which I have to decide is whether I will accept the confirmation, under the circumstances, in a spirit of conciliation, or reject it, on the principle that the Senate is bound to take the whole in the form in which it is submitted. It will be very gratifying to me to have your sentiments on the subject. You may recollect whether any circumstance of this kind ever took place before.

I send you also a copy of a letter from Mr. Taylor from Mexico,[2] giving interesting details of events there, the result of which has been to place Iturbide in the supreme direction of affairs. The prospect is discouraging for the present, but I have no doubt that he will find it necessary to change his course, & relinquish all pretention to hereditary power, or be finally driven from it, & perhaps from the country. I will thank you after perusing to return to me this latter paper, retaining a copy if you think it worth the notice.

You will have seen the proclamation arranging the difference with England as to Colonial trade, founded on the act of Parliament. Congress may reciprocate the duties if it should be thought advisable. Thus two important objects, the trade with France, and that with England are adjusted on conditions which will I trust be advantageous & satisfactory to our country.

Mrs. Gouverneur has added a son to our family,[3] & both mother and child are doing well. The whole family desire their best regards to be presented to you & Mrs. Madison.

Printed in Hamilton, *Writings of James Monroe*, 6:295–96.

1. *In the Senate of the United States, April 30, 1822, Ordered, That the Injunction of Secrecy be Removed from the Following Proceedings and Documents, and That They be Printed* (Washington, 1822; Shoemaker 10894).

2. The enclosure was William Taylor to John Quincy Adams, 6 June 1822, describing the events surrounding the elevation of Agustín de Iturbide as emperor of Mexico (DNA: RG 59, CD, Veracruz, vol. 1).

3. James Monroe Gouverneur (1822–1885) was born deaf and mute. He attended the New-York Institution for the Instruction of the Deaf and Dumb and succeeded to the extent that his parents solicited President James K. Polk for a federal clerkship for their "unfortunate" son, though apparently without success. He died at Spring Grove Asylum in Catonsville, Maryland (Ammon, *James Monroe*, 548–49; Roswell R. Hoes to John B. Larner, 4 Nov. 1911, ViU: Pleasonton Collection, Special Collections; *Eleventh Annual Report of the Directors of the New-York Institution for the Instruction of the Deaf and Dumb . . .* [New York, 1830], 15; Herbert Weaver et al., eds., *Correspondence of James K. Polk* [11 vols. to date; Nashville, 1969—], 11:465, 475, 488).

From Benjamin Joy

SIRE BOSTON 27th Augt 1822

I had the honor of receiving yesterday your favor of the 12th Inst[1] inclosing a letter for my brother George Joy. I have inclosed it agreeably to your request, and it will be sent him by the first vessel from this port for England. Permit me to express the high respect & esteem with which I am your very obedient & hble Servant

B. JOY

RC (DLC: Rives Collection, Madison Papers).

1. The letter has not been found, but the enclosure was JM to George Joy, 10 Aug. 1822.

From George Joy

DEAR SIR, N. 13 FINSBURY SQUARE 27th August 1822

I have not seen Mr: Rush since the Packet Liverpool was a missing Ship; but Mr: Maury whom I met here at dinner on sunday last had seen him that morning and was informed by him that there was a long arrear of information due to him from Washington; and we are now advised that the abovementioned packet was sunk by the Ice on the Banks of Newfoundland.

It would be against the doctrine of Chances, in god knows what proportion, that two packets, at two such distant dates as the Albion & the Liverpool should take to the bottom original and duplicate of the same Dispatchs—certainly not less than ten thousand to one; and yet, I strongly suspect it will be found to have been the case—the Letters ℔ Liverpool are all lost—the crew and Passengers are saved, and arrived at Bristol—some, I understand, have reached London this day, and report that they were reduced for six days in the Boat to an allowance of a Biscuit a day ℔ man.

I wrote you that Mr Rush's dispatches ℘ Albion were not among the Letters that were drifted ashore from that ship; and this will apprize you that anything you may have favoured me with ℘ the Liverpool has met no better fate.

You are aware how happy I am on all occasions to hear from you, and will I trust indulge me with a repetition of any thing you may have written on either of the above occasions. I rest always, very faithfully, Dear sir, Your friend & Servt.

G. Joy

You would be delighted to see Mr: Maury after so long an absence—he is certainly no longer young; but very sprightly, and full of anecdote. In all the time that I have known him he has observed the rule that Swift laid down for himself in middle life to govern him in *riper* years—"not to tell the same story a second time to the same person"[1]—and this tho' he is not so silent as when I first knew him—he occupies a large portion of what Chesterfield calls the joint stock of Conversation;[2] and leaves every one present to regret his suspension of it. We had on the above occasion some very entertaining Notions of what he saw and heard at the Capitulation of Yorktown.

RC (DLC). Docketed by JM.

1. "Not to tell the same story over and over to the same people," Jonathan Swift, "Resolutions: When I Come to be Old," in Walter Scott, ed., *The Works of Jonathan Swift* . . . (19 vols.; Edinburgh, 1814), 9:429.

2. "Most long talkers single out some one unfortunate man in company . . . to whisper, or at least in a half voice, to convey a continuity of words to. This is excessively ill-bred, and, in some degree, a fraud; conversation-stock being a joint and common property" (Philip Dormer Stanhope Chesterfield, *The Works of Lord Chesterfield: Including His Letters to His Son* . . . [New York, 1838], 223).

From an Unidentified Correspondent

Sir, Pennsylvania September 1. 1822.

"Nulla dies sine linea."[1]

Upwards of seven years have elapsed, since you had plunged the United States into *flagranti bello:*[2] and, as you were the Author of that War, & responsible for the consequences, mediate and immediate; you will pardon me, for the feeble attempt, I shall make, in the narrow compass of a Letter to remind you of a few of the probable consequences all which and many more were at its commencement (and then had been with prophetic wisdom) foretold you with a warning voice, by some of the now departed heros* and fathers of our Liberty & Independence: and all which and many more have since been realized by sad experience! Suffer me, Sir, to bring to your view some of the most prominent of those *consequences.* You cannot, most assuredly, be insensible to the deplorable condition of our common Country. If I could be persuaded of this, I would ask leave to direct and fix your attention to the dismal Contrast which arises to the View, on drawing a comparison between the two periods antecedent and subsequent to the memorable era, the 18 June 1812.[4] You, Sir, in common with every other person must be convinced of the miserable state of the country. The unparalleled complication of calamities arising immediately from natural political and commercial causes, that has afflicted the people of the U States ever since that unfortunate day cannot be otherwise accounted for than by tracing them to that War into which you without necessity without policy without prudence and without preparation plunged the nation. A war that has not only inflicted an incurable wound into the Constitution, but sap'd the Basis of it. A War, professedly waged for the vindication of maritime rights, the violating of which even admitting the alledged fact, never did by the Laws of nations & of nature's god, constitute a cause of war or shedding of human blood: the fact of a Sailor being compelled even against his will into the exercise of his proper employment and duly remunerated for his service, could in no sense under those circumstances be called Imprisonment; nor the vessels in which he was so constrained and employed, "*prisons*" or "*floating dungeons!*" But it was well calculated to inflame, and ultimately to serve your purpose. For the presidential office was then shortly to be newly filled and one hundred thousand dollars (4 years salary) was a prize worth drawing out of the political Wheel; and it should seem, that although it was to be "the price of blood" it proved a tempting *Bait.* Accordingly you were tempted by its charms, and rashly & regardless of all consequences, swallowed it. You next accepted the bloody sword and after roling up the Sleeves of your Garments and laying bare your feeble arm, you plunged it in the Bosoms of thousands of your fellow men!

And now mark the multifarious distresses and calamities that have afflicted the Country ever since. Is it necessary, Sir, to particularize these? It is not. If you have heretofore held a deaf ear to them, but are now willing to hear their recital, ask your Slaves; even they can inform you. If you are too high minded to stoop so low, inquire of James Munro who was your colleague in Butchery!!

You are now like myself considerably advanced in years & according to the law of nature, in such case, cannot expect to live many more. It is high time, therefore, that you should take a serious view of the aspect of your

* Washingtons Advice. Col. Chronicle Sep. 27. 1814.[3]

hands and the State of your Conscience. Turn & lift your Eyes to the Father of Mercies, and supplicate him to enable you to wash away the bloody stains of the one and assuage the remorse of the other. The murders that were committed, directly and indirectly, during that unjust, unnecessary and wanton War, must as in all other cases of even private murder be answered by a proper atonement. Yes Sir, if one man in case of murder, or causeless shedding of human blood of another, must answer at the Bar of Heaven; so must many; so must a nation. That you might have prevented that War or shortly after its commencement stop'd its Career, are demonstrable facts. Consequently, inasmuch as you did not do either you must in fact and truth be the Father of *it.*†

You Sir, it was that butchered thousands of human beings and in doing it wasted millions nay hundreds of millions of our money! Do you not admit these facts as solemn serious and sad Truth? Can you deny them? No: you dare not. What justification excuse or palliation can you offer? None. Do you not often hear the voice of the blood of our slaughtered Citizens, crying to heaven, from the Plains of Bridgewater Erie or Bladensburgh for Vengeance? Do not their Shades often visit your pillow, in the silent hours of the night, "at the glimpses of the Moon,"[6] and disturb your slumbers, by appearing to you in your dreams? What says your Conscience; is all right there?!

Again, I beseech you, Sir, to look around you and observe how insulted and injured heaven is pouring out the "Phials of its wrath["] upon our once happy country! See the complication of calamity that is chastising us? See our country visited from year [to year] by a state of things closely bordering on Pestilence and Famine? Why is all this? Was this so before that period, that unfortunate era when you received one hundred thousand pieces of silver, "the price of blood?" No. No, never!

Behold ever since that ill fated day when you wrote your name in that unhallowed statute (Oh! had you while writing it drop'd a Tear on it and blotted it out for ever)—a Statute written with the blood of our fellow mortals—a Statute which it was amply and completely in your power, as it was your solemn duty, to have interposed your disapprobation and forbade the opening of the Sluices of human blood and consequently averted those distresses and disasters which appear to be entailed on the country.

Behold I say, good Sir, these States? And mark the annual visitations of Heaven in the form of droughts diseases and deaths, even from the Close of the war and that ridiculous Farce, played off at the. city of Ghent! Even until the present calamitous season; when many people, formerly in affluence and opulence, can neither procure bread or water, at many places but at great expence or hardship. To be more particular is needless. A word to

† qui non prohibet cum prohibere possit jubet[5]

the wise is always sufficient. But the News papers will detail the sad and deplorable condition into which you have brought a once free and happy nation. Yes, Sir, they are the marks of the just vengeance of an angry & offended Diety, visited upon our Nation, as a punishment for Murder of the blackest and deepest dye, among the perpetrators of which you stand, the chief among millions. Yes, Sir, you deliberately and for the price of four times twenty-five thousand dollars placed yourself at the head of bloody monsters. The mark of Cain is in your forehead.

Again, Sir, after having been, the prime author of death and slaughter, it became a matter of course, that you should be the plunderer of the property of those who survived the bloody conflict. Hence the enormous public debt you have created is become so burthensome that in numerous instances, it had been the lesser evil, if they had been numbered among the slain. How, Sir, is this debt to be paid? When your impolitick course has deprived the people of the ways and means of paying even their private debts. Behold the long lists of Insolvencies and Bankruptcies, The failures and suspension of all business. Where is the trade and commerce, the credit, public and private, the circulating medium in specie and par-paper that was once in such general circulation amongst us? Where the agriculture that pervaded every part of the nation? And all before the 18 June 1812. They are all gone. Your impolitick and cruel and vicious war swept them away or impaired what still remains to such a degree that they only enable the people to linger out an existence, that had better in innumerable instances have been terminated in the general wreck. Yes, Sir, the people are taxed, but you have by the inevitable result of your desperate measures, while you wielded the national sword and were filling your Coffers, deprived them of the means of paying those Taxes. It is an incontrovertible fact that this heavy debt would never have had any existence but for your cruel unjust & unnecessary war; nay all our public debt, which you have increased to somewhere about 100. millions might, if the real honor and interest of the nation had been consulted, long since have been discharged. But instead of paying off the old debt, which was about 35 millions, you chose rather to add an increase of 100 millions to it; as also 100 thousand dollars to your private coffers! Instead of owing nothing as might have been the case if wise and prudent measures had been pursued, the nation at present owes as I observed already, 100 millions. Your Case reminds me of a traitor who from the sordid motives of avarice and ambition betrayed his Master:[7] with this difference, that you betrayed the lives of millions of people.

I would recommend it to you to reflect on these things and if possible to repent. But if the compunctions of your Conscience (if you have any) should be too poignant you might peradventure find more speedy relief, by having recourse to the same or similar means as your Prototype. For certain it is some Atonement ought nay must be made to an offended God! Hark!

Methinks I hear the voice of thousands of your victims—the victims of your avarice and desperate ambition—whose blood calls aloud, to heaven, for a propitiatory sacrafice. Who so suitable as yourself to step forth, and become voluntary peace offering.

Before I close this letter I must observe to you that the writer of it is not an old Tory: far from it. But who on the contrary, served his country by fighting the Battles of our Independence, in the war of 1776. But all the fruits and benefits of which you have been so instrumental in impairing if not destroying altogether; for certainly, a people so Bankrupt so insolvent so out of Credits, without Money or commerce, destitute of the means of paying their debts public & privat⟨e⟩ deprived of the conveniences and in thousand instances the necessaries of Life—so afflicted from year to year with droughts & diseas⟨es⟩ a people so circumstanced, it is perfect mockery to call them free and independent. But such was not their situation before the 18th June 1812.

History will furnish ample testimony that nations must answer for murder, as well as individuals. The Greeks who sacked Troy paid dearly for their victory. And their King, Agamemnon atoned for that iniquitous war. But is it necessary to cite history to prove the impolicy and ruinous consequences of unjust Wars? It is not. But if it were Europe furnishes ample proofs. Besides Principle and the light of Reason are amply sufficient, independent of holy writ: And remember a truth as clear as axiom, That a republick which does not rest upon the basis of Virtue is like a house built upon Sand. Alas! Ours is falling. The immortal Washington had placed it on solid foundations but James Madison, sapt its foundation for ever. To conclude Well might the patriot exclaim in the language of that inimitable passage of the scriptures, not altogether unapposite to the Subject. "O Jerusalem, Jerusalem, thou that killest the Prophets and stonest them that are sent unto thee ⟨how often⟩ would I have gathered thy children together even as a ⟨hen⟩ gathereth her chickens together under her wing, & you ⟨would⟩ not. Behold your *house* is left unto you *desolate*."[8] Yours respectfully,

ROBERTS

☞ NB. The act of *rejecting* a treaty without laying it before the Senate[9] is also a distinguished link in the Chain of causes and effects that brought the Country to the present miserable Condition, Independent of Embargos, non Intercourse & non Importation laws; when fortune and good policy, in combination offered to throw into our nation's lap the benefit of Trade & Commerce enable us by Duty on imports & tonage to throw off the burthen of the revolutionary debt and become what we contended for, realy & truly free and independent!

RC (DLC: Jefferson Papers). Letter addressed to JM and marked "(Copy)" below signature. Cover addressed to Thomas Jefferson and marked "mail.," although there is no postmark.

Cover docketed by Jefferson "Anonymous (Roberts) Angloman recd aug. 24. 24." Damaged by removal of seal.

1. *Nulla dies sine linea:* no day without a line.

2. *Flagranti bello:* a raging war.

3. The article "Roberts" referred to was "Washington's Opinion of a British War," printed in the Philadelphia semiweekly *Freemans Journal and Columbian Chronicle*, 27 Sept. 1814. After positing that it had long been "a favorite object of the present ruling party, to get this nation at war with Great Britain," the writer quoted from a letter written by Secretary of State Timothy Pickering (according to the article, at President Washington's behest) to U.S. minister to France James Monroe on 12 Sept. 1795, in which Pickering spelled out the consequences of such a war. The entire letter is printed in Preston, *Papers of James Monroe*, 3:447–51.

4. "An Act declaring War between the United Kingdom of Great Britain and Ireland and the dependencies thereof, and the United States of America and their territories," 18 June 1812 (*U.S. Statutes at Large*, 2:755).

5. *Qui non prohibet cum prohibere possit jubet:* whoever does not forbid when he could forbid, abets.

6. "What may this mean, / That thou, dead corse, again in complete steel / Revisits thus the glimpses of the moon": Shakespeare, *Hamlet*, 1.4.51–53 (*Riverside*).

7. "Roberts" referred here to Judas Iscariot and his betrayal of Jesus Christ, and suggests that JM should, like Judas, commit suicide.

8. Matt. 23:37–38 (AV).

9. For the 1807 rejection by the Jefferson administration of the treaty negotiated with Great Britain by James Monroe and William Pinkney, see Ketcham, *James Madison*, 448–50.

To Ira Barton

Sepr. 5. 1822

J.M. with his respects to Mr. Barton returns the thanks for his Oration,[1] which are due as well to its merits, as to the Politeness of Mr. B.[2] in forwarding a Copy.

Draft (DLC).

1. Ira Barton, *An Oration, Delivered at Oxford, on the Forty-Sixth Anniversary of American Independence* (Cambridge, Mass., 1822; Shoemaker 7968).

2. Ira Barton (1796–1867) graduated from Brown University in 1819 and practiced law in Oxford, Massachusetts, 1822–34. In 1834 he moved to Worcester, where he served as judge of probate for Worcester County, 1836–44. He was a member of the state legislature several times (William A. Benedict and Hiram A. Tracy, *History of the Town of Sutton, Massachusetts, from 1704 to 1876 . . .* [Worcester, Mass., 1878], 600–601).

From William Crawford

DR SIR LOUISA Sept. 6th. 1822

Capt. Payne[1] informed me some Time last spring that you would be so good as to let me have a Ram of your Cape breed of Sheep.[2] In consequence of my having been from home for several Weeks past, I fear I may have defered too long sending for him; If not you will let Abram the bearer hereof, have such as you can spare. Respectfully yr. Most obt. St

WM. CRAWFORD[3]

RC (DLC). Docketed by JM.

1. This was Dolley Madison's brother, John Coles Payne, who served as a captain in the U.S. Army, 1813–15 (Heitman, *Historical Register*, 1:777).

2. The sheep of the Cape of Good Hope were a long-legged broad-tailed breed (William Youatt, *Sheep: Their Breeds, Management, and Diseases; To Which is Added the Mountain Shepherd's Manual* [London, 1837], 117–18). JM had a flock of broad-tailed sheep from about 1806–7, to which he added a separate flock of merino sheep in 1811 (JM to William Madison, 11 Jan. 1811, and to Richard Peters, 15 Mar. 1811, *PJM-PS*, 3:116, 222).

3. Rev. William Crawford (ca. 1771–1858) was rector of Trinity Parish, Louisa County, Virginia (Ann Pamela Cunningham, "Ecclesiastical Register," *American Quarterly Church Review and Ecclesiastical Register (1858–1870)* 11 [1858]: 343; "Journals of the Conventions of the Protestant Episcopal Church in the Diocess of Virginia. From 1785 to 1835, Inclusive," in Francis L. Hawks, *Contributions to the Ecclesiastical History of the United States of America* [2 vols.; New York, 1836–39], 1:second 152).

From Thomas Potts

SIR, NEW YORK Septr. 7th. 1822

When at London in Feby. last a small parcel (said to contain a Book or Books) was entrusted to my care by a Mr. Joy, which was addressd to you[1]—on my arrival at Baltimore in April, I left the said parcel at Mr. Williamson's, Fountain Inn, Light Street—where I believe it still remains. I would have forwarded it immediately, but had no opportunity during my short stay in that place, and since that, having been much engagd in business & in moving from place to place it had intirely escapd my memory until this morning, when in perusing some papers, I found Mr. Joy's Memo.

By authorizing any one to call on Mr. Williamson, the parcel will be delivered. I am sir very respecy. yrs.

THOS. POTTS[2]

RC (DLC). Docketed by JM.

1. For the parcel, see George Joy to JM, 2 Feb. 1822, and n.

2. Thomas Potts was the captain of the merchant ship *Henry Clay* (*Baltimore Patriot & Mercantile Advertiser*, 15 Apr. 1822).

To Clara Baldwin Bomford

MONTPELLIER Sepr. 8. 1822

J Madison with his best respects & many thanks returns Mrs Bomford's manuscript copy of the History of Arnold's plot by Mr. Marbois,[1] which has been so long detained for want of a good conveyance. He had erroneously supposed that the history contained some incidental mention of Napoleon's motives for parting with Louisiana to the U.S. with which Mr. Marbois must have been particularly acquainted, having been the negociator of the Treaty.[2] J.M. is still under an impression that Mrs. B. possessed some paper from Mr. Marbois which related to that subject. Should this be the case J.M. will take as an additional kindness a communication of it, if no objection be felt to it.

RC (NjP: Crane Collection); draft (DLC). Addressee not indicated on RC or draft; assigned based on the description of the RC for sale in Walter R. Benjamin, the *Collector* (1949), No. 682, item 531, as an autograph letter, signed, dated Montpelier, 8 Sept. 1822: "To Mrs. Bumford, returning a manuscript copy of Marbois' 'History of Arnolds's plot.'" Minor differences between the copies have not been noted.

1. For this volume, see JM to Richard Cutts, 12 Oct. 1817, *PJM-RS*, 1:139–40 and n. 2.

2. The remaining part of the sentence that begins "with which Mr. Marbois must have been particularly acquainted . . ." was omitted from the draft.

From Edward W. DuVal

MY DEAR SIR, WASHINGTON, Sepr: 8. 1822.

I have been prevailed on, by some of my friends, in this place, to become a Candidate for the Clerkship of the House of Representatives, now vacant by the death of Mr. Dougherty; and as the gratification of success, as well as the chance of it, must, with me, materially depend upon my possessing the good wishes of those to whom I have long been known, I have, not without the hope of receiving your's, presumed to address to you this Communication. Altho' I could neither ask, nor expect, the direct aid, and exertion of your influence, with those by whom the Election will be made, I am not unaware how important, and need not add how very acceptable, the manifestation of a favorable disposition by you, towards me, would be, at any time preceding the choice.

In the election of the present Congress so many of those that were members of the preceding were left out, as greatly to diminish the number and strength of my acquaintances in the House. There are yet, however, many in it to whom, I have every reason to believe, it would afford the most unfeigned pleasure to contribute to my advancement, and whose zeal for my welfare will be evinced by their activity and good offices on this occasion. But this can only appear & be made effective after the Members have arrived here, and but a day, at most, before the Election. In the mean time, my competitors, whoever they may be, may, and probably will, unless I procure and use the means to prevent it, obtain, through their friends, with Representatives to whom I am unknown, an impression in their favor.

To say nothing in extenuation of this trespass on your attention, of a subject which, in its nature, may be considered as, in some degree, connected with public concerns, would imply a measure of insensibility which justice to my own feelings and respect and veneration for your character would equally disclaim. A sense of the reluctance with which I have committed it, I should vainly endeavor &, therefore, will not attempt to convey to you. Relying, as I do, upon that characteristic kindness in which other intruders have found indulgence & pardon, I will only add, that, nothing but a deep solicitude for the interest of my family (considerably enlarged within the last five years) could have prevailed over the serious objections, which arose in my mind, to interrupting, with the alloy of entreaty, the even and perpetual enjoyment of that tranquillity and happiness which I am persuaded & trust will ever be your's.

To Mrs. Madison, the recollection of whose benevolence and virtues will never cease to inspire, in our domestic circle, the most grateful feelings, please to present the kind regards and best wishes of my Sister, Mrs. Duval & myself; and believe me, my dear Sir, to be always sincerely & most Respectfully, your's,

E: W: DUVAL[1]

RC (DLC). Addressed by DuVal to JM at Orange Court House, and franked. Docketed by JM.

1. Edward W. DuVal (ca. 1790–1830), a nephew of Supreme Court justice Gabriel Duvall, was trained as a lawyer and served as clerk in the Navy Department, 1813–16. He was appointed agent for the Cherokee Indians west of the Mississippi River in 1824 and served in that post until 1829 (Philadelphia *Columbian Star, and Christian Index* 3 [27 Nov. 1830]: 352; McKee, *A Gentlemanly and Honorable Profession*, 18–19; *Baltimore Patriot & Mercantile Advertiser*, 4 Apr. 1829).

To Edward W. DuVal

Dear Sir Sepr. 13. 1822

I have just recd. your letter of the 8th. instant. The course which I have found it neccessary to adopt would involve me in inconsistency were I not to decline a recommendatory interposition for the vacancy to which your thoughts have been turn'd; and I am glad to infer from the candour & delicacy of your ideas that you view the subject in the light to be wished. I avail myself of the occasion, nevertheless to assure you of the very favorable sentiments which could not but be impressed by every thing which I have known of your character & qualities.

Mrs. M. receives the kind expressions of Mrs. D. & your Sister, with a request that I would offer every proper return for them. To yourself, she repeats the acknowledgment of her obligations for the polite attentions she experienced at the difficult moment which occurred in 1814.[1] With friendly respects

J.M.

Draft (DLC).

1. According to Secretary of the Navy William Jones, who recalled the events on the day of the British attack on Washington: "I left the Navy yard at about half past three Oclock accompanied by Mr. Duval and not long after learned that our army was rapidly retreating and that of the enemy advancing rapidly. We proceeded to Georgetown where I met my family and that of the Presidents at the house of Charles Carrol Esqr. of Bellevue and received a message from the President requesting that I would join him at Foxalls Works. At about 5 Oclock I set out in company with the family of the President, of Mr. Carrols and my own with Mr. Duval and proceeded through Georgetown to join the President but found he had crossed at masons ferry" (Memorandum of Secretary of the Navy Jones, 24 Aug. 1814, William S. Dudley, ed., *The Naval War of 1812: A Documentary History*, [3 vols. to date; Washington, 1985—], 3:214–15).

From Robert H. Rose

Dear Sir Huntsville Sept 13th 1822

I had the honor to receive your letter of the 26th Ultimo[1] on wednesday. I write so soon to allay the apprehensions of your brother. The Securityship alluded to has entirely escaped the recollection of your Sister and myself. I have hopes that I have obtained the deposition of Mr John Hilliman of Knoxvill⟨e⟩ (as witness to the Bond) that will place the transaction in a proper point of view and will induce the Court to give me a Perpetual Injunction. At any rate I shall send on a sum to cover the amount; and if it should not be applied to McClelland's Debt you will pay it in part discharge of my Bond due your brother. He may rest assured that I will not let him suffer on my account. The Crops in this State are excellent and we have not suffered for rain a single moment. Corn is worth a Dollar per Barrel. Pork may be had in Tennessee on the Cumberland for nine shillings per hundred weight. Cotton will probably not be more than from ten to twelve cents. Lands in eligible situ⟨a⟩tions from twenty to twenty five Dollars per acre. Rent for cleared land of good quality from two & a half to three Dollars per acre; producing on an average from eight to ten Barrels of Corn per acre and from eight to twelve hundred weight of seed Cotton per acre. Our family still continue to enjoy uninterupted health except your Sister whose general health is much improved. Her Cough is still very troublesome but I hope it is only symtomatic and will soon cease of itself. I have rented a Plantation for six years eighty miles below on the Tennessee River opposite Mr. Armstead, on the condition of clearing three hundred acres, which is the work of one year, only, and the Corn made on it will reimburse me for clearing. It is belting[2] and fencing only. It is also adjacent to the Indian [. . .] where I can raise Stock to any extent & without the necessity of feeding them in the Summer or Winter & the Cows can be purchased at 6 & 8 Dollars per head, Steers of six & eight hundred weight at ten & twelve Dollars. I saw a Gentleman who w⟨as⟩ at Mr Armsteads five days ago. They were all well; ⟨h⟩e has however lost fourteen negroes. I will thank you to tell your good Lady that I have not been unmindful of her ⟨New?⟩ Orleans Snuff some of which she will receive soon. With the best wishes for you and yours I am yr friend & Sert

Robert H. Rose

PS It is only a few days ago that I began to ride which is my apology for the badness of writing.

RC (NN: Arents Tobacco Collection). Docketed by JM. Extensively damaged.

1. Letter not found.
2. Belting: girdling a tree (*OED Online*).

From James Monroe

Dear Sir Washington Sepr 16. 1822

I send you here with the 10th vol: of the journals of our revolutionary Congress,[1] the one which you intimated, was deficient in your collection. I have a complete set, with several other odd vols., form'd out of my own collection, & that of our old estimable friend Judge Jones, so that if you should want any other, it is probable, I might supply you.

I send you also a detailed copy of the proceedings of the Senate, on the renomination of Cols: Towson & Gadsden,[2] and on the nomination of other officers, which involvd a principle connected with theirs. I shall be glad to receive any views which you may take of the subject, & which I need not mention shall be confidential.

We have nothing new from Europe, to vary the state of things, presented by the gazettes, except that the disorderly proceedings at Madrid, have been exaggerated, to the disadvantage of the Cortes. Every thing, however, imputed, to the misconduct, of the King, is confirmd, by Mr Forsyth.

Mrs. Monroe's health continues to be very delicate—that of the rest of my family is good. They all desire their respectful regards to you & Mrs Madison. Your friend & servant

James Monroe

I send you also a copy of a letter from Mr Taylor from Mexico,[3] which gives distressing accounts of proceedings in that quarter. Return it to me, it being the only copy I have.

RC (DLC: Rives Collection, Madison Papers).

1. *Journal of the United States in Congress Assembled: Containing the Proceedings from the First Monday in November, 1784* (Philadelphia, 1785; Evans 19316). This was volume ten of the thirteen volumes of the *Journals of Congress* (1774–88).

2. See Monroe to JM, 25 Aug. 1822, and n. 1.

3. The enclosure was William Taylor to John Quincy Adams, 4 Aug. 1822, describing the coronation of Iturbide, the poverty and misery of the people, and warning of the country's descent into civil war (DNA: RG 59, CD, Veracruz, vol. 1).

To James Monroe

Dear Sir Montpellier Sepr. 24. 1822

The mail of saturday brought me your favour of the 16th. The letters inclosed in it are returned. Accept my thanks for the odd vol:[1] Congl. Journals.

As I understand the case presented in the other paper inclosed, it turns on the simple question, whether the Senate have a right, in their advice & consent, to vary the *date* at which, according to the nomination of the President an appointment to office is to take effect.

The subject continues to appear to me in the light which I believe I formerly intimated. The power of appointment, where not otherwise provided by the Constitution, is vested in the President & Senate. Both must concur in the Act: But the Act must originate with the President. He is to nominate, and their advice & consent are to make the nomination an appointment. They cannot give their advice & consent without his nomination, nor of course differently from it. In so doing they would originate or nominate so far as the difference extended; and it would be his, not their advice & consent, which consummated the appointment. If the President should nominate A to be an officer from the 1st. day of May, and the Senate should advise that he be an officer from the 1st. day of January preceding, it is evident that for the period not embraced by the nomination of the President, the nomination would originate with the Senate & would require his subsequent sanction to make it a joint act. During that period therefore it would be an appointment made by the nomination of the Senate, not of the President; and with the advice & consent of the President, not of the Senate.

The case is not essentially changed by supposing the President to nominate A to be an officer from the 1st. day of January, and the Senate to confirm from the 1st. day of May following. Here also the nomination of the President would not be pursued, and the Constitutional order of appointment would be transposed. His intention would be violated, and he would not be bound by his nomination to give effect to the advice & consent of the Senate. The proceeding would be a nullity, nor would this result from mere informality. The President might have as just objections to a postponement of the date of an appointment,[2] as good reasons for its immediate commencement. The change in the date might have an important bearing on the public service; and a collateral or consequential one on the rights or pretensions of others in the public service. In fact, if the Senate, in disregard of the nomination of the President, could postpone the commencement of an appointment for a single day, they could do it for any period, how ever remote, and whatever might be the intermediate change of things. The date may be as material a part of the nomination as the person named in it.[3] Health & success

James Madison

RC (DLC: Monroe Papers); draft (DLC). RC docketed by Monroe. Minor differences between the copies have not been noted.

1. In the draft "of" is added here.

2. In the draft "for three months" is added here.

3. Following this sentence in his draft JM wrote an additional paragraph but crossed through it: "We are still suffering under the intense drought of which you witnessed its encreasing effects. *Ten* weeks have now passed since we had any rain of sensible value. On some of our farms it may be sd. there has been none at all. Our crops of Corn, notwithstanding, w[h]ere they were *forward* were so favored by the early part of the Season, as to promise support till the next summer harvest. The Tobo. crop is in a sad plight, and no weather now can repair it. Your neighborhood in albemarle, I understand, has fared much better."

From James Monroe

Dear Sir Washington Sepr 26th. 1822.

My affairs in Albemarle, requiring my attendance there, again, before the meeting of Congress, & the Phisician deeming the exercise useful to Mrs Monroe's health, we have resolvd to set out thither in a few days, & to call on you & Mrs Madison on the route. If we go by Loudon, which is not decided, it may be the last of the week (next) before we see you; but if we go direct, about the middle.

We have had a proposition from the strongest party in *Cuba (in great confidence) to join our union*, & to take measures to that effect promptly, on an intimation that they will be receiv'd.[1] I have no doubt that such a measure, at this time, would shake our system, whatever might be the advantages, likely, or sure to attend it, if all the States would unite in it. On this subject however we will confer when I have the pleasure to see you. Your friend & servant

James Monroe

RC (DLC: Rives Collection, Madison Papers). Docketed by JM.

1. For the proposal of Cuban agent Barnabé Sanchez and cabinet discussions on its merits, see John Quincy Adams's diary entries for 26 and 27 Sept. 1822 (MHi: Adams Papers [microfilm ed.], reel 6); and Bemis, *John Quincy Adams and the Foundations of American Foreign Policy*, 372–74.

To James Maury

Dr. Sir Sepr. 28. 1822

I have lately recd. yours of July 20. That of June 24. enclosing the Act of Parlt. relating to the W. Inda. trade, was also duly recd.

I am glad to find that the Brit: Govt. has at length made that change in its Colonial policy. It augurs well for greater harmony in the intercourse between the two Nations. The U.S. will I believe be always ready to meet G.B. as well as other nations in a liberal & *reciprocal* System; and it may be hoped notwithstanding the enveloped motives which preface the Act of Repeal, that the late restrictive contest has sufficiently shewn not only that this Country will be satisfied with nothing short of reciprocity, but that in relation to the Brit: Colonies at least, such a Contest has a ruinous influence on their prosperity, & their value to the parent Country.

I have heard nothing as yet of your Eldest son. Your request was not necessary to ensure him a kind reception whenever he may give us the opportunity. Should your other son repeat his trip across the Atlantic, he will not doubt of an equal welcome.

The past Season has been very unfavorable to most of the Crops in the Atlantic States. The drought has been more or less distressing to all; in the earlier part of the Season, the Eastern, and during a later period, the middle & some of the Southern States. We have just had here a plentiful rain, after an intense drought for *ten weeks*. It is too late to be of sensible use to any of our Staple Crops, even to our Tobo: which is now either in the House, or so scorched in the field, as to be little susceptible of amendment, if a probable frost were less at hand. As far as I have learned, this crop will be very limited, especially what is of first quality. The crop of Indian Corn is also very short, but fortunately the intensity of the drought was not felt, till a certain proportion of it had, in some degree, as we say, made itself. The Wheat crop throughout the U.S. is in the aggregate remarkably short, tho' of a quality generally good. I can say nothing of the Cotton crops. In the Western Country the crops, I understand have suffered from rather too much rain, with the exception probably of the Indian Corn which rarely suffers from that cause.

I am sorry to add that much Sickness prevails in most parts of the U. States. In this particular region we enjoy our usual exception from Summer & autumnal complaints. I have presented your kind remembrance to my mother, who is still in good health & desires me to express the proper returns to you. From the rest of us accept our best respects & good wishes.

Draft (DLC).

From Mathew Carey

SIR Oct 3 1822

By this day's mail, I take the liberty of sending you a pamphlet on the policy that prevails in our intercourse with foreign nations[1]—a policy which renders us hewers of wood and drawers of water[2] to the manufacturing nations of Europe. We give the labour of 30, 40, or 50 farmers & or planters for that of one cotton manufacturer.

The low price of the produce of the earth, & the glutted markets, the cause of that low price, prove that we have too many farmers & planters. And the enormous amt. of our importations of manufactures proves that we have too few manufacturers. Hinc illa lacryma.[3] This is the true source of all embarrassments & difficulties—& the restoration of the equilibrium between the different classes of society can alone insure us the prosperity & happiness to which our inestimable advantages entitle us.

Your name wd. be a tower of strength in any good cause—& if on a mature consideration of the subject, you think our policy radically wrong, it wd be worthy of your illustrious career to come forward, & proclaim the truth to aid the efforts of those who, however benevolent their views, & how ever salutary their policy find their efforts in vain, from the want of influence.

In all the pains I have taken, & the great expense I have incurred in this important cause, I have never regarded myself as the advocate exclusively of the manufacturers—No—I have been equally pleading the cause of the farmers, planters & merchants—indeed of the nation at large. Very respectfully Your obt. hble servt

MATHEW CAREY

RC (DLC). Addressed by Carey to JM at "Monticello Va." Docketed by JM.

1. This was probably a copy of Mathew Carey, *Address to the Citizens of the United States on the Tendency of Our System of Intercourse with Foreign Nations. No. 1* (Philadelphia, 1822; Shoemaker 8253).

2. "Now therefore ye are cursed, and there shall none of you be freed from being bondmen, and hewers of wood and drawers of water for the house of my God" Josh. 9:23 (AV).

3. *Hinc illae lacrymae:* from hence these tears.

Minutes of the Board of Visitors of the University of Virginia

Octob. 7. 1822.

At a meeting of the Visitors of the University of Virginia at the said University on Monday the 7th. of October 1822.

Present Thomas Jefferson Rector, James Breckenridge, Joseph C. Cabell, John H. Cocke and James Madison.

Resolved that the Proctor be instructed to enter into conferences with such skilful and responsible undertakers as he would approve, for the building of the Library, on the plan heretofore proposed, and now in his possession, and to procure from them declarations of the smallest sums for which they will undertake the different portions of the work of the said building, each portion to be done as well, in materials, manner and sufficiency, as the best of the same kind of work already done in the preceding buildings, or as well & sufficiently as shall now be agreed on; that (omitting the capitels of the columns, which would be procured elsewhere) the several other portions be specified under such general heads and details as may be convenient to shew the cost of each, and by whom undertaken, fixing also the time within which each portion shall be compleated: and that his agreements be provisional only, & subject to the future acceptance or refusal of the Visitors.

Resolved that the Committee of Superintendance be authorised to employ a Collector to proceed to the collection of the monies still due on subscriptions, under such instructions and agreement as they shall approve.

Resolved that the examination and report of the accounts of the Bursar of the University of Virginia, from the 1st. day of Octob. 1820. to the 31st. of March 1821. and from the 31st. of March 1821. to the 27th. day of November 1821. made by John H. Cocke, at the request of the Rector, by his letter of the 1st. of December 1821. be hereby ratified as done under authority of this board; and that the said John H. Cocke be, and he is hereby appointed to examine & verify the accounts of the said Bursar, from the 27th. of November 1821. to this date and make report thereof to this board.

Resolved that George Loyall[1] esq. now a member of this board, appointed on the resignation of Robert B. Taylor, be added to the Committee for settlement of the Bursar's and Proctor's accounts, with authority to the Committee to act singly or together, as convenience may admit.

The following Report was then agreed to.

To the President and Directors of the Literary fund.

In obedience to the act of the General assembly of Virginia, requiring that the Rector and Visitors of the University of Virginia should make report annually to the President and Directors of the Literary fund (to be laid before the legislature at their next succeeding session) embracing a full account of the disbursements the funds on hand, and a general statement of the condition of the University the said Rector & Visitors make the following Report.

The Visitors considering as the law of their duty the Report of the Commissioners of 1818. which was made to the legislature, and acted on by them, from time to time subsequently, have compleated all the buildings proposed by that Report, except one; that is to say, ten distinct houses or Pavilions containing each a lecturing room, with generally four other apartments for the accomodation of a Professor & his family, and with a garden and the requisite family offices; six Hotels for dieting the Students, with a single room in each for a Refectory, and two rooms, a garden and offices for the tenant; and an hundred and nine Dormitories, sufficient each for the accomodation of two students, arranged in four distinct rows between the Pavilions & Hotels, and united with them by covered ways; which buildings are all in readiness for occupation, except that there is still some plaistering to be done, now in hand, which will be finished early in the present season, the gardens grounds and garden walls to be compleated, and some columns awaiting their Capitels not yet recieved from Italy. These buildings are mostly paid for by the monies which have been recieved, and it is still expected they would be compleatly so, by the subscriptions due, were they in hand. But the slowness of their collection will render it necessary to make good their deficiencies, in the first instance, out of the annuity of the ensuing years, to be replaced to that fund again by the subscriptions as they come in.

The remaining building, necessary to compleat the whole establishment, & called for by the Report of 1818. which was to contain rooms for religious worship, for public examinations, for a Library, & for other associated purposes, is not yet begun for want of funds. It was estimated heretofore by the Proctor, according to the prices which the other buildings have actually cost at the sum of 46,847. Dollars. The Visitors, from the beginning, have considered it as indispensable to compleat all the buildings before opening the institution; because, from the moment that shall be opened, the whole income of the University will be absorbed by the salaries of the Professors, and other incidental and current expences, and nothing will remain to erect any building still wanting to compleat the system. They are still of opinion therefore that it is better to postpone, for a while, the commencement of the institution, and then to open it in full and compleat system, than to begin prematurely in an unfinished state, and go on, perhaps for ever, on the contracted scale of local academies, utterly inadequate to the great purposes which the Report of 1818. and the legislature have hitherto had in contemplation. They believe that, in that imperfect state, it will offer little allurement to other than neighboring students, and that Professors of the first eminence in their respective lines of science, will not be induced to attach their reputations to an institution, defective in it's outset, and offering no pledge of rising to future distinction. Yet the Visitors consider the procuring such characters (and it will certainly be their aim) as the peculiar feature which is to give reputation and value to the Institution, and to constitute it's desirable and important attractions. But the present state of the funds renders the prospect of finishing this last building indefinitely distant. The interest of the sums advanced to the institution now absorbs nearly half it's income. A suspension of interest indeed, for three or four years, would give time for erecting the building with the established annuity; but the subsequent repayment of the principal from that annuity would remove the opening of the Institution to a very remote period.

On this view of the condition of the University, the Visitors think it their duty to state that, if the legislature shall be of opinion that the sums advanced to the University, in the name of loans, from the general fund for education, have been applied to their legitimate object, and shall think proper to liberate the annuity from their reimbursement, it will suffice in three or four years to compleat the last building, and the institution may be opened at the end of that term. And further that if the requisite sum can be supplied from the same or any other fund, then the University may be put into as full operation, as it's income will admit, in the course of the year ensuing the present date, and while the remaining building will be proceeding on such supplementary fund. This however, or whatever else their wisdom may devise, is subject to their direction, to which the Visitors will in willing duty conform.

In the same Report of the Commissioners of 1818. it was stated by them that "in conformity with the principles of our constitution, which place all sects of religion on an equal footing, with the jealousies of the different sects in guarding that equality from encroachment or surprise, and with the sentiments of the legislature in favor of freedom of religion, manifested on former occasions, they had not proposed that any professorship of Divinity should be established in the University; that provision however was made for giving instruction in the Hebrew, Greek, and Latin languages, the depositories of the Originals, and of the earliest and most respected authorities of the faith of every sect, and for courses of Ethical lectures, developing those moral obligations in which all sects agree. That, proceeding thus far, without offence to the Constitution, they had left, at this point, to every sect to take into their own hands the office of further instruction in the peculiar tenets of each."

It was not however to be understood that instruction in religious opinions and duties was meant to be precluded by the public authorities, as indifferent to the interests of society. On the contrary, the relations which exist between man and his maker, and the duties resulting from those relations, are the most interesting and important to every human being, and the most incumbent on his study and investigation. The want of instruction in the various creeds of religious faith existing among our citizens presents therefore a chasm in a general institution of the useful sciences. But it was thought that this want, and the entrustment to each society of instruction in it's own doctrines, were evils of less danger than a permission to the public authorities to dictate modes or principles of religious instruction, or than opportunities furnished them of giving countenance or ascendancy to any one sect over another. A remedy however has been suggested of promising aspect, which, while it excludes the public authorities from the domain of religious freedom, would give to the Sectarian schools of divinity the full benefit of the public provisions made for instruction in the other branches of science. These branches are equally necessary to the Divine, as to the other professional or civil characters, to enable them to fulfil the duties of their calling with understanding and usefulness. It has therefore been in contemplation, and suggested by some pious individuals, who percieve the advantages of associating other studies with those of religion, to establish their religious schools on the confines of the University, so as to give to their students ready and convenient access and attendance on the scientific lectures of the University; and to maintain, by that means, those destined for the religious professions on as high a standing of science, and of personal weight and respectability, as may be obtained by others from the benefits of the University. Such establishments would offer the further and great advantage of enabling the Students of the University to attend religious exercises with the Professor of their particular sect, either in the rooms of the building still to be erected, and destined to that purpose under impartial regulations, as proposed in the same Report of the Commissioners, or in the lecturing room of such Professor. To such propositions the Visitors are disposed to lend a willing ear, and would think it their duty to give every encoragement, by assuring to those who might chuse such a location for their schools, that the regulations of the University should be so modified and accomodated as to give every facility of access and attendance to their students, with such regulated use also as may be permitted to the other students, of the library which may hereafter be acquired, either by public or private munificence, but always understanding that these schools shall be independant of the University and of each other. Such an arrangement would compleat the circle of the useful sciences embraced by this institution, and would fill the chasm now existing, on principles which would leave inviolate the constitutional freedom of religion, the most inalienable and sacred of all human rights, over which the people and authorities of this state individually and publicly, have ever manifested the most watchful jealousy: and could this jealousy be now alarmed, in the opinion of the legislature, by what is here suggested, the idea will be relinquished on any surmise of disapprobation which they might think proper to express.

A committee of the board was duly appointed to settle finally the accounts of all reciepts and disbursements, from the commencement of the Central college, to the entire completion of the four ranges of buildings of the University. They found it necessary to employ a skilful Accountant to make up a compleat set of books, in regular form, wherein all the accounts, general and particular, should be stated, so as that every dollar might be traced from it's reciept to it's ultimate expenditure, and the clearest view be thus exhibited of the faithful application of the monies placed under the direction of the board. This work has taken more time than expected; and altho' considerably advanced, is not entirely compleated. Until it's completion however, the committee cannot proceed on the final settlement with which they are charged. The Bursar's accounts for the year preceding this date are rendered herewith; as are also the Proctor's for the first six months; but his books and papers being necessarily in the hands of the Accountant, his account for the last half year could not as yet be prepared. The settlement by the committee, when made, will be transmitted, as a supplementary document, to the Literary board, as well for it's regular Audit by their Accountant, as to be laid before the legislature.

And the board adjourned without day.

TH: JEFFERSON Rector

Ms (ViU: Jefferson Papers, Special Collections). In Jefferson's hand.

1. George Loyall (1789–1868) of Norfolk, Virginia, graduated from the College of William and Mary in 1808. He served in the Virginia House of Delegates, 1818–27, in the U.S. House of Representatives, 1830–31, and 1833–37, and as navy agent at the port of Norfolk, 1837–61 (with the exception of a hiatus of two years). Loyall was a member of the University of Virginia Board of Visitors, 1823–28 (*Manual of the Board of Visitors of the University of Virginia, 1998*, 73).

From Peter Minor

DEAR SIR RIDGEWAY Oct. 9th. 1822.

Prefixed, I have the pleasure of forwarding to you an extract from the proceedings of the Agricultural Society, at its meeting on monday last. You will percieve the request of the Society that, you would undertake to prepare the circular address to the other Societies in the state. If you comply with the wish thus expressed, & will send me the address, I can have it expeditiously, copied, [. . .] printed, & sent without delay to each Society [. . .] the state. An early transmission of the address, is rendered the more expedient, from a belief that the most or all of them, hold a fall meeting, which will generally take place in a month or two from this time. Respectfully yr. Obt Sert

P. MINOR

[Enclosure]

Extract from the proceedings of the Agricultural Society of Albemarle.

Monday Oct 7th. 1822.

The following preamble & Resolutions were adopted.

"Whereas the establishment of a Professorship of Agriculture in one of the principal seminaries of Learning in this State is a measure eminently calculated to hasten & perpetuate the march of Agricultural improvement, already so happily commenced; and whereas there are grounds to believe that such an institution may be incorporated into the University of Virginia, a position at once the most advantageous & convenient to every part of the state; And whereas this Society could not make an appropriation of its funds, more conducive to the permanent attainment of the primary objects of its institution; and, as it is reasonable to expect that all the Agricultural Societies, the Farmers & planters of the State generally, will cheerfully contribute to an establishment of such universal Interest, Therefore

Resolved, That one thousand Dollars of the sum now in the hands of the Treasurer of this Society, be appropriated to the establishment of a fund, the profits of which shall go to the support of a professorship of Agriculture at the Univers[i]ty of Virginia.

Resolved that for the furtherance of this design, & to encrease this fund, the president of this Society be requested to prepare a circular address to the other Agricultural Societies of this state, requesting their co-operation in this scheme—And further to promote the same object, that a Committee be appointed to solicit donations, not to exceed one Dollar, from Individuals in every County of this commonwealth.

Resolved, That the aforesaid appropriation, together with whatever may accrue under the foregoing resolutions, be loaned to Individuals on good personal Security, or to Corporate bodies; & that when the sum loaned to any one individual shall amount to one thousand Dollars or upwards, Landed security shall be required; that the Interest shall be payable semiannually, & shall be reinvested, untill the yearly profits of the fund shall be sufficent to afford an income equal at least to a professorship in the University.

Resolved That the funds above refered to, together with donations of every description be, with the permission of the Legislature, transferred to the Rector & Visitors of the University in their Corporate Capacity.["]

(Extract from the Minutes). P. MINOR SEC.

RC and enclosure (DLC). RC cover addressed by Minor to JM "now at Monticello," which has been crossed out and "Montpellier near Orange C. H." interlined in Jefferson's hand; franked. Docketed by JM. RC damaged by removal of seal. The enclosure was later printed as an enclosure to JM's circular letter to the presidents of other agricultural societies in Virginia (see JM to Peter Minor, 21 Oct. 1822, and n.).

From John Quincy Adams

DEAR SIR WASHINGTON 11th October 1822.

In requesting your acceptance of the copy herewith transmitted of a Collection of Documents recently published by me,[1] I think it necessary to ask of your indulgence to overlook that part of it which is personally controversial. The transactions to which it relates having occurred during your Administration and the discussion involving in some degree sanctioned by you, I have thought they would not be without interest to you, on that account as well as because they are of no inconsiderable moment to the permanent welfare of the Union. I have much satisfaction also in being thus offered the occasion of tendering anew the grateful sense I entertain of that public confidence with which you honour'd me at a time when, as now appears, there were not wanting efforts then unknown to me to shake it. I remain with great Respect, Dear Sir, your very faithful and humble servant

Letterbook copy (MHi: Adams Papers). RC listed for sale in Parke-Bernet Catalogue No. 2763 (1968), item 4.

1. John Quincy Adams, *The Duplicate Letters, the Fisheries and the Mississippi. Documents relating to Transactions at the Negotiation of Ghent* (Washington, 1822; Shoemaker 7740). This pamphlet was an answer to an attack on Adams by Jonathan Russell over proposals made during the Anglo-American negotiations at Ghent on the subject of the navigation of the Mississippi River. Adams's rebuke was so overwhelmingly successful that thereafter to destroy someone's reputation before the public was known as to "jonathanrussell" someone. For a full discussion of this issue, see Bemis, *John Quincy Adams and the Foundations of American Foreign Policy*, 498–509.

To Richard Cutts

Dear Sir Montpr. Ocr. 14. 1822

Yours of the 12th.[1] came to hand this morning. I regret most sincerely, the circumstances which compel you to take the step you meditate, as the only resort under the pressure of your debts. I wish it were more in my power to aid you in your distress.[2] Short crops, low prices, and other causes limit my present means, & suggest caution as to future engagements. I have determined nevertheless to risk a purchase of the House & lots from the Bank as is proposed; it being understood that the first payment is not to be due till the end of one year; and the title of course to be clear & unexceptionable; and that you will appropriate a reasonable portion of your Salary to a discharge of the debt to the Bank. Send me therefore a conveyance properly executed, & with it the proper notes to the Bank to be signed & returned. With respect & good wishes

James Madison

RC (MHi).

1. Letter not found.

2. For Cutts's "distress," see Madison and Richard Cutts's Financial Difficulties, Editorial Note, March 1820.

To Edward Coles

Montpellier Ocr. 19. 1822

As you are about to assume new motives to walk in a straight path, and with measured steps,[1] I wish you to accept the little article* enclosed, as a type of the course I am sure you will pursue, and as a token of the affection I have so long cherished for you.

* a Pedometer

RC (NjP: Edward Coles Papers); draft (DLC). RC docketed by Coles. Filed with the RC is a separate sheet with the following, in JM's hand: "The Pedometer is to be put into a Watch pocket, fastened by the hasp, and the string passed through the bottom of the Pocket over the Knee, and hooked to the knee band or garter. The bend of the knee at every Step will then move the Indexes, which count units. &c &c.

When out of order any Watchmaker can readily put it to rights."

1. Edward Coles was the newly elected governor of Illinois.

From J. F. Daniel Lobstein

Lebanon Pennsylvania
October 19. 1822.

Honourable & Respected Sir!

To address so distinguished a personage is in a stranger a liberty perhaps unpardonnable, but it is from a conviction that any effort, however feeble, that has a tendency to remove the unfavourable and erroneous impressions Europeans have imbibe of this Country, will meet your approbation, and induce you to pardon the writer for transmitting you the Contents of his contemplated Work—A Topography of the City of Philadelphia,[1] in which the Author has sedulously endeavoured to convince them that their information respecting the Character of the Americans & the Government of the United States is incorrect and emanated from the most sordid and impure motives and that the said Government is the only one on the Globe where is tolerated genuine Liberty in every sense of the word. The collection of materials for my said work since my arrival in this Country has engrossed the major part of my time, and during my residence in America I have had the pleasure of contracting an acquaintance with the most eminent of my profession, especially with the learned Doctor *Hosack* of New York who has evinced much friendship for me. I flattered myself ere this period to have had it printed, but I find it will be more advisable for me to return to Europe and to have it there published, as the printing in this Country is too expensive. After its publication I will do myself the honour of presenting a copy to you, which I trust, may prove acceptable. I had yesterday the gratification of receiving from the venerable Ex-President of the United States Thomas Jefferson a letter,[2] in which he expressed much pleasure in the appearance of such a work. I have the honour to be Respected sir with the highest consideration and personal regard your most obedient & humble servant

Lobstein M.D.[3]

RC and enclosure (DLC). Addressed by Lobstein to JM, and franked. Cover sheet docketed by JM. For enclosure, see n. 1.

1. Lobstein enclosed a four-page, hand-written title page and table of contents for his proposed two-volume "Topography of the City of Philadelphia and Observations of the United-States of North-America," and listed six works he intended to publish in future on a separate page. The latter included treatises on dysentery, yellow fever, leprosy, and the present state of medicine in North America.

2. Jefferson to Lobstein, 10 Oct. 1822 (DLC: Jefferson Papers).

3. Johann Friedrich Daniel Lobstein (1777–1840) was born and practiced obstetrics in Strasbourg, Alsace, before undertaking further study in Paris. He served as a physician in the French army during the Napoleonic Wars. Lobstein returned to his native city, where he wrote or translated a number of medical treatises, but subsequently went bankrupt and immigrated to the United States, where he settled in New York City (*Biographisches Lexikon der hervorragenden Ärzte aller Zeiten und Völker* [6 vols.; 1929–34; reprint, Munich, 1962], 3:813).

To Peter Minor

Dr Sir Ocr. 21. 1822

I was prevented by a prolonged absence, from recg. yours of the 9th. inclosing the late Resolns. of the Socy. untill the 16th. and I have since barely found time for the hasty sketch of the required address which I now inclose. I wish it may have seized the precise views of the Society, which not being present I may not fully have comprehended. Should any corrections or additions occur to you, do not scruple to make them, without the delay of further communication with me. I hope the box of seeds from Paris left at Monticello found its way to you, and that you will be good eno' to give a proper answer to the worthy correspondent to whom the Society is indebted for such favors.

[Enclosure]

Sir Ocr. 1822

The enclosed Resolutions of the Agricultural Society of Albemarle explain the wish of the Society to provide for Agriculture, the advantage of a Professorship to be incorporated into the University of Virginia; the means proposed for making the provision, and the hope entertained of a general Co-operation in the scheme.

The present seems to be an important crisis[1] in the Agriculture of Virginia. The portions of her Soil first brought into cultivation have for the most part been exhausted of its natural fertility, without being repaired by a meliorating system of husbandry: and much of what remains in forest, and can be spared from the demands of fuel and other rural wants, will need improvement, on the first introduction of the plough.

These truths are now sufficiently impressed on the Public attention; and have led to the establishment of the Agricultural Societies among us, which are so laudably promoting the work of reform.

As a further means of advancing the great object, it has occurred to the Albemarle Society, that a distinct Professorship in the University of the State if sanctioned by the proper Authority, might be advantageously appropriated to the instruction of such as might attend, in the theory & practice of rural economy in its several branches.

To the due success of agriculture as of other Arts, Theory & practice[2] are both requisite. They always reflect light on each other. If the former without the test of the latter be a vain Science, the latter without the enlightening precepts of the former, is generally enslaved to ancient modes however erroneous or is at best but too tardy & partial in adopting salutary changes. In no instance perhaps is habit more unyielding, or irrational practice more prevalent, than among those who cultivate the earth: And this is the more to be lamented as Agriculture is Still so far below the attainments to which it may fairly aspire.

A professorship of agriculture in the University[3] might derive special advantages from the lights thrown out from the Chair of Chemistry in that Institution. This Science is every day penetrating some of the hidden laws of nature, and tracing the useful purposes to which they may be made subservient. Agriculture is a field on which it has already begun to shed its rays, and on which it promises to do much towards unveiling the processes of nature to which the principles of Agriculture are related. The professional Lectures on Chemistry which are to embrace those principles could not fail to be auxiliary to a professorship having lessons on Agriculture for its essential charge.

The fund contemplated for the support of such a professorship is to consist of a sum drawn from unexpended subscriptions, from special donations, and from a diffusive contribution not exceeding a dollar from an individual. It is hoped, that for a purpose of such general utility, the number of contributors will more than make up for the smallness of the respective sums: and that with the other resources, means may be gathered not only adequate to the immediate views entertained; but justifying an enlargement of them.

Should this prove to be the case, it will be an improvement of the plan of Agricultural instruction to provide and place under the superintendance of the Professor a small farm in the vicinage, to be cultivated partly as a pattern farm illustrating practically a system at once profitable & improving; partly as an experimental farm, not only bringing to the test new modes of culture & management, but introducing new plants & animals deemed worthy of experiment. In obtaining these, aid might be found in the patriotic attention of the public & private naval commanders in their visits to foreign Countries: And it might well happen that occasional successes in rearing new species or varieties, of peculiar value, would yield in seeds & stocks a profit defraying the expences incurred on this head.

A farm exhibiting an instructive model, observed as it would be by occasional visitors, and understood as it wd. be in its principles & plans, by students returning to their dispersed homes, would tend not a little[4] to spread sound information on the subject of Agriculture & to cherish that spirit of imitation & emulation which is the source of improvement in every Art & enterprize.

You will oblige, Sir, the Society of Albemarle by laying this communication before that over which you preside; and by transmitting its sentiments thereon; which will afford particular pleasure if they should accord with the views of this Society and promise so valuable a co operation in carrying them into effect.

By order of the Society.[5]

Draft and draft of enclosure (DLC). The draft of enclosure (4 pp.) was later sent as a printed circular, enclosing the 7 Oct. 1822 resolutions of the Agricultural Society of Albemarle, to the presidents of other agricultural societies in Virginia. An RC survives of the printed circular and enclosed resolutions (Vi: Collection F.–N.F. Cabell Manuscripts relating to the History of Agriculture in Virginia), addressed to Joseph C. Cabell, Warminster, Nelson County; postmarked 28 Nov. 1822; and redirected to Williamsburg. Docketed by Cabell: "Resolutions and Mr. Madison's circular respecting a Professorship of Agriculture." The circular and resolutions were printed in the *Daily National Intelligencer*, 30 Nov. 1822, and the *American Farmer* 4 (22 Nov. 1822), 273–74, and in other newspapers. Replies to this circular from James M. Garnett, president of the Fredericksburg Agricultural Society, and John Faulcon, president of the Agricultural Society of Surry County, were acknowledged at the 6 Oct. 1823 meeting of the Agricultural Society of Albemarle (True, "Minute Book of the Albemarle Agricultural Society," printed in *Annual Report of the American Historical Association for . . . 1918*, 1:300). Minor differences between the draft of enclosure and printed copies have not been noted.

1. In the draft of enclosure JM first wrote then crossed through "a critical stage" before interlining "an important crisis" here.

2. In the draft of enclosure JM first wrote here "ought both to be regarded" then interlined "are both requisite." The printed copy has the latter phrase here.

3. The printed copy does not have "in the University" here.

4. In the printed copy "not a little" was deleted here.

5. The printed copy is signed "James Madison, *Pres't.*"

To John Quincy Adams

DEAR SIR MONTPELLIER [October] 24. 1822

I have received with your favour of the 11th. a copy of the "Collection of Documents" which you had recently published.

The Treaty of Ghent forms a prominent epoch in our National History; and will be a lasting monument of the Ability and patriotism with which it was negociated. Incidents elucidating the transaction, can not therefore but be interesting, and they are made the more so by the eloquent strain in which they are presented. Accept my thanks Sir for the little volume containing them, with assurances of my continued esteem and cordial respects.

JAMES MADISON

RC (MHi: Adams Papers); draft and FC (DLC). RC month not indicated; supplied from draft. FC in John C. Payne's hand.

To Mathew Carey

DR. SIR Ocr. 25. [1822]

An absence from home with some pressing avocations since my return have delayd. thus long my acknowledgment of your's of the 3d. inst; and of the pamphlet on our commercial policy, which is another proof of your disinterested zeal on an important subject.

You have placed in a strong light the evils necessarily resulting from the excess of our importations over our exportations, and the expediency of restoring an equilibrium.

I wish the remedy were as easy as the malady is distressing. The malady does indeed like some physical ones, carry *in some degree* its cure within itself. The amount of purchases, must be controuled by deficient means of payment. But as long as a foreign credit is given, a limited balance may be kept up, producing a drain of the circulating metals and embarrassment in our internal affairs.

How a remedial equilibrium in our foreign trade is to be brought about is the problem?

Our Imported articles are of 2 Classes. 1. Such as are or may be provided at home. 2. Such as can not, either at all, or for a long time, be otherwise obtained than from abroad.

With respect to the first, an encouragement to home products results from a declension of foreign demand, for our articles of export, and from the profitableness of transferring labour from these to manufactured articles. In the policy of favoring this transfer, within the reasons, heretofore intimatd I entirely concur.

I fear however that this source of relief would fall short of the object. Whatever might be gained by such a transfer of labour as would diminish our imports in a greater proportion than it would diminish our exports, the remaining class of imports which can not be provided at home, and which has in fact, been a main source of the unfavorable balance might still keep the scale agst. us. It is the class consisting in great part of luxuries, which the habits of our people are prone to call for when they can be obtained from indulgent Creditors. Whilst foreign capital gives a credit to our importing Merchants, which enables these to do the same to the retail Merchants, who are thus induced to extend it to the consumers, experience has shewn the danger that the consumption will not be measured by the rules of economy. The trade of this Country in its Colonial State was always a trade of Credit, and the Country, as a consequence always under the pressure of debts to Brith: Merchants, and perplexed in its pecuniary affairs. Hence the resort to paper currencies, and hence the amount of British debts at the commencement of the revolutionary war. Since the peace of 1783, the like cause & the like effects have marked our situation, which has been not a little aggravated by the abuses of the Banking system.

Our difficulties would seem then to have deeper roots than many suppose. On the disposition of G. B. to avail herself of her great mercantile capital in her commerce with us we have neither a power of controul nor a right to complain. And over the habitual propensities of our own Citizens, there could be no adequate controul but by sumptuary prohibitions; to which they are averse as well from a sentiment of liberty, as on the score of enjoyment.

Must we then despair of our situation? Far from it. Progressive alleviations at least may fairly be looked for, which may prepare the way for the desired State of things. Among our misfortunes have been unusual failures of some of our Staple crops which reduced the quantity in greater proportion than they raised the price. Future seasons may be less unpropitious. Our growing manufactures, which may be still further fostered by public patronage, will abridge the excess of our imports. The harrassing consequences of improvident consumption, may be expected to check in individuals an indulgence in foreign superfluities. Reforms in the Banking System may put an end to the lavish credits which have conspired to produce extravagant habits. A like tendency will result from a more prompt and exact administration of justice, where relaxations or aberrations have crept into it. All these causes together must have a healing influence that will be felt in the general condition of the Country. Nor is it a premature consideration that the young nations which are entering into the commerce of the world, and which are still more agricultural than the U.S. will by narrowing the room for our present staples in foreign Markets, hasten & extend the application of our industry, to manufactured articles which their own growing markets will call for, & of which our comparative vicinity will favor supplies from our workshops. Whatever advantage therefore may accrue to a nation from a combination of manufacturing with agricultural industry will in our case be forwarded by the Independent rank assumed by our fellow inhabitants of this Hemisphere. Finally we are not to lose sight of the material fact, that an insufficiency of our exports to balance our imports, must *of necessity*, restrain or reduce the latter within certain limits; and co-operate powerfully with other means of promoting an equilibrium. Among the persuasive means, it is not an empty compliment to class the impressive statements and sound admonitions which your pamphlet addresses to the good sense & interest of all who have contributed to the evils of an unfavorable balance of trade, by their inconsiderate use of imported merchandizes. Of all the remedies for our embarrassments, economical habits are the most desirable & the most effectual. If individuals live within their incomes the nation must do so.

Such is the view of the subject which at present occurs to me. I am aware that it may not in some respects receive your approbation. Of the frankness with which it is given I am sure you will not disapprove. With sincere esteem & respect

J.M.

Draft (DLC: Rives Collection, Madison Papers). Year supplied at a later date in pencil in JM's hand.

To J. F. Daniel Lobstein

SIR MONTPR. OCr. 28. 1822

I have recd. your letter of the 19th. inclosing a specification of the contents of a work you are about to publish. The topics you have selected will afford ample scope for information and observations on the State of this Country. An eye which is aquainted with Europe will be best able to mark such features of America, as will present a comparative view doing justice to one without injustice to the other. I wish you success in the task you have undertaken. With respect

J.M

Draft (DLC).

From Edward Coles

My dear Sir Washington Oct: 30 1822

It was my intention, as you know, to have remained here but two or three days. But altho' I have made every effort in my power to complete sooner the little business I had to attend to, I have found it impossible to do so, and indeed I have not even yet done so. But I am now compelled to hasten off in the morning, and to ride very rapidly, by the most direct route, to reach Illinois in time for the meeting of the Legislature.

When I arrived here I found Mr. Cutts confined to what is called the bounds. He seemed rather reserved and not much disposed to converse freely, on the subject of his embarrassed situation. He assured me there was no lein or encombrance whatever on his house and the four Lots attached to it, and that the Bank had a good and perfect title. This account has been confirmed to me by the officers of the Bank, by Col: Bumford, Mr. Ringgold &c, all of whom agree too in saying that the property is richly worth the sum the Bank asks for it. I have seen the title papers from Mr. Cutts to the Bank. They consist of a Deed dated Nov: 1818 from Mr. Cutts to Mr. Geo: Sweeny in trust for the benefit or rather security of Th: Munroe, who had endorsed for Mr. Cutts to a considerable amount in the Bank. Mr. Cutts having failed to pay, Mr. Munroe was called on by the Bank, and the Bank having agreed to receive from him the property in question in payment of the debt, George Sweeny as trustee made a Deed to the Bank. These Deeds have all been recorded, and are now in the possession of the Bank. Mr. Smith,[1] the Cashier, informed me that the Board of Directors had agreed to let you have the property for 5750$ to be paid by instalments with interest, and on the receipt of your notes would give you the obligation of the Bank to make you a perfect title to the property on the payment of your notes—or that the Bank would make you a Deed at once on your giving it a mortgage on the property to secure the ultimate payment of it—or that the Bank would make the Deed on your giving your notes with a good endorser in the City of Washington. I requested him to make his propositions either directly to you or through Mr. Cutts—this he promised to do. It is therefore unnecessary for me to state them more formally.

Mr. Th: Munroe, who also thinks the property has been valued very low, and that the title to it is perfectly good, informs me that the Deed from the heirs of Davidson to Mr. Cutts was dated the same day with the Deed of Trust from Mr. Cutts to Geo: Sweeny viz: Nov. 1818. And of course there could not be any liens from Mr. Cutts on the property.

I have had several conversations with Mrs. Cutts on the subject of her Husbands situation—she will act with perfect prudence and propriety.

It is unnecessary to add more on the subject as she will write all the details to her sister.

Mr. Monroe and family are all well. I have experienced particular gratification from the unusually kind and friendly manner which he has recd: and treated me during this visit to Washington. It is now very late at night and I have yet my clothes to pack up in order to setout by sunrise in the morning. I must therefore beg you to excuse this hasty letter—to accept my thanks for the Pedometer which I shall always highly prize as a token of your friendship for me—and with a tender of my affectionate regards to Mrs. Madison and Payne accept assurances of my great respect and sincere regard

EDWARD COLES

RC (ICHi). Addressed by Coles to JM at "Orange C. H.," and franked. Docketed by JM.

1. Richard Smith was cashier of the branch bank of the Second Bank of the United States at Washington, 1817–36, and then the Bank of the Metropolis. He was a friend of Dolley Madison, and her trustee in old age (William Tindall, *Standard History of the City of Washington; From a Study of the Original Sources* [Knoxville, Tenn., 1914], 546, 548; Mattern and Shulman, *Selected Letters of Dolley Payne Madison*, 412).

From Mathew Carey

DEAR SIR, PHILADA. NOV. 1. 1822

I have duly recd your favour of the 25th ult. and have read it with the attention to which the writer & the subject are entitled.

You will pardon me for stating that I think you have greatly overrated the difficulties in the way of a sound system of policy for this Country, wh. would cure all its evils, & place it on the exalted ground, to which its immense advantages, natural moral, & political entitle it, instead of wasting its resources in the support of the industry & governments of Europe. We exhibit to the world the shocking spectacle of imbecility & folly, in submitting, without retaliation to the exclusion of the third (formerly the first or second) staple of the nation—& why? Because a few merchants, regardless of the interests of the country, and really blind to their own, clamour against any alteration of the tariff, reecho the cuckoo note—*let-us-alone*—while they have, from the commencement of the government, been almost constantly goading the government for restrictions on foreign Commerce; & retaliations of all measures that restrained or injured our commerce. Your administration affords a thousand proofs of the justice of their claims of peculiar privileges & protection.

I shall take the liberty of resuming the subject, at no distant day. Meanwhile I request you will accept the assurances of the most sincere esteem & regard of Your obt. hble. servt.

MATHEW CAREY

PS. I enclose two numbers of Hamilton.[1]

RC (DLC). Addressed by Carey to JM at "Monticello Va.," and franked. Docketed by JM.

1. Carey published five essays under the pen name "Hamilton," attacking the "let us alone policy of our government," and supporting a protective tariff. They appeared in the *Daily National Intelligencer* on 4 and 17 Sept., 3 and 23 Oct., and 8 Nov. 1822, and were also published in pamphlet form. JM's copies of numbers 2, 4, and 5 are in the Madison Collection, Rare Book and Special Collections Division, Library of Congress.

To William Rufus Devane King

DEAR SIR MONTPR. Novr. 3. 1822

Mr George Conway[1] of this State is about to become with his family, inhabitants of Alabama. As he will be there an entire stranger, he very naturally wishes to be made known to some one whose acquaintance & countenance may be valuable to him. Though not a very remote kinsman, I have personally a slight knowledge only of him: but I am well assured that his character is in every feature a worthy & amiable one. It is on this ground that I take the liberty of giving him an introduction to any friendly attentions it may be convenient for you to shew him; tendering you at the same time assurances of my esteem and my cordial respects.

J.M

Draft (DLC). William Rufus Devane King (1786–1853) was born in North Carolina, attended the University of North Carolina, and served in the U.S. House of Representatives, 1811–16, as a supporter of JM. In 1818 he moved to Alabama, participated in the state's constitutional convention, and became one of its first U.S. senators, serving terms in 1819–44 and 1848–52. He was appointed U.S. minister to France, 1844–46, and was elected vice president of the United States in 1852.

1. George Conway (1789–1827), the son of Francis Conway of Port Conway, Virginia, was a great-nephew of JM's mother, Nelly Conway Madison. President Monroe appointed him receiver of public money for the district east of Pearl River in Alabama in 1824 (Hayden, *Virginia Genealogies* [1973 reprint], 254, 255, 256, 263, 264; James Monroe to JM, 27 Mar. 1824, DLC; *Senate Exec. Proceedings*, 3:354).

To [James Monroe?]

private

DEAR SIR MONTPELLIER NOVR 3 1822

My neighbour & your Acquaintance Mr Richard Taliaferro[1] is desirous that one of his sons[2] should receive a military education at West Point. His progress in the preparatory studies is certified by his present Tutor, and I have myself had a slight opportunity of witnessing that he has some knowledge of Latin. Of his general character I know nothing which is not favorable. If there be no bar to the admission of the youth as a Cadet, from the distributive or any other established rule, your dispositions towards the father will ensure attention to the just pretensions of the son.

I make this a *private* letter the rather, as my declining interposition in some other cases, might subject me to dissatisfactions where I do not wish them to be felt. The truth is, I promised Mr. T. to drop you a few lines without taking this obstacle into consideration; his request being made in a transient interview. Health & every other happiness

JAMES MADISON

Printed facsimile of RC (Superior Galleries, The Moreira Collection Sale, Part 3 and Other Important Properties Auction and Mail Bid Sale January 29, 30, 31, 1989 Catalogue [Beverly Hills, Calif.], item 5078). Addressee not indicated; most likely to James Monroe owing to the complimentary close.

1. Richard Henry Taliaferro was the proprietor of Ashland, a plantation in Orange County, Virginia (Miller, *Antebellum Orange*, 121).

2. Peachy R. Taliaferro was accepted as a cadet at West Point in 1823 but was discharged from the academy in 1824 (John Gilmer Speed, *The Gilmers in America* [New York, 1897], 188; Peachy R. Taliaferro to John C. Calhoun, 10 Mar. 1823, Robert L. Meriwether et al., eds., *The Papers of John C. Calhoun* [28 vols.; Columbia, S.C., 1959–2003], 7:512, 8:526 n.).

To Charles Tait

DR. SIR MONTPR. NOVR. 3. 1822

Mr. Geo: Conway being on his way to Alabama, where he is about to establish himself & family, and where he will be an entire stranger, I take a liberty which I hope you will excuse, of introducing him to any kind attentions which may be convenient to you. Tho' a kinsman in a degree not very remote, I have little personal acquaintance with him; but I have sufficient grounds for my confidence that he will be found in every respect worthy of them. I avail myself of the occasion to assure you Sir of my high esteem and my friendly respects.

Draft (DLC). Charles Tait (1768–1835) was born in Louisa County, Virginia, and settled in Augusta, Georgia, where he became a law partner of William Harris Crawford. He served as judge of the state superior court for the western circuit of Georgia, 1803–9, and as U.S. senator, 1809–19, where he strongly supported JM and naval operations during the War of 1812. Tait helped secure the admission of Alabama to the Union in 1819, and after moving to the new state, was first federal judge of the district of Alabama, 1820–26 (Charles H. Moffat, "Charles Tait, Planter, Politician, and Scientist of the Old South," *Journal of Southern History* 14 [1948]: 206–33).

To Richard Cutts

DEAR SIR MONTPR. NOVr. 4. 1822

I recd. yours of Ocr. 31.[1] on saturday but not in time to answer it by the return mail. Inclosed are the papers from the Bank, with my name to the promisory Notes. Not wishing to resort to an Indorsor in the City, I embrace the alternative of accepting a bond for the conveyance of the lotts, for the reason you suggest. Be so good as to have the Bond executed on the delivery of the Notes, and forward it to me. With respects & best wishes

JAMES MADISON

RC (MHi).

1. Letter not found.

From Peter Minor

DEAR SIR, RIDGEWAY NOV. 5. 1822

I now have the pleasure of sending you by Mr Macon, some printed copies of the late resolutions of our Society, & the circular address.[1] It has been delayed some time, by a week or two's absense from home when your letter arrived.

I have directed to all the societies, that I know of in the state, & I have thought it proper to send them to you, to obtain your Frank. I have also sent some extra copies, which you can direct to any others, whose existence in the state you may know, or be informed of. Some errors of the press have occurred, which in those that are addressed, I have corrected with the pen. The scheme I find is popular, wherever I have heard it mentioned, & I have no doubt will succeed thro'out the state, if we can but select active & zealous individuals in the different counties to push it forward.

I have not yet recd. the Box of seeds from Monticello, but can get it at any time. I feel much at a loss to decide what would be a *suitable* answer to the presents of Monr. Thouin, seeing that he has sent us mostly, the weeds of our own country. Shall we pay him in kind or not? With great respect yrs.

P MINOR

If you wish more copies of the address &c. to send to distinguished agriculturali[s]ts of yr. acquaintance I will send them to you on request.

PM

RC (DLC). Docketed by JM.

1. See JM to Minor, 21 Oct. 1822, and n.

From Virgil Maxcy

SIR, TULIP HILL, NEAR ANNAPOLIS, MD NOV. 10. 1822.

I take the liberty of inclosing you a pamphlet written in Defence of the Maryland Resolutions relative to Appropriations of Public Land for the purposes of education, and in answer to objections, which have been raised against them[1]—and cannot but hope that a Proposition, promising if carried into effect, important results in favour of the stability of our Institutions, will meet with the approbation of one, whose great talents have been devoted through life to the interests of Freedom & good Government. I have the honour to be With the greatest Respect Sir, Yr. Mo: Obt. Hble. Servt.

V. MAXCY[2]

RC (DLC). Docketed by JM.

1. [Virgil Maxcy], *The Maryland Resolutions, and the Objections to Them Considered* (Baltimore, 1822; Shoemaker 9444).

2. Virgil Maxcy (1785–1844) graduated from Brown University in 1804 and read law with Robert Goodloe Harper of Maryland. He served in the Maryland legislature, as solicitor of the U.S. Treasury, and as U.S. chargé d'affaires to the court of Belgium. He died in the gun explosion on the U.S.S. Princeton, 28 Feb. 1844 (Jonathan Maxcy, *The Literary Remains of the Rev. Jonathan Maxcy, D. D. . . . with a Memoir of His Life* [New York, 1844], 29–30).

From Mathew Carey

DEAR SIR, PHILADA NOV 12. 1822

I enclose you some numbers of Hamilton—& hope, when you have given the subject a full and complete consideration, that you will agree that there is but one way to insure the prosperity & happiness of the Country, and that is by adopting the restrictive and protecting system which has elevated Great Britain to the towering height where she has stood for half a century, so far beyond what her population or natural resources entitle her to and which has restored France to prosperity after her horrible sufferings in 1815, 16, & 17. With the great volume of European experience before them, our rulers are unpardonable for making such a horrible shipwreck of our prosperity & happiness as they did after the close of the war. If any thing could add to the disgrace of their ungrateful & heartless abandonment of the Manufacturers to destruction, it would be the contemptible & false pretence of extortion during the war. What abhorrence must every man of sound head and pure heart feel for a Randolph, who sold his tobacco for 30 cents per lb.—a Lowndes who sold cotton at 33—and a Wright who sold Wheat at 2 Dollars per bushel[1]—cawling & railing at a miserable manufacturer of woollens, who sold his goods at 12 or 14 Dollars per yard, instead of the peace prices of 7 or 8, when the farmers had raised the raw material from 75 cents to 3 & 4 Dollars per lb.!! It sickens me to think of it—& will be an eternal blot on the escutcheon of the fourteenth Congress—as the callousness with which the sufferings of the devoted manufacturers were regarded in 1817, 1818, & 1819 will be on that of their successors. The stain is indelible, & will remain as long as the history of those times shall endure. If no one else transmits it to posterity, my endeavours shall not be wanting.

Enough, however, of this lamentable subject. What is past is irreparable. It is our duty to try to rescue the vessel of state from the quicksand on which she has been thrown by want of skill. *We furnish nearly all our food. Let us supply but three fourths of our own clothing*—& distress & embarrassment will be banished from the land. Our citizens will all be profitably employed. Specie will flow in upon us in a full tide. We shall then be really and truly independent—& no longer be "*hewers of wood & drawers of water*" for foreign nations, for the support of whose industry & governments our resources are at present so prodigally lavished.

Excuse the freedom I take—& the warmth I display. Feeling the magnitude of the cause as I do, it is impossible for me to restrain myself at all times within due bounds. Your obt. hble. servt

MATHEW CAREY

RC (DLC). Addressed by Carey to JM at "Monticello." Docketed by JM.

1. Carey was referring to the U.S. representatives John Randolph of Virginia, William Lowndes of South Carolina, and Robert Wright of Maryland.

From Edwin C. Holland

SIR, CHARLESTON Novr. 15th. 1822.

Under cover of this, I take the liberty of presenting to you a Pamphlet that I have recently published.[1] It is upon a subject deeply interesting to us, in this section of the Union, more particularly from the excitement that now exists among us. The important public services that you have rendered to our common Country endear you to the affections of every American and to none more since[re]ly than to Yr. obdt. Servt. & fellow Citizen

EDWIN C. HOLLAND[2]

RC (DLC). Docketed by JM.

1. [Edwin C. Holland], *A Refutation of the Calumnies Circulated against the Southern & Western States. Respecting the Institution and Existence of Slavery among Them.* . . . (Charleston, S.C., 1822; Shoemaker 9037). For a summary of this proslavery tract, see Larry E. Tise, *Proslavery: A History of the Defense of Slavery in America, 1701–1840* (Athens, Ga., 1987), 59–61.

2. Edwin Clifford Holland (1794–1824) was the editor of the *Charleston Times* and a writer of poems and plays (Oscar Wegelin, *Early American Plays, 1714–1830* . . . [1900; reprint, New York, 1970], 54).

From John S. Skinner

DEAR SIR BALT: POST: OFF: Nov 18. 1822

This conveyance will bear to you a beautiful & very perfect specimen of northern corn—exhibited at the late Agricultural exhibition at Brighton.

I sincerely rejoice at your prospect of adding a *Professorship of Agriculture* to your university, as it will enlighten & dignify the most useful of all occupations.

If I could be justified in so far trespassing on the leisure which you ought to be allowed to enjoy, after so many important services to your country, I would entreat occasional communications on the leading topicks which the American Farmer was established to discuss & illustrate. With sincere respect & regard Your obt. ser

J. S. SKINNER

RC (DLC). Docketed by JM.

To Virgil Maxcy

MONTPELLIER NOVR. 20. 1822

J. Madison presents his respects to Mr. Maxcy, with thanks for his pamphlet in defence of the Maryland Resolutions proposing grants of public land for the purposes of Education to the States which have not received them. Of the publication less can not be said than that it has taken a very able & interesting view of the question.

RC (NN); draft (DLC). RC addressed and franked by JM to Maxcy at "Tulip Hill near Annapolis Maryland." Postmarked 26 Nov. at Orange Court House. Minor differences between the copies have not been noted.

From Thomas Jefferson

DEAR SIR MONTICELLO NOV. 22. 22.

The person who hands you this letter is an interesting subject of curiosity.[1] He was taken prisoner by the Kickapoos when he supposes he must have been about 3. or 4. years of age, knows not whence taken nor who were his parents. He escaped from the Indians at about 19. as he supposes, & about 7. years ago. He has applied himself to education, is a student of Medecine, & has assumed the name of Hunter as the translation of that given him by the Indians. To a good degree of genius he adds great observation and correct character. He has been recieved with great courtesy at N. York & Philade. by the literati especially and also by the gens du monde. He has been long enough in this neighborhood to be much esteemed. He is setting out for the Medical lectures of Philade. & asked me to give him a letter to you which I do, satisfied that the enquiries you will make of him, and to which he will answer with great willingness will gratify you to the full worth of the intrusion. He has prepared a very interesting book for publication.

Ten days ago I incurred the accident of breaking the small bone of the left fore-arm, & some disturbance of the small bones of the wrist. Dr. Watkins attended promptly, set them well and all is doing well. He tells me I must submit to confinement till Christmas day. I had intended a visit to you shortly, but this disappoints it. Dawson[2] has finished the account books very ably. Genl. Cocke has been 3. days examining them. The vouchers wanting are reduced to about 4000. D. which can be got immediately the persons being in the neighborhood. He thinks there will be scarcely a dollar unvouched. I salute mrs. Madison and yourself with constant affection and respect.

TH: JEFFERSON

RC (DLC).

1. John Dunn Hunter (ca. 1797–1827) published the story of his life as *Manners and Customs of Several Indian Tribes Located West of the Mississippi* . . . (Philadelphia, 1823; Shoemaker 12897). Soon thereafter he visited England, where he was lionized and his book published as *Memoirs of a Captivity Among the Indians of North America* . . . (London, 1823). Though celebrated in Europe, Hunter was described as a fraud by fellow Americans Lewis Cass, Henry R. Schoolcraft, Thomas L. McKenney, and Peter Stephen Du Ponceau. On his return to the United States in 1824, Hunter exchanged letters with JM (15 Oct. 1824, and JM's reply of 20 Oct. 1824 [DLC]), and went to the Southwest, where he and others attempted to establish the independent Republic of Fredonia, a union of Indians and whites centered at Nacogdoches. As the experiment came to a violent end, Hunter was killed by a paid assassin (Richard Drinnon, *White Savage: The Case of John Dunn Hunter* [New York, 1972], 3–10, 15–21, 27–29, 56, 61–67, 121–24, 201–11, 216–22).

2. Martin Dawson (ca. 1772–1835), was a merchant of Milton, Virginia, who as commissioner of accounts for the University of Virginia, annually examined the accounts of the bursar and proctor from 1822 to 1834 (Bruce, *History of the University of Virginia*, 2:389–95).

¶ From Richard Cutts. Letter not found. *22 November 1822*. Acknowledged as received by JM in John C. Payne to Richard Cutts, ca. 25 Nov. 1822, where it is described as enclosing an account with the Second Bank of the United States and a deed for a house and lots mentioned therein.

From Mathew Carey

DEAR SIR, PHILADA. NOV. 25. 1822

By this mail, I send you two copies each of No. 2 & 3 of Hamilton, new series. No. 1 was forwarded some time since.

For the sake of your country and your reputation, I beseech you reflect deeply on this subject—& I hope you will see there is but one course can save our country—that is, adopting the policy which has wrought wonders for Great Britain, France & every country which has followed their example. The weight of your name, openly & decidedly given, wd be a tower of strength in this great cause, on which "the wealth, power, and resources" of the U.S. depend. With great respect, Your obt. hble. servt

MATHEW CAREY

RC (DLC).

From Horatio Gates Spafford

ESTEEMED FRIEND, JAMES MADISON: TROY N.Y., 11 MO. 25, 1822.

Providence sometimes blesses us with necessary chastisements. The untoward events that drove me from my Cabin in the wilds of Western Pennsylvania, restored me again to society, led to the performance of a necessary literary task, a second edition of my Gazetteer, & to the completion of another task, on which, during 20 odd years, I had expended, hitherto to no profit, a great deal of time, thought & money.

I have now fully realized the truth of a theory, of great importance in the arts & to the country, long since conceived; & what has so very long been theory, struggling in the birth, is now mere mechanical demonstrations, & may be taught by practise in a few minutes! How, now, shall I avail myself of the benefit of the discovery? I ask thy advice.

The theory was, that all Iron, perfectly pure, is uniformly good; that pure Iron, duly & equally carbonized, makes good Steel; & it embraces modes of operation conformable to this theory, designed to make perfectly pure Iron, & Cast Steel, a pure carbonate of Iron. The system is all new, & perfectly succeeds, equal to the high expectations I had formed of it. The Steel is of the quality called Cast Steel, has been thoroughly & severely tried, by the best artists & mechanics, & is pronounced decidedly superior to any ever imported. I make it from the ores of Iron, Pigs, Bar Iron, &c. & with such facility that it affords profit enough for a good business. A company is formed for manufacturing Steel, men of business, with a half million of dollars' capital, bound to make so much as to supply the demand in the United States, giving to me one third of the clear profits. Such is the confidence of capitalists, that were it possible to carry on the manufacture & keep the process a secret, I could sell the invention for almost any sum that could be named. It is my intention to apply to Congress for a special law, permitting the specifications to remain *sealed papers in the department of State*, for 14 years. Were this done, I could sell the Steel Patent for an annuity of 5000 dollars, for that term of time.

The system embraces the making of Iron, as well as Steel, & is secured to me by 2 Patents.[1] I have stated to the Patent Officer my intention to apply for such a law, & have requested him, if permitted by the laws, to keep the specifications private until the meeting of Congress. Of all men living, I hate lawyers & lawsuits the worst. My desires as to money are moderate. I wish the government would buy the discovery; say pay me one third of what good judges should say it would be worth, perfectly securred, for 14 years, & make it a public benefit. I should then only want to stipulate that the Iron & Steel, made conformably to my theory, should be stamped with my name, Spafford Iron, & Spafford Cast-Steel, let the world call it vanity, or what it please, & give myself no farther any concern about it. It has cost me enough of care. The thing is now perfected; I want to dismiss it from my mind.

Now, one of the two things I have named is very desirable. Pray give me thy opinion whether Congress would grant me such a law; & also, whether, in thy opinion, the goverment, being fully satisfied of the truth of what I state, it would purchase the discovery on some equitable terms?

I can make the very best of Cast-Steel, from our native ores, at about the expense of making refined Bar Iron, by the old process; & can make pure Bar Iron, Castings, &c. for half what they are made, in any country, by the old method. In a few weeks I will send thee, should I have opportunity, some cast-steel plough-shares, for trial, cast, as the cast-iron ones are.

Bar Iron is now worth, per cargo, 80 dolls. a ton; Cast Steel, 500. The Contractors on three half miles of the Erie Canal, have used 3 tons of cast-steel this year, at 28 cents a pound. The best English cast-steel is a carburet, not perfectly pure; mine is all of one quality, a pure carbonate of Iron; iron saturated with carbon. As a discovery, none of modern times exceeds it in importance; and it is all American, all new; no patch-work system; nothing borrowed from the old, the work of 20 centuries. If the goverment would act wisely, we could soon stop the importation of Iron & Steel, save our Millions of dollars at home, & tell Europe, as Europe tells us, we consider self-preservation the first law of nature: We are as independent as you are. I should be obliged by thy advice, & am, with great consideration & regard, thy friend,

Horatio Gates Spafford

RC (DLC). Addressed by Spafford to JM, and franked. Docketed by JM.

1. The two patents were issued on 30 Oct. 1822. For more on Spafford's invented process, see Julian P. Boyd, "Horatio Gates Spafford, Precursor of Bessemer," *Proceedings of the American Philosophical Society* 87 (1943): 47–50, 49 n. 5.

John C. Payne to Richard Cutts

Dr. sir. [ca. 25 November 1822]

From the indisposition of Mr. Madison he directs me to acknowledge the rect. of your favor of the 22d. inclosing the account of the Bank of the U.S. shewing the payment of the balance due that institution & the deed from Mr. Smith as Trustee for the house & lots therein mentioned. From the slight view which his health allows him to take of the latter he supposes it is drawn up in that form which is best & safest, but he suggests for your consideration the propriety of shewing it to Mr. Jones before it is recorded to see that it is fully guarded against any flaw of which unjust advantage might be taken. The deed is returned.

Draft (DLC: Dolley Madison Papers). Undated; conjectural date supplied from internal evidence.

From David Porter

MERIDIAN HILL Novr. 28th. 1822

Captn. Porter presents his compliments to Mr. Madison, sends him the right Voln. in place of the one returned,[1] and hopes the work may afford him some amusement.

It will be the source of great gratification to Captn. P. if the Preface should meet Mr. Madisons approbation.

RC (DLC). Docketed by JM.

1. David Porter, *Journal of a Cruise Made to the Pacific Ocean, by Captain David Porter, in the United States Frigate Essex, in the Years 1812, 1813, and 1814*, 2d ed. (2 vols.; New York, 1822; Shoemaker 9978). In a long preface, Porter took issue with and answered at length the critics of the first edition of the *Journal*, noting that during the war he had suffered "personal wrongs and outrages" (ibid., v) and "that the terms 'Pirate, Freebooter, Bucanier,' &c. were the epithets with which he was usually honoured by the British prints and British partisans; and that the usual language of both was, that 'the scoundrel Porter deserved to be hanged alongside of the scoundrel Madison'" (ibid., iv).

From John Browne Cutting

DEAR SIR, WASHINGTON 30 Novr 1822

Thomas Law Esqr:[1] who resides on a farm in this vicinity has by letter, requested that I woud in his name inclose you his last essay on a very thorny subject:[2] a severe domestic calamity has for the last month drawn me near to him. But even were this otherwise, any function of friendship woud be rendered to me additionally pleasant, that gave me occasion to assure you & Mrs Madison of that true and respectful regard, with which I shall long remain her and your very obedt Servt

JOHN BROWNE CUTTING[3]

RC (DLC). Docketed by JM.

1. Thomas Law (1756–1834), a former administrator for the British East India Company, who immigrated to the United States in 1794, was a Washington real-estate investor and gentleman of leisure who wrote on political and economic topics. He married Elizabeth

Parke Custis, a granddaughter of Martha Washington, in 1796, but the couple later separated (*PJM*, 17:52 n. 1, 53 n. 7).

2. [Thomas Law], *Additional Facts, Remarks, and Arguments, Illustrative of the Advantage to the People of the United States, of a National Circulating Medium* (Washington, 1822; Shoemaker 7741). JM's copy is in the Madison Papers, Special Collections, University of Virginia Library.

3. John Browne Cutting (1755?-1831) was a native of Boston, a Revolutionary War veteran who served in the Hospital Department and as apothecary general, and a resident of Washington (L. H. Butterfield et al., eds., *Adams Family Correspondence* [10 vols. to date; Cambridge, Mass., 1963—], 7:122 n. 8; Francis J. Sypher Jr., *New York State Society of the Cincinnati: Biographies of Original Members & Other Continental Officers* [Fishkill, N.Y., 2004], 112).

To Edwin C. Holland

MONTPR. NOVR 30. 1822

JM. presents his respects to Mr. H. with thanks for the copy of his pamphlet; which is made particularly interesting by some of the views given of the subject discussed.

Draft (DLC).

To Philip P. Barbour

DEAR SIR MONTPELLIER Decr. 1. 1822

The enclosed letter[1] not having come to hand before your departure for Washington, I cannot so well comply with the request of the writer as by forwarding it for your perusal. Should you think his object a reasonable one, or entitled to a fair consideration, a word of explanation from you to the Secy. of war & the Attorney General, if proper at all, may be more so from you than from me and can not certainly be of less avail. I am indeed without the least information on the case, beyond what is gathered from the letter itself. Of the character of the writer, tho' my personal knowledge is of old date, I am authorised by all the evidence short of it, to speak favorably. He has been ever represented as remarkable for an honest frankness, and a warmth of good feelings; and as a firm patriot through all the vicissitudes of the times, from the commencement of the Revolution to the present. I have understood too that his present distress is the consequence of no fault but that of a liberality and benevolence, indulged beyond the limits of prudence. With this view of Mr. Ts character & situation, I can not but wish him success in his pursuit, if within the rules by which Congress are of necessity to be gover[n]ed.

Draft (DLC).

1. This letter has not been found, but it was likely from Richard Taylor Sr. of Kentucky, who had been struck off the pension list "on account of his being a Publick defaulter." Taylor had an invalid pension due to wounds suffered as a captain in the Virginia navy during the Revolutionary War, but there is no evidence that he held public office or was in a position to disburse public moneys (David White to Samuel L. Southard, 9 Apr. 1824, DNA: RG 15, Revolutionary War Pension and Bounty-Land Warrant Application Files, 1800–1900; Taylor to JM, 26 Sept. 1816, DLC).

To John G. Jackson

DEAR SIR MONTPELLIER Dcr. 1. 1822

The inclosed is an answer to your late letter to Mrs. M.[1] I have only to add to it, that I shall fully share with her in the pleasure of the promised visit from her neice, and that we shall both feel a further gratification in seeing you as her escort. Cannot Mrs. Jackson avail herself of the opportunity of fulfilling her promises also? Health & every other happiness

JAMES MADISON

RC (InU: Jackson Collection).

1. Dolley Madison to John G. Jackson, 29 Nov. 1822, Mattern and Shulman, *Selected Letters of Dolley Payne Madison*, 247.

To Bushrod Washington

Decr. 1. 1822

I return under cover with this the 2d. parcel of my letters to Gl. W. which you were so obliging as to send me. I am sensible of the delay in fulfilling my promise; but it is of late only that I could conven[i]ently have the desired copies taken, and I ventured to suppose that the certainty of the return of the Originals was the only circumstance to wch. any attention wd. be given.

Having found in these papers several particulars which I wished to possess, and seeing by references in Genl. Washingtons letters to me, to which I may add my own recollection that there must be other letters from me to him, which might have been put on his files, I can not but hope that a further search by the Ch: J. or yourself, may procure for me the oppy. of looking into their contents; for which I shall feel a great addn. to the obligation your kindness has already laid me under.

Draft (DLC).

To Horatio Gates Spafford

Dr. Sir — Decr 5. 1822

I have recd. your letter of the 25. Ult: in which you state your discovery of a process which gives a greater purity & cheapness to Steel & Iron than any yet known.

Iron is the metal and even the article which has been justly considered as causing more than any other, the civil[iz]ation & increase of the human race. Every improvement therefore in the preparation & uses of it has been deemed a benefaction to the World. If the discovery you have made be found on extensive & thorough trials, to justify your expectations from those already made, it will be well entitled to the merit claimed for it, and the author to the pecuniary as well as honorary recompense due to public benefactors. In what mode it may be most advisable to seek the former, I know not that I can say any thing that would be of service to you. On the general question on which you ask my opinion, whether Congs. would grant a special law securing your patent right, I can only give a general answer that it is a fair presumption that Congress will be disposed to give all constitutional encouragements to useful inventions. I have no doubt there may be cases in which a purchase on behalf of the public might be preferable to the grant of monopoly; but on a recurrence to the enumerated powers of Congress, it is observable that the one relating to the encouragement of useful arts is confined to the mode of granting to inventors exclusive rights for limited times. If there be cases in which any other mode be authorized, the authority must be found, if at all, to be an incident to some other power, necessary & proper to the exercise of it. Such a peculiarity is not suggested in your case. From this view of the subject, you will be sensible that instead of advice I can only offer the good wishes which I beg you to accept that you may be gratified with all the success on which you count in making your discoveries beneficial to your Country, and a source at the same time of liberal compensation for the labor & merit of introducing them.

Draft (DLC).

To John Browne Cutting

Dear Sir — Montpellier Decr. 7. 1822

I have recd. with your note of the 30th. Ult: the little tract of Mr. Law forwarded by you at his request; and I take the liberty of conveying thro' the same channel, my respects & thanks to him. If my sympathies with his domestic afflictions could be of any avail, I should add the expression of them with great sincerity.

I have always regarded Mr. Law as a man of genius as well as of singular philanthropy; and as uniting with other intellectual acquirements, a particular familiarity with questions of finance. In his occasional publications relating to them, I have observed many sound principles, and valuable suggestions. I most [*sic*] own at the same time that I have never had the confidence he has felt in his favorite plan of putting an end to the evils of an unfavorable balance of trade, and the fluctuations of an exportable currency. There would seem to be much danger at least that the disposition to borrow the paper issuable by a public Board would bring an excess into circulation; and that this instead of reducing of interest, would have the effect of depreciating the principal. With friendly respects

James Madison

RC (Forbes Magazine Collection, New York, N.Y.); draft (DLC).

To David Porter

Dr. Sir Montpr. Decr 7. 1822

I have recd. with your note of the 28. Ult: the right volume of your Journal; and have looked over the preface. Less cannot be said of it, than that it has taken an able and judicious view of its subject. The severity of its retaliations can not be complained of by those who so wantonly provoked them. There can be no danger that your Enimies whatever be their motives or modes of attack will ever impair your title to the niche assigned you by your Country among the distinguished of her naval heroes, or deprive you of the esteem commanded by your private and social virtues.

Draft (DLC); letterbook copy (DLC: David D. Porter Papers). Minor differences between the copies have not been noted.

From Philip P. Barbour

Dear Sir, Dec. 10th. 22.

I received your letter with the one from Mr. Taylor enclosed;[1] I fear it will be not practicable to effect his object. It seems to have been the opinion of the Attorney General, that a pensioner once stricken from the roll, cannot be re-instated by the Secretary of War; there are many in this situation; the subject was before the house at the last session, & will I think be resumed at this; individual cases will therefore abide the general result; I have mentioned the subject to Mr. Breckenridge[2] (the member from Mr. Taylor's district) who has promised to attend to it. There is nothing here of a public nature worthy of communication; you will have seen by the papers that we have done little else than organize ourselves. Resp'ly your obdt. Servt.

P. P. BARBOUR

RC (DLC). Docketed by JM.

1. JM to Barbour, 1 Dec. 1822.

2. James Douglas Breckinridge (d. 1849) was a Louisville, Kentucky, lawyer who served in the Kentucky legislature, 1809–11, and the U.S. House of Representatives, 1821–23 (John E. Kleber et al., eds., *The Encyclopedia of Louisville* [Lexington, Ky., 2001], 115).

From Junius Johnson Jr.

RESPECTED SIR, RICHMOND Dec. 10th. 1822.

Permit a stranger to take the liberty of asking a favor at your hands. Aware of your devotion to literature and the improvement of your country's youth, I know that you will grant it with the utmost cheerfulness.

I am about to commence the study of a course of history, preparatory to that of the law; and having seen the one selected by yourself, am anxious to obtain it.[1] The only means, at present suggested by which it can be done is by an application to you, which I now respectfully make. I am Sir, yours with the highest veneration and esteem

JUNIUS JOHNSON JR.

RC (DLC: Rives Collection, Madison Papers). Docketed by JM.

1. This may have been the plan of reading JM shared with his nephew, Edgar Macon (see Macon to JM, 12 Sept. 1818, *PJM-RS*, 1:355).

From Benjamin Waterhouse

DEAR SIR, CAMBRIDGE 12th. Decr. 1822

I have just read in one of the Boston News-papers, a paragraph to this effect—that through the agency of the late President Madison, a *Professorship of Agriculture* was about to be established in the University in Virginia. It directly occurred to me to send you some publications of mine on that highly important subject.

By the "Heads of Lectures," and by the "*Botanist*," you can see how far we have progressed here, and make your improvements accordingly.[1] I broke up the ground, & sowed the seeds of this branch of Science first in the college at Providence in 1786, and then in the University here in 1788; and laboured incessantly in it, while a Professor of physic, *seventeen years*, or, until the lectures became very popular, and in some measure, profitable; when the *Junto* took the business out of my hands, & gave it to one of their own clan; principally, because I would not join them in their gross abuse of your predecessor. It was *Naboths* vineyard over again; both as it regarded *Ahab*, and the *sons of Belial*.[2] They are *all* in their graves but two, the *District Judge*, & one clergyman.

You will see my reason for giving the subject a popular dress. Those subjects were new to our countrymen. No lectures on botany-agriculture, or mineralogy were ever known in our country prior to those just mentioned.

That Agriculture, with every other beneficial establishment—whether physical moral, or political, may go on prospering among you is the ardent desire of Sir your obt. servt.

BENJN: WATERHOUSE

RC (DLC). Docketed by JM.

1. The enclosures were Waterhouse's *Heads of a Course of Lectures, Intended as an Introduction to Natural History* (Providence, R.I., [1788?]; Evans 45406), and *The Botanist. Being the Botanical Part of a Course of Lectures on Natural History, Delivered in the University at Cambridge; Together with a Discourse on the Principle of Vitality* (Boston, 1811; Shaw and Shoemaker 24380).

2. Ahab's desire for Naboth's vineyard led him to elicit the false testimony of the sons of Belial against Naboth, which led to Naboth's death and Ahab's possession of the vineyard (1 Kings 21 [AV]).

To Junius Johnson Jr.

SIR [ca. 13] Decr. 1822

I have recd. your letter of the 10th. & should comply with its request but that I have no copy of the historical course of reading to which it refers; nor do I recollect even the person to whom it was recommended. On application to him you will doubtless obtain a copy, for which this will be a sanction, if he should happen to be scrupulous without one. I ought to remark at the same time, that the gentleman whoever he may be, under whose auspices you commence the study of law will probably be able to point out the historical works preparatory to it, more fully & appropriately than was done in the paper you have seen. With friendly respects & wishes

J.M.

Draft (DLC). Day of month not indicated; conjectured day assigned based on Johnson to JM, 10 Dec. 1822.

From Benjamin L. Lear

DEAR SIR, WASHINGTON, 14 Decr. 1822.

At the request of my friend Captain Hull[1] of the navy, I have been Endeavouring to settle, at the Treasury Department, the accounts of his uncle, the unfortunate General Hull, once Governor of Michigan, and have Effected a settlement, of all I believe, excepting the charge made by him for his salary as Governor of Michigan, from 1st of April 1812 to the 1st of March 1814, at $2000 per annum. This charge is resisted at the Department, upon the ground that he was not Entitled to receive his salary as Govr. of Michigan while he was receiving pay as a Brigr. Genl. of the Army. But Genl. Hull adheres to this charge as perfectly fair & just, because, he says, it was not only understood by the Executive, but Expressly stipulated by him as a condition of his acceptance of the office of Brigr. Genl. that he should continue to hold that of Govr. of Michigan & shd. receive the pay of both, and this he considers sanctioned by the Examples of Genl. St. Clare,[2] Genl. Wilkinson & others. The present Secretary of State knows, of course, nothing of the understanding between Genl. Hull and the Executive on this subject, and the present President, with whom I have conversed on the subject, thinks that no such understanding Existed with regard to the pay, altho' he is certain that both the offices were to be held by Genl. Hull. Mr. Attwater,[3] the Secretary of the province, performed the duties of Governor, during Genl Hulls absence on command, but received no additional compensation for it, & the appropriation of the Gove[r]nor's salary was regularly made by Congress during the whole time. Genl. Hull has forwarded a letter from Mr. Bradley,[4] who was in the Senate at that time, & who states, that his understanding, & he believes that of the Senate & of the Executive at that time, was accordant with Genl. Hull's recollection on the subject, & the Genl. further states that some members of the Senate told him then, that they shd. vote agst. his nomination, because he was to receive the Pay of both offices.

Under these circumstances, Sir, I have been advised at the Treasury Department, to request the favor of you, to say what is your recollection on the subject, and whether it was stipulated or understood that Genl. Hull was to receive the pay of both offices?

I am sure, sir, that you will readily Excuse the liberty I have taken of writing to you on the subject, since it is desired by the accounting officers of the department as well as by Genl. Hull, to Effect a just settlement of the accounts between them, and to serve a man, who, whatever may have been his public defection, is Estimable in private life & overwhelmed with misfortunes.

My mother,[5] being informed that I am wri⟨ting⟩ to you, begs to avail herself of the occasion to assure Mrs. Madison of her particular respect & affectionate remembrance, to which permit me to add, Sir, the sincere respect for her & yourself, of Your most obedient servant,

Benjamin L. Lear[6]

RC (DLC). Docketed by JM. Damaged by removal of seal.

1. Isaac Hull (1773–1843) was a naval officer who served in the Barbary Wars and the War of 1812. Promoted to captain in 1806, he commanded the frigates *Chesapeake*, *President*, and *Constitution* in succession, and in the latter, defeated the British frigate *Guerrière* in 1812 (*PJM-PS*, 5:266 n. 2).

2. Arthur St. Clair (1736–1818), a major general in the Revolutionary War, was a member of Congress, 1785–87, and first governor of the Northwest Territory, 1787–1802. As governor, St. Clair retained his rank in the army until his resignation in 1792 (*PJM*, 3:267 n. 5; Carter, *Territorial Papers, Northwest Territory*, 2:386–87).

3. Reuben Attwater (1768–1831) of Vermont was secretary for the Michigan Territory, 1808–14 (Clarence M. Burton et al., eds., *The City of Detroit, Michigan, 1701–1922* [5 vols.; Detroit, Mich., 1922], 2:988; Carter, *Territorial Papers, Michigan*, 10:211, 480–81, 491).

4. Stephen Row Bradley (1754–1830), a Yale graduate, lawyer, and a veteran of the Revolutionary War, represented Vermont in the U.S. Senate, 1791–95 and 1801–13.

5. Frances Dandridge Lear (1779–1856), the third wife of Tobias Lear, and Martha Washington's niece, was a good friend of Dolley Madison's (Thomas L. Tullock, "Colonel Tobias Lear," *Granite Monthly, A New Hampshire Magazine* . . . 6 [1882]: 6; Mattern and Shulman, *Selected Letters of Dolley Payne Madison*, 294).

6. Benjamin Lincoln Lear (1792–1832), the son of Tobias Lear and his first wife, Mary Long, was a Washington lawyer (Tullock, "Colonel Tobias Lear," *Granite Monthly* 6 [1882]: 6–7).

To Benjamin L. Lear

Dr. Sir Decr 19. 1822

I have recd. your letter of the 14th. requesting me to say, according to my recollection whether it was stipulated or understood that Genl. Hull, was to receive the salary of Govr. as well as the pay of Brigadier after his acceptance of the latter appointment.

After giving Sir to the subject the proper attention I find myself obliged to say that my memory furnishes no evidence relative to the question, which ought to influence the decision of it.

Mrs. M. desires me to offer to Mrs. Lear, affectionate returns for her kind remembrance. Be so good Sir to add my best respects: & to receive for yourself my esteem & good wishes.

Draft (DLC).

To James Monroe

Dear Sir   Montpellier Decr. 20. 1822

I have recd. from Mr. Lear engaged in settling the accounts of General Hull, a request of what I may recollect on the question, whether there was a stipulation or understanding, that the General was to receive his salary as Governour, as well as his military pay. I have simply answered that my memory does not furnish any evidence which ought to influence the decision of the question. As the war Department was the proper depository of such a fact, and the then Secretary is now on the spot, I conjecture that his recollection is not favorable to the claim. In a legal point of view, it would seem that if the two appointments were compatible, and the Civil appointment was neither revoked nor superseded, the salary would be an incident to it, unless a stipulation or understanding to the contrary should have taken place. This is a remark which I have not made to Mr. Lear, because I wished neither to go beyond his enquiry, nor to meddle with the point of law in the case.

I take this occasion to thank you for the copy of your Message;[1] which could not have been better fitted for its purposes. I am constrained however, to enter an exception to the latitude given to the authority to appropriate money. The able & extended view taken of the subject in a former Message[2] did not satisfy me that I have been wrong in considering the authority as limited to the enumerated objects in the Constitution which require money to carry them into execution. If an authority to appropriate without respect to that limitation, be itself a substantive one in the list, it would seem, like the others, to be entitled to "all laws necessary & proper to carry it into execution,["] which would be equivalent to a power to "provide for the general welfare." A general power merely to appropriate, without this auxiliary power, would be a dead letter; and with it an unlimited power. Considered as itself an auxiliary power incident to, as being necessary & proper for the execution of the specified powers, it comes fairly & safely within the purview of the Constitution. But enough & more than enough on that subject.

You have not I presume lost sight of Marbois's intention to compile a history of the Louisiana Convention. It is of public importance that the motives of Bonaparte to make the Cession should be authenticated, and other developments may be expected not without some interest. Health & every other happiness

James Madison

RC (DLC: Monroe Papers); draft (DLC). RC docketed by Monroe. Minor differences between the copies have not been noted.

1. *Message from the President of the United States, to Both Houses of Congress, at the Commencement of the Second Session of the Seventeenth Congress. Dec. 3, 1822* (Washington, 1822; Shoemaker 11011).

2. JM referred to the lengthy rationale Monroe added to his short veto message of 4 May 1822, entitled "Views of the President of the United States on the Subject of Internal Improvements" (Richardson, *Compilation of the Messages and Papers of the Presidents*, 2:711–52).

From Thomas Cooper

DEAR SIR, COLUMBIA SOUTH CAROLINA 21 Dec. 1822

I take the Liberty of inclosing you a report concerning ⟨the⟩ State of our College.[1] I remain always with the ⟨highest?⟩ respect, Dear Sir Your obedient Servant

THOMAS COOPER MD
President of the South
Carolina College

RC (DLC). Docketed by JM.

1. The enclosure may have been the one-page *Report of the Committee on the College, on So Much of the Governor's Message as Relates to the College, Also on the Presentments from Chester and York. Wm. J. Grayson Chairman* (n.p., 1823? [1822]; Shoemaker 14174).

From Creed Taylor

DEAR SIR, NEEDHAM 21st. decr. 1822.

Will you permit me to avail myself of the return of Mr. Stringfellow,[1] to his friends in the county of Culpeper, to submit to your consideration, a copy of the journal of the law- school,[2] to enable you to form, a more correct opinion of the merits of that institution: and, to ask, if you please, at your liesure, your opinion in relation to it: and, be assured, that in asking this, I am most sensibly alive, to all the apprehensions, so natural to the author of every new institution. But still, from the confidence, which I hold, in your justice and wisdom, I have prevailed upon myself thus far, to trespass, upon your time. Allow me to say, as I could not attend to the operations of the press, more errors, than my own, are to be found in the work. They will not escape your eye; nor is any other apology necessary. I submit with great deference, to your consideration; not from your practical; but general knowledge of our laws; whether it might not be regarded, as some improvement to our country, if our professional gentlemen, were to conform, in their professional duties, to one uniform system of precedents, even such, as are to be found, in the humble pretentions of the journal of the law-school, if no better can be had, than to go on, as at present, without any system at all.

Allow me also to add, that I have not forgotten, your very friendly & polite invitation, at the Rock fish gap,[3] to visit you, and my promise to do it. This visit, I have not, as yet, had in my power to make; but, I anticipate it, with pleasure: and, I will, before very long, make it.

Permit me, if you please, to present to Payne, (who was with us at the gap) through you, my best respects: and, for yourself accept, the very high considerations of your most obedient Servant

CREED TAYLOR[4]

N.B. I should be much gratified, if my efforts to be useful, shall meet Mr. Madison's approbation, to be at liberty, to make it known, or not, as occasion may require. January & february I shall be in Richmond.

C.T.

Excuse the erasements, as I have no one to copy for me, and the stage can not wait.

C.T.

RC (DLC). Docketed by JM, with his note: "Recd. Mar. 1 1823."

1. This may have been Robert or Henry Stringfellow, cousins who lived in Culpeper County, Virginia (George Harrison Sanford King, "Copies of Extant Wills from Counties Whose Records Have Been Destroyed," *Tyler's Quarterly Historical and Genealogical Magazine* 27 [1945]: 42–43).

2. Creed Taylor, *Journal of the Law-School, and of the Moot-Court Attached to It; At Needham, in Virginia . . .* (Richmond, 1822; Shoemaker 10414).

3. For the Report of the Rockfish Gap meeting, 4 Aug. 1818, see *PJM-RS*, 1:326–39.

4. Creed Taylor (1766–1836) served in the Virginia Senate, 1798–1805, and was a judge of the High Court of Chancery for the Richmond district, 1806–31. Taylor established a law school at his home, Needham, near Farmville in 1821 (W. Hamilton Bryson, ed., *Essays on Legal Education in Nineteenth Century Virginia* [Buffalo, N.Y., 1998], 39).

From Charles Yancey

DEAR SIR, RICHMOND December 21st. 1822

I have taken the liberty of enclosing for your perusal a prospectus of a Newspaper about to be printed here by Mr. Crawford,[1] a gentleman well recommended; I lately sent one to the President and received for answer "which as I approve it you will subscribe my name." Will you be so good as to write to me, if one may be sent to you. Please to accept assurances of my great respect & believe me to be yr. frd. & most Obedt. Servt.

CHARLES YANCEY[2]
of Richmond Va.

RC (DLC). In a clerk's hand, signed by Yancey. Addressed in an unidentified hand to JM at "Orange County Va.," and franked. Docketed by JM.

1. *Proposals for Publishing by Subscription, in the City of Richmond, a Semi-Weekly and Daily Newspaper to Be Called the Virginia Times by Samuel Crawford. Dec. 12, 1822* (n.p., 1822; Shoemaker 8463). JM's copy of this broadside is in the Madison Collection, Rare Book and Special Collections Division, Library of Congress.

2. Charles Yancey (1766-ca. 1825) of Albemarle County, Virginia, a local magistrate, colonel of the county militia, 1806–15, and sheriff, 1821–23, served in the Virginia House of Delegates, 1814–17. He also owned a tavern, store, mill, and distillery in the area known as Yancey's Mill (Looney et al., *Papers of Thomas Jefferson: Retirement Series*, 2:405 n.).

From James McKinney

SIR MADISON MILLS 23. Dec. 22.

In conversation with Gen. William Madison relative to the purchase of your Mill[1] I told him that I would write you as soon as I could make my Arangements. I have three sons that is Millwrights that has several gangs of hands now at work between the waters of James & the Roanoak rivers; principally on the Nottaways & Meherrin rivers; & their branches, known in that section of Country as the firm of James McKinney & Sons, it was therefore Necessary that I should Make them Acquainted with this business before I entered into any contract, for several reasons Viz—1st. Whether they could Make the Necessary repairs & Alterations immediately without interfering with their other engagements—2d Whether they could furnish some Money & how Much—3d Where plank, Scantling, Coggs, rounds, &c. &c &c. could be procured & at what price. The Object with me was to put the Mill in complete order to Make flour of the very best kind for the supply of the Neighbourhood (which in My Opinion would support such an establishment) say family & if all could Not be vended in the Neighbourhood a load or 2 Might be sent to Market Occationally, the Object would be to keep the Mill pretty well imployed when there was no grist to grind but to pay good Attention to what is Usually calld. Country work.

Now Sir Please to inform me when you find a convenient time, the price, the payments, & when possession could be had & you shall have an Ansr. immediately on receipt thereof With many wishes for your health & happiness I am yours very respectfully

JAMES MCKINNEY[2]

Perhaps you would have no Objection to retain the half of the property.

J McK

RC (DLC). Addressed by McKinney to JM. Docketed by JM.

1. This was the plantation gristmill on Madison Run to the southeast of Montpelier. It was acquired by James Madison Sr. and maintained by the family through JM's lifetime, though rebuilt many times. The sale to McKinney apparently never took place (Orange County Court Order, 22 Oct. 1804, *PJM-SS*, 8:201 and n. 3; JM to Richard Cutts, 13 Sept. 1824, MHi). This mill should not be confused with the commercial mill that James Madison Sr. built in partnership with his sons in the 1790s, which was sold in 1808 (*PJM-SS*, 2:125–26 n. 1).

2. James McKinney (b. ca. 1773), a miller from Brooke County, Virginia (now West Virginia), had partnered with Thomas Mann Randolph to operate Thomas Jefferson's manufacturing mill at Milton, Virginia, in 1810 (Looney et al., *Papers of Thomas Jefferson: Retirement Series*, 1:92 n.).

From William Zollickoffer

Respected Sir — Middleburg 25 Dec: 1822 Maryland

It has always afforded me an infinite source of pleasure, to have it in my power, to present literary gentlemen with such information: as I conceive of practical utility, as relates to the alleviation of the sufferings of mankind; induced by disease: and under the influences of an impression of this kind, I with much pleasure, forward on to you two copies of my little treatise on the use of Prussiate of Iron in intermitting and remitting fevers[1]—which you doubtless will receive at the time this letter reaches you. I shall consider myself highly honoured by receiving a letter from you, by way of acknowledging that they have come safe to hand. I have the honour, to be Respected Sir Your most obt. Sert.

William Zollickoffer[2]

RC (DLC). Docketed by JM.

1. William Zollickoffer, *A Treatise on the Use of Prussiate of Iron, (or, Prussian Blue) in Intermitting and Remitting Fevers* (Frederick, Md., 1822; Shoemaker 11504).

2. William Zollickoffer (1793–1853), who received his medical degree from the University of Maryland in 1818, was a lecturer there on "medical botany, materia medica and therapeutics." He published *A Materia Medica of the United States* in 1819 (Kelly and Burrage, *American Medical Biographies* [1920], 1284).

To Benjamin Waterhouse

DEAR SIR MONTPELLIER Decr. 27. 1822

I have received your favor of the 12th. instant, and with it the "Botanist," and the Sheets containing "Heads of a Course of Lectures."

A glance over them has satisfied me that the Volume on Botany very happily opens the door to the subject, and gives enough of an Inside view to attract curiosity, and guide investigation. From the heads selected for the Lectures, they must have embraced a larger field, which, I doubt not, became in your hands a fruitful one.

It is among the proofs of Mr. Adams' comprehensive patriotism, that he called the attention of his country, at so early a day, and in so impressive a mode, to the subject of Natural History, then so little an object of American Science; and you have done an Act of Justice only, in the conspicuous notice you have taken of the fact.

I perceive by the newspaper paragraph you cite that more than justice is done to me in the notice taken of the proposed professorship of Agriculture in the University of Virginia. The printed sheet inclosed, shews that the resolution of the Agricultural Society originated with General Cocke, a highly respectable member, and that I but executed an order of the Society, in preparing an Address on the subject, to the other Societies in Virginia, taking the liberty only of bringing into view a small cultivated farm as a sort of apparatus to the professorship.

The principles of Agriculture have been sometimes embraced in other professorships, and are so, in that of Chemistry in the University of Virginia. The object of the Society of Albemarle was to give to Agriculture the importance as well as the advantage of a distinct professorship exclusively charged with it; which was not known to have been done in any other instance. With much esteem & every good wish

JAMES MADISON

RC and enclosure (MBCo); draft (DLC). The enclosure (3 pp.) is a copy of JM's printed circular to the presidents of Virginia agricultural societies, 21 Oct. 1822, and the accompanying resolutions from the 7 Oct. 1822 meeting of the Agricultural Society of Albemarle. Minor differences between the RC and draft have not been noted.

¶ To George W. Erving. Letter not found. *30 December 1822*. Noted in the *Numismatist* 35 (1922): 143, as exhibited by George H. Blake at the New York Numismatic Club: "a case of seven bronze medals presented to President James Madison by George W. Erving. Accompanying the case and enclosed in it is a letter of acknowledgement, dated December 30, 1822, thanking Mr. Erving for his gift." Erving sent JM two, probably identical, sets of seven bronze medals, one for himself and another for Thomas Jefferson. Jefferson's set included representations of George Washington, Benjamin Franklin, William Augustine Washington, John Eager Howard, Christopher Columbus, John Paul Jones, and Thaddeus Kosciuszko (Jefferson to Erving, 11 Apr. 1823, DLC: Jefferson Papers; Susan R. Stein, *The Worlds of Thomas Jefferson at Monticello* [New York, 1993], 245–47). The two parcels were delivered to JM by Hazlewood Farish (Erving to Anna Cutts, 19 Dec. [1822], ViU: Richard Cutts Papers).

To James McKinney

Sir Jany 3. 1823

I have recd. your letter of the 23. Ult. Not having since found it convenient to examine all the circumstances affecting the value of my mill in its present state, I can not name precisely the terms of sale: with respect to which also, I should be glad previously to know the payments it would be convenient to make. If you cd. ride up at an early day, we could view the premises together. You know I presume that 50 acres of ground are attached to the mill, about one third or ¼ of which I believe is uncleared. The whole was originally rich, and with the exception of a few gutted spots & gulleys, the cleared part tho' worne might be cultivated with profit. As to the plank & scantling, that might be wanted I can say no more than that there is a sawmill at a small distance where it is probable the articles might be obtained at the usual prices; viz. about a dollar a hundred feet & ca. Coggs of the best sort & ready seasoned I can furnish myself; & the rounds also of the best wood. A miller havg. been engaged for the current year, the time of delivery will involve that consideration; but it will occasion no serious difficulty. Please to let me know whether I may expect to see you & at what time.

Draft (DLC).

To Charles Yancey

Sir [4 January 1823]

I have recd. your letter of the 21st inclosing a prospectus of a Newspaper about to be printed at Richmond. I have for a considerable time found it convenient rather to reduce than extend my receipts of Newspapers; and have no farther lost sight of that object, than by taking, in one or two instances a new Gazette for *a single year*. Under that limitation the paper in question may be forwarded to me; for which the payment in advance is inclosed, & a return of a rect requested. With friendly respects

J M

Draft (DLC). Undated; conjectural date assigned based on comparison with Yancey to JM, 21 Dec. 1822 and 9 Jan. 1823. Filed after Samuel L. Gouverneur to JM, 2 Jan. 1833, in the Madison Papers, Library of Congress.

To Thomas Cooper

Dr Sir, Montpellier, January 5th, 1823.

I have received the "Report" on the state of the South Carolina College, covered by your favor of December 21. I have read it with very sincere pleasure as the harbinger of days happy for yourself, as well as prosperous for the Institution. You are not, I perceive, without an adversary of the same family which raised its cries against you elsewhere. The triumphs of education under your auspices may prove an antidote to the ambition which would monopolize the fountains of knowledge, which is another name for power.

Our University is still at a halt. Whether the present Representatives of the people are as blind as their predecessors, is yet to be learnt. I have as many fears as hopes.

I enclose a little tract, of which I have just received a couple of copies from the author.[1] It will be at least a harmless duplicate, if you should be otherwise possessed of one. If it has any good pretensions, you will be more able to do them justice than I am.

I take this occasion, though aware of its lateness, to thank you for your Introductory Lecture on Chemistry; of which the merits certainly never had a more persuasive illustration. With great esteem and cordial regards.

Printed copy (Madison, *Letters* [Cong. ed.], 3:291).

1. This was probably the pamphlet by William Zollickoffer enclosed in his letter to JM of 25 Dec. 1822.

From George W. Erving

Dear Sir Washington Jany. 5. 1823

I am highly flattered by the very obliging manner in which you have condescended to receive the small articles which I took the liberty of offering to you;[1] I wish that I could devise more adequate means of expressing my respectful & grateful feelings towards you & Mrs Madison: You still augment my obligations by your joint good wishes for my happiness, but alas! that to which Mrs Madison more particularly refers is beyond my reach "past praying for."[2] I have recourse to philosophy; an author who is a favorite of yours, & a teacher of gospel for me, says "nous nous preparons des peines touts les fois que nous cherchons des plaisirs," & again "moins nous desirons plus nous possedons," & again "Le bonheur est au dedans de nous meme, il nous a ete donné, le malheur est au dehors et nous l'allons chercher."[3] These apothegms of St. Pierre I find ingenuity enough to apply "tant bien que mal"[4] to my solitary propensities, for I do not know how to understand Socrates, who when asked by one of his pupils whether it were better to marry, or to remain unmarried, answered, "do which you will, you will repent;"[5] yet I bear in mind as throwing some light on the paradox—that his wife was none of the best.

Mrs Bomford has searched all her papers without success for that which you desired to have, viz. the Exposé of Marbois of the motives of the french government in the sale of Louisiana; she does not recollect that she ever had such a paper, but concludes that the matter in question may possibly be contained in Marbois's preface to his manuscript entitled "*Complot d'Arnold et de Henry Clinton;*" the manuscript she has, but the preface, which was a detached paper, she has lost.

I find amongst my own records a very interesting, & as it may be hereafter a valuable historical document; the speech of the famous Louvel who killed the duke of Berri; it is of undoubted authenticity, as Mr Gallatin from whom I had it assured me; indeed its genuine character is plainly marked in Every sentence of it; I am not aware that it has otherwise found its way to this country, or that it has even been communicated confidentially to the Secretary of State by Mr Gallatin; he himself received it sub rosâ as I believe. I take the liberty of herewith enclosing a copy of it,[6] persuaded that you will esteem it as a curiosity, tho' you may not think that it merits the importance which I attach to it; Louvel, according to me, was one of the most Extraordinary men of our time, a solitary Example of what we term "*Roman* virtue:" Europe has carbonari, illuminati, & philosophers of all sorts in abundance, but practical men of Louvels character, none: many under the influence of pride or vanity, of ambition or avarice, have in falling, merited the apotheosis of patriotism, but Louvel with a simple unsophisticated mind, unbiassed by any personal interest or passion, not urged forward by any personal wrongs, calmly sacrificing himself to *his* sense of the publick good—this is a miracle in the morality of the 19 century, so much vaunted. Dear Sir With very sincere & respectful attachment your most ob St

George W Erving

I pray you to present me to Mrs Madison.

RC (owned by Charles M. Storey, Boston, Mass., 1961).

1. See JM to Erving, 30 Dec. 1822.

2. When Prince Hal says "Pray God you have not murd'red some of them," Falstaff replies, "Nay, that's past praying for, I have pepper'd two of them" (Shakespeare, *1 Henry IV*, 2.4.189–92 [*Riverside*]).

3. These quotations are taken from Georges Louis Leclerc, comte de Buffon's *Histoire naturelle:* "Thus, when we search for pleasure, we create to ourselves pain; we are miserable from the moment we desire to augment our happiness. Good exists only within ourselves, and it has been bestowed on us by Nature; evil is external, and we go in quest of it. The peaceable enjoyment of the mind is our only true good: We cannot augment this good, without the danger of losing it: The less we desire, the more we possess" (*Natural History, General and Particular, by the Count de Buffon, Translated into English*, 2d ed. [9 vols.; London, 1785], 3:241).

4. *Tant bien que mal:* with moderate success.

5. Valerius Maximus, *Memorable Deeds and Sayings: One Thousand Tales from Ancient Rome*, trans. Henry John Walker [Indianapolis, Ind., 2004], 239).

6. The document has not been identified, but at his trial for the assassination of the duc de Berri in 1820, Louis Pierre Louvel ostensibly made a speech in his own defense, "which was considered a repetition of the crime, and which was, therefore, never allowed to be published" (*Edinburgh Annual Register, for 1820* 13 [1823]: 243–44; David Skuy, *Assassination, Politics, and Miracles: France and the Royalist Reaction of 1820* [Montreal, 2003], 114–16, 168, 189–90).

From Thomas Jefferson

Dear Sir Monticello. Jan. 6. 23.

I send you a mass of reading, and so rapidly does my hand fail me in writing that I can give but very briefly the necessary explanations.

1. Mr. Cabell's letter to me & mine to him which passed each other on the road will give you the state of things respecting the University,[1] and I am happy to add that letters recieved from Appleton give us reason to expect our capitels by the first vessel from Leghorn, done of superior marble and in superior style.

2. Young E. Gerry informed me some time ago that he had engaged a person to write the life of his father, and asked for any materials I could furnish. I sent him some letters, but in searching for them, I found two, too precious to be trusted by mail, of the date of 1801. Jan. 15. & 20. in answer to one I had written him Jan. 26. 99. two years before.[2] It furnishes authentic proof that in the XYZ. mission to France, it was the wish of Pickering, Marshall, Pinckney and the Federalists of that stamp, to avoid a treaty with France and to bring on war, a fact we charged on them at the time and this letter proves, and that their X.Y.Z. report was cooked up to dispose the people to war. Gerry their colleague was not of their sentiment, and

this is his statement of that transaction. During the 2. years between my letter & his answer, he was wavering between mr Adams & myself, between his attachment to mr. Adams personally on the one hand, and to republicanism on the other; for he was republican, but timid & indecisive. The event of the election of 1800–1. put an end to his hesitations.

3. A letter of mine to judge Johnson & his answer.[3] This conveys his views of things, and they are so serious and sound, that they are worth your reading. I am sure that in communicating it to you, I commit no breach of trust to him; for he and every one knows that I have no political secrets for you; & from the tenor of his letter with respect to yourself, it is evident he would as willingly have them known to you as myself.

You will observe that mr. Cabell, if the loan bill should pass, proposes to come up with mr. Loyall, probably mr. Johnson, and Genl. Cocke to have a special meeting. This is necessary to engage our workmen before they undertake other work for the ensuing season. I shall desire him, as soon as the loan bill passes the lower house (as we know it will pass the Senate) to name a day by mail to yourself to meet us, as reasonable notice *to all the members* is necessary to make the meeting legal. I hope you will attend, as the important decision as to the Rotunda may depend on it.

Our family is all well and joins in affections to mrs Madison and yourself. My arm goes on slowly; still in a sling and incapable of any use, and will so continue some time yet. Be so good as to return the inclosed when read and to be assured of my constant and affectionate friendship

TH: JEFFERSON

FC and draft (DLC: Jefferson Papers). Minor differences between the copies have not been noted.

1. Jefferson to Joseph C. Cabell, 28 Dec. 1822, and Cabell to Jefferson, 30 Dec. 1822, Cabell, *Early History of the University of Virginia*, 260–65.

2. Elbridge Gerry to Jefferson, 15 and 20 Jan. 1801, Boyd, *Papers of Thomas Jefferson*, 32:465–69, 489–94, and Jefferson to Gerry, 26 Jan. 1799, ibid., 30:645–50.

3. One topic discussed in the exchange of letters between Jefferson and William Johnson was the practice of U.S. Supreme Court justices issuing one majority opinion, rather than each justice giving his opinion seriatim, as Jefferson and JM preferred (Jefferson to Johnson, 27 Oct. 1822, and Johnson to Jefferson, 10 Dec. 1822, DLC: Jefferson Papers).

From James McKinney

SIR MADISON MILLS Jan 6th. 23.

I recd. yours this Morning & Observe the contents.[1] I will call & See you as Soon as I can Which I hope will be Soon. Mr. Fray[2] goes to Fredericksburg in the Morning & will be gone nearly all the week. We cannot both leave the place at the Same time. I beg you to Accept My Sincere respects

James McKinney

RC (DLC). Addressed by McKinney to JM, and marked "Zachary."

1. JM to McKinney, 3 Jan. 1823.

2. John Fray (1787–1880) was born in Madison County, Virginia, to Ephraim Fray, a miller. In 1810 the father sold his mill on Deep Run, known as Speedwell Mills, to John. Justice of the peace in Madison County in 1826, John Fray moved to Albemarle County in 1833 and established a mill and a general store on the north fork of the Rivanna River at Fray's Mill, now Advance Mills (Florence Virginia Fray Lewis, comp., *A History & Genealogy of John Fray (Johannes Frey) of Culpeper County, Virginia . . .* [Ann Arbor, Mich., 1958], 15–17).

From Charles Yancey

Dear Sir, Richmond 9th. January 1823

Yours of the 4th Instant has been Recd. & I feel much honored in Communicating it to Mr. Crawford, the Editor of The Va. Times: shortly to Issue from here. He will be here in a few days, & I shall take his Rect. for $5. enclosed by you, for the paper in question to be sent on &c. I sincerely hope it May prove satisfactory. Yours truly & sincerely

Charles Yancey of
Richmond Va.

RC (DLC). Addressed by Yancey to JM, and franked.

To Thomas Jefferson

Dear Sir Montpellier 15. [January] 1823

I have duly received yours of the 6th. with the letters of Mr. Cabell, Mr Gerry, and Judge Johnson. The letter from Mr. C. proposing an Extra Meeting of the Visitors, & referred to in yours was not sent, and of course is not among those returned.

The friends of the University in the Assembly seem to have a delicate task on their hands. They have the best means of knowing what is best to be done, and I have entire confidence in their judgment as well as their good intentions. The idea of Mr. Cabell, if successful will close the business handsomely. One of the most popular objections to the Institution, I find is the expence added by what is called the ornamental style of the Architecture. Were this additional expence as great as is supposed, the objection ought the less to be regarded as it is short of the sum saved to the public by the private subscribers who approve of such an application of their subscriptions. I shall not fail to join you on receiving the expected notice from Mr. Cabell, if the weather & my health will permit: but I am persuaded it will be a supernumerary attendance, if the money be obtained, and the sole question be on its application to the new Edifice.

The two letters from Mr. Gerry are valuable documents on a subject that will[1] fill some interesting pages in our history. The disposition of a party among us to find a cause of rupture with[2] France, and to kindle a popular flame for the occasion, will go to posperity [*sic*] with too many proofs to leave a doubt with them. I have not looked over Mr. Gerry's letters to me which are very numerous, but may be of dates not connected with the period in question. No resort has been had to them for materials for his biography, perhaps from the idea that his correspondence with me may contain nothing of importance, or possibly from a displeasure in the family at my disappointing the expectations of two of them. Mr. Austin the son in law[3] was anxious to be made Comptrouller instead of Anderson,[4] who had been a revolutionary officer, a Judge in Tennessee, and a Senator from that State in Congress; and with equal pretensions only had in his scale the turning weight of being from the West, which considers itself without a fair proportion of national appointments. Mr. Austin[5] I believe a man of very respectable talents, & had erroneously inferred from Mr. Gerry's communications, that I was under a pledge to name him for the vacancy when it should happen. Thinking himself thus doubly entitled to the office, his alienation has been the more decided. With every predisposition in favor of young Gerry, he was represented to me from the most friendly quarters as such a dolt, that if his youth could have been got over, it was impossible to prefer him to the place (in the Customs) to which he aspired. I have reason to believe that some peculiarities in his manner led to an exaggeration of his deficienc[i]es, and that he acquits himself well eno' in the subordinate place he now holds.

Judge Johnson's letter was well entitled to the perusal you recommended. I am glad you have put him in possession of such just views of the course that ought to be pursued by the Court in delivering its opinions. I have taken frequent occasions to impress the necessity of the seriatim mode; but the contrary practice is too deeply rooted to be changed without the injunction of a law, or some very cogent manifestation of the public discontent. I have long thought with the Judge also that the Supreme Court ought to be relieved from its circuit duties, by some such organization as he suggests. The necessity of it is now rendered obvious by the impossibility, in the same individual, of being a circuit Judge in Missouri &c. and a Judge of the Supreme Court at the Seat of Government. He is under a mistake in charging, on the Executive at least, an inattention to this point.

Before I left Washington I recommended to Congress the importance of establishing the Supreme Court at the Seat of Govt. which would at once enable the Judges to go thro' the business, & to qualify themselves by the necessary studies for doing so, with justice to themselves & credit to the nation.[6] The reduction of the number of Judges would also be an improvement, & might be conveniently effected in the way pointed out. It cannot be denied that there are advantages in uniting the local & general functions in the same persons if permitted by the extent of the Country. But if this were ever the case, our expanding settlements put an end to it. The organization of the Judiciary Department over the extent which a Federal System can reach involves peculiar difficulties. There is scarcely a limit to the distance which Turnpikes & Steamboats may, at the public expence, convey the members of the Govt. & distribute the laws. But the delays & expence of suits brought from the extremities of the Empire, must be a severe burden on Individuals. And in proportion as this is diminished by giving to local Tribunals a final jurisdiction, the evil is incurred of destroying the uniformity of the law.

I hope you will find an occasion for correcting the error of the Judge in supposing that I am at work on the same ground as will be occupied by his historical view of parties,[7] and for animating him to the completion of what he has begun on that subject. Nothing less than full-length likenesses of the two great parties which have figured in the national politics will sufficiently expose the deceptive colours under which they have been painted. It appears that he has already collected materials, & I infer from your accts of his biography of Green which I have not yet seen, that he is[8] capable of making the proper use of them. A good work on the side of truth from his pen will be an apt & effective antidote to that of his Colleague[9] which has been poisoning the public mind, & gaining a passport to posterity.

I was afraid the Docr. was too sanguine in promising so early a cure of the fracture in your arm. The milder weather soon to be looked for, will doubtless favor the vis medicatrix[10] which nature employs in repairing the injuries done her. Health and every other happiness

James Madison

RC (DLC); draft (DLC: Rives Collection, Madison Papers). Month not indicated; conjectural month assigned based on Jefferson's docket on the RC: "recd Jan 19." Draft dated 5 Jan. 1823. Minor differences between the copies have not been noticed.

1. The draft has "must" here instead of "will."

2. In the draft, JM added "Revolutionary" here.

3. James Trecothick Austin (1784–1870), of Boston, a graduate of Harvard College, studied law with William Sullivan and was admitted to the bar in 1805. He was attorney for Suffolk County, Massachusetts, 1807–32. JM appointed Austin a commissioner under the forty-first article of the Treaty of Ghent in 1816. He was attorney general for Massachusetts, 1832–43. Austin married Catharine Gerry in 1806, and he published a two-volume

biography of his father-in-law, Elbridge Gerry, in 1828–29 (*The Necrology of Harvard College, 1869–72* [Cambridge, Mass., 1872], 5–7).

4. Joseph Inslee Anderson (1757–1837) was born near Philadelphia and enlisted in the Continental Army in 1776, rising to brevet major in 1783. He was appointed territorial judge of Tennessee by President Washington in 1791, attended the Tennessee constitutional convention in 1796, and served in the U.S. Senate, 1797–1815. JM appointed Anderson First Comptroller of the Treasury in 1815, and he served until 1836 (Fay E. McMillan, "A Biographical Sketch of Joseph Anderson (1757–1837)," *East Tennessee Historical Society's Publications* 2 [1930]: 81–93).

5. In the draft, JM added "is" here.

6. For JM's recommendations, see *PJM-RS*, 1:98 n. 4.

7. Johnson had written: "I was also informed by Judge Todd at the last Session, that Mr Madison was engaged on some Work in that Period, which, I have flattered myself was upon the same Subject, or some one intimately connected with it. If so, it would be presumptuous in any other to attempt it. He is now, except yourself, the only Man living who could do Justice to it" (William Johnson to Thomas Jefferson, 10 Dec. 1822, DLC: Jefferson Papers).

8. In the draft, JM added "very" here.

9. For John Marshall's biography of George Washington, see JM to Bushrod Washington, 14 Oct. 1820, and n. 2.

10. *Vis medicatrix naturae:* the healing power of nature.

To Benjamin Bell and William Tapscott

GENTLEMEN MONTPR. Jany. 19. 1823

It is so very long since payments were due from both particularly one of you for the land purchased of Mrs. Willis & myself[1] without our having recd. even a line on the subject from either, that you cannot be surprized at being now reminded of your obligations, and called to discharge them. I am not unaware of the circumstances which may have embarrass[ed] pecuniary transactions, but they cannot, especially as prices have risen with the fall in the value of the currency outweigh the protracted indulgence, and the serious inconveniences which have been experienced from it. We hope you have not failed to keep in view our just expectations, & that you have been gradually making preparations to satisfy them. Creditors to whom interest has been paid, are now in urgent want of the principal; and we rely on receipts from you, towards meeting their demands. The 10th. of Apl. next terminates the 5th. year from the date of the Contract and the 4th. since part of the debt accruing has been unpaid. By that time we hope to hear satisfactorily from you. The whole payment with the accumulated interest will then be very desiriable [*sic*]. Should that be impossible, we count on a considerable part, and must observe that the receipt of balance will be indispensable by the 10th day of Sepr in the present year. With respect.

Draft (owned by Charles M. Storey, Boston, Mass., 1961).

1. For the sale of the Kentucky land owned by JM and his niece, Nelly Conway Madison Willis, see JM to Benjamin Bell, 22 Dec. 1817, *PJM-RS*, 1:176, 177 n. 1.

To James Monroe

Dear Sir Montpellier Jany. 27. 1823

The Speaker of the H. of R.[1] the particular friend of my nephew Edgar Macon has intimated to him that a Clerk will soon be wanted for a Board for executing the late award of the Emp: of Russia, and has advised him to be a candidate. Of his qualifications for such a service Col: Barbour can speak with much more knowlege than I can, having been the patron of his professional studies, and individually, closely acquainted with him. Of his integrity & estimable dispositions, I have every reason to be satisfied. With these impressions, I can not refuse to express what might be presumed, the pleasure I should feel in his success in any case where the public interest would coincide, & no injustice be done to the pretensions of others. With the highest respect

James Madison

RC (DLC: Monroe Papers). Docketed by Monroe.

1. Philip P. Barbour.

From George Joy

Dear sir, [30 January 1823]

Neither Captn. Pott, nor his Broker could refer me to any Bookseller that was shipping by the Henry Clay, or I should have got him to add the Books for you to his Invoice and instruct his Correspondent to transmit them to you. Mr Rush had made no Ceremony of sending a Book occasionally to a public Character thro' the Department of State in a Letter. Colo: Aspinwall said that Books were often sent in Letters by the Mail; and the Captain believed that, small as the parcel was, he should be allowed to add it to his manifest, remembering the like of small parcels received onboard after Clearance of the ship. I therefore sent it to his Brokers, (Hopkins & Glover,) engaged the latter to pay him, on his return, any expences he might have incurred; and sent the Note of which I subjoin a Copy to the Captain. The Clerks at the Brokers remember the parcel with my name at the corner, and think it was sent in the Letter Bags but Mr Glover thinks it was delivered with a number of similar Parcels to the Captain—(I think he said in a Trunk)—there is no doubt of the Captain having received it and Mr Glover has little (judging from past experience) that it will be found in the Custody of the Collector at Baltimore; which will be more probable, if the Captain has forgotten to change the direction.

If this should cost you the trouble of a Letter to the Collector of Baltimore, as, in the case of Mrs Hutchinson's History,[1] to him of Norfolk; it will be the very trouble that I wished you to avoid: but it is hardly worth your while; for I have a Duplicate which I shall send by the Liverpool to Richmond to the Care of Messrs Warwick; and, to make it a package of sufficient bulk for the ship's Manifest, I shall accompany it with a pair of prints; for which, if you have no better Copies, I hope you will find room at Montpellier. They are Impressions, for which I was an early subscriber, of the Battles of Bunker's Hill and Quebec; and have had the honor, if it be one, to grace the Walls of a student at Oxford; where such subjects are not often studied; and I have held them since to adorn any Hall of State for which my pious Countrymen might discover me to be a proper Inmate—but there is such a want of discernment among them, that, with all my inordinate ambition, I find I shall make no figure till the next transmigration, to which I shall therefore defer it.

Taking down these Books by the way, to examine their Condition; I find them unworthy of such Company: the first volume has actually fallen open by accident at the 124th page; and the first passage that has struck my eye is "Ce plaisir (de la Vengeance) est celui des Dieux et *des femmes*"—a sarcasm that I cannot forgive in the Author; tho' in casting my eye upward I find him saying "la parole d'une femme suffisait deja a la galanterie française["]; and tho' a few of the last Leaves are physically sweetened with Sirop of Capillaire[2]

DEAR SIR, BRIGHTON 30th Janry 1823

The above was written in Octr: on receipt of your obliging Letter of the 10th Augst thro' Mr Benjn Joy; when I was suddenly called into the City, and met with a Contusion of my Arm which was followed by the Mistake of a Chymist in giving me the wrong Medicine, which has made me an Invalid ever since. I am here for the benefit of the Saltwater Baths, and other advantages of this royal residence, and am to be the better for it, if I can believe the medical men; but I have a want of faith from my ignorance how a man can be better than well. Every man's Complaints are worse than every other's; and my shoulder being the seat to which all my fires were directed, was covered with an inflammatory Eruption which could of course only be compared to "the raging fire That burns in Etna's breast of flame."[3] I have been skilfully treated however, and see nothing to prevent my becoming as well as heretofore; but my progress has been much slower than I anticipated. The greatest *inconvenience* I have suffered has been in the difficulty of using my pen; and the greater as while my disorder has been kept stationary and topical the constitutional Cacoëthes remained: but I found the Liverpool was not returning to Richmond, and that I should not have an opportunity of sending the package abovementioned till sometime in february.

I remember very well what I was going to write, and among other things, tho' it was little in favor of my prophetic powers, that I did not believe any heads could be found in Europe—even crowned heads—so ideotic as to involve the nations in war. The train of reasoning that led to this Conclusion may now be spared. The sword of divine right is unsheathed, or at least the Duc d'Angoulême has laid his hand upon it, and it will soon be flushed in the Martyrs of freedom, if they have flesh and blood to oppose it.[4] The King of France is surely in his dotage. I began to think that adversity had at length taught him wisdom. I still think him a good hearted man; but he has no sway over his Counsellors, and most unhappily and faultily, he has now less than ever in his Chambers the true link between him and his people. Here is then a state of things on which a man must be a bold dealer in prognostics to hazard an opinion. Will the Duc d'Angoulême "blow them all from the face of the Earth?" Buonapartè could not do it. Is the Spaniard so imbued with the Principles of Civil Liberty as to enlist his enthusiasm in the Cause? Between the tardy progress of those principles in general and the information we have of their corresponding societies, and in the absence of that personal intercourse by which a better Judgement could be formed; who can decide this question? Will they oppose France in the Onset? A single battle may decide their fate à la Naples—or a single instance of good fortune in the beginning may enable them to endure the alternations of success and defeat that may follow. Will none of the french Army take sides with them; or will none of the combustible matter they leave behind take fire in their absence; and if it should burst into a flame, what will be the rate of premium for insuring the throne of a Bourbon in any part of Europe for ten years? The late state papers, and this thing called a speech of the King of france have developed two objects of great importance. Whatever doubts may have been heretofore entertained on the subject, it is no longer doubtful that Russia has been plotting the subjugation of So America, and the Gauntlet is fairly thrown down between Legitimacy and the Rights of Man. These last too, I apprehend, are better understood in Germany than in Spain or France either; and now that the views of the sovereigns are no longer a secret, are no perturbations to be looked for in that quarter? The worst of the alternatives of Görres,[5] whom you have read no doubt, seems fast approaching; yet I cannot but think the best was practicable. Even now, if Ferdinand would produce a project, somewhat devious from the present Constitution—which is capable enough of amendment, God knows—a Constitution that would insure a fair representation of the people—and boldly and unequivocally assert his assent to it—the hand of the destroying angel might be stayed. But I am not there to nudge him; and I suppose he will be employed in unkenneling Santiago with his white horse to betray his Army to the worshippers of St Louis. Your Saints are all Legitimates. Really the thing is too farcical to be serious, and too serious to be farcical, upon. I never doubted the Patriotism, or the Philanthropy, which is a better thing, of Mr: Adams or Mr: Jefferson. Their difference lay in the one viewing man as he is, the other, as he ought to be. The Smellfungus[6] of the one and the nihil humani[7] of the other influenced their opinions, which neither ought to have done in their stations in life; for why are we endowed with reason, but to controul our erroneous propensities. I too believed with the latter that a gleam of light was bursting on the world; and I cannot let go the hope even now that some progress is making in the human understanding—that there is a remote prospect of amelioration. Yet if the question were reduced to a wager to be ⟨sealed?⟩ in the year 2000 I would bet large odds on Mr: Adams—for Man is Man—at best a learned Pig, and must feed on acorns.

In the other sheet, as it lay in my Portfolio, I found a slip in shorthand, which I believe made part of a Letter to Mr Benjn: Joy on his advising me of some interlocutory Judgement in the Case of the Eliza and Rising Sun,[8] and was intended to be incorporated in what I was then writing to you. It is as follows.

"This was precisely the Case contemplated in Mr. Madison's Invitation to the Owners to bring forward their Claims.[9] When the ships sailed from England the Colonial Governments had invited such trade. On arrival at Rio Janeiro the supercargo was informed that he might still carry it on under certain modifications. These he pursued with the best advice he could get. To say that after the Owners had gone to all this expence, and even entered the port of Montevideo, they must go back because of a new Order from Spain, of which they could know nothing when they incurred the Expence, and from continually shifting their Counsels and detaining the ships for further orders, and finally depriving them of the benefit they had a right to expect at the outset, was in fact ensnaring them into Loss and ruin."

I shall only add on this subject at pres[e]nt that I shall be greatly obliged if you can furnish Mr: Benjn: Joy with, or advise him where he can find, the Document here referred to. It is not in Wait's Collection. I hope this will find you quite well, and rest always very faithfully and sincerely yours

G. Joy

RC (DLC). Addressed by Joy to JM.

1. See Joy to JM, 1 Mar. 1820, and n. 3, and JM to Joy, 25 Nov. 1820.

2. *Ce plaisir (de la Vengeance) est celui des Dieux et des femmes:* this pleasure (vengeance) is that of gods and women. *La parole d'une femme suffisait deja a la galanterie française:* The word of a woman sufficed for French gallantry. *Sirop de capillaire:* syrup of maidenhair fern. For the volume from which Joy was quoting, see Joy to JM, 2 Feb. 1822, and n. 1.

3. "But mine was like the lava flood / That boils in Ætna's breast of flame": George Gordon Byron, "The Giaour," *The Poetical Works of Lord Byron*, ed. Thomas Moore et al. (London, 1847), 74.

4. In April 1823 Louis-Antoine d'Artois, duc d'Angoulême, led a French army into Spain to support Ferdinand VII and reverse the Revolution of 1820, which had established a constitutional monarchy (Carr, *Spain, 1808–1975*, 138–46).

5. Johann Joseph von Görres (1776–1848), a German newspaper editor and political writer, had published *Teutschland und die Revolution* in 1819, a work that reflected the dismay of those who had expected great democratic change following Napoleon's defeat (Christopher John Murray, ed., *Encyclopedia of the Romantic Era, 1760–1850* [2 vols.; New York, 2004], 1:437).

6. Smellfungus: grumbler (*OED Online*).

7. *Nihil humani:* short for, nothing human is alien to me.

8. For the case of the *Eliza* and the *Rising Sun*, see Joy to JM, 16 Apr. 1804, *PJM-SS*, 7:70–71.

9. See JM to Stephen Higginson and others, 6 Sept. 1802, *PJM-SS*, 3:549–50.

From Charles Yancey

Dear Sir. Richmond Va. 30 Jany. 1823

Your letter enclosing a $5 Note for the Va. Times to you one year, Was duly Recd.[1] & I delay'd the answer for Mr. Crawfords arrival which is hourly expected. So soon as he comes a Rect. will be forwarded to you. I have the pleasure to say to you, that your old fellow servants Messrs Jefferson, & Monroe have made a similar request. I avail myself of this opportunity, to assure you, that I hold in gratefull Remembrance, the Many Years hard Labour you have spent in the service of your Country, & sincerely hope you may enjoy a long & peacefull retirement. I am your friend & Mo. Ob. Sert.

Charles Yancey

RC (DLC).

1. JM to Yancey, 4 Jan. 1823.

From Tench Coxe

Gentlemen Jany 31. 1823.

The extraordinary operations against the cause of self government is manifest in the old world, and the unprecedented combination against Liberty under name of the holy alliance, together with guarded but effective cooperation with them on the part of Great Britain, and some of the minor powers appear to threaten the world, in which we must prosper or suffer and act with many trying circumstances even in the current year. Our internal situation (and particularly in respect the movements in the course of the presidential election, which will be made 1823 & 4,) has in my opinion a real great and dangerous relation to those foreign operations against republican governments, and even such shares of pure popular representation as the French and English lower houses would be were the electors of the same de[s]cription as those who chuse the houses of representatives of those five or ten of our populous states whose constitutions most effectually for the electors rights, religious and civil [*sic*]. The manifest adoption as a candidate for the Presidency of Mr. J.Q. Adams by the worst of the federalists of 1797 to 1801, and by their successors (considerably identified as far as alive) and by all those, who openly or in disguise are unfriendly to our institutions, after openly treating him for years as an unprincipled contravener of his unaltered political faith, and the Union with these of a great portion of *republican* interest of Massachusetts & Maine, with other circumstances, which discuss[i]on will develope and display convince me that Mr. John Quincy Adams had on the 1st. day of this year a less divided federal and Massachusetts standing than Mr J. Adams senr. had either in 1796 or 1801. Decidedly averse to a change of the principles of the constitutions of the U.S. on their proper merits; *and* as decidedly averse to the various and manifold evils of a revolution in them and on our organation [*sic*], I have been drawn to the consideration of such measures as may be most effectual for the peaceable prevention. It is impossible to turn my heart & understanding into that ground, without an hundred recollections of your names from the first measure of œconomical reform, which led to the convention at Annapolis in 1786 to the present hour. I have therefore determined to address this *uncopied* joint letter to you with the general view of opening the subject, and with the intention of offering any specific measures or particular requests for consideration or grant. Did my circumstances admit I would spend a week or more as occasion might recommend in your vicinities, for the benefit of such conferences as have heretofore taken place between us, and which are more eligible in their nature, and more consistent with the convenience of your increased years, and especially with those of your elder name.

After this introduction permit me [to] state that from the time that I have given one deliberate reading to the Essays of Publicola of 1791,[1] I have assimilated him in my own mind to Genl. A. Hamilton than to his father Mr. Adams senr with whom however, as his preceptor governor, and predecessor in political career I think it just and prudent to connect the son, in prudent consideration. I therefore took up the subject by indicating to two [of] our daily gazettes copies of Publicola's essays in the pamphlet form (as reprinted in London & Dublin with the name "John Adams Esqre." in the title pages)[2] and in the news paper form in John Fennos gazette of the U.S. in 1791 in 11 numbers, from which last authority the whole were reprinted. I prepared six papers under the signature of Greene, for the American Sentinel *here*,[3] which were published after Publicola to show the predecession of Mr. Adams senior (in London in 1797.8 & in N. York in 1790 in his "*defence*" and his Discour[s]es on Davila[4] in 1790) to Mr. Adams junr. in his Publicola's of 1791, and the succession of Mr. Adams junr. to his fathers labors, to the same end; the setting up the British, and the undermining the principles and character of our Constitution. While Greene was in the course of publication, I prepared another series under the signature of Sherman,[5] (a name of republican esteem in the East) in five numbers, which will be continued, if I will. These are in Binnss democratic press. At the same time I published another series more strictly on the demerits and evils of Publicola, of which No. 4 has appeared to day.[6] They will be continued. I send nine of the Greene's, the Sidneys & the Shermans, all I have by me: also two numbers of Publicola, all that I have out of pamphlet. You will collect from these broken papers some of my views on the case; and ⟨treat?⟩ the great case now & till its close [as] you think fit. All these papers have appeared in the Dem: Press and Sentinel since the 5th. of Jany. currt. and were in Washington in 36 hours, & in Boston in 70 hours. But not a syllable has been published in attack, or in explanation, justification, extenuation or reply from either place, from Boston to Washington down to the 27th. from Boston and to the 28th. from Washington, whither many copies go in papers taken by the members of the two houses, by the President & the Heads of Depts including Mr. Adams, and by the Washington Editors, and a number of the citizens. The republication, & commentaries (Publicola, & the strictures on him) as so recd as far as I learn, as to leave no doubt that Mr Adams will be unsupported in Pennsa. by our electoral vote.

There is a matter of great importance which I beg leave to state. In the course of the history of republican & anti-republican exertions, since 1786, there are many public facts, many public evidences, many published papers or papers not confidential which would be [of] great use if they were collected here in an accessible Situation. Among these are

Mr. Adams senrs. Defence of the Constns.[7]
his Discourses on Davila
his answers to addresses—
Mr. Adams junrs. Publicola
Mr. John Langdons letter to
Genl. S. Ringgold[8]
Genl. Washington's answer to Mr.
Adet's address on the delivery of the
Colours of France Jany 1. 1796[9]
all of which we have here in our collections.

But there [are] many important things which we have not, tho we remember them, and many which we do not remember & yet may have. I should be glad therefore to have, to receive in such confidence as may be prescribed any thing that will bear upon the facts of endeavours to convert the public mind from our institutions, or to oppose, or change or discredit them. One paper I much want is a copy of a letter from Mr. John Adams senr. to Mr. Samuel Adams dated AD 1790[10] in which he states (if my memory is true) that he Mr. J A. senr. never was in favor of republicanism further than as a government in which people should have "*a Share.*" I trust in your excuse for this hasty letter on a solemn subject, and beg you to exercise your recollections & revise your files as to any such materials as can be with propriety confidentially imparted, or lent. The time requires effectual measur[e]s of appeal to the public mind. I have the honor to be yr. mo. respectful Servt.

TENCH COXE

RC (DLC). Unaddressed; joint addressees Thomas Jefferson and JM determined by comparison with Coxe to Jefferson and JM, 1 Feb. 1823. Enclosed in JM to Thomas Jefferson, 19 Feb. 1823.

1. The eleven "Letters of Publicola," written pseudonymously by John Quincy Adams, were published in the Boston *Columbian Centinel*, 8 June–27 July 1791. For JM's comments on them, see JM to Jefferson, 13 July 1791, *PJM*, 14:46–47. JM's copies of the newspaper clippings of the articles republished by Tench Coxe in 1823 are in series 7, box 2, of the Madison Papers, Library of Congress.

2. *An Answer to Pain*[e]*'s Rights of Man. By John Adams, Esq.* (London, 1793).

3. Coxe's "Greene" essays have not been found (Cooke, *Tench Coxe*, 517 n. 20).

4. "Discourses on Davila," a series of articles written by John Adams, were published anonymously in 1790–91 in the Philadelphia *Gazette of the United States.*

5. The six articles "To the American People," signed by "Sherman," on the subject of the "Letters of Publicola" were published in the Philadelphia *American Sentinel* in January and February 1823. JM's copies of the newspaper clippings of these articles are in series 7, box 2, of the Madison Papers, Library of Congress.

6. The series of essays written by Coxe entitled "To the Friends of the Principles of the Constitution of the United States," and signed "Sidney," were published in the Philadelphia *Democratic Press* in January 1823. JM's copies of the newspaper clippings of these articles are in series 7, box 2, of the Madison Papers, Library of Congress.

7. John Adams, *A Defence of the Constitutions of Government of the United States of America* (Philadelphia, 1787; Evans 20176).

8. John Langdon to Samuel Ringgold, 10 Oct. 1800. Langdon wrote: "In the conversation held between Mr. Adams, Mr. Taylor, and myself, Mr. Adams . . . hoped, or expected to see the day when Mr. Taylor, and his friend Mr. Giles, would be convinced that the people of America would not be happy without an hereditary chief magistrate and senate, or at least for life" (John Wood, *The Suppressed History of the Administration of John Adams, [from 1797 to 1801,] as Printed and Suppressed in 1802 . . . Now Republished with Notes, and an Appendix, by John Henry Sherburne* [Philadelphia, 1846], 136–37). For the history of this book, originally published in 1802, see Sowerby, *Catalogue of Jefferson's Library*, 1:247–49.

9. See Reply to the French Minister, 1 Jan. 1796, Fitzpatrick, *Writings of George Washington*, 34:413–14.

10. "Whenever I use the word *republic* with approbation, I mean a government in which the people have collectively, or by representation, an essential share in the sovereignty" (John Adams to Samuel Adams, 18 Oct. 1790, Charles Francis Adams, ed., *The Works of John Adams, Second President of the United States: With a Life of the Author, Notes and Illustrations* [10 vols.; 1850–56; reprint, New York, 1971], 6:415).

From an Unidentified Correspondent

Alabama Jany 31. 1823

"Nothing sells high but land which is kept up to an extravagant price from the particular situation of that article. All the valuable land in the State is either forfeited to Govt or in the hands of individuals who calculate on this situation, & do not expect a sale of the forfeited lands for many years, when they will have disposed of their land, at a high price to the Emigrants to this State: & it is supposed there are at this time at least three hundred families who have removed to this State, & can not procure land to settle on, till Govt. may please to sell some of the forfeited land. The current rent per acre for open land is from three dollars to four & half. If the Executive should not determine to sell some of those lands soon, the Monopolizers will get off their lands at extravagant prices on those families, and be in a situation to purchase again at the public sales, and the price of land of course will be raised higher than a reasonable man ought to give.

"N.B. The statements I have made above in regard to the situation of the land and emigrants to this State, is disinterested & true: for I have no intention of settling here, or owning a foot of land in the State. The land forfeited, in many instances, is still held by the former owner & cultivated, and much injured or rented by him for his benefit, that the sooner they are sold the better, or they will be ruined if possible. And as to that portion of land on which eight years credit has been taken, they will be ruined as far as it is possible, and will be abandoned at the end of that period. The latter portion of lands on which a credit of 8 years is given must be eventually ruined, but the former portion can be saved by an immediate sale, otherwise they will be divested of everything that is valuable. For instance, a Speculator has purchased a section of land. He will forfeit all but 80 acres on which is his Gin, Dwelling house, & Spring; and he will keep in possession 2 or 3 hundred acres of cleared land which he will rent at three dollars per acre, or ruin by cultivating if he can, & save his own land adjoining, he will cut down every tree on the forfeited part to prevent any one from purchasing. If these lands are not immediately taken out of the hands of the former Owner & sold the loss will be very great to the U.S. And there have been forfeited at the Huntsville Land Office alone four hundred & ninety five thousand acres; nearly the whole of which is deemed first rate land, lying mostly adjacent to Tennessee River."

JAMES MADISON

Extract (owned by Herman Blum, Philadelphia, Pa., 1959). In JM's hand; from a letter from an unidentified correspondent. Probably enclosed in JM to James Monroe, 4 Feb. 1823.

From Tench Coxe

GENTLEMEN PHILA. Feby 1. 1823

I took the liberty on the 31st. Ulto. to address a letter to you, which was covered, with some parts of news papers, to Mr Madison. In the dusk of the evening, two packets on my table were closed and, inadvertently, that to you was closed before revision, and taken to the post office. The direction at bottom to both of you was omitted, which you will be pleased to consider the same as this; and you will be so good as to allow for imperfections in a letter not revised.

Papers, which have been published, of the character of the letter to Mr. *Samuel* Adams of 1790,[1] are deeply important, as are such as may be published, bearing on the subject. The case of J. Henry the Govr. Sir J. Craig of the Canadas,[2] must be attended with many important evidences facts, & pieces which it is a duty, as far as proper, to use, since they are giving us Mr. H. G. O.,[3] as Govr. of Mtts. & Mr. J. Q. A. as P. U. S. I am duly impressed with the allowances, in regard to public and to laborious exertions of Gentlemen of your respective ages, long services and standing; but since the times are most dangerous to the cause of liberty, religious & civil, in Europe, and since a total failure (by power, numbers, arms and corruption) *there*, will endanger us and our system, *in the two Americas*, I do not doubt, that all *convenient* aid will be afforded by you both, to preserve our internal tranquility and freedom, by protecting the inviolability of our principles and institutions. The letter, of 1822, from Mr. Jefferson to Lieutt. Govr. Barry,[4] written without reference to this election, has been of great importance in this year of action. The recognition of the sappings and more open violations of our principles and constitutions down to 1801, and of an actual recovery of the ground from our opponents, and of "*a civil revolution*" from wrong to right, has supported the firm, open and solemn warnings, which the adoption of a monarchical candidate had previously drawn forth, from Jany 1822 and thro the subsequent time; particularly since the failures of the regeneration of Naples & Piedmont, the neglect of the Greeks, the menaces to Spain & Portugal, and the falling off of the popular power in France & the Netherlands, together with the persecutions of the reformers in Great Britain.

It would be useful, in this season, if the Demc. Press, the American Sentinel, & the Boston Statesman were seen in your parts of the country, as I believe they will contain much of those current views, which will be taken of this great case, till Decemr. 1824: the time of action of the boards of Electors.

I suppose the most convenient direction of letters to Mr Jefferson is *M.*, near Charlotte[s]ville Va. and to Mr. Madison, Montpr. near Orange Court House, Va. Your agricultural or other Societies near Monticello, and Montpellier, would find much useful matter in those three papers in relation to Agriculture, and the whole circle of the arts, that minister, at home & abroad, to its indispens[a]ble prosperity. Tho I most sensibly feel the obligation of apologizing for these two letters, yet, my venerable friends, I cannot but confess the concurrent feelings, which the view around us, at home & abroad, irresistibly suggests to a sound discretion & to a paramount temporal duty. Knowing well your hearts and understandings I rest, in ease of mind, yr. faithful servant

Tench Coxe

RC (DLC). Addressed jointly to JM and Thomas Jefferson. Enclosed in JM to Jefferson, 19 Feb. 1823.

1. For John Adams's letter to Samuel Adams of 18 Oct. 1790, see Coxe to JM, 31 Jan. 1823, and n. 10.

2. For the John Henry affair, see Elbridge Gerry to JM, 2 Jan. 1812, and nn., *PJM-PS*, 4:116–17.

3. Harrison Gray Otis.

4. Thomas Jefferson to William T. Barry, 2 July 1822, DLC: Jefferson Papers, which was published in the newspapers and in *Niles' Weekly Register* 23 (15 Feb. 1823): 376.

¶ From James Monroe. Letter not found. *3 February 1823*. Described as a three-page autograph letter, signed, listed for sale in the Charles Hamilton Catalogue No. 103 (24 Feb. 1977), item 161, summarized and abstracted as follows: "dealing with a post for Madison's nephew, a constitutional matter concerning grants of power in which he is in apparent disagreement both with Madison and Jefferson, and about Poinsett and his recent return from Cuba and Mexico.

'. . . Among the last pursuits in which I should engage would be a difference with you, or Mr. Jefferson, in a construction of any of the grants of power in the constitution . . .' The issue concerns appropriation of money for road construction, 'and the right of appropriation. On great consideration I was satisfied, that that construction was sound & the safest for state rights, that could be adopted. I well know that the subject is not free from difficulty. . . . I am well aware that Congress cannot of right, apply money to other than national objects, that they can not, for example, build court houses, for counties in a state, but I think that the lack of that power turns pretty much on the same principle, with the want of it, in a state, to tax its people, to make like improvements in another state, as fortifications at its own expence for the union. . . .' Monroe pursues the subject at great length, and concludes that it was wise to construct the Cumberland road by appropriation of money, 'with the consent of the states through which it passes. . . .' As to the reports of Mr. Poinsett, Monroe relates his view that although Mexican Emperor Iturbide has the support of the clergy and the military, 'his dominion will not be permanent. . . .'"

To James Monroe

DEAR SIR Feby. 4. 1823

Having just recd. a letter stating the circumstances in the extract enclosed,[1] I have thought it not amiss, that they should be known to you. You will be able, or can be enabled to judge how far they merit attention. Some of them, if there be no error in the statement, seem to require & admit of correction. You will observe that the information is from a source professing & I believe truly to be disinterested: and the dexterity, with which even the indulgences of the Govt. are often turned to unfair advantage, gives but too much credibility to examples of the abuse. Yours

JAMES MADISON

RC (NNPM). Docketed by Monroe.

1. The enclosed extract was probably from an Unidentified Correspondent to JM, 31 Jan. 1823.

From Littleton Dennis Teackle

CHAMBER OF THE HOUSE OF DELEGATES
SIR, ANNAPOLIS 4 Feby 1823

As chairman of the Committee of Publick Instruction, I take the liberty of transmitting a bill reported for that purpose,[1] and beg the favour of your views upon the System proposed, and that you will be pleased to note its defects, and to suggest Amendments.

Presuming upon a knowledge of your liberal and Philanthropick disposition, I venture to Essay this claim upon your time, and attention. I have the Honor to be with the highest respect & Consideration Your Ob'd Svt.

LITTLETON DENNIS TEACKLE[2]

RC (DLC). Addressed by Teackle to JM. Docketed by JM "recd. Feby. 9."

1. *An Act to Provide for the Public Instruction of Youth throughout This State, and to Promote the Important Interests of Husbandry and Agriculture* ([Annapolis, 1823]; Shoemaker 13225). JM's copy is in the Madison Collection, Rare Book and Special Collections Division, Library of Congress.

2. Littleton Dennis Teackle (ca. 1776–1848), a resident of Somerset County, Maryland, was a merchant and entrepreneur who served in the Maryland House of Delegates, 1824–36, as an advocate of public education. Teackle was president of the Bank of Somerset and projected a railroad for the Eastern Shore in the 1830s (*Daily National Intelligencer*, 20 Nov. 1848; Jason Rhodes, *Somerset County, Maryland: A Brief History* [Charleston, S.C., 2007], 39–40, 47, 61; Robert J. Brugger, *Maryland, A Middle Temperament, 1634–1980* [Baltimore, 1988], 250–51).

From Stephen Van Rensselaer

SIR WASHINGTON Feby 4th. 1823

Pardon the liberty I take of troubling you with the enclosed address[1] and beg the favor of your opinion of the project. Any improvements that may occur to you will cheerfully be adopted. We look up to you as the great Patron of Agriculture. In our State we propose establishing an Agrictr School & I have offered a farm to the Board of Agriculture for a pattern farm if the Legislature will sanction it. A Bill is reported to the Assembly which I hope will pass into a Law.[2] I am very respectfully Your ob St

S. VAN RENSSELAER

RC (DLC). Docketed by JM.

1. Amos Eaton, *To the Gentlemen Residing in the Vicinity of the Erie Canal* (Troy, N.Y., 1822; Shoemaker 8589). JM's copy is in the Madison Collection, Rare Book and Special Collections Division, Library of Congress.

2. The bill was unsuccessful, but in 1836 the legislature passed an act incorporating the New York State Agricultural School, the money for its support to be raised by public subscription. Though several attempts were made to raise the necessary funds, the school never got off the ground (Harry J. Carman, ed., *Jesse Buel, Agricultural Reformer: Selections from His Writings* [1947; reprint, New York, 1972], xxiv–xxv).

From George Joy

Dear sir Brighton 5th Febry. 1823.

I wrote you on the 30th Ult: to take the first Conveyance from London or Liverpool; and I now find my Letter will go by the Packet of the 8th Inst. from the latter port, for which this may possibly be in time. I ought to have added, as I had here no Copy of my Letter to Captn. Pott, that my Instructions to him were to change the direction of the parcel from his name to yours and either send it forward carefully himself or leave the Collector to do it, as he should be advised; or to that effect.

The Speech of the King of france[1] must have been in Liverpool in time for the packet of the 1st Inst: and I do not grudge to my friend Maury the Credit and Eclat of a first Communication; which you will probably receive from him. I like to be useful in this way; but I like better that you should be early advised on an interesting topic.

By the packet of the 8th you will also receive the Speech of the King of England;[2] and if we are rightly informed here the Amendments to be proposed, in the House of Lords by Lord Lansdown, and in the Commons by Mr Brougham; which will supercede all anticipatory Speculations on these subjects. And 'tis well—for between the plain course which the Policy and Necessities of the Country call for, and the Bias to Error, it would be difficult to form an opinion of the measures to be adopted.

I wish the Spaniard & the Portuguese may settle down with a Constitution in which Security blended with liberty may give a spring to Industry—partial pecuniary Interests might suffer from it for a time; but the aggregate even of these would be benefitted, and the approximation of the triumph of freedom promoted; but I am far from approving the Canningisms and Cobbetisms that appear in their Correspondence with the foreign Ministers. Say even they were provoked—a contrastic style were better. There is a want of Dignity in their responses which savours too much of the Bully for men of moral valour; and it was the less to be expected from the moderation in fact with which they have hitherto conducted the revolution.

The subjects of the Speech have been kept with more than ordinary Secrecy—probably, because "They could not tell us what they did not know." There has undoubtedly been much vacillation in the french Cabinet, and it should seem that the Duc de Villele[3] had promised not to oppose the war if his proposal to the Spaniard should be rejected. The discussions here are as lively and entertaining as if a few hours would not settle the question—the discrepancy between the professions of the government and the scope of the govt: Newspapers creates a glorious puzzle; yet Mr Vansittart[4] said a year ago in the House that there had been many things in the Courier, which is the cheif of them, that he could not approve, and the palpable evidences of stockjobbing, which it has lately exhibited, are as disgusting as a Lottery puff. The short history of the Congress at Verona, as respects this Country, I take to be this. The Duke of Wellington, who was never the Marquis Wellesley, was sent, in ill health and with un⟨connected?⟩ Ideas, to meet the other mighty men of valour; who found his military notions of discipline and subjugation not uncongenial with their autocratical—when this was perceived instructions were sent him by Lord Liverpool (Mr: Frederick Robinson,[5] who does not favor Legitimacy against Liberty abroad, being of the Counsel) not to be quite so pliant—and he followed orders. I believe there is some truth in the anecdote of his Conversation with the King of France, which terminated in the Compliment from this last that he liked him too well as a friend to wish to see him an enemy. Whether his ⟨love?⟩, or his instructions extended to the provisions of the treaty of Utrecht does not appear; but he ought to have said that England would never see France, Buonapartical or Bourbonical, in quiet possession of Spain.

Mais revenons à nos moutons.[6] On the subject of the Eliza and Rising Sun, on which I have already troubled you more than once, it may be proper that you should know that no secret instructions were given to the super Cargo—against the Laws of trade in any Country I never did act, nor did I ever authorise a breach of them in any other person; save that where an article has been prohibited, and no tax would admit it, I have bought it for use, as medicinal, but not for sale— a few pounds of Boston Chocolate, for example, which is purer and better than any money will buy here. I think smuggling to defraud the revenue or injure the fair trader, a breach of the 8th Command.[7] But whe⟨n⟩ a small potentate, like the Emperor of Russ⟨ia⟩ is compelled under duresse to adopt a system of general exclusion, and afterwards allows an Artic⟨le⟩ of the first necessity to the poorest of his subjects to be imported; I have no scruples. This is the whole head and front of my offending. In the Case of the E. & RS. my Instructions were plainly written, and afterwards plainly printed. I had great Dependence on the supercargo but gave him no latitude inconsistent with these principles. He was moreover largely interested in the voyages; and could have no inducement on his arrival at Rio Janeiro, (where unquestionably he did not find the express permission that my instructions contemplated,) to adopt any other measures than what the safety and profit of the Concern required, under the Circumstances in which he found himself. Thus much I have thought it necessary to say for your satisfaction; that whatever may result from the perverse technicalities of the Law, you may be assured that everything was fairly intended by me and the Owners in Boston; and the measures adopted by the supercargo when he found his hand in the Lions mouth, were à notre insçu,[8] and entirely his own.

Here is the Speech just arrived, and our Sanhedrin (we have many politicians in this house) pronounce it milk and water; but you will see it before you receive this, or at the same time. It says more on the main point than was expected in this shape. The Newspapers are usually here some hours before the return of post; but owing to the length of the Debates they were not out in time for the morning Coaches. You will receive them then without any Comments from me, on which I congratulate you; and hope you may not have as much fatigue in reading this, as I have with my lame arm in writing; being always very truly, Dear sir, Your friend & Servt.

G. Joy

The Copy of my Letter to Captn: Pott will be sent from London with this; or in the package with the Prints and duplicate of the Books on my return to town.

RC (DLC). Addressed by Joy to JM. Damaged by removal of seal.

1. The speech of the king of France delivered at the opening of the session of the two chambers, 28 Jan. 1823 (*Annual Register for 1823*, 149–51), noted France's preparation for war with Spain, among other topics.

2. The speech of the king of Great Britain, read by the Lord Chancellor in the king's absence, was delivered on 4 Feb. 1823 (ibid., 4–5), and disclaimed all interest in intervening in the internal affairs of Spain.

3. Joseph, comte de Villèle (1773–1854) was born in Toulouse, served in the navy, and established himself as a landowner on the Île de Bourbon (now Réunion). He returned to France in 1807. Villèle joined the ultra-royalist party and in 1815 was elected to the Chamber of Deputies. In 1821 he was named minister of finance, and the following year president of the council, a post he held until his resignation in 1828. In 1823 Villèle sent French troops into Spain to quell a revolution and restore the monarch (Jean Guillaume Hyde de Neuville, *Notice historique sur M. le Comte de Villèle* [Paris, 1855], 1–4, 7, 9, 13, 16, 71, 93–95, 182–84, 205).

4. Nicholas Vansittart (1766–1851) was a member of Parliament, 1796–1822, and chancellor of the exchequer, 1812–22. In 1823 he was created baron Bexley of Bexley.

5. Frederick John Robinson (1782–1859) was a member of Parliament, 1806–27, and was appointed to a number of government positions, including president of the Board of Trade (1818), where he was a member of the cabinet. He was chancellor of the exchequer, 1823–27, and briefly, prime minister, 1827–28. Robinson was created Viscount Goderich of Nocton in 1827, and first Earl of Ripon in 1833.

6. *Mais revenons à nos moutons:* let us get back to the subject.

7. The eighth of the ten commandments is "Thou shalt not steal."

8. *À notre insu:* without our knowledge.

From Robert Mackay

Dr Sir Fredericksburg Feby 6. 1823.

Under cover herewith you receive your account, Shewing a balance in my favour of $17.24 Which you will no doubt at Some early day desire to be paid. With esteem,

Robert Mackay

RC (DLC). Docketed by JM.

To Stephen Van Rensselaer

Dr Sir Montpr. Feby 11. 1823

I have recd. your favor of the 4th. inst. inclosing the address of Mr. Eaton relating to a geological & agricultural survey of the vicinity of the Erie Canal. As far as my judgment extends, his instructions are ably drawn up, & give an adequate scope to the researches & observations most likely to be scientifically and practically useful. In the execution of the task objects not foreseen may doubtless occur to an enlightened observer increasing the stock of information obtained. I wish every success to the Survey which can reward the patriotic bounty of its projector & patron.

I wish equal success to the proposed Agricultural School, in aid of which you generously offer a pattern Farm. To perfect Agriculture as an Art, it must in the hands of some at least; be a Science also. Such a Farm under a proper cultivation, besides other uses, may serve as a kind of apparatus to the professorship.

It wd. seem that I have much more credit with some as a farmer than I deserve. I have the zeal of a votary, with very scanty pretensions beyond it.

J M.

Draft (DLC).

To Littleton Dennis Teackle

Sir. Montpellier 12. February 1823

I received a few days ago your letter of the 4. Instant, enclosing the copy of a bill to provide for the public instruction of youth, and to promote the interest of Agriculture; and requesting observations thereon. I wish I were less incompetent to a satisfactory compliance with the request.

The wisdom of providing a system of diffusive education must at once, be universally approved. Of the proper organization and details of it, which must be accomodated to local circumstances, to popular opinions and habits, and perhaps to co-existing institutions and arrangements, those only can judge who can apply these tests. And after all such is the difficulty of the task, that experience alone can give the system its desired improvement. It will be well therefore in such cases instead of requiring too much perfection in the outset, to trust to the lights which must quickly be furnished from that source.

It is easy to observe generally that such a system ought to be made as little complicated and expensive as possible, that its structure should render its execution regular and certain, and that it should guard particularly against the abuses incident to monies held in Trust or passing thro' different hands. But it is not so easy to frame or judge of the precise regulations necessary to obtain these advantages; especially where the population is thin, and local changes of various sorts are constantly going on, and where the difficulty is much greater than in a more compact and settled population where the duties to be performed, lie within a narrow space, and within the reach of every eye.

The plan proposed by the Bill appears in its outline to have been well conceived. A single Superintendant held in adequate responsibility, may be preferable to a Board. The inconveniences of the latter justify the experiment at least. The Levy Courts are entitled doubtless to the confidence placed in them. Whether the chain of agencies might not be shortened by dropping that link and making the Commissioners appointable by the people at County elections for other purposes is a question I do not venture to decide. Unless the extent of the Counties forbid, it might be a question also whether the Commissioners might not suffice without the Inspectors associated with them. The Trustees whose agency is connected with the arrangement of the taxes and the immediate application of the funds, are very properly to be elected by the people of their districts, whose interests are at stake, and who will of course have an eye to the due expenditure of their money. In contracting with the Teachers, they are to have, I presume, a discretion to make the amount of their wages depend in part on the number of pupils. This may be influenced more or less by the conduct of the Teacher; as this again will be by making the amount of his income dependent on it.

I observe that the Commissioners and Trustees are made Corporate Bodies for receiving and holding property granted for the Schools without limitation and without any authority over it reserved to the Government.

It may be thought very nugatory to guard at this time against excessive accumulations in such hands, and abuses growing out of them. But if the Schools are to be permanent, and charitable donations be unalienable, time must produce here what it has produced elsewhere. The abuses which have been brought to light in old countries in the management of Elemosinary and Literary endowments accumulated by a lapse of time, are a sufficient warning to a young one to keep the door shut against them.

The provision made in the Bill in behalf of Agriculture, is an example highly creditable. But why restrict the professorship to the Chemical source of instruction? Ought it not to be at large on a subject abounding in others, many of them still more appropriate to it.

You will readily beleive that I have sketched these remarks because some were expected, and not because they present ideas not obvious or not likely to occur in the discussion of the Bill: and viewed in that light, you will as readily pardon my request that they may be received as a *private*, and not a public communication. With great respect

James Madison

RC (NjP); draft (DLC). RC in an unidentified hand, signed by JM.

To James Monroe

Dr Sir Montpr. Feby. 13. 1823

I have rcd. your favor of the 3d. I am much obliged by the kind manner in which you speak of my Nephew. I hope you will always consider expressions of my good will in such cases as perfectly subordinate to public considerations, and superi[o]r pretensions. In the present case I am not sure that the appt. of my nephew to the place in question ought to be desired even by himself, unless Col: Barbour, who knows him well & who has a nearer view of the duties to be performed, thinks him adequate to them, and sufficiently balancing the Clerk on the other side, it might ultimately be more of an obstacle than an advance in his career.

Nothing was farther from my purpose than to draw a word from you on the constitutional question regarding Canals &c. I have as little doubt of your sincerity in the view taken of it, as of the ability with which it was maintained. I have always regretted that the Const: did not give more power on the subject than your construction of it claims.

I had noticed the call of the H. of Rs. which among other cases wd touch that of Mr. Cutts. He is very fortunate in having friendly dispositions where his fate must be finally decided, because they ensure him every thing consistent with justice & propriety. I can say nothing but that I shall feel much pleasure, on many & obvious accts. if the loss of his fortune shd. not be followed by that of his character & station.

Draft (DLC).

From Elisha Callender

Dr Sir Boston Feby 16 1823

Your favor of 16 April[1] came in due cource to hand, a leisure moment now offers, to notice the contents; I have Sir, a full view of your Just observations, on the cultivation of the olive in your State, which I greatly regret. On mature reflection, Since writing you, I have had my doubts, whether the climate of your State, was not two intemperate, to indulge much hope of Success. I flatter my Self, that the fumigating Bellows, with the preparation for distroying insects, & &c, will prove, on fair trial useful, as well as the Olive Press, in Situations where there utility, can be tested; how far, and how much, merrit if any, is attached to the projector, lies in the Sphere of others to Judge. I have embraced for many years past, much time in Study, and writing; having at all times, a full view of being useful to my Country, has invited me, to an active Spirit, for general good; nature has done much for me, and I have endeavor'd to cultivate her rich gifts, by active and Studious industry, in the various paths of Sceience, both military, & naval; in different inventions, proved by models, and by drawings, with a mass of Miscelanious writings, nearly five hundred pages, on writing Paper reversed 14 by 6 Inches, full Sheets, Such as Bottony Astronomy, Anattomy &c &c. I have kep[t] them from the Eye of observation, untill I have a Suitable time of leisure, to give them punctuation, and recopy them in a fair & handsome manner—altho I possess, like most others, more or less, of the tincture of vanity, but in this case, I will divest my Self of it, & plainly assert, that whoever reads my manuscripts, will be satisfied; and I flatter my Self, that they will conceive me, for what I am. Fully persuaided my time could be Spent, much more profitable in the Service of my Country, than to remain where I now am Situated for my natural & acquired talents, are perfectly hid; and can be of no use either to my Country or Society.

I beg leave to transmit a drawing for your State, by the name of the Virginia, Agricultural College; should it be errected, either by the State or Individuals, it will be I Presume, the first in the Union; and as I Judge your State as Such, has induced me to forward it for your inspection, with liberty to make what use of it, you may think propper. The Building to be either of Brick or Wood, as may be Judged for the best; the length to be 90 feet, and the breadth 50 feet; runing East and West, a Cellar under a part, or the whole, the first floor to have Suitable & Spacious apartments proportionate, to the Building. The Second Story may be a little contracted, in the Plan, which will give more chambers, and that of the third intended for Sleeping Rooms of the Scholars, to run the intire length of the House, each one, will be by dimention 12 by 10 feet. Passage way 10 feet wide, the Doors to be opposite each other, with a Small Window, of 4 Squares of Glass, on a line with the top of the passage Door, for the convenience in Warm Weather, that there Should be a draft passing both Chambers, by a current of Air, communicating to north and South View; in case it may not be agreeable, to have there Doors open direct in face of each other. The Small Window will be convenient: one person is only to Sleep in a Room, which is conducive to health; I have no opinion, of crowded places where they inhale, each others Atmosphere: it will be found not wholsome, unless a Ventalator is in the Room, fixed in the top Square of a Window. This mode, gives a revival, and rejects impure Air it will be of great Service to refresh the Room. It will be of the highest importance in establishing this Building or Seminary, for instruction and improvement, to make choice of three able well informed, Sceientific Men, masters in there Business, and qualified to each department required. Such will make the institution, what it is intended for, profitable & Respectable, as will be Seen by the following Order. 1st A master Professor, in the various branches of Bottany, teaching by instruction, the growth, qualities, properties, and name of each Plant; for what use, & purpose in medicin, or weather for mere imbelishment, to please the fancy or gratify the taste which the rich Gift of nature, So profusely bestows, here, he will walk: in the Smooth and lovely path, parading, and difusing Sceientific knowledge to all around; more particular, his pupils, displaying in the fullest manner, the hues & tints of each flower, taking care at the same time, to make a propper, and exact division, betwixt the male, & female; lecturing on nutritive qualities, and how produced, conducting the nourishment, cause[d] by the Earth, through the pores of the Stamina, to various parts of the Limbs, reaching the calax, of the flowers, and the artiries and vanes of the Leaves, producing life and beauty in the whole, the Bottinist will have a wide and rich field, to act in, which must afford him, the highest gratification; when he conceives, he is rendering his Country, and Public, the most important Services. This must be a proud Solace, emminating from a refined & exalted mind; he surveys the admirable Scenery, of nature, and looks up to natures God, with unspeakable gratitude & Satisfaction. He must be careful, in laying out his ground in perfect order, intersecting his Beds with bordering Plank, or Slabs of Sawed Stones, inserting them, a Suitable debth in the Earth, in order to admit a passage to, & arround each plant either for inspection, or instruction: he will bring forth his judgement, in the construction of a

Hot House for his Plants, & Shrubery, in order that they should receive no injury, from the inclement Season of winter, let it be elevated fifteen or twenty feet from the Base, a Sloping Roof, South aspect, with glass windows fixed on the same, perfectly tite. Stoves of Cast Iron, will be required one or more, intented to produce a temperature, perfectly congenial, to the vitality and nature of the Plants. Here the master in this retreat, can find an equal Scope for instruction, as he would display in the Garden, or field. Here the rich garment of nature, with its Beauty, will unfold its Self, and open her bosome with warmth, to the kind and fostering hand of the cultivator; whoes love, and attention, to the Supreme order displayed, by the hand of nature, will give his mind, a full share of adoration, & praise the author of every good. All the leisure time the Scholars have, during both Seasons, I should advise there immediate attention to Study, in whatever branch of Sceience Suits there genious & Taste, either Husbandry, Bottany, Mechanic Arts, or History, and if they feel a wish to vary there hours in Writing, Cyphering, or Spelling, let them enjoy this privilidge, for all, and every part will be highly useful & Benificial to them; prepareing them, to be valuable members in Society. There must be a minute attention to there clenliness; and let them be well fed, and well clothed if possible, in every respect, with American Manufactures, as a proud emblem, of the rise & progress of Genious, and interpriseing Industry.

2ly. A master Professor, of Husbandry, in general, his business will call his active attention, to the quality of the Soil, giving the cause of all Produce, originating therefrom, by the attention of the cultivator, introducing when required, and at a propper Season, manure to enrich, in the highest manner the quality of the Earth; he must exercise his Judgement, and give a full display of his knowledge; what Sort of Seed, will be required for this, or that Soil, wether Strong, Dark, light, luminous, or Sandy; he will embrace every occation, either by Study, or experiment, the best manner of producing the first quality, and the most abundant Crop, he will view minutely, at the time of planting, that his Seed is Sound and of the first quality, and by no means touched by insects; here is a caution, worthy of observation, and must be Scrutinised with the utmost attention; thin crops has often been the result, in this case, by car[e]lessness. The master will now proceed to lay the bosome of the Earth open, with his Plow, giving a propper Depth, & Length, to his furrows; this mode of Planting Corn, will be much facilitated, by covering the Seed, at proper distances with the Hoe. He will now proceed to the Planting of Grain, such as wheat, Rye, Barley, & oats, the Plow of cource, will be made use of in the Same manner; I would advise him, to follow my Plan, of sowing, which is thus, put a Horse in a Common cart, fix a Cylinder made of thin wood, at the extreme part of it, fix a pivot at each end of the same, with a gruve Truck, place one other on the Hob, of the Cart wheel, with a double turn of Line to both. In this manner it will revolve, with an equal motion of the Horse. In feading the machine, it will be necessary to have Baggs of Grain in the Cart, a Harrow will be attached at the extreme end of the Same, either by chain, or Cord, and must be rather wider than the carriage, and of equal width to the Cylinder, whoes holes will be as close together, as the nature of the machine will admit, and will be made thus, here will be Seen, and known, the most perfect & exact mode of Planting, that can possibly be introduced by this new order.

Let us now pause, for the winter is passed, and the beauties of Spring, opens her Self, with mild Seerinity, pouring from her Swelled Bosome, her intented luxurious reward. Now Professor, your time and exertions are wanted; is your Earth, well manured, and your fences in due Order, if so, pay your attention to your Fruite Trees, let the Trunk of them, be well Scoured, with a stiff Brush, giving them the composition of Strong Brine, mixed with Tobacco Juice. By this means, it will clense the Stem from the Eggs of Insects, and will prove very Servisable. Let the Earth, be raised one foot in debth, round the Stem of the Tree, and place in the hole, so raised, a Small quantity of Horse, Cow, or Hogg manure therein, & recover the Same. We are all of us, extreamly fond of grasping the Fruites, but greatly inatentive to its proper nourishment; why should these Trees be so neglected. They certainly possess valuable properties, and add much to our comfort. Let it be known, by this indifference, the quality and quantity of the Same, are & is greatly diminished, and as far as the Roots extend, they will in the cource of time, draw intirely the nourishment of the Earths, best qualities. How often do we See the Tree, weare a Sickly appearance, pine and drupe, and is visible to the Eye; the cause and effect is Seen, by the failing verdure of its Leaves. My opinion, is, that it wants to be nourished, by the observation Stated above. Should the Tree be infected, while in Bloom, or after, with insects, make use of the fumigating composition, as given to you by directions some time past; take a short Iron Pan 14 Inches long, & 6 wide & 4 Inches deep. Let there be a Socket handle, direct in the center of the bottom. Insert in the Same, a handle of wood, in proportion to the heigth of the Top part of the Tree, and for the lower and middle Branches, you may insert a Short handle, entering the Socket, in the Same manner. You may then commence to fumigate, the different part[s] of the Tree, with the greatest effeect and by the strongest mode, of destroying the insects in the most rapid manner.

I shall now commence, and advise, a new mode of ingrafting Stone Fruite Trees with Scions of different Stone fruite, and also the different Seed fruite, with the Seed, as I am well convinced the Seed fruite, will not engender with the Stone. I shall hold this conception, untill proof is given to the contra. In preference to lascerate the Tree, with a Knife, or other sharp instrument, I should make use of the Center Bitt, which cutts an orifice, in the Limb of the Tree, round and smooth, and wants no bandage. Simular to the other mode, cut the Sceion a little pointed, at the end, and Slit it cross ways, in Order, that it may imbibe, the nutritive qualities of the Tree, so inserted in. Open the gash, and place a leafe from the Tree of the Sceion cross ways. As soon as the buds put forth, or the Tree, is in leaf, I would execute—in either case, it will promise success. Here we must know and calculate the attractive power of the Sun, pouring forth its vehement rays, on the top and middle Branches of the Tree, extending power by extraction, its congenial heat thereto, all the propper movements that I could request, in this case, to crown my views with expected, and desired Success. The most carefull attention will be required, in giving them water at the Stem, either Trees or Plants when required. The Earth now, and then, should be loosened round the Stem, in a manner necessary, to give expansion, to the absolute demand, of promoting there Health and which stimulation, will add much to there improvement. All animated Bodys, which are contracted by pressure, or confinement, will in all cases, produce a very bad effect. Natures Laws must be perfectly free, and whoever violates them, must introduce an injury to the worst effect, which time and experience will prove. When the most p[r]opper, and Suitable Season arrives, to gather the moison,[2] due attention must be observed, that the weather is clear, & the wind Dry. You have then nothing to fear, or further to do, but fill your garners, and continue your work from time to time, through the winter; observing with humanity and care, your Cratures are well fed & rubed. Give them gentle exersise daily. By this means, you will have them in good condition, and perfect order, able if required, to go through any fatigue; it would be well and highly requisit, that there should be attached to the concern, a Cuting machine, and Corn Mill. They are both of them, in this case, of great use. When the fodder is cut fine, and the Corn cracked or ground, the Same, these mixed together, no better nourishment can be given them. Once a week or fortnight it would be very propper to give in there food, a Small hand full of fine Salt united with a much less quantity of Sulpher. This is intended to clense the interior, promote health, with a continued appetite. This food, may be given every morning, or oftener as the case may require, but free from the Salt, & Sulpher, only at stated times, once every other Day, cintinued for the Space of a fortnight. The proof of there thriving will test the utility.

3ly A master Professer, in promoting the Breed of different kind[s] of annimals. He must be acquainted with there Pedigree knowing in general there qualities as to Blood, form, & movements, wether for the race, Saddle, or common use. There cannot be a more usefull, gentle, & kind annimal ever given to man, than the noble Beast, called the Horse; to esteem his great qualities, is to know wether we can do without him in all & every case. The great usefulness of the Cow, can only be appreciated, but by her usefull product. The Milk she produces is a Luxury, and is exceptable to all classes, as highly nutritive, and in all cases very much esteem'd. Where can you find a fluid, equal in comparison, to its perfect & Benificial use. The Ox must be considered very useful not only for draft, but for provisions either fresh or Salt. Altho slow in his movements, yet he possesses much power, and is considerd servicable by his Labour; he is nourished with much ease, and very little expence. He is in all cases where power is required, next to the Horse, docile, Obedient, and usefull, and I should advise the incouragement & improvement of his Breed; not loosing by neglect this valuable consideration. Next in consideration and which will prove of much importance, and profit, will be the incouragement of raising Mules, part for home use, and part for Shipping to the West Indias, where there value is well known. In the cource of a few years they will difray the expence of the college. They are a hardy, Tuff, Strong, but Stubborn annimal, and are nourishd with uncommmon ease. They will exist on almost any thing, and mentain a Life to great extent. It would be well, to procure 3 or 4 of the first rate Jacks, to accommodate the Mares, whoes number I should advise, not to be less than fifty or Sixty, and each one, not to cost more than Forty Dollars, or a little over. We must not look for Beauty, in the Breed of this animal, but actual, and well known Servises which they are capable of performing. Nerves and Sinnows to the Backbone, tho Small in Statu[r]e, nothing can Surpass there Surprising viewing; his form as to Ears, legs, & tail, I cannot conceive a more indifferent annimal on Earth. However the value of all things, ought not be juged by looks, but tested by there intrinsic worth, and I do believe, take them weight for Size, there is no odds to match them. They are capable of drawing on a good Road, from one to one & half Ton weight, with great ease. I recommend every attention in raising this annimal, to a great extent, as they will always meet, both a ready and quick Sale, in the different parts of the west India Islands, commanding generally Speaking, a very handsome price at all times, and every preference is given to what may be deemed a good Horse.

I will now reflect, on the practibility of improving the Breed of Swine, whoes properties are valuable, and much esteemed, as to its wholsome nutriment, either fresh for the Table, or salted & Barreled for exportation; it would be adviseable, to procure a Suitable number of the first rate Boars, communicating them with the female swine. This plan will give high expectation of profitabl views. The best improved Breed, is called the White Boar, whoes khine is uncommonly thin, and has very short hair as well as leggs. One of this kind brought from England, Some time Since Cost $60.00. His Piggs Six Weeks old, brings three Dollars a piece with a quick Sale. I should advise in preference to Let them run at large, would be to have commodious Pens, which Shall, or may, be constructed & fixed on Rolers, capable to move to different Spots, where the benifit of the manure, may inrich the Earth. Let one end of the inclosure have a coarse covering, to keep them from being exposed, from the Sun, in warm weather, and from bad weather in Winter. Let the Stye be kept clean at all times, and in Summer heat, the Hoggs may be washed by throwing water over them, once or twice a Week. Scrubing them with a Stiff Brush, after washing, will be found very useful; the food which will constitute there nourishment in part, is Simple and Sane. All the savings from the college, should be carefully attended to. Even the Boilings of a Meat Pot, ought not be neglected. Uniting the Same with the pareings of Potatoes, Turnips, Cabage leaves & all other refuse of vegitable will nourish and fatten, many Hoggs ℔ annum. I wish to be indulged in my further views on a much larger Scale, as to food in extent of Numbers, on the Same Plan. Give them Pumpkins cut fine, also squashes, Turnips, Potatoes Carots or mellons, and in fact, all kinds of Vegitables, mix'd with Ground or cracked Corn, three times a Week, or ofener as will best suite by observation there thriving. It will be found by this treatment a just and ample reward.

I shall now view with extended and Just calculations on the best Breed of Sheep. This annimal in its full view demands the highest consideration, as to there valuable properties. In many respects we are fed and clothed, by there useful products; being fit for the Table, giving the most wholsom nourishment not to epicures, but to men of reason and plain Living, valuing health & Strength, in prefference to effeminate dainties, whose continued Luxuries advances a full share of debility. See the many thousands, who procure a living by his fleece convey'd to manufactures, going through there various process, and finally producing the finest and best of Covertures, for the comfort and convenience of man. Master Pro[fe]ser, you as well as my Self, know the value and great usefulness of this harmless annimal. Let me advise you by all means, not to turn them out of the fold, or inclosure, before the Sun, is at least two hours high on the Earth, either in Spring, Summer, or Autumn. The Noixous and fowl vapours, with there bad quality, produced by the Night Air, falls on the spire of the Grass, whose bad effect, continue, until the Sun by its power, consume this great detriment and at the Same time, give both nourishment to the Spire & Root, being Sweet to there taste, not deviating from the view I have here laid down, for I believe it Just. How often has the sheep been infected with the distemper commonly called the Rott, which has proved distructive and fatal, to many: it will be seen, & known when they are distemper'd, with this complaint, by a collection of matter runing from there Nostrills, and who will loose there appetite by this Sickness, pine away, and are finally Loss't. I should in this case, make use of the fumigating preparation, which will be noted in its propper place. The full Blooded are held in this State, as well as others, in high estimation, particularly for the fineness of there fleece, and are Sold When but Six weeks old, for five Dollars ℔ piece;

there product in Wool brings from 75¢ to 100¢ ℔ pound. This most Superior flock of Sheep as well as the White Boar, belong to a Gentleman in Brighton, about four miles from Boston.

I cannot say much about Goats, for they are out of my Lattitude, intirely, and are under the particular care, of the moral & Religious Societies; many profess to be very Sanctified, and were the sacr[e]d covering for a mantle, but the Horns are two often Seen through it. All good men I highly esteem but hypocrites and deceivers I must neglect.

Stewart & Libranian [*sic*]. It is expected he can execute each office, with much care, and do the duty of both to the satisfaction of all parties. He will be furnished at proper and stated times, with sufficient funds, advanced, from the Trustees, of the College, purchasing all Supplies, of a good quality, and use the utmost means, in the view of a just oeconomy, keeping uniformly an exact and perfect account, of all expenditures for the Sole use of the College, from Day to Day; paying of[f] weekly, monthly, or Quarterly, as may be convenient, to all who may be any ways, connected with this institution, provided, if pressing wants, & unforeseen accidents Should oblige, the furnisure to call for his pay before the stipulated time, let him have it, by consent of the Trustees, reporting at all times, the State, and nature of the demand. It will be highly requisit, and most advisable, that his accounts should without any neglect, be revised & liquidated Quarterly, and not to exceed that time: he will embrace a steady view, to the department of the Library, and at the period of being furnished, with a Suitable, & Suffitient Supply of useful Books; his duty will call him to note them in Order, by taking an exact, catalogue, of all and each Number, on different Subjects. He will be parti[c]ular to cover them, with Brown or other Strong Paper, with neatness, and secure them, with Sealing Wax or Wafers, inside the Cover, labeling & Lettering each front outside top Edge, with description of the work, and to be placed in Alphibettical Order. No Books, shall be lent out [o]utside the Seminary, which must be made known to the Schollers, and any infringment contra to this order, the transgressor shall not only pay for the Book, but receive a just and Severe reprimand, or the Librarian shall pay for the Same. Let there be no turning down of Leaves, in the Book, nor reading with unclean hands, to deface and injure the Book. There must be caution in this respect. It will and must be the duty of the Librarian, to call in his Books once a week, in order to See what is missing, and to adjust and keep the whole, in perfect order.

I would wish, and do most warmly recommend, that a Farier & Hortographer may be attached to the College. A man of this description, with proved qualities in his profession, will be highly usefull, not only for Shoeing the annimals, but of various kind of work, which will be required in this establishment, whose repares in many cases, will much want his attention and aid. I should advise, provided a person can be procured, who is capable and adequate to fill both stations, that he may receive a Liberal reward, suffitient to enliven his views, and incourage him to perform and execute his duty, when required, either early or late, and in all weathers. I should advise him whenever he Sees the simptoms of distemper, commonly called the Horse ail, which will be Seen, by a discharge of matter, from the nostrills, a Loss of appetite & of flesh, he will then proceed knowing the cause, to fumigate. Halter or Bridle him, in any manner, So as to keep his head a little de[c]lined. Take then a common Shovell, place therein live coals of fire, Sprinkel thereon, a Small quantity of flour of sulpher, with a Pinch or two, of common Feathers. Hold the Same to his nostrills, not more than three or four Seconds. Draw back, and Stop a minute, or two. Return again to the Same procedure, and follow it three different times, every morning for a week. By this treatment, it causes the Horse to Sneeze and at each effort, releives the Head by the passage of the Nostrills, with great quantiti⟨es⟩ of matter; mix also in there food, which will be of ground, or cracked Corn, united with Bran, if to be had a Small quantity of sulpher, with fine Salt. Let his nourishment through the Day & Night, be Hay or Fodder. Give them, or him, gentle exercise a short distance, and Stable him the rest part of the time. This treatment, in this case, will save a valuable Horse. The same treatment, or application, but of less quantity, will answer for Sheep, distempered with the complaint called the Rott. There is many complaints in annimals, originating from various causes, most generally from bad food, and; a great neglect of clensing by medicin there interior. It will be often Seen when the annimal is infected with worms which complaint is commonly called the Botts, whoes foot hold is on the Morr, or vital part of the crature, they will throw there head aside, and often bite there Side with pain. There nostrills will Sink in, and there Eyes ware a languid and dim appearance. Hesitate not and let it be done immediately, by drenching them. Make use of a common Junk Bottle, charged with Milk Hunney, or Molasses, and insert the Same in there Mouth. Give them the whole contents & while feasting on this preparation, which they are fond of, apply in a few minutes after, while taking there refreshment on the first preparation, a Second dose of Spirits of Turpentine, at Least, one half pint in quantity. By this means, it will put a full Stop to there voracity, and cut them in the most prompt, and decisive manner, to attoms of distruction. In case a Horse is over Strain'd by hard riding, and the ignorance or carelesness of the rider, who Should give him two much Corn in that state, not proceeding with caution, and bate him before he is in a state of Coolness, or partly so, the risque is great, and often proves the Horse injured, by being foundered. If a quagmire, or Swamp is not at hand, make use of common Clay, if to be had, or Earth. Take his Shoes of[f], and envelope his hoofs with a course Cloth up to his Knees charged with the Same and let it be so attached that it will keep its position. The Earth or Clay must be constantly wet with Vinagar & water or salt and water. Diet him low, and give him gentle exercise a few Rods twice a Day. This mode of treatment will cure him in a Short time. The cause of his being disabled is being over heated which desends to his hoofs which makes them tender, and is Simular to the gout in men. Had I time which I could call my own, I would inlarge on the advantages which your State, is capable of producing, in the manufactureing Line, both of Cotton & Wool. You would be surprised, and look with astonishment, at the rapid Strides they are making in this State, as good Cloth as can be imported, and as fine Cotton Shirting as any man need ware. The Interest on there Capital, is from sixteen to twenty ℔ Cent. Your State offers great advantages, from its fine Situation, and its my opinion can raise and produce, as good a Breed of Sheep, as else where; you are as I may say, next door neighbour to the Cotton Planter, which, raw material, you have close at hand and could I have not a doubt, Succeed well in these two Branches of manufactures. Enterprize, and Capitol, is only wanted to insure Success.

You will pardon me Dr Sir, for these tedious and lengthy writings, and I indulge a hope, you will be as pati[e]nt in reading, as, I have in Studying and writing them; more particularly when we have in view, any Services we can render our Country, or fellow Citisens, undoubtedly will make us proceed, in the most cheerful manner; on my part, to crown these views with Success, I have not been Idle night or Day, and have Stept forward, with full determination to be useful, if possible, in all and every respect. A few observations, in continuance, I shall then draw to a close; I beg Sir, you will tender my warmest regards to your Niece. I have heard much of her exalted talents: invite her to continue improvement; that she may be perfect hereafter. Except my respectful, and great regards, for you & family, and believe me at all times, your friend & obet Servant,

E. CALLENDER

RC (DLC). Docketed by JM.

1. Letter not found.
2. Moison: quantity (*OED Online*).

From Thomas Jefferson

DEAR SIR. MONTICELLO Feb. 16.—23

You already know that the legislature has authorised the literary board to lend us another 60.000 D. It is necessary we should act on this immediately so far as to accept the loan, that we may engage our workmen before they enter into other undertakings for the season. But the badness of the roads, the uncertainty of the weather and the personal inconvenience of a journey to the members of our board, render a speedy meeting desperate. Mr Cabell and Mr Loyall have by letters to me expressed their approbation of the loan & that they will confirm it regularly at our april meeting. If you think proper to do the same, Genl. Cocke and myself will authorise the engagement of the workmen and they will be satisfied to begin their work immediately and to provide materials for the library. The sooner you can conveniently give me your answer, the sooner the operations may be commenced. Accept my affectionate esteem & respect.

TH: JEFFERSON

RC (DLC); draft (DLC: Jefferson Papers). RC in Virginia Jefferson Randolph's hand, signed by Jefferson. Draft docketed by Jefferson "Madison James Breckinridge Genl. / Feb. 16. 23."

From George W. Spotswood

DEAR SIR, 17th. Feby. 1823

The Legislature of Va. having appropriated a sum of money to be applied to the finishing of the University, I presume that Institution will be in operation the next year. I will take the liberty, of again, soliciting your Friendly influence in my behalf, in obtaining a Stewartship, and if the request should not be considered unreasonable, I beg your goodness, in naming the subject to Mr. Jefferson. I have been induced to make this early application, as I have reason to believe, there are others, who have in contemplation becoming candidates for a like situation in the College, and hope, Sir, you will pardon me for being thus troublesome, and will only plead as an appology, the anxiety of a parent, whose slender fortune, will not enable him to give, Six Sons (in his present situation) such an Education as he could wish; should there be an appointment of a head Stewart, I should wish to be considered a Candidate for the Office, & should spare no exertions to give general satisfaction, should I succeed in obtaing the situation. I am Sir, very Respectfully, yr. Obd. Servt.

GEO. W. SPOTTSWOOD[1]

RC (DLC). Docketed by JM.

1. George Washington Spotswood (d. 1844) of Orange County, Virginia, was commissioned a midshipman in the U.S. Navy in 1799 and dismissed in 1803. He served as a lieutenant in the Virginia militia during the War of 1812. His request for a position at the University of Virginia was eventually answered and he spent the years 1825 to 1829 as a hotel-keeper there. He left Charlottesville and settled first in Charleston, then Kanawha County, Vir-

ginia (now West Virginia). About 1836 Spotswood moved to Springfield, Illinois, where he owned various businesses, including a hotel and a tavern. He was appointed postmaster of Springfield in 1841 (Nathaniel B. Curran, "General Isaac B. Curran: Gregarious Jeweler," *Journal of the Illinois State Historical Society* 71 [1978], 273–74; Callahan, *List of Officers of the Navy*, 515; Scott, *History of Orange County*, 244; Bruce, *History of the University of Virginia*, 2:222–24; Spotswood to JM, 4 July 1829, ViU: Madison Papers, Special Collections; JM to Spotswood, 21 June 1831, and Spotswood to JM, 11 Nov. 1833, DLC).

To Edward Everett

DEAR SIR MONTPELLIER Feby. 18. 1823.

I have received your favour of the 9th. inst:[1] and with it the little pamphlet entitled "Notes &c."[2] forwarded at the request of your brother; for which you will please to accept and to make my acknowledgments.

The pamphlet appears to have very ably & successfully vindicated the construction given in the Book on "Europe," to the provision article in Mr Jay's Treaty. History, if it should notice the subject,[3] will assuredly view it in the light in which the "Notes" have placed it; and as affording to England a ground for intercepting American supplies of provisions to her Enemy; and to her enemy, a ground for charging on America a collusion with England for the purpose. That the British Government meant to surrender gratuitously a maritime right of confiscation, and to encourage a Neutral in illegal supplies of provisions to the Enemy, by adding to chances of gain an ensurance against loss, will never be believed. The necessary comment will be that Mr. Jay, tho' a man of great ability & perfect integrity,[4] was diverted by a zeal for the object of his Mission, from a critical attention to the terms on which it was accomplished. The Treaty was fortunate in the sanction it obtained & in the turn which circumstances gave to its fate.

Nor was this the only instance of its good fortune. In two others it was saved from mortifying results; in one by the integrity of the British Courts of Justice, in the other by a cast of the die.

The value of the article opening our trade with India depended much on the question whether it authorised an *indirect* trade thither. The question was carried into the Court of King's Bench, where it was decided in our favour;[5] the Judges stating at the same time, that the decision was forced upon them by the particular structure of the Article, agst. their private conviction as to what was intended. The decision was confirmed by the twelve Judges.

In the other instance, the question was, whether the Board of Com[m] issioners for deciding on spoliations could take cognizance of American claims which had been rejected by the British Tribunal in the last resort.

The two British Commissioners contended that G. Britain could never be understood to submit to any extraneous Tribunal a revision of cases decided by the highest of her own. The American Comrs. Mr. Pinkney and Mr. Gore, argued with great & just force against a construction; which, as the Treaty confined the jurisdiction of the Board to cases where redress was not attainable in the ordinary course of Judicial proceedings, would have been fatal, not only to the claims which had been rejected by the Tribunal in the last resort, but to the residue, which it would be necessary to carry thither through the ordinary course of Justice. The 4 Comrs. being equally divided, the lot for the 5th. provided by the Treaty for such a contingency fell on Mr. Trumbull, whose casting vote obtained for the American sufferers the large indemnity at stake.[6]

I speak on these points from memory alone. There may be therefore, if no substantial error, inaccuracies, which a sight of the Archives at Washington or the Reports of adjudged Cases in England would have prevented.

The remarks on the principle "free ships—free goods," I take to be fair & well considered. The extravagance of Genet drove our Secretary of State to the ground of the British Doctrine: and the Government finding that it could not depart from that ground, witht. collision or rather war with G. Britain, and doubting at least, whether the old law of nations on that subject did not remain in force, never contested the practice under it.[7] The U. States in their Treaties however have sufficiently thrown their weight into the opposite scale: and such is the number & character of like weights now in it, from other powers, that it must preponderate; unless it be admitted that no authority of that kind, tho' co-inciding with the dictates of reason, the feelings of humanity, and the interests of the civilized world, can make or expound a law of nations.

With regard to the rule of 1756[8] it is to be recollected that its original import was very different from the subsequent extensions & adaptations given to it by the belligerent policy of its parent. The rule commenced with confiscating neutral vessels trading between another belligerent nation and its colonies, on the inference that they were hostile vessels in neutral disguise; and it ended in spoliations on neutrals trading to any ports or in any productions of belligerents, who had not permitted such a trade in time of peace. The author of the "notes" is not wrong in stating that the U.S. did in some sort acquiesce in the exercise of the rule agst. them; that they did not make it a cause of war; and that they were willing, on considerations of expediency, to accede to a compromise on the subject. To judge correctly of the course taken by the Governmt. a historical view of the whole of it would be necessary. In a glancing search over the "State papers" for the document from which the extract in the pamphlet was made (it is referred to in a wrong volume & page, being found in Vol VI p. 240; the extract itself being not free from one typographical change of phrase) my eye caught a short letter of Instructions to Mr. Monroe (Vol VI p. 180–1)[9] in which the stand taken by the Government is distinctly marked out. The illegality of the British principle is there asserted; nothing *declaratory* in its favor, as applied even against a neutral trade *direct* between a belligerent country & its colonies is permitted; and a stipulated concession on the basis of compromise, is limited by a reference to a former instruction of Jany: 1804 (See Vol. VI p. 160-1-2) to that in the Russian Treaty of 1781;[10] which protects all colonial produce converted into neutral property. This was in practice all that was essential: the American Capital being at the time adequate and actually applied to the purchase of the Colonial produce transported in American vessels.

"The Examination &c" referred to in the letter to Mr. Monroe as being forwarded, was a stout pamphlet drawn up by the Secretary of State.[11] It was undertaken in consequence of the heavy losses and loud complaints of the Merchants in all our large seaports, under the predatory operations of the extended rule of 1756. The pamphlet went into a pretty ample & minute investigation of the subject, which terminated in a confirmed conviction both of the heresy of the British doctrine, and of the enormity of the practice growing out of it. I must add that it detracted much also from the admiration I had been led to bestow on the distinguished Judge of the High Court of Admiralty:[12] not from any discovery of defect in his intellectual powers or Judicial eloquence; but on account of his shifting decisions and abandonment of his Independent principles. After setting out with the lofty profession of abiding by the same rules of public law when sitting in London, as if a Judge at Stockholm, he was not ashamed to acknowledge that in expounding that law he should regard the orders in Council of his own Gover[n]ment as his authoritative Guide. Those are not his words, but do him, I believe no injustice. The acknowledgment ought to banish him as "Authority" from every prize Court in the world.

I ought to have premised to any remarks on the controversy into which your brother has been drawn, that I have never seen either the review in which his book is criticized, or the pamphlet in which it is combated. Having just directed the Brit: Quart: Review now sent me, to be discontinued, and the North A. Review to be substituted, with the back numbers for the last year, I may soon be able to do a fuller justice to his reply.

On adverting to the length of this letter I fear that my pen has received an impulse from awakened recollections, which I ought more to have controuled. The best now to be done is not to add a word more than an assurance of my cordial respect & esteem

JAMES MADISON

RC (MHi); draft (DLC). RC docketed by Everett. Minor differences between the copies have not been noted.

1. Letter not found.

2. Alexander Hill Everett, *A Few Notes on Certain Passages Respecting the Law of Nations, Contained in an Article in the July No. of the North American Review, upon the Work Entitled "Europe, By a Citizen of the United States." By the Author of That Work* (Boston, 1823; Shoemaker 12481). JM's inscribed copy is in the Madison Collection, Special Collections, University of Virginia Library.

3. The draft has "fact" in place of "subject" here.

4. The draft has "rectitude" in place of "integrity" here.

5. JM referred to article 13 of the Jay Treaty (Miller, *Treaties*, 2:255–56). For the 1798 decision in *Wilson v. Marryat*, which gave the widest possible construction to the article, see Holden Furber, "The Beginnings of American Trade with India, 1784–1812," *New England Quarterly* 11 (1938): 249–50.

6. According to John Trumbull, the fifth commissioner, this question was submitted to the Lord Chancellor, who ruled in favor of the American position. See John Bassett Moore, ed., *International Adjudications, Ancient and Modern, History and Documents . . .* (6 vols.; New York, 1929–33), 4:81–87.

7. For Secretary of State Jefferson's 1793 comments on contraband, see the review of Everett's *A Few Notes* (see n. 2 above) in the *North American Review* 17 (1823): 165–67.

8. The rule of 1756 denied neutral ships permission to trade with foreign colonies in times of war, if that trade had been denied them in times of peace (Bemis, *John Quincy Adams and the Foundations of American Foreign Policy*, 43).

9. JM to James Monroe, 13 Jan. 1806, *State Papers and Publick Documents of the United States, from the Accession of George Washington to the Presidency, Exhibiting a Complete View of Our Foreign Relations since That Time*, 2d ed. (10 vols.; Boston, 1817), 6:180–81.

10. JM to James Monroe, 5 Jan. 1804, ibid., 160–62. These observations and instructions on article 4 of the proposed convention between the United States and Great Britain are printed and annotated in *PJM-SS*, 6:300–301. For the Russian Treaty of 1781, in particular, see ibid., 307 n. 15.

11. [James Madison], *A Memoir, Containing an Examination of the British Doctrine, Which Subjects to Capture a Neutral Trade, Not Open in Time of Peace* ([Washington, 1806]; Shaw and Shoemaker 10777).

12. William Scott, Baron Stowell (1745–1836) was the judge of the High Court of Admiralty from 1798–1828, and as such, his decisions profoundly affected U.S. commerce and the rules of neutral trade (*PJM-SS*, 3:414 n. 2).

To Thomas Jefferson

Dear Sir Montpellier Feby. 19. 1823

The inclosed letters & papers being addressed to you as well as me,[1] I am not at liberty to withold them, tho' I know the disrelish you will feel for such appeals. I shall give an answer, in a manner for us both, intimating the propriety of our abstaining from any participation in the electioneering measures on foot.[2]

I congratulate you on the loan, scanty as it is, for the University; in the confidence that it is a gift masked under that name; and in the hope that it is a pledge for any remnant of aid the Establishment may need in order to be totus teres atque rotundus.[3]

Can you not have the hands set to work without the formality of a previous meeting of the Visitors? I have recd no notice from Richmond on the subject. Health & every other happiness

JAMES MADISON

Partial RC (DLC); partial RC (ViU: Jefferson Papers); partial Tr (ViU: Jefferson Papers). First partial RC docketed by Jefferson as "recd. Feb. 23." A note on the second partial RC reads: "Taken off for an autograph for Mrs Judge White March 18th. 1838." Partial Tr is a tracing of the partial RC (ViU: Jefferson Papers), with the following note: "The orignl in the Livingston Collection. N.B. Mrs. Livingstons grandmothr who made this collection was a Miss Peyton and married Senr. White of Tennessee."

1. JM enclosed Tench Coxe's letters of 31 Jan. and 1 Feb. 1823 to himself and Thomas Jefferson.

2. The first partial RC ends here; the rest of the letter is taken from the second partial RC.

3. *Totus teres atque rotundus.* Horace, in his Satires, II vii. 86, says that a man indifferent to desires and honors is "in se ipso, totus, teres, atque rotundus," that is, whole in himself, smoothed, and rounded (*Horace: Satires, Epistles and Ars Poetica*, Loeb Classical Library [1970 reprint], 230–31). Note JM's clever play on words: the Rotunda was the last piece left in building the University of Virginia.

From Jedidiah Morse

SIR, NEW HAVEN (CON.) Feb. 20. 1823

I have just read, in Niles' Register, your letter to Lt. Governor Barry, on the subject of a "general system of Education.["][1] The sentiments you have expressed in this Letter, are so just & excellent, & comport so well with the present state of the World, & specially of our own favored country, that I cannot but thank you for them, & express my hope, that, from the influence you have acquired from the succession of high civil offices you have been called to fill, they will have extensive circulation & lasting good effects. In no way can the wisdom of our aged Wise men be more usefully employed, than in devising & recommending to their Successors in office, the best methods of educating the *whole body* of the youth of our country, rich & poor, in all branches of useful knowledge adapted to their ages & circumstances in life. In no better way can our admirable form of government be preserved, & "*liberty with order*" effectually secured, than by a *universal* & *thorough good* education of our youth. A nation untaught, or badly taught—ignorant or vicious, must, of necessity, consist of a *few tyrants*, & a *multitude of slaves*. They would be incapable of enjoying the blessings of freedom. A free people must be an enlightened people: & an enlightened people will always be free. They will prefer death to slavery.

It is gratifying to witness the gradual diminution of those sectional feelings & prejudices, which, in times that are past, have afflicted us by dissipating & weakening those energies, which should have been combined for the good of the nation, & by lessening our respectability abroad. The in[c]reased intercourse between men of influence from the different States, the adoption of similar modes of education, & the mingling of citizens from different sections of the Union, in our old, & especially in our new settlements, have all conduced to bring about this most desirable effect. Your liberality in recommending the plans of popular education now in successful operation in "*the Eastern States*," as "*examples*" worthy of the attention of other states, will have a very conciliating effect on the people of the east, the south & west, as far as the fact shall be made known.

Your just remarks on the importance of the study of Geography & Astronomy, by the youth of our Country, you will readily suppose, must have been gratifying to me, who have been, for nearly *forty* years attending particularly to these sciences, & preparing elementary books for the instruction of our youth in them. My age & infirmities remind me, that it is time for me to retire from this wide field of arduous labor; & I have, accordingly, resigned it to two of my three sons. The first efforts of the eldest of the two, I take the liberty to transmit to you from him,[2] with his respects, for your acceptance. He has received approbations of a high cast, of both his books, from men of high respectability, & it will be peculiarly gratifying both to him & myself, if he shall have yours. With great & very sincere respect, I am, sir, your obdt servt

JEDH MORSE

RC (DLC). Addressed by Morse to JM, and franked. Docketed by JM.

1. See JM to William T. Barry, 4 Aug. 1822.

2. Sidney Edwards Morse, *A New System of Modern Geography, or A View of the Present State of the World. . . . Accompanied with an Atlas* (Boston, 1822; Shoemaker 9560).

To Tench Coxe

DEAR SIR MONTPELLIER Feby. 21. 1823

Since I recd. your two letters of [1] I have hitherto been prevented from acknowledging them first by some very urgent calls on my time, and afterwards by an indisposition which has just left me.

I have forwarded the letters with the printed papers to Mr. Jefferson. I know well the respect he as well as myself attaches to your communications. But I have grounds to believe that, with me also, he has yielded to the considerations & counsels which dissuade us from taking part in measures relating to the ensuing Presidential Election. And certainly if we are to judge of the ability with which the comparative pretensions of the candidates will be discussed, by the samples sent us, the public will be sufficiently enabled to decide understandingly on the subject. I know you too well to doubt that you will take this explanation in its just import, and will remain assured that it proceeds from no diminution of confidence or regard towards you.

I have made a search for the documents of which you wish the loan, but without success. I am not sure that some of them were preserved in my collection. If they were, it is probable they were among bundles which, during my long exile from private life, and alterations in my dwelling, were removed into damp situations, where they perished: or included in parcels carried to Washington in order to be assorted & bound, where they had the fate of many other articles in 1814. With a continuance of my esteem & my best wishes

James Madison

Facsimile of RC (Heritage Auction Galleries [www.ha.com], Auction #658, 2007, Lot 25080); draft (DLC). Draft dated incorrectly 1828.

1. Left blank in RC and draft. JM was acknowledging the receipt of Coxe's letters of 31 Jan. and 1 Feb. 1823.

From Mason Locke Weems

Charleston. S.Ca. [21 February 1823]

Mi Suavissime Rerum![1] Most Honord of friends,

This is just to tell you that the Life of Wm. Penn is launchd. and, thank Heaven, nearly half seas over,[2] of the 1st. Edition. It is not for me to open my lips about it—but I am happy to know that sundry great men—of the Bench, also, to my huge amazement, of the Pulpit, are pleasd to say of it, as Mr Monroe at first reading of it said of my Marion—that, it is a book that *will travel.* However be that as it may I have taken the liberty to send you a copy of it for Mrs. Madison,[3] who I have been told was brought up a "*Friend.*" I had hopes of coming myself to bring it to you—and for the same reason have all this time neglected to ask for the small ballance due of a little Religious Book Agency wherin Mrs. Madison was so public Spirited as to aid me two years ago, viz

2 Hunters Sacred Biogy.[4]	22
1 Life of Washington[5]—for the Miller Broun	1
1 Copy Stevens French Wars[6]—subscribd for by Mr. Todd—& sent to him by the *Stage*	16
	39

Now If you coud be *so good* as to order this to be paid by some friend of yours in the Federal dist. or Dumfries—or Fredericksburg—or Richmond—givg. one single line of notice of the same to my son Jesse Ewell Weems Dumfries,[7] you will very singularly & seasonably Oblige, yours, With the Utmost Resp. & Esteem

M.L. WEEMS

10,000 good wishes to Mrs. M & Mother &c.

RC (DLC). Undated; conjectural date supplied based on JM's docket. Addressed by Weems to JM, and franked.

1. *Mi Suavissime Rerum:* this is a variant of the common greeting "dulcissime rerum," translated as "my dearest fellow." Here Weems uses "suavissime," which can be translated as agreeable, charming, or pleasant (Edward P. Morris, ed., *Horace: The Satires* [New York, 1909], 122 n. 4).

2. Half seas over: halfway towards a goal (*OED Online*).

3. Mason Locke Weems, *The Life of William Penn, the Settler of Pennsylvania, the Founder of Philadelphia* . . . (Philadelphia, 1822; Shoemaker 11390).

4. See Weems to JM, 22 Jan. 1819, *PJM-RS*, 1:404 and n. 3, and Weems to Dolley Madison, 22 July 1813, *DMDE*.

5. See *PJM-RS*, 1:404 and n. 2.

6. Alexander Stephens, *The History of the Wars Which Arose Out of the French Revolution: To Which is Prefixed, a Review of the Causes of That Event* (2 vols.; Philadelphia, 1804; Shaw and Shoemaker 7305).

7. Jesse Ewell Weems (b. 1799), the eldest son and third of Weems's ten children, was associated in business with his father (W. A. Bryan, ed., "Three Unpublished Letters of Parson Weems," *WMQ* 23 [1943]: 274 n. 10).

To Richard Peters

DEAR SIR MONTPELLIER Feby. 22. 1823

I have recd. the copy of your Agricultural Address in Jany. last,[1] which I have read with much pleasure, and as always, not without finding instructive ideas. You have done very right in taking occasion to record the fact which shews that your Society is the Mother of the American family, and to present a fair view of its public services; with respect to which you might say, tho' you will not say "quorum pars Maxima fui."[2]

You will pardon me for noting an error in the reference to the Resolutions of the Albemarle Society, as requesting the co-operation of the

Societies in *other States.* The request was addressed to the *other Societies* in *this State.* I must take the blame in part at least to myself. I ought to have let it appear, when I forwarded you a Copy, that it was a friendly only not an official Communication. With my continued esteem & all my best wishes

JAMES MADISON

RC (WHi); draft (DLC). Addressed and franked by JM to Peters in Philadelphia. Postmarked 25 Feb. at Orange Court House. Docketed by Peters "Ansd. 4 March." Minor differences between the copies have not been noted.

1. Letter not found. Richard Peters, *Address Delivered before the Philadelphia Society for Promoting Agriculture, at Its Annual Meeting, on the Twenty-Third of January, 1823* (Philadelphia, 1823; Shoemaker 13738).

2. *Quorum pars maxima fui:* of which I was the greatest part. Aeneas, in Virgil's *Aeneid* 2.6, says about the events of the Trojan War, "quorum pars magna fui," that is, "whereof I was no small part" (Loeb Classical Library [2 vols.; Cambridge, Mass., 1934], 1:294–95).

From Thomas Jefferson

DEAR SIR MONTICELLO Feb. 24. 23.

I have read mr. Cox's letters and some of his papers, which I now return you. It is impossible for me to write to him. With two crippled hands I abandon writing but from the most urgent necessities; and above all things I should not meddle in a Presidential election, nor[1] even express a sentiment on the subject of the Candidates. As you propose to write to him, will you be so good as to add a line for me of the above purport? It will be a great relief to me; as it hurts me much to take no notice of the letter of an old friend.

The acceptance of the loan being now approved by five of us I shall proceed immediately to have the workmen engaged. As there are some very important points to be decided on previously to embarking in such a building, I sent to request Genl. Cocke to join me in setting the thing agoing. But he had engagements which prevented his leaving home; and as the case admits no delay, I shall proceed according to the best of my judgment, with the aid of mr. Brockenbrough, and with all the caution the case admits. Ever & affectionately yours

TH: JEFFERSON

RC (DLC); draft (DLC: Jefferson Papers). Minor differences between the copies have not been noted.

1. The draft has "never" in place of "nor" here.

From Peter Perpignan

RESPECTED SIR PHILADA. Feby. 26th. 1823

Inclosed you will find the smallest representation, of our departed patriot Genl. Geoe. Washington, that has ever been presented to our Countryman.[1]

Should you be pleased to accept it, your answer, to its reception, will Serve Your friend and fellow Citizen

PETER PERPIGNAN[2]

RC (DLC). Docketed by JM.

1. Enclosure not identified.

2. Peter Perpignan was a watchmaker and jeweler who had a shop at 356 North Front Street, Philadelphia, and whose home was in the Northern Liberties section of the city. He was active in Democratic-Republican politics and his Masonic Lodge, and served in the Pennsylvania state militia during the War of 1812 (Philadelphia *Franklin Gazette*, 23 Mar., 10 June, and 1 Oct. 1819; Joshua L. Lyte, comp., *Reprint of the Minutes of the Grand Lodge of Free and Accepted Masons of Pennsylvania* [12 vols.; Philadelphia, 1895–1907], 4:172; Scharf and Westcott, *History of Philadelphia*, 3:2082–83).

Index

Note: Persons are identified on pages cited below in boldface type. Identifications in the first volume of this series are noted within parentheses. Page numbers followed only by n (e.g., 272n) refer to the provenance portion of the annotation.

INDEX